THE TECHNIQUE
of the
SOUND STUDIO

Alistair Collins
October 1977

f

THE LIBRARY
OF COMMUNICATION TECHNIQUES

THE TECHNIQUE OF THE

SOUND STUDIO

For Radio, Television, and Film

by

ALEC NISBETT

Communication Arts Books
Hastings House, Publishers
New York 10016

*Recorded on tape by the State Service for
The Blind of Minnesota U.S.A.*

First Edition 1962
Second Impression 1965
Third Impression 1966
Fourth Impression 1967
Fifth Impression 1969
Second Edition, Revised and Enlarged 1970
Third Edition, Revised 1972
Eighth Impression 1972
Ninth Impression 1974
Tenth Impression 1974
Eleventh impression 1977

Printed in Great Britain by A. Wheaton & Co., Exeter

CONTENTS

6

8

9

INTRODUCTION TO THE THIRD EDITION

THE principles guiding the sound balancer and recordist do not change. But the equipment does: each year the range increases—and the revisions in this volume take account of some of the advances that have occurred since the second edition was written. The new equipment offers greater flexibility; this in turn implies the need for greater precision in description of the alternatives that are available. Where they are essential, such changes in the text have been made.

But there is a danger in this. The increasing complexity of technical equipment could all too easily be reflected in more complex technical descriptions. I have tried to avoid falling into this trap, for this would defeat the original purpose of the book which is to explain the subject simply, in terms that will be acceptable both to the creative people in production—including writers and performers —and to those who, more technically orientated, deal with the balance and recording of sound and with its engineering aspects. By exploring the ground common to both groups, the work of each may be interpreted to the other.

For those who use this book in University or College courses on Communications, it is obviously undesirable to make large structural changes to the layout so soon after the second edition (itself virtually a new book) was published. So the arrangement of the text has been kept as close as possible to that of the second edition: subject and page references should still be the same, though the matter may sometimes be a little different.

The basic approach has remained unaltered from the first edition. Its emphasis is on general principles rather than rule-of-thumb, though the shorter routes to high quality results are not neglected. It still insists on the paramount importance of subjective judgment—of learning to use the ears properly. Above all else, the sound man needs well-developed aural perception that is allied to a strong critical faculty. So, in this book, studio and location techniques are described in terms of what each operation does to the sound and why—*and what to listen for*.

INTRODUCTION TO THE SECOND EDITION

FOR the second edition, this book has been expanded: there are many new sections, and much of the earlier material has been extensively revised and brought up to date.

In the first edition, I wrote about the principles underlying the techniques of using sound; I took nearly all of the examples and applications from radio, but said that they could be applied almost equally in other media—particularly, of course, in the production of records, but also in television and film. In this volume those underlying principles remain the starting-point, but it is now shown by example how they apply in all of the different media.

The similarities are greater than the differences: curiously, single-channel sound in radio, television, and film have more in common with each other than the two branches of radio itself: mono and stereo (descriptions of which are now also integrated into this book).

In recent years the programme content and organizational structure of radio broadcasting in Britain have both changed—becoming closer, many have said, to the American model. But there remain very large differences, the most important of which is that in Britain the main instrument of broadcasting remains, in both radio and television, the public service BBC. Here the broadcaster's service is filtered not through the needs of the advertiser (as it largely must be in the United States); nor, it must be emphasized, through the State (as it has been in France). The BBC's contract is directly with its audience, subject only to the restraints that are imposed on broadcasting in any country (in Britain these are, surprisingly, less restrictive than those of the FCC in America). The existence of a strong commercial television network and the establishment of commercial radio in Britain do not alter this. Also, certain programme types have been retained in existence, which in the U.S. have diminished in importance or vanished completely; this is particularly true in radio.

To American readers I must say that in defining this difference I am not attempting to enter a plea for public service broadcasting: what is much more important within the terms of reference of this book is that it has given rise to the largest single body, with by far the largest amount of home-produced output at all levels (central, regional, and local) and of all types in the English-speaking world.

This gives rise to a body of knowledge of techniques which is probably unique. It is an environment within which I have been privileged to learn a variety of crafts (of which the use of sound is only one). Both the knowledge available to me and the opportunity to put it into practice have been as great as—indeed possibly greater than—might have been provided in any other broadcasting organization or, for that matter, place of learning.

This book remains largely what it originally set out to be in the first edition: a description of operational techniques based on personal experience and observation gained over a wide range of productions in different media. Starting as a "studio manager" in sound radio, I became a producer in the BBC's North American Service (providing transcription material for American, Canadian, and other English speaking stations throughout the world). Then I moved to television, producing and directing both studio and outside broadcast programmes, and also directing and supervising the editing of films for television. This direct experience has been augmented by study of the many "Technical Instructions" and other information sheets assessing equipment and techniques that are available within an organization the size of the BBC. To the many (often anonymous) authors of these notes I am deeply indebted, and also to the many individuals whose specialized expert knowledge I have consulted in a variety of fields. Where something is a matter of opinion, the opinion is usually my own (it will be clear where it is not!). In other cases the book reflects either a consensus or the opinion of an individual whose judgment I trust.

This book assumes a need and a desire for high standards, both of technique and programme content. These may be attained with apparent ease by the large network with time and money to spend— but is a knowledge and understanding of these high standards of value at the ground-roots level, in a small-town one-studio radio station with a transmitter on a rack in the corner?

I think it is, because high-quality work sets a standard by which all other work may be measured. Sometimes—particularly for the freelance—it may make all the difference between success and failure: if you want to sell a product it helps if the quality is at least as high as (and preferably higher than) the buyer can achieve by his own efforts—particularly if that quality can be achieved with apparent ease (and certainly without "fuss").

The whole point of this book is that high standards are *not* just a matter of having good equipment: just as important is knowing how to use it.

Wee have also Sound-Houses, *wher wee practise and demonstrate all* Sounds, *and their* Generation. *Wee have* Harmonies *which you have not, of* Quarter-Sounds, *and lesser* Slides *of* Sounds. *Diverse* Instruments *of* Musick *likewise to you unknowne, some* sweeter *then any you have; Together with* Bells *and* Rings *that are dainty and sweet. Wee represent* Small Sounds *as* Great *and* Deepe; *Likewise* Great Sounds, Extenuate *and* Sharpe; *Wee make diverse* Tremblings *and* Warblings *of* Sounds, *which in their* Originall *are* Entire. *Wee represent and imitate all* Articulate Sounds *and* Letters, *and the* Voices *and* Notes of Beasts *and* Birds. *Wee have certaine* Helps, *which sett to the* Eare *doe further the* Hearing *greatly. Wee have also diverse* Strange *and* Artificiall Eccho's, Reflecting *the* Voice *many times, and as it were* Tossing *it; And some that give back the* Voice Lowder *then it came, some* Shriller, *and some* Deeper; *Yea some rendring the* Voice, Differing *in the* Letters *or* Articulate Sound, *from that they receyve. Wee have also meanes to convey* Sounds *in* Trunks *and* Pipes, *in strange* Lines, *and* Distances.

From *The New Atlantis* by Francis Bacon
1624

1

THE SOUND MEDIUM

SOME readers of this book will already have a clear understanding of what sound is. Others will know very little about the physics of sound, and will not wish to know, their interest being solely in how to *use* the medium. "Do you have to know how paint is made to be an artist?" they might ask.

These two groups of readers can skip this chapter and go straight on to read about the operational techniques, the creative applications, and the practical problems and their solutions which are the main theme of this book.

The non-technical reader should have no difficulty in picking up as much as he needs to know as he goes along (perhaps with an occasional glance at the glossary). In other chapters most of the terms used are either understandable from their context, or are defined as they first appear. But for the sake of completeness, and for those who prefer their raw materials—or ideas—to be laid out in an orderly fashion before they begin, this chapter gives a very brief introduction to the physics of sound. It also includes an account of some of the basic concepts of stereophony (see p. 38).

The nature of sound

Sound is really a very simple thing. It is caused by vibrating materials. If a panel of wood is vibrating, the air next to it is pushed to and fro. If the rate of this vibration is somewhere between tens and tens of thousands of excursions per second the air has a natural elasticity which we do not find at slower speeds. Wave your hand backward and forward once a second and the air does little except get out of its way; it certainly doesn't bounce back. But if you could wave your hand backward and forward a hundred times every second the air would behave very differently. It would have no time

15

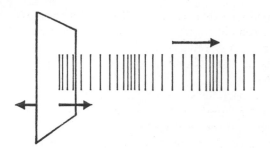

SOUND WAVE. A vibrating panel generates waves of pressure and rarefaction: sound. A tuning fork is usually used for this demonstration, but in fact tuning forks do not make much noise—they slice through the air without moving it. A vibrating panel is more efficient.

to get out of the way. It would instead compress as the surface of the hand moved forward and rarefy as it moved back.

In such circumstances the natural elasticity of the air takes over. As the surface moves forward each particle of air pushes against the next, which pushes against the next in turn, so creating a pressure wave. As the surface moves back the pressure wave is replaced by a rarefaction which is followed by another pressure wave, and so on.

It is a property of elastic media that a pressure wave passes through them at a speed which is a characteristic of the particular medium. The speed depends not only on the material itself but on the closeness with which its atoms or molecules are packed together. In the case we are considering—the speed of sound in air—it depends on the temperature, as well as on the nature of air. In fairly average conditions it is 1120 feet per second.

The speed is quite independent of the rate at which the surface generating the sound moves backward and forward. We suggested 100 excursions per second, but it might equally have been 20 or 20,000. This rate at which the pressure waves are produced is called the frequency, and is measured in cycles per second. (In fact, it is convenient for physicists and mathematicians to consider frequency not as a derived function but as an entity. So cycles per second are usually called Hertz. 1 cps = 1 Hz. You can then talk about things like changes in sound intensity with frequency without getting into a terminological tangle.)

To go back to the hand shaking backward and forward at 100 Hz, it is clear that it is not a perfect sound source: some of the air slips round the sides as the hand moves in each direction. To stop this happening with a fluid material like air the sound source would have to be much larger. Something the size of a piano sounding board would be much more efficient, losing far less round the edges. But if a hand-sized vibrator vibrates very much faster the air simply doesn't have time to get out of the way. For very high frequencies indeed quite tiny surfaces are efficient radiators of sound.

In real life sounds are produced by sources of all shapes and sizes, vibrating sometimes in extremely complicated ways. In addition, the pressure waves bounce off any reflecting surfaces. Already this begins to belie the statement that sound is really a very simple thing.

But consider a single air particle somewhere in the middle of this sound field. The various pressure waves passing by cause it to move in various directions, to execute a dance which faithfully describes every characteristic of all of the sounds passing through. Faithful it must be, or it would not be able to pass the information on to the air next to it.

All we need to know to be able to describe the sound at that point completely is what a single particle of air is doing. The size of the particle is not critical so long as it is small compared with the separation of the successive pressure waves which cause the movement. We don't have to go *very* small. Indeed, we would certainly not want to go down to the size of individual molecules of air, even if it were practical without grossly disturbing the motion of the molecule being measured. We want to measure an *average* movement which is sufficiently gross to even out all the random tiny vibrations of the molecules, and irregular movements that occur because one molecule may be struck harder than another in the advance of the pressure wave.

What is so delightfully simple about sound is not what happens at each end of the chain, the production of the sound and its perception by the brain, but what happens in the middle. All we need to know about sound is stored in the motion of a single particle, complex though that motion may be.

Equally satisfactory is the fact that it doesn't have to be an impracticably small (or large) particle of air. A short cut to seeing what size is needed is merely to consider the size of the human eardrum. *That* has been designed by evolution to be a suitable size. Consideration of the ear leads us to another simplification. A single ear does not bother with *all* the different directional movements of the air particle; it simply measures the air pressure, which leads us to the idea that a continuously operating pressure-measuring device with a diaphragm approaching the size of the eardrum would be a good instrument for describing just about all we need to know about sound in practical audio-engineering terms. Slightly more complex calculations (involving wavelengths, etc.) confirm this, as does practical experience. For what we have described is the first requirement of a high-quality microphone.

Wavelength

Pressure waves of a sound travel at a fixed speed for a given medium in given conditions, and if we know the frequency of a sound, i.e. the number of waves per second, we can calculate the distance between corresponding points on successive waves, i.e. the wavelength.

Taking the speed of sound to be 1120 feet per second, a sound frequency of 1120 Hz (or cycles per second) has a wavelength of one foot. Sometimes it is more convenient to think in terms of frequency and sometimes wavelength.

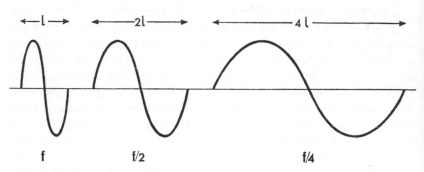

FREQUENCY AND WAVELENGTH. All waves travel at the same speed, therefore, as the wavelength (l) increases, the frequency (f), the number of peaks passing a given point in a second, will decrease in inverse proportion.

Because the speed of sound varies substantially with air pressure, any relationship between wavelength and frequency which doesn't take this into account is only approximate. But for most practical purposes, such as calculating what thickness of sound absorber will be needed to absorb a particular range of frequencies, or estimating whether a microphone diaphragm is small enough to "see" very

MUSICAL NOTES, FREQUENCY, AND WAVELENGTH

Note on piano	Frequency (Hz)	Wavelength
—	14,080	1 in.
—	7,040	2 in.
A^{iii}	3,520	$3\frac{3}{4}$ in.
A^{ii}	1,760	$7\frac{1}{2}$ in.
A^i	880	1 ft. 3 in.
A	440	2 ft. 6 in.
A_i	220	5 ft.
A_{ii}	110	10 ft.
A_{iii}	55	20 ft.
A_{iv}	27.5	40 ft.

The velocity of sound is taken to be 1100 ft/sec—as it might be in cool air.

high frequencies, an approximate relationship is adequate. Particular frequencies also correspond to the notes of the musical scale.

The first thing to notice from this is the very great range in sheer physical *size* these different frequencies represent. Two octaves above the top A of the piano the wavelength is about one inch (or rather less). As it happens this is about the upper limit of human hearing; and the corresponding size is reflected (indirectly) in the dimensions of high-quality microphones. At the lower end of the scale we have wavelengths of forty feet and more. The soundboard of a piano can generate such a sound, though not so efficiently as the physically much larger pipes in the lower register of an organ.

The second point to notice (and the reason for the first) is that for each equal interval, a rise of one octave, there is a doubling of frequency (and halving of wavelength).

Much less obvious is the fact that as the pitch of a sound depends on the size of the object making it, and that size remains nearly constant as temperature increases, then because the velocity of sound is increasing, the pitch goes up. The strings of violins can be tuned, but the vibrating column of air in most wind instruments cannot. So a flute, for example, sharpens by a semitone as the temperature goes up 15° C.

Waves and phase

Still considering a pure, single-frequency tone, we can define a few other variables and see how they are related to the pressure wave.

First we have *particle velocity*, the rate of movement of individual air particles. As this is proportional to air pressure, the wave forms for pressure and velocity are similar in form. But not only that: where one has a peak the other has a peak; where there is no excess of pressure, there is no velocity, and so on. The two identical waveforms are said to be in phase with each other.

The next variable is *pressure gradient*; the rate at which pressure changes with distance along the wave. Clearly, this must have a waveform which is derived from that of pressure, but where pressure is at a peak (maximum or minimum) its rate of change is zero. Again it turns out that the waveform is the same, but this time it has "moved" a quarter of a wavelength to one side. The two waveforms are said to be a quarter of a wavelength *out of phase*.

Another variable, again with a similar waveform, is that for *particle displacement*. This is a graph showing how far a particle

19

of air has moved to one side or the other of its equilibrium position. (This is, in fact, the equivalent in sound of the wave we see on a water surface.) Displacement is proportional to pressure gradient, and is therefore in phase with it. It is directly related to *amplitude*.

These terms are all encountered in the theory of microphones. For example, most microphones are *constant-velocity* or *constant-amplitude* in operation. These names are confusing: they actually

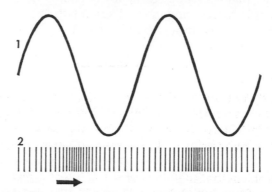

WAVES. Pressure waves are usually represented diagrammatically as lateral waves, as this is very convenient for visualizing them. This also clearly shows the characteristic regularity of the simple harmonic motion of a pure tone. With distance from the sound source shown on the horizontal axis, I represents displacement of individual air particles from their median position. As the particles are actually moving backwards and forwards along the line that the sound travels, the actual positions of layers of particles are as shown in 2 (which also shows the travel of pressure waves). In these diagrams, note that pressure is proportional to particle velocity and pressure gradient is proportional to particle displacement.

mean that the electrical output of the microphone is equal to a constant *times* the diaphragm velocity, or to a constant *times* the displacement amplitude. Constant-velocity microphones include moving-coil and ribbon types; constant-amplitude microphones include electrostatic, crystal, and carbon types. From the point of view of the operator these descriptions are not particularly important: there are high- and low-quality microphones in both categories; the terms are mentioned here only because they may be met in manufacturers' literature. They are, of course, very important to the microphone design or service engineer.

A great deal more will, however, be heard of "pressure-" and "pressure-gradient" operation, as these characteristics of a microphone's action lead to important differences in the way it can be used.

The phase of the signal as it finally appears in the microphone

WAVEFORM RELATION-
SHIPS. 1. Pressure wave.
2. Displacement wave. 3.
Pressure gradient. 4. Particle velocity.

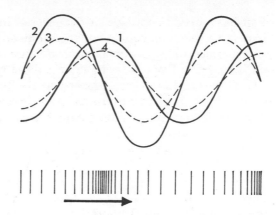

output is clearly not always the same as that of the sound pressure measured by the ear. Fortunately the ear is not usually interested in phase (but see p. 40), so for most purposes the phase of the microphone output is immaterial, and microphones may be interchanged at will.

The only problem that might occur is when two signals which are very similar in form but different in phase are combined. In an extreme case, if two equal pure tones exactly half a wavelength out of phase are added together the output is zero. Normally, however, sound patterns are so complex and different from each other at different points (even in the same studio) that microphones of completely different types may be used together, and their outputs mixed, without too much danger of the differences of phase having any practical effect.

So far we have considered simple tones. If several are present together a single particle of air can still only be in one place at one time: the displacements are added together. If many waves are superimposed the particle performs the complex dance that is the result of adding all of the wave patterns. Not all of this adding

ADDING SOUND PRES-
SURES. At any point the
sound pressure is the sum of
all pressures due to all waves
passing through that point. If
the simple waves A and B are
summed this results in the
pressure given by the curve C.
At 1 there is partial cancellation; at 2 the peaks reinforce.
The resultant curve is more
complex than the original.

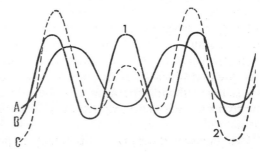

21

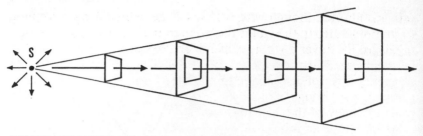

SOUND INTENSITY is the energy passing through unit area per second. For a spherical wave (i.e. a wave from a point source) the intensity dies off very rapidly at first. The power of the source is the total energy radiated in all directions.

together actually results in increased pressure. At a point where a pressure wave is superimposed on a rarefaction the two—opposite in phase—at that point partially (or if they are exactly equal, completely) cancel each other out.

Energy, intensity—and resonance

There are one or two more concepts that we need before going on to consider the mechanics of music.

First, the *energy* of a sound source. This depends on the *amplitude* of vibration: the broader the swing, the more *power* (energy output per second) it can produce. The sound *intensity* at any point is then measured as the acoustic energy passing through unit area per second. But to convert the energy of the sound source to acoustic energy in the air we have to ensure that the sound source is properly coupled to the air, that its own vibrations are causing the air to vibrate with it. Objects that are small (or slender) compared to the wavelength in air that is associated with their frequency of vibration, things like tuning forks and violin strings, are able to slice through the air without giving up much of their energy to it: the air simply slips round the sides of the prong or the string.

If a tuning fork is struck and then suspended loosely it goes on vibrating quietly for a long time. If, however, its foot is placed on a panel of wood the panel is forced into vibration in sympathy and can transmit to the air. The amplitude of vibration of the tuning fork then goes down as its energy is lost (indirectly) to the air.

If the panel's natural frequency of vibration is similar to that of the tuning fork the energy is transferred and radiated much faster. In fact, wooden panels which are fixed at the edges may not appear to have clear specific frequencies at which they resonate: if you tap them they do not usually make clear musical sounds, but instead rather dull ones, though with perhaps some definable note seeming to predominate. In the violin the wooden panels are very irregular, to ensure that over a whole range of frequencies no single will be emphasized at the expense of others. The string is bowed but transmits little of its energy to the air. Instead, it is transferred through the bridge which supports the string to the wooden radiating belly of the instrument.

At this stage an interesting point arises: the radiating panels are not only much smaller in size than the strings themselves but also considerably smaller than some of the wavelengths (in air) that the strings are capable of producing. The panels might respond well enough to the lowest tones produced, but they are not big enough to radiate low frequencies efficiently. And this leads us to consider several further characteristics of music and musical instruments.

Overtones, harmonics, and formants

Overtones are the additional higher frequencies that are produced along with the fundamental when something like a violin string or the air in an organ pipe is made to vibrate.

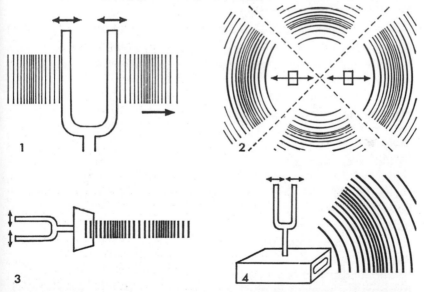

TUNING FORK. 1 and 2. Each fork vibrates at a specific natural frequency, but held in free air radiates little sound. 3. Placed on a wooden panel, the vibrations of the tuning fork are coupled to the air more efficiently and the fork is heard clearly. 4. Placed on a box having a cavity with a natural resonance of the same frequency as the tuning fork, the sound radiates powerfully.

23

On some instruments, such as bells, it may be a problem in manufacture to get the principal overtones to have any musical relationship to each other (the lowest note of a bell is not even distinguished by the name of a fundamental). In others, such as drums, the fundamental is powerful and the overtones add richness without harmonic

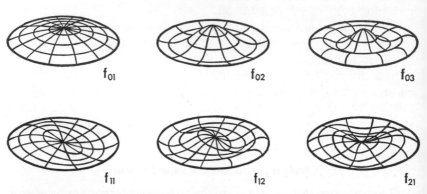

VIBRATION OF A DRUMSKIN (stretched circular membrane clamped at the edges). The suffixes refer to the number of radial and circular nodes (there is always a circular node at the edge of the skin). The overtones are not harmonically related. If $f_{01} = 100$ Hz, the other modes of vibration shown here are as follows: $f_{02} = 230$, $f_{03} = 360$, $f_{11} = 159$, $f_{12} = 292$, $f_{21} = 214$ Hz.

quality; in others again, such as triangles or cymbals, there is such a profusion of tones present that the sound blends reasonably well with almost anything.

But on a string the overtones are all exact multiples of the fundamental, the lowest tone produced. It is this lowest tone which, as with most of the musical instruments, defines pitch. If the string were bowed in the middle the fundamental and odd harmonics would be emphasized, as these all have maximum amplitude in the middle of the string; and the even harmonics (which have a node in the middle of the string) would be lacking. But the string is, in fact, bowed near one end so that a good range of both odd and even harmonics are excited.

There is one special point here: if the string is bowed at approximately one-seventh of its length it will not produce the seventh harmonic. So this is a good point at which to bow, because as it happens the seventh harmonic is the first that is not musically related to the rest—though the sixth and eighth are both members of the same musical family, and there are also higher harmonics produced in rich profusion to give a dense tonal texture high above

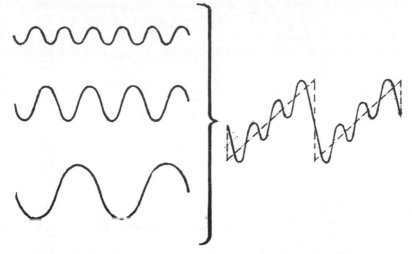

COMPLEX WAVEFORMS. Pure tones may be added together to produce a composite form. In this case the first two overtones (the second and third harmonics) are added to a fundamental. If an infinite series of progressively higher harmonics were added, the resultant waveform would be a "saw-tooth". When the partials are related harmonically, the ear hears a composite sound having the pitch of the fundamental and a particular sound quality which is due to the harmonics; but when the pitches are unrelated or the sources are spatially separated the ear can generally distinguish them readily; the ear continuously analyses sound into its components.

the fundamental. These are all characteristics of what we call string quality, irrespective of the instrument.

The quality of the instrument itself—violin, viola, 'cello, or bass— is defined by the qualities of resonator; and most particularly by its size. But clearly, the shape and size of the resonator superimposes on the string quality its own special *formant* characteristics. Some frequencies, or range of frequencies, are always emphasized; others are always discriminated against. Formants are very important:

THE FIRST EIGHT STRING HAR-
MONICS. (The fundamental is the first harmonic; the first overtone is the second harmonic, etc.) They are all notes in the key of the fundamental, except for the seventh harmonic which is not a recognized note on the musical scale (it lies between G′ and G♭′). If the violinist bows at the node of this harmonic (at one seventh of the length of the vibrating string) the dissonance will not be excited. The eleventh harmonic (another dissonant tone) will be excited, but is in a region where the tones are beginning to be clustered together to give a brilliant effect.

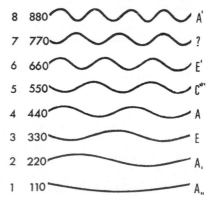

8	880	A′
7	770	?
6	660	E′
5	550	C♯′
4	440	A
3	330	E
2	220	A,
1	110	A,,

25

obviously, in music they are a virtue—but in audio equipment the same phenomenon would be called "an uneven frequency response" and would be regarded as a vice.

There are many other essential qualities of musical instruments.

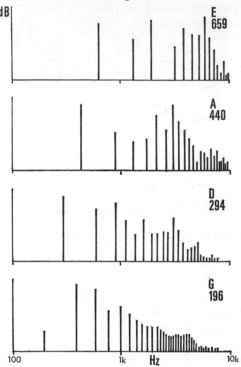

THE OPEN STRINGS OF THE VIOLIN: relative intensities of the harmonics. The structure of the resonator ensures a very wide spread—but is unable to reinforce the fundamental of the low G, for which it is physically too small. Note that there is a difference in quality between the lowest string (very rich in harmonics) and the highest (relatively thin in tone colour).

These may be associated with the method of exciting the resonance (bowing, blowing, plucking, or banging); or with qualities of the note itself, such as the way it starts (the attack) or changes in volume as the note progresses (its envelope). The importance of these is examined in another context on p. 362.

Air resonance

Air may have dimensional resonances very much like those of a string of a violin—except that whereas the violin string has transverse waves, those in air, being composed of compressions and rarefactions, are longitudinal. And whereas radiating sound moves through the air forming *progressive waves,* dimensional resonances stand still: they form *stationary waves.*

These stationary or standing waves can again be represented diagrammatically as transverse waves, though here the waveform chosen is usually that for displacement amplitude. At nodes (e.g. at solid

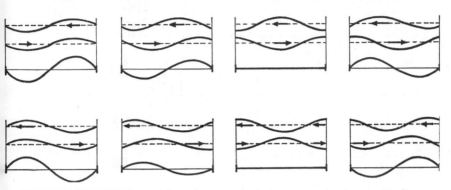

STATIONARY WAVE formed from two progressive waves moving in opposite directions.

parallel walls if the resonance is formed in a room) there is no air-particle movement. At antinodes (e.g. half-way between the walls) there is a maximum movement of the air swinging regularly backwards and forwards along the particular dimension concerned. Harmonics may also be present. Standing waves are caused when any wave strikes a reflecting surface at right angles and travels back along the same path. In practice, not all of the wave is reflected: the result—in effect—is a mixture of progressive waves and stationary waves. In practice, too, little of any sound striking a surface is reflected back exactly along the same path; instead, the crossing paths form a complex interference pattern.

The air in a narrow pipe (such as an organ pipe) can be made to resonate. If it is closed at both ends there are reflections, as at any other solid surface. The fundamental (twice the length of the tube) and all of its harmonics may be formed.

But if the pipe is open at one end resonance can still occur. If the pipe is narrow in comparison with the wavelength the sound has difficulty in radiating out into the outside air. The energy has to go somewhere: in practice, what happens is that a pressure wave reflects back into the tube as a rarefaction, and vice versa. The difference in this case is that only the fundamental (the wavelength of

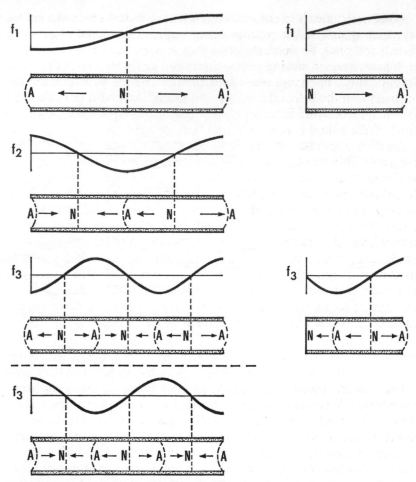

VIBRATION OF AIR COLUMNS. *Left*: for an open pipe, f_1, the fundamental frequency, is twice the length of the pipe. There is a node N at the centre of the pipe and antinodes at the open ends. The second and third harmonics are simple multiples of the fundamental: $f_2 = 2f_1$; $f_3 = 3f_1$, etc. *Left below*: the third harmonic, half a cycle later. Air particles at the antinodes are now moving in the opposite direction, but the air at the nodes remains stationary. *Right*: a pipe closed at one end (i.e. stopped). The wavelength of the fundamental is four times the length of the pipe. The first overtone is the third harmonic; only the odd harmonics are present in the sound from a stopped pipe: f, $3f$, $5f$, etc. In both types of pipe most of the sound is reflected back from an open end for all frequencies where the aperture is small compared with the wavelength of the sound.

which is four times the length of the tube) and its odd harmonics are formed. The tone quality is therefore very different from that of the fully enclosed space, or again, from that of the pipe which is open at both ends.

Wind instruments in the orchestra form their sounds in the same way, the length of the column being varied continuously (as in a slide trombone), by discrete jumps (e.g. trumpet and French horn), or by opening or closing holes along the length of the body (e.g. flute, clarinet, or saxophone). Formants are varied by the shape of the body and the bell at the open end—though for many of the notes in instruments with finger holes the bell makes little difference, as most of the sound is radiated from the open holes.

Another important way in which air resonance may be important is where a volume of air is almost entirely enclosed and is connected to the outside through a neck. Such a device is called a *cavity* or *Helmholtz resonator*. It produces a sound of a single, distinct frequency, an example being the note that can be obtained by blowing across the mouth of an empty bottle. In a violin the cavity resonance falls within the useful range of the instrument and produces a "wolf-tone" which the violinist has to treat with care, bowing it a great deal more gently than other notes. Going back to the example of the tuning fork, boxes may be made up with volumes which are specific to particular frequencies. These make the best resonators of all—but each fork requires a different box.

The voice

The human voice is a great deal more versatile than any musical instrument. This versatility lies not so much in the use of the vocal cords to vary pitch as in the use of the cavities of the mouth, nose, and throat to impose variable formant characteristics on the sounds already produced. It is as though a violin had five resonators, several of which were continuously changing in size, and one (the equivalent of the mouth) so drastically as to completely change the character of the sound from moment to moment.

These formant characteristics, based on cavity resonance, are responsible for vowel sounds and are the main vehicle for the intelligibility of speech. Indeed, sometimes they are used almost on their own.

For the effect of robot speech the formants are extracted from the human voice or simulated by a computer and used to modulate some simple continuous sound, the exact nature of which is chosen to suggest the "personality" of the particular machine producing the sound. (In practice, it is a great deal cheaper to use a real voice as the original and leave computer speech to the machines themselves.)

In addition to the formants, a number of other devices are used in speech: these include sibilants and stops of various types which, together with the formant resonances, provide all that is needed for high intelligibility. A whisper, in which the vocal cords are not used, may be perfectly clear and understandable; in a stage whisper intelligibility carries well despite lack of vocal power.

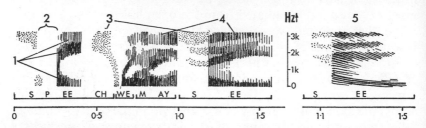

HUMAN SPEECH analysed to show formant ranges. 1. Resonance bands. 2. Pause before plosive. 3. Unvoiced speech. 4. Voiced speech. These formants arise from resonance in nose, mouth, and throat cavities. They are unrelated to the fundamental and harmonics, which are shown in the second analysis of the word "see" (5): the vocal harmonics are falling as the voice is dropped at the end of the sentence, but the resonance regions are rising as the vocal cavities are made smaller for the "ee" sound.

The vibrations produced by the vocal cords add volume, further character—and the ability to produce song. For normal speech the fundamental may vary over a range of about twelve tones and is centred somewhere near 145 Hz for a man's voice and 230 Hz for a woman's. The result of this is that, as the formant regions differ little, the female voice has less harmonics in the regions of stronger resonance; so a woman may have a deep-toned voice, but its quality is thinner (or purer) than a man's.

For song the fundamental range of most voices is about two octaves—though, exceptionally, it can be much greater.

The human ear

The part of the ear that senses sound is a tiny spiral structure called the cochlea. It is a structure which gets narrower to one end of the coil, like the shell of a snail. But unlike the shell, it is divided lengthways into two galleries which join only at the narrow "inside" end. The entire structure is filled with fluid to which vibrations may be transmitted through a thin membrane or diaphragm called the oval window. The acoustic pressures may then travel down one side of the dividing partition (the basilar membrane) and back down the other, to be lost at a further thin diaphragm, the round window.

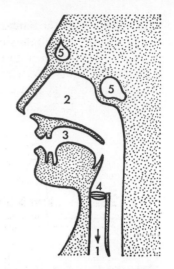

VOCAL CAVITIES. 1. The lungs. 2. The nose. 3. The mouth. (This is the most readily flexible cavity, and is used to form vowel sounds.) 4. The pharynx (above the vocal cords). 5. Sinuses. These cavities produce the formants which are characteristic of the human voice, emphasizing certain frequency bands at the expense of others.

All along one side of the basilar membrane are hairs which respond to movements in the surrounding fluid. Each hair standing in this fluid acts as a resonator system designed to respond to a single frequency (or rather, a very sharply tuned narrow band). The hairs therefore sense sound not as an air particle sees it, as a single, continuous, very complex movement, but as a very large number of individual frequencies. The hairs are so arranged as to give roughly equal importance to equal musical intervals in the middle and upper middle ranges, but the separation is poor at very low frequencies: it is difficult to distinguish between very low pure tones. So (apart from indicating this lack of interest in low notes) a study of the mechanism of hearing confirms that we were right to be concerned with intervals that are calculated by their ratios rather than on a simple linear scale.

This means that for almost any purpose when we are drawing diagrams that involve a wide range of sound frequencies it is best to adopt a scale which gives each doubling up equal space. A regular scale of this sort is called *logarithmic*. The converse of a logarithm is an exponential: something which grows (for our purposes it will be either in time or space) by doubling up at equal intervals. Engineers use exponentials and logarithms as a precise mathematical tool that helps them describe and make calculations about things which behave in this way, but in this book I will use the terms only in a qualitative way: exponential is something which grows in a certain way, and a logarithmic representation is one which converts that growth into a linear (and much more convenient) form.

31

Sound volume and the ear

In considering the ear we have not yet done with exponentials and logarithms: frequency is not the only thing that the ear measures logarithmically.

When the hairs on the basilar membrane vibrate they do so in different degrees, depending on the loudness of the original sound.

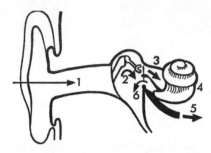

THE EAR. 1. Sound enters via the outer ear and the auditory canal. This channel has a resonance peak in the region 3–6 kHz (the effects of this may be seen on the hearing curves). At the end of the auditory canal is the eardrum, which vibrates in sympathy with the sound. But for low frequencies this is not well adapted to following large excursions. 2. The sound is now transported mechanically from the eardrum across the middle ear via three small bones, the ossicles. These are an impedance matching device: they convert the acoustic energy of the air to a form which is suitable for transmission through the fluid of the tiny delicate channels of the inner ear. The middle ear contains air: this permits the free vibration of the ear drum, and avoids excessive damping of the motion of the ossicles. The air pressure must be equalized (through the Eustachian tube, a channel to the nasal cavity) or the excess pressure on the eardrum will prevent satisfactory vibration. 3. The sound is pumped into the inner ear via a membrane called the oval window. 4. The inner ear is formed as a shell-like structure. There are two channels along the length of it, getting narrower until they join at the far end. Distributed along the upper channel are fine hairs which respond to particular frequencies: when the hair is bent, a nerve impulse is fired. The further the hair is along the canal the lower the frequency recorded. 5. A bundle of 4000 nerve fibres carries the information to the brain, where it is decoded. 6. Pressures in the cochlea are equalized at another membrane to the inner ear: the round window.

And they measure this not by equal increases of sound intensity but by ratios of intensity.

It is therefore convenient to calculate all changes of intensity logarithmically, and the measure that is used for this is the decibel (or dB).

The unit the decibel is derived from is the bel, representing a tenfold change in intensity. But this is an inconveniently large unit, as the ear can detect smaller changes than this. So an interval a tenth of the size has been adopted.

The ratio of intensities in 1 decibel is about 1·26:1. (1·26 multiplied by itself ten times equals 10.) This is just about as small a difference in intensity as the human ear can detect in the best possible circumstances.

As it happens, the ratio of intensities in 3 dB is 2:1. This is convenient to remember, because if we double up a sound source we double the intensity (at a given distance). So if we have one soprano bawling her head off and another joins her singing equally loudly the sound level will go up 3 dB (not all that much more than

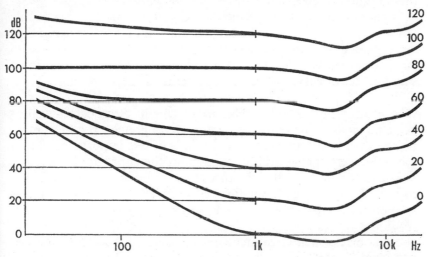

EQUAL LOUDNESS CONTOURS (Fletcher-Munson curves). The scale on the left is intensity: that on the right is loudness; the two are equal at 1 kHz. These typical contours are usually described as "for normal ears", but hearing that is regarded as normal may differ substantially from this (though the threshold of hearing should be reasonably close to the lowest curve). Note that the ear can less easily distinguish differences in volume at low frequencies—except at very high volumes, where an increase in physical pain makes it easier.

the minimum detectable by the human ear). But to raise the level by another 3 dB two more sopranos are needed. Four more are needed for the next 3 dB—and so on. Before we get very far we are having to add sopranos at a rate of 64 or 128 a time to get any appreciable change of volume out of them. To increase loudness by increasing numbers soon becomes very expensive: if volume is the main thing you want it is better to start with something that is louder to start with, such as a pipe organ, a trombone, or a bass drum.

Loudness, frequency, and human hearing

The ear does not measure the volume of all sounds by the same standards. Although for any particular frequency the changes in

33

volume are heard more or less logarithmically, the ear is more sensitive to changes of volume in the middle and upper frequencies than in the bass.

The range of hearing is about 20–20,000 Hz for a young person; but the upper limit falls with age to 15,000 or 10,000 Hz. Sensitivity is greatest at 1000 Hz and above: the auditory canal between the outer ear and the eardrum helps here by having a broad resonance in the region of 2000–6000 Hz

Obviously loudness (a subjective quality) and the measurable volume of a sound are not the same thing—but for convenience they are regarded as being the same at 1000 Hz. Perceived loudness in *phons* can then be calculated from actual sound volume by using a standard set of curves representing average human hearing.

Figures for such things as the noise levels are also *weighted* to take hearing into account. This may refer to electrical as well as acoustic noise. For example, some microphones produce more noise in the low-frequency range: this is of less importance than if the noise were spread evenly throughout the entire audio range.

The lower limit is called the threshold of hearing. It is convenient to regard the average lower limit of human hearing at 1000 Hz as zero on the decibel scale. (There is no natural zero: absolute silence would be minus infinity decibels on any practical scale. The zero chosen corresponds to an acoustic pressure of 2×10^{-5} Newtons per square metre.)

The upper limit to hearing is set by the level at which sound begins to be physically felt. This upper limit is called the threshold of feeling or the threshold of pain.

The ear and audio engineering

At all times when we are dealing with the techniques of sound we will bear in mind the capability of the human ear. The objective measurements of the engineer are meaningless unless we interpret them in this way.

When we fall short of what the ear can accept we should be aware of the fact and be able to give good reasons why. Usually the reason is that the difference in cost would be too great for the difference in subject appreciation.

One question that must be asked is, what is a reasonable upper limit for audio equipment? An individual may be happy to spend money on equipment which has a frequency response which is substantially level to 20,000 Hz (claiming, perhaps erroneously, that his hearing is that good). But for a broadcasting organization this is too high. For most people hearing is at best marginal at 15,000 Hz; it is a waste of money to go above this figure—particularly as costs do not observe the same logarithmic law that the ear does.

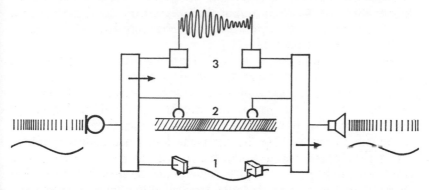

ELECTRICAL AND MECHANICAL ANALOGUES OF SOUND. Recording and transmission systems all use analogues of the original sound wave. 1. Disc. 2. Tape. 3. AM radio.

The octave between 10,000 and 20,000 Hz is by far the most expensive.

On the other hand, one thing the ear does not do is to distinguish phase. So within certain limits phase changes in lines and equipment are unimportant. (This does not, however, apply to the relative phase of the two channels in stereo; these must stay close together.)

A microphone is simply a device for converting sound into electricity in such a way as to retain the information content. The simplest way of doing this is quite adequate: *changes in pressure become changes in voltage; the electrical waveform is the analogue of the acoustical waveform.* The shift in phase that occurs with some microphones should not be important.

The electrical signal can be used to magnetize iron oxide particles on a moving strip of tape, or drive a cutter that will physically inscribe a waveform on a disc. But in these cases the exact waveform will not do. In the case of the disc, assuming that the amplitude of the middle frequencies is about right, the low frequencies would be too big and occupy too much space on the disc. Accordingly, they are reduced in amplitude. The high frequencies, on the other hand, would be of a size comparable to the tiny irregularities in the wall of the groove which are heard as noise. To improve the signal-to-noise ratio the high frequencies must be emphasized.

Provided that these changes are the same for every record, there

35

is no problem: the inverse characteristic is included in the amplifier of each record player, and the original signal is thereby reconstructed. (Actually, in certain crystal pick-ups this is not necessary: the characteristic of the crystal itself is sufficiently close to the recording characteristic that for low- to medium-quality reproduction money may be saved by omitting equalization.) Recording and reproducing characteristics are the same on all modern records and most high-quality record reproducers.

For tape, too, a recording and reproducing characteristic are chosen which are suitable to the physical conditions of tape. Unfortunately, Britain and Continental Europe, on the one hand, and the United States and Japan, on the other, have adopted different standards, so that it is necessary when handling foreign tapes or equipment to ensure that the right characteristic is chosen. These are CCIR in Europe and NARTB in America.

On film, magnetic recording systems are now widely used, but for some purposes optical tracks are still regarded as satisfactory. The big problem here is noise due to scratches or dirt on the film; and again high-frequency pre-emphasis has been used to combat this.

For radio, amplitude-modulation transmission is given no special pre-emphasis—which is perhaps just as well, as the wavebands are so crowded together that the high frequencies often overlap. In

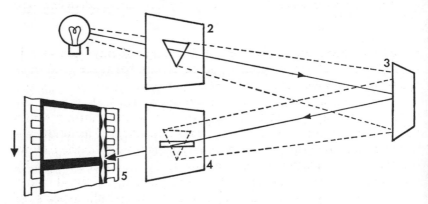

VARIABLE AREA OPTICAL SOUND TRACK—recorded by projecting a lamp (1) first through a wedge shaped aperture (2) (or double wedge in the case of the double track system). The beam is then deflected by a pivoted mirror (3) through a slit (4), and is focused on to a continuously moving film (5). The mirror is attached to a galvanometer measuring sound intensity: its slight movements cause different parts of the wedge to be projected through the slit, thereby producing variations in the width of the sound image. In the absence of sound the mirror comes to rest not in the centre position, but tilted to the end of the wedge. This keeps the clear film area (and therefore noise due to dust and scratches) to a minimum.

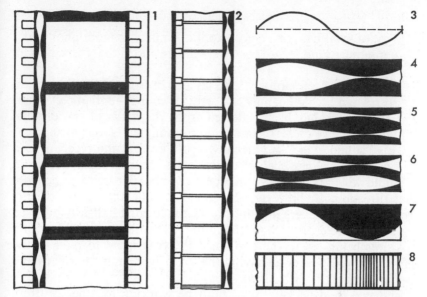

OPTICAL SOUND TRACK. 1. 35-mm film. 2. 16-mm film. 3. Original sound signal shown in optical recordings 4–8. 4. Bilateral variable area track. 5. Double bilateral variable area track. 6. Push–pull track (a special sound reproducing head is required for this. 7. Unilateral, or 50/50 track. 8. Variable density track. The principal problem with optical sound is noise due to dirt and scratches on the track; also distortion in early optical recording systems. For reproduction a lamp is projected through a slit which is then focused on wanted section of film. The transmitted light is picked up by a photocell. Other systems are also available. For the replay of old films on television a 5-kHz filter is often used.

frequency modulation, however, a true high-fidelity response is possible; but HF pre-emphasis is used to combat noise, and once again this is compensated for in every receiver.

Note, however, that this book is not concerned with engineering aspects of the equipment used for recording or transmitting sound information except in so far as they affect operational techniques—although brief descriptions are given, where necessary, in the following chapters. In particular, see Chapter 13 (in which sound quality is discussed in relation to different recording media) and the glossary.

A special engineering problem which affects all aspects of operation is the efficient conversion of electrical signals back to sound energy—in other words, the design and construction of loudspeakers. This problem (also considered briefly in Chapter 13) is probably the principal limiting factor in most sound systems, and should be studied by those with an interest in audio engineering, but is aside from the main theme of this book.

Stereophonic sound

Most of what has gone before applies equally to monophonic and stereophonic sound. A little extra should be added that is specifically about stereo.

The object of stereophony is to lay out in front of the listener, in a natural and lifelike manner, an array of sound—both direct sound and that which has been reflected from the walls of the original studio—which re-creates some real or simulated layout in space.

This "sound stage" is normally reproduced at the receiving end by two loudspeakers, each of which has a separate signal fed to it. A sound which is heard on one speaker only appears to come from that direction. If, however, the sound is split and comes equally from the two speakers it sounds as if it is located half-way between the two. Other directions on the sound stage are simulated by other mixtures being fed to the two speakers. It is usual to refer to the left-hand loudspeaker as having the "A" signal and the right-hand one as having the "B" signal.

The two loudspeakers must both be working together in every sense. But the very minimum requirement is that, if the same signal is fed to both, the cones of both loudspeakers move forward at the same time; in other words, the loudspeakers must be wired up to move in phase with each other. If they move in opposite senses an effect of sorts is obtained, but it is nothing like that intended: for a start, a sound intended for the centre of the sound stage, the most important part, is not in the centre, but is of indeterminate position.

A second requirement is that the loudspeakers be matched in volume and frequency response. If the volume from one is greater than from the other the centre is displaced and the sound stage distorted. If the difference is as great as 20 dB the centre is displaced to the extreme edge of the sound stage. The exact matching of frequency responses is less important to the average listener. Of a number of possible effects, probably the most important is that the differences could draw attention to the loudspeakers themselves, thereby diminishing the illusion of reality.

In the studio, operational staff need to work in fully standardized conditions, sitting on the centre line of a pair of matched high-quality loudspeakers placed about eight feet apart.

It is recommended that the home listener should have his loudspeakers between six and twelve feet apart, but it is accepted that he is quite likely to be off the centre line. The listener who uses a

STEREO BY RECONSTRUC-TED WAVEFRONT. Sound pressures at many points in a large surface, 1, are reproduced at corresponding points in a similar surface, 2. The biggest practical problem in this arrangement is the very large number of channels of communication required.

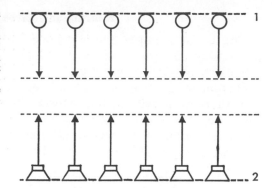

stereogram (with speakers only, say, four feet apart) will also get some stereo effect, but little can be done to compensate him for his choice of less than ideal conditions. Anything that is done for the listener with loudspeakers properly spaced will benefit him too, though to a lesser degree.

Headphones must not be used for monitoring, as the essence of the two-speaker system is that both signals reach both ears from a pair of points somewhere to the front and also that the sound stage is static. Neither of these conditions is satisfied by "stereo" headphones.

Stereo by wave reconstruction is a theoretical alternative to the two-speaker system for the production of stereophonic sounds. In this the wave front in the studio is sensed at a large number of points so that it can be reconstructed at a similar number of points in the listening room. This would require a large number of microphones, transmission lines, and loudspeakers, so in its fullest application the idea is clearly impractical. However, a modified multi-loud-speaker system is used for stereo in cinemas—though for audience near the front individual groups or pairs of loudspeakers dominate.

In *four-channel stereo* there are two further signals which are fed to loudspeakers on the wall opposite to the normal A and B speakers. Early recordings used all four speakers for direct sound, but this is unnatural for all existing music except for rare compositions such as the quartet of brass bands in the Berlioz *Requiem*. The real value of four channels is that *indirect sound*, i.e., reverberation, can be spread in a natural manner to envelop the listener in a way that cannot be achieved by small room acoustics. Experimental work written specially for such a system is another matter; but existing music demands that direct sound comes from one side only.

39

Hearing and stereo

This is not a subject that is completely understood, as in part it depends on interpretation by the brain in the light of experience. There are, however, some clues.

Obviously, differences in signal received at the two ears have something to do with it. For signals off the centre line of the head there are differences of path length resulting in differences of phase which at certain frequencies can be used to give a fairly sensitive measure of angle. This is most effective at frequencies about 500 Hz.

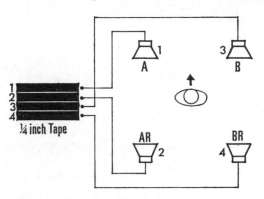

FOUR-CHANNEL STEREO from $\frac{1}{4}$-inch tape. Tracks I and 3 feed the front A and B loudspeakers. Tracks 2 and 4 feed the rear AR and BR loudspeakers. This layout gives the greatest compatibility with existing $\frac{1}{4}$-inch tape systems. (Again for reasons of greater compatibility, the narrower tape used in cassettes should have the front A and B signals on tracks I and 2.)

The head itself begins to produce a screening effect at frequencies about 700 Hz, resulting in differences of amplitude in signals received from one side or the other. Head movements are a further aid to direction finding.

In the two-speaker stereo system it is fairly easy to see how signals from a particular sound source which reach the two loudspeakers *in phase* can simulate this condition fairly well.

Assume first that the source is in the centre of the sound stage and that the listener is on the centre line. The A signal reaches

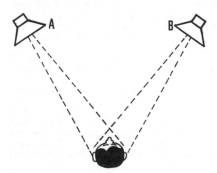

STEREOPHONIC REPRODUCTION USING TWO LOUDSPEAKERS. The position of apparent sources is perceived by phase differences between signals received by the left and right ears. The phase of sounds at the two ears is always the sum of the sounds arriving from the A and B loudspeakers.

TWO LOUDSPEAKER STEREO. The signals from the A and B loudspeakers are equal; the B signal takes longer to reach the left ear, and the A signal takes longer to reach the right. But the combined signal C is exactly in phase: the image is in the centre.

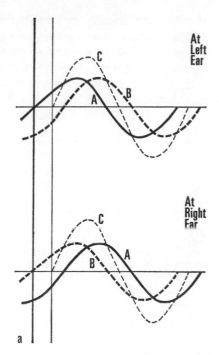

At Left Ear

At Right Ear

a

Signal A is increased. The effect of this is to make the peak in the combined signal C at the left ear a little earlier, and that at the right ear, later. There is therefore a slight delay (t) between the two signals C; this phase difference is perceived as a displacement of the image to the left of centre.

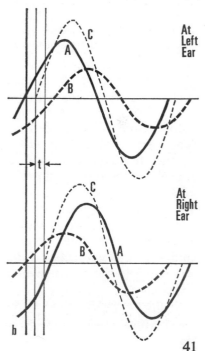

At Left Ear

At Right Ear

b

In these diagrams it is assumed that the listener is on the centre line between A and B, and facing forwards. If, however, he turns his head this will cause the phase difference at his ears to change —but in such a way as to keep the image roughly at the same point in space. If the listener moves away from the centre line the image will be distorted but the relative positions of image elements will remain undisturbed. (These arguments apply in their simplest form only to sound derived from a co-incident pair of microphones.)

41

the left ear slightly before the B signal, and for middle and low frequencies the two combine to produce a composite signal which is intermediate in phase between them. For the right ear the B signal arrives first, but the combination is the same. The brain, comparing the two combined signals, finds them to be the same and places the source in the centre. If the amplitude of the sound from one speaker is now increased and the other reduced the signals

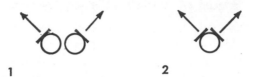

1   2

STEREOPHONIC MICROPHONE. The method of picking up stereophonic sound that will be recommended in this book is the co-incident pair: two directional microphones very close together (1) or in a common housing, usually one above the other (2). The second symbol (as 2) will generally be used. The microphone elements will not necessarily be at 90° to each other.

combine at the ears as before, but the resultant signals differ from each other in *phase*—in effect, it appears as though the same signal is arriving at the two ears at slightly different times. This was one of the requirements for directional information.

If the listener moves off the centre line (or if the volume controls of the two loudspeakers are not set exactly the same) the sound stage is distorted, but there is still directional information that matches the original to some reasonably acceptable degree.

For the basic stereo signal the BBC uses almost exclusively techniques which provide signals at the loudspeaker which are in phase with each other throughout the frequency range, directional information being provided solely by differences in signal amplitude. These are called *co-incident microphone* techniques. The two microphones feeding the A and B information are usually mounted one above the other and are directional, so that the A microphone picks up progressively more of the sound on the left and the B microphone progressively more on the right. Both pick up equal amounts of sound from the centre, the line half-way between their directional axes. Such techniques are relatively simple in theory and work well in practice. BBC stereo programmes have been widely praised; and the advice given in this book is largely based on BBC experience.

If the rear speakers in a four-channel stereo system are used for reverberation only, the delays involved in this will ensure that they do not contribute to the positional information. But for special effects there is clearly scope for interplay between direct sounds from other pairs of speakers. Except for the benefit of the express-train-through-the-living-room brigade of hi-fi enthusiasts such effects should nearly always be used with subtlety. The eternally over-whelming rapidly loses its effect.

Spaced microphone techniques for stereo

An alternative system which is widely used is based on spaced microphones. The original reason for this technique may have been an idea that the sound at two points in the studio was being re-produced at two comparable points in the listening room. The reader is not advised to try to follow the logic of this line of argu-ment: it is both confused and confusing. What really matters is what happens at the point where the listener is sitting. And at that point there is a very complex situation indeed.

Because microphone A is physically nearer to side A its signal is greater in amplitude than that from microphone B: so far, so good. But in addition there are phase differences from subjects that are off-centre, due to the separation of the microphones: these are bigger the farther off centre the subject is. In addition, the phase

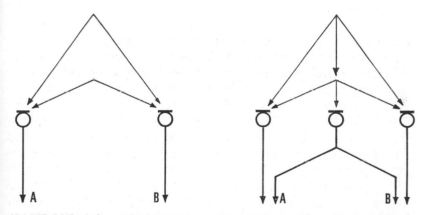

SPACED PAIR. *Left*: a technique which was sometimes used in the early days of stereo. However, for subjects along the centre line the apparent distance from the front of the audio stage is greater than for subjects in line with the microphones; and the farther forward the subject is, the more pronounced this effect is. It is called "hole-in-the-middle". *Right*: the introduction of a third microphone in the centre does a great deal to cure "hole-in-the-middle". Some record companies still use this balance, but it has been discarded by the BBC as lacking the clarity of the co-incident microphone tech-nique. (A and B are the left and right stereo signals.)

differences vary systematically all the way throughout the audio-frequency range.

The theory does not bear thinking about in detail, but clearly there is a great deal of directional information of one sort or another still being offered to the listener, a lot of it being in apparent mutual contradiction. The remarkable fact is that the brain can still sort some sense out of all this, and that spaced microphones can be and are used successfully by many record companies.

The only test that can be applied is the practical one: does it sound all right? It was soon discovered that with pairs of spaced microphones it did *not* sound right: there was "a hole in the middle"; the centre subjects appeared to be much farther away than the outer ones. In order to combat this the usual technique is to add a third microphone in the centre, the output of which is split between the A and B channels.

No theory can adequately support these spaced microphone techniques: the only thing that practitioners can do is to call it an art and learn by experience. The fruits of this experience are valuable to record companies and are rarely disclosed to outsiders. Nevertheless, co-incident microphone techniques work perfectly satisfactorily and the secrets do not have to be handed down from father to son!

Dummy head techniques

Another technique that has been used is a "dummy head" with two pressure microphones in the position of the ears. The analogy is obvious, but less obvious is what this has to do with true stereo. There is indeed some spatial effect, because the signals are very slightly different, especially in high frequencies at which the real head is best at discriminating position. The best test is whether it really works in practice—and the answer is that it does not, certainly in comparison with other stereo techniques.

In France a technique called the "dummy head" is still used, but

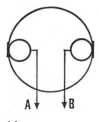

"DUMMY HEAD" stereo technique. Microphones mounted in a solid baffle of head size were tried in the early days of stereo. When used in combination with a two loudspeaker system this cannot be justified on theoretical grounds. A hangover from this is to be found in techniques where a near-coincident pair is spaced at head-width—but this spacing is not necessary.

this now employs directional microphones at head spacing (17 cm). The phase distortion effects are thereby limited to high frequencies, above those at which phase is of importance for direction finding. The positive advantages of such spacing are, however, difficult to see: so, again, the technique is disregarded in favour of co-incident microphones.

Compatible stereo

If the outputs of the two stereo microphones are added together they should provide an acceptable monophonic signal. In fact, the A and B channels can easily be combined electrically into two new signals, A + B and A — B. The first of these is taken as the derived mono signal and the second contains the information that is needed to convert it back to stereo.

There are advantages to using A + B and A — B signals when recording on disc and for radio transmissions.

If a disc is recorded so that A + B corresponds to lateral displacement the mono signal can be picked up on a mono record player without difficulty. To this extent *all* stereo records are compatible. However, the groove is so constructed that a stylus of smaller tip radius and lower playing weight is required—and if the second of these conditions is not met by a mono record player the record is likely to be damaged. The A — B signal is recorded in the vertical plane, by hill-and-dale signals: a mono stylus simply rides up and down but has no means of converting this information into an electrical signal.

For stereo reproduction it is not necessary to separate the signals electrically: it can be done mechanically, as the A and B signals are in effect inscribed in the respective walls of the groove, which are at 90° to each other. The pick-up has two elements, one responding to movements at 45° to the vertical on one side and the other on the other side at a similar angle: these produce A and B signals directly.

Similar advantages are obtained from using A + B and A — B signals in radio. The A + B signal occupies the place in a waveband normally occupied by a mono signal; the A — B signal can then be modulated on to a subcarrier above the main A + B band. It is beyond the scope of this book to give engineering details, but briefly: frequency modulation is generally used, with a subcarrier at 38 kHz; and a pilot tone at 19 kHz is used to stabilize phase relationships (which are very important in this case). Signal-to-noise ratio is slightly (but not appreciably) poorer for a compatible mono signal than for pure mono; the stereo information has, in principle, a substantially poorer signal-to-noise ratio, but as it starts off from such a high standard in FM, the loss does not matter in practice.

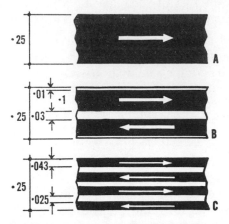

QUARTER-INCH TAPE: standard widths of recording track. A. Full track. B. Half track mono (for twin track stereo and film recording with sync. pulse, the two tracks are recorded at the same time and in the same direction). C. 4-track recording; this is not used professionally for double twin-track stereo (i.e. as shown here, with pairs of tracks recorded in opposite directions by turning round the tape). But with all four tracks recorded in the same sense, using a stacked head, this configuration can be used for 4-track stereo. This is a facility offered by the use of tape which cannot so conveniently be matched by disc (which is otherwise cheaper for the production of large numbers of copies of a recording).

Magnetic stereo recordings

The normal method of recording stereo on magnetic tape is to put the A and B signals side by side on separate tracks. A full-track head will reproduce both together, or alternatively the combined signal can be obtained electrically by adding the two outputs from separate heads.

Two standards are used for width of track. The one which is now more commonly used has a wider unrecorded guard track in the centre to minimize crosstalk. The two standards are compatible.

Quarter-track tape has a pair of stereo tracks in each direction. These are not adjacent: tracks 1 and 3 are recorded in one direction and 2 and 4 when the tape spool is turned over. This is not a mechanically compatible system. But it is in any case not used professionally.

There are several standards for magnetic recordings on film (depending on the number of outputs required). Generally, however, on combined magnetic recordings (i.e. where sound and picture are on the same roll) the master track, recorded where the normal mono track would be, generally gives the equivalent of an A + B signal. Other tracks may then carry separate A and B tracks.

Further details of both magnetic and disc recording systems are given on pages 396 and 407.

Four-channel stereo recordings use a stacked head so that the four signals lie side by side on the tape. Ideally a four-channel system should be compatible with existing two-channel and mono replay equipment; and the microphone techniques used should permit the derived signals to provide acceptable sound when used in the "wrong" equipment.

2

SOUND CONTROL

THROUGH years of intimate daily contact with the problems of the medium, through spending hours each day consciously and critically listening, the professional sound man in the radio or recording studio, in television or film, builds up a considerable body of aural experience, an awareness of subtleties and nuances of sound that makes all the difference between an inadequate and a competent production, or between the competent and the exciting. He hears details that would pass unobserved by the untutored ear. At the same time he develops the ability to handle sound and to mould it into the shape that he requires.

In recent years the tools for recording sound have improved enormously. It is now much easier to acquire the necessary skills; individual operations have become simpler. But because of this there is more that *can* be done. Using tape, complex editing jobs can be tackled. Using lightweight portable recorders or tiny radio transmitters sound can be obtained from anywhere men can reach and many places he cannot.

The tools have not only improved in quality, they have also become much more widely available. It is now possible to find recorders of good quality which may cost only two or three times as much as the cheapest domestic equipment, and yet give technical quality close to that obtained from the best professional equipment.

The easy acquisition of tools, however, does not obviate the necessity for a well-trained ear. Each element in a programme has an organic inter-dependence with the whole; every detail of technique contributes in one way or another to the final result; and in turn the desired end-product largely dictates the methods which are to be employed. This synthesis between means and end may be so complete that the untrained ear can rarely disentangle them—and even critics frequently disagree.

The thing to remember here is that faults of technique are nothing like so obvious as those of content. A good microphone balance in suitable acoustics, with suitable fades, pauses, mixing, editing, and so on, can make all the difference to a programme—but at the end an appreciative listener's search for a favourable comment will probably land on some remark about the subject matter. So it is important to develop a faculty for listening analytically to the operational aspects of a production.

In radio, television, or film the investment in equipment makes slow working unacceptable. Each recording, with its individual problems, has to be technically sound on the first "take". And although each member of the production team is concentrating on his own job, this is geared to that of the team as a whole. The major concern of everyone is to raise the programme material to its best possible standard, and to catch it at its peak.

Studio operations

On the operational side of sound studio work, or in the sound department of the visual media, the various jobs can be listed as follows:

   (i) Microphone balance: selecting suitable types of microphone and placing them to get the most satisfactory sound from the various sources.

  (ii) Mixing: combining the output from the microphone or microphones, tape or disc replay machines, echo chamber, distant studios ("outside sources"), etc.

 (iii) Control: ensuring that the programme "level" (i.e. volume in relation to the noise and distortion levels of the equipment used) is not too high or too low, and uses the medium— recording or radio transmission—efficiently.

 (iv) Creating special effects ("spot effects") in the studio.

  (v) Playing tape and disc into programmes: this includes recorded effects, gramophone records, interviews and reports, pre-recorded sequences, etc.

 (vi) Recording: ensuring that the resultant mixed sound gets on to the tape without any significant loss of quality.

In small American radio stations one additional responsibility may be added to this: supervising the operation of a transmitter which may also be housed in the studio area. Certain minimal technical qualifications are required.

The man responsible for balance, mixing, and control may be a balance engineer or programme engineer; in BBC radio he used to

49

be called a studio manager and is now a programme operations assistant; in television he may be a sound supervisor with sound assistants; in film, a sound recordist or, at the dub, a dubbing mixer. Although in many parts of the world the man doing some of these jobs is an engineer, BBC experience indicates that in radio—and for some posts in other media—it is at least equally satisfactory to employ men and women whose training has been in other fields, because although the operator is handling technical equipment, his primary responsibilities are artistic.

Whatever his designation, the sound supervisor has an overall responsibility for sound studio operations and advises the producer on technical problems. Where sound men are working away from the studio (e.g. on outside broadcasts or when filming on location), a higher standard of engineering knowledge is required. This is true also in small radio stations, where a maintenance engineer may not always be available.

The sound man in the radio studio may also be responsible for recording items if no separate monitoring is required—though for complex recordings (and always in television) a separate recording engineer is employed. In film, recording is a primary function of the sound man around which all of his other activities revolve. The sound man may have one or several assistants: in radio these may deal with effects in the studio, and may play tapes and gramophone records. Assistants in television and film may also act as "boom-swingers", positioning microphones, just out of the picture.

The sound control room

In considering the physical layout that is needed for satisfactory sound control let us look first at the simplest case: the studio used for sound only, for radio or recording.

The nerve centre of any broadcast or recording is the control desk. It is here that all the different sound sources are mixed and controlled. In a live broadcast it is here that the final sound is put together; and it is the responsibility of the programme operations assistant to see that no further adjustments of any sort are necessary before the signal leaves the transmitter (apart, perhaps, from the occasional automatic operation of a limiter to protect the transmitter from overloading).

Apart from the microphones and control desk, the most important single piece of equipment in a studio is a high-quality loudspeaker. For a radio or recording studio is not merely a room in which sounds are made and picked up by microphone; it is also a place where shades of sound are judged and a picture is created by ear.

So the main thing that distinguishes a "studio" from any other place where microphone and recorder may be set up is that two acoustically separate rooms must be used; one where the sound may be created in suitable acoustics and picked up by microphone, and one where the mixed sound may be heard. This second room may be called the "control cubicle" (in BBC radio terminology a "control room" is a lines switching centre).

Tape and disc reproducers, and the staff to operate them, are also in the control cubicle, as are the producer (usually here rather than in the studio with the performers) and the production secretary (who checks the programme timing, etc.).

In television the term "sound control room" has more rationally been applied to the sound area in the gallery of an individual studio. The physical layout is much the same as for sound radio, but with several obvious though relatively minor differences.

The television sound supervisor needs to listen to the programme sound (while viewing it on two monitors—one for programme and one for preview) in a cubicle which is separate from the main control area. This is because the director and his assistant are giving a continuous stream of instructions on an open microphone, which means that the programme sound loudspeaker has to be set at a lower level than is satisfactory for good monitoring.

Studio layout for recording

It is no good finding a recording fault ten minutes after the artist has left the studio. So an important rule in studio work is that every recording must be monitored *from the tape* as it is being made. On the simplest recordings—straight talk programmes in which there are no cues to be taken—programme operations staff can do both jobs, operating the recorder and monitoring the output from a separate replay head.

When the tape is monitored in this way, there is a delay of perhaps a fifth of a second (three inches between recording and reproducing heads at 15 ips) or two-fifths of a second (at $7\frac{1}{2}$ ips). This delay makes it unsatisfactory to combine the two jobs when the programme has any degree of complexity. A fifth of a second does not sound very much—but in fact it can completely destroy the sound man's sense of timing. The perfect fade on a piece of music, for example, may have to be accurate to within a twentieth of a second.

51

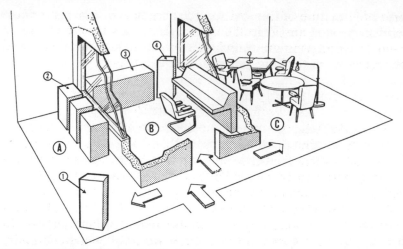

STUDIO LAYOUT FOR RECORDING. Showing recording room (A) combined with studio suite (B and C). All three sections are acoustically separate. Equipment includes 1. Recording engineer's loudspeaker, reproducing output from tape recorders 2 (also used for playing tapes into programme). 3. Gramophone bank. 4. Loudspeaker for monitoring control, mixing, etc. (Small radio studio for magazine programme with interviews, etc.)

These requirements mean that there may be a third acoustically separate room in which the recording engineer can check the quality of the recorded sound. The most convenient plan is to group together the studio, control cubicle, and recording room as a suite. Many programmes use such an arrangement, rehearsing and recording section by section. Each few minutes of the programme is separately discussed, run through, and then recorded; and the results are cut together afterwards. This is probably the quickest way of doing the job, and for many purposes the finished product is perfectly acceptable.

An alternative arrangement is based on the belief of many radio producers that the dramatic contour of a programme is likely to have a better shape if it is fully rehearsed and then recorded as a whole, leaving any faults that occur to be corrected by retakes at the end. Then a more economic arrangement is to divide studio time into two parts, with the recording session limited to a relatively short period. This technique is based on the way studio time is organized for live transmissions. In such cases the recording rooms are remote from the studios, but can easily be linked to any of them at will.

There are various other arrangements, such as that used for certain topical and miscellany programmes which go on the air in the form of a mixture of live and recorded segments. Here last-minute items may be recorded in the control cubicle, with the recording engineer monitoring on headphones for an immediate check, and subsequently on the loudspeaker if time allows.

The broadcasting chain

In broadcasting, the studio suite (studio and control cubicle) forms only the first link in a complex chain. The next link is a continuity suite where the entire programme service is assembled. Part of the material to be presented (or, in some cases, most of it) is played in from tape or disc at this stage.

The output of individual studios is fed in "live", and linked together by station identification and continuity announcements. In the "traditional" system an announcer on duty in the continuity studio is also usually given executive responsibility for the service as a whole, and must intervene if any contribution under-runs, over-runs, breaks down in the middle, or completely fails to materialize. He also presents programme trailers and (in many countries) spot commercials.

In large networks the basic service is put together in the same way, but with greater emphasis on precision of timing, and the output of the network continuity appears as a source in the regional (or local

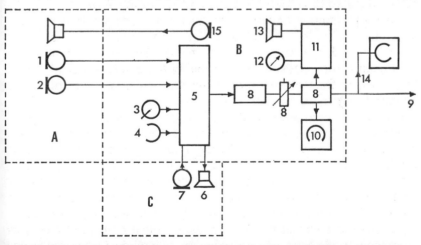

THE STUDIO CHAIN. Block circuit diagram of studio (A) cubicle (B) and echo chamber (C). Showing: 1, 2. Microphones. 3. Disc reproducer. 4. Tape reproducer. 5. Mixer. 6, 7. Echo loudspeaker and microphone. 8. Main gain amplifiers and control fader. 9. Studio output. 10. Tape recorder. 11. Monitoring amplifier. 12. Programme meter. 13. Monitoring loudspeaker. 14. Feed to external recording room. 15. Talkback circuit.

station) continuity which feeds the local radio transmitter. The links between the various centres may be landlines or radio links.

In television the broadcasting chain is substantially the same as for sound radio, except that in the presentation area there may be

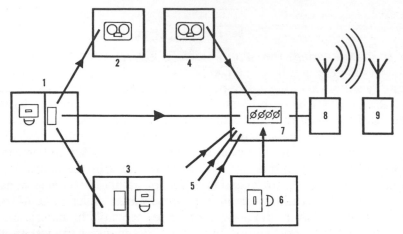

THE BROADCASTING CHAIN. The studio output may go to a recording room or it may provide an insert into a programme compiled in another studio—or it may be fed direct to a programme service continuity suite. Between studio, continuity, and transmitter there may be other stages: switching centres, boosting amplifiers, and frequency correction networks on landlines, etc. The diagram shows: I. Studio suite. 2. Tape recording room. 3. Remote studio. 4. Tape reproducing room. 5. Other programme feeds. 6. Continuity announcer. 7. Continuity mixer. 8. Transmitter. 9. Receiver. This diagram shows the chain for sound radio, but the television chain is similar, though it may be a little more elaborate. For example, the presentation studio (7) may have both a small television studio and a separate sound studio for an out-of-vision announcer.

both a small television studio and a separate—usually very small—sound booth for out-of-vision announcements. Use of the sound booth means that rehearsals of more complex material in the main studio do not have to be stopped completely for routine—or unscheduled—programme breaks.

Broadcast automation systems

But it is the side of broadcasting which deals with the transmission of programme material (as distinct from its creation) that has seen the greatest changes in recent years. The introduction of broadcast automation systems at many stations has meant the elimination of a large amount of routine work which can be taken over by machines under the control of a switching unit or, for the more ambitious systems, a small on-line computer. The computer is not unduly expensive; indeed, taking staff costs into account, it may actually

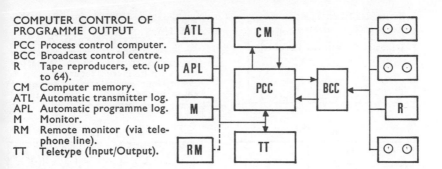

COMPUTER CONTROL OF
PROGRAMME OUTPUT
PCC Process control computer.
BCC Broadcast control centre.
R   Tape reproducers, etc. (up
     to 64).
CM   Computer memory.
ATL Automatic transmitter log.
APL Automatic programme log.
M   Monitor.
RM   Remote monitor (via tele-
     phone line).
TT   Teletype (Input/Output).

be cheaper than automated machinery. Routine operation of the computer is simpler than that of the control unit.

Automation could, in principle, clear the way for a higher proportion of the jobs that remain in broadcasting to be creative in nature. In practice, however, it is equally possible for such systems to be used as an almost complete replacement for creative effort, because once they are set in operation they are capable of providing a simple basic service to a standard format with a minimum of computer programming.

Sound control desks

Sound control desks used professionally have become progressively more complicated with time; and television desks are even more complex than those used in radio. This is partly because television is so much more complicated in its operations; for example, movement within a single scene may require a performer to appear on a number of different microphones where in sound radio he might work to one only. In addition, television studios cannot be so

TYPICAL 15-MINUTE SEQUENCE
using simple automatic broadcast control system.

Number	Event
4	"Personality" tape: opening or "mood" announcement
1	Musical item from "show opener" tape
6	Spot commercial
2	Musical item from second tape
5	Time check
3	Music (third category)
9	Fade-in of closing music
6	Spot commercial
5	Time check and station identification
10	Switch to network

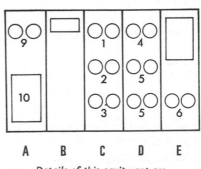

Details of this equipment are shown on pp. 56–57

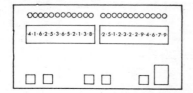

This uses manual switching on a main control unit (*left*) and on several of the items that are used with it. Here a sequence of up to twenty-four events may be set up in advance; and recycling may be started at any predetermined time.

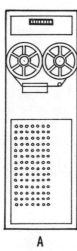  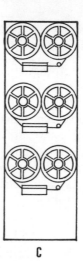 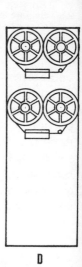

A   B   C   D

A. AUTOMATIC NETWORK SWITCHING. This unit has (at the bottom) a bank of switches which may be preset for times at which the local station must switch to and from the network. (When computer control is used, this bank of switches is not required, as the information is held in the computer memory.) Below this is a fill tape which starts automatically at a given time before network switching: it starts mute (on "dead-roll" or "prefade") and fades up when other programme material ends. At the top of the rack is a digital clock: this cues the switching operations.

B. CONTROL UNIT: *see above*.

C. PLAYBACK MACHINES. Each tape contains a series of items—musical items or speech segments. In normal use one item only is played, at the end of which 25-Hz signal cues the control unit to make its next selection (or in the event of failure, a silence sensor in the control unit exercises the same function). The tape then automatically sets up at the start of the next item.

D. AUDIO CLOCK. Two tape transports are used: one has prerecorded announcements for every even minute of the programme day; the other covers the odd minutes. Time is given to the nearest half minute. Each replay machine in turn is on standby for a minute, then automatically moves forward to the next announcement.

Besides giving the time, the audio-clock announcements may include station identification and prerecorded musical backings. Tapes with suitable voice and music (e.g. guitar or harp) can be supplied with the equipment. From the same source, a service of music programme tapes can also be supplied (often with built-in announcements over music). These are used in the automatic reproducers appearing in different combinations so that the same sequence is not precisely repeated. The station may (if it so wishes) record its own local "personality" items on a separate tape.

This (or the computer controlled system) is ideal for "streamed" radio programming in which each station produces a narrow range of material interspersed with commercials, with or without network switching. Minimal talent is required, except for local news and sports coverage, and for locally produced commercials.

AUTOMATIC BROADCASTING SYSTEMS:

II: COMPUTER CONTROL. A teletype or IBM typewriter input is used with a very simple computer language (using plain-language radio terminology). The computer is "conversational", that is, it gives an immediate response to each instruction.

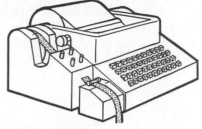

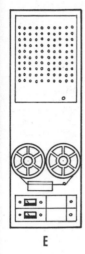 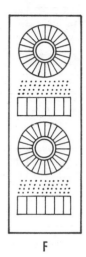 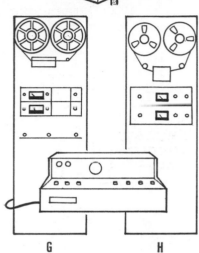

| E | F | G | H |

E. RANDOM SPOT LOCATOR. The tape contains up to a hundred items. The fifty pairs of switches allow up to fifty Items to be selected in any order (including repeats). The main use for this is to allow spot commercials to be introduced into the programme material in an order that is predetermined by manual switching. After playback of each selection the next in sequence is automatically set up.

F. CARTRIDGE CAROUSELS. Each wheel holds up to twenty-four cartridges, and a sequence of fifty-two playbacks can be set-up manually. Again, the main use is for the replay of spot commercials.

G. RECORDING UNIT (mono or stereo) with (inset) remote recording panel.

H. STATION LOG. Very low speed recorder notes time and transmission details.

When used with computer control instead of the control unit the pre-set switching panels on items E and F are not required; this information is stored in the computer. For use with computer control fast retrieval systems are also available: a pair of multi-track broad tapes (of the type also used for computers) are fitted in a single rack, and any item (which may be up to 70 seconds long) can be located and set up for replay in 15 seconds. This allows continuous replay from random access.

The computer used is a specially developed real-time (process control) machine. It has a fairly large requirement for information storage, but as it does not require facilities for high-speed handling of large amounts of material it need not be expensive. Depending on the size of the memory either a day or two's programming or a whole week can be held in the computer at one time. Where day-to-day working is adopted, each day's schedule can be retrieved on punched tape, then re-inserted and up-dated a week later.

Computer control gives great facility for commercial operations: in particular, once a given number of commercial slots has been programmed into a day's schedule, the computer can at any time be asked for information about what spots are still available; further, this information can be requested from a distance, using normal telephone circuits.

specialized as those in sound radio; a smaller number of very much more expensive studios must each be capable of producing a wider range of programmes. As there is a huge financial investment both in the studio itself and in its equipment for producing pictures, there

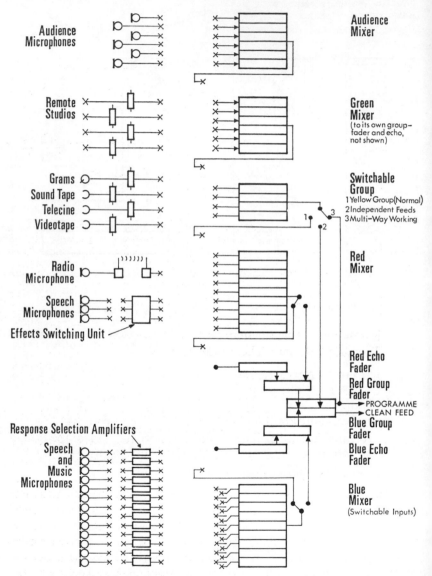

STUDIO SOURCES, SWITCHING AND CONTROL DESK. This would be a complex desk for a radio studio, but very simple for television.

can be no question of production capacity being hampered by any lack of versatility on the sound side. The equipment (and the staff) must be capable of handling a very wide range of problems.

In a typical BBC television studio the capacity of the mixing

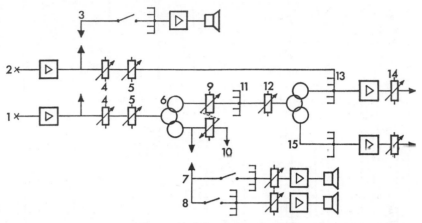

CONTROL DESK: FACILITIES ASSOCIATED WITH FADERS. 1. Normal microphone input. 2. Independent microphone (signal to be mixed in after group faders). 3. "Prehear" side chain. 4. Microphone balance attenuator (preset). 5. Channel fader. 6. Hybrid transformer, splitting the signal. 7. Foldback side-chain (to studio floor loudspeakers). 8. Public address side-chain (to audience loudspeakers). 9. Echo mixture switch. 10. Echo feed. 11. Star mixer combining a group of sources. 12. Group fader. 13. Star mixer combining groups and independent sources. 14. Main gain control. 15. Clean feed chain (supplying feed of all groups except independants).

desk is conditioned by the number of possible sources—though not all will be used at once. There may be available:

(i) Up to 60 microphones.
(ii) 4 disc reproducing desks.
(iii) 2 tape machines.
(iv) 1 reverberation plate (and access to 3 echo rooms).
(v) 16 outside source lines (from telecine and videotape sound reproducers, other studios, outside broadcasts, overseas circuits, the public telephone system and so on).

Sound radio has sources of all of these types, though with less microphones and perhaps more disc and tape reproducers. As sound radio studios are more specialized, so too, are the desks.

The latest equipment adopted by the BBC is of modular construction, with units which can be used in either radio or television desks (or, with the addition of a few supplementary controls, for stereo). For each source there is a separate amplifier-fader channel

59

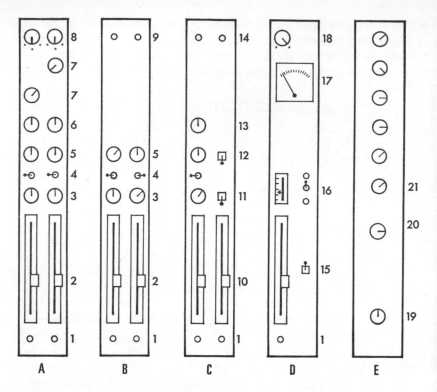

MODULAR UNITS FOR SOUND OR TELEVISION CONTROL DESK. (Note that as each module carries two channels the basic units can be also modified for stereo sound. In this case the fader knobs will be clipped together in pairs.) A. Individual source module (two channels). 1. Prehear buttons. 2. Quadrant faders. 3. Public address volume control. 4. Selector switch: p.a. before or after fader. 5. Feedback volume control. 6. Echo feed control. 7. Preset attenuator for coarse setting of volume from source. 8. Group selector switch. B. Group control (accepts all individual faders switched to it, plus group echo output). 1–5. Controls as for A. 9. Emergency change-over push button for group amplifier (using public address feed amplifier as spare). C. Master control module. 10. *Left*: clean feed fader. 10. *Right*: main fader. 11. Public address feed "cut" switch. 12. Foldback feed "cut" switch. 13. Pre-hear overall volume control. 14. *Left*: main amplifier emergency change-over push-button. 14. *Right*: "split working" push button—permits the two channels to operate independently, different groups being selected to each. (In this condition the desk is working, in effect, as two separate control desks.) D. Echo control module (see "Echo" chapter). 15. Echo "cut" switch. 16. Echo plate controls (to change reverberation time), with scale. 17. Peak programme meter, indicating volume of signal sent to echo room or plate. 18. Switch selecting output from one of two groups as echo feed. E. Audience Mixer. 19. Volume control for loudspeakers in audience area. 20. Group fader for audience microphones. 21. Six carbon track faders for audience microphones (this is a low level mixer in which the relative levels should be preset, if possible). A–E represent only a selection of facilities available on a modern desk used by the BBC. However, many control desks will have less facilities than this.

which in the most recent version is very versatile and can, by pre-setting the amplifier gain, be adjusted to accept sources which differ in level by as much as 90 dB. Ancillary controls mounted in line with their respective quadrant faders provide a range of additional facilities:

Pre-hear: press-button operation allows circuits to be heard on a small auxiliary loudspeaker before being faded up. Outside sources need to be checked in this way, and also microphones which may have been replugged during the programme. If a microphone has been knocked or is otherwise suspect, it can be checked.

Echo mixture: a switch controls the ratio of direct and echo feeds (see p. 336).

Foldback: a switch (which may be pre-set and left) feeds the output of the fader (in combination with any other faders selected) to a studio loudspeaker for cue (or possibly mood) purposes. Levels are adjusted to avoid a degree of pick up on open studio microphones which is sufficient to produce coloration of the sound, unless such coloration is required.

Public address: like foldback, this allows a selection of sources to be fed to the studio, in this case to loudspeakers in an audience area. The loudspeakers used are often of the "line-source" type, radiating most of their power in a plane at a right-angle to the line, and so can be directed to avoid excessive pick up by open microphones.

Group selection: for convenience of handling, individual channels

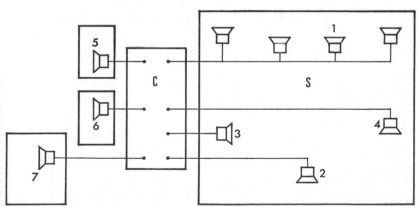

LOUDSPEAKERS IN A TELEVISION MUSICAL PRODUCTION. C. Sound control room. S. Studio. 1. Audience (public address) system. 2. Foldback of recorded sound effects. 3. Special feed of vocalist's sound to conductor. 4. Special feed of rhythm group to vocalist. 5 and 6. Echo feeds. 7. Remote studio.

are gathered into "groups", each controlled by its own sub-master fader. The groups are designated by different colours, such as yellow, green, red, blue, and orange. The group selection switches are used to choose the routing required. The manner in which such routings can be selected is complex, and varies from design to design. Facilities are also provided for some of the channels to be able to by-pass all of the group channels to become independent channels, or even the main control, in which case they can be used for *multi-way working* with *clean feed*—see p. 311. Other facilities commonly provided include *equalization* or *response-selection* circuits (see pp. 351–353). On the BBC desk described there are sufficient (pluggable) response selection units for about a third of the available channels, but on other types of mixer (and particularly in popular music studios and dubbing theatres) there is one on every channel. A number of *effects units* (see p. 349) and *compressor/limiter* units (see p. 429) may also be available.

On a typical television desk there may be provision for 40 sources of various kinds, *plus* three separate echo channels, *plus* a six-channel low-level submixer for audience coverage. For television only, the desk also incorporates a *telephone effects switching unit* (see p. 348) which can be used to ensure that telephone quality is always on the out-of-vision end of a telephone conversation.

A facility that is also available on BBC television control desks (although very rarely used) is a *prompt-cut*. This is push-button operated from the studio floor by an assistant floor manager acting as a prompter. It can be used in dramatic productions to cut the output of all of the main studio microphones but leaving tape, grams, and outside sources unaffected. To avoid a "dead" period during the prompt, studio atmosphere from a distant open microphone (or from a tape loop) is cut in at the same time to bridge the pause.

Faders

The fader is the principal means of control provided by a mixer desk. It is the one item that is in continuous use, as the operator monitors the relative levels of the sounds from different sources, and at the same time keeps up a running compromise between the desire for a dramatic or natural contrast in levels and the need to make the best use of the medium by keeping the overall volume as high as possible (for example, by keeping the percentage modulation of a radio carrier wave to as close to 100 per cent as possible).

62

Such continuous use rules out certain types of design. For example carbon resistance faders (for many purposes perfectly satisfactory) cannot be used because all too soon they become worn and subject to occasional crackles as the slide contact moves along the carbon track; and wire-wound resistors, given a little more time, are subject to the same fault. But in any case it is not particularly easy to make them work logarithmically over a wide range—and this is an essential feature of any fader used for the precise control of audio signals.

High-quality faders have separate studs which the sliders move on to in turn; and between each successive pair of studs there is a fixed

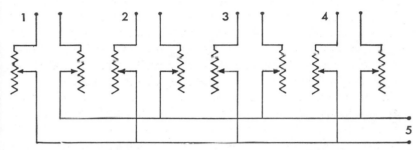

SIMPLE LOW LEVEL MIXER (an even simpler type has the fader on one wire only). 1–4. Inputs. 5. Output. One disadvantage of this layout is that the channels cannot be controlled independently: as fader 2 is opened, the signal on channel 1 finds an alternative path and is reduced.

network of resistors. Even with the most expensive faders the mechanical design has been the most difficult part: to create studs and sliders with surfaces which give good contact, with low wear, and which are unaffected by dust, moisture, and other contaminants from the atmosphere.

A very large number of geometric configurations of resistances is possible in stepped faders. Some of the simplest designs have been used in low-level mixers (i.e. those in which there is no pre-amplifier, and where there is no integrated circuit design involving both faders and amplifiers), but the results have been regarded as unsatisfactory because as a second or third channel is faded up in a mixer it provides an alternative path for signals from the other sources. In consequence, the faders are not independent in operation: as fader 2 is brought up, there is a slight loss in signal 1, so that its fader must be adjusted to compensate for this. As a result, the next requirement for channel faders used in mixers has been that they present a constant (and preferably rather high) resistance to other signals "looking back" into them.

One layout which does this is the "bridged-T"—which in its time has been the main type of fader adopted for professional equipment. Other characteristics of the bridged-T are that it also presents a constant impedance to the source and—as relatively high resistances are involved—it requires more amplification in the circuit than do more simple faders. The bridged-T was combined with high-level mixing so that the chain now consisted of microphone, pre-amplifier, channel fader—after which the signals from the mixers

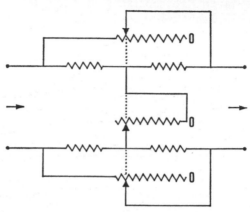

BRIDGED-H FADER. A complex 3-slide balanced fader that was used for many years in BBC sound equipment. The three slides move together on a common shaft: when they are at O the fader is closed. A simpler design is the Bridged-T fader: in this, one of the wires follows a straight-through path and the effect on the signal paths is unbalanced.

were combined to pass through the first of the main gain amplifiers, the main control, and then via the second main amplifier to line.

The main type of fader used for many years by the BBC was a rotary bridged-H fader (a balanced bridged-T, i.e. one with faders in both wires of the two-wire line from the microphone); this required three sliding contacts, three sets of studs, and three resistance networks. It was, needless to say, very expensive, and—perhaps at least partly because of the large number of studs—not always free from noise.

Current BBC designs have simplified the fader itself, but made it more complex in its co-ordination with the associated amplifier. A quadrant fader with two stud-by-stud potentiometers is used (as may also be used for a bridged-T), but here the operational ranges of the two are displaced so that they are effective at different input levels; and one of the two components (that which is used for most of the lower part of its range) actually operates *between* two successive stages of the channel amplifier, so that for a high input signal

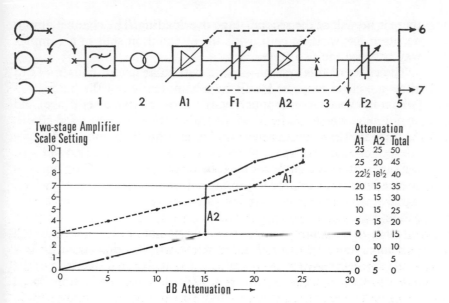

Two-stage Amplifier
Scale Setting

dB Attenuation →

A1	A2	Total
25	25	50
25	20	45
22½	18½	40
20	15	35
15	15	30
10	15	25
5	15	20
0	15	15
0	10	10
0	5	5
0	5	0

Attenuation

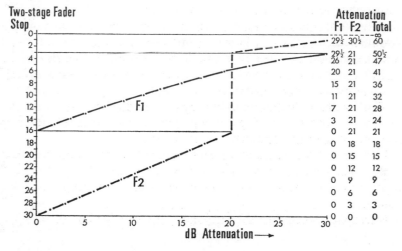

Two-stage Fader
Stop

dB Attenuation →

Attenuation

F1	F2	Total
29½	30½	60
29½	21	50½
26	21	47
20	21	41
15	21	36
11	21	32
7	21	28
3	21	24
0	21	21
0	18	18
0	15	15
0	12	12
0	9	9
0	6	6
0	3	3
0	0	0

COMPLEX FOUR STAGE CHANNEL AMPLIFIER-FADER COMBINATION (A1–F1–A2–F2) that has now been adopted as standard for BBC sound equipment. It is shown (*top*) in combination with other elements used with it in a microphone channel: 1. RF filter. 2. Balancing transformer. 3. Insertion jackfield (for response selection amplifier, compressor, limiter). 4. Public address and pre-hear feeds. 5. Public address, pre-hear and foldback feeds. 6. Echo feed. 7. Direct signal (to group fader). A1 and A2 are parts of a single amplifier. Attenuation is applied first to stage 2, then to stage 1, then to both together. The channel can accept both high-level and low-level sources. F1 and F2 are two tracks on a single quadrant fader: for a channel fader, F1 and F2 also operate at different settings, as shown. This extends still further the useful range of input levels that the channel will accept without distortion. (But for group and main controls F1 and F2 both operate over the whole range of the fader.)

65

there is no risk of the second stage overloading. The channel amplifier itself has variable gain, with the attenuation split in a complex way between the two stages.

The effect of this system—in the particular layout chosen—is to allow a control range of 90 dB by a combination of the fader itself (which in effect is continuously variable over a narrower range) and an amplifier which can be preset at 5-dB steps over a range of 50 dB. As a result, the same channel can be used not only for an ordinary microphone picking up a sound of normal or low volume but also for the high-level signal from a tape or disc reproducer or outside-source line; or again, for anything in between, such as a high-level signal from a microphone balancing a trombone section or a bass drum.

In many older mixers high and intermediate level signals are fed to a mixer channel through attenuators which reduce them to low level: the newer system avoids this. A particular characteristic of the former BBC equipment was that 600-ohm junctions were used throughout, but this has now been abandoned in favour of high-impedance fader module outputs working in to low-impedance desk inputs: this means that the operator can link any number of channels in to a group without appreciably affecting the levels in the circuit, and as a result the desk is very much more flexible.

In most faders the studs are separated by about $1\frac{1}{2}$ dB over the main working range, perhaps increasing to 2 dB over the lower half of the range, with broader spacing still for the two or three steps at the bottom end (to avoid too sharp a drop as the signal is cut off completely). A difference in level of $1\frac{1}{2}$–2 dB is only just appreciable on pure tones in the middle and upper middle frequency range, so nothing more precise than this is really necessary for

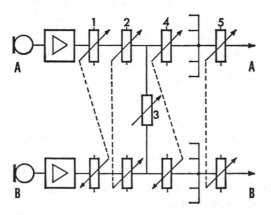

STEREOPHONIC CHANNEL. 1. Preset control to balance output between microphone elements. 2. Ganged fader. 3. Image width control. 4. Channel offset control (this displaces the complete, spread image). 5. Group fader.

TWO MONOPHONIC CHANNELS USED AS A STEREO CHANNEL. 1. Faders clipped together. **2.** Panpots: these will be preset to give the correct scale of width for the source covered (i.e., they are being used not as panpots, but as width and offset controls).

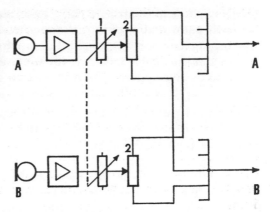

ordinary working. (However, for those who think it is, in mono an intermediate setting can be found as the sliding contact bridges successive studs. But note that this position of the slider is more critical than for the on-the-stud position, and should in any case be avoided for stereo.)

The stereo channel

A stereo channel into which the output of a coincident or spaced pair of microphones is fed has separate paths for the A and B signals, but with the principal faders ganged, so that the signals are automatically faded up and down together. However, in high-quality equipment the faders are stepped at intervals of about 1½–2 dB between successive contacts. If the slide on one side makes contact with a stud a fraction of a second before that on the other, the image will momentarily shift laterally. This is called fader "wiggle" or "flicker". Higher standards of engineering design are called for in stereo than in mono, but even this will not eliminate the occasional particle of dust that may be present on one side or the other. The operator must therefore move the fader smoothly and never too slowly from stud to stud; and he must be aware by the feel of the fader where the danger points are between each successive pair of studs.

Additional controls are used on stereo sound channels:

(i) Image width control. This cross-links the A and B signals, feeding controlled and equal amounts of the A signal to the B channel, and vice-versa. As this cross feed is increased the image width narrows. However, if at the same time the phase is reversed the image width is increased.

67

(ii) Displacement control. This is a ganged pair of faders, one on each path, and working in opposition to each other, so that turning the knob has the effect of moving the whole of the image on this particular channel sideways. This control can also be used to give apparent movement to a static but spread source.

In a stereo channel the main pair of faders and the width control could also be put into the circuit in a different way: by first converting A and B into M and S signals and operating on these. When M and S signals are faded up or down there is no "wiggle"; instead, there might be minor variations in image width—but this is less objectionable. In addition, image width can now be controlled simply by changing the proportion of M to S signal. In particular, image width can be increased without change of phase. However, after passing through the channel fader and the width control the M and S signals must be converted back to the A and B form before passing through the displacement faders.

Monophonic channels in stereo: the panpot

When monophonic sources are introduced into a stereo mixer their output has to be "steered" or "panned" to a particular position

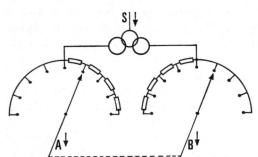

PANPOT. A signal (S) from a monophonic source is split and fed to two potentiometers (shown here in simplified form). The ganged faders attenuate one of the signals only. When these are fed to the A and B channels the image of the source is displaced accordingly —in this example to the right of centre.

in the stereo image. For this a panoramic potentiometer or "panpot" is used. In films with stereophonic sound this is used to follow the movement of individuals whose speech has been recorded in mono.

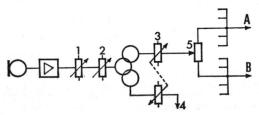

PANPOT USED WITH MONO-PHONIC MICROPHONE IN STEREO BALANCE 1. Preset control. 2. Fader. 3. Echo mixture switch. 4. Echo feed. 5. Panpot.

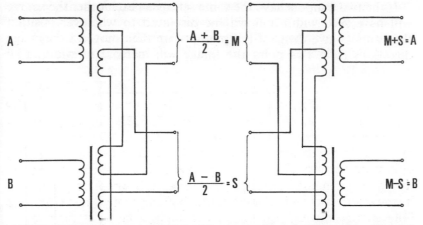

STEREO SIGNALS: an electrical method for converting A and B signals to M and S, and vice versa. "M" is equivalent to the signal that would be obtained by directing a single suitable monophonic microphone towards the centre of the audio stage. It therefore gives a mono output which can be used by those without stereo loudspeakers. The balance between centre and side subjects, and between direct and reverberant sound will not necessarily be as good as for a normal mono balance. "S" contains some of the information from the sides of the audio stage.

Where full stereo equipment such as that described earlier is not available, two monophonic channels with panpots can be linked together in pairs to form a stereo channel into which A and B microphone signals can be fed. The two channel faders are generally physically linked: adjacent quadrant faders are clipped together. Image displacement and width are then controlled by the relative settings of the two panpots.

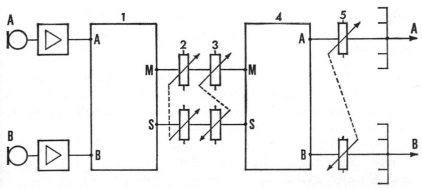

STEREOPHONIC CHANNEL WITH CONTROL ON THE M AND S SIGNALS. I and 4. Signal conversion circuits. 2. Channel fader. 3. Image width control. 5. Offset control. This arrangement is less subject to fader "wiggle"—a momentary displacement of the image which occurs when the studs of A and B faders are not reached simultaneously.

If the two panpots have the same setting as each other the source will have zero width and will be displaced to whatever position the panpots give them. If the panpots are then moved in opposite directions from this point the image will increase in width. Full

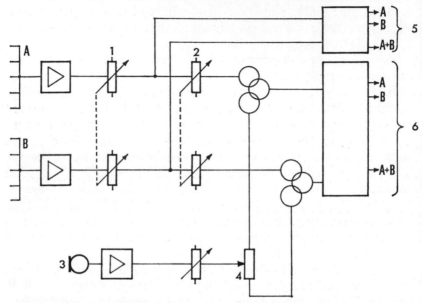

STEREO CONTROL DESK: clean feed and output arrangements. 1. Master control. 2. Main control. 3. Separate microphone (e.g. for announcer). 4. Panpot. 5. Clean feed (i.e. without sound from separate feed, 3 and 4). 6. Fully mixed control desk output. A + B signals are generated in order to check the quality and volume of the compatible mono signal.

width is given by steering one of the signals to the A side and the other to the B side in the mixed signal; but this can, of course, be done without a panpot at all.

Studio communications

In both radio and television there are sound circuits which are used for local communication only. The equipment and circuity involved in this can be surprisingly complex; in the BBC Television Centre studios have loudspeaker talkback from six positions in the control gallery and headphone talkback from seven.

The use of headphones carrying an independent talkback circuit between control cubicle and studio may also help a recording session or radio transmission. Their use may range from the full-scale relaying of instructions (as occurs in television productions), through supplying a list of questions to an interviewer, to monitoring a feed of some separate event in order to give news of it.

In radio studios there can sometimes be quite complex systems of talkback (to the studio) and "reverse talkback" (an independent feed from the studio, sometimes associated with a "microphone cut" key, so that a speaker can cut himself off the air and ask for information or instructions).

When a studio microphone is faded up it is usually arranged that the studio loudspeaker is cut off (except for talkback purposes during rehearsal). This can be done automatically by having a relay-operated switch which can only be "on" if all the faders are turned right out. Convenient though this arrangement is, it may mean that an artist in the studio does not hear the last second or so of his cue to speak. For most purposes this will not matter, but when the man in the studio is a regular broadcaster with a good sense of timing it will be possible to dispense with signals (hand or light) and let him take his own cues—listening to the music or other recordings on headphones. This leaves the artistic control of the timing of the programme to one person, which is always desirable.

In the automatically operated system used in radio this means that the studio loudspeaker is always live when all the microphones are out, but for television positive action is needed to feed anything to studio loudspeakers.

In television the complexity of the communication systems is so much greater, partly because there are so many more people involved, each with a different job to do, and also because they need to occupy about half a dozen acoustically separate areas, including the studio itself and the main control gallery where the director sits and the vision is mixed. The director speaks to the floor manager over a local VHF radio circuit; the floor manager hears him on a "deaf-aid" type of single earphone; the cameramen and others in the studio hear him on headphones.

In his separate room the sound supervisor can hear high-level and high-quality programme sound. In addition, on a second much smaller loudspeaker (so that it is distinctly different in quality) he will hear the director's instructions and reverse talkback from his own assistants on the studio floor.

Lighting and camera control also generally have a (third) acoustically separate area. They will have their own talkback system to appropriate points on the studio floor; and cameramen in their turn have reverse talkback to them. In the control gallery itself the technical manager has in front of him what is in effect a small telephone exchange for communication with all points concerned technically with the programme: this includes control lines to outside sources, and also to the videotape recorder and telecine operators (who, in their own areas, hear the director's circuit as well as programme sound or their own output).

Television outside broadcast vans sometimes have sound control, director and camera control all in the same tiny area of a vehicle, as a result of which adequate monitoring may not be possible where high-quality sound (e.g. of a musical event) is required. In these cases sound is "de-rigged" and set up in some convenient room; or alternatively, a separate sound control van may be used.

In both radio and television outside broadcasts the sound man provides communication circuits between the various operational areas (e.g. commentary points) and the mobile control room. This often takes the form of local telephone circuits terminating at special multi-purpose boxes which also provide feeds of programme sound and production talkback. (On television outside broadcasts the latter is particularly for the stage manager.) Additionally, field telephones may be required at remote points.

3

PLANNING AND ROUTINE

How much detailed planning should go into the technical handling of a radio or television production? The answer to this question will vary with every script and every producer or director who enters the studio.

In general, the right amount of planning is that which ensures that all of the necessary technical facilities are available; and the right amount of operational instructions marked on the script is that which indicates in a general way the necessary fades, mixes, effects, echo, and so on for a preliminary run through. Experienced operators (under clear direction) will be able to continue from there.

What follows applies particularly to radio or television studio work, whether for recording or broadcast, and also (with a few minor changes of terminology) to gramophone record recording sessions. Film dubbing is similar, but involves additional techniques which are described later (p. 488).

During the first run-through of a complex programme the programme operations assistant or sound supervisor will glance ahead down each page of script, quickly estimating what will be needed; he will see that the right microphones are up and will get the "feel" of the overall and relative levels and such things as fades and mixes. At this first attempt the results will probably not be exactly right, but each operator will quickly note down anything out of the ordinary on his script in some sort of personal shorthand: it might be the level of a recorded effect, perhaps, or the setting for the first words that are to be heard in a fade in. In radio, a few extra words may have to be written in for a fade, or a small adjustment made to an actor's distance from the microphone: questions which will be referred to the producer. But in television, the sound man will be more inclined to try to solve his problems with the minimum of reference to the director. Often the

73

difficulties here will be more severe; generally revolving around the question of how to get adequate sound coverage without the microphone getting in the picture or throwing shadows.

Nothing should ever be too precisely set prior to the recording or transmission: in a play, for example, actors' emphases and levels may be substantially different on the "take" as they let loose their final reserves for a performance.

Where difficult sequences or unusual ways of doing things have to be fitted in, pre-rehearsals and perhaps pre-recordings of the complicated parts will be necessary; but these themselves can be rehearsed and recorded in the same not-too-calculated way. It is merely a question of breaking up awkward material into tractable segments.

Many radio and television programmes are, of course, still broadcast live. The live broadcast seems to have a greater sense of occasion: the once-for-all feeling brings out the best in many people, and repeated takes for a recording may never reach the same standard. And if things do go wrong in a big way, as occasionally they must ... well, the audience delights in and treasures the moments that show the efficient machine on the other side of the box is run by fallible human beings.

Planning: radio or sound recording

In comparison with television, the planning that is necessary prior to the arrival of the production and sound staff and performers in the radio or recording studio is simplicity itself.

When there is a number of studios available (and sometimes even when there is not) the request for the allocation or booking of a sound studio will normally be accompanied by a brief description of the use to which it will be put: e.g. the number of speakers or musicians, and if necessary a brief indication of the type of balance: e.g. "discussion—6 people" or "novelty sextet with vocalist".

Except for the very simplest programmes, the production office will prepare a running order or script which (except for very topical material) will be sent to the programme operations staff in advance. Many productions follow an established routine such that the minimum of discussion is necessary before arriving in the studio; but if there is any doubt, or any unexplored aspect to the production, the sound staff should contact the producer in advance.

For example, before a recording session involving an unfamiliar musical group the balancer should discover from the production office what instruments are to be expected and what sort of balance

74

the producer wants to hear: if, for example, it were required to sound like an existing record the balancer would have to listen to it. He would want to know whether the music is to be featured, or for background use; whether it is to be brilliant and arresting in its sound quality, or soft and undisturbing; or whether it is to be heard with announcements at certain points within it, or applause (which would thicken the texture of the sound).

The recording arrangements will also be discussed: the probable duration, whether it is to be stop–start or single take, the tape speed that will be used for the recording and the number of copies required; and any special arrangements for handing over the tapes, or for transfer to magnetic film stock.

Any unorthodox or experimental layout will have to be discussed with the musical director in sufficient time for studio attendants to be given a plan showing the provision of chairs, music stands, acoustic screens and other furniture; and studio instruments such as the piano. The balancer will also set up the microphones (or check their layout) and arrange their output on his desk, working out and plugging up a suitable grouping of channels, with frequency correction units, compressors and limiters in the appropriate circuits and echo and tape delay or any other devices ready for use.

And finally, before the musicians arrive in the studio he will check that all of the facilities that he is likely to use are actually in working order: this also includes things like the talkback and any foldback circuits and the levels of the loudspeakers associated with them. At which point he should be ready to greet the players as they arrive, and to show them their positions.

The television planning meeting

Whereas in radio most problems prior to the studio day can be dealt with without special meetings, in television it is normal for the director and some of the technical staff to meet several weeks before a programme. The size of such meetings varies. For a simple programme it may involve the director, the lighting man, the technical manager (who is in direct overall charge of all technical services other than lighting and sound); and for all but the most straightforward productions the sound supervisor. More complex programmes may also require the presence of the floor manager, senior cameraman, the costume and make-up supervisors, and other people dealing with house and studio services, such as audience management, the assessment of fire risks, allocation of dressing

75

rooms, and dealing with any special problems in catering that might be posed by breaks at unusual times or the arrival of distinguished guests.

From this planning meeting, and from subsequent contact with the director and the production team—and perhaps even from direct observation of outside rehearsals—it is the sound man's responsibility to assess what will be required from his own particular department, and to arrive in the studio with all non-standard equipment and facilities booked and available, knowing how the sound coverage is to be obtained, and ready to set up the microphones and other equipment to go ahead with the rehearsal on schedule.

But the planning meeting also serves a secondary purpose: it is a forum within which ideas can be proposed and discussed and then either adopted or abandoned. Often there will be conflicts of interest as each department tries to do its best for the director, conflicts that must be resolved in compromise and co-operation. As the director listens to the various suggestions that are made, he will generally arbitrate rapidly between conflicting aims. Sometimes he will make slight modifications to his original ideas to make things easier for everybody; but if in a complex situation he does not, it is usually the sound man who has the trickiest problems to solve— many more television directors put picture first and sound second than the other way round. Sound men who make light work of complex problems are therefore valued members of any production team—but those who accept unsatisfactory compromises and then explain after the programme that poor sound was an inevitable result are not likely to be thanked.

At the planning meeting the sound supervisor starts to build—or re-establish—a working relationship with several other members of the team that will carry on throughout the term of the production.

The sound supervisor and the television director

The sound man will meet various types of director (and producer). Some will be able to outline their needs concisely and precisely— and once they have said what they want they will stick to it. Such directors are easy to work with and are not likely to waste others' effort, demand extra staff who are not used or cause the sound supervisor to requisition equipment and resources which in the event are not needed.

Another director may have a few of these obvious virtues, but still be worthy of all the help the sound man can give him. This is the type who likes to maintain as much flexibility as possible up to a late stage in the preparation of a production. As a result, he will then be able to take full advantage of elements of the production that turn out better than could reasonably have been expected, and cut his losses on ideas that do not shape up well. In these circumstances the sound man may have to plan his resources by intelligent anticipation, expecting some degree of wasted effort. With this sort of director the means can be justified by the results.

Inexperienced directors will also need a great deal of help from the sound man, but should be persuaded towards simpler solutions so that things are less likely to go wrong; and also so that if (or, perhaps, when) they do the resulting situation is relatively easy for everyone (including the director himself) to cope with.

For certain types of production (in particular, plays) the sound supervisor will have read a script even before the planning meeting, and will already have a number of questions that he wants to ask the director—who for his part will probably be ready to give the answers without even being asked. The director will probably start by giving a general outline of what the programme is about, and what his own production attitude is to this. His descriptions may be technical or artistic in style. In the first case he may not be very accurate (but do not assume that this will always be so!); in the other the technical staff may require a fertile imagination to turn far-fetched analogies in to concrete requirements.

The sound supervisor should pay particular attention to descriptions of the visual style: a "strong" style with fast cutting, mixtures of close and wide shots, unusual angles and split focus (which may be adopted to establish an appropriate psychological mood or simply to jazz up a weak story line) could require different sound coverage from a simple and more logical visual style. As he listens to this he will be looking at plans—scale drawings of the studio layout—which should already be available to show the areas in which the action will take place.

At this stage the director may welcome advice on sound coverage. Effective solutions to some of the more difficult problems may, indeed, involve him in extra effort before arriving in the studio—by making pre-recordings, for example—or extra expense for additional equipment or staff; and the director should have the opportunity to decide whether the effect he is seeking is worth this.

Even before the planning meeting the studio sound supervisor may have been consulted on ways of linking film to studio. If this is done before film is shot, mismatches of background sound or voice quality can sometimes be avoided.

The basic running order for rehearsal and recording is also settled at the planning meeting: here the director will need to hear whether there is sufficient time allowed for the various things that he is asking for, or whether (for example) a recording break will save equipment and staff and therefore perhaps money. (But to bring a television studio to a halt for ten minutes for the lack of one man may be an expensive economy.)

Sound and the television designer

It is the job of the television designer to produce the scale plan of the proposed studio layout. The sound supervisor will need to be expert in interpreting such plans, to which symbols for his own equipment (booms, slung and stand microphones, and loudspeakers) will be added later by the director after their positions, boom tracking lines, etc., have been discussed with the sound man.

Rostra, ceilings, doors, archways, and alcoves will all be accurately marked on the plan, as will features such as tree-trunks or columns which may obstruct a boom arm, or areas of floor which are covered with materials which make it impossible for sound equipment to follow. Stairs and upper working levels will also be shown. Scale models are sometimes made up for complex productions; these can be of considerable assistance in providing an immediate interpretation of the plan.

But at this stage the plan will not be final: a ceiling may be redesigned to be made of an acoustically transparent material so that a microphone can "see" down from above; a tree may be chopped off at 7 feet 6 inches so that a boom can swing over it; or a potted plant may be strategically repositioned so that it can bear improbable fruit in the shape of a concealed microphone.

Certain types of set reflect and therefore reinforce sound: this is particularly true of flattage built of wood. Such flats may help musicians or other performers, but can cause trouble if they are arranged in a semicircle so that they focus sound. The extra difficulties in the placing of performers and microphones can generally be overcome, but an added complication is that such a setting will also focus reflected noise from other parts of the studio.

Scenic projection equipment such as that for back projection of film or television pictures (the latter derived from the output of telecine, videotape replay, or other live cameras) may itself be noisy.

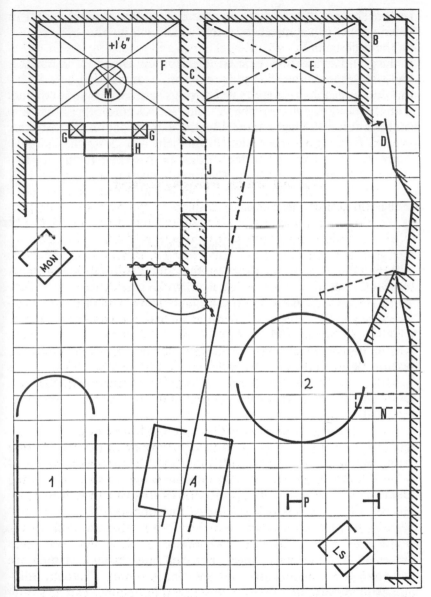

STUDIO PLAN. Corner of set in a television studio, including cameras (1 and 2), boom (A), loudspeaker (LS) and Monitor (MON). These are drawn exactly to scale as they would be on a standard $\frac{1}{4}$ inch to the foot studio plan. Here, Camera 1 is a small motorized tracking camera (other cranes require much more space). Camera 2 is a pedestal camera: the circle represents the working area it requires. The boom is capable of further extension (to reach beyond the back wall of the set) if required. Details of set: B. Single clad flattage. C. Double clad flattage. E. Ceiling over (broken lines). F. Rostrum, 6 × 4 feet, at 1 foot 6 inches above studio floor level. G. Columns. H. Steps. J. Arch. K. Drapes on gallows arm. L. Swinger (flat which can be pivoted in and out of position). N. Bracket. P. Lighting barrel over (these will be shown all over the plan). M is a slung microphone which has been hung in this corner because the high columns make it difficult for the boom to reach.

The positioning of such equipment and the need or otherwise for it to be blimped is yet another matter which will involve both sound man and designer.

Floor and other surfaces used in television are often painted or made up to look other than they really are. Consequently, footsteps are often a problem: there may be footsteps that are audible (and wrong) when they should not be heard at all, and others that are wanted but for which the natural sound is quite inappropriate to the picture. Here again the designer can help sound by the suitable choice and treatment of surfaces. This is discussed further in the chapter on sound effects, as are the sound-effects treatment of wind, rain, and fire in television, and also "practical props", such as telephone and intercom systems.

Planning microphone coverage

In planning television sound coverage the first question is almost invariably: can it be covered by a boom? The microphone which can be swung or moved in and out on its telescopic arm, and then turned to any horizontal or downward angle, is with its operator a "microphone with intelligence" which can cope with so many situations without appearing in vision that it must be regarded as the principal method of sound pick-up in television.

Static or "personal" microphones may also be used to augment booms, or in place of them. Also, for many types of television programme, microphones may appear in vision. The conventions that govern this, the details of different types of microphone that conditions their choice, and also the techniques for their use for speech and music are all described in chapters 4–7.

At the planning stage the sound supervisor must decide how many booms are required and how they must be moved about the studio to cover the various sequences, remembering that some sequences may require more than one boom. At this stage, too, it is necessary to anticipate minor changes in the script which could have a big effect on the sound man's ability to cover a scene. For example, it may seem reasonable to plan for speeches by two performers who are separated from each other to be covered by a single boom because the script indicates there is a few seconds between the two during which the boom can be swung. But supposing that at a late stage it becomes apparent that dramatically a pause is wrong at this point and must be cut? If that happens, the sound man may find himself in a very difficult position: he is the one person who is standing in the way of a good performance. Once in a lifetime is usually enough to convince any sound man that this is a problem which he must plan to avoid.

A boom may require no operator (if it is simply to be placed in relation to a performer who does not move), one operator (for normal operation), or two (if it must be tracked at the same time). The

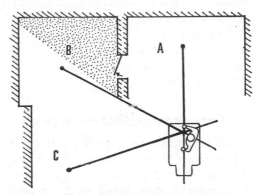

BOOM OPERATOR IN DIFFICULTIES. If the operator of a boom positioned for use in area A is immediately asked to swing to area B, he is blind to all action which is obscured by the wall, and so cannot judge the angle and distance of his microphone. If the action continues to area C, again without movement of the dolly, the operator is now supported only by his boom and a toe-hold on the platform. Alternative provision must be made for coverage of B and C before the position for A is decided; this requires planning as camera positions and lighting are also involved.

initial booking of this staff, and their management throughout the rehearsal and recording will be a responsibility of the sound supervisor.

He must ensure that an operator is not placed in such a position that he is unable to follow the action properly because the performers move into a corner of the set which he cannot see in to. He also has a responsibility for the operator's safety: he must arrange that the boom pram does not get angled so that as the operator swings the arm he runs out of platform to stand on; with certain types of boom this can happen very easily.

He must agree with the senior cameraman on the relative positions of cameras and boom pram; and particularly in the case where large camera mountings such as cranes need freedom of movement.

Above all, he must plan to ensure that lighting will not throw shadows of microphones or booms on to performers or visible parts of the set.

81

Booms and lighting

To see how shadows may be caused it is necessary to understand a little about television and film lighting.

Performers are generally lit by two frontal lights. One, the "key", is the main light: it is the strongest, and casts sharp-edged shadows. The second frontal light is the "fill": ideally this should be from a source that has a lower power, but a large area (e.g. an array of relatively weak lamps) so that it does not cast a hard-edged shadow. In addition there is "rim" lighting from the rear to outline the figure and separate it from the backing (which is lit separately).

For portrait close-ups the camera and the key light will not be widely separated in their angle to the subject (though they must be far enough apart to give satisfactory modelling to a face). If the boom were also to come in from somewhere about the same angle there would obviously be a danger of a shadow being cast down on the subject's face. So the first rule for boom placing is that *the boom should come in from the side opposite to the key light* (perhaps at 90–120° to it).

Provided that the same camera is not used for wide-angle shots, there should be no danger of the shadow being seen against the backing. This leads us to the second rule: *long shots should if possible be taken from an angle well away from the key light.* Then, if the boom is coming in from roughly the same angle as the long-shot camera the shadow will be thrown to the side of the shot and not into it.

In television, lighting often has to serve several purposes in order that a scene can be shot from a number of different angles. For example, it is often arranged for a light that is used as a key for one

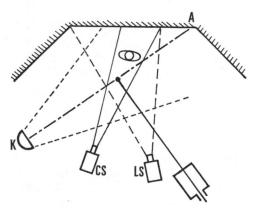

LIGHTING, CAMERAS AND MICROPHONE: the ideal situation. The close-shot camera has near-frontal key lighting (from K). The microphone shadow is thrown on to the backing at point A where it appears in neither picture. Few cases are, however, as simple as this.

person to become the rim for another standing close to and facing him.

But as scenes become more complex in their camera coverage, what may be relatively easy to arrange in shot-by-shot filming may become tricky in television, and compromises must be made. A third rule (which will generally make things easier) is that *plenty of separation should be allowed between the main action and the backing*, on to which a boom shadow could easily fall. This is, in any case, desirable for good back lighting.

As a corollary to this, note that the boom arm should not be taken close to a wall or any other vertical feature of the set that will appear in vision. If the arm is close enough, even the soft fill lighting will begin to cause shadows. Slung microphones may also cause shadows; again, the danger will be greater if they hang close to a wall.

Occasionally there is no convenient way round having a microphone shadow, perhaps from the fill light, in vision: it may be the only way to get close enough for good sound. In this case the shadow is less likely to be seen if the microphone is kept still on the particular shots concerned and also if it is arranged to fall on a point of fussy detail rather than an open plain surface.

In the planning stage, if the action seems to be getting too close to the backing, the lighting and sound supervisors are likely to join together in an appeal for more room to work. To such a strong demand the director will usually accede. The director may have several courses open to him: he may change the action or the timing of the words spoken; he may move action props away from the wall; or he may arrange with the designer for the working area to be physically enlarged.

In practice, shadow problems rarely result from bad planning:

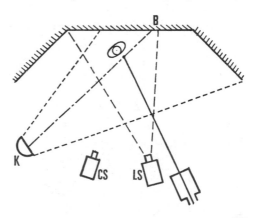

LIGHTING, CAMERAS, AND MICROPHONE: Problems. The actor has now moved 18 inches closer to the backing, and the microphone, to get good sound, has followed. With the key light and long-shot camera in the same positions there is now a shadow visible at B in the long shot.

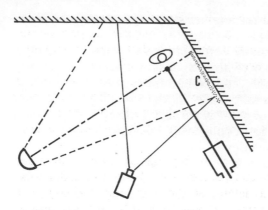

BOOM SHADOW. With a boom close to a long wall there is a danger of a shadow along it (C) on wide shots. If the boom is very close, even soft "fill" lighting will cast a shadow.

they are such a headache to everyone in a team that several people are likely to be on the lookout for any such possibility. But they can result from last-minute changes of plan on which consultation is impossible, or as a result of a series of minor compromises which finally build up to a big one. In such situations the normal cooperative spirit between sound and other departments may wear thin.

Standard routines for the recording session

Before considering individual techniques in greater detail there are a number of more or less related aspects of studio organization which should be touched on first. Apart from the placing of microphones and checks on balance and level there are a variety of other routines and practices which help to keep a recording session running smoothly.

Here are some of the main elements of these:

(i) The line-up procedure: this is to check that for a standard signal at the start of the chain all meters read the same, showing that nothing is being lost or added on the way. When extra equipment is introduced into the system this too must be lined up. For example, when a recording session or transmission follows a period of rehearsal, time must be set aside for line-up tests before the "take" or live show. A sound studio schedule will normally allow some ten or fifteen minutes for this. Television line-up (involving similar procedures for the video signal) will last much longer, so there will be adequate time for sound line-up within this. (However, in the more complex television desks provision can also be made for line-

84

up tone to be sent to line without disturbing normal sound rehearsal circuits.) Where a recording machine is part of the studio equipment, or permanently linked to it, the line-up procedure may be abbreviated.

(ii) Timing the programme: a constant check is kept on timing, using either a script, a timed cue-sheet, or the recording form. All recording faults are noted on this, as is any other information which may be useful in editing, including all details of retakes.

(iii) Documentation: this is a chore, but may save time and avoid confusion later. On quarter-inch sound tapes a leader tape (giving summarized details of the contents) and a trailer (several feet of coloured tape—preferably red—to give a visual indication of the end) may be cut on to the recording.

(iv) Cueing: in radio a system of signals and other methods of liaison must be established at an early stage in the proceedings. This will save time during the recording, when as much of one's attention as possible should be given to the programme; being able to pass directions to the studio may also save retakes. In television these are passed through a floor manager or studio manager who will be permanently on headphones. (In a television studio—as distinct from an outside broadcast location—it is best for these to be fed from a radio transmitter, with a single "deaf-aid" earphone replacing headphones.) Reverse talkback from studio floor to director is also needed. All these are, of course, sound engineering responsibilities.

(v) The management of applause. This may seem an odd subject to include as a "standard routine", but in fact in programmes

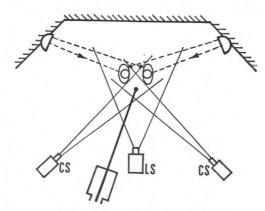

REAR KEY LIGHTING. Here two people facing each other are both satisfactorily lit, and there is no danger of microphone shadows as these are thrown to the front of the set. But this solution is less satisfactory for colour television than it was for black and white, as more light is needed than for frontal keying.

with an audience, reaction in the form of applause or laughter can be an unknown quantity which can vary from one group of people to the next in a totally unpredictable way—despite the fact that in any invited audience there are many people (perhaps most) who much prefer to be told what is expected of them rather than to produce a spontaneous and "genuine" reaction. To leave such people to work out whether they are supposed to applaud all the time or not at all is simply perverse.

Each of these subjects will be discussed in detail in the following sections.

Line-up

Each organization has an established routine, and so must the individual person working on his own; but the exact details may vary.

The procedure adopted for a BBC sound radio recording illustrates the form that such routines may take. At the end of the rehearsal, and a few minutes before the scheduled recording time, the programme operations assistant rings the recording room on the "control line" (in fact an ordinary telephone circuit, but called a "control line" to differentiate it from the broad-band "music line" along which the programme is fed). Details of the recording are checked, and the equipment is lined up on a standard 1000 Hz tone sent from the studio. The standard used is 1 milliwatt in 600 ohms: this is called "zero level" and is equivalent to 40% modulation at the transmitter (so that 100% is about 8 dB above this). At all stages in the chain the tone should give the same steady reading on all meters, and some of it is recorded on the tape, so that this process can be repeated when the tape is replayed.

Then "level" is given: someone in the studio is asked to read a few lines. This gives the recording engineer an additional check on quality, the last he will hear direct from the studio, for, just before he starts recording, he must switch over to monitor the output of his own recorder.

After a final check that everybody is ready, the programme operations assistant announces over the studio talkback (which also goes to the recording room), "We'll be going ahead in ten seconds from … now!" He switches on a red light (which indicates to people outside the studio that a recording or transmission is in progress); he fades up the studio, flicks a green cue-light—and the recording is under way.

In television the procedure is a little more complicated. In the line-up period video and sound lines are tested (again the BBC uses "zero level" tone for sound line-up). At the start of the actual recording a VT clock mounted on a board giving programme details is shown for the thirty seconds or so prior to the start of the required material. On an open microphone the floor manager calls "30 seconds ... 20 seconds ... ten–nine–eight–seven–six–five–four–three ..." and then both sound and picture are faded out for the last three seconds. As an additional sound check, ten seconds of tone (lined up to zero level at the studio control desk) is sent to line between the counts of 20 and 10, and this, too, is recorded on the tape as a final reference level.

At the end comes the reckoning: the duration is checked, and possible retakes discussed. If these are necessary further cues are given and they are recorded at the end of the main programme tape, to be edited later. Apart from documentation, the recording session is now complete.

A live transmission differs from a recording in several details, but principally in that just before the studio goes on the air the end of the preceding transmission is monitored. The sound man hears his cue and once his own transmission is under way he switches back to studio output (and since at every stage between studio and transmitter everyone is listening to the programme as it leaves his own point in the chain, the source of any fault can be rapidly located). The same switching procedure is adopted at the end of the transmission.

BBC stereo is lined up slightly different from mono: each channel is lined up 3 dB below zero level. This is convenient in that at all points where the combined A+B signal is fed to mono equipment, line-up tone appears at the normal mono zero level.

The main thing to be noticed in these cases is that nothing is haphazard, though the routine may be got through in a casual and relaxed sort of way; and nothing is inessential.

Programme timing

By "timing" we mean two things: the tyranny of the stop-watch over broadcast programmes, and the artistic relationship in time of the various elements of a programme. In much radio work, particularly in America and other countries where commercials have to be fitted into the schedules with split second precision, and also where there is networking, each second must be calculated. An

American director once described himself as "a stop-watch with an ulcer".

Today the stop-watch is probably no longer in his hands, but for some purposes is built in to the operation of an automatic control unit or possibly a computer. For the purely mechanical business of getting programmes, short items, music, commercials, time checks, and station identification announcements on the air many stations are now almost entirely automated, leaving the staff formerly occupied in this work free for more useful work, such as (according to the manufacturers of one broadcast automation system) selling more air time to advertisers, or giving news stories on the spot coverage.

Or perhaps that director still has both his ulcer *and* his stop-watch—for the segments from which programmes are built still have to be created, and often to a strict overall duration: automation can—so far—only build transmission schedules from material which already exists.

But this preoccupation with the value of time is not always such a bad thing. It reminds us to tighten up our programmes and make sure that every part counts (though whether we always take this hint is a different matter). The amateur is rarely under this sort of pressure, and it is perhaps no coincidence that the professional quality most often lacking in amateur work is that other aspect of time, a good sense of timing.

Although "time" and "timing" are two separate things—which are often enough at odds with each other—they are closely interconnected. Differences between rehearsal and transmission timings may explain a fault of pace. The relative lengths in time of different scenes or sections of a programme may throw light on faults in overall shape. So we see that the one obvious and overwhelming reason for timing radio programmes is not the only one.

When timing an item, the usual practice is to set the stop-watch going *on* the first word and not before it (not, that is, when the cue is given); and the watch is stopped after the last word is complete. The reason for doing it this way is that if various timings are to be added together in sequence, we shall want to count the pause between successive items once only—and it is obviously better to calculate a pause at the end than to add in an indeterminate stretch of dead air at the start.

There are various ways of marking the rehearsal and recording timings on a script. It can be done at minute or half-minute intervals, at the bottoms of pages, paragraph by paragraph, or by scenes or parts of scenes. Working in round figures makes calculation easier; but marking the time at natural junctions in the programme probably has more actual value.

If a programme is being timed in rehearsal or recording and a fluff occurs, so that it is necessary to break off and either go back on it at once or stop to sort the matter out, the first thing to do before dealing with anything else whatsoever is to stop the watch and mark in the script the point at which this was done, even though this is after the fluff. And then when the same point is reached again, the watch is restarted. Even if there is quite a long overlap, the true duration will probably be substantially as shown on the stop-watch, despite the fact that it is the first take which has been timed, and not the second.

Where a programme consists of various individual elements—as in a magazine programme—two (or more) watches may be used, including one for the "overall" and one for "individual" timings. In television this is done for videotape or film inserts, and the production secretary keeps everybody informed over talkback how many more minutes there are (useful if moves or microphone changes have to be made in the studio) and counts down the last ten seconds.

Another way in which a stop-watch may be used in radio is to give a speaker his "last minute" of air time. A stop-watch is started by someone in the studio and placed in front of the speaker, who knows that as it ticks up to one minute he must stop. (It is a curious and very professional-looking accomplishment to be able to extemporize perfectly to the last second—and yet in radio circles people who can do this are by no means rare.)

Documentation

After a recording is complete it is necessary to write up various details for later reference. Some of these are technical responsibilities and some production (and it must be clearly understood who does what). They may include:

(i) Name and address of owner and recordist, title, reference number, date, and place of recording, etc. The sample recording report on page 91 shows a layout for a quarter-inch sound tape recording. Similar forms are used for videotape and film sound recording.

(ii) Technical notes. Besides details of equipment and tape (including reel number where more than one used—e.g. "reel 2 of 5") the report should indicate which track was used and the position at which material is to be found (if not at the start); also details of any technical imperfection, fault in balance, etc.

(iii) Full details of contents with durations: e.g.—

(*a*) Names and addresses, etc., of interviewees.

(*b*) Music information: composer, writer, performer, copyright owner, record numbers, etc.

(*c*) Identification of material which is not original.

(iv) Timed script or cue-sheet, with editing notes; and details of the current state of the editing process.

(v) Details required for programme costing.

(vi) Any extra information related to the programme, e.g. source of material used, contacts, etc.; and material which may be needed for publicity, etc.

In addition to this summaries of the programme details are written both on the leader of the tape itself and on the spine of the box in which it is kept. The contents of the tape can then be identified immediately, whether the tape is lying loose or stacked away in its box on a shelf. For sound radio programmes the BBC uses printed leader tape: "British Broadcasting Corporation" followed by spaces for the title of the programme, its reference number, reel number, tape speed, duration, and date of recording. On the spine of the box the reference and reel numbers, title, and speed are repeated. When the tape is finally wiped and reclaimed the leader is removed (as well as the trailer and any spacers), and a new strip of tape is stuck down the spine of the box ready for re-use.

Radio and television stations usually log their output as it is broadcast: in the United States this is a requirement of the FCC. Such a log can be used—among other things—to check the total duration of commercials per hour, or the proportion of "sustaining" (unsponsored, public service) material in a schedule. But since the effort involved benefits no one at the station directly, it is not surprising that even its storage space is grudged. However, stations using broadcast automation systems can now have a low-speed ($\frac{1}{6}$ ips) recorder for the automatic logging of programme details to comply with FCC regulations: the tapes take up only $1\frac{1}{2}$ cubic feet of space for two year's information. In computer-controlled versions the log is teletyped on demand, giving accurate times from the computer's digital clock (see pp. 54–57).

OWNER				SOUND RECORDING REPORT
ADDRESS				
TITLE			REF. NO.	
SUBTITLE			REELS USED	
DATE	PLACE OF RECORDING		EQUIPMENT	
Type of Tape	Reel Size	Tape Speed	1/2/4 Track	Mono/Stereo

Report on Quality of Incoming Programme

REPORT ON QUALITY OF RECORDING/EDITING AND COPYING NOTES

Reel No.	Duration		Cues	Technical Notes
	Mins	Secs		
TOTAL			RECORDED BY	

SAMPLE RECORDING REPORT for a quarter-inch sound tape recording. Similar forms are used for videotape and film sound recording.

Cueing systems

The sound man in radio may be directly or indirectly involved in cueing performers; in television he may be responsible for equipment for doing so.

There are two principal systems of communication between director and performer. These are the cue-light system (used by BBC radio and adopted by many other radio organizations which are modelled on the BBC and also in film dubbing theatres), and the hand-signal system (favoured in American radio and universally in television).

BBC radio studios are equipped with green cue lights. These are operated by switches which are set in the control desk close to the faders. A separate cue light is provided for each studio area (or table) and is placed so that the artist does not have to turn away from the microphone to see it. Some hand signals are also used.

One green flick means "go ahead". It is held on long enough for the least observant speaker to see it, but not so long as to hold up the person who thought you said "when it goes off". This convention is standard for all types of programme except one, the fast-moving news and actuality programme. For this the narrator is given a steady green "coming up" cue, ten or twenty seconds (as agreed) before the actual word cue is expected, the narrator goes ahead when the cue light is switched off.

The equivalent hand signal for "go ahead" is to raise the arm for "get ready" and then to drop the arm, pointing at the performer.

For radio talks, cue lights are also used to help regulate timing and pace. A series of quick flicks means "hurry up", and a long steady means "slow down". A mnemonic for this is "Quicker-flicker, slow-glow". These instructions may not be solely to adjust the programme to fit the scheduled time, but also to stop an unpractised speaker from gabbling or to get him moving. The equivalent hand cues are: hand and forefinger rotating in a small circle, fairly rapidly—"speed up"; hand, palm down, gently patting the air—"slow down". These are both used extensively even when cue lights are available. In television the director gives the cue via the production talkback circuit to the floor manager, who signals it to the performer.

In discussion programmes the chairman may wish to use these signals and others for precise information about timing—e.g. two steadies at two minutes before the end, one at one minute to go, and flicks at thirty seconds. To give the signals by hand the director must stand where he is clearly visible, and then indicate "minutes to go" by holding up the appropriate number of fingers; and "half" by crossing the forefinger of one hand with the forefinger of the other.

Other hand signals which are sometimes used are: pulling the hands apart repeatedly—"stretch". (But have care, as it might also be taken for "move back from the microphone"; as moving the hands together may be used to indicate "get closer"—either to the microphone or to another speaker.) Waving the arms across each other, palms down in a horizontal plane, can be used for "stop"; and the side of the hand drawn across the throat predictably means "cut". This last signal probably ought to be explained before use—as indeed should most of the others.

Crowd noise in a television play may be waved out; but in radio a series of quick flicks may be used to indicate "the studio is faded out—everybody stop" and can be followed quite soon by the single flick for the start of the next scene.

There is one special case in radio: when the speaker is blind. The director (or an assistant) must stand behind the blind person's chair and give the various cues by laying a hand on his shoulder or arm. Quite complex cues can be given in this way, if arranged beforehand. The blind often take more easily to broadcasting than the sighted.

The management of applause

The management of audience applause is important to many radio and television programmes.

In most ordinary cicumstances an audience will wait politely until the end of a sentence and then (if what they have heard seems to call for it) they will clap or shout or do whatever seems appropriate. Through uncertainty as to whether they should interrupt the proceedings or not, the applause may be delayed a second or two, or apparently (or actually) be half-hearted. They may even completely fail to applaud (particularly if the speaker is inexperienced in this branch of stagecraft, or does not wish to appear to be too obviously attempting to produce a response). In any of these cases the effect will be a lack of warmth and a failure to generate the feeling of an event with unity of location and purpose. For the home audience, the people who are watching in the studio might just as well be as far away from the action as they are themselves; as a result, there is no one with whom the viewer or listener can identify himself, to feel vicariously that he, too, is invited and actually a participant.

At the other extreme of audience reaction the studio applause may be excessive to the extent of breaking the flow of a programme in too many places. If applause is injected one sentence before the best point, then either that point will not be applauded at all (and might just as well be dropped), or it will be given reduced applause (and appear as an anticlimax), or it will receive a totally excessive reaction which simply holds up the programme in time, while alienating the home audience.

Certain types of excessive applause may be inappropriate in their programme context, or simply unsatisfactory for sound—for example, young people stamping their feet on the wooden or metal rostra which support the seating in many television studios.

In Britain the overt management of applause is viewed with disapproval by many intelligent members of the public. It is, however, necessary in all of the cases already mentioned where the programme becomes clumsy without it; it is particularly necessary in the case of small audiences of, say, a hundred or less, which may lack enough of those people who in any given situation help to start a crowd reaction; and it may be useful where "atmosphere" demands that applause continues unnaturally long, such as at the close of a programme, behind closing music and titles or announcements, until sound (and where appropriate, vision) finally fades out. The management of applause is right and proper where it leads the local audience to react in places where reaction would in any case be natural, where such applause helps to interpret the material to which it is a reaction, and where it helps by "pacing" a programme and allowing the home audience time to absorb and assess what has gone before.

The behaviour of the audience may be partisan, either in the sense of being composed of admirers of a particular performer, of a participating team, or of a political party: in any of these cases it is reasonable to show the outward trappings of an existing genuine relationship. In all of these cases applause must be handled with responsibility towards both truth and intelligence.

In Britain a failure to do so will alienate an important part of the audience; and this may also be true in many other countries.

Audience cueing

There are three stages in the management of applause. These are:

  (i) Getting the audience in to the right frame of mind; persuading them that they are, in fact, invited to participate in this way.

 (ii) Telling the audience the ground rules of the game; showing them the signals that will be used, and perhaps trying them out as various people are introduced before the programme.

(iii) Actually using the signals in the programme.

Appropriate signals (in television from a floor or stage manager) might be as follows:

For "start applauding", with the hands high above his head, the stage manager starts clapping—but not for the first few claps very loudly, or one person will be heard all too clearly starting ahead of the main body of applause. The stage manager must be very clearly visible to all of the audience, and it may help to draw attention to the action if he has his folded script in his hand as he goes through the motion of clapping. If his applause is audible he must take care not to be too close to a live microphone.

For "continue applauding", the same action may continue, or be replaced by waving the script in a small circle, still well above the head (this adds variety to the stimulus and allows the other hand to be used for cueing). Both hands high, palms inwards, will also keep it going. But turning the palms outwards will bring the applause down, and waving the hands downwards at the same time, or if necessary more violently across the body, will bring it to a stop.

Other signs may be used: the only requirement is that the audience understands and follows. But avoid the ludicrous "applause" signs that are sometimes shown in old films. It is better to lead an audience than to direct it.

For natural, warm applause it is often best if there is a slight overlap between speech (or music) and applause. This implies careful timing and clear understanding by the sound supervisor as to whether the last words must be intelligible or whether it is permissible for them to be partly or completely drowned. He must also know whether the first words of a new cue starting over applause require moderate or high intelligibility (ideally, for "warmth", it should be the former, with redundant information in the words spoken until such time as the applause has almost completely died away).

The "warm up" is an essential part of any programme with an audience. Often music of an appropriate kind should be played until the warm-up proper, which consists of speeches giving information about the programme and the audience's important role in it. For a comedy show it is essential to start off with an audience that is reacting well right from the start. In a theatre it is to be expected that for the first few minutes the performers will have to work very hard to bring the audience together and establish communication. This is not, however, natural on radio or television: the previous programme was the previous act on the bill—or, even if the home audience has just switched on, he has not had all the business of travelling and settling in to unfamiliar surroundings that a studio audience has had. Also the viewer or listener at home is very likely to have established an attitude (a pseudo-relationship) to the performer which can be readily picked up. The studio warm-up must take account of this by inducing a readiness to laugh and clap right from the start.

Warm-up entertainers, specialists in breaking the ice, may be employed to tell weak, old jokes that generate affectionate amusement. But they must not, of course, be funnier than the main performers—which may in itself be something of a constraint, such is the quality of many comedy programmes.

The feeling in Britain is that laughter should be natural and unforced, sympathetic and genuinely related to the real content in humour of the programme of which it is part.

Dubbed laughter and applause is therefore frowned upon in general, and in particular where it is used to suggest that a performer is being funny or otherwise talented when all he is impressing is a machine.

Microphone techniques for applause are described on p. 240.

Film sound recording

A film unit includes a director, a cameraman, a sound recordist, and an electrician (for lighting), plus as many assistants in each of these departments as is necessary for efficient operation or to observe union rules. But using modern equipment, there are few occasions when a sound recordist actually *needs* an assistant for television film location work, except as a mobile microphone stand for certain types of dramatic subject.

The sound recordist generally has a high-quality lightweight quarter-inch tape recorder which can be used to record both the output from his own microphones and a reference signal which is related to camera speed. In countries where the electricity supply frequency is 50 Hz, 25 fps has been adopted as the standard television film speed, and the pilot tone is 50 Hz; but where the mains frequency is 60 Hz the film industry standard of 24 fps has been retained for television work, and a pilot tone based on 60 Hz is used for film recorders.

Many ingenious systems have been devised for combining the two signals on the one tape, of which the main aim is often to achieve the highest possible signal-to-noise ratio for the main sound recording. The system adopted by the BBC, on the other hand, has the great advantage of simplicity: the two signals are recorded side by side, each occupying a half track as recorded by a standard stereo head. This results in a reduction of the signal-to-noise ratio of about 3–5 dB less than the theoretical maximum, but this is not in practice important if a high-quality recorder is being used—particularly as in most practical film-recording situations the ambient noise level is much higher than in, say, most sound radio studios.

The other apparent objection to using a stacked head (i.e. one with the recording gaps in line one above the other) is the danger of cross-talk. BBC experience is that this is negligible if the pilot tone is a pure 50-Hz signal (i.e. a simple sine wave) recorded at 8 dB below the full modulation level of the programme sound, and using a normal HF bias to assist the recording (low frequencies are, in principle, difficult to record without such assistance: see p. 397). Cross-talk from low-frequency signals of this sort is some 38 dB below programme sound, and this is not audible unless harmonics of the 50 Hz are present—which they are not to any significant degree.

The system adopted by recordists in other parts of the world will depend on what equipment is available for the transfer of the quarter-inch tape to 16- or 35-mm magnetic film stock for editing: it is this transfer equipment which matches the speed of tape and magnetic film by scanning the pilot tone, so that the picture and sound tracks that are presented to the editor are perfectly in register, sprocket hole to sprocket hole, whatever the duration of the take. In practice, the pilot tone "invisible sprocket hole" and the associated transfer systems are very reliable: provided that his equipment is working correctly, this is one of the least of the sound recordist's worries.

97

It will be evident that unless the camera and tape are controlled to a common standard speed (e.g. by the mains supply or by a crystal frequency standard in self-powered equipment), some means must be found for passing a signal from the camera to the recorder to indicate what the shutter speed actually is so that the 50- or 60-Hz pilot signal can be varied slightly in accordance with this. Two systems are used: a cable (a "sync. lead") or a VHF radio link. (The latter is also used on modern camera and sound-recording systems for the identification and start marking of takes.) A sync. lead does not usually cause any difficulties, but for perhaps one shot in a hundred in normal use, or rather more when a camera is hand held for high mobility, it is inconvenient for the cameraman and recordist to be umbilically connected in this manner. The type of production which the crew is likely to be involved in will determine which type of equipment is taken as standard.

Two other systems of recording are in use:

One employs a magnetic stripe on the film itself and is suitable for news and other situations where the extreme mobility of a one- or two-man team is required. The sound is recorded in the camera itself, but displaced by about a second from the relevant picture.

The remaining system is a hang-over from before the days of quarter-inch tape: a single unit acts as both camera and sound recorder, but using sprocketed magnetic film stock to run in mechanical interlock with the picture.

I have used this "double-headed" camera for recordings that require extensive and fast editing, for example, in a February the twenty-ninth "vox pop" in which a reporter asked a number of girls to tell him how they would propose marriage to him. Editing points were marked up in sound only while the film was being processed, so that a rapid and precise editing job could be done on its return. The system permitted a marginal saving of time which was useful in view of the relatively high shooting ratio required to get a really amusing four-minute magazine item.

The film sound recordist's microphones and his techniques for using them are described in later chapters. And many other techniques which will be discussed primarily in terms of the studio are equally applicable in location filming.

Filming routine

Rehearsal for a film shot will normally allow the recordist to obtain a microphone balance and set his recording level. In a full

98

rehearsal the action, camera movement, and lighting will be close to those to be adopted on the actual "take", so the recordist will have a final chance to see how close in he can get his microphone without this appearing in vision or casting a shadow. He will then be able to judge the ambient camera noise levels in realistic conditions.

When the rehearsal is complete and the performers are ready the camera will normally be set up for some form of identification of the shot, and the lights (where they are used) will be switched to full power. While this is going on, the recordist will be listening for any rise in noise level due to traffic or aircraft, or people who are so carried away by the informality of the occasion as to be chatting happily but audibly in the background. If he feels that the director is likely to go ahead before any of these extraneous noises have been stopped or have died away he will warn him, ask for a delay, or possibly resort to direct action to get the offending noise stopped. When the director has checked with each department—often very informally—the camera assistant will (in the conventional start to each shot) hold up a clapperboard to the camera, and the sound recordist or his assistant will direct a microphone towards it.

On the director's instruction "turn over" the tape starts: the recordist runs his tape and almost immediately the camera operator runs the film; the recordist checks that he is receiving the sync. pulse, while the cameraman checks that the film has run up to speed: when it has, the camera assistant is told to "mark it".

Marking the shot ("boarding" or "slating" it) consists of stating clearly the shot and take numbers: "one–two–seven take three" while holding the board up to the camera with the bar open. The board is then clapped, the assistant and the camera operator both taking care that the action of the board closing is still clearly in vision, and the recordist noting that the clap is identifiable and distinct from other sound that it could be confused with. If any fault is observed, a second board can be called for: the camera assistant will put the board back in shot, this time saying something like: "one–two–seven take three, sync. to second clapper". He then clears the shot quickly but quietly, while the cameraman checks his framing and (if necessary) focus, and the recordist checks his microphone position for the start of the take and gives a final thought to noise problems—as the director himself may also be doing at this time.

The director will check that his performers are absolutely ready, wait for a signal that the cameraman has framed up and his assistant has settled himself and that there are no new shadows that will affect the start or a later part of the shot. When he is finally satisfied he will call "action" ... and the whole of this procedure so far may have taken only six or seven seconds.

At the end of the take the director will call "cut": the camera will stop running first, and as soon as he has, the recordist will stop too (or if there is some continuing noise, he may signal for everyone to hold positions while he records extra sound for a fade: the director's cue might later be deleted in the editing).

If an event occurs without warning, so that camera and sound have to be run without a board (and the director should be very clear in his instruction to do this) the cameraman and recordist should continue to run after the end of the filmed action until the assistant can reach a place to mark the film, adding to the shot identification the words, "board on end".

Mute shots, i.e. picture filmed without sound, is marked with an open board (and perhaps held in such a way that it obviously could not be shut without chopping off a few fingers).

Wildtracks are recordings made without a picture. The best way of identifying them is to relate them to particular shot number (the director or his assistant will have to say which this is): "Wildtrack extra background of car interior with gear change for slate one–two–eight" or "wildtrack commentary for one–three–two onwards." Another system is to give them letters: "Wildtrack B: atmosphere quiet classroom."

The recordist should make a separate recording of the characteristic continuing sound of each different location unless specifically told it will not be wanted; and should rerecord important effects that can be improved by a balance in the absence of the camera, unless this is likely to hold up the proceedings. There may also be specific additional noises the director wants.

Where the scene that is being filmed would be unduly disturbed by the standard procedure for marking shots, it can be simplified by starting each sync. take with a picture of the recordist speaking the shot number and tapping his microphone: here, exaggerated lip movements are more important than a loud voice, and the tap should be visually clear as well, with the fingers left touching the casing for a fraction of a second after the tap. With this system it is important not to get confused in the order of shots and never to repeat any number for a "take two": all this is to help the editor when putting sound and picture together later.

In some modern systems it is not necessary to identify each shot with a board: the camera control system itself produces a "mark"

100

for both picture and sound which (in one example) numbers from one to ten then over and over again (there are no "retakes" marked as such on this system: each shot uses a new number). Despite this facility, it is still useful to show a board at the start of each roll of film, and then intermittently within a long roll—and certainly if there is any changing backward and forward between rolls.

Film documentation

The director's assistant, the camera assistant, and the recordist or his assistant each have their own documentation to complete. The main (director's) shot list should include the following for each shot (this is my own preference for documentary work):

(i) Roll number (of film).
(ii) Board and take number.
(iii) A suffix "s" or "m" to the shot number to indicate sync. or mute; also "b.o.e." for the board on end if appropriate (this use of suffixes is not general, but is convenient for quick reference—which is what shot lists are mostly used for).
(iv) Shot description with brief indications of opening frame (on start of action); the action within the shot (including camera action: pans, tracks, or zooms, timed if possible); continuity points; faults or errors, including sound problems; and the overall duration of significant action. All of this should be kept very brief and selective.
(v) Overall duration or footage of film used.
(vi) "P", "OK", or a tick for a shot to be printed; "NG" for a shot that is not worth printing.

Also:

(vii) Sound roll numbers as new rolls are started.
(viii) Wildtrack details (inserted in the shot list between the sync. takes where the sound itself is to be found).

The film sound recordist's own report should include as many technical details of recordings as may be useful later. Each board for which sound was recorded will be listed, followed by a list of takes. A convenient way of indicating which takes should be transferred is to put rings round those particular ones but not round the others (these should be as agreed with the director and cameraman). Restricting the transfer will save the director and editor time later

101

(as well as magnetic stock costs). Wildtracks will be included in the same order in which they were recorded, and notes on quality will be added where relevant.

In addition, the recordist will have identified each new roll of tape over the microphone, with a standard list of details which might include the name of the director, costing details, date, location, recorder type and number, and camera speed (in countries where this might be at either 24 or 25 fps).

The recordist will be responsible for getting the tapes back for transfer within the shortest convenient time unless otherwise agreed: the simplest arrangement is for them to be despatched with the film (which is generally sent for overnight processing) and then forwarded with the rushes for transfer while the picture is being viewed without sound). If so required, the synchronized rushes could then be viewed later the same day. This schedule assumes a fast, routine operation in which there is no special haste; but in a slower schedule the rush print would still be viewed for technical faults as soon as possible, though the sound would not be synchronized with it until later—perhaps at the start of the editing.

Choosing film locations

A final word about film routine takes us back to the planning stage, and the choice of suitable locations—an important first step in avoiding sound problems which may prove expensive in the loss of working time or may even make it quite impossible to record anything satisfactorily.

Surveys should establish that aircraft are not likely to disturb the proceedings too much. Direct observation is a good start on this, but in addition a glance at an air traffic control map of the area concerned will show what type of disturbance there might be—jet airliners along the main airways and in the terminal control zones, and light aircraft elsewhere. The survey should also ensure that traffic noise is not obtrusive (or, if traffic is accepted as a visual element, that it is not excessive), and that machinery noise from factories, building sites, or road workings will not create difficulties —and so on.

If the investment in good sound is high a visit to the site at the same time of day in the appropriate part of the week is a useful precaution. The story is told of a production assistant who went out on a Sunday and found a delightfully idyllic secluded rural location for a period drama—and it was not until the film unit had actually arrived and the camera was ready to turn over that the first roar of a jet engine started up on the other side of the nearest hedge. It was a busy military airfield which had just happened to be closed down for the Sunday. (In this case it would also have helped if the production assistant had looked over the hedge.)

Good survey work includes asking the right questions, reading the local papers, and so on ... but even had I done all of this, I still might have missed the notice of the bell-ringing practice—apparently the first in months—that nearly wrecked my coverage of a union meeting specially arranged in the picturesque setting of an old public-house in the centre of Wigan in the North of England—and standing right under the bell tower of the parish church.

For interiors, acoustics as well as noise will be surveyed: what can be done to convert an interior "location" to something approaching a studio is considered later in the next chapter.

4

STUDIOS

THIS chapter deals with studios: their purpose and layout (seen in terms of the operations that must be carried out in them); their acoustics, and treatments that can be used to modify the acoustics; and their furnishings. These are described both for radio studios and for television. Film studios are similar to but perhaps simpler than television studios: the output of a television studio is very high, and demands a high investment in equipment and working space.

How many studios, and what sort?

Before considering how studios are planned to fulfil their function, it would perhaps be better first to consider what are the needs for countries, regions, or communities of various sizes. Not until we do this can we see whether studios must all be for general (and perhaps limited) purposes or whether it is possible to design studios for particular specialized purposes.

The cost of television is such that the number of studios that can be supported by any given population is very limited.

If we take as our basic unit a regional population of 5–8 millions we find that this will be sufficient to sustain two centres (perhaps in competition with each other), each with about three studios for:

    (i) major productions (including drama);
    (ii) general purposes (including entertainment, with audience);
    (iii) speech only (presentation and news);

and also an outside broadcast unit.

Population at or below the lower end of this scale will have difficulty in sustaining even this number: there may be only two studios or even one. But there will also be less use for an outside broadcast unit, so this may be taken for part of its time to a "drive-in" studio—something like a film studio which is converted for television by the addition of the outside broadcast mobile control room, electronic cameras, videotape recorder or radio links, and so on.

Such a studio centre would not be self-sufficient: it would use networked material or film for the greater part of its output, unless special local conditions required a high proportion of low-cost local material.

At the lower end of the scale towns serving areas of a million or so may have single-studio stations (again perhaps two, in competition). But these studios will be small, big enough for only two or three setting areas of moderate size.

A national population the size of Britain or the United States is sufficient to sustain three or four national networks. At the main studio centres for these there will be a range of studios that is wide in size and purpose, and greater in number than for a region only. Very large conurbations can sustain both network centres and smaller local stations, particularly if the smaller stations specialize to take substantial minorities which are disregarded by the main networks.

In radio (living, in most countries, in the shadow of television) a more confused situation exists. In the United States there is a radio station to every 25–30,000 population. Many—a very large number indeed—broadcast to very small audiences and can survive only by using records for the greater part of their output; "good music" stations, in particular, can be run at very low operational costs. The studio in such a small station may be little more than a fairly sound-proof room, perhaps with some acoustic treatment, together with a microphone, turntables, and tape decks.

But looking again at our region with 5–8 million people, we now have a population which can sustain a full range of studios for all of the specialized functions that the current purposes of radio permit. These are likely to be fewer in the United States, where radio has become more limited, than in Britain, where a regional centre may have the following studios:

(i) speech only (several);
(ii) pop music;
(iii) light and orchestral music;
(iv) light entertainment (with audience);
(v) general purpose, including drama and dramatized educational programmes

Smaller regions (100,000–1 million population) are capable of sustaining vigorous, but more limited, radio stations. National

105

populations are capable of sustaining networks in about the same number as for television (though these are much more fragmented in the United States than in Britain, where they all reach almost the entire population). The BBC has about sixty radio studios in London alone, though many are for overseas broadcasting. Some are very highly specialized—for example, one has been acoustically adapted for the production of major non-musical features in stereo (though such productions are not common).

Studio design: keeping noise out

In designing or choosing buildings for the installation of radio or television studios there are a number of points to consider right from the start.

(i) Do not build near an airport.

(ii) Prefer massive "old-fashioned" styles of construction to steel-framed or modern "component" architecture.

(iii) In noisy town centres offices that are built on the outside of the main studio structure can be used as acoustic screening. These outer structures can be built in any convenient form, but the studio must be adequately insulated from noise from *them*.

(iv) The best place to put a studio is on solid ground.

(v) If a radio studio cannot be put on solid ground the whole massive structure, concrete floor, walls, and roof can be floated on rubber or other suitable materials. The resonance of the whole floating system must be very low: about 10 Hz is reasonable (1 inch of glass fibre or expanded polystyrene gives resonances at about 100 Hz, so care is needed). An alternative technique is to suspend the structure like a leaf from a tree.

(vi) Airborne noise from ventilation is a major problem. Low-pressure ducts are broad enough to cause resonance problems if not designed with care: they also require acoustic attenuation within them to reduce sound from one place to another. Grilles can also cause air turbulence and therefore noise.

(vii) High-speed ducts have been suggested as an answer to some of the problems of airborne noise, but would also require careful design, particularly at the points where the air entered and left the studio.

(viii) Double doors with a pressure seal are needed.

(ix) Holes for wiring should be designed into the structure and be as small as possible. They should not be drilled arbitrarily at the whim of wiring engineers.

(x) Windows between studio and control area should be double and of different thicknesses (say $\frac{1}{4}$ inch and $\frac{3}{8}$ inch). Contrary to what might be expected, it does not seem to matter if they are parallel. Insulation to higher standards than this is not necessary, as the higher levels of sound will be the same in both places.

(xi) Windows to areas outside the studio area *or to the control area if the loudspeaker is to be switched to replay during recordings* should be triple. Measures to avoid condensation will be necessary only in the case of windows to the outer atmosphere, where there will be temperature differences.

(xii) Any noisy machinery should be in a structurally separate area, and should be on anti-vibration mountings.

Even acknowledged experts can make errors: The BBC's own had problems with studios in the basement of a steel-frame building next to an underground railway. Calculations for studio structures floating on rubber proved to be 10 dB wrong, and the only practicable answer was to bear the noise and wait for the introduction of continuously welded rails.

Although massive structures have been recommended, *extremely* massive structures may be more expensive than their improvement warrants. *Doubling* the thickness of a brick wall from $4\frac{1}{2}$ to 9 inches gives an improvement of only 5 dB.

For television studio roofs the limiting thickness for single-skin construction is about 10 inches: this gives an average attenuation of 60 dB over the range 100–3200 Hz. BBC research indicates that for noisy jet aircraft flying at 1000 feet a minimum of 65 dB attenuation is desirable. Even low-flying helicopters are less of a problem than this (provided they do not actually land on the studio roof!), but supersonic aircraft producing a sonic boom with overpressures of 2 lb/ft² require 70 dB attenuation—particularly at low frequencies.

Since a double skin is in any case desirable for more than 60 dB attenuation, it may be wisest to adopt the higher standard—70 rather than 65 dB attenuation. This results, in fact, in a structure which is little heavier than a 60-dB single skin.

As part of the BBC experiments there were subjective tests using both types of aircraft noise attenuated as if by various roofs and

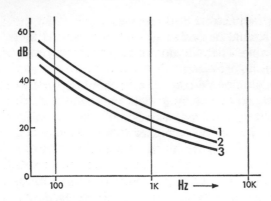

PERMISSIBLE BACKGROUND NOISE IN STUDIOS. I. Television studios (except drama and presentation). 2. Television drama and presentation studios; sound radio: all studios except those for drama. 3. Sound radio drama studios.

added to television programme sound at quiet, tense points in the action. In the limiting case the action may be part of a period drama, in which aircraft noise would be anachronistic.

Obviously, permissible noise levels depend on the type of production. For example, in television drama background noise from all sources (including movement in the studio) should ideally not exceed 30 dB at 500 Hz (relative to 2×10^{-5} N/m²). For light entertainment the corresponding figure is 35 dB. However, in practice, figures up to 10 dB higher than these are often tolerated.

Reverberation

So far all we have for our studio is a bare empty box of concrete (or some similar hard and massive material). It will reflect most of the sound that strikes it; and this will be almost independent of frequency—though very broad expanses of flat thin concrete may resonate at low frequencies and mop up some of the low bass.

When normal furnishings are placed in a room they will include carpets, curtains, soft chairs. These (together with people) act as *sound absorbers*. Other furnishings will include tables, hard chairs, and other wooden and metal objects. These reflect much of the sound striking them, but break up the wave fronts. They act as *sound diffusers*. Some things do both: a bookcase will diffuse sound and the books will absorb it.

The absorption or diffusion qualities of objects vary with frequency. In particular, the dimensions of an object will condition how it behaves. A small ornament will diffuse only the highest frequencies; sound waves that are long in comparison to its size will

108

simply pass round it. The thickness of a soft absorber will affect its ability to absorb long wavelengths, and so will its position. At the hard reflecting surface of a wall there is no air movement anyway. So an inch of sound-absorbing material will reach out into regions of substantial air movement (and damp them down) only for the highest frequencies; to have any effect on lower frequencies it must be well away from the wall.

Sounds in an enclosed space will be reflected, many times, with some (great or small) part of the sound being absorbed at each reflection. The rate of decay of reverberation defines a characteristic for each studio: its *reverberation time*. This is the time it takes for a sound to die away to a millionth part of its original intensity (i.e. through 60 dB). Reverberation time will vary with frequency, and a studio's performance may be shown on a graph for all audio frequencies. Or it may be simply given in round terms for, say, the biggest peak between 500 and 2000 Hz; or at a particular frequency within that range.

Reverberation time will depend on the number of reflections in a given time, so large rooms will generally have longer reverberation times than small ones. This is not only expected but also, fortunately, preferred by listeners.

Colouration

In a large room an *echo* may be detected. If there is little reverberation in the time between an original sound and a repetition of it, and if this time gap exceeds an eighteenth of a second (which is equivalent to a sound path of 60 feet) it will be heard as an echo.

In a small room *colouration* may be heard. This is the selective emphasis of certain frequencies or bands of frequencies in the reverberation. It will often be the result of hard parallel wall surfaces which allow many reflections backward and forward along the same path: at each reflection absorption always occurs at the same frequencies, leaving some frequencies still clearly audible long after the rest has decayed.

Parallel walls will also give rise to *eigentones*, the natural frequencies of air resonance corresponding to the studio dimensions. If the main dimensions are direct multiples of, or in simple ratios to each other these may be reinforced.

The rate of absorption in different parts of a hall may not all be the same, giving rise to anomalous decay characteristics. For

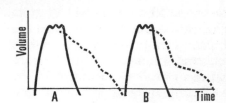

HOW SOUNDS DIE AWAY. A. In a good music studio the sound dies away fairly evenly. B. In a poor music studio (or with bad microphone placing) the reverberation may decay quickly at first, and then more slowly.

example, sound may die away quickly in the partially enclosed area under a balcony, but reverberation may continue to be fed to it from the main hall. More unpleasant (though less likely) might be the reverse of this, where reverberation was "trapped" in a smaller volume and fed back to a less reverberant larger area.

Resonances may interchange their sound energies: this happens in the sounding board of a piano and is one of the characteristics which we hear as "piano quality". In a room it may mean that a frequency at which the sound has apparently disappeared may recur before decaying finally.

Not all of these qualities will be bad if present only in moderation. They may give a room or hall a characteristic but not particularly unpleasant quality: something, at any rate, that can be lived with. In excess they are vices that may make a room virtually unusable, or usable only with careful microphone placing.

The answer to many of these problems—or at least some improvement—lies in theory in better diffusion. The more the wave fronts are broken up, the more the decay of sound will become smooth, both in time and in frequency spectrum.

In practice, however, if acoustic treatment has been carried out and panels of the various types that may be necessary for adequate sound absorption have been distributed about the various walls and on the ceiling, little more generally needs to be done about diffusion.

Studios for speech

Studios that are used only for speech will often be about the same size as a living-room in an ordinary but fairly spacious house. But where demands on space result in smaller rooms being used, the result may be unsatisfactory: awkward, unnatural sounding resonances will occur which even heavy acoustic treatment will not kill . . . and, of course, acoustic treatment that is effective at low frequencies will reduce the working space still further.

110

Colouration, which presents the most awkward problem in studio design, is at its worst in small studios, because the main resonances of length and width are clearly audible on a voice which contains any of the frequencies which will trigger them off. An irregular shape and random placing of the acoustic treatment on the walls help to cut down colouration. But in small rectangular studios treatment may be ineffective, and one is forced to work closer to the microphone. Using ribbon microphones means that bass correction circuits are required; and in the smallest speech studios at the BBC they are usually built in as standard equipment.

But colouration, as I have said, is not necessarily a bad thing; a natural sounding "indoor" voice always has some. But it has to be watched carefully, at least on single-channel "monophonic" recordings. Remember that even on a single voice there is a world of difference between mono and stereo: with mono all of the reverberation and studio colouration is collected together and reproduced from the same apparent source as the speech.

The answer might at first sight appear to be to do away with reverberation entirely and try to create entirely "dead" studios. Then the only acoustics to apply would be those of the listener's room. But listening tests indicate that most people prefer a moderately "live" acoustic.

What is the ideal reverberation time for a speech studio? The experience of the BBC suggests that, for normal living-room dimensions, something like 0·4 seconds is about right with a ribbon microphone. A smaller room would need a lower time—a quarter of a second, perhaps. And whereas the former would be the sort of figure to be expected in the home, the latter is not. So that for recording speech under home conditions big rooms are probably best, provided, of course, that they are fairly well furnished—from the sound-absorption point of view.

Remembering that reverberation time is the time it takes for a sound to die away through 60 decibels you can use a hand-clap to give a rough guide to both duration and quality. In a room that is to be used as a speech studio the sound should die away quickly, but not so quickly that the clap sounds muffled or dead. And there must certainly be no "ring" fluttering along behind it.

Listening rooms and sound-control cubicles should have similar acoustics: 0·4 second is just about the maximum. BBC listening rooms are acoustically engineered for a response of 0·4 second up to 250 Hz, falling gradually to 0·3 second at 8000 Hz.

General-purpose sound studios

In Britain there is still a need for studios in which a variety of acoustics is used for dramatic purposes. In some other countries such facilities can hardly be justified by their use (except, perhaps,

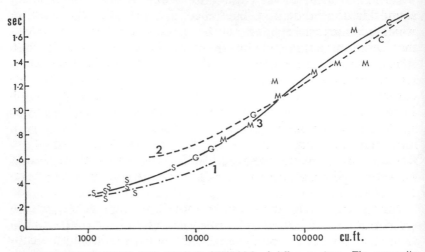

REVERBERATION TIMES FOR SOUND STUDIOS of different sizes. The generally accepted optimum reverberation times (Beranek) are: I. Speech studio. 2. Music studio with "natural" acoustics. BBC experience of good studios is shown by the central line, 3. S. Speech. G. General purpose. M. Music (natural acoustics). C. Concert halls. (However, studios for recording popular music may be deliberately designed to be as dead as is practicable. Artificial reverberation may then be added in different proportions to the output of the microphones.)

to add interest to commercials). They may also be used for special projects to be issued as records. This studio type is therefore still important, though much less so than when radio was the principal means of broadcasting.

There are two main working areas, usually separated by no more than a set of curtains. One end, the "dead" end, has a speech acoustic that is rather more dead (by about 0·1 second) than would be normal for its size. The other end is "live", so that when used for speech the acoustic is very obviously different from that of the dead end. If the curtains are open and microphones in the dead end can pick up sound from that direction the resonance of the live end can sometimes be heard on speech originating in the dead end. This parasitic reverberation will generally sound unpleasant unless there is a good reason for it, so the normal position for the curtains will

112

be such as to cut off the live end (i.e. at least partly closed). However, useful effects can sometimes be obtained near the middle of the studio.

The live end can also be used for small musical groups working with speech in the dead part of the studio.

There may also be a very dead area; though if this is small it may sound like the inside of a padded coffin rather than the open air which it is supposed to represent. For good results the type of treatment used in anechoic chambers for sound testing would be best. These have wedges of foam extending out a metre from the walls. (But it would not be necessary to have this on the floor; a normal carpet would be adequate. After all, the open air usually has ground underneath it.) However, some performers find it unpleasant to work in such surroundings.

If there is a fourth area this may be very live. Again, limitations of space may cause this to sound like the inside of a bathtub. It may be better to dispense with this and use an echo chamber or reverberation plate.

Studios for stereo speech will be more dead than other general-purpose studios. The reason for this will be seen later: where coincident microphones are being used, voices must be placed physically farther back than for mono; otherwise any movement will be exaggerated.

The music studio

The foremost characteristic of a studio, and one which will make or mar its performance, is its reverberation time. Preference tests indicate that, for any given size of studio, music requires longer reverberation than speech does. These preferences are not absolutes; but they are valid for the music and musical instruments played in them during the tests, i.e. for music which we have come to regard as the normal. But it must be remembered that both music and instruments as we know them in the West today have developed in a very specialized way: in particular, our orchestral and chamber music is developed from that played in rooms of large houses in the Europe of the seventeenth and eighteenth centuries. The original acoustics has defined the music—and our music now, in turn, defines the acoustics needed for it.

That these instruments and this music are not the only forms possible should be fairly obvious—but it is only necessary to point to the majority of Eastern music, which is designed for performance in

113

the open air, and to church music, which is at its best in highly reverberant surroundings, to show that we are dealing with a form which has been ruled somewhat arbitrarily by the acoustic conditions available. And it is interesting to note that some "modern" music is now written for drier acoustics than those which sound best for Beethoven. Nevertheless, the acoustics which we have been accustomed to have led to the design of instruments for which music of great beauty and power has been composed; and so the studios we look for have certain specific qualities which can be judged by these subjective tests.

Listening tests are not always the best indication of true value: they measure what we like best at the time of the test, and not what we could learn to like better if we took the trouble to change our habits. Nevertheless, several clear results appear when such tests are applied to music studios.

It turns out that the ideal (i.e. preferred) reverberation time varies with the size of the studio: small studio—short reverberation; large studio—long reverberation. For the very smallest studios (e.g. a room in a private house set aside as a music room) the ideal is between three-quarters and one second. This is what might be expected if the room has no carpet and few heavy furnishings.

Some authorities suggest that there should be a slight rise in the bass; but the BBC has a response that is "flat" at all frequencies.

An interesting sidelight on reverberation is that for monophonic radio and recording work, reverberation times about a tenth of a second lower than those for live music are preferred. The emergence of the reverberation from the same apparent source as the direct sound means that less is required. And in any case the reverberation of the listening room is added.

Apart from this, the principal quality of a good hall is good diffusion; i.e. the sound waves are well broken up and spread throughout the hall. There should be no echoes due to domes, barrel vaults, or any other concave architectural features.

Dead pop music studios

The studio acoustics play no part in much of today's popular music. The internal balance of the orchestra is deliberately surrendered in exchange for electronic versatility.

A celeste, piano, or flute may be given a melody and may be expected to sound as loud as brass, and various other effects may be

114

sought which can be achieved only if the sound of the louder instrument does not spill to the microphones set at high amplification for quiet instruments.

Microphones are placed as close as may be practicable, and their directional properties are exploited to avoid picking up direct sound from distant loud sources, and also to discriminate against reverberation from the open studio. But acoustics must also play their part.

The answer is to make the studio dead—more dead than is required for a speech studio. It is not just a question of cutting down reverberation. There must be substantial attenuation at a single reflection from any wall. This means that much less of the sound of the brass will strike the walls and reach the flute or celeste microphone from directions that cannot be discriminated against.

There is one aspect of acoustics which is very important to pop music, not for its presence but again for its absence; this is the attenuation due to air transmission.

At frequencies below about 2000 Hz absorption by the air is negligible. But for 8000 Hz, air at 50% relative humidity has an absorption of 0·028 per foot. As one BBC pop-music balancer points out, this means there will generally be something of the order of a 30-dB loss at a distance of 100 feet for high frequencies. For damper air the loss is a little lower, but for very dry air it rises sharply and begins to affect lower harmonics (4000 Hz) appreciably. This may make a great deal of difference between two performances using a distance balance in the same concert hall, but it does not affect close-balanced pop music, except to make instrumental quality *different* from that which may be heard normally: substantially more of the higher harmonics of each instrument are heard.

Television and film studios

Studios for television and film (and particularly the larger ones) are usually made very dead for their size. The primary reason for this is that if they are not to appear in vision, microphones must be farther away from their subjects than for other types of balance. But it also helps to reduce inevitable noise from distant parts of the studio. A major production may require 200 kW of lighting power; ventilation has to be provided to remove the heat produced, and this ventilation cannot be completely quiet. In various parts of the studio scenery may have to be erected or struck during the action or props

115

set in. Close to the action cameras will be moving: this movement itself is fairly quiet, but the cables dragging behind them are not. Scenic projection equipment is often noisy (in particular, equipment for back projection of film).

The floor of a television studio must allow the smooth movement of heavy equipment. Accordingly, it is acoustically highly reflective, whereas the rest of the surfaces have to be very absorbent.

Sound which radiates upwards at any angle will be reflected several times before it can reach a microphone, but sound travelling horizontally may be reflected only once. For this reason the most effective place for the absorption of sound is the lower parts of the walls; more of the treatment is concentrated here rather than higher up.

The set itself is not likely to have much effect on the overall reverberation time, but it may have unpredicted effects on the local acoustics. Such considerations are not normally allowed to enter much into the design of scenery and choice of furniture and "props" for television, except sometimes in the case of music productions.

Television studios have acoustics approaching those used in "dead" music studios; they are therefore suitable for music techniques of this type. For serious music, however, they are basically

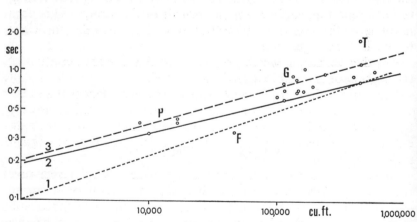

REVERBERATION TIMES OF TELEVISION STUDIOS (maximum values between 500–2000 Hz). 1. Lowest practicable limit. 3. Highest acceptable figure. 2. Normal design aim. The examples shown are all BBC television studios. Those above the upper line are too live (though mostly only marginally so). Group P. Presentation and small news studios. Group G. General purpose studios. F. A converted film studio: unusually dead. This deadness has been obtained at the expense of a poor balance of frequency content. T. A converted theatre. The sound is too live for convenient use in television, but satisfactory for the audience present.

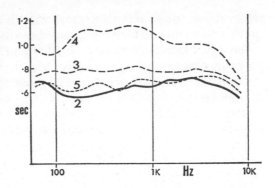

FOUR TELEVISION STUDIOS: frequency response (variation in reverberation time with frequency). BBC Television Centre Studios 2 and 5 are both 116,000 cu. ft; studios 3 and 4, 357,000 cu. ft. Studio 4 was designed primarily for musical entertainments, for which it is very satisfactory; it is a little live for plays.

unsuitable, and artificial echo must be applied liberally to compensate for this. But this does not solve the problem of the musician who finds the surroundings acoustically unpleasant.

In particular, string players need reflected sound to satisfy themselves that they are producing a good tone quality at adequate power. In its absence they are apt to bow harder, changing the internal balance of the orchestra and making its tone harsh and strident. The timing of ensemble playing also suffers. An orchestral shell helps all of the players, but the brass players (who do not need it) more than anyone else: a full shell turns a balance inside out and should not be used. In fact, the best solution is to design the setting to have reflecting surfaces for the benefit of the strings. This does nothing for the overall reverberation time, but helps the musicians to produce the right tone.

Another technique which does this *and* changes the acoustics at the same time is "ambiophony": see p. 125.

Film studios have in the past tended to be even deader than television studios. In addition to the other problems, the cameras are, by the nature of their intermittent action, noisy things which are difficult to silence really effectively—though there have been very great improvements in recent years.

Television sound control rooms and film dubbing theatres have the same characteristics as their counterparts in radio: 0·4 second at 250 Hz to 0·3 second at 8000 Hz. But the main production and lighting control areas should be as acoustically dead as is practicable in order that the director and his assistant and the technical director shall be clearly audible on open microphones in an area that also has programme sound. In fact, these areas will not be very dead: the large areas of hardware and glass see to that.

Other technical areas, such as those for telecine and videotape,

117

will need acoustic treatment: both machines can be noisy in operation; and both areas have loudspeakers for programme sound and two-way talk-back circuits. If machines are grouped in partly open bays acoustic partitioning will be necessary; in the case of telecine a 20-dB separation between one bay and the next is a suitable level to aim for.

Acoustic treatment

Three basic types are available:

Soft absorbers. These are porous materials which are applied to walls: their action depends on loss of sound energy, as air vibrates in the interstices of the foam, rockwool, or whatever it may be. The

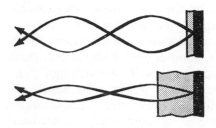

SOUND ABSORBERS. Padding which is close to a reflecting surface is efficient only for sufficiently short wavelengths. Screens with (say) an inch of padding are poor absorbers at any but the highest frequencies. For greater efficiency in absorbing a particular wavelength the absorber should be placed at a quarter wavelength from reflecting surfaces.

method works very well at high and middle frequencies, but for efficiency at low frequencies needs to be about 4 feet thick. As this will not be required over the whole surface of a wall (or the room would be too dead), there would be large and awkward projections of absorber into the studio; clearly this is going to waste a lot of valuable space.

So it is reasonable to lay these at thicknesses which are efficient down to about 500 Hz and then become less so. Many different types are commercially available. Control of high frequencies (for which absorption may be excessive) is provided by using a perforated hardboard surface: with 5% perforation much of the "top" will be reflected; with 25% much of it will be absorbed. Different surfaces may be alternated.

Helmholtz resonators. Cavities which are open to the air at a narrow neck resonate at particular frequencies. If the interior is damped they will absorb at that frequency. Broad-spectrum low-frequency absorption can be achieved with banks of such resonators; but while this may be quite successful, it is a specialized technique and has not gained wide acceptance. It is, however, useful for attacking dimensional resonances of sound radio studios.

This is not a problem that should be overstated, however. Only

118

about seven out of a hundred BBC studios seem to be affected; and in these it may not be the ideal solution, as it requires treatment to be fitted either at particular places which may be already occupied or some of the only places which are not.

Membrane absorbers. These are often used to cope with the low frequencies. But if the low frequencies are a problem, so, too, can be the absorbers themselves. The idea is simple enough: a layer of some material or a panel of hardboard is held in place over an air space. The material moves with the sound wave like a piston; but its movement is damped, so that low-frequency sound energy is lost. So far so good.

Unfortunately, there are as many variations on this and similar ideas as there are experts on the subject. And there are, it seems, experts at each of the major studio centres throughout Western Europe, all of whom have methods which they can demonstrate to work well. Unfortunately, however, there is one other matter which also seems to be universally agreed: that although their own methods work, no one else's do. The BBC Research Department tried most of the membrane absorbers used in the studios of Continental Europe and found that *none* of them worked as well as might be desired. Low-frequency absorption techniques, they concluded wryly, do not travel unless the designer travels with them.

A practical all-purpose absorber

For some years the BBC used a mixture of soft absorbers and specially designed membrane absorbers which gave satisfactory results, and many of the BBC's sound radio and television studios now have these. But more recently a much simpler type of treatment has been devised, which has several virtues:

(i) The units are of a standard size: 2 feet × 2 feet × 7 inches deep.

(ii) They are easy to construct and to install; this can be done by building contractors without constant supervision by acoustic engineers.

(iii) A level response can be obtained by ringing (literally) superficial changes on a single design. This single basic design therefore serves all purposes.

The box is made of plywood, with a plywood back. The interior is partitioned into four empty compartments by hardboard dividers 6 inches deep. Over this airspace, and immediately behind the face

119

of the box, is 1 inch of heavy density rockwool. The face itself may be of perforated hardboard or other perforated materials. If the open-area perforation is very small (about 0·5%) there is a resonance peak of absorption at about 90 Hz. If the perforation area is large (20% or more) a wideband absorption is achieved, but with a fall-off at 100 Hz and below. So by using one lot of boxes with two lots of facing it is possible to achieve level reverberation curves.

Using sound absorbers

If the acoustics of a sound studio are fully designed, then a mixture of absorbers is likely to be needed; and the majority of existing studios have a mixture of different types of absorbers.

The *coefficient of absorption* at a particular frequency is the proportion of sound at that frequency which is absorbed by the material. The absorption qualities of an area of wall can be calculated (total absorption is taken as unity).

For relatively small areas and at particular frequencies absorbers may have a coefficient that is greater than the unity. (The explanation for this apparent contradiction is that it is caused by diffraction effects.)

Larger objects have been described as the number of "open window units" (their equivalent in the number of square feet of total absorption) that they represent. People rate about 4½ on this scale (at lower-middle to high frequencies); orchestral musicians with all their equipment rate two or three times this, and a padded sofa may have ten times the effect of the man sitting on it. Tables of these values are available: in addition, they give values for the studio structure itself and for the volume of air within it. The calculations are complex.

There are, however, a number of rule-of-thumb ideas which can be applied whether on a major acoustic adventure or more simply when attempting to correct the performance of a given room:

(i) Apply some of each type of absorber to surfaces affecting each of the three dimensions.

(ii) Try to ensure that no untreated surfaces remain to face each other, remembering that a surface that is treated at one frequency may be reflective and therefore effectively untreated at another.

(iii) Put the high-frequency absorbers at head level in speech studios.

For the floors of speech studios it is worth noting that the cheapest and best treatment is a good-quality carpet and underlay (though the roof will need compensation in the bass). Wooden blocks are good on the floor of a (live) music studio.

As for the general furnishings of sound studios: it is obviously unwise to get the acoustics right for the studio when it is empty and then bring in a lot of items (particularly large soft absorbers) which subsequently change it. Such things must be included in the calculations from the start. But apart from this, it is not worth worrying too much about problems until you actually hear them: for example, if there is enough treatment in a room to get the reverberation low and level, and if the main rules for the layout of absorbers have been observed, the diffusion of sound is probably going to be all right anyway. So you can arrange the furniture with aesthetic and other considerations in mind: for how it looks best, makes the occupants feel happy, and gives the most convenient layout of working areas.

The use of screens

Very often the acoustics which are built in to a studio are not exactly those which are wanted for a particular programme, so ways of varying studio quality have been devised. Sometimes the acoustic treatment of a studio is set in hinged or sliding panels, so that with little effort an absorber can be replaced by a reflecting surface. But such half-and-half arrangements rarely prove satisfactory: it is difficult enough getting a studio's acoustics right for a single particular type of programme, without introducing extra uncertainties into the design problem.

But there is one method which is widely used, despite occasional frowns from purists, and this relies on various layouts of studio screens.

Screens are basically rather unsatisfactory absorbers. In order to be easily movable, they must be light in weight; and not more than about three feet wide. Screens are effective only for sound of short wavelengths: low-frequency sound flows round and past them as though they were not there. This means that individual screens have little effect on wavelengths longer than three feet, i.e. on low and middle frequencies. Grouping screens together improves things somewhat, but even so, the small depth of absorber normally available makes the screen very inefficient at low frequencies.

Various types of screen have been designed, the most common consisting of a panel of wood with a layer of padding on one side.

Such screens have the advantage of being dual purpose: used dead side to the microphone, they will damp down the highs: with the bright side forward, the highs will be emphasized, and the ambient sound in the studio somewhat reduced by the absorbent backs. Other types of screen that have been tried include near-hemicylindrical wooden constructions with padding across the diameter (theoretically better, but very cumbrous): and, in "pop" recording studios, large free-standing sheets of perspex or wood.

Whatever the type, the effect of all screens is basically the same in several important respects.

(i) There are shorter path lengths between reflections of the sound in the studio: there are more reflections and more losses in a given time. This means, in general, a lower reverberation time for the studio as a whole.

(ii) Sound from distant sources is reduced; but sound which does get round the screens is usually lacking in top. This includes any appreciable reverberation from the open studio.

(iii) Colouration can be introduced by careless layout. If there are two parallel screens on opposite sides of the microphone a standing-wave pattern will be set up. On the other hand, such distortion effects may be used constructively—though this is more often done by placing a microphone close to a single screen.

(iv) For the purposes of multi-microphone music balances the separation of a large number of individual sources which are physically close together can be made more effective. Important enough in mono, this is vital in stereo.

In any studio it helps to have a few screens around—you never know when they may come in useful. They may be wanted to produce subtle differences of voice quality from a single acoustic, or to screen off a light-voiced songster from the "big" accompaniment, or in a serious music studio for backing and reinforcing the horns.

Altering the acoustics of concert halls

Two examples of halls which have had their acoustics physically altered are the main concert halls in London.

Ever since it was built in Victorian times, the Royal Albert Hall has inflicted severe echoes on large areas of seating and its unfortunate occupants. This was partly due to the shape and partly due to the size of the hall. Being very large, for some seats the path the order of 100 feet, resulting in a delay of nearly 0·1 second. Ideally, to be absolutely sure that the reverberation is not distinct from the direct sound this interval should be 0·02 or less. However, many halls have an appreciable delay between direct sound and the earliest reflections: whether this is acceptable or not depends on the nature of those reflections.

This is where the shape of the Albert Hall comes in: it was designed as a drum shape with an elegant dome surmounting the interior. Such concave surfaces mean that there are bound to be focused reflections at many points: unfortunately some of them coincide with the seating. Apart from the gallery, where the sound was clean, though distant, there were (regular concert-goers claimed) only about two places in the hall which were satisfactory—and those who knew about them booked early and kept their mouths shut.

Some types of music were affected more than others; obviously, staccato playing, including percussion and particularly the piano, were special problems. Also, the natural reverberation time of the hall is long. As a result, the range of music which could be played to really good effect was limited virtually to one type: romantic music with long flowing chords—and for this the warmth of tone of the hall was excellent; sufficiently so, in fact, to ensure that concert-goers returned to the hall time and again to endure its echo.

Half-hearted attempts to improve matters without changing the appearance of the hall too much have provided a continuing saga over several decades. But the problem was eventually tackled drastically, by suspending flights of "flying saucers" 6–12 feet in diameter below the dome. One hundred and nine of these hang just above gallery level; taken all together, they define a new ceiling, slightly convex towards the audience and filling about 50% of the roof area.

These polyester-resin-impregnated glass-fibre diffusers (some of them with sound-absorbent materials on the upper or lower surfaces) have largely solved the problem of echo from above and at the same time have reduced the reverberation at 500 Hz to more reasonable proportions for a wider range of music. Before, it would have been impossible to broadcast without the acoustic aid of an audience. Now something with reasonably large forces—say *Verdi's Requiem* —could be.

In London's post-war Royal Festival Hall the error was in the opposite direction. Musicians had been asked in advance what acoustics they would like to have, "tone" or clarity. The answer came, "tone"—but unfortunately what they actually got instead was a quite remarkable degree of clarity. The sound was much more dead—and particularly in the bass—than had been expected, largely due to the construction of far too thin a roof shell. Minor measures, such as taking up carpets from walkways and making surfaces more reflective, had insufficient effect. While a cough sounded like a close rifle shot, the bass reverberation remained obstinately at about 1·4 seconds. How, short of taking all the seats out and sending the audience and orchestra home, do you lengthen a reverberation time?

The answer was novel and like the hall, twentieth century in style: "assisted resonance". Cavity resonators were used, but not in their normal form: these contained microphones, which were thereby tuned to respond to narrow bands of frequencies present and to re-radiate sound through individual loudspeakers. A hundred channels could each have a separate frequency; allocating each a band of 3 Hz, the whole range of up to about 300 Hz could be boosted. In this way, resonance was restored at surfaces at which, previously, sound energy had begun to disappear. A reverberation time of 2 seconds was now possible; but this could now be varied and actually "tuned" at different frequencies.

The treatment was not as cheap as the Albert Hall's flying saucers, and—alas! it was less satisfactory in dealing with matters other than duration: in particular, when the brass opens up or tympani start rolling, the other players are still overwhelmed and blotted out. As a result, very few seats have a really good balance for all music; and the Hall still remains at its best when used for modern works with a "dry" sound.

In both of these places, however, the BBC had been able to get good or fairly good sound before the alterations by suitable choice of microphone and careful placing; and the balance problems (other than for reverberation *time*) have hardly been affected.

Recording companies working with London's many first-rate orchestras have found their own solutions. Audiophiles all over the world may not know it, but the acoustics *they* generally hear on record are not those of the well-known concert halls, but obscure suburban town halls at places like Walthamstow, Wembley, Watford, and Hammersmith—in buildings that were not originally intended for such a use at all. The moral of this story is that science, so far, is not doing quite so well as happy chance, the fortuitous combination of circumstances that gives perfect blending. Search until you find it.

Not all stories of concert halls and studios have happy endings.

In radio, making the right choice of hall is important, but the occasional use of a bad one is not likely to put the radio organization out of business (and it may help to make the people of the town in which the hall is situated feel wanted). But when recording for sale on disc or tape, the choice of studio is vital: it may affect the recorded quality to such an extent as to affect the reputation of the issuing company if sold at top price.

Ambiophony

So far, almost all of this discussion on the alteration of acoustics has assumed that the studio is constructed as a shell which is basically over-reverberant and that the purpose of acoustic treatment is to reduce this, tailoring it to the required response. The case of London's Royal Festival Hall has, so far, appeared as the only exception to this; and here the extension of the original acoustics has been carefully limited.

But a much more drastic technique than this is needed if large but relatively dead studios, such as those for general-purpose television and film use, are to house orchestras or other musical groups requiring a natural acoustic balance. The addition of artificial "echo" is only a half-solution, because of the effect of the acoustics on the players themselves: the string and some other players may tend to force their tone to "hear" themselves as they think they should be, thereby marring both the internal balance of the orchestra and the overall orchestral quality. Another problem for the musicians is that more distant sections that can normally be heard clearly may not be, so that ensemble playing is more difficult.

A solution which has been offered is called ambiophony. It employs a subsidiary microphone and loudspeaker system which to some extent replace the missing reflecting surfaces. A large number of loudspeakers is required: say, fifty or more in a studio of moderate size.

The microphone and multi-loudspeaker circuit cannot be used in its simplest form for several reasons. One is that the acoustic path lengths are necessarily shorter than the actual size of the studio would suggest: the total distance, musicians to microphone, plus loudspeaker to listener is less than a first reflection path via the position of the loudspeaker. If, however, a delay is introduced into the circuit this problem is overcome and the apparent reflective surface can be made, in effect, to recede to a point beyond the actual distance of the wall. In practice, a much more satisfactory result is

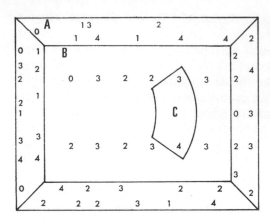

AMBIOPHONY. A. Gallery level. B. Grid level. C. Orchestral area below. 0–4. Loudspeakers with different delay times: 0. No delay. 1. 30 and 60 ms delay. 2. 90 and 150 ms. 3. 120 ms. 4. 180, 210, and 240 ms. This is a typical layout, but each actual case will be different.

achieved by introducing not a single delay system but four (plus some loudspeakers relaying undelayed sound). The four systems are·derived from combinations of the outputs of eight replay heads situated at intervals on a tape loop. This produces a much more rapid break-up of the sound, as it passes repeatedly through the ambiophony microphone and multi-loudspeaker system, diminishing as it does so. In addition, there is variable feedback within the tape delay loop itself, introducing some degree of artificial echo.

The ambiophony microphone needs to be placed close to the sound source; preferably not more than 6 or 8 feet away if there is to be good separation between sources and loudspeakers. This may be closer than is convenient for reasonable coverage of the whole source, so that several microphones may sometimes have to be used, or alternatively, the microphone may have to be moved back to a less favourable position. The use of several close microphones may be visually unsatisfactory in a television studio, even using the small, neat microphones that are available today—so a compromise may be necessary. And if the compromise means that the ambiophony microphones are placed at a much greater distance than the ideal special measures may have to be taken to avoid howl-round when the loudspeakers are set at sound volumes loud enough for the system to work well.

Given a particular array of microphones, amplifier feeds, and loudspeakers, individual levels may be set by taking each loudspeaker in turn, raising its volume until a howl-round occurs, then setting back a little from this. The overall master volume control must, of course, be left at the same setting throughout this whole process.

126

This setting then becomes the maximum at which the system may be used.

It is characteristic of such systems that instability is likely to set in at a particular frequency (which is likely to be a quality of the studio, rather than microphone, amplifier, or loudspeakers). To achieve the highest possible output for the loudspeakers, a response shaper consisting of a system of octave (or more closely spaced) filters may be included in the circuit. Using this, the response may be modified not only to reduce "peaks" of instability at particular frequencies but also generally to improve the quality of the ambiophony.

The whole system may be very critical, and may even be affected by a change of tape in the loop: for this reason any change must be made before the final run-through so that there is time for any necessary adjustment to be made, and to allow time for the tape to become well polished as it circulates through the system, so that the relationship between recording and reproducing characteristics is not likely to change.

The ambiophony circuit must, of course, be kept completely separate from that for the main programme, as the microphones used will be much too close to get a good overall balance—though with certain types of control desk a sub-mixer can be isolated and used to drive the system.

The primary purpose of ambiophony is to create conditions in which musicians can work comfortably, as in natural acoustics. There is no doubt that this is achieved—but in addition a reasonable simulation of music studio acoustics is produced, one which gives a sound that is very satisfactory given the initially unfavourable conditions. However, ambiophony would certainly not be preferred to the balance of an orchestra in a good, natural concert hall acoustic.

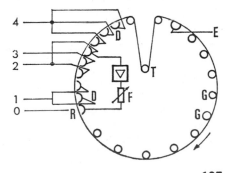

AMBIOPHONY. R. Recording head, fed from ambiophony microphone, plus feedback loop, F. E. Erase head. T. Tension pulley. G. Tape guides. D. Delay heads. 0–4. Feeds to loudspeakers with different delay times (see opposite).

The final pick-up of the resulting sound will normally be made using an omnidirectional microphone placed high up (as described in the chapter on microphone techniques for music), with the variation that the microphone is balancing direct sound against a system of apparent acoustics that is itself variable in frequency response, in reverberation time (by varying feedback within the tape delay system itself) and to some extent in overall volume. The first two of these techniques are discussed further in the chapter on echo and distortion techniques.

Once a particular distribution of loudspeakers, each with its own delay, is worked out, this will be specific to a particular position of the sound source for which it was calculated. As a result, if additional sources are introduced (say, singers in other parts of the studio) the system may be unbalanced. In particular, ambiophony cannot be expected to work satisfactorily where a boom microphone is to be used for a moving singer. Obviously, different loudspeakers will be favoured as the microphone is swung to different angles. But with experiment—and care—solutions may be found to particular problems.

5

MICROPHONES

In the simplest terms, the job of a microphone is to convert sound energy into electrical energy, and to do so without changing the sound information in any important way.

A microphone must therefore do three things:

(i) For normal sound levels it must produce an electrical signal which is well above its own electrical noise level.
(ii) For normal sound levels the signal it produces must be substantially undistorted.
(iii) Together with its associated equipment, it should, for a particular sound source, respond almost equally to all significant audio frequencies present (within whatever range subsequent equipment is capable of handling).

With today's high-quality microphones the first two objectives are fairly easily met—though to achieve a signal which can even be transmitted safely along the microphone lead, a transformer or amplifier is often required so close to the head as to be regarded as part of the microphone itself.

The third requirement is more modest, and deliberately so. Indeed, until the advent of FM broadcasting there was no call in radio for microphones that could pick up the full audio range. To have demanded this would have been a waste of money. And even today it may still be unnecessary to use a microphone with a full-range frequency response for a source which does not have this: for example, in multi-microphone music balances it is desirable to match the microphone response to the instrument—and not just to save the cost of having large numbers of expensive very high-quality microphones, though it may do this too.

Microphones differ from each other in the way that movement of the diaphragm is converted into electrical energy. The most important types in present-day professional use are moving-coil, electro-

129

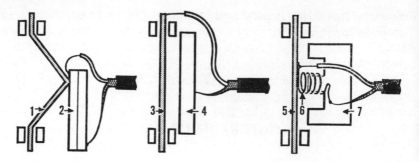

TYPES OF MICROPHONE. Crystal (*left*). 1. Light rigid diaphragm. 2. Crystal bimorph. Condenser or electrostatic (*centre*). 3. Foil diaphragm. 4. Backplate. Moving coil (*right*). 5. Diaphragm. 6. Coil fixed to diaphragm. 7. Permanent magnet.

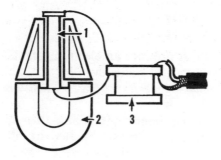

RIBBON MICROPHONE. 1. Aluminium foil ribbon. 2. Permanent magnet (with pole pieces extending above). 3. Transformer.

static (condenser), and ribbon types. Crystal microphones are used in cheaper equipment and carbon types in telephones. Other microphones include inductor, moving-iron, magnetostriction, and electronic types. The latter will not be described here; several of them have practical disadvantages which have limited their development.

Microphones also differ from each other in the way in which air pressures are converted into movement of the diaphragm. These variations show themselves as differences in directional characteristics (or "polar diagram"), and they are of great importance to the user.

However, although the output of a microphone may be deliberately designed to change with the angle from a given axis, the frequency response, ideally, should not. But unfortunately this is an almost impossible demand, so it is usual to define the "useful angle" within which this condition is, more or less, met; or to devise ways in which the deficiency can be turned to advantage.

Sensitivity is also an important quality: this is the strength of the electrical signal that is produced by a microphone. In practice, most professional microphones have sensitivities within a range of only a few dB of each other (though this level may be at the output of a microphone head amplifier). Characteristically, rather more than 70 dB (further) amplification will be required to reach a level which is suitable for input to a high-level mixer or for transmission by line between studio and radio transmitter—though at the bell of a trombone a microphone may also have to respond without distortion to levels which are 60 dB higher than that for which it is rated.

Other properties that may be of importance are:

(i) *Robustness.* Moving-coil microphones in particular stand up well to the relatively rough treatment a microphone may accidently suffer when used away from the studio. Electrostatic (condenser) microphones require greater care.

(ii) *Sensitivity to handling,* e.g. by pop singers. Again moving-coil types score. If microphones are to be handled while in use the cables and cable connections must not be subject to handling noise either.

(iii) *Sensitivity to wind pressures.* Ribbon microphones may be bad in this respect, and may therefore not be suitable for outdoor work.

(iv) *Shape, size, or weight.* Appearance matters a great deal in television, and size and weight in microphones that are held or attached to clothing.

(v) *Cost.* Crystal microphones are very cheap, and good moving-coil microphones moderately so; electrostatic microphones are relatively expensive. The cost of high-quality microphones has, however, been reduced very considerably in recent years.

(vi) *Suitable impedance.* Nominally a microphone should be rated appropriately for the impedance of the system into which its signal is fed, otherwise the interface between components

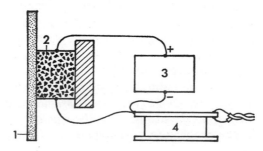

CARBON MICROPHONE. 1. Light rigid plate. 2. Granular carbon button. 3. Battery. 4. Transformer.

reflects some of the signal and may affect the frequency response. However (within limits), a low-impedance microphone may be used with a high-impedance system following it, e.g. a 60-ohm microphone plugged in to equipment rated at 300 ohms may behave perfectly satisfactorily. Microphones are often available in several versions, each having a different impedance.

In a given situation any one of these points may be dominant, severely restricting or even dictating the choice of microphone.

The conditions of use may also determine the way in which a microphone is used. For example, television often demands that no microphone be visible even in a wide picture. Or in a very noisy location, such as by the side of an aircraft that is about to take off, the only place for a microphone so that speech can be heard is right by the mouth of the speaker. In these and many other cases the first criterion must be clarity.

But if clear speech is possible in more than one limiting position of the microphone (or with more than one type) we have a series of choices that we can make. These are the choices that are open to us in *microphone balance*.

Microphone balance

Returning to the start of the chain, we have the studio and, placed somewhere in it, the microphone. The exact placing of the microphone in relation to the source and the studio acoustics is called microphone balance.

There are two main objects of balance. The first of these is *to pick up the required sound at a level suitable to the microphone and recording set-up; and at the same time to discriminate against unwanted noises.*

In professional practice this means deciding whether one microphone is necessary to cover the sound source adequately, or several, and choosing the best type of microphone, with regard to polar characteristics (i.e. response to signals coming from various directions: see p. 134) and frequency characteristics. In addition, it will often be possible to choose the position of the source or degree of spread of several sources.

The second aim of a good balance is *to place each microphone at a distance and angle which will produce the right degree of reinforcement from the acoustics of the studio.*

The proper use of reverberation is fundamental to good balance, the aim being to achieve an appropriate ratio of direct to indirect sound.

To take two extremes: a distant balance will give a very full account of studio characteristics; whereas a very close balance will give predominantly direct sound, and acoustics may have no effect.

Acoustic reinforcement may, however, be replaced by artificial reverberation which is mixed in to the final sound electrically. In this case each individual sound source can be individually treated. For this reason, and because picking up a sound on a second more distant microphone will reintroduce the effect of the studio acoustics, we have as an alternative aim of microphone balance: *to separate the sound sources so that they can be treated individually*.

For the man working on pop music the term balance means a great deal more than this: it includes the treatment, mixing, and control functions which are integral parts of the creation of his single composite sound. In this chapter, however, I shall deal only with microphone placing, the element of balance which has most affected their design.

The balance test

Good sound is not just a matter of "going by the book". It is a subjective quality, and can be judged only by listening, with objectivity and detachment, under the best conditions that the listening audience is likely to use. The only way to be sure of getting a good balance—or at any rate the best balance with the available studio and microphone—is to carry out a balance test.

The man working in a studio, having a separate monitoring cubicle, is able to use a high-quality loudspeaker to listen to the balance from the soundproof studio direct. But where these ideal conditions are not available, and artistic quality is both important and possible, balance tests should take the form of trial recordings— if necessary, a whole series of them—so that comparisons can be made on playback.

Since the recordist uses these trial runs to judge how he can use the acoustics of the studio to the greatest advantage (or to the least disadvantage, if the reverberation is excessive or highly coloured), he must use reasonably high-quality equipment for playback. It must be remembered that a tape recorder's internal speaker will generally have colourations (peaks and troughs in its frequency response, due to resonances, etc.) which will often be severe enough to mask those picked up by the microphone.

A film recordist or radio man working on location may be at a particular disadvantage here; a disadvantage which will not be viewed sympathetically back in the studio. So skill—or in the absence of experience, very great care—is needed here.

A fully equipped studio makes the balance test a very simple business—deceptively simple perhaps. For music, by far the best way to find a good balance is to put up two microphones in likely positions and make a direct comparison of the two by listening to each in turn. The microphone giving the better sound is left where it is, and the other is moved—and the process repeated until no further improvement is found.

For speech, the method of achieving an ideal balance is much the same. If your speaker is sitting at a table it will probably be easiest to let him settle into a comfortable position and then, using two microphones, make a series of direct comparison tests.

A skilled operator working in familiar surroundings and with little time to spare may proceed by experience and rule of thumb. This should not deceive the newcomer to the medium.

There is no way of getting round the necessity for properly conducted tests, where an artistic balance is required. Such methods as walking about a studio, finding a spot that "sounds good" and putting the microphone there, just don't work. (Although for music this may be a useful guide to a starting-point.) For reportage, an unchecked balance will generally yield results which have an adequate documentary value. But for all other purposes it would be better to assume that any defects of balance will diminish the listeners' appreciation of the programme.

Directional response

A great deal depends on the choice of microphone. These fall into several main groups, according to their directional characteristics. The descriptions given below are introduced mainly in order to define the various terms that the reader will meet, here and elsewhere. The basic types will be treated in greater detail later.

Omnidirectional microphones. These, ideally, respond equally to sounds coming from all directions. Basically, they are devices for measuring the *pressure* of the air, and converting this into an electrical signal. Most designs of moving-coil and crystal microphone work in this way, as do some electrostatic microphones. The diaphragm is open to the air on one side only.

OMNIDIRECTIONAL RESPONSE. The electrical signal is independent of microphone angle. (In a polar diagram such as this the curve indicates the output of the microphone for a given sound arriving from any angle.)

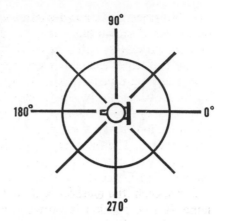

Bi-directional microphones. These measure the *difference in pressure* (pressure gradient) at two successive points along the path of the sound wave. If the microphone is placed sideways to the path of the sound the pressure is always the same at these two points and no electrical signal will be generated. The microphone is therefore "dead" to sound approaching from the side and "live" to that approaching one face or the other.

Moving round to the side of the microphone, the response becomes progressively smaller; and since a graph of the output looks like a figure-of-eight, this term is sometimes used to describe this type of microphone. The "live angle" is generally regarded as being about 100°.

Moving round to the back of the microphone produces a signal which is equal in strength to the one at the front, but 180° out of phase (antiphase) to it.

Ribbon microphones most often work in this way, responding to the difference in pressure on the two faces of a strip of aluminium

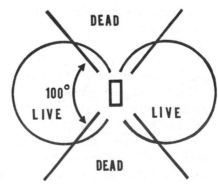

BI-DIRECTIONAL RESPONSE. "Live" and "dead" sides of the ribbon microphone. At 60° from axis response drops to half: the "live" angle is generally taken to be rather less than this (total angle 100°).

135

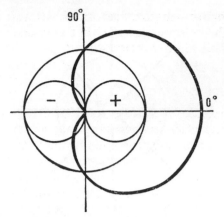

CARDIOID RESPONSE. Is the sum of omnidirectional and figure-of-eight pick-up: on one side of the microphone the two are in the opposite sense, and so cancel out. Such a microphone is therefore sometimes called unidirectional.

foil. Single-diaphragm electrostatic microphones work in this way if the air pressure can reach both sides of the diaphragm equally.

Cardioids—sometimes called *unidirectional microphones*—have a heart-shaped response. This is obtained if the output of a pressure gradient (e.g. ribbon) microphone is joined with that of a pressure microphone (e.g. moving coil). Some cardioid microphones actually contain a ribbon and a moving coil within a single case.

The output of the two is added together for sounds at the front; but at the back the two are antiphase and cancel out. At the side there is no output from the ribbon, but the omnidirectional element retains its normal output. So there is a substantial pick up of sound on the front and right round to the side, but beyond this very little.

Cardioids are complex microphones, having either two diaphragms or a single diaphragm with a complicated acoustic network feeding the rear face.

Some microphones of this type may also be switchable to an

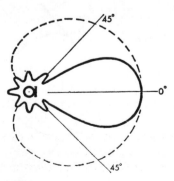

HIGHLY DIRECTIONAL MICROPHONE. The unbroken line shows the polar response for medium-high audio frequencies (at very high frequencies the beam is narrower). At low frequencies (broken line) the response degenerates to the normal response for the microphone type being used (in this case cardioid).

omnidirectional or figure-of-eight response, and possibly also to intermediate conditions. A particularly important one is the *hyper-cardioid* or cottage-loaf response: this is bi-directional, but with a relatively broad lobe in front and a smaller, somewhat weaker lobe at the rear.

Highly directional microphones. These are substantially dead to sound from the side or rear. They are characterized by their size: either a large parabolic dish to concentrate sound for a microphone placed near the focus or, more commonly today, a long tube extending forward from the main unit. The frequency response is a narrow forward lobe at high frequencies, but this degenerates into a broader response at wavelengths greater than the major dimensions of the microphone.

The frequency response of practical microphones

Practical, high-quality professional microphones rarely have a response that is anything like flat. Peaks and troughs of the order of 3–4 dB are common and are to be found even on extremely expen-

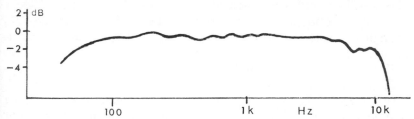

FREQUENCY RESPONSE of a good ribbon microphone. Note that variations in the frequency response of microphones is generally described in decibels of *voltage*, dB (V). Each dB (V) corresponds to *two* decibels of *acoustic* power, db (A); i.e., I dB (A) = 2 dB (V). There are good mathematical reasons for this, but it is confusing and can make microphone performance look worse than it actually is. In the case illustrated above, the frequency range of the microphone is less than $2\frac{1}{2}$ dB (V) between 55–1100 Hz. Such a small variation—corresponding to $1\frac{1}{4}$ dB (A)—will not be noticed.

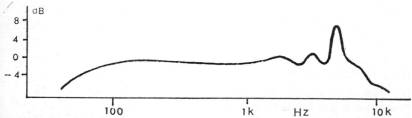

ERRATIC RESPONSE of an inexpensive omnidirectional microphone with a large diaphragm. Minor variations have been disregarded, but the peaks in the h.f. response will be clearly audible. Such unrealistic peaks can, however, be used constructively to provide "presence".

137

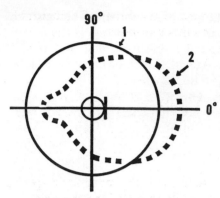

PRACTICAL MICROPHONES. Typical degeneration of frequency response of omnidirectional microphone with large case. While response is maintained at all angles for low frequencies (I), the output falls off at the rear for high frequencies (2).

sive microphones. This is not bad workmanship: it is simply that it is extremely difficult to design a microphone for a level response at all audio frequencies. In addition, individual samples may vary by 2 dB or so from the average for its type. Fortunately few people notice variations of this order: in a reverberant balance they will probably be overshadowed by variations due to the acoustics, anyway. But a broad peak of 6 or 7 dB in the top response of a close speech microphone will certainly be noticeable.

Some microphones have a response which falls away in the bass enough to make them unsuitable for particular orchestral instruments (or for that matter a full orchestra). But much more common is loss of top—from about 10 kHz (or even below) on some professional microphones and from 12 kHz on many of high quality. A very few go well beyond this, but the angle at which the microphone is used may be critical: the axis of the diaphragm should point directly at the sound source.

The most common defect of microphones—and a serious one for high-quality work—is an erratic response in the upper-middle range. Except in individual cases where a *continuous* trace of the frequency response is provided with each microphone, manufacturers tend to publish data and diagrams which somewhat idealize the performance of their products. So this defect may not be apparent from publicity material.

The size of a microphone affects its frequency response. In general, the larger the diaphragm and the larger the case, the more difficult it is to engineer a smooth extended top response (but the easier it is to obtain a strong signal).

Also, having the rear of the diaphragm enclosed (as with omnidirectional microphones) creates difficulties in the upper middle response. Some designs have been developed to smooth out this

138

effect, but a ribbon microphone (open at the back) of comparable workmanship is likely to have a smoother response.

Omnidirectional microphones

Many microphones which are nominally omnidirectional are truly so only at low frequencies. A microphone measuring about two inches across can be expected to show marked directional qualities above 7,000 Hz. This happens in many inexpensive crystal microphones, and even in some larger professional moving-coil microphones. Very often these have a rise in the high-frequency response along the axis, but are much "flatter" at about 45° to the axis.

Used with care, this allows some control of the frequency characteristics of a recording. In this case a balance at an angle of something like 45° will be preferred (experiment will indicate the angle at which the smoothest response will be obtained), but if the microphone is used for interviewing in a noisy location an on-axis balance will "lift" the intelligibility of the speech out of the background.

Very small microphones avoid this sort of pattern in their response.

Studio techniques using omnidirectional microphones for speech will be dealt with in Chapter 5, but in fact the type is also widely used outside the studio—held in the hand for reporting and interview work.

Bi-directional microphones

Figure-of-eight microphones have much to recommend them for indoor work of all kinds. Their directional qualities give the balancer a great deal of control over such things as the ratio of direct to indirect sound; and they have a useful ability to discriminate against unwanted sound.

An important characteristic of ribbon and other bi-directional microphones is that if they are placed too close to the source— less than about 2 feet—the bass frequencies are emphasized; and this becomes progressively more severe as the microphone is moved still closer to the source of the sound. Close to a source, sound levels change in intensity a great deal within a short distance. At 2 feet from the source the intensity is a quarter of that at 1 foot. Pressure gradients are therefore emphasized—but more so in the bass than at higher frequencies (for which the effect is masked by the greater change of phase between front and rear of microphone). This result of close working is called bass tip-up.

139

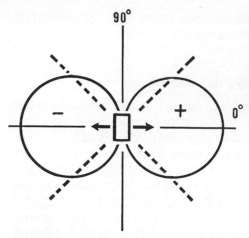

FIGURE-OF-EIGHT RESPONSE. As a sound source moves round to the side the microphone's output is gradually reduced. At 90° there is no signal due to direct sound. At the back of the microphone the output once again increases but in the opposite sense.

There are a number of points to note when using ribbons, particularly if the studio conditions are such that fairly close working seems necessary:

(i) Bass tip-up is more troublesome with some voices than others. Women, for example, can often speak at less than the usual recommended distance without distortion being apparent.

(ii) Using a suitable correction circuit (e.g. a pre-amplifier with a tone control), some degree of bass correction can be introduced for working closer than normal. Experiment will indicate suitable settings and distances.

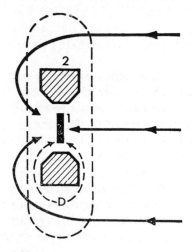

PRESSURE GRADIENT OPERATION. The effective path difference (i.e. the extra distance travelled by the wave to reach the back of the ribbon 1) is equivalent to the distance D round the magnet pole-piece 2.

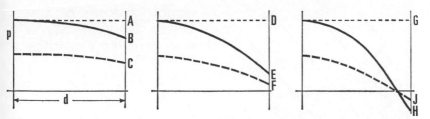

BASS TIP-UP in pressure gradient microphone. In each diagram the unbroken line represents the pressure waveform at the front of the diaphragm; the broken line represents the reduced pressure in a spherical wave as it has travelled a further distance d to reach the other side of the diaphragm. *Left*: the pressure difference, which would be AB in an unattenuated wave, has been increased to AC. *Centre*: for a shorter wavelength the pressure difference DE has again been increased (to DF) but the change is proportionately much smaller than for the long wave. *Right*: for a very short wavelength the effect could in principle be reversed; the pressure difference GH might actually be reduced to GJ. But this third case is hypothetical. In fact, for short waves the rear of the diaphragm is shadowed and the microphone is operated by pressure on the front alone.

(iii) It is unwise to move about too much. At normal working distances six inches of movement backward or forward will produce a big enough change in intensity to be obvious. If the level is controlled to compensate for this there will still be a change in the ratio of direct to indirect sound, and therefore a change of quality (this is true of other types of microphone as well, but with ribbons the effect may be emphasized by some variation in the amount of bass).

(iv) The changes in volume and frequency characteristic that go with any change in distance are even more noticeable when a microphone with bass correction is used for close working.

(v) It is sometimes possible to work very close to a ribbon for whispers but it is advisable to speak across the face of the microphone in order to minimize the effect of "popping".

When two bi-directional microphones are placed close together a check should be made that the two are *in phase*. If they are not, cancellation of direct sound will occur for sources which are equidistant from the two (although normal reverberation will be heard) and severe distortion may be apparent for other positions of the source. The cure, with ribbon microphones, is to turn one of them round. Otherwise, it is the leads which must be reversed.

When two microphones are needed to pick up separate sources, ribbons are very often used with each microphone dead-side-on to the other source. This gives better control in mixing.

The polar response of ribbons varies very little with frequency in

141

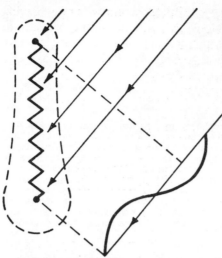

VERTICAL RESPONSE OF RIBBON MICROPHONE. At oblique angles, there is partial cancellation of very short wavelengths (i.e. high frequency) sounds along the length of the ribbon.

the horizontal plane, but there is some variation in the vertical plane; the degree of loss of top depends on the size of the microphone—it is due to partial cancellation along the length of the ribbon.

Cardioid and hypercardioid microphones

With true cardioid microphones the useful angle is a broad cone including at least 120° on the live side—but which may be taken as extending round to the sides up to a total included angle of about 180°, though so far round to the side the overall response is noticeably lower and the high-frequency response will be nothing like so good as that on the main axis. Going round to the back of the microphone the response should in theory simply diminish gradually to nothing, but in practice the output, though at low level, is very uneven, with an erratic frequency response.

Because of the directional properties there is some bass tip-up with close working; and although this is only about half of that of figure-of-eight types, it is quite enough to cause trouble if the microphone is hand-held close to the mouth.

Coverage being broader than with a figure-of-eight, a cardioid microphone can be used where space is limited. For similar distances of working it will give a fuller account of the surrounding acoustics, but being directional, still gives the balancer a good measure of control over studio conditions.

The most obvious way of producing a cardioid, by connecting up an omnidirectional moving coil in parallel with a bi-directional

142

ribbon, has already been mentioned. But a second way of achieving the same result is much less obvious: to allow the sound pressure to reach the back of the diaphragm (which may be moving-coil, electrostatic, or ribbon) but with a *change of phase*. To make this

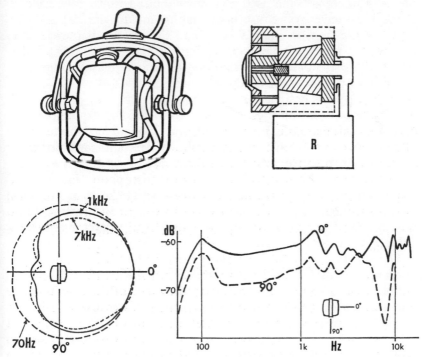

MOVING COIL CARDIOID MICROPHONE suitable for television boom operation. A complex system of acoustic labyrynths is built in to the microphone housing: the air reservoir R (shown in the simplified sectional diagram) provides the damping for one of three resonant systems which are used to engineer the response of the microphone.

work satisfactorily over a range of frequencies, a complicated phase-shifting network of cavities and narrow tunnels is needed.

Most users accept the result, and do not worry too much about the theory—but such a system can be described mathematically in terms of acoustic resistances, capacitances, and inertiances. Using these quantities, the pressures on both sides of the diaphragm can be calculated for a range of frequencies arriving from different directions, so that working back from the desired result—a cardioid response reasonably independent of frequency—it has been possible to define a suitable acoustic network at the back of the diaphragm. Microphones have been designed in this way and work well.

143

An electrostatic microphone with two diaphragms on either side of a central base-plate will also work as a cardioid. In this case there is a polarizing charge between one of the diaphragms and the base-plate; but the other plate has the same charge as the base, so only one diaphragm is being used as a normal electrostatic microphone element. Sound waves cause both diaphragms to vibrate; and the resulting pressures in the cavity behind the second diaphragm are transmitted through holes perforating the base-plate: these holes are of such a size and number that they produce a phase change, and this in turn produces the cardioid response.

In recent years designers have produced a range of professional microphones based on these and similar ideas: for example, twin-diaphragm electrostatic, moving-coil, and ribbon microphones have all appeared. Not all of these microphones are pure cardioid: it is, for example, possible to arrange for a broad cardioid response, which is rather like an omnidirectional microphone but with a somewhat reduced output at all frequencies at the rear. Another type is "cottage-loaf", or hypercardioid, i.e. it is bi-directional but with a relatively broad lobe at the front, and a narrow one with reduced volume at the back.

This last type may be particularly useful for close work in multi-microphone music balances. One that is commercially available—a double ribbon—has a bass output which falls off below 200 Hz: this is automatically compensated for on close working.

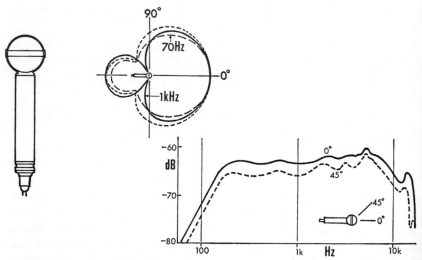

DOUBLE-RIBBON HYPERCARDIOID MICROPHONE: polar and frequency response curves.

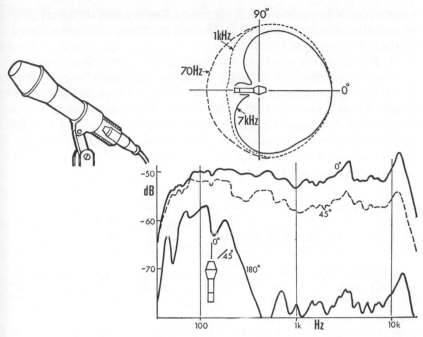

DOUBLE MOVING COIL CARDIOID MICROPHONE: polar and frequency response curves.

In one example of double moving coil the response is a broad cardioid derived partly from the double-diaphragm operation and partly from phase shift. It also has a built-in wind-shield of porous metal ("sintered bronze") at the front, which protects it in close working from blasting by explosive consonants. Here again, a deliberately permitted gradual degeneration of the low-frequency response allows close working without bass tip-up.

Both the double-moving-coil and the moving-coil phase-shift microphones are suitable for mounting on television booms, though for music, electrostatic cardioids are to be preferred.

Switchable microphones

A microphone in which the cardioid response is directly derived from two microphones, one omnidirectional and one figure-of-eight, can be made switchable between the three conditions, and in principle also to intermediate ones, by combining the outputs of the two microphones in various proportions. However, early microphones of this type underwent so much compromise at the design

145

stage in order to optimize their cardioid response that their performance in the omnidirectional or bi-directional condition is not so good as that of separate microphones.

In a switchable electrostatic microphone one diaphragm is constantly polarized and the other can have its polarization changed. If the two diaphragms are polarized in the same sense the microphone operates as a pressure capsule, as would two single-diaphragm electrostatic microphones placed back to back and wired to add outputs. But if the polarizing current on one diaphragm is decreased to zero (and the centre plate has suitable perforations) the polar response will become cardioid.

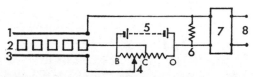

DOUBLE-DIAPHRAGM ELECTROSTATIC MICROPHONE: Variable polar response. 1. Front diaphragm. 2. Rigid centre plate (perforated). 3. Rear diaphragm. 4. Multi-position switch and potentiometer. 5. Polarizing voltage. 6. High resistance. 7. Head amplifier. 8. Microphone output terminals. When the polarization is switched to position "O" the voltage on the front and back diaphragms is the same, and above that of the centre plate: the capsule operates as an omnidirectional (pressure) microphone. At "B" the capsule measures pressure gradient and is bi-directional. At "C" the polar response is cardioid.

Taking this process a stage further, if the polarizing current is now increased in the opposite sense, so that the voltage on the centre plate is intermediate between those of the two diaphragms, the mode of operation of the microphone will become pressure-gradient and its output bi-directional. That it would do so might have been expected: this is very similar to the symmetrical layout in which a central diaphragm is balanced between two oppositely polarized perforated plates. Indeed, looking at it this way, the cardioid can be seen as the expected intermediate stage between the omni- and bi-directional conditions.

Despite their fragile construction, the diaphragms stand up well to overloading, though the head amplifiers may not. It is in this latter field that much recent work on electrostatic microphones has been concentrated, and types using several different principles for converting the changes of capacitance to a usable electrical signal are now available.

Even with a very high-quality double-diaphragm microphone of this type some compromises have to be made. In a particular case the cardioid response is excellent and the intermediate positions

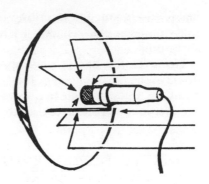

MICROPHONE IN PARABOLIC RE-FLECTOR. For wavelengths greater than the diameter of the bowl the directional qualities degenerate. The reflector gives a gain of about 20 dB on axis; in comparison, the gun microphones described on the following pages give none. The parabolic reflector therefore gives a better intrinsic ratio of signal to amplifier hiss.

useful; the omnidirectional condition is good, but the bi-directional condition has a broad peak in its high-frequency response.

However, for many purposes this broad peak may be no disadvantage—and other attributes of the capacitor microphone may outweigh the possible disadvantages of the peak.

Highly directional microphones

The method by which the parabolic microphone achieves its directional properties is obvious; equally obviously these directional properties will degenerate at low frequencies for which the sound waves are too long to "see" the dish effectively. So although high frequencies may be picked up well at a considerable distance, low frequencies are not: for a reasonably manoeuvrable reflector of 3–4 feet in diameter the directional response will be less effective below 1000 Hz. Also, the microphone is subject to close unwanted noises at low frequencies, unless a bass cut is used. This microphone

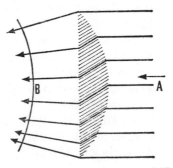

SOUND LENS. The slatted structure transforms the plane wave A into a convergent wave B, providing high acoustic amplification for a microphone at the focus. A sound lens is effective only at wavelengths which are less than its diameter.

147

has found favour for recording birdsong and certain other specialized purposes, but has never been widely used, if only because of its sheer bulk.

However, this and other focusing techniques (e.g. the sound lens) do have the advantage that they can be concentrated almost to pinpoint accuracy at high frequencies, or defocused slightly to give a broader lobe of pick-up. Also, they work just as well indoors as out,

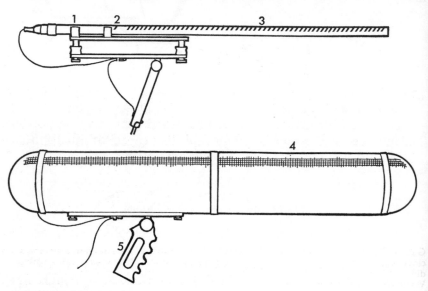

GUN MICROPHONE. 1. Head amplifier of condenser microphone. 2. Electrostatic capsule (cardioid operation). 3. Acoustic interference tube (with entry ports along upper surface). 4. Windshield for open air use. 5 Handgrip.

which other types may not; however, their shape is against them here too.

More useful (because less awkward to handle) are "gun" microphones. Early designs had many narrow tubes of different lengths forming a bundle with the diaphragm enclosed in a chamber at the base. When these tubes are pointed directly at a subject sound pressures passing along the different tubes all travel the same distance, so (apart from acoustic impedance effects) the pick-up in this direction is normal.

But for sound approaching from an oblique angle many different path lengths are travelled, and as the pressures recombine in the cavity before the diaphragm there is cancellation over a wide range of frequencies. The further round to the side or rear, the more

148

efficient this cancellation becomes; for sound from the rear the path lengths vary by twice the length of the "barrel" of the "gun". But there is still a limit to effective cancellation, and therefore to the directional response itself—and again this depends on the physical size of the attachment to the microphone.

In more recent gun microphones the many tubes have been replaced by a single narrow barrel, to which the sound has access at many points along the length. In some of the early "rifle" micro-

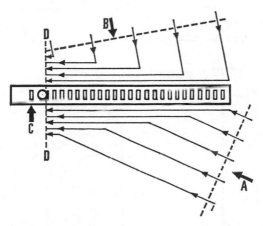

GUN MICROPHONE: phase cancellation effect. Wave A approaching from a direction close to the axis reaches the microphone front diaphragm D by a range of paths which differ only slightly in length. There will be cancellation only at very high frequencies. Wave B reaches the diaphragm by a much wider range of path-lengths. Cancellation will be severe at middle and high frequencies. Normal sound reaches the back of the diaphragm via port C. The polar diagram of the capsule without the acoustic delay network is cardioid; with the tube it becomes highly directional.

phones, the slot is filled with porous material (e.g. felt), so that once in, a substantial part of the sound pressure stays in and is transmitted to the microphone.

An older microphone of this type has a tube 6 feet 8 inches long, and is therefore highly directional; indeed, as an acoustic engineering aid it has been used to pinpoint the sources of echoes in concert halls. Similar microphones have also been used for picking up voices at a distance; for example, reporters in a large audience at Presidential press conferences. But the sound obtained in this way is far from high quality, and the operation of the microphone is itself aurally distracting, as it is very obvious when it is being faded up or down, or panned to find a person who is already speaking. Speech at a distance has a harsh, unpleasant quality—but is, at least, clearly

149

audible. One difficulty with this arrangement is that sound travels slower along the tube than in the outside air, so that for such a long microphone even sound along the axis is subject to partial cancellation.

The next generation has been a much shorter gun microphone, with a tube length of about 18 inches on one side of a cardioid-response electrostatic capsule. It retains much of the larger instrument's directional response at high frequencies, but has a high-

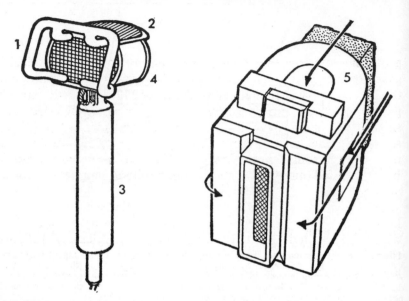

LIP RIBBON MICROPHONE. The mouth guard 1 is placed against the upper lip and the stainless steel mesh 2 acts as a windshield below the nose. The handgrip 3 contains a transformer. Within the housing 4 the microphone assembly is mounted with the yoke of the magnet 5 towards the mouth, and the ribbon away from it. The sound paths are marked.

quality performance in the direction in which it is pointing. This has found favour with many film recordists for location work and has been used very satisfactorily for television documentary films that I have directed. It is sensitive to low-frequency noise from the sides, but if bass-cut can be applied (as it often can be for exterior work) this will reduce traffic rumble considerably.

In these microphones the acoustic interference tube is completely open internally, but has a light mesh covering the entry ports: this obstructs any continuous air flow and larger dust particles.

In one example there is a pistol grip below the microphone and

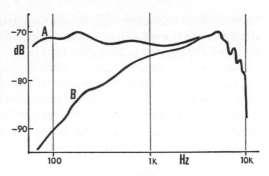

RESPONSE OF LIP-RIBBON MICROPHONE. A. Response to spherical wave at approximately 2½ inches (i.e., the user's voice). B. To plane wave (ambient sound), on axis. This effect is achieved by equalization, without which B would be flat and A would be very high at low frequencies, due to extreme bass tip-up at such a close working distance.

projecting at a convenient angle. For outdoor work a windshield is generally used, but this may be very bulky, so that if it obtrudes into the picture it is very obvious. But even with a windshield, strong, gusting wind can cause break-up of the signal even when the windshield itself is protected by the body of the recordist and other screens. In this respect, however, there is little to choose between this and "personal" microphones (which will be described later); but when used out of doors the gun microphone is preferable for its quality.

In a normal room indoors the microphone will suffer partial loss of its directional qualities, as much of the reverberation will be out of phase and will not be subject to cancellation. Indoors, therefore, the response may not be better than a hypercardioid, and a sound off the axis is likely to be unpleasantly reverberant.

Noise cancelling microphones

There are several ways of getting rid of noise: one is to put the speaker—a sports commentator perhaps—into a soundproof box. But against crowd noise such commentary boxes tend not to be soundproof at low frequencies, and in any case are bound to introduce unpleasant resonances if they are small. Another technique is to use an omnidirectional microphone close to the mouth; but in very noisy surroundings this may still not provide the ideal balance between the voice and the background sound—while the man who is controlling the sound level will have no direct means of correcting the mixture.

To allow the best results in any situation like this, the voice and background need to be almost completely separated. The one

151

broadcast-quality microphone that will do this in almost any circumstances, even for a commentator speaking in a normal voice with the roar of the crowd all around him, is a "lip-ribbon".

The microphone, as its name implies, has its ribbon very close to the mouth of the speaker. As the ribbon is working in its pressure-gradient mode, it is, in fact, subject to very heavy bass tip-up for sound from such a close source; there will, however, be no bass tip-up on ambient sound arriving from distant sources. If a specific distance is chosen, say a little over 2 inches, for the separation

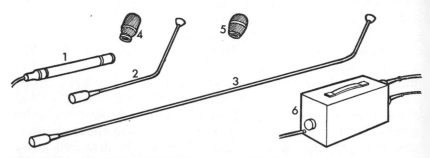

AN ELECTROSTATIC MICROPHONE, supplied with alternative capsules for cardioid and omnidirectional operation. 1. Head amplifier and capsule. 2 and 3. Extension pieces (these are fitted between head amplifier and microphone capsule). 4 and 5. Windshields. 6. Power supply unit.

between lip and ribbon, and equalization is introduced which makes the microphone response to the voice flat for a sound source at such a distance, this will also reduce the ambient bass noise level by the same amount. Obviously, the closer to the mouth the ribbon is, the better—so long as the explosive sounds in speech, and streams of air from the mouth and nose can be controlled. With a distance of $2\frac{1}{8}$ inches (exactly measured by placing a guard against the upper lip) these factors can be controlled by windshields (which, as they are so close to the mouth or nose, need to be made of stainless steel or plastic), and by cupping the ribbon itself *behind* the magnet.

Some versions have a variety of equalization settings for different degrees of bass; but in general the reduction of noise is about 10 dB at 300 Hz, increasing to 20 dB at 100 Hz. A high-frequency response of up to about 7 kHz is all that is needed for speech in these conditions, so above that frequency the sensitivity of the microphone falls away. These figures are, of course, to be added to those for discrimination due to the extremely close working, and (for noise from particular directions) the figure-of-eight response.

It is possible that even more efficient noise-cancelling microphones could be devised. But this one—though not visually attractive because it obscures the mouth—has proved sufficient for almost any conditions of noise yet encountered in broadcasting.

Microphones for use in vision

Everything within a television or film picture, as much as everything in the sound, adds to the total effect; and a microphone which may be in the picture or a series of pictures for a long time is an

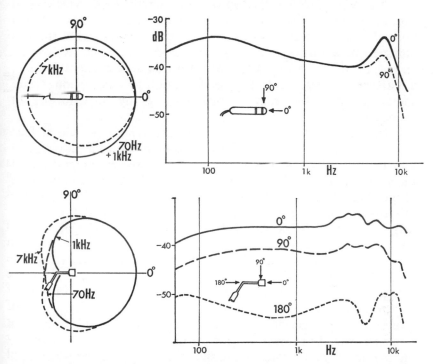

ELECTROSTATIC MICROPHONE of type shown opposite. Response curves *above* for omnidirectional head fitted directly to head amplifier (i.e. without the extension pieces); *below* for cardioid head fitted together with extension piece.

important visual element. Accordingly, some modern microphones have been designed specifically for good appearance as well as high-quality performance. The design problem extends to the mounting as much as the microphone itself.

Table microphones. The condenser microphone lends itself to suitable design. A pencil shape perhaps half an inch or more in diameter has room for a directionally sensitive capsule pointing

153

along the axis of the tube; the body of the pencil houses the head amplifier.

Other neat microphones have also been designed: for example, a ribbon with a magnet layout that fits into a small rectangular case.

The mounting, if it is to be relatively heavy and stable, and is to protect the microphone from vibration, cannot also be made small. However, this, too, can be given clean lines and can sometimes be concealed from the camera.

Microphones on floor stands. For someone standing up, a microphone may be placed at the top of a full-length stand, which again should be reasonably strong and have a massive base. It will normally be telescopic. Whatever happens, in a long shot there is going to be a vertical line very obviously in the picture, but the cleaner this is, the better. The means for holding the microphone at a particular height and the clip holding the microphone itself should be neat but easy to operate (e.g. by a performer in vision).

Microphones have been devised which have no capsule at face level, but instead a hollow column leading down to a moving-coil unit at floor level. Such a column must be designed integrally with the microphone capsule it is to work with, as the acoustic impedance of the tube is bound to affect the signal reaching the diaphragm. For this reason the tube cannot be varied in length, and this makes height adjustments inconvenient. Sensitivity is not high, and in particular the port at the top of the tube has to be properly terminated to stop it acting like the end of an organ pipe and reflecting most of the sound energy.

But if you are going to have to flare the top of such a tube anyway, why not put a small capsule in it? And this, in fact, is what more recently designed in-vision microphones do—using an electrostatic capsule. Such a microphone requires a head amplifier, but in this design it is removed to the other end of a narrow column, and the capacitance of the wiring is taken into account in the design. One such microphone kit comes with a choice of capsules for omnidirectional or cardioid response and two different lengths of "swan-neck" column. It is suitable for floor use with seated speakers without a table, or alternatively may be stood on a box so that only the neck and capsule projects into vision.

Hand microphones. These generally have a "stick" shape so that they can be held easily. They require an omnidirectional response at low frequencies, as their distance (except in the case of the lip microphone) cannot be controlled. For sensitivity without the need for pre-amplification, a good diaphragm size is required, which means some broadening at the tip is desirable for normal speech. However, for singers, proximity and sheer volume of sound can be relied on to compensate for lack of microphone sensitivity, so a neater, parallel-sided "stick" can be used for this purpose.

With a particular example, the most level response is obtained by speaking directly along the axis, but this would be uncomfortable for the user, and visually bad, as the lips and chin would be partly

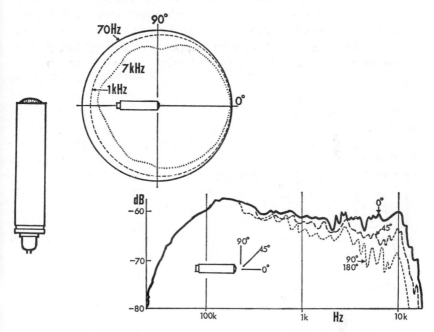

MOVING COIL, OMNIDIRECTIONAL MICROPHONE suitable for pop-singer: polar and frequency response curves.

obscured by the hand. At an angle of 45° there is a slight fall-off in top response, which may have to be compensated electrically, perhaps to produce a broad peak of "presence" at 2–3 kHz and somewhat reduce the effect of a wide lower-middle-frequency plateau if this gives a "chesty" quality to a particular singer. (With the control desk normally used for this type of programme it should be a simple matter to change the frequency response in this way: see pp. 58 and 351–353).

Neck or lanyard microphones are sometimes also called *lavalier* or *personal microphones*, though strictly, the hand microphone is also

155

an example of the latter. Typically, the microphone rests not at the neck as the name implies, but against the chest of the user. It may be in vision or concealed beneath a tie or other clothing.

A lanyard microphone should be onmidirectional at low frequencies, because though it is situated fairly close to the mouth, it is not at a predetermined distance. Commonly, a small moving-coil unit is used: it can be pinned to the clothing or slung on a cord round the neck.

Such microphones work reasonably well because the pattern of radiation from the mouth is also essentially omnidirectional; though there is some loss of high frequencies reaching the microphone, particularly if it is hidden behind clothing. Microphones of this type, therefore, have a strong, broad resonance between 2500 and 8000 Hz, produced by cavity resonance in the housing above the

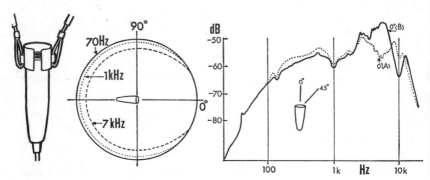

LANYARD MICROPHONE: omnidirectional moving coil. With the clip lowered (0° curve A) this is a general purpose omnidirectional microphone. With the clip raised (0° curve B) the 7-kHz peak makes it suitable for a lanyard position below the chin.

diaphragm, which compensates for this but which makes it suitable for speech only, and not very satisfactory in other possible uses for a small unit of this type—e.g. held in the hand, or hidden in scenery to cover an otherwise inaccessible position in a set—unless the cavity resonance can be eliminated.

However, one example has a rather more level response for normal studio use; but also has a sleeve which can be raised around the top rim of the unit: this gives the broad "presence" peak that may be required.

Lanyard microphones must be light in weight (one example is $1\frac{1}{4}$ oz, another $2\frac{1}{4}$ oz), robust—they are more likely to be sat on or knocked about than some other microphones—and should not be sensitive to conduction noise. Both in the studio and on location a personal microphone may be used with either a cable or a radio link.

Also available are high-quality electrostatic microphones with a very small diaphragm in an assembly which can be clipped unobtrusively to a tie or lapel. Unobstructed by clothing, the quality may be very good. The head amplifier is connected to the diaphragm capsule by a thin cable and can be slipped into a side pocket.

Personal radio-microphones

In radio or television the user of a personal microphone may need to be completely free of the cable because:

(i) In a long shot the cable may be seen to drag; this is completely unacceptable in drama and is distracting in other programmes.

(ii) In a sequence involving a number of moves the cable may get caught on the scenery, or completely tangled up; or movement may be unduly restricted to avoid this.

(iii) The performer with a neck microphone may have to move about so much in the intervals between the various rehearsals and "takes" that it may be more desirable to give him complete freedom of movement than to keep plugging or unplugging his microphone.

In these cases the cable may be replaced by a battery-powered radio transmitter and aerial. The transmitter pack should be small enough to be slipped into a pocket, pinned to the inside of the clothing, or, more likely, simply hung at the waist beneath the jacket. In trouser or jacket pockets the transmitter may be shaken about, possibly causing signal bumping. If a side-jacket pocket is used a hole will have to be cut through the lining for the cable. In other positions the transmitter is held firmly against the body in places where it is not likely to get leaned on: a pouch of the exact size, with pairs of 24-inch tapes at top and bottom, is useful for this. If an external aerial is used (as in outside broadcast or film work) the aerial, approximately a quarter wavelength long, may perhaps be allowed to hang inside a trouser leg. For studio use the screening of the microphone lead can itself be made the right length and used as an aerial.

The receiving aerial is usually a simple dipole placed so that there is an unobstructed electromagnetic path between performer and aerial. The equipment can "see" through sets made of wood and other nonconductive material, but is likely to be affected by metallic objects (including large camera dollies, which will, of course, move around during the production).

When setting them up, i.e. before giving the transmitter to the performer, checks should be made that the receiver aerial is suitably placed. This needs two people: one walks in all the places in the set or location to which the performer will go (and other places where he might), talking over the circuit to a second person who listens for dead spots, or places where interference affects reception. A variety of positions for the aerial may have to be tried before a suitable one is found.

Alternatively, a second aerial may be used to fill in the dead spot. Note that the transmitter must be battery-powered, and that the voltage will generally drop suddenly when the battery is exhausted. A log of duration of use should therefore be kept and batteries discarded well within their expected life-time.

Exceptionally, there may be other equipment in the studio which is likely to cause interference at the frequencies used by radio microphones: an obvious possibility is when radio-controlled special effects or other equipment is being used. Such problems can often be anticipated, so that alternative transmitter packs using different frequencies can be held ready for possible trouble. One obvious frequency to avoid is that used for production talk-back to the studio floor manager.

A practical disadvantage of early radio-microphone links was that as the transmitter had to be preset it could easily be overloaded (or undermodulated). This can now be avoided by introducing some degree of compression at the transmitter, or by the use of a simple limiter which is inoperative at normal speech levels.

Radio-microphones can be used in filming (particularly in documentary work or current affairs reporting); for roving reporters in television outside broadcasts; by comperes of studio programmes, and for a variety of other purposes. But it must not be forgotten that although the quality of the radio link itself may be high, it is compromised by that of the neck microphone. So alternatives should be considered: in the studio a boom, and on location a gun microphone.

Radio links can also be used with hand-held microphones, though in this case the sight of a cable disappearing into the clothes and not coming out again may be distracting to the audience, particularly in the case of lady singers in tight clothing.

158

Contact microphones

A device which is used to pick up sound vibrations from a solid material, such as a reverberation plate or the sounding board of an electric guitar, is called a contact microphone. For the conversion of acoustic energy to an electrical signal, any of the methods used in microphones and record pick-ups (and conversely in loud-speakers) could in principle be used. Indeed, a record-player pick-up head could be adapted to accept the vibrations if these were presented to it at the appropriate amplitude and sense. (A plate or sounding board vibrates transversely, whereas the mono element of a record groove is lateral.)

Contact microphones often have to be placed where it would be inconvenient to anchor them to a rigid bridge or massive arm. They are therefore supported only by the surface to which they are attached so that the casing moves with the surface. An "active mass" inside is, however, subject to inertia and free to move relative to the casing.

This mass reacts against, say, a piezo-electric device (e.g. the ceramic, barium titanate) to generate the electrical signal. The microphone measures the acceleration of the air particles as they are moved by the sound wave and is therefore frequency dependent, but as with other acceleration microphones, this is allowed for by equalization.

Miscellaneous microphone equipment

Windshields are supplied to fit many microphones. Sometimes these may be needed even indoors to reduce breath effects in close working. Generally, however, their purpose is to cut down noise due to wind turbulence at sharp edges, or even corners that are too sharply curved. To reduce wind effects proper, a smooth airflow round the microphone is required. The ideal shape, if the direction of the wind were always known and the same, would be a tear-drop, but in the absence of this information it is a sphere; eddies may be formed in the lee of the shield, but these should be relatively unimportant, as they do not flow over the surface very much.

Practical windshields are usually either spherical or a mixture of spherical and cylindrical sections (though those whose purpose is to protect against breath noise need not be rounded off at all). The framework will generally be of metal or moulded plastic, with a fine and acoustically transparent mesh, often of wire and foamed

159

plastic, covering it. In fact, windshields do make a very slight difference to the frequency response, but with careful design this can be used constructively.

Antivibration mountings. Certain microphones, particularly ribbons with compliant (i.e. relatively floppy) diaphragms, are very sensitive to vibration at resonant frequencies and benefit from the use of mountings which will absorb these frequencies. Most microphones will benefit from some degree of protection from mechanical vibration.

Power units. Microphones with head amplifiers are usually supplied with power units in a separate box. These may also provide the polarizing voltages for electrostatic microphones. Often a special cable must be used with extra wires to carry the power for the head amplifier, but modern, low-power devices, such as the field-effect transistor unit, do not. In this design a phantom circuit may be employed: for one direction the current is split equally between the audio leads; for the reverse the screen surrounding them is used.

Plugs, etc. In plugs and sockets, like the colour coding of wiring and the impedances chosen by different organizations for different purposes, there has been little standardization in the past; and as high-quality equipment is drawn from a wide international field, this may lead to—to say the least—inconvenience. The vastness of the range of connectors available is the worst feature of this.

Mountings. In addition to the equipment already described, there are a number of other standard ways of mounting microphones, including a variety of booms. In concert halls several modern microphones may be slung by their own cable from the roof of the hall— though guying may be necessary for the accurate final choice of position and also for control of angle.

In television a simple hand-held boom—a "fishing rod"—gives some of the advantages of the full-scale sound boom and can sometimes be used from directions which are inaccessible to the larger booms. It can be held braced under one arm for substantial periods, or in exceptional circumstances (and by healthy, strong sound assistants) with both arms braced over the head. Directors should expect this only for short takes.

Microphone connections. In sound and television studios, microphone cables may be plugged into sockets at convenient places in the studio walls. In television it is necessary to route sound cables round or through the set (which may include extensive backings) at suitable points, and to avoid camera tracking lines and areas of

160

the studio floor that will appear in vision. So here a very large number of points is provided: one BBC studio has over a hundred; several have over fifty. Mostly these are distributed around the walls in groups, but some are in the studio ceiling, so that cables can be "flown", or microphones suspended from above. Some terminate

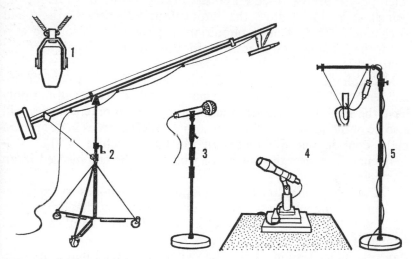

METHODS OF MOUNTING MICROPHONES (used in professional studios). 1. Suspension by adjustable wires, etc. 2. Boom (adjustable angle and length). 3. Floor stand (with telescopic column). 4. Table stand (but 1, 2, or 5 are better for table work if there is any risk of table-tapping by inexperienced speakers). 5. Floor stand with bent arm. All methods of mounting have rubber shock absorbers or straps.

in the gallery area itself. It is convenient to have several multi-way single-socket outputs at the studio walls so that a single cable can be run out to a terminating box on the floor, to which, say, ten microphones can be routed.

Jackfield. In the sound control room for television and all but the simplest radio control cubicles the microphone channels are wired to a jackfield at which each microphone is routed (by crossplugging) to a convenient fader. So, for example, it can be arranged that all of the main speech and singers' microphones appear at the desk in one group with audience as a sub-group, and the orchestra in another block with rhythm as a further sub-group. In some cases response selection units might be included in the fader channel, as would echo feeds; in other cases these, and other specialized equipment, such as telephone-effects filter units, would have to be cross-plugged.

Microphones for stereo

For stereo an important technique for giving positional information is the co-incident pair of microphones. This is the method
generally used by the BBC in preference to spaced pairs: the reasons
for this are given in Chapter 1. Other individual monophonic
microphones are also used for close working, positions subsequently
being allocated by dividing the output electrically between the A and
B channels. Pairs of monophonic microphones are also used at a
distance for adding reverberation: for this purpose the pair need not
be together.

Microphones which are used as a pair (whether spaced or co-
incident) to define position are usually matched. They will not only
have the same polar and frequency response; in practice, they will
also be of the same manufacture—as minor differences in design can
make considerable differences in the fine structure of the high-
frequency response, the effects of which will be emphasized in an
unmatched pair.

Co-incident pairs may be separate microphones or double-
element instruments. In the double microphones the diaphragms are
generally placed one above the other, with the end capsule arranged
so that it can be rotated on a common axis with the other. Sometimes the polar responses may be switched between figure-of-eight,
hypercardioid, cardioid, and broad cardioid conditions (as well as
omnidirectional, which has no direct use in stereo).

Directional characteristics of co-incident pairs

A co-incident pair of figure-of-eight elements set at 90° to each
other will have their phases the same (positive or negative) in two
adjacent quadrants. The overlap of these will allow a useful pick-up
angle of 90°. Outside of this the elements will be out of phase, so that
directional information will be confused and meaningless to a
listener, except at the back, where there is a further angle of 90°
within which the elements are in phase once again. The front and
back are therefore both useful areas, whereas no sound source
should be placed at the sides (other than for a special effect).

The sound stage as heard by the listener will not coincide with its
physical layout because:

(i) The 90° included angle of the microphones will become the
included angle from listener to his loudspeakers (often 60°;
sometimes less).

162

(ii) Sound sources at the rear of the pair will be introduced in mirror image into the sound stage that the
listener has in front of him. Thus physically incompatible
objects could appear to be occupying the same point in
space.

In a hypercardioid pair (crossed cottage-loaf response) the
frontal lobes must again be in phase. With the diaphragms still at
90° to each other, the useful pick-up angle will now be about 130°
at the front. The corresponding 50° at the back will not now be
much use for direct pick-up, as the frequency response of the
individual microphones is degenerate in these directions. However,
if a source that is being picked up on a separate microphone is
placed in this angle at least its position will not be distorted by the
out-of-phase pick-up that would be found at the side.

Crossed cardioids have a maximum usable angle of 270°, but for
direct pick-up the useful angle is about 180°, as the frequency
response of the microphone which is turned away from the sound
source degenerates at angles that are farther round to the side than
this.

These three examples are members of a family that is, in principle,
continuous.

There are two ways of looking at the polar response of a co-
incident pair. One uses the normal response curves for the A and B
microphones. The other considers their combined signals, the A + B
and A − B signals. The A + B signal is sometimes also called the
M signal: this stands for "main" (not "mono", though mono
usually is taken as A + B). Similarly, A − B is sometimes called
the S signal ("side", not "stereo"; stereo information requires
both M and S signals—though "S" represents the *extra* information
required for stereo).

If the M and S diagrams are examined it will be seen that they
correspond to the polar responses of another pair of microphones
that could in principle have been used to obtain them directly—a
"main" one which has a range of different polar diagrams and a
"side" one which is figure-of-eight. Sometimes A + B and A − B
stereo information has been taken directly from main and side
microphones, thereby cutting out several items of electrical equipment. But a disadvantage of this is that the combined frequency
response is at its most erratic at the most important part of the sound
stage: close to the centre—though the effect of this gets less as the
S contribution gets smaller.

163

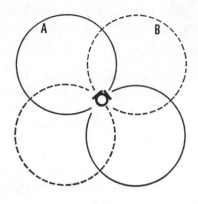

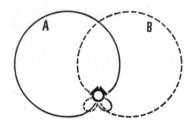

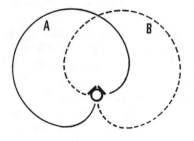

Polar diagrams for co-incident pairs of microphones at 90°.
Top: crossed figure-of-eight.
Middle: crossed cottage-loaf.
Bottom: crossed cardioid. The M and S diagrams corresponding to these are shown opposite. Note that although the subject of crossed microphones is introduced here in terms of elements set at 90°, a broader angle is often better for practical microphone balances. 120° is commonly used.

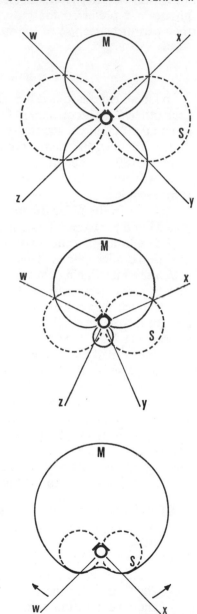

M and S diagrams for the co-incident pairs of microphones shown opposite. *Top*: for crossed figure-of-eight the useful forward angle (W–X) is only 90°. Sound from outside this (i.e. in the angles W–Z and X–Y) will be out of phase. The useful angle at the rear (Y–Z) will (for music) be angled too high for practical benefit.

Middle: crossed cottage-loaf microphones have a broader useful angle at the front (W–X).

Bottom: the crossed cardioid has a 270° usable angle (between W and X, forwards) but only about 180° is really useful, as to the rear of the elements the response is erratic.

As will be seen later, crossed cardioid or near-cardioid microphones are preferred for most practical professional balances, as they permit better use of the studio space.

Cardioids back-to-back

So far we have assumed that the crossed pair were angled at 90° to each other. This is convenient for looking at the diagrams, but is not essential: it is only a starting-point for possible combinations.

In particular, the elements may both be cardioids and face outwards at 180° to each other (though not physically "back-to-back", as this could introduce standing waves in the high-frequency responses).

Here again the polar diagrams produce interesting and recognizable M and S curves. The M signal will pick up sound equally from any direction—in other words, it is the equivalent of an omnidirectional microphone. This is exactly the same diagram which we saw when introducing cardioid response for the first time: we saw that by adding pressure and pressure-gradient operation, perhaps physically as separate elements in the same case, a cardioid could be achieved. Now we see that by adding (and subtracting) two cardioids we can get back where we started. Indeed, if the only cardioids available actually were combination microphones it would seem a little perverse (in this one case) to use these for stereo, rather than try a good omnidirectional plus a good figure-of-eight. It also follows that even in the absence of a matched pair quite acceptable stereo can be obtained by anybody with an omnidirectional microphone plus a figure-of-eight which would be placed sideways on to that part of the studio which is to be the centre of the sound stage. (Similarly, a hypercardioid plus a figure-of-eight could be used.)

The cardioids back-to-back layout has two possible advantages:

(i) The whole area of a studio is usable (though certain positions have poor frequency response on one microphone or the other).

(ii) Most of the reverberation will be included in the M signal, so that if reverberation is right for stereo it is more likely to be right for mono than cases where the S signal contains most of the reverberation and the M signal is relatively dead.

A small problem with this layout is getting everything in exactly the right place when 360° is reduced to about 60°. Also, if the

166

cardioids are more directional at high frequencies than at low the centre of stage may be the weakest point. This would again be the case if the signal were derived from omnidirectional and figure-of-eight microphones.

Intermediate angles have also been used successfully: in Holland

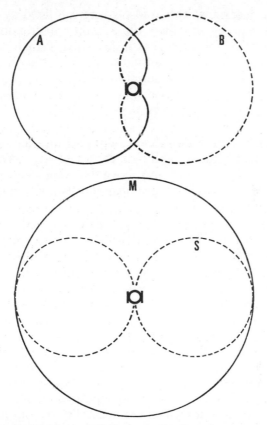

CARDIOIDS BACK-TO-BACK. This arrangement makes the best use of the space in a small studio with low reverberation. There is no out-of-phase position. To build the correct audio picture, careful positioning of sound sources is required: if the whole area is used, this will be unlike any "natural" layout.

120° and in France 110°—the latter with a 17-cm "dummy head" spacing, the positive value of which is difficult to see, but which does no obvious harm.

Microphones with two capsules in a single housing are constructed so that it is possible to swivel the end capsule (in its immediate housing) relative to the other, and on a common axis with it.

167

Lining up a stereo pair

If coincident microphones do not have the same output level the positional information will be distorted. Here is a line-up procedure that can be carried out in a few minutes by two people, one at the microphones and one at the monitoring end.

(i) First check that the loudspeakers are lined up reasonably well, e.g. by speaking on a mono microphone (or one element of the pair) that is fed equally to A and B loudspeakers. The sound should come from the centre.

(ii) If they are switchable select identical polar diagrams for the co-incident pair. These may be the ones which will subsequently be used operationally, or if this is not known, figure-of-eight.

(iii) Visually set the capsules at about 90° to each other. Check and identify the left and right capsules in turn. Where microphones are mounted one above the other, there is no agreed standard on which capsule should feed which channel.

(iv) Now visually set the pair at 0° to each other, ensuring with microphones of symmetrical appearance that they are not in fact back to back (there will always be some identifying point, e.g. a stud on the front, or the mesh at the back of the housing may be coloured black).

(v) Listen to A − B only—or if there is no control to select this, reverse the phase of one microphone and listen to A + B.

(vi) While one person speaks in to the front of the microphones, the other adjusts for minimum output. If possible, this should be on a preset control for one microphone channel or the other; most conveniently, this may be a separate microphone balance or "channel balance" control.

(vii) Restore the loudspeakers to normal stereo output (restoring the phase reversal to normal if necessary). Speech should now be approximately midway between the speakers whatever the position of the speaker. Disregarding minor variations when the speech is from near the common dead axis or axes of the microphones, if there are any major shifts in image position as the person speaks from different places there is something wrong with the polar response of one of the microphones; the test must be started again when the microphone has been corrected. Note that if there is, the earlier part of the line-up procedure is invalid. Also,

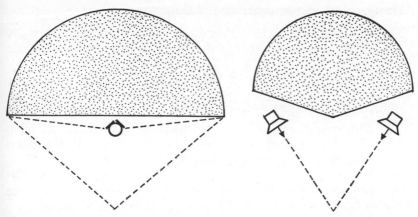

COMPRESSION OF SCALE OF WIDTH. A sound source which might be spread over 90° or more in real life (*left*) will be compressed on the audio stage to a standard 60°.

note that as the person walks round loudness should vary in a way that coincides with the polar characteristic chosen.

(viii) Restore the angle between the capsules to 90° (or whatever angle is to be used operationally) and identify left, centre, and right once again.

Stereo microphone balance

Microphone balance has the same objects in stereo as in mono—but with one major addition: *to find a suitable scale of width.* Remember that whereas indirect sound will occupy the whole sound stage, it may be quite acceptable that direct sound should occupy only part of it.

A large sound source such as an orchestra should obviously occupy the whole stage, and for even this to be realistic must be set well back by the use of adequate reverberation. On the other hand, a string quartet with the same reverberation should occupy only part of the stage, say the centre 20° within the available 60°; anything more would make the players appear giants. The same quartet could, however, be "brought forward" to occupy almost all of the sound stage, that is, provided that the balance itself were sufficiently "dry". In either case, whatever reverberation there was would occupy the whole available width.

169

Image width can be controlled in three ways:

(i) The microphone may be moved closer or farther from the sound source. Moving farther back narrows the source and also increases reverberation, as with mono.

(ii) The polar response of the microphone elements may be changed. Broadening the response from figure-of-eight out towards cardioid narrows the image. It also reduces the long-path reverberation that the figure-of-eight picks up from behind and permits a closer balance. There is therefore, overall, a considerable reduction in reverberation.

(iii) The ratio of A + B to A — B may be changed electrically: if the A — B component is reduced the width is reduced. If the A + B component is reduced the width can be increased a little. (There are two ways of doing this, one of which does not involve converting the signal to the M and S form first) (see p. 67).

Reverberation may also be added by using additional distant microphones.

Close microphone techniques for stereo

Individual sources for which no appreciable image width is required can be balanced on monophonic (or "spotting") microphones. The balance must be close enough (or the studio dead enough) to avoid appreciable reverberation, or there will be a "tunnel" effect: extra reverberation beamed from exactly the same direction as the sound source. This effect (very common in films with

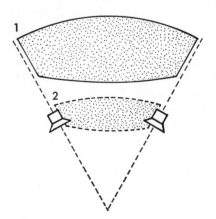

ORCHESTRA IN CORRECT SCALE OF WIDTH. A broad subject will need enough reverberation to make it appear a natural size (1); if the reverberation is low the subject will appear close and under-sized or cramped together (2).

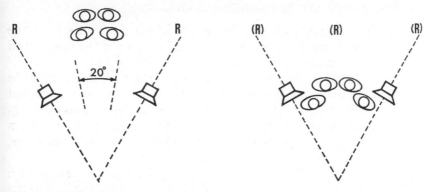

A QUARTET IN STEREO. *Left:* the quartet uses only a third of the audio stage, but reverberation fills the whole width. *Right:* The quartet occupies the whole of the space between the loudspeakers. Here the reverberation must be low in order to avoid the players appearing gross: such reverberation as there is appears from behind them.

stereophonic sound) produces a characteristic unpleasant quality and impairs the stereophonic illusion.

It does not matter if there is too little reverberation, as this can be added in the form of stereo artificial "echo".

A position on the sound stage may be established by "steering" or "panning" proportions of the signal to the A and B channels. If the source can already be heard, though perhaps in insufficient volume, then the proportions should be adjusted to coincide with its existing position—unless a special effect is sought. If it is not already present on the sound stage it can be allocated any position within artistic reason.

But take care that the two monophonic microphones do not pick up the same source unintentionally. If they do, they will form a spaced pair, giving a position of the source that will probably disagree with its proper position; what is more, this false information will change if the level of one of the microphones is changed. Close balance, directional characteristics, layout of sources in the studio, and screens may all be used to make sure this does not happen.

Monophonic spotting techniques cannot be used for subjects which have obvious physical size—such as a group of instruments or singers, a close piano, or an organ. In this case two monophonic microphones may be used to form a stereo pair.

6

SPEECH BALANCE

ONE might expect speech recording to be a simple operation. But making a really good recording of speech can be quite a struggle. In a good balance the voice should be clear and natural sounding, reinforced and brightened a little by the acoustics of the room that is being used as a studio. And the listener should hear no distracting sounds.

The three factors upon which speech balance depends are the voice itself, the microphone, and the surrounding acoustic conditions.

In a radio station each studio has acoustically treated walls and a carefully measured reverberation time and frequency characteristic. Studios for different purposes may be very different in design, but one for speech and discussion programmes will be about the size of a fairly large living-room.

There will be a good carpet on the floor; and treatment on the walls to absorb more or less the same amount of sound as the curtains and furniture of your own sitting-room.

The type of microphone to be used influences the choice of acoustics to a certain extent. A discussion where six speakers are grouped round a cardioid or omnidirectional microphone requires deader acoustics than one with a smaller number of speakers and a ribbon microphone. The latter, being directional, discriminates against the studio reverberation and any colouration that goes with it.

The ribbon microphone: one or two voices

A good ribbon microphone has a flat response throughout the frequency range of speech. It is, in BBC radio, the most widely used studio microphone for speech.

The working distance may be anything from eighteen inches to three feet. Use a balance test, as described earlier (p. 133), but keep such tests to a minimum for people unused to having their voices

172

MICROPHONE POSITION. Showing a good position for speech, with head well up (and not too close). Script also held up and to side of microphone.

recorded. A series of complicated microphone adjustments can be very disconcerting.

The best way of getting a good signal-to-noise ratio is to speak clearly and not too quietly. A natural vice of the British is to speak too quietly; not to open the mouth wide enough. Some other nationalities, e.g. Americans and Australians, are less inclined to mumble. But whatever the nationality, very quiet speech is to be discouraged.

Balancing two speakers on opposite sides of a ribbon is little more difficult than a single voice, unless the two speakers have radically different voice levels. (In an interview, the interviewer can sometimes help by adopting a suitable voice level to ensure that the two voices balance.)

It has sometimes been suggested that an interviewer's voice should be slightly lower in volume than that of the interviewee. If this can be managed without the whole discussion becoming too subdued it will generally succeed, the primary aim of an interview being—as it is generally understood by the listener—to bring out the views and personality of the interviewee. The interviewer can normally express himself with adequate clarity at this relatively low volume; but in any case this is a useful discipline for all interviewers.

If the relative loudness of two voices does not sound right on the balance test it should help if the microphone is moved slightly to favour one or the other. But watch out for any tendency for the more distant voice to sound acoustically much brighter than the other; rather than allow this to happen it will be necessary to introduce some control (i.e. adjustment of the gain)—just a slight dip in level as the louder speaker opens his mouth to speak.

Random variations in loudness are much less tolerable when heard over a loudspeaker than when listening "live" in the same room, so if nothing can be done to stop people rocking backward and forward, or producing considerable changes of voice level

173

(without, for example, breaking the flow of a good spontaneous discussion) some degree of control will have to be resorted to.

It may help if the microphone is less obtrusive, e.g. mounted in a well in a table between interviewer and interviewee. Sight lines will be better, but paper noise from notes lying on the table may be worse.

Omnidirectional microphone: one or two voices

Since omnidirectional microphones require a close balance, they are best used hand-held for commentary or interview work outside the studio. In the studio they will normally be mounted and used by individuals for close work—as also will certain cardioids which become omnidirectional at low frequencies.

For example, certain disc jockeys prefer a close, intimate style of working, with very little of the studio acoustic in the sound. It is possible that the wish to work very close to the microphone is partly also psychological: the performer is helped if he can feel that he is speaking softly in the audience's ear. A disc jockey with a soft, low voice does not improve matters by "creeping in" to an uncorrected directional microphone and accentuating the bass elements in his voice, particularly when he is compering pop records which have what in other fields of recording would be regarded as an excess of top. In many omnidirectional (and cardioid) microphones the middle-top response is erratic, giving the voice an edgy quality which may be no disadvantage when linking pop music, for otherwise the contrast can sound unpleasantly marked.

Another use for the omnidirectional microphone in the studio is matching studio questions to actuality material recorded on location.

Using an omnidirectional microphone in the hand for interview work, three basic balances may be adopted:

(i) With the microphone at or just above waist level, so that its presence is unobtrusive. This balance is sometimes used for television work or where it is felt that the interviewee will take fright at a closer technique. Unfortunately it generally gives very poor quality, with either too much background sound or too reverberant an acoustic. In television, however, the picture distracts conscious attention from the sound quality, so that provided speech is clearly intelligible it may be accepted.

(ii) Between the two speakers at chest or neck level, the face of the microphone pointing upwards.

174

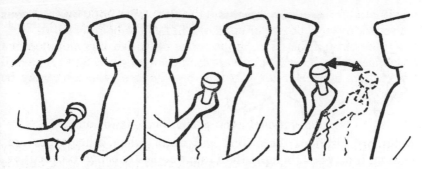

INTERVIEWING TECHNIQUES. Position 1. Microphone at waist or chest height. Sound quality: poor. Position 2. At shoulder or mouth level. Sound quality: fair; or good if interviewer and interviewee are close together in acoustically favourable and quiet surroundings. Position 3. Moving the microphone from one speaker to the other. Sound quality: good.

(iii) Angled towards the mouth of each speaker in turn, the distance being judged according to background acoustics or "atmosphere". This, the only balance in which the microphone is moved in between each question and answer, may be a little distracting to the interviewee, but gives by far the best quality.

The interviewer should get close to the subject. This may best be done by standing at about 90° to him or sitting side by side.

Three or more voices

When three or four people are taking part in an interview or discussion—again, in good studio conditions—the ribbon microphone remains the best for the purpose. Although a "round-table" layout is not possible—four speakers must be paired off two-a-side, and three divided up two and one—sound of very satisfactory quality is consistent with a fair degree of comfort for the speakers. The microphone can be moved a few inches, or angled slightly, to favour the lighter voices; and two speakers on the same side of the microphone should be encouraged to sit shoulder to shoulder so that there is no tendency for anyone to get off-microphone. If possible, the seating should be arranged so that those sitting side by side are more likely to want to talk to the speakers across the table. The change in quality which occurs when one of a pair turns to his neighbour can be quite marked, and if he leans back in his chair at the same time the effect will be magnified.

Whereas "figure-of-eight" microphones are used very widely by

175

ROUND TABLE DISCUSSIONS. Showing six speakers working to a cardioid microphone.

radio organizations, occasions will occur when other types are chosen. It may be that more than four people are being recorded; or that a three-and-one arrangement is wanted; or that it is felt that the atmosphere of a discussion will be improved if speakers are allowed to sit around in a circle; or simply that a "pencil" microphone just peeping out of a well in the centre of the table, or suspended just above the level of the speaker's heads, is considered less obtrusive than a ribbon which has to be at about mouth level.

But it is not at all easy to get a good balance of a group of people recorded in this way. Bearing in mind that the quality of many omnidirectional microphones and most cardioids varies more with direction than the names imply, it is best to place the microphone face up (or hang it face down) and distribute the people in a circle round it—the idea being to keep all of the speakers at about the same angle (probably about 45°) to the axis of the microphone.

A specially made table may have a well in the centre with a flexibly suspended platform on which a microphone may be placed.

Since it is usually difficult to crowd a group of seated people very close to the microphone, and since it is often necessary to place the microphone at some distance above or below mouth level, pick-up of unwanted studio "atmosphere" will often be much greater than with a ribbon. And even more care must be exercised over extraneous noises made by speakers.

A balance for four people taking part in a quiz game is shown opposite.

Studio noise

Whether "background" noises are acceptable or not depends on the purpose of the recording. For many purposes (e.g. studio narration, "straight" talks, plays, etc.) they are not. The answer, once again, is to make a trial recording to see the problems that have to be faced—and from then on, just watch as critically as possible for any troublesome sounds. The trial recording should show whether room "atmosphere" itself is obtrusive. "Atmosphere" means the ambient noise which pervades even the quietest of rooms; and some check is needed to see whether voice-level or balance will have to be changed to reduce it. Some noise may have to be tolerated with a directional microphone. Close working will introduce bass tip-up, whereas the alternative of using more voice may be against the best interests of the programme. (The sort of voice quality which stands out really effectively against background noise is more suitable for a hard-sell commercial than ordinary talk—so beware!)

Troublesome noises may find their way into your studio from outside. Even in the studios of radio stations built to discriminate against these things, difficulties can occur: ventilation systems may carry noise from other parts of the building, or may themselves sound noisy when quiet speech is being recorded—simply due to the flow of air. Structure-borne noises are almost impossible to eliminate, and rebuilding work is complicated by the need to avoid all noisy work when nearby studios are recording or on the air. But however much care is used, there will still be the odd "one that got away". (See Chapter 3 for a further discussion of studio noise.)

The recordist must always watch for noises made by the speaker himself. A lightly tapping pencil may sound like rifle-fire. A slightly creaky chair or table may sound as if it is about to fall to pieces. And if they are not noticed at the time of recording, sorting out the source of these sounds can prove to be a very puzzling business. Many people have small nervous habits which come to light when they are being recorded: for example, retractable ball-point pens can be a menace—people will fiddle with them, and produce a sharp, unidentified click every ten or fifteen seconds.

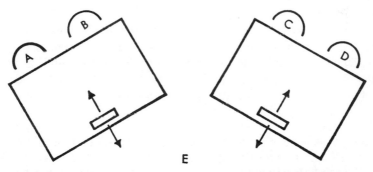

BALANCE WITH TWO MICROPHONES. Voices A and B are on the dead side of microphone 2 and vice-versa: this is a useful balance for quiz-games, etc., recorded before an audience. (A voice at E would be picked up on both—provided the two were in phase.) This technique is very useful in a wide variety of balances—and particularly for music.

Lighting a cigarette is not quite so bad as some of these other noises, because it is at least identifiable—although a match lit carelessly close to the microphone can be quite alarming. A few smokers in a discussion programme can sound more like an opium den or firework display than a group of sober and respectable people in conversation.

There are several things which make these noises so irritating. The first is that most people listen to broadcast or recorded speech at a level which is much louder than real life; and a quiet talker is allowed much the same volume at the loudspeaker as someone who almost shouts. So the extraneous noises are loud too.

And not only are the noises actually louder than they should be, but, heard monophonically, they appear to come from the same point in space as the speech. This is important, because, as I have already indicated, it is part of the process of hearing that we can discriminate against unwanted sound coming from a different direction from the main sound. This is called the "cocktail party" effect (whereby a pair of ears can selectively listen to one voice in a crowd).

A third reason for noise being irritating is that, whereas a visually identified sound slips immediately into place in the mind and is accepted, the unidentified one does not. Many practised broadcasters realize this and take it into account. The compere of a magazine programme will notice that a speaker's movements are not absolutely silent and say, "And now, just coming to join me, is ..." and the noise is given a reason and thereby reduced to its proper proportions—so that it will not be consciously noticed by the listener.

Handling a script

A frequent source of extraneous noise at the microphone—and a particularly irritating one—is paper rustle; a few comments by the producer on the handling of scripts or notes is common practice at the start of any recording or broadcast where these are used, and where the speaker is not thoroughly versed in the business. Here are a few general rules about this:

    (i) Use a fairly stiff paper (duplicating paper is quite good). Do not use a copy that has been folded or bent in the pocket. Thin paper (e.g. airmail paper or flimsies sometimes used for carbon copies) should be avoided.

    (ii) If you are sitting at a table, take the script apart by removing its paper-clip or staple. It is very difficult to turn over pages

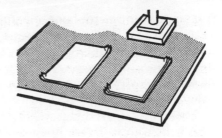

AVOIDING SCRIPT NOISE. Corners of script turned up to make it easier to lift noiselessly to one side.

quietly, so it is a good idea to turn up two corners of the script, and then each page can be lifted gently to one side as it is finished with. Any sliding of one page over another will be audible.

(iii) If possible, place the script so that it is not necessary to turn or drop the head in order to read.

(iv) Standing at a microphone (necessary for actors with moves to make) the script can be left clipped together. The pages should be turned well off-microphone—in the case of a bi-directional microphone this means on the dead side.

(v) When there are several people in a studio (as in a play), do not all turn the pages together. If actors remember to stagger the turnover, they will also remember to turn quietly.

(vi) If there are only a few sheets of script they may perhaps be slipped inside clear plastic envelopes of a suitable size.

I myself prefer to hold a script up, a little to the side of the microphone. This is certainly the best when standing at the microphone, and can often be tried when sitting at a table. It is bad to lay the script flat on the table between speaker and microphone, as reflections from the script interfere with sound taking the direct path

SCRIPT RACK. No reflections from script can reach microphone, but speaker may still drop his head at foot of page. Note that rack (as well as table surface) may be made of acoustically transparent mesh.

from mouth to microphone. In addition, as a speaker reads down to the bottom of the page there is a gradual change in voice quality due to the movement of the head, with a sudden jump back as the top of the next page is reached. Slight changes of volume can be made to compensate for this. But no compensation can be made for changes of quality, so it is better to avoid this effect altogether.

One device which is sometimes used is a script-rack. Sloping up towards the microphone, this avoids awkward reflections, but it does not prevent a persistent offender from dropping his head. Indeed, since he will be speaking more directly into the microphone at the top of the page, results may be worse than without the rack.

Studio acoustics used for dramatic purposes

So far we have been considering microphone balance for speech largely in terms of microphone type, distance, and angle. We now have to consider the effect of the studio itself, for a balance can be very considerably changed in quality by altering the acoustic "furniture" of a studio.

It is even more important to be able to provide acoustics of different characteristics where dramatization is to be attempted; indeed, in BBC drama studios a wide range of acoustics is built in, and screens, curtains, etc., are provided so that finer shades of differentiation may be obtained.

In Britain and many other countries radio drama still has a life twenty or more years after it died in America; indeed, as will be seen later, stereo versions have been developed. It must be emphasized that this continued existence into the 1970's can be justified on audience size alone—let alone the statistically measured high appreciation of the audience. Radio drama could therefore survive in a fully commercial environment were it not for the difficulty of the many interruptions that are necessary. It is notable also that in a situation where television can cater for the less demanding audience, quality drama—the individual play—has done quite as well as the soap opera serial.

The microphone techniques used in radio drama also have their applications for out-of-vision recordings for film or television (including post-synchronization), although they are regrettably rarely used for these purposes.

We have already established that the basic acoustic required for speech balance is that of an average "living-room", the sound from

180

which will not differ greatly from that of the listener's own living-room.

In fact, the most important quality of this acoustic is that it should have no special virtues or vices, nothing to call the audience's attention to it. This is also the basic acoustic required for radio drama; and if called upon to define the location of such a scene a listener would probably just look blank—that "the action takes place in a room" (unless evidence is offered to the contrary) is too simple and obvious a reply to be worth offering.

Realistic use of acoustics

A studio suite may be divided into areas having different amounts of sound-absorbent or reflecting treatment; each area providing a recognizably different quality of sound. And these may give fairly realistic simulation of the actual conditions they are supposed to represent. Dead acoustics, on the other hand, are rarely dealt with realistically—as will be shown later.

It is important to recall, in considering live acoustics, that size is conveyed not so much by reverberation time as by reverberation quality. Small rooms sound small because certain frequencies are picked out and emphasized in the dimensions between the walls, etc. A combination of reverberation time and quality will suggest both size and the acoustic furniture of a room: a sound with a reverberation time of one second may originate from a small room with little furniture (and therefore rather bright acoustically) or from a very large hall with a rather dead acoustic. The two would be readily distinguishable.

For example, a "bathroom" acoustic would be provided by a small room with strongly sound-reflecting walls, and can be used for any other location which might realistically have the same acoustic qualities. Similarly, a part of the main studio (or a larger room) with a live acoustic can be used to represent a public hall, a court-room, a small concert-hall, or anything of this sort—and indeed, when not needed for drama, this area can be used as a small music studio. When going from one type of acoustic to another, balance (i.e. distance from the microphone) can be used to help to differentiate between them; for example, the first lines of a scene set in a large reverberant entrance hall can be played a little farther from the microphone than the main body of the action which follows—it would probably be too hard on the ears if the whole scene were played with heavy reverberation.

181

The first complication arises if we have a narrator as well as the "living-room" action to cope with. The two must be recognizably different, especially if the narrator is extensively used. There will, of course, be differences in the style of acting between the two: the reflective, narrative link should contrast with the here-and-now

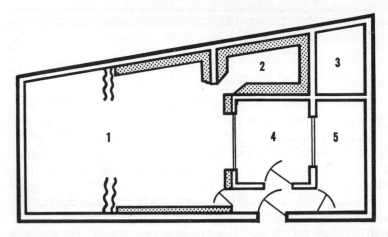

DRAMA STUDIO SUITE. This is typical of the specialized studio layouts adopted for broadcast drama in the days when radio was at its peak of popularity. Many such studios still exist (as at the BBC) and are used for their original purpose. The principles involved in the layout remain valid for many other purposes. The main areas shown are: 1. Main acting area: the "live" and "dead" ends of the studio can be partially isolated from each other (and their acoustics modified) by drawing double curtains across. 2. "Dead" room, with thick absorbers on walls. 3. Echo chamber. 4. Control cubicle. 5. Recording room. In this example a virtue has been made of the irregular shape of the site. The use of non-parallel walls avoids standing wave colouration.

action of the scene. Nor will the fades be the same. But acoustics can also be used to emphasize the differences: if the scene is played well out into the open studio with an average working distance of about three feet from a ribbon microphone the narrator can be placed somewhere nearer to one of the walls at a working distance of, say, twenty inches.

So far, so good—unless the narrator figures as the first voice in the scene, in which case this arrangement, in a fair-sized studio, may require him to do some smart moving between microphones. Here, a more comfortable way of doing things is to have a second microphone of a different type in the same acting area as the first: a ribbon for action within the scene, and an omnidirectional microphone for the narration. The two microphones can be so placed that the only move necessary to get from one to the other is a slight turn.

The ribbon will have a smooth, realistic quality; the omnidirectional may (depending on choice) have slightly more colouration in the top, giving a somewhat harder, more mechanical quality to the voice— just enough to make it sound like the printed page speaking, as against the eavesdropping-on-the-event quality of the ribbon. It may

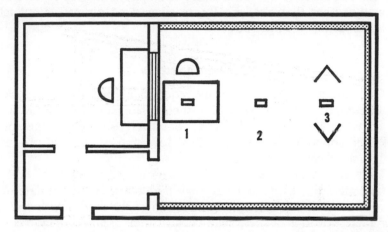

SIMPLE LAYOUT FOR DRAMA. A simple set-up using three ribbon microphones for dramatic work. Mic. I. Narrator (close to window). Mic. 2. "Open"—for normal indoor acoustics. Mic. 3. "Tent"—to represent outdoor quality. This is a much less versatile layout than can be obtained in a multiple acoustic studio, and the results will sound more stylized. It can be argued that this is all that is necessary for broadcasting directed to schools, because: (a) school audiences often have poor listening conditions and will only hear a limited range of acoustic differences; (b) casts for a variety of reasons are small and do not need much room; and (c) educational broadcasting generally has a low budget, so studio space allocated to it will accordingly be small.

help to provide a satisfying contrast if there is a screen near the narration microphone.

It is sometimes necessary to mix acoustics—to have two voices in acoustically different parts of the same studio. There is a great deal of scope for ingenuity here; and the big problem lies in avoiding spill, particularly where the voice in the drier acoustic is as loud as or louder than the other. Much can be done by using directional microphones, but these may not prevent the spill of reverberation from the live acoustic to the dead one. Double curtains running out from the walls may help to trap the sound—or screens may be used for the same purpose—but in extreme cases separate studios are needed. Spill is an even greater nuisance in simulated telephone conversations, so methods of avoiding it are considered in more detail in a later chapter (p. 347).

Screens can be used to lend realistic touches to a scene. For example, the interior of a car consists of a mixture of padded and reflecting surfaces: a "box" of screens, some bright, some padded, will give a very similar quality of sound. But perhaps the most common arrangement of screens, a double-V of two (or more) screens on the two sides of a bi-directional microphone is used representationally rather than realistically, to suggest an almost completely dead acoustic—the open air.

Open-air acoustics

Open-air acoustics, frequently required in dramatic work, are characterized in nature by an almost complete lack of reverberation. Even when there are walls, etc., to reflect some of it, the total reflected sound at the source will be low, and is likely to produce only a small change in quality.

How are we to represent these conditions in the studio?

One method which has been tried in Germany is to simulate this quality realistically by building a section of the studio with almost completely dead acoustics, i.e. a "dead-room". (To do the job completely, acoustic treatment about four feet thick would be needed.) At first sight it would seem that the use of such a dead-room as an "open-air" studio presents some very definite advantages—and it is worth noting these carefully, because no other methods have them, and their absence certainly makes things tricky:

(i) It would provide the best possible contrast to other acoustics in use, thus making a wider range of sound quality possible.

(ii) The muffling effect of the treatment would cause the performer to lift his voice and use the same amount of edge on it as he would in the open air.

(iii) Effects recorded outdoors would blend in easily.

(iv) Off-microphone voices and spot effects could be blended with on-microphone voices by using positions round towards the dead side of a ribbon microphone.

(v) The amount of space round the microphone would be greater than that within a tent of screens.

Unfortunately, there are also disadvantages:

(i) Such an acoustic is very uncomfortable to work in, and for those with any tendency to claustrophobia the term "dead-room" takes on a second and more unpleasant meaning, for the atmosphere rapidly seems to become oppressive and unreal.

(ii) Completely dead sound is difficult to balance: the transient peaks tend to over-modulate, even if the general level is kept low.

(iii) It is unpleasant to listen to completely dead sound for any length of time.

In fact, the true dead-room is not a practicable proposition, and some sort of a compromise solution has to be found. Just how far away our representational "dead" acoustic must be from true outdoor deadness depends on just how much "open-air" there is required by the script. Where a script is set almost entirely out of doors, it is more convenient to go for a formalized style of production with an acoustic which is hardly less reverberant than a normal speech balance. On the other hand, if there are only a few isolated lines set outdoors, something fairly close to the dead acoustic may be used. In other words, apart from exceptional cases, one should usually try to set the "average" acoustic demanded by the script as one which is fairly close to a normal speech balance, and arrange the others relative to this.

Tent acoustics

Of the various possible sound-deadening systems, it is best to try to avoid those which give a padded-cell effect. This is, very literally, what a thinly padded dead-room sounds like, and the same sort of sound can all too easily be obtained by laying out a cocoon of screens.

But probably the most satisfactory arrangement is that which employs two Vs, one on each side of a ribbon microphone.

Here are some points to remember with this layout:

(i) Keep the screens as close to the microphone as is conveniently possible; try to persuade the actors to accept a little restriction on their movements. This layout will keep the path

USE OF SCREENS. Double reflection of sound in a V of screens set at an acute angle. For any particular path there will be some frequencies which are poorly absorbed, but these will be different for the various possible paths. Sound that is reflected back to the region of the microphone is less coloured with this arrangement than with a broad V.

185

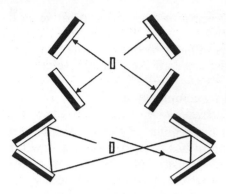

lengths short and damp out reverberation (and colouration) as quickly as possible.

(ii) Avoid setting the screens in parallel pairs. In fact, keep the V of the screens fairly acute. This helps to reduce bass as well as top; certainly it seems to me to provide a cleaner sound than a broad V. Also, actors should avoid standing too far back into the apex of the V.

(iii) Exit and entry speeches can be awkward. In nature, distant speech is characterized by a higher voice level arriving at a lower final volume. In the studio, a voice moving off is likely to be characterized by a sudden increase in studio acoustic. The only answer is to stay inside the screens at all times, and even then to avoid directing the voice out from the edge of the screens into the open studio.

(iv) Off-microphone (i.e. "distant") speeches may be spoken from the screens, speaking across the V. And if this is still too loud to mix with other voices, the actor should change his voice quality, giving it less volume and more edge. He should not try to deaden his voice by turning to face right into the angle of the screens: the only result from this will be a cotton-wool muffled quality.

All in all, the effect of screens is not that of the open air. But it is not a normal live acoustic, either. It is just different: half measures, perhaps, but acceptable as a convention. If the results seem to sound more boxy than they should it won't necessarily improve matters to play in a record of birdsong: this may just contrast with and emphasize the deficiencies of the methods.

In the more extreme cases of stylization, e.g. the sort of imaginative feature in which a character is making "a journey through life" (radio scripts in which the action is set in a predominantly open-air setting often seem to boil down to just this), a fairly open layout is satisfactory, with, say, three screens on each side of the microphone —and the studio floor may be left uncarpeted.

An example of the sort of set-up which can be adopted in this type of studio is one where no less than six microphones were used for a quarter-hour playlet:

The main action was a trial scene in a criminal court at the Old Bailey, and this took three bi-directional (ribbon) microphones in the livest part of a drama studio. Counsel and witnesses worked to microphone 1 at various distances, and slight "echo" was added. The people working farther away were picked up also on microphone 2, which was about five feet above microphone 1 and given a stronger dose of echo: perspective effects were made more real by this arrangement. A record of courtroom "atmosphere" completed the picture by providing an occasional cough or shuffling noise. An intermittent whispered discussion in the gallery had to be superimposed on the main action; for this, microphone 3 was ten feet to the side of microphone 1. No echo was used on this, and the actors worked at about eighteen inches.

Flashbacks to the scene of the crime took us to microphone 4, in a tent of screens representing the open air ("outside a garage"). Microphone 4 could also be used with a filter switched in circuit for the far end of a telephone conversation. Microphone 5 was for the car door (a real car door mounted on a frame) and "body" falling (not a real body; there were no volunteers! Instead, we used a piece of metal tubing, wrapped in thick cloth.) Taken on the same microphone as the action, the car door would have been too loud and the "body" too soft and distant. Microphone 6, at the end of the studio that had normal "living-room" acoustics, represented a room in a suburban house.

Use of these six microphones gave a very wide range of acoustics, and varying the combinations of microphones and echo made "tracking shots" possible.

In this recording, a "one-shot" technique was used, i.e. the whole programme was taken as a continuous sequence. However, this is not the only way of doing things. For the vast majority of recordists another method has to be adopted. This second method is that of the

SPEAKING OFF MICROPHONE. No actor should go farther off than this, or turn farther into the screens. More "distant" effects must be achieved by changes of voice quality, or by adjusting the microphone fader.

film: sections of the play are recorded at different times in different locations (i.e. different studios or rooms where the acoustic furniture is appropriate to the action being recorded). Special effects are cut in as required, and the whole is finally joined together on the work-bench.

The two techniques have more in common than may at first appear, for, despite differences in methods of assembly, the problems presented by a play at each stage in the course of production may be answered in very similar ways.

Visual conventions for microphones

In film and television the normal criteria for the placing of microphones for good balance still apply, but in addition a second set, based on what is visually acceptable, must also be considered.

One important convention concerns the match of sound and picture perspectives for speech. Obviously, a close picture should have close sound. Also, if possible, a distant picture should have sound at a more distant acoustic perspective. However, the need for intelligibility may override this: a group walking and talking across a crowded room may be clearly audible in a relatively close perspective, whereas nearer figures may be virtually inaudible; again, a reporter seen in long shot may be audible in close-up. In neither case will the audience complain—because they want to hear, and they can.

Other conventions concern whether microphones may appear in vision or not.

For dramatic presentations, the microphone should always be unseen, as its presence would destroy the illusion of reality.

For television presentations where such total "suspension of disbelief" is not required of the audience, microphones may be out of vision or discreetly in vision. In-vision microphones are used where better or much more convenient sound coverage can be obtained in this way; but because much of television consists of programmes in which microphones *may* appear in vision they may be seen a great deal without being noticed. However, their very ubiquity is a point against them: there is visual relief in getting rid of them if the opportunity allows.

For film, including television films, where the illusion of reality is not required, microphones may appear in vision; but the reason needs to be stronger than that required in a television studio; and the use even more discreet. This is because most film is shot in

188

places where microphones are not part of the normal furniture; so that to show a microphone may remind the audience of the presence of all of the technical equipment (including the camera). Also, in a film there may be greater variety of picture, or a more rapid rate of cutting than may be possible in the studio; in these circumstances a microphone that is constantly reappearing is more intrusive.

In certain circumstances the microphone may be introduced as a primary element of the picture. In public affairs the microphone has become and is sometimes deliberately used as a symbol of either authority or inquiry. The microphones surrounding politicians or statesmen, or those thrust into the faces of newsworthy people, all have a pictorial significance—again by convention. The commentator's hand microphone has visual associations with both authority and inquiry—but he should beware: the illusion can all too easily be changed by a misplaced word or emphasis to that of the self-indulgent popular entertainer, whose image may also include a microphone close to the mouth.

In the intermediate range of television programme, where the microphone in vision is otherwise acceptable, there may be cases where the symbolism of the obvious microphone is not wanted. Perhaps authority would be overstated and appear as arrogance; or perhaps the spirit of inquiry is already fully established visually by the studio setting and the fact that air time has in fact been allocated for this particular purpose. In this case the microphone is in the picture because that is where it can get the best sound (particularly as some of the speakers may not control their voices as actors can), but it must be subject to the pictorial rules imposed on all incidental picture elements.

The techniques for speech balance with microphones out of vision are as different from those where these may be seen as are the microphones themselves.

Boom operation

For studio work where the microphone must not be seen, the studio boom is the most important and common means of picking up sound. From a particular position the boom arm can be extended telescopically to cover a wide area between its minimum and maximum radius, and it can be moved with relative ease to new positions. In addition, the operator can turn the microphone (pointing it down at an angle, in its cradle at the end of the arm) to favour sound from any one direction, or to discriminate against any other.

189

The boom operator has a script (where one is available) and generally turns his microphone to present its axis towards whoever is speaking or expected to speak. It may be asked why, when he is using a cardioid with a good response over a wide range of directions, he needs to move the microphone at all for most work, instead of splitting the difference between two people and leaving it.

The answer to this is that there is a 2- or 3-dB high-frequency loss at about 45° to the axis, increasing to perhaps 5 dB at 60°. The microphone will be dropped as close to the performers as the picture allows (in rehearsal he will from time to time dip his microphone into picture to locate the edge of frame), and this closeness accentuates any angle there may be between speakers. This means that by proper angling there can be not only the best signal-to-noise ratio for the person speaking but automatic balancing in favour of the person speaking to discriminate against the person who is not. If both speak it may be decided to let this balance ride to favour the person who has the most important lines, or it may be decided to cover both equally.

The position for the microphone must be a compromise between the positions of the various speakers, and if they become widely separated, or one speaker turns right away, the split may become impossible to cover by a single boom. In this case a second microphone may be used, perhaps on a stand out of vision, or suspended over the awkward area, or concealed within the picture. Sometimes a second boom might be used, though this is liable to cause lighting problems.

For "exterior" scenes in plays produced in the studio the microphone must be kept as close as the limits of the picture allow. To provide a contrast with this, interiors may have a slightly more distant balance or a little added reverberation. (The 0·8 second minimum setting for the reverberation plate is very different from the 0·8 of the studio: the plate gives many more reflections in that time.)

Because a number of different types of microphone may be used for a single voice, the control desk in a studio must have frequency correction which can be used to make microphones match as closely as possible. If correction is needed, the boom microphone will usually be taken as the standard and the other microphones matched to it.

Another justification for the boom is that given suitable (rather dead) acoustics, it automatically gives a perspective appropriate to

190

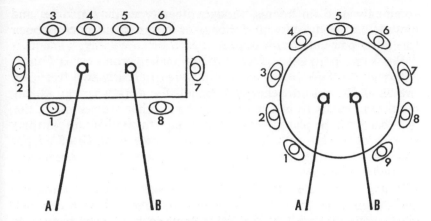

BOOM COVERAGE of a large television discussion (e.g. board meeting in a play). *Left*: Boom A covers speakers 4–8, B covers 1–5. *Right*: Boom A covers speakers 5–9 (with 1 and 4 at low level); B covers 1–5 (with 6 and 9 at low level). Cardioid microphones are used.

the picture: close shots have close sound; group shots have more distant sound. The boom operator uses the monitors on the studio floor to check his limits (the edge of frame) during rehearsal. Then by taking a sight line again on the far backing he is able to remember the position of the microphone for the main programme. In the days before the widespread introduction of zoom lenses it was also easy for him to see at a glance what width of shot each camera was set up for; now he has a more difficult task.

However, in television the sound supervisor can call the boom operator (and his other staff on the studio floor) over his own circuit, which cuts in on the director's circuit to the operator. (The BBC procedure is for this to be preceded by a tone-pip warning to tell them that this message is specifically for them.) During rehearsal and at such times in recordings or transmissions as the studio sound is faded out, the boom operator can reply to or call his supervisor on a separate sound talkback circuit. A boom therefore has a multicore cable, permitting communication as well as transmitting programme sound.

Boom prams are also convenient mounting positions for loudspeakers that have to be introduced in to the set. Such loudspeakers will usually be line-sources radiating in a horizontal plane: this gives the microphone the best available separation from sound from the loudspeakers.

Moving-coil cardioid (or broad cardioid) microphones are

191

commonly used on booms, though other types may also be employed, e.g. bi-directional ribbons, or electrostatic microphones (the latter particularly for music).

For some purposes a highly directional microphone is better. Although the high inertia of a gun which is nearly two feet long overall makes it a little clumsy to handle for work where gross and rapid movements from one direction to another are necessary, the fact that it can be placed farther back helps to compensate for this: some programmes of talk (particularly where a series of people turn directly to the viewer rather than to each other) are regularly covered in this way.

Where two people are having a "face-to-face" discussion, but are far enough apart for a boom operator to have to turn a cardioid microphone through a considerable angle to cover each in turn, it may be best to use two microphones pointing outwards at about 90° to each other. The overall effect is a very broad cardioid which is suitable for low close working. In a play such an arrangement would restrict the use of the boom for other scenes, so in a similar situation—or, for example, for a number of people sitting round a large table, two booms might be brought in.

A boom can cover action taking place on rostra built up to a height of about six feet (provided that the performers keep within about ten feet of the front of the high area), but the boom pram should be positioned as far back as possible so that the angle of the arm is kept reasonably low. For scenes on acting areas above this height it may be necessary to hoist the boom up on to rostra at a similar level (as a result of which it will, of course, be lost for scenes in the more distant parts of the studio to which it could normally be taken).

Another possibility is to de-rig the microphone boom arm and attach it to fixed scaffolding. The arm will require rebalancing, and the operator will need rather more time in rehearsal to get used to the unfamiliar conditions.

Microphones in vision

The presence of a microphone in vision must be natural and undistracting. A boom microphone (for example) which was actually visible in the top of the picture could be very disturbing, particularly if it moved from time to time to point to a different person.

Microphones used in vision are either *personal*, slung round the

192

neck or held in the hand, in which case they are moved around by the performer, or they are *static*, on table or floor stands.

For a speaker who is not going to move a fixed microphone in the picture will give by far the best sound. But to do its job properly it must generally be angled to point at the speaker (or may be split between two): if this deliberately chosen angle conflicts with the designer's choice of "line" within the picture the microphone may be more noticeable, as it will also be in a simple uncluttered design. This may not matter, but it should never be unexpected.

The base, for stability and to cushion shocks, needs to be reasonably large and can therefore sometimes appear more obtrusive than the microphone itself. Sometimes it may be recessed into a desk, but such a cavity needs to be designed with care: a fully boxed-in cavity would perhaps modify the local acoustics noticeably, so one or more sides of the recess should be left open. The microphone capsule itself should in any case stand well clear of such a recess, so in a shot showing the table it will have to be clearly in vision, unless hidden behind something standing on or in front of the table—which in turn may be a more obtrusive or unattractive element of design than the microphone itself.

A microphone placed to one side will be neater than one immediately in front of a speaker; normally a speaker will be more likely to turn one way than another, so the microphone could be placed on that side. However, if the person does turn the other way he may be right off microphone; it will therefore be useful if the next person's microphone can also pick up his voice.

Where there is a number of people spread over a large area of studio, a microphone will often be used for every individual. Even when there are pairs who are close together, the sound man may prefer to balance them individually, provided that he always knows who is going to speak, either from the script or because names are used. This is necessary because good quality demands that as few microphones as possible be open at any one time.

In a practical example: in a particular quiz there are three questioners and three teams, each of which may consist of anything up to six or even more people. Each team is examined in succession, but for each the questioning is limited to two of the judges, who may, however, butt in on each other at any point. In addition, the answers are limited to four spokesmen from a team (in fact, only these four have microphones), and they are always identified by name in the question.

Thus the balancer has only six microphones to handle, which

193

is just about possible without his being caught napping too often.

In other situations, where two people are sitting together and may be talking together a great deal, a single microphone may be used for both, but it must be arranged that if they are both likely to look off in a certain direction it will still pick up both voices adequately.

Using hand microphones in vision

The use of hand microphones has long been established as an accepted convention of television (and television film) reporting. This is because it is very convenient for the two-man, reporter plus cameraman combination; and because the microphone can be always used closer if the surroundings become noisier. In two-man operation it is recorded directly on to a magnetic stripe on the film. Even if there is a sound man in the crew, the reporter may still prefer to use a hand microphone for interview work (the techniques have been described on pp. 174–5) or in excessively noisy conditions.

I have used two stick microphones for a discussion taking place by an electric-arc steel-melting furnace, the microphones being held very close to the lips of the two speakers. This achieved a satisfactory balance with the noise of the furnace, and was exciting to listen to. The only difficulty was a non-technical one—the two people had more difficulty in hearing each other than making themselves heard to the audience.

In extreme circumstances lip microphones may be used in vision: one was used for the commentary, at the airfield itself, for the maiden flight take-off of Concorde, and gave excellent separation of speech and engine noise. On this occasion the microphone was passed from hand to hand between commentators.

But hand-held microphones can easily be overused, particularly where they make a person look unduly dominating and aggressive: for this reason they should probably not be used by women interviewing men. (In one film interview set-up in a particularly noisy situation which had been chosen for the sake of the picture, I once found myself forced to use this technique as the only one giving adequate sound. But I received complaints from the otherwise charming interviewer and from one viewer who commented caustically on the perverse symbolism of this use of a stick microphone.)

Alternative techniques, which for most purposes should be preferred, are the use of personal (lanyard) microphones, or (for exterior work) gun microphones.

Using gun microphones

The virtues and limitations of the short gun microphone have already been described (p. 149).

It is very useful for filming out-of-doors. It is held just outside the edge of frame and is pointed directly at each speaker in turn. Careful working between cameraman and sound man is required to avoid the microphone getting in to picture: its windshield is very obtrusive even when still, and is even more so if it moves.

An advantage of this microphone is that it allows very considerable movement (but not of course for the subject to turn right away from the microphone while speaking).

Accidentally off-microphone sound will be at low level in exterior work, and very bad quality in interiors. I have, however, used the microphone successfully in the relatively dead surroundings of a television studio (in an area well away from strongly reflecting surfaces), for picking up voices at a distance. But in general its directional qualities are not trustworthy in normal interiors or even reverberant exteriors.

The gun microphone is the first design that can be used with reasonable success where actually attached to a camera and pointing along its line. It is subject to mechanical noise from film cameras if these are not well blimped, and for any camera makes handling a matter for even greater care than normal. It will pick up sound effects adequately within the field of a normal wide angle. However, for all but the simplest shows there are few occasions when artists always work directly to a single camera; so this arrangement is unlikely to replace other techniques to any great extent, except perhaps for one-man news-film coverage.

Whether attached to the camera or not, when a highly directional microphone is used to cover effects such as tap dance, or to follow the action in an outside broadcast of some sport (to which it adds great realism), it is often best to filter out frequencies below about 300 Hz.

A gun microphone with bass cut has sometimes been used in conjunction with other microphones to cover the press-conference type of situation, supplying "presence" that other distant microphones lack.

Using lanyard microphones

Lanyards or "lavaliers" are another very useful type of microphone for location work: one is hung round the neck of each person who might speak.

The microphone itself can often be hidden behind a tie (though some "silk" ties cause crackling), while a thick tie will result in a correspondingly woolly response. If it is concealed it is best to ensure that the means of suspension is also invisible—for example, by using a cord which is of the same tone or colour as the shirt or other clothing against which it may otherwise be seen. Many recordists do not bother with this: the results can be untidy. A microphone which is not concealed may also sometimes merge in to the tones of a tie and not be too distracting.

These microphones, being very light in weight (of the order of an ounce or two), can be pinned to clothing of moderate thickness to prevent too much swinging against the body when the subject moves. Even so, care will be needed in large or sudden movements: leaning forward, in particular, may produce noise; and some actions which disturb the hang of clothes (as sitting down or standing up does with a jacket) may have to be done in a pause in speech so that the microphone can be faded down, or so that any noise which occurs can later be replaced in film editing by "atmosphere". However, the subject should not be discouraged from normal movement unless this is absolutely necessary; indeed, an advantage the lanyard has over the hand-held stick microphone is that it leaves both hands free for demonstration work. Also, if the speaker turns right away from the camera he may be heard clearly—though if he turns his head to look over one shoulder this may cause speech to be off-microphone. However, pinning the microphone on the lapel, or simply limiting the movement, may accommodate this.

The cable may be hidden beneath a jacket: for a tight mid-shot (which probably does not warrant the use of a neck-microphone anyway) this will be enough. However, in the more general case the cable will have to continue on its path beneath the clothing, down a trouser leg, or inside a skirt. This cable should ideally have a connector not too far from the feet, so that the wearer can easily be disconnected during breaks.

If the subject is going to walk it is best to attach the cable (and connector) to one foot, perhaps tying it in to a shoelace. Walking dragging a considerable length of cable is awkward, and may be visibly so.

Personal microphones have a characteristic quality. Once a sequence starts with such a microphone the speaker should continue on it until there is either a marked change of location (e.g. exterior to interior) or a very long pause before the same voice

196

recurs. (This is true also for many other microphones, though to a lesser degree.)

They are good (on a short lanyard) in fairly noisy surroundings, or in acoustics that are brighter than usual for television. The sound quality gains a little from good reflected sound.

When considering the use of neck microphones it is worth remembering that most viewers assume much more spontaneity in television than can in fact be the case. And even though the amount of work involved in putting a microphone round someone's neck may be trivial compared with the care that will often be taken with lighting or camera or subject position, the presence of a visible microphone will, by drawing attention to technique, diminish the illusion. Also, a person seen to be wearing a neck microphone should be unequivocally (in the mind of the viewer) a willing victim. In confrontations the victims should not be visibly lassooed in this way, though they may be perfectly prepared to be.

It must be recognized that some people do not like wearing technical equipment; for example, an actor in a play may feel that his mobility is restricted by it. A disadvantage of personal microphones when compared with booms is that there is no change of aural with visual perspective. This is more important in plays than in other programmes.

As an example of a possible use for a lanyard microphone in a play, the case of a death scene in a four-poster bed has been quoted. In the best of circumstances, action in such a setting is difficult to cover by a boom, as the director will normally wish to start with an establishing wide shot. A static microphone might be concealed in the hangings for speech at normal volume, but for the death scene this will not be close enough—hence the personal microphone concealed in the bedclothes, which in such a scene are not likely to be moved so roughly as to produce noises on the microphone.

In very long shots the possibility of using radio microphones may have to be considered even in plays (where they would be wrong for perspective unless the sound is treated with care); the radio microphone is for this purpose better than the cabled lanyard, as in plays there can be no question of trailing microphone leads in view. But there will be far greater use for radio microphones, as for all lanyard microphones, in documentary and current-affairs programmes, and light entertainment.

Co-operation between sound man and wardrobe department may be necessary for fitting the microphone and transmitter, and care will be required in establishing the field within which pick-up is satisfactory. For notes on both of these points see p. 157.

Using low-quality "actuality" microphones

There may be occasions when the output from certain low-quality microphones may be wanted: for example, actuality intercom in an aircraft, for a documentary film. In this case a feed can generally be taken from the distribution system (a suitable plug—or temporary lash up—will be required; and impedances may need to be matched). But there will still be some question as to whether the resulting recording will actually be intelligible to anyone but the air and ground crews who are used to making sense of such quality. This sort of exercise is not usually tried unless no alternative exists for the recordist.

A special, but very wide, group includes transducers which can pick up sound from media other than air.

A case in point was an underwater sync. interview I filmed at the bottom of the English Channel. The subject of the film was the method of communication used in this interview. So, as the film unit itself was to be used to illustrate the story, we had an underwater (aluminium) clapper-board made, and even a metal-framed folding chair labelled "Director".

In the standard underwater communications equipment being used a small microphone in the face mask fed speech to a waterproof 10-watt battery-powered moving-coil loudspeaker strapped to the air-cylinder back pack. Unaided underwater ears were used to pick up the sound. A microphone switch was used, both to conserve the batteries and to cut down on transmissions of heavy bubbling by both the interviewer and the director/clapperboy, who, in this case, had limited underwater experience.

A further part of the equipment was a "boat set": another similar transducer used alternately as loudspeaker and microphone. The sound recordist (sitting comfortably in the boat) was able to take a feed from this. The recording was moderately intelligible though marred on one take by the location film sound recordist's most common difficulty: engine noise from a passing aircraft, which could be clearly heard underwater.

The sound-conducting medium itself was, in principle, no problem, as water is a good conductor of sound; but future underwater film-makers should beware: the sea is a noisy place.

198

Speech in stereo

Much speech for stereo radio transmissions is, in fact, balanced on monophonic microphones. In particular, announcements are normally taken mono, and are generally placed in the centre, so that listeners can use this to balance the two loudspeakers. If the announcement is in a concert hall a monophonic microphone is still used with a relatively close and dead balance, but with a stereo pair left open at a distance to add stereophonic reverberation. The announcer and microphone are so placed that little direct sound is picked up in stereo; if it were (and were not central) the position of the announcer would be offset.

One reason for avoiding a stereo pair for speech balances where movement is not expected is that any slight lateral movements close to the microphone are emphasized and become gross on the sound stage.

The growth of stereo in radio has coincided with the decline of radio drama, and more particularly has coincided with reductions in the amount of money available for radio in comparison with television, and for the spoken word in comparison with music. Nevertheless, the BBC has gained experience in stereo drama: some of this has also been issued on records. (And BBC transcriptions have been broadcast on stereo channels in America.)

Co-incident microphone techniques for stereo drama

In BBC studios co-incident pairs are almost invariably used for the main stage; and crossed cardioid or near-cardioid gives best use of the space. The studio floor is marked up with strips of white adhesive tape on the carpet showing the main limits of the acting area, together with any special positions or lines of movement. Movement across stage (a straight line on the sound stage) will be movement along an arc of the studio: the acting area should therefore be defined by an arc at its centre, or by arcs roughly limiting it. Such arcs can be drawn either as having constant radius—for convenience—or alternatively at distances which give constant A+B pick-up. The latter is better for more complex situations, such as group or crowd scenes in which the relative distance of different voices is important. From the microphone polar diagrams it can be seen that for a crossed cardioid this arc will be farther away at the centre line and will loop in closer at the sides. In addition, the studio itself will have an effect: unless the acoustic treatment is evenly balanced, the line may "pull" closer to the microphone on one side than on the other. Indeed, sound stage positions may also be offset laterally from studio positions: the whole studio may seem to "pull" to the left or right.

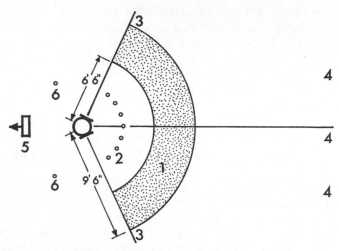

A STEREO SOUND STAGE LAYOUT FOR SPEECH. Most of the action takes place within the shaded area, 1. "Intimate" speech may, however, be closer, 2; but movement at this distance will be exaggerated and the stereo effect will be partly lost as rever-beration will be low. If the layout is such that the studio walls are closer at the sides (3), than at the front of the stereo pair long approaches will be limited to frontal paths. The narrator has a mono microphone (5) centred behind the stereo pair. Positions 6 are for speech "in the speakers".

Positions "in the speaker" on the two sides may be marked: for crossed cardioids, these will be on (or about) the 270° limits of the theoretically available stage, though for equal apparent distances these, too, may be different in actual distance from the microphone. In practice, much less than the full 270° is used—stereo is what lies between the loudspeakers, not in them; so working limits of 160°–200° will probably be established except for special cases.

In mono a long approach from a distance can be simulated by a relatively short movement by the performer, who simply walks slowly round from the dead to the live side of the microphone as he comes in to it. In stereo this space-saving technique cannot be used: long approaches, if they are required, really will have to be long, and must be carefully planned in terms of what space is available. They may, for example, be laid out to the sides, or in other particular directions from the microphone: a decision on this in advance will probably determine studio layout.

If a microphone with capsules one above the other, in the same housing, is used the difference in the height of the two capsules may cause problems in close working: a tall actor will be nearer the top capsule and will "pull" one way; a short actor will be nearer the low one and will "pull" in the other direction. Working side by side, a short and tall actor may be either separated more or shifted to the same position.

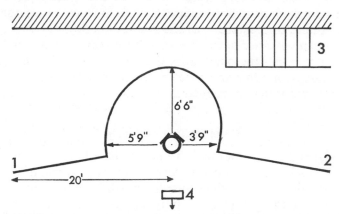

A STEREO SPEECH LAYOUT EMPHASIZING EXTREME SIDE POSITIONS and allowing long approaches from left (1) and right (2). This is taken from an actual layout in a BBC Studio where, due to assymmetry in acoustic treatment, the minimum distance for normal working was closer on the right then on the left. The positions were judged by ear and marked on the floor accordingly. Use was also made of an existing studio staircase (3) for actors to approach from mid-right, making their own footsteps. 4. The announcer, as usual, is centred.

But in any case it has been found that balances which are more distant than those that are normal for mono are necessary in order to avoid movements being exaggerated: for safety the nearest part of the real stage in which much lateral movement will occur should be at least as broad as the sound stage. In consequence, the studio must be somewhat deader than for a comparable scene in mono, and reverberation added if brighter-than-average sound is required.

For this, either stereo echo or a second stereo pair within the studio may be used. If a co-incident pair is chosen, this should be placed perhaps four feet above the first pair (this is a little like the technique described for mono and provides some degree of automatic compensation as a speaker moves in close: see pp. 343 and 345). An alternative arrangement is to use a spaced pair pointing back to the end of the studio that is away from the stage.

Whereas a studio for drama in mono may have several acting

201

areas, the same area if used for stereo may have room for only a single stage (this allows for a reduction in reverberation and an occasional need for deep perspective). Therefore there may be good reason to record all scenes with one basic acoustic before resetting the studio for the next, eventually editing the programme in to the correct running order. If very different acoustics are required in the same scene—e.g. a distant open-air crowd scene including studio "open-air" voices, mixed with close "interior" conversation—a pre-recording will have to be made, the studio reset, and the second part dubbed in to a playback of the first.

To simulate exterior scenes in a studio it may be unavoidable to use the same basic studio acoustic. Cutting bass on the microphone output may help, but the result will depend on the particular coloration of the studio acoustic.

Stereo drama problems

New dramatic conventions have had to be established for stereo sound productions: the most important is that movement (or other sound) should occur during speech, or while other sounds—e.g. footsteps—are being made; certainly, moves should never be made in a short pause between two speeches, except for "blind man's buff" comic or dramatic effects—which could easily be overused.

Problems that are met in mono drama may be greater in stereo. For example, extraneous noises are worse because:

(i) There is no dead side of the microphone.
(ii) Because of the more distant balance of voices, the signal at the microphone will be at a lower level. Channel gains will be higher and therefore noise amplified more.
(iii) Noises may be spatially separated from other action, and therefore more distinct.

Particular difficulties are raised by a need for artistic compatibility between stereo and mono.

Consider, for example, a conversation between two people trying to escape unnoticed through a crowd: they talk unconcernedly as they move gradually across the stage until eventually they are free of the other actors and can exit at the side. The mono listener to the stereo play will need as many positional dialogue pointers as he would be given if the production were not in stereo. Indeed, in mono the microphone would probably stay with the main subjects and other near voices would drift in and out of a clear hearing dis-

202

tance; in stereo this convention, too, could perhaps be established—though with greater difficulty. In such a case the producer must imagine or listen to both stereo and mono versions of his chosen convention and must decide whether changes could or should be made for the benefit of one group or the other; or whether he will disregard potential mono listeners.

A more extreme case might be a telephone conversation: a theoretical possibility would be to "split" the stage, putting one actor "in" to each loudspeaker. This might work well in stereo, but for mono would be meaningless. In this case artistic compatibility does not just suggest, it *demands* another technique: one of the actors must be on "distort", as in mono (see p. 347). The distorted voice could still be put "in" one of the loudspeakers, but the other, undistorted voice would probably be closer to the centre of the sound stage and in a normal stereo acoustic ambience, but offset to balance the distorted voice. Here a stereo convention has been determined by that which is necessary for mono.

Recordings using speech from the theatre stage will generally not work in stereo any better than they do in mono—because the acoustics are likely to be far too bright for the distance of the microphones. Recordings of broadcasts of opera performed before an audience can be balanced using spaced microphones along the footlights (see p. 238), but this cannot satisfactorily be done for normal speech.

Other techniques used in conjunction with speech balance in stereo are dealt with in other chapters: in particular, layout for monitoring (p. 390), mixing (p. 67), control (p. 436), and echo (p. 342).

Speech for stereophonic film is generally recorded in mono and panned to its proper stereo position at the dubbing session (p. 68).

7

MUSIC BALANCE

THERE are two basic types of music balance.

One is the "natural" balance, which uses the studio acoustics for reverberation: this is generally preferred for "serious" music. For a single instrument or for a group having perfect internal balance a single microphone may be sufficient. However, perfect balance is rare: a singer may be overwhelmed by all but the quietest of pianos; an orchestra may be (and often is) dominated by its brass. So "natural" balance often has to be extended to two microphones.

This first type of balance has two subdivisions: mono and stereo. As I have already made clear, co-incident rather than spaced pairs will be recommended as the basis of "natural" stereo balances. And though the position of the microphone, the relative angle of the elements, and the choice of their polar diagrams should give sufficient control over all of the variables, it may in practice be easier to set up a second stereo pair (which may or may not be co-incident and control reverberation separately). In addition, individual mono microphones may still be used to modify a given internal stereo balance.

The second type of balance uses many close microphones and artificial "echo" instead of natural acoustics. It is preferred for popular and much light music. Mono balance techniques are generally used for both mono and stereo, with stereo positioning, like "echo", being introduced synthetically.

In this chapter the problems of each of these types of balance will be considered in general terms; then taking individual instruments and groups of instruments in turn, I will show how they are applied.

What to listen for

The balance test has already been considered in some detail. Speech balance is a specific type of balance that presents special problems; for the more general case of music balance we must look at a broader pattern of wanted and unwanted effects. Here are the main things to listen for:

(i) Wanted direct sound, i.e. sound radiating from part of the instrument where the vibrating element is coupled to the air. It should comprise a full range of tones from bass to treble, including harmonics, plus any transients which characterize and define the instrument.

(ii) Unwanted direct sounds: e.g. hammer (action) noises on keyboard instruments, pedal operation noises; piano-stool squeaks, floor thumps, page turns, etc.

(iii) Wanted indirect sound: reverberation.

(iv) Unwanted indirect sound: severe colourations.

(v) Unwanted extraneous noises.

When trying out a balance, listen to check that bass, middle, and top are all present in their correct proportions, and sound in the same perspective. If they do not, it may be the fault of the studio, in that certain frequencies are emphasized more than others (so changing both proportion and apparent perspective; or it may be more directly the fault of the balance in that a large instrument is partly off-microphone (this can happen with a close piano balance).

"Natural" monophonic balance

In a monophonic balance which is taken basically on a single microphone, its distance will depend on both the polar response of the microphone chosen and the acoustics of the studio.

When using a good music room or hall, or in fact any place where the acoustics are both lively and clean, it is probably worth starting the balance tests with a bi-directional microphone. For some instruments or groups a good ribbon microphone will be satisfactory, but in the more general case a condenser (electrostatic) microphone will often be used. Try various distances and listen carefully to the results: the balance to seek is one where you get plenty of reverberation, but not so much that the sound becomes muddy or coloured.

A close balance sounds more dramatic; it is ear-catching, arresting. Such a balance can, in fact, help to sell a record—but may be difficult to live with. However, where the acoustics are difficult it may well be necessary to accept the brilliant close balance whatever one's personal preference, perhaps making a kind of virtue of necessity. As the balance gets closer it will probably help to have a field of pick-up which is broader than the normal figure-of-eight (this is certainly so for orchestral balance). A condenser microphone which can be switched between figure-of-eight and cardioid, and has intermediate conditions available as well, is particularly useful for this purpose.

But bear in mind that when they are listening on high-quality loudspeakers many listeners prefer—quite definitely prefer—a more distant and therefore more blended sound than those which many balancers enjoy. But for listening on poorer equipment, greater clarity helps to make up for some of the deficiencies: if you can't hear everything, at least you can hear the main elements of the music. For this reason (and also because it helps to motivate close-ups), a "drier" balance is preferred in television.

Music studio problems

In a "natural" balance we are recording the characteristics of the studio just as much as those of the player.

It is rather as though the studio were an extra member of the orchestra. With stringed instruments, very little of the sound we hear is directly from the strings; what we are actually listening to is the radiation from a sounding board to which the strings are coupled. And the individual character of the instrument depends heavily on the shape and size of that radiator.

In the same way, the studio acts as a sort of sounding board to the instruments: its shape and size gives character to the music. By uniformity of design, the character of all instruments of one particular type is roughly the same. But music rooms, studios, halls, and so on differ widely in character: no two are the same.

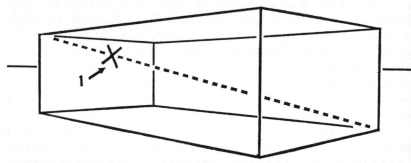

MICROPHONE PLACING. A good place for a monophonic microphone in a large hall with good acoustics may be fairly well back along one of the diagonals.

CURVED SURFACES. Concave architectural features can cause echoes. Microphones should not be placed within the radius of a vault such as this.

In broadcasting studios theory suggests that a monophonic directional microphone should be angled to pick up reverberation equally from all three main dimensions. Further, a central position is generally avoided: this can be justified theoretically on the grounds that in the middle of the room the even harmonics of the eigentones—the basic resonances of the room—will be missing, thereby thinning out the acoustic response of the room.

Fortunately, in practice, the number of studios where this really matters—where there are serious eigentone problems in music balance—is small. (Stereo microphones are usually placed on the centre line of concert halls and rarely with ill effect; though admittedly concert-hall eigentones are very low pitched.)

Nevertheless, there is no harm in playing safe: a microphone position which works well for a music balance in mono can often be found somewhere along one of the main diagonals of the room. The first attempts at balance are usually tried with such a position. Then, using comparison tests, proceed by trial and error—remembering that if the sound is wrong wherever you put the microphone it may help to move the sound source.

In a studio which is comparatively dead for its size an omnidirectional microphone may help. But there are times when even a distant balance with an omnidirectional microphone does not do enough. Some percussive instruments, such as tympani, continue to sound for some time, and have decay characteristics which are somewhat similar to those of reverberation. These may therefore stand out in too dead a hall. When this begins to happen, artificial reverberation may have to be considered.

The average television or film studio is the dead studio on the grand scale. But the same problems may also arise in microcosm when one or two singers or instruments are being recorded "on location"—perhaps in a domestic living-room which is not designed for music making. Here the answer is different, for taking the microphone to the other side of a small room with heavily damped acoustics will only emphasize their inadequacy. In this case the only effective solution may be furniture removal: if it is possible to get rid of heavily padded furniture—armchairs and so on—take these out first; but, in any case, carpets should be rolled up and soft drapes pulled aside. And avoid having too many people in the room.

For monophonic balance, a directional microphone will give the greatest control in cases where acoustics cause difficulty, as it allows an extra dimension for experiment: the angle can be varied, as can the distance from the source and position within the room. In stereo this facility is, however, lost: a good "natural" stereo balance is therefore even more at the mercy of studio acoustics than is monophonic balance.

Stereo music balance

The stereo music balances recommended in this chapter will be based primarily on co-incident pairs of microphones with cardioid elements angled at 90°. This may be modified in practice by changing the polar diagram, or by changing the relative angle of the elements: this will have the results described in Chapter 5 (pp. 162 to 167).

In particular, the double figure-of-eight will not be used, and for two reasons. The most important is the poor compatibility with mono: there are bound to be some listeners to a stereo broadcast

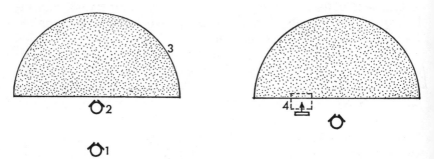

ORCHESTRAL BALANCE IN STEREO. 1 and 2. Two stereo pairs with different polar diagrams but giving the same stage width to the orchestra (3). Microphone 1 is double figure-of-eight; microphone 2 is double cardioid: a mixture of the two can be used to control and change reverberation where there is such a wide dynamic range that a great deal of volume compression is necessary. For a soloist (4) a spotting monophonic microphone will be used, steering this to the same position as it appears on the audio stage established by the stereo pair.

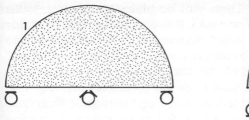
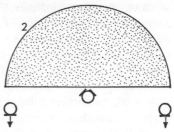

STEREO ORCHESTRAL LAYOUTS. 1. With a spaced pair to "pin down" the corners of the orchestra (e.g. harp on left and basses on right). 2. With a spaced pair used to increase reverberation. This layout can be readily adapted for use in four-channel stereo.

or disc who will hear it in mono, and if the A—B signal is very large they will lose a significant part of the information. (What happens, in fact, is that they lose far too much of the reverberation: this is very strongly represented in the A—B component of a double figure-of-eight). The second problem is that reverberation is picked up on both back and front of the microphones in roughly equal proportions, so that at low frequencies there is a phase-cancellation effect which takes some of the body out of the stereo reverberation, making it thin and harsh. This will be noticeable in a concert hall and very marked in the more reverberant surroundings of, say, a cathedral. Switching the polar diagram even a quarter of the way towards cardioid reduces this effect significantly.

It is assumed, then, that a first attempt at balance will be made

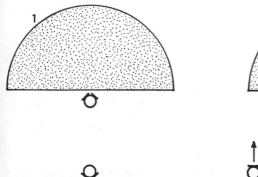
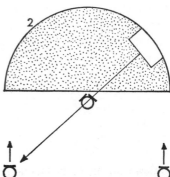

STEREO ORCHESTRAL LAYOUTS. 1. A second co-incident pair with reversed output used to control reverberation separately: can also be used for four-channel stereo. 2. WRONG: A forward-facing spaced pair set back into the hall may give false information from the brass, which, directed towards the microphone on the opposite side, may suddenly appear to be in the wrong place.

with co-incident cardioids. These will be placed to control width rather than reverberation: for a subject that is to occupy the major part of the audio stage the microphones will look down from one edge of the pick-up area. For an orchestra that is to occupy about two-thirds to three-quarters of the sound stage, they will be high over and perhaps a few feet back from the conductor.

Reverberation may be added by a variety of means. One is to have a second co-incident pair set back from the first and facing towards the empty part of the hall or studio. Another has a spaced pair of cardioids at the sides of the hall, well forward again, but looking back along it. In either of these cases the two microphones must be steered to their correct sides of the studio, as some direct sound will arrive at these microphones, and even more by short-path first reflections.

These two layouts also offer the prospect of good sound in four-channel stereo in cases where the rear loudspeakers are used only for reverberation—which is more aesthetically pleasing than feeding direct sound to all four speakers. References to stereo in this chapter will generally assume two channels, but can readily be adapted to four in this way. Other four-channel systems have been used experimentally; in particular, one with four omnidirectional microphones set in the auditorium with very roughly the same configuration and spatial layout as the speakers in the listening room. But such an arrangement does not stand up to close analysis: although it does produce a sound field which envelopes the listener, this is not closely related to the field in the concert hall itself. So despite the fact that this balance has been used for concerts by the Boston Symphony Orchestra and broadcast by two local stereo stations working together to produce a four-channel signal through two receivers, it is not the main type of balance to be recommended here. It could, however, be used where a sound that is more thrilling than realistic is required.

A further layout has a second co-incident pair of microphones, but this time figure-of-eights looking forward and set back to such a distance that the positions of the various parts of the image roughly coincide. For an orchestra this distance may be about ten feet. This arrangement has the additional advantages that the balancer can work between the two pairs to handle extreme changes of volume, and that the second pair gives an automatic stand-by facility in the event of failure or loss of quality of the first pair during a live transmission (this is very rare, but such a facility is, none the less, desirable; two pairs of microphones are in any case needed for balance comparison tests). Phase cancellation on the back of the second pair remains a problem, however.

Additional mono microphones may be used for "spotting" individual instruments or small groups.

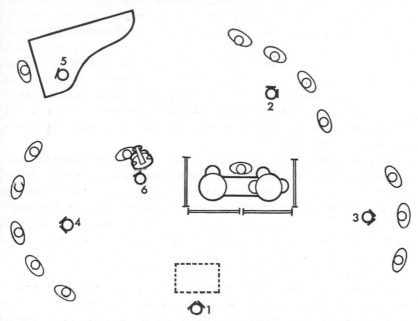

SHOW BAND IN STEREO, using a basic "natural" balance on microphone I, above the conductor. But this is reinforced by extra stereo pairs for the trumpets (2), trombones (3), and woodwind (4), which are steered to their corresponding positions and widths; while for the piano (5) and bass (6) monophonic spotting microphones are used.

Artistic compatability: mono and stereo balances

If an item recorded or broadcast in stereo is likely to be heard by many people in mono it is obviously desirable that the mono signal should be artistically satisfying. This may mean modifying the stereo version somewhat. There are several problems which may occur:

Loudness. Whereas a sound in the centre will appear equally loud in both channels, those at the side will be split between the M and S channels. As the S information will be missing in mono, such subjects may be lower in volume than is desirable.

Reverberation. The S signal has a higher proportion than does the M; the mono version may therefore be too dry. A possible way

211

round this is to make the main stereo balance drier still, and then add more reverberation on the M channel.

Aural selectivity. Individual important sound subjects may not be clearly heard in the mono version when in stereo they are quite clearly distinct because of spatial separation. It may be necessary to boost such subjects or so place them (towards the centre of the stage) that in the mono version they are automatically brought forward.

Phase distortion. Spaced microphone techniques may not adapt well to mono, as the subjects to the side will have phase-distortion effects: systematic partial addition and cancellation of individual frequencies which will no longer vary with position.

In addition, there are things which are less of a nuisance in mono than stereo. For example:

Extraneous noises. Noises which are hardly noticed in mono may be clearer in stereo because of the spatial separation. Moving noises (e.g. footsteps) may be particularly distracting unless they are part of the action and balanced and controlled to the right volume, distance, and position.

One microphone or many?

The alternative to studio acoustics and the natural blending of sounds is the multi-microphone balance, in which an essential, but not necessarily conventionally natural, quality is sought from each instrument or group and blended together electrically. Neither technique is any more "right" than the other, but after a period in which orchestras could have many microphones and big bands sometimes only one, opinion has tended to polarize to the view that most classical or "serious" music written up to the mid-twentieth century (and some written since then) is best balanced on one or, at most, a few microphones; and that popular music demands many.

There is a rightness about this: the "simpler" microphone technique for classical music reflects the internal balance of the orchestra and existing acoustics that the composer wrote for; whereas the top-twenty hit of the moment generally reflects the acceptance of the opportunities for experiment that are open to today's arranger.

This leaves several gaps. The modern serious composer has tended to go out on a limb technically: some of the avenues that he has explored are discussed in Chapter 12. But popular music—at the time of writing—has yet to influence serious music in the

212

way that, for example, jazz and blues did in the first half of the twentieth century. When it does, the question, "one microphone or many?" will reopen in serious music.

Meanwhile, the question *is* still open in a number of areas lying between the extremes of orchestra and pop group: somewhere in the region between light orchestra and showband there is room for this to be a practical question.

Before choosing a single-microphone balance one has to consider how the sound source is distributed. And if the acoustics are suitable, can it be arranged that the sound source falls within the pick-up field of a single microphone? Given that the instrumental layout is suitable, careful placing can ensure that the distance between the microphone and each source is exactly right.

But in the multi-microphone situation the balance problem is divided up into stages.

A very broad range of techniques is drawn together: techniques for mixing several microphones, for handling "echo", for creatively distorting sound, and for building up a recording by adding track upon track; all these are considered later in their separate chapters. The number of variables under the control of the balancer is enormous, and the only way to deal with them all is to develop the sort of mind which is constantly analysing the sound, selecting each of these variables in turn, and checking it against the others.

The multi-microphone sound

In this technique, what happens after the microphones have been positioned is as important as that which goes before. More detailed descriptions will follow in later chapters, but here are brief notes:

Equalization. Nominally this means restoring a level response to a microphone which has inherently or by its positioning an uneven response. Certainly, this is one part of the job; but in this case why do balancers deliberately select microphones with responses which are not level? Equalization, as with all of the following procedures, is done by ear: "What *sounds* right, *is* right." Generally it is simply a second stage in the creative distortion of sound—the response of the microphone in its chosen position being the first. Equalization, whether in a separate RSA (response selection amplifier) or incorporated into an integrated fader–amplifier unit, has controls for bass response, "top" response, and midlift. Some BBC units have four bands of midlift, centred on 1·4, 2·8, 4·0, and 5·4 kHz, and each

213

with two switched levels of increase. Other RSAs offer different facilities, e.g. 2, 3, 5, and 8 kHz with a wider range of increased levels. There may be advantages to the closer spacing, and certainly an 8-kHz peak has its uses. (See pp. 351–353.)

"Echo" (see p. 336). This replaces the natural reverberation given by conventional acoustics. Greater control is possible, as feeds taken from individual microphones can be set at different levels. Equalization can be applied to echo, too, perhaps to give the high harmonics of direct sound greater clarity by having less echo in the "top".

Compression (see p. 429). Reduction in dynamic range may be used to maintain a high overall level (in order to ensure the strongest possible recorded or broadcast signal), or it may be applied to single parts of a backing sound which would otherwise have to be held low in order to avoid sudden peaks blotting out the melody, or to the melody itself, which might otherwise have to be raised overall, and as a result become too forward. Limiters as well as compressors are used for this.

Tracking. This is the building up of a complete sound by additive recording. For example, the instrumental backing may be recorded first; then the soloist listens to a replay on headphones and adds his contribution, the mixed sound being recorded on a second machine. Or, for a particular item, an extra instrumental track may be required from a musician who was already playing in the original recording.

Mixing (see Chapter 2). For almost every purpose there are advantages in high-level mixing—that is, raising the level of the electrical signal by up to 70 dB before combining one sound with another. However, in pop music some microphones are working at acoustic intensities which are 30 dB or more above their nominal level. So for the balance of popular music there are strong objections to normal high-level mixing using preamplifiers of fixed gain.

Post-balancing. Some recording studios prefer to use half- or one-inch tape in order that a number of additional synchronized tracks can be retained until after the recording session is over. Experiments with balance, i.e., in the treatment and combination of the sounds, can then be continued in the absence of the musicians themselves.

In *multi-microphone stereo* these elements of balance change hardly at all. Almost invariably mono microphones are used, and the stereo is created in the mixer. However, for instruments which are to be spaced apart on the sound stage even higher standards of separation are required than in mono.

214

Instruments of orchestra and pop group

Orchestral players and pop musicians play instruments that have a great deal more in common than in difference. All orchestral instruments are fair game for popular music; but there are instruments in pop or novelty groups which rarely make the journey in the opposite direction, notably the electric guitar but also some of the older sounds such as the piano accordion or banjo.

For all types of music balance we are therefore dealing with the same basic sound sources, which can be treated in a range of different ways, but for which the various possible treatments required in different types of music overlap. An orchestral balance may require reinforcement of a particular instrument; a stereo balance may require individual mono "spotting": both of these demand close microphone techniques which approach those used in multimicrophone balance. In serious music a distance of several feet is "close" or even "very close", depending on the instrument; for pop music closeness may be measured in inches: there may be slight differences in terminology.

But there is no difference in the basic problems and possibilities. In the following sections these are explored in terms of individual instruments, sections, and combinations; and full orchestras and bands.

The instruments to be examined will be divided into the following groups:

(i) *Strings*: plucked, bowed, or struck, and coupled to a sounding board acting as a resonator (or from which vibrations are derived electrically and fed to a loudspeaker).

(ii) *Wind*: where the resonator is an air column excited by edge tone, vibrating reed, etc.

(iii) *Percussion*: where a resonator (often with an inharmonic pattern of overtones) is struck.

This far from exhausts all possibilities: mouth organ and accordion, "wind" machine and musical saw are further variations; as are the instruments devised in France which use longitudinal vibrations in glass rods (which are excited by stroking them with wet fingers) to cause lateral vibrations in metal rods, which are transmitted to the air by metal resonators of novel design.

These last, and many others, will not be considered in detail. For any instruments which have not previously been met it is useful to determine (or guess) the radiation pattern for different frequen-

215

cies and try microphones in different directions and at different distances accordingly, using (wherever possible) comparison tests to find the preferred balance for a particular purpose.

It is as well also to remember that such a balance will be for a particular player and a particular example of the instrument: some players and some instruments produce very different sounds from others of the same apparent style or type (this is notably true of double basses and their players). It will be a balance also for the particular microphone or microphones used, and in all but the closest balance, for a particular studio—and perhaps even for particular weather conditions.

A humid atmosphere might be expected to affect balance, as high frequencies are transmitted better by damp air. However, in controlled experiments conducted by the BBC no consistent relationship has been found between musical quality (including frequency content) and humidity. Other factors may be its effects on musical instruments and human ears, and—perhaps even more important—subjective judgment.

The string family

A violin radiates its strongest concentration of upper harmonics in a markedly directional pattern; and therefore it is to be expected that, for all but the lower frequencies produced, much of the sound goes in to a lobe directed over the heads of the audience. A great deal of harsh quality, squeak, and scrape that even good players produce is thereby also lost to an audience. So it must be recognized that an audience normally hears little of the high-frequency sound that is produced, as even in the reverberation it may be heavily attenuated in the air. At its lowest frequencies the radiation pattern is omnidirectional, but the violin is an inefficient radiator of sound at low frequency owing to its size: the lowest notes are heard mainly in their harmonics.

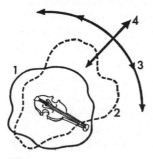

RADIATION PATTERN AND MICRO-PHONE POSITION FOR VIOLIN. 1. Low frequency radiation. 2. High frequencies. 3. Move along this arc for more or less high frequencies. 4. Move closer for clarity; more distant for greater blending. (See also p. 26.)

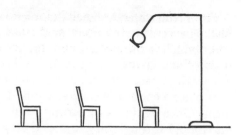

For a concert balance the microphone will be placed well back from the instrument to add studio reverberation; and the frequency content can be controlled by movement in an arc over the instrument. The upper harmonics are heard at their strongest a little off the axis, towards the E string (i.e. the "top" string on the violin).

To make a *close* violin sound pleasant requires more than the art of the balancer; it requires a modified style of playing in which the unpleasant but normally acceptable components are much reduced. But very close working for pop music work may be limited by the athleticism of the player. In ordinary circumstances three feet is about the limit, for during pizzicato passages there is some danger of the bow hitting the microphone, though some players are capable of encircling it with the right (bowing) arm. The lowest string of the violin is G, of which the fundamental (at 196 Hz) is weak, so bass tip-up is not a serious problem with directional microphones; indeed, a bass filter at 220 Hz may be used to discriminate against low-frequency sound from other sources. A high-quality ribbon microphone can give a very satisfactory response (though possibly requiring some reduction in "top").

For a close balance on a violin section the players may sit in their normal arrangement of two at a desk, with the desks one behind another. The microphone is then slung directly over and slightly behind the first two players. This will still favour the leader sufficiently for solos, but will not lose the rear players as a close balance farther forward would. If this balance is still too distant for adequate separation in, say, a dance band balance in live acoustics, a microphone may be placed over each desk. But some roll-off of high frequencies will be required to counter the harsher quality.

For a stereo balance either a mono or stereo set-up may be used. But a mono microphone *must* be used for close working, as the slightest movement near a co-incident pair will become gross. In this case the instrument will have to be steered to its appropriate position on the sound stage (for a soloist on his own, in the centre) and stereo echo added to fill the full width with reverberation.

217

For a true stereo balance the microphones must be more distant. Slight movements of body and instruments will then produce an effect which is pleasant, unless these substantially alter the proportions of sound reaching the microphones. This could happen very easily with spaced microphones, but may still do so with a coincident pair: a change in reflected sound may produce spurious movement. Once again, reverberation must be adequate in quality and distributed throughout the sound stage.

Violas may be treated in the same way as violins, except that *very* close working on directional microphones may produce bass tip-up, and that a filter at 220 Hz cannot be used, as this is well inside the frequency range of the instrument.

'Cellos and basses differ from violins and violas in that they are much more efficient as radiators in the lower register, because they have a much larger area of resonator to drive the air. The high, extended spectrum of resonance, which made the violin shrill and "edgy" if heard directly above the instrument, is scaled down to the upper middle frequencies in the case of the 'cello. In order to get the full rich sonority of this instrument's upper harmonics, it becomes necessary to place the microphone more directly in line with its main radiating lobe. Again with these lower strings we have a tool to aid us in balance—if we merely want to add depth to a fuller orchestral sound we may be content to balance near-sideways-on to the instrument, but if we want richness we turn the instrument to the microphone, as a 'cello is turned to the audience in a concerto.

For popular music the bass, or double bass—plucked rather than bowed—is one of the three basic instruments of the rhythm group; the others are piano and drums. Of the three, the bass is the most difficult to separate: a very close balance is essential, as the level is low.

Pop music balancers are disinclined to recommend any single balance that will always work, pointing out that there are great differences between one bass or bass-player and another.

The following are suggested:

(i) A cardioid, "cottage-loaf" or figure-of-eight microphone a few inches in front of the bridge looking down at the strings.
(ii) A similar microphone directed towards the f-hole at the side of the upper strings.
(iii) A "personal" or small studio microphone suspended from the bridge, with the diaphragm pointing directly upwards to face the bridge.

STRING QUARTET. Viola 1, 'cello 2, violins 3 and 4. Similar arrangements may be made for wind and larger chamber groups.

(iv) A "personal" microphone wrapped in a layer of foam plastic, suspended by its cable *inside* the upper f-hole. This gives virtually total separation.

One "cottage-loaf" microphone which may be used for (i), (ii), or (iii) has a response which falls away in the bass so that correction for close working (though variable with distance) is automatic. Most figure-of-eight microphones used for (i) or (ii) will, however, require a great deal of low-frequency equalization to compensate for bass tip-up.

In general, (i) has the most to recommend it, as it will hear the percussive attack quality from the string itself as it is plucked, and there can be fine control over the ratio of this to the resonance of the body of the instrument. In contrast, (iv) gives a heavy "hanging" quality which will have to be controlled to a lower level than the other balances.

In stereo pop balances the bass is always taken mono and steered to its appropriate position.

Other stringed instruments, such as the (acoustic) guitar and the banjo, the violin's predecessors (the viol family), and so on, all radiate their sound in ways similar to the instruments already discussed, and the control that the balancer has over the ratio of top to bass is much the same. Groups based on stringed instruments are also balanced in a similar way.

The string quartet is a simple group to balance: if the players sit in two rows of two, the microphone can be placed in front of them at any suitable distance. Imagine a line extending forwards and upwards at about 30° from the middle of the group, and try a microphone position somewhere along this. Then check that distance, angle, and position within the studio are right for taking full advantage of the acoustics. Listen to each instrument in turn as though it were a soloist, and make sure that the 'cello can "see" the microphone. The quality of sound to listen for is one which

219

combines clarity and brilliance on individual instruments with a resonant well-blended sonority for the group as a whole.

As more instruments are added, a similar "natural" arrangement may be retained, moving the microphone back if necessary in order to keep all the instruments within its field. In this way we progress through the various types of chamber group or wind band to the small orchestra.

"Electric" stringed instruments

There is, of course, an alternative way of picking up the signal from the resonating panel, and this is to attach a contact microphone to it. This is what happens with the electric guitar and similar instruments, the output of which is converted into "live" music by feeding the amplified signal to a loudspeaker. There is no absolute necessity for this loudspeaker to be of high quality; many are not. The character of the instrument is derived from a combination of the frequency response of the loudspeaker and those of the panel at any points where microphones are situated.

How are we to balance the electric guitar family? Or perhaps the first question is, *why* balance it? Why not feed the electrical output direct to the recorder? There are several reasons which favour a normal balance, and the first is that a performer needs to hear his own instrument and the way it blends with others: do not forget that more than half the job of balance is done before the sound reaches the microphone. The second reason has already been indicated: that the loudspeaker provides part of the composite formant characteristic of the instrument.

The loudspeaker of the pure electric guitar should be treated like any other instrument, though for the fullest high-frequency response the microphone should be exactly on the axis of the cone. A "cottage-loaf" microphone like that described above may be used for a close balance.

In many cases the guitar will serve double purpose as an acoustic and electric instrument. In this case the amplifier unit is placed on a box or chair opposite the player, with the microphone between loudspeaker and instrument. The player himself can now adjust the overall amplifier level, comparing it with the direct, acoustic sound: he will have control of the loudspeaker volume from moment to moment by means of a foot control. A ribbon microphone may be used for this balance, with any bass equalization that may be necessary at the distances involved. Picking up sound equally on the two sides, it will not distort the balance between acoustic and electric output set by the player himself.

The piano

The piano radiates in a similar manner to the smaller stringed instruments: the vibration is fed to the soundboard, and almost the entire wanted sound is due to radiation from this.

The radiation pattern from the soundboard allows a reasonable degree of treble and bass control: in particular, the bass is at its strongest if the microphone is placed at right-angles to the length of the piano; and the extreme top is clearest if it is directed at the "top" end of the soundboard.

So we have an arc extending from top to tail of the piano, the balance with the most powerful bass being that at the end of this arc closest to the top of the keyboard. As the microphone is moved round, the bass is progressively reduced until it is at its minimum at the tail. For very powerful concert pianos this tail position may be best, but there is a slight disadvantage in that there is a loss of definition in the bass, as well as reduced volume. For most purposes, a point somewhere in the middle of this arc is likely to give a reasonable balance—and this is as good a starting-point as any for studio tests.

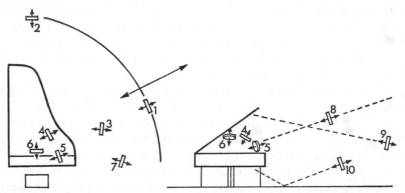

PIANO BALANCE. The best balance for a grand piano is usually to be found somewhere along the arc from the top strings to the tail. A close balance gives greater clarity; a distant balance gives better blending. Of the positions shown, 1. Often gives a good balance. 2. Discriminates against the powerful bass of certain concert pianos. 3. Picks up strong crisp bass. (A mix of 2 and 3 can be very effective.) 4. Close balance (with lid off) for mixing into multi-microphone dance band balances (pointing down towards upper strings). 5. Discriminates against piano for pianist/singer. 6. (Angled down towards pianist) as 5. 7. One of a variety of other positions which are also possible: experiment rather than rule-of-thumb will indicate best balance. 8. Concert balance "seeing the strings". 9. By reflection from lid. 10. By reflection from floor.

The height of the microphone should allow it to "see" the strings (or rather, the greater part of the soundboard) which means that the farther away it is, the higher it should be. However, if this is inconvenient, other balances are often possible: for instance, you can use reflections from the lid. This is the balance which an audience generally hears at a concert. For the very lowest notes, the pattern of radiation tends to the omnidirectional; but for the middle and upper register, and the higher harmonics in particular, the lid ensures clarity of sound.

Another possible balance (provided there is no carpet) is by way of reflection from the studio floor. And the reader may find that an even more unorthodox-seeming position provides a perfectly adequate balance in his own studio. Indeed, in some studios it does not seem to make much difference where the microphone is placed.

So far I have assumed that we have been using a ribbon microphone and a grand piano; but the problems are essentially the same for all types of piano balance. If you are using an omnidirectional microphone the solution may not be quite so easy. You will have to work a little closer to the piano to adjust the proportion of direct/indirect sound, and you will have less effective control of direction of pick up.

The closer one gets to an open piano, the more the transients associated with the strike tone will be apparent; at their strongest and closest they may be difficult to control without reducing the overall level or risking momentary distortion on the peaks. Action noise—the tiny click and thud as the keys are lifted and fall back—may be audible, and in balance tests this and the noises from pedal action, etc., should be listened for.

When a close balance is employed for pop music the lid is always removed.

A balance suitable for a piano in a rhythm group may be as close as six inches above the top strings. Surprisingly, a bi-directional ribbon microphone can still be used, as the bass tip-up at this distance will actually help to rebalance the sound. The exact position finally chosen will vary with the melodic content of the music being played: one criterion is that the notes played should all sound in the same perspective (the manner of playing may also affect this). For a percussive effect the microphone could be slung fairly close to the strikers, and if a baffle—perhaps a piece of cardboard—is fastened to the upper surface of the outer casing of a ribbon microphone, this will further emphasize and "harden" the higher frequencies, and especially the transients.

222

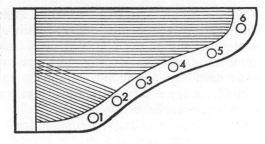

PIANO HOLES. The focusing effect of the holes in the frame of a piano can be used for a pop music balance. Microphones may be used either singly (usually over hole 2) or in pairs.

An alternative is to use the focusing effect of the holes in the iron frame of some pianos: the different sounds can easily be heard by listening close to them. A microphone two or three inches above the second hole from the top gives the best overall balance, though for particular effects the holes on either side may be used. An interesting mixture can be obtained with two microphones, by using the top hole in combination with the fourth, fifth, or sixth hole.

Distortion (particularly of the percussive transients) due to overloading has to be avoided, and may require attenuation before the first preamplifier. Microphones with head amplifiers (including electrostatic microphones) are at a disadvantage here.

Certain older types of ribbon microphone may be unsatisfactory, too. A long ribbon of low compliance may sag to the edge of the gap between the magnet pole-pieces when the microphone is laid on its side: this can result in a distorted signal. There is, however, no problem with modern ribbon microphones.

The piano is the first instrument that we have considered for which stereo spread is a real advantage. In pop music, where two microphones are used, these will be picking up different parts of the instrument and can be steered to different positions; but in a true stereo balance a co-incident pair will generally be placed fairly well back from the piano, and reverberation will be controlled to provide a matching perspective. While a concert grand piano *could* fill the space between the stereo loudspeakers, few people would normally wish to hear it that close. Even a width of a half of the stage brings it close enough for most people, and a more distant balance may be preferred.

For upright pianos, listen again for each of the wanted and unwanted sounds that I have listed, again watching to see that the balance remains the same over the whole scale (except for the cases —with lighter styles of music—when you may prefer to have "not too much left hand").

Lift the lid and try the microphone somewhere on a line diagonally up from the pianist's right shoulder—a good balance can generally be found in this position. But remembering that it is the soundboard that is radiating, an alternative is to move the piano well away from the wall and stand the microphone on a chair at the back (for a close balance), or diagonally up from the soundboard (for a more distant one).

One of these will also be suitable for balancing a "jangle-box" (this is the type of piano that is specially treated, with leaves of metal between hammer and strings to give a tinny strike action, and with the two or three strings for each note of the middle and top slightly out of tune).

A similar balance may be used for the celeste; though this, even more than the jangle piano, is subject to mechanical noise on a close balance. In either case it is usually possible to find a position where this noise is not obtrusive. An alternative microphone position for the celeste is to the front of the instrument and below the keyboard, on the treble side of the player's feet at the pedals (and keeping well clear of them).

Piano and soloist

The piano is fundamentally a much more powerful instrument than the human voice, and it is part of an accompanist's job to see that a singer (or any other sort of soloist) is not swamped by the piano sound. But the accompanist's judgment of this is valid only for the "live" concert hall; when recorded and heard through a single loudspeaker, the level of the accompaniment must be lower still, as the ears are no longer able to discriminate spatially between the two sounds.

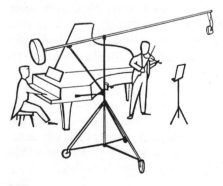

PIANO AND VIOLIN. Balance for piano first and then balance soloist on same microphone. A two-microphone technique for the same instruments is shown opposite.

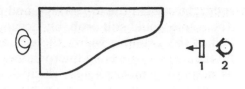

PIANO AND SOLOIST SIDE BY SIDE. I. Mono microphones. 2. Microphones used in stereo.

In practice, this is a problem which is usually solved easily enough with a single microphone—simply by adjusting the relative distances. In many cases it will be best to get a good piano balance first (with the microphone not too high) and then place the second source accordingly. It may prove necessary to have the piano lid in its lower position; but apart from this, you should find that if the musicians themselves are in good balance your worst difficulties will be half resolved before you even set up your microphone. A balance with the second performer placed in the curve of the piano looks good, and may sound good, but remember that the musicians often need to see each other's faces, so a balance on opposite sides of the microphone will often be preferable.

In order to discriminate against the piano, a directional microphone may be turned until it is partly or completely dead-side-on to the piano. But this is not an ideal solution, for two reasons. For a start we have a direct sound balance on the soloist, while the accompanist sounds miles away. The piano sound is muddy and unattractive. The second reason is that this device may not work anyway, particularly in small studios; and instead of a close overwhelming accompaniment we have a distant overwhelming accompaniment.

A third balance, again using two microphones, can work better than either of these, and is very good in stereo as well. Here, the soloist and accompanist are placed side by side, facing the same way, so that they can both be heard on the main microphone, which is so placed as to give good piano balance: on a concert grand it may be in line with the tail. The soloist is then given a relatively close directional microphone, which is brought up to a volume which is high enough to give him adequate presence when heard against the piano. This close microphone is dead side on to the piano and picks up little of its sound.

In stereo precisely the same balance can be used: the main microphone is replaced by a co-incident pair which locates, from left to

225

right, the soloist, the top strings, and the bass strings of the piano. The whole would still probably occupy not much more than about half of the available width, though reverberation would, as usual, fill the stage. The second microphone, that for the soloist, now acts as a spotting microphone, which is steered to coincide with the soloist's position on the main balance, and then brought up in volume, as before, to give adequate presence.

More complex piano balances

In a studio with suitable acoustics it is possible to get good separation by turning the soloist's microphone dead-side-on to the piano and mixing in the output of a second microphone which is arranged to pick up a little of the piano. In carrying out your balance tests with the two microphones, first get a good sound from the soloist, and then gradually fade in the second microphone until it just brings the piano into the same perspective. In small studios this minimum setting will often be quite loud enough.

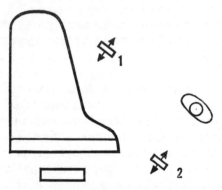

A TWO-MICROPHONE BALANCE. Separate balance of piano I and soloist 2. Particularly loud or soft passages can be controlled individually.

An alternative technique is to employ a backing track (this requires an extra tape machine for replay, and a mixer, but only one microphone). The soloist listens to the pre-recorded piano on headphones, and the levels can be adjusted at will at the mixer. This method is employed a great deal in the recording of popular music—but very rarely indeed for serious music.

A slightly more tricky balance is one where the pianist himself also speaks or sings. In many such cases a singer will wish to take advantage of the opportunity to use less voice than would be possible without a microphone. A more "intimate" effect is achieved, but at the expense of losing internal balance. Here a suspended microphone becomes essential. If a ribbon microphone is used it should be placed about twenty inches from the singer (as for a speech balance), with its dead side towards the soundboard of the piano. It may be in front of the singer (tilted down) or round to

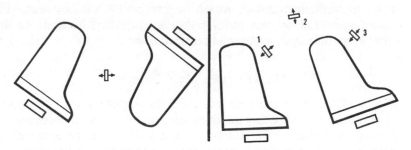

BALANCE FOR TWO PIANOS. *Left:* two pianos on a single microphone. *Right:* two pianos on individual microphones 1 and 3 or on a single microphone 2.

his right. An omnidirectional microphone will require a much closer balance of the voice in order to discriminate against the piano.

A two-microphone balance can sometimes be employed for this arrangement as well, using microphone 2 for piano presence. But a great deal of care should be used if either is to be faded, as the quality can change considerably.

The best way of balancing two pianos on a single microphone will depend on studio layout—and this in turn is a matter where the wishes of the pianists should be observed if possible. With the pianos placed side by side, a single ribbon at the tail should suffice. The equivalent two-microphone balance would use two ribbons, each in the curve of one of the pianos: these can be a shade closer than the single microphone, and will give a marginally greater degree of control over the relative volumes and frequency pick-up. But one microphone should provide an adequate balance with this arrangement as it does with a tail-to-tail layout.

Other keyboard stringed instruments may be treated in much the same way as the piano. The direction of pick-up for a harp is not critical. Indeed, quite a good balance—and one which cuts down mechanical (pedal) noises—can be found with a microphone behind the harpist's head.

But for a close balance when the harp is being used as a novelty instrument in popular music, separation is achieved by having a directional microphone pointing down directly at the sounding board.

Wind instruments

Each of the wind instruments has its own directional pattern of radiations. For brass, the main axis of the bell carries the main stream of high harmonics, though few, if any, of an audience will be able to hear these at any time. For woodwind with fingered or keyed holes the bell may make little difference to the sound: the main radiation is through the first few open holes. It follows that, unless we go close, we have considerable freedom in balancing woodwind and brass; in general, a microphone placed somewhere in front of and above the player will prove satisfactory.

For wind, as with other sections of the orchestra, the transient, the way in which a note starts, is of considerable importance in defining the instrument for the listener and giving it character: as also is the breathy edge tone that we hear with the flute. These sounds must be clear but not exaggerated. The closer the balance, the stronger are the transients in comparison with the main body of the sound. Listening at an ordinary "concert" distance, the sharp edges of the notes are considerably rounded off. Listening to a flute at two feet, it sounds like a wind instrument with a vengeance! In close balances it is occasionally advisable to resort to "tricks" such as placing the microphone *behind* a flautist's head. This will reduce the high-frequency mouth noise and edge tones without affecting the sound radiating from the other end of the instrument.

The range of volume from woodwind and brass is very wide, but there should be no trouble with this except where the output of a close balance on heavy brass is fed through pre-amplifiers of fixed gain; this can result in overloading and consequent distortion. Care should therefore be taken when the pre-amplifier comes before the volume control.

The balancer should not rely on rehearsal levels of "big band" brass players he does not know, but should allow for as much as a 10-dB rise in level on the "take", which if it were a live broadcast could be disastrous. Not only might he be left without an adequate working range on the faders, resulting perhaps in distortion of the sound, but also he could find himself facing new and unrehearsed problems of separation.

A close balance on trumpets or trombones is difficult to control, but it will help if the players themselves are prepared to co-operate by leaning in to the microphone on quiet passages with mutes, and sitting back for the louder passages. The microphone must be near enough for them to reach for close work but far enough back to pick up several players equally. Players are also well aware of the directional properties of their instruments and will play directly towards the microphone, or not, as the music requires; though some bands which have done little work in studios and more in dance halls may take this to extremes—perhaps by playing soft passages in to the music stand. Here the balancer needs to remind them that a cleaner sound can be obtained if some of the control is left to him.

The height of the microphone should be such that it may be on the axis of the instruments as they can be comfortably played—though with the trombones this is a little awkward, as the music stands get in the way of the ideal position. However, the leader of the section will say whether he prefers the microphone above or below the stand.

The answer will probably depend on how well the players know the music. In a band where the music played is part of a limited and well-rehearsed repertoire the trombones will often be held up; but musicians faced with unfamiliar music will, understandably, wish to be able to look down to see it.

Brass is one section of the orchestra which benefits from midlift, an increased response of 5 dB or more, in this case at somewhere about 6–9 kHz. But certain microphones have peaks in their response in this region and produce the effect without much need for help from an equalizing amplifier.

In the orchestra French horns are generally placed where their sound will reflect from a wall or from other surfaces behind them. Such an arrangement—with a microphone looking down from above at the front—will be suitable in almost any circumstances; though exceptionally, for complete separation and a strong, rather uncharacteristic quality, a microphone can be placed behind the player and in line with the bell.

In popular music a commonly used "woodwind" section consists of up to five saxophones. These are frequently balanced by placing three players on one side of a ribbon microphone and two on the other, with the microphone raised on a box to a height such that it will be in line with the bells of the instruments. The lowest saxophone (usually a baritone) should in this arrangement be at one end of the row of three. Players in this section may double on flute or clarinet, which will often also be played to the same microphone.

However, for this balance on the saxophones, separation is less than it could be, as there has to be compensation in volume for the angle of the bell of the instrument; besides which the microphone is well placed to pick up sound reflected from the walls of the studio.

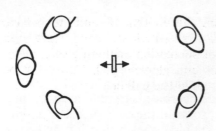

WOODWIND in dance band. Saxophones arranged in a group in a multi-microphone balance. The microphone stands on a box to raise it above the bell of the instruments.

So other arrangements have been suggested. One particularly successful balance uses the same grouping of the players, but with two "cottage-loaf" hypercardioids angled down towards the centre of each side. This layout is very flexible and allows a precise adjustment of the balance.

An alternative arrangement which some balancers prefer is to place this section in a line or arc, with one microphone to each pair of musicians. This helps particularly where saxophone players doubling woodwind fail to move in for their second, quieter instrument, and also allows the height of each microphone to be adjusted more precisely to the needs of the second instrument. For a close balance on a clarinet, for example, it should be lower than for a flute.

The woodwind section (and particularly saxophones) may benefit from midlift at about 2·5–3 kHz.

In informal popular music the balancer will probably have no score to guide him (even if the players have), so he will not necessarily know whether a player has the melody or part of the backing. In an extreme case a woodwind player may to all appearances have an important part, which when the balancer lifts it so that it can be heard, turns out merely to be fingering—the musician doubling another player at low level. The balancer may reasonably expect the musical director to indicate where the melody lies: this is especially important where particular instruments have figures or lines that are introduced into pauses in a vocal.

Several layouts are possible for brass or military bands. In one the various groups are laid out in an arc round the conductor in the same way as a string orchestra; in the other the performers form three sides of a hollow square, with the cornets and trombones facing each other on opposite sides. In this way the tone of the horns and euphoniums at the back will not be blotted out by the full blast of the other, more penetrating instruments. The microphone may be placed a little way back from the square, and off the centre line of the studio.

230

The military band differs from this in that it tends to behave rather more like a small orchestra from which the strings have been omitted. There is usually plenty of percussion, including such melodic instruments as the xylophone and glockenspiel. Care must be taken that these are given full value in the balance.

Percussion, drums

Most percussion instruments can be recorded with ease. However, some percussion sounds will register more easily than others, and on all but the most distant microphone set-up it is as well to check the balance of each separate item with care.

The only sounds in the percussion section which warrant the full hi-fi treatment (in the sense, that is, of extended frequency response) are the triangle, cymbals, and gong. The character of these instruments lies in their ability to fill in the gaps and extend the sound spectrum laid out by the rest of the orchestra; and they need that last half octave up to 15 or 16 kHz as much as any other. Just as in the field of sound effects jingling keys or clinking money sound twice the size and made of lead if the high frequencies are missing, the cymbals and triangle can sound dull and uninteresting for the same reason.

In popular music percussion shows itself mainly in the form of the drum set: this will include a snare drum, bass drum (foot-pedal operated), a cymbal (or several), a hi-hat (a foot-operated double cymbal), a large tom-tom, and perhaps a small one as well.

In the simplest balance for these a single microphone (which also requires a good high-frequency response) points down at the snare drum. But any attempt to move in for a close balance from the

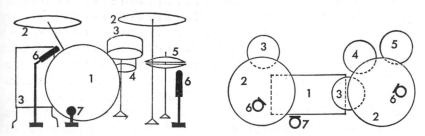

TYPICAL DRUM KIT for dance band or pop group. 1. Bass drum. 2. Cymbals. 3. Tom-toms. 4. Snare drum. 5. Hi-hat. 6. Microphones with good high frequency response used in two-microphone balance. 7. Additional microphone (moving coil) for more percussive bass drum effect (used in some pop music).

231

same angle will increase the dominance of the nearer instruments over the bass drum and the hi-hat. (The hi-hat radiates most strongly in a horizontal plane, in comparison with the up-and-down figure-of-eight pattern of the top cymbals.)

A good close balance employs a wide-frequency-range cardioid microphone at the front of the kit and at about the level of the hi-hat. For an even tighter sound this can be moved in closer still to the hi-hat, also favouring the left-hand top cymbal or cymbals and some of the snare and small tom-tom, together inevitably with some bass drum; a second cardioid microphone is then moved in over the other side of the bass drum to find the other cymbal or cymbals, the big tom-tom, and again, perhaps, the snare drum. Changes of position, angle, polar diagram, or relative level give considerable control over nearly every element except clarity of the bass-drum sound. This may also be required to fill in the texture of some pop music and can be obtained by facing the diaphragm of a moving-coil microphone towards the front skin and close to its edge, where a wider and more balanced range of overtones will be present than at the centre. This is one place where one of the older, more solid-looking microphones with a limited top-response is as good as a modern high-quality microphone (which might in any case be overloaded).

In stereo, width can be introduced by steering the various microphones to slightly separate positions.

Singers: solo and chorus

What counts as a close balance for a singer depends on the type of music. For a "pop" singer it may be four inches: for an operatic aria it is more like four feet—but whatever the music, a monophonic recording will almost invariably present the soloist in much closer perspective than you hear in the concert hall or theatre.

In the opera house or concert hall, good balance is possible only when the orchestral accompaniment is delicately soft-pedalled—or when the singer bawls. But if a closer microphone is used for the soloist, there is more freedom to create brilliant orchestral backings which can be interwoven and contrasted with a subtle and varied vocal line—as our best modern popular arrangers have found.

A bi-directional microphone is often used: figure-of-eight or hypercardioid. For serious music a clean, flat response is all that is necessary; a high-quality ribbon at three or four feet is excellent. But for lighter styles of music a closer balance is used, and com-

232

pensation for bass tip-up will be needed when working closer than two feet on a ribbon microphone.

For closer balances still and where the backing is loud the hyper-cardioid discriminates slightly more against the background and may allow the singer to come in closer. One double-ribbon hyper-cardioid has a reduced bass response such that a singer can work at a matter of inches without noticeable tip-up (indeed, if the singer moves back, bass may have to be added). A singer working very close does in any case produce less of the chest tone which in serious music is used to deepen and strengthen the sound.

Hand-held microphone techniques have already been described (p. 154).

In pop music balances a singer is often given presence by adding mid-lift at about 1500–2500 Hz.

Individual singers are never balanced in stereo (except where action is taken from an operatic stage). Mono microphones are used and steered to a suitable position in an overall balance.

With choral groups, clarity of diction is the thing to aim for. The microphone must be far enough back to get a well-blended sound, but the limit for this is the lower limit of intelligibility. If a ribbon microphone cannot be placed far enough back to see the group as a whole, then a cardioid may be the answer. With an omnidirectional microphone, the singers can be placed in a complete circle.

The cardioid is very useful for light music choral groups: a closer balance than that for the more serious works is needed, and the singers can spread themselves out sideways more than with a ribbon; and yet it is still possible to discriminate against an instrumental group or orchestra.

For stereo a large chorus could in principle be grouped round a co-incident pair in a rough semicircle. But in practice this may be inconvenient: most choruses prefer to arrange themselves in a straight line or shallow arc, and fixed seating for choruses normally also follows this pattern. So here, three, or perhaps even four, spaced cardioid or near-cardioid microphones *are* used. Spaced microphones also make it easier to steer a chorus to a suitable position behind an orchestra on the sound stage.

There is no special virtue in clear separation of sopranos, altos, tenors, and basses into separate blocks: the stereo effect may be good, but the musical quality of a layout which blends all sections may be better. As an alternative to the block layout a chorus may be arranged in rows (here even more than in the other cases the microphones need to be high up in order to balance all of the

233

voices). Or better still, the singers may all be mixed up together. Opera singers must be able to do this, and so can some choirs. A high order of musicianship is required: when a group can and want to sing like this the stereo balancer should not try to discourage them.

The orchestra

Our next individual "instrument" is the full orchestra. And, indeed, an orchestra may rightly be considered to be an individual instrument if it is well balanced internally. For such an orchestra the general principles already outlined apply: the reverberation offered by the studio acoustics is balanced against direct sound from the orchestra (mono, see p. 206; stereo, see p. 208).

The detail of orchestral layout is far from standardized, but the strings are always spread across the full width of the stage, grouped in sections around the conductor, and with the woodwind behind them in the centre. In the older form of string layout the violins are divided, with the first violins on the left and second on the right, and with the violas and 'cellos between them and the double basses also in the centre. For stereo this has the advantage that the violin sections are clearly separated, and the weight is in the middle. But that the upright instruments ('cellos and basses) face forward is unnecessary for microphone or audience, as they are virtually omnidirectional radiators anyway; and there is also the slight disadvantage that the high-frequency radiation from the second violins is directed backwards away from both audience and microphone. The more modern layout has the sections placed, from the left: 1st violins, 2nd violins, violas, 'cellos; and raised behind the 'cellos on the right, the basses.

Apart from the woodwind, which are always across the centre, there are further variations in the rest of the placings: brass, tympani, percussion, horns, piano, or harpsichord (as orchestral instruments, not soloists); all of these may appear in different places. The resident conductor of an orchestra may have strongly expressed reasons for his particular distribution of sound, but from the point of view of the balancer who sees many different layouts in a single hall the strongest common reason may appear to be whim.

While his job is generally to reflect what is offered to him as well as he can, a well-established and experienced balancer may also offer suggestions for improvement. Indeed, a conductor who is thorough will consult the balancer not only on matters of detail in

234

placing but will also ask how the internal balance sounds. Many conductors, however, will concentrate solely on musical qualities, so that if, for example, there is too much brass it will be left to the balancer to sort it out, if he can—though in fact the problem will be virtually insurmountable.

In stereo an interesting possibility is offered by a pair of spaced microphones that are used to add reverberation. It will be recalled that these are normally placed to face *away* from the orchestra. But an alternative is to use a pair of omnidirectional (or broad cardioid) microphones placed at the outermost front edges of the orchestra, or a little forward from it. With a "modern" orchestral layout the left-hand one will pick up harp and part of the 1st violins; the right-hand one will pick up the basses: these corners can then be "pinned down" and perhaps drawn towards the loudspeakers, so broadening the sound stage a little.

Any microphone that is set up in addition to the main pair and facing towards the orchestra (or a "bright" reflecting surface) may give false information about the position of the brass, if significant direct or strong first-reflection sound can reach it. The trumpets are likely to be directed over the heads of the strings and may be picked up on any microphone in line of fire on the *opposite* side of the studio. There is then an extra trumpet signal, pulling the section across the sound stage, perhaps to a position occupied by other instruments.

A weakness of numbers in any section can sometimes be rectified in part by putting a microphone over it and giving it more presence. But in stereo such a microphone will have to be close. For example, woodwind spotting must be done in such a way as to avoid spill from neighbouring and louder instruments—in particular, once again, the brass.

Quiet, unusual instruments such as the mandolin need to be brought well forward, right under the conductor's nose. If this is done it may not have to be spotted for stereo, but if it should prove to be necessary, in this position it can easily be arranged.

If a *pipe organ* is used with orchestra there is a danger (in stereo) that its distance will cause its image to be too narrow.

In fact, as a good organ is laid out in the hall, it should have some width (indeed it is bound to), but not so much that the spatial separation of the various voices are marked: like a choir, an organ tone is better blended than broken up into obvious sections. However, in stereo excessive width (such as that of the Royal Festival Hall in London) will be narrowed by the microphones to something more reasonable; and a good average width may appear rather narrow. A pair of microphones at such a distance that they "see" the organ as a whole can be used to broaden the sound stage. These should be placed to pick up as little orchestra as possible; and the orchestra microphone itself may have to be angled to discriminate against direct sound from the organ.

Orchestra with soloists or chorus

Concert works with solo instruments can often be taken on a single microphone. Soloists are usually placed on the conductor's left, and the microphone may be off-centre to this side in order to favour them. But a greater degree of separation is obtained if the solo instrument is placed out to the side of the orchestra with a separate microphone (taking care, as usual, to present the dead side of the solo microphone to the orchestra). Or alternatively, the soloist may be placed with his back to a side wall.

When two or more microphones are used the apparent reverberation will be increased. The main microphone will need to be a little closer than if it were the only one in use. This means that the soloist's microphone must not be faded in or out suddenly, or the change in perspective on the orchestra will be noticed.

In mono these techniques will work well for instruments or singers who need to be boosted a little to hold them clear of the orchestral backing. (For pianos this is rarely a problem.)

But for concert-hall balances or for most stereo this form of separation will not work: the soloists must be at the front of the platform. In both cases the soloist is likely to benefit from spotting: remember in all of these cases the primary balance of the soloist remains on the main microphone, and the subsidiary microphone is used only to provide a little additional presence; that is, not only a little more volume but also more of the enhanced high-frequency content that only a close balance can give. It is the latter, a change of quality, giving increased clarity that the balancer is listening for as he brings up the solo microphone. In stereo this must, as usual, be steered to its proper position on the audio stage.

If there are several soloists, as in a double or triple concerto, or several solo singers, these need to be placed with a thought for lay-out on the sound stage. Spotting microphones cannot be used to move them to more convenient places, as their positions are already defined in the main balance. So if four singers, say, are to appear regularly spaced across the audio stage this means that they cannot

236

ORCHESTRA AND CHOIR. A. Orchestra. B. Choir or soloist. C. Alternative position for choir or soloist. I. Microphone position for orchestra only. This balance is acoustically similar to 2 plus 3 (or 2 plus 4) for orchestra plus chorus or soloist.

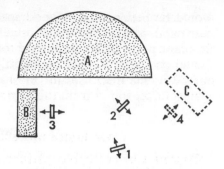

stand all on the conductor's left: such an arrangement, with adequate spacing, would be satisfactory for mono, but for stereo would produce a very tight echelon formation on one side.

A piano concerto in stereo raises a different problem. With a co-incident pair in its normal position, over and behind the conductor's head, the question is not how to get more of the soloist but how to get less of him. The apparently facetious suggestion "spot the orchestra" does in fact provide the answer. The main microphones can be moved back a little (and their polar diagram narrowed) and an additional pair, very broadly angled, set in high over the piano but shielded from the full blast by the lid. If anything, this pair is favouring the woodwind.

When a chorus is introduced this is normally placed behind the orchestra. If it is already weaker than the orchestra this position does not help; and moving the microphone in (as for stereo) only makes the orchestra stronger in comparison with chorus. Several spaced directional microphones are therefore added to give presence to the choir. These are set on very high stands (or suspended) at the back of the orchestra. As they look down at the choir, giving it increased body, presence, and intelligibility, their dead side will be towards the orchestra. This works well in stereo too; and the spread can be increased if on the main microphone they appear to be bunched too close together. (In this case their actual position as indicated on the main pair does not matter much, as this is expected to be a spread and not positionally defined source.)

There are further problems in stereo when the chorus is supplying not words but orchestral texture, as in Ravel's *Daphnis and Chloë* (the difficulty here is to get sufficient spread when spotting microphones would bring the chorus too far forward), or in the last movement of Beethoven's Ninth Symphony (where the soloists

237

would be better placed for perspective at the back, but prefer to come and stand at the front). I will not give detailed suggestions to fit every possibility—except for one further important technique for singers, chorus, and orchestra, which in a number of different variations the BBC uses for most studio performances of opera.

Opera

Opera may be recorded or broadcast in concert form; or it may be taken from a public stage performance. A good layout for the first is as follows:

The orchestra is balanced normally (for stereo or for mono: I assume stereo in the following). The chorus is placed on the left-hand side of the studio, in rows, and balanced on a row of about four microphones, to which the soloists also work. As the right-hand one of these overlaps the left-hand end of the orchestra, this microphone is steered to the left-hand side of the sound stage. The other microphones are then steered to positions progressively farther to the right.

The result is that the chorus and orchestra now occupy the full width of the sound stage with the soloists at the front, but that all of the singer's positions have been transposed left to right.

For stage opera good balance is not easy.

In mono it is customary to use a high microphone to get a good balance on the orchestra and a row of cardioids in the footlights (dead side towards the orchestra) to pick up the singers. If the singers are reasonably well back there is no problem of balance between several voices (though they may appear a little distant). But if a singer comes down stage very close to a microphone his footsteps could become gargantuan: he is therefore balanced on the next microphone along (depending which way he is facing). If two singers are working together and one is well down stage of the other the best microphone to balance them may be on the opposite side of the stage: this will be equidistant from both, and should still see the face of the downstage singer even if he turns partly away from the audience.

It might be supposed that this will not work in stereo, but the fact is that it can and must. In stage opera *good musical quality is more important than the correct positional information.* As the opera progresses the balancer may produce what is in effect a completely new set of movements, sometimes working singers on

238

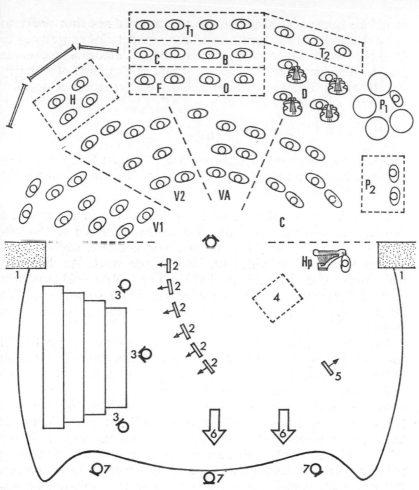

STUDIO OPERA LAYOUT in which the chorus and soloists are reversed left to right and superimposed on the orchestral stage. A converted theatre is used in this example, with the proscenium arch (1) in front of the orchestra. The stage is extended into the main auditorium for soloists (2) and chorus (3), conductor (4), and announcer (5) whose microphone can also be used for spotting effects (e.g. castanets, which can be steered to represent the movement of a dance). An offstage chorus can be placed underneath the balcony without a microphone (6) and the audience is above (7). The orchestral layout is as follows: VI. Ist violins, V2. 2nd violins. VA. Violas. C. 'Celli. D. Basses. H. Horns (with reflecting screens behind). F. Flutes. O. Oboes. C. Clarinets. B. Bassoons. TI. Trumpets. T2. Trombones. PI. Tympani. P2. Other percussion. Hp. Harp. Note that the harp is "in" or near the right-hand speaker, and that the left-hand side of the orchestra and the side of the chorus and soloists nearest to it will be picked up on each others' microphones and *must* therefore be arranged to coincide in the audio stage. For the singers, examples of positioning for particular scenes using this layout are as follows: i. Part of chorus left; principals centre; off-stage chorus, right. ii. Duet at centre solo microphones; harp figures, right. iii. Quartet at four centre solo microphones. Note that as their seating and music stands restrict quiet movement, any major repositioning of sections of the chorus must be done in recording breaks.

239

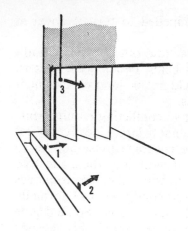

MICROPHONE POSITIONS IN THE THEATRE (E.G. FOR OPERA). 1 and 2. A pair of (cardioid) microphones in the footlights. Though very close to the orchestra their response discriminates sufficiently against this. 3. A single microphone placed high in the auditorium—but well forward. Cardioid response again favours singers.

pairs of microphones which may be on a different side of the stage from their actual position. Obviously, the movements must be handled with care; and major changes in relative microphone settings must be made to coincide with moves on the theatre stage. And finally, the overall effect must be at least credible, which means that at least some of the tricks that the mono balancer would resort to cannot be used. Sometimes the stereo balancer will just have to let a problem ride.

The novice, coming to stereo balance of opera without ever having learned to handle it in mono, may be tempted to do it the "easy" way, simply taking the whole work on a row of open microphones. This, even apart from producing many ugly perspectives, can still produce odd effects. A character may project his voice across the stage, or he may be blocked off from the microphones on his own side, either of which will mean that incorrect positional information is given, this time quite unintentionally.

The techniques described for mono opera are also usable for plays *televised* from the stage as outside broadcasts. A television audience will come to accept actors' projection after a while. But the technique is not suitable for stage plays recorded or broadcast in sound only, whether in mono or stereo, as the theatre acoustics will be far too lively.

Applause

The main problem with applause for serious music is one of level. Prolonged applause at high level is unacceptable: it must be held at such a level that the listener is not impelled to turn it down in irritation.

For all types of programme, applause (and other forms of audience reaction) must be clear, without being unbalanced, that is, individual pairs of clapping hands should not be loud or dominant enough to draw attention to themselves.

In order to achieve such a response two conflicting requirements must be met: the audience must be reasonably large (ideally, several hundred strong); and the microphone coverage must not be so distant as to lose the desired clarity. In addition, there must be adequate separation between audience and other microphones which may be live at the same time. These conditions will normally be satisfied only if a number of microphones are used. Some degree of directional response will often be desirable, though this depends on factors such as the relative position of performers and audience, the studio acoustics, and the use of public address. What is *not* necessary is a set of high-quality microphones and expensive mixing apparatus: this can sometimes be a job for obsolescent but still usable equipment. High-level mixing is not necessary. Many modern mixer desks on which all of the main channels are mixed at high level have a simple six-channel low-level submixer supplying audience as an internally balanced single source to a single channel on the main mixer.

The problems of even balance are not necessarily reduced by having a small audience; indeed, the fewer the number present, the more important it is to get full value by means of a balance which loses nobody.

In stereo applause is best spread across the full sound stage. It must be picked up on the main, its own, and any announcer's microphone only in such a way that controlling the level of the applause does not pull it to one side.

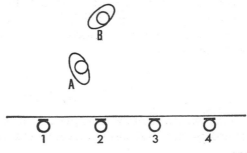

MONOPHONIC OPERA BALANCE FROM STAGE PERFORMANCES. Singers A and B, well down stage, are balanced only on microphone 4, and not on 2, which is closer. For stereo such a balance would also be better, if the reconstruction of the position on the sound stage can be tolerated or managed.

Popular music groups

Having worked up to some of the largest and most complex layouts for classical music, we can now take some of the same—or similar—components and put them together again in a contrasting style.

For absolute contrast to the last musical theme, and linked to it only by the rapturous applause that is common to both, I will start with a combination that reached the peak of its development in the sixties: one drum kit and three electrical guitars, plus the voice of one of the guitarists.

For this, a suitable studio layout has the three loudspeaker cones on a common axis and all pointing the same way and three bidirectional microphones on those axes.

To the side of this array and on the dead side of the microphones lies the drum kit, with low screens to separate it from the amplifiers. For even better separation the two main drum kit microphones can be on the far side of the drums, that is, behind them and on either side of the drummer. A bass drum microphone will also be used.

For many numbers this would be enough to take at one go: the vocal would be recorded to playback of the backing track. However, it may sometimes be taken at the same time. For this, use a directional microphone equalized for very close working, apply presence at 2–3 kHz and perhaps compression as well if the voice is intended to blend in to the backing. If the vocal is compressed the backing can be brought up tighter behind it—though this, too,

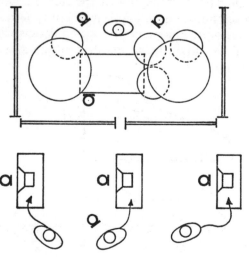

POP GROUP with 3 electric guitars, drums and vocalist. Maximum separation has been achieved by screening the drummer heavily: there are two low screens in front of him, high screens at the sides, and a further screen bridged across the top. The two main microphones for the drums are at the rear, and the bass drum microphone is separated from the skin only by a layer of foam plastic. The vocal will often be recorded to replay of the remainder of the sound.

might be limited to hold excessive peaks and to permit the highest possible overall recording—or broadcast—level.

For stereo, the monophonic elements can be steered to any arrangement of the producer's or balancer's choice, e.g. guitar—drums—guitar and vocal—guitar.

A more traditional element of popular music is the piano trio, i.e. piano, bass, and drums, which forms the nucleus of most larger and more versatile groups. To this may be added, stage by stage, guitar (acoustic/electric), brass, woodwind (primarily saxophones), vocalist, and other instruments for particular effects: these might include celeste, violin, horn, harp, electric organ, or any other instrument that interests the arranger. Once again, mono balances will normally be used throughout for stereo—though there have been experiments with the use of stereo pairs on three sections: trumpets, trombones, and woodwind.

Normally the studio will be dead, but sometimes bright surroundings may be all that is available. In this case some spill may be inevitable, and it may be best to modify the ideal fully separated balance. For example, if the brass is going to spill on to the vocalist's microphone come what may, it is worth considering whether to make it good-quality spill by using the same microphone: the vocalist sings at three inches and the brass blows at six feet. This surprising balance has been used quite successfully—though for mono; in stereo spatial separation of brass and vocal would be desirable.

Even in the best of conditions there may be enough spill in the studio to dictate some elements of the layout of the stereo sound picture. However, certain relationships will appear in both the real layout and its image: for example, the piano, bass, and drums will always be close together. These might be steered to centre and left

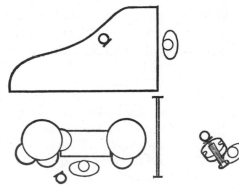

RHYTHM GROUP. The drum kit and bass are separated by a low acoustic screen. A range of positions is possible for each microphone.

243

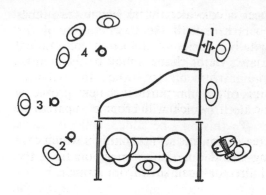

SMALL BAND. Rhythm group with 1. Guitar (acoustic/electric); 2.Trumpet; 3.Trombone; 4. Woodwind (saxophones). Rhythm group microphones not shown

of centre with electric/acoustic guitar near the left speaker, vocalist and woodwind right centre, and brass on the right. The actual layout in the studio is governed not only by the need for separation (so that this or some other stereo picture can be achieved, and so that all of the sounds can be individually treated), but also by a number of practical considerations—such as whether the players can hear or see each other.

Multi-microphone layout

When the musicians arrive in the studio they will expect to sit at positions already arranged for them, with chairs, music stands, screens, piano, boxes for such things as guitar amplifiers, and microphones all (at least roughly) laid out. They will have been set according to the balancer's instructions; and in the case of the microphones he or an assistant will have actually placed them himself. What guides the balancer in the various choices he can make in his layout?

Three different situations may occur:

(i) The group may already have a layout used for stage shows. In this case the balancer will find out in advance what this is and vary it as little as possible (but as much as may be necessary for good separation) with the co-operation of the musical director.

(ii) The group may have done previous recordings or broadcasts with the same organization. The balancer will find out what layout was used before, and if it worked well use it as a basis for his own layout. The group will not expect to be in different positions every time they come to the studio. However, minor changes for the purposes of experiment, or to include

244

ideas that the balancer is convinced work better than those already used may be tried—with the co-operation of the individual instrumentalist, leader of a section, or musical director, as appropriate. Major changes may be dictated by the use of additional instruments (of which the balancer should have been informed), or particular new problems created by the music itself (which will become apparent in rehearsal).

(iii) The group may be created for this session only, in which case the balancer—having found out the composition from the producer or musical director—can start from scratch.

Even starting from scratch, the balancer will apply certain rules that make the musician's job easier. For example:

(i) The bass player may wish to see the pianist's left hand, to which his music directly relates. This is particularly important if there may be improvisations.

(ii) The drummer, bass-player, and pianist form a basic group (the rhythm group) who will expect to be together.

(iii) In a piano quartet the fourth player can face the other three in the well of the piano; everybody can see everybody else. But a guitar player may be working particularly with the bass, so could be placed at the top end of the piano keyboard so he can see across the pianist to the bass player.

(iv) When the bass player has fast rhythmic figures he will need to hear the drums, particularly the snare drum and hi-hat; these can be heard well on the drummer's left.

(v) Any other two players who are likely to be working together on a melodic line or other figures will need to be close together.

(vi) Where players double, e.g. piano with celeste, the two positions will be together.

(vii) All players, including a saxophone (and woodwind) group which may be split with up to three and two facing each other, will need to see the musical director or conductor.

(viii) The musical director may also be a performer playing a particular instrument. But if it has been arranged that all players can see each other, condition (vii) will still be satisfied.

This may appear to make the original idea of building up a layout according to good principles of separation less feasible. But in fact, although compromises may be necessary here and there, careful use of directional microphones and screens should make a good —or very good—sound possible.

But the studio acoustics may still enter into the problem. An

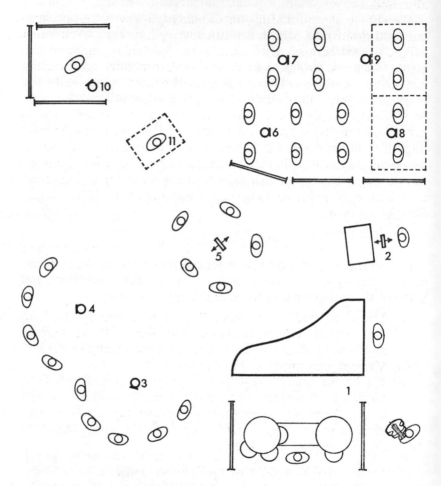

SHOW BAND WITH STRINGS. 1. Rhythm group. 2. Electric/acoustic guitar. 3. Trumpets. 4. Trombones. 5. Woodwind. 6. 1st violins. 7. 2nd violins. 8. Violas. 9. 'Celli. 10. Vocalist. 11. Musical director. Variations must be made for acoustic difficulties: in one regularly used BBC layout it was found necessary to bring the bass forwards to the tail of the piano and separate him by acoustic screens from brass, drums, and woodwind (the trumpets having been moved farther away). Additional forces will also complicate the layout still farther. For example, the pianist may need an additional keyboard for organ or celeste: this could be placed to his right and the guitar moved forwards. A wide range of different microphones will be used: see the notes on individual instruments for details of type (including frequency and polar response) and position (distance, height, and angle).

example is one BBC studio regularly used for multimicrophone work. The basic layout had to be modified because the woodwind (saxophone) group said they could not hear the bass. So the bass has been brought up to the tail of the piano and heavily screened all round.

Screens. In the normal layout suggested, a low screen between bass and drums will help to acoustically separate the two; another will be needed between drums and brass. Particularly quiet instruments, such as strings, celeste, etc., will probably also require screens. A vocalist may be provided with a tent of screens well away from the players, but so positioned that he can see them.

In a relatively live studio more screens may be needed—and in particular for the drums, which may end up with full screens on either side and behind, and another resting across the top. In front, the treatment is limited to half screens so that the drummer can peer over the top occasionally to see what is happening in the outside world—and so that the players out there can still hear something of his beat.

Serious music in vision

For serious music, a television picture makes only a little difference to the type of balance that is sought. But getting a good balance of any type is a little more difficult, because:

(i) Television studios are generally too dead (see pp. 115 and 125): concert halls or sound music studios are therefore to be preferred in all cases where they can conveniently be used.
(ii) Microphones must not be obtrusive (see p. 153).
(iii) The layout must be visually satisfying; but a good rule is to adopt a layout which is as close as possible to that of a concert performance. (Sometimes more open layouts have been adopted to get better visual separation of players, but these are now out of favour in Britain.)

What is *not* needed is any attempt to make sound follow picture: where the camera zooms in to a close-up of the oboe the sound remains at the concert perspective (note that this is the exact reverse of what may be done with speech). The big close-up in sound would be permitted only for a special effect; if, for instance, someone were talking about the role of the oboe in the ensemble, or alternatively, if this were a drama and we were hearing, as we were seeing, from a position within the orchestra. Even in these cases the overall orchestral sound would be distorted as little as possible.

247

The slight difference in balance that is desirable for television is marginally greater clarity at the expense of the tonal blending that many people prefer for sound radio and records. This permits individual instruments or groups to be heard just clearly enough for close shots to be aurally justified. This does not necessarily mean shorter reverberation, but simply that the attack on each note must be heard with reasonable clarity: this is usually enough to identify individual instruments. A technique which can be used successfully to produce this effect is to mix the outputs of two microphones, one closer and one more distant than would be used for a single microphone balance. (It is interesting to note that this type of balance is also used with great success for stereo.)

A balance with this extra degree of clarity also takes into account the different listening conditions that may exist in the home: the sound quality of loudspeakers on the majority of television receivers is rather lower than that used for radio and records by many people who enjoy listening to serious music; for this lower quality of sound reproduction a clear balance is better than a tonally blended quality.

For *ballet* performed in the television studio it is often difficult to get both the dance settings and the orchestra into the same studio: this may be a blessing in disguise, however, as the solution is to take the orchestra away to a music studio (with "outside broadcast" cameras, if required). The music can then be replayed to the dancers over loudspeakers.

Limitations (due to cost) on orchestral rehearsal time means that orchestra and dancers really need to be rehearsed separately; if this also means that the orchestra can be prerecorded the tempi are then set, and the dancers will know from then on precisely what to expect. Ideally, of course, the principal dancers will have attended the recording. Piano transcriptions may have to be used for rehearsal, however, and it may be a sound responsibility to make and replay a recording of this too. The dancers must have clear sound replay at all places where the action takes them, so the action studio must be liberally supplied with suitable loudspeakers. In some cases in ballet the dancers start before the music; where this happens it is up to the tape operator to be as precise and accurate as an orchestral conductor in timing the start of the music to match the action.

Effects microphones—usually cardioids slung above the action and angled to discriminate against loudspeakers—are needed in the studio to add just sufficient noise of movement (the dancers' steps,

248

rustle of costume, etc.) to add conviction to the pictures of the dance.

For *singers*, the type of balance depends on whether a microphone may appear in vision or not. If it may, there should be no serious problems; if not, a boom will probably have to be used. This introduces separation problems if ordinary microphones are used on the boom: orchestral spill on to the singer's microphone can modify the balance to a noticeable degree. Where this occurs, a high-quality gun microphone could conceivably be used on the boom; but normally, electrostatic cardioid microphones would be preferred.

One marginal advantage of the relative deadness of television general-purpose studios is that when reverberation is added it can be added differentially—not simply by adding different proportions of echo but (where facilities permit, such as in a large studio centre) by adding echo of different durations to different parts of the sound: in general, singers require less than the orchestral music which may accompany them.

An important part of any singer's performance lies in his use of vocal dynamics. In sound radio some degree of compression may be necessary; in television the problem is made more complex by movement of both the singer and the microphone and by variation in the distance between singer and microphone to accommodate the size of shot. It is important to realize that in these circumstances even more of the responsibility for interpretation of the artist's role may be given to the sound man than is normal: he must be thinking all the time not only about problems of coverage but also—along with the director and the singer himself—about the overall artistic intention.

Where singers and accompaniment have to be physically separated, time-lag problems may hinder the performance, and fold-back loudspeakers will be needed to relay sound from the musician to the singer; the conductor, too, will need to hear how the singer's contribution fits in to the ensemble.

For wide shots pre-recordings may have to be used: timing this to work in with live action will require careful planning and rehearsal. Often the second track of a twin-track recorder will be used for cues which are fed to performers but not to line.

The problems of dealing with both singers and orchestras are at their most severe in televised opera: and it is for this that some of the most sophisticated arrangements used in television sound have been devised.

Televised opera

There are several different ways of presenting opera on television:

(i) From the stage.
(ii) With actors miming to music performed in another studio (if the music is pre-recorded the actors may include some of the singers themselves).
(iii) With singers in a television studio and orchestra in a sound studio.
(iv) With both singers and orchestra in some hall of suitable (large) size with good musical acoustics.

For stage performances a normal monophonic sound balance is virtually all that is necessary: this has already been discussed (p. 238). Balance using the normal facilities of some outside broadcasting mobile control vans is unsatisfactory, as all the other functions of direction, camera, control, etc., are going on noisily all around, and because the loudspeaker and acoustics are unsuitable to work of the highest sound quality. So it is usual either to de-rig the sound equipment and set it up in more sympathetic surroundings or to use a larger, special mobile sound control room which has good loudspeakers, a reasonable volume of space, and suitable acoustic treatment.

Miming opera is a technique that has in the past been extensively used in Continental Europe; sometimes with results that, to say the least, have been undistinguished. That it can work well has, however, been demonstrated a number of times, for example by one superbly effective and moving *Madame Butterfly* produced by the BBC in the fifties. The technique employed is similar to that described for ballet above, care being taken to pick up sound effects clearly—and also any spoken passages in such operas as have them (though there are problems of matching both acoustics and voice quality).

The turning point was at a UNESCO congress of opera and ballet in 1959 at which the BBC, NBC, and CBC productions, which were not mimed, were generally acknowledged to carry more conviction and spontaneity than all the others for which the singing had been pre-recorded.

For a decade the BBC then used only the third technique, and did so with considerable success. This is complex, but in essence it uses a combination of two studios, each appropriate to the job that has

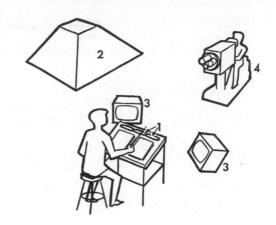

OPERA OR BALLET IN THE TELEVISION STUDIO: layout for conductor with orchestra in separate sound studio. 1. Line loudspeaker along top of music stand. 2. Hood loudspeaker over conductor's head. 3. Monitor for conductor to see action. 4. Camera to relay beat to repetiteur in television studio

to be done in it. The orchestral studio has good musical acoustics; the action studio has all of the normal facilities for the visual and sound coverage of dramatic action. It goes without saying that in this type of production the original grand, and deliberately unrealistic style of stage opera is modified to that of music drama (the more theatrical style of presentation can, in any case, be adequately represented in direct relays from opera houses). The singers are therefore covered by boom (and, where necessary, other microphones) in a way which is basically similar to that for a play, while at the same time trying to maintain many of the pure musical qualities of a concert performance.

Several of the problems that have had to be solved are relatively straightforward technical problems of intercommunication between the studios that may be several miles apart. Picture is easiest to deal with: the conductor has a monitor for the action, and a camera on him to relay his beat back to the action studio where a repetiteur takes it from a monitor and relays it to the singers. The latter, apparently complex arrangement presents no problems for the musicians: an identical arrangement is used in nearly every opera house.

Sound communication is a little more complex. The orchestral sound is relayed to the action studio floor by using directional loudspeakers mounted on the front of the boom prams. As the booms themselves are moved around to follow the action, so automatically will be the 6-foot column (line source) loudspeakers that are used with them. Since such a line source is directional at middle and high frequencies, radiating primarily in a plane intersecting the line at

251

right-angles, good separation can be achieved. Relaying the voices of the singers to the conductor has been done in several ways: one employs a "hood" (a pyramid-shaped baffle 4 feet square and 2 feet high) with a loudspeaker in the apex and above the conductor's head. The wide brim of the hood helps to separate the loudspeaker from the orchestral microphone above. But if the conductor is to appear in vision (for other than the repetiteur) such a hood restricts the television lighting and may otherwise be visually unsatisfactory. The alternative is to equip the conductor with a line-source loudspeaker along the top edge of his music stand. In practice, three 3-inch eliptical speakers set in a line have been used. Such a loudspeaker will produce little bass and will be directional at high frequencies, so once again separation is possible.

Even using this technique, it may be necessary to pre-record or film some scenes in advance. To employ an orchestra for such a short sequence may be disproportionately expensive, so a system using guide tracks may be used. Here the pre-recorded (or filmed) scenes are accompanied by a sound track consisting of bar counts or a piano version of the music, plus any useful verbal instructions such as warnings of impending changes of tempo. This guide track is fed to the conductor only (by headphones in this case). Orchestral sound is then added at the main recording.

If singers' voices are included in the pre-recording this can itself be used as the guide track or, better still, twin track sound can be used with one track for each purpose. Videotape has a separate "cue" track available, and for film a combined optical or magnetic track can be used for cue and a separate magnetic track for the sound.

Where singers' voices are pre-recorded in sound only (so that miming can be used—e.g. as the only means of satisfactorily covering very long shots), a guide track can again be accommodated if a twin-track $\frac{1}{4}$-inch tape recorder is used.

So much for the third system of presenting televised opera. Despite its complexity, this is now well established—but as with any compromise, some people are bound to find it cumbersome. And so it was that in 1969 the composer and conductor Benjamin Britten (disliking his remoteness from the action) persuaded the BBC to try an opera recorded with orchestra and singers in the same place. Accordingly, an opera was mounted with the two elements at opposing ends of the same concert hall. In this sort of production, some of the communications systems used with separate studios are still needed: for example, the time lag between the ends of the hall

252

still requires the use of the conductor's music-stand loudspeakers. Separate rehearsal, one of the advantages of twin studios, is lost; but in its place is an enhanced unity of purpose.

Popular music in vision

At the other end of the musical spectrum, visual considerations may result in slightly greater differences in sound balance than for serious music. Obviously the recording-studio layout for pop music cannot be adopted in vision—though a band wholly or largely out of vision certainly can, and probably will use it.

But apart from layout—which may produce some problems of separation—all other elements of the balance and treatment will be as close as possible to that of the recording studio, which after all, provides the standard by which the television sound will be udged.

Low microphones, in among the instruments are generally not obtrusive; indeed, they are readily accepted as part of the pop paraphernalia. Microphones at about or just above head height (particularly if they would be between the cameras and the front line of players) are avoided if possible; as are large microphone booms and stands. Indeed, there are more differences in mountings than in microphone position.

A microphone may be obvious if it is an accepted part of the action. For the pop singer the hand microphone is accepted as a "prop" and not merely something to sing into—though some experienced singers also use it to balance themselves with skill. Equally, for the less mobile singer a stand microphone is an accepted convention—though to move to and from a stand is a formal act acknowledging that the singing of the song is more important than any other part of the act.

For any popular music television programme it is essential for the control desk to have all of the equalization, compression, and echo facilities of the recording studio. Today most television studios have these available on a sufficient number of channels as a matter of course.

Television has to a large extent adapted its pictures to the sound needs of popular music, rather than the reverse; nevertheless, occasions still occur where a singer must appear without a microphone in vision—so booms are still used, but perhaps with a high-quality gun microphone to improve separation.

Where separation cannot be achieved by these means or in com-

253

plex song and dance acts the music is pre-recorded and vision is shot to playback of sound.

Miming to playback of records is a cheap and easy way of creating television—though many would qualify this by describing it as cheap and nasty: the sense of occasion about any particular performance is almost inevitably lost. In Britain this (by one of the more merciful edicts of the Musician's Union) is no longer practised. The result has been a marked improvement in this type of television programme.

Music on film

Most of what has gone before applies also to music on film (including film for television); though generally there will be a somewhat greater effort to eliminate microphones from the picture than in the television studio.

Although multiple-camera techniques have, at times, been used, close-ups are normally shot separately, taking sound, but only as a guide to synchronization with a master recording. More is shot than is actually required, so that actions before and after the cuts will match. Occasionally film shot in sync. for one sequence will eventually be synchronized to the sound from another part of the work. Here the beat or action (e.g. drum beat) will be marked on the track and matched to a close-up of the action. Or, for example for a marching band, the beat in two different sections may be synchronized and the film transposed from one part of the music to the other, provided that the right players are doing the right things in the picture.

Largely due to the technical problems involved, stereophonic music on film has rarely achieved its full potential. A single song— superb in every department—from *Seven Brides for Seven Brothers* stands out and will serve as an example of what can be done in the way of combining picture, song, and musical effects (chopping logs) in vision. The whole number was, incidentally, filmed in a single extended mobile shot.

254

8

SOUND EFFECTS

SOUND effects are of three basic types, "spot" effects, "library" recorded effects, and actuality recorded effects.

Spot effects are those which are created live in the radio studio at the same time as the performers speak their lines, out of vision in a television studio, or live in a film dubbing theatre to match action on the screen. They include such noises as doors, telephones, bells, tea-cups, letters being opened, crashes, bangs, squeaks, footsteps, and even that old standby, horses' hooves. They include sounds it just isn't worth recording, and sounds which are so much part of the action that to have them anywhere but in the studio would leave the actor confused and uncertain of his timing.

Recorded effects consist principally of those which cannot conveniently be created in the studio: cars, aircraft, birdsong, weather, crowd chatter, and so on. Their field overlaps with that of spot effects in many instances: for instance, as an alternative to coconut shells, a recording of real horses' hooves may be used. But curiously enough, some of the most realistic horses' hooves that I know were actually recorded using coconut shells!

It may seem odd that an effect may be created by an apparently— and in the case of coconut shells, even ludicrously—inappropriate sound source. But it is important to realize that the purpose of sound effects is not, in general, to re-create actuality, but to *suggest* it. Realism is not always necessary to this, and indeed at times may even be detrimental to the final result, in that some inessential element of the "real" sound may distract the listener.

Library effects are those which are already available on disc or tape; actuality effects are those which are specially recorded (more often for film than for any other medium).

For any radio production in which effects appear, it is probable that both spot and recorded effects will be needed, and a brief examination of the script will indicate into which category most cues fall. The division of labour will probably work out about fifty-fifty, with most sounds obviously belonging in one group or the other. In a few cases the final decision will depend on factors such as whether the studio is equipped with the heavier pieces of spot effects furniture or whether a particular recording is available.

In a big organization such as BBC radio it is easy to feel spoilt for choice. Spot techniques developed in the 'thirties are still remembered and handed on to newcomers to the business, and there is an impressive store of noise-making equipment which has been built up over the years. On the other hand, the BBC also possesses an enormous recorded effects library which is constantly being added to, and from which many hundreds of sounds are used in broadcasts each day. Inevitably this library duplicates many of the sounds which have formerly been imitated by spot effects—which means that in many of the less-complicated programmes for which effects are needed they can all be done by one person (probably mostly from records, with an occasional excursion into the studio).

For smaller organizations and individuals the situation may be different. So far from having a duplication of methods, there may be a vast region in which no methods at all are immediately at hand. Many spot effects require specially made-up equipment, and the commercially available libraries of sound effects records may not provide the exact noise that is wanted. It is when working under these conditions that sound effects become an exciting challenge; and each new sound that is needed presents a problem whose solution demands inventiveness and resource. Magazines for amateur recording enthusiasts frequently print the modern adventure stories of their readers—from which it is clear that for many, capturing or creating just the right sound can give as much sense of achievement as hunting big game or composing a piece of music. And, of course, this is not so inappropriate an analogy, for many recordists do go out to record the sounds of wild life, and many others stay at home to involve themselves in the intricacies of *musique concrète* on the workbench.

The semi-realistic use of effects

Effects are rarely used in a strictly realistic way—and even when this is attempted, it is generally a heightened realism which owes a great deal to art. This is true enough in film or television; it is particularly the case in radio.

As an example of what I mean, I will instance an occasion when I wanted an eye-witness account of a "Viking Raid". This was the highlight of a traditional festival on the Isle of Man. The tape I received was not usable in the form in which it had been recorded. The reporter had, very rightly, concentrated on getting good speech quality, so that the background noises were too low. There were some good shouts, screams, and crowd noise, but when the words "You can probably hear the clash of their swords now" came up it took a bit of ear-straining to make them out. Also, there were breaks in recording, mostly due to the fact that loudspeakers were being used to explain the scene to onlookers, and whenever these were switched on the atmosphere of the event was lost.

To re-create the event in a form acceptable to the listener, the tape had first to be cut together into the form of a continuous narrative (at the same time removing such remarks as "I've never seen anything so realistic as this, even on the films", because the report conveyed the enthusiasm of this without the necessity for words).

In the actual programme the first sound heard was a recorded sound effect, heavy breakers on the beach (the report referred to gusts of wind up to forty miles an hour), and these were held behind the studio narrator as he quickly sketched in the necessary background information. Towards the end of this the actuality screams were faded in, and the tape report took over. The effect of sea-wash was gradually lost as the description of the invasion brought the Vikings on to and up the beach, but an occasional angry-sounding seagull was touched into the clamour to keep the sense of location strong. After the first reference to swordplay the sentence starting "You can probably hear ..." was cut and in its place the clash of swords was inserted in a much closer perspective. The final result was highly realistic: an actual event (with the actual shouts and screams) had been brought into sharp focus by a little touching up on the sounds which could not have been recorded at the same time without an array of microphones dotted about the beach, and a complicated piece of mixing.

So much for the neo-realist technique, one which is well suited to the sound medium when a programme consists largely of edited actuality. But where the programme is created entirely in the studio, we must live by a series of highly artificial—but effective—conventions; and as far as effects are concerned, we rarely strive after the sound that would be found in a recording of an event "as it happened".

257

The conventional use of effects

Sound effects are usually held quite deliberately to an unrealistically low level. There are many reasons for this, apart from the risk of overmodulation. One is that, for many listeners, sudden loud noises are unnerving or irritating, and not just "dramatic".

A second reason for holding effects back—and a very important one for all continuous effects—is the masking that is caused by even moderately quiet background sound.

The "cocktail party effect" is often quoted as a demonstration of one of the basic qualities of binaural perception: this is the ability of the ear and brain to fasten on a single sound source in a crowded room, rejecting and almost ceasing to be conscious of the excessive surrounding noise level. But if a monophonic link is introduced into the chain (microphone, recorder, or loudspeaker) a great deal of this ability to discriminate is lost, and the effort to concentrate on the main stream of dialogue becomes a very conscious one.

I wanted to demonstrate this in a programme about hearing aids, so I borrowed one from a very deaf user and plugged it into my recorder to pick up a discussion between half a dozen people in a half-empty bar. As readers who have tried this sort of thing themselves will expect, the din as it appeared on the tape was appalling, with only a word here and there intelligible. It was clear to me why my deaf friend preferred to switch it off and lip-read.

This, then, is the cocktail-party effect in reverse. Set up an open microphone in a noisy location without attempting to discriminate against the background and you will be lucky if you can make out more than an occasional fragment. Record in stereo and the situation is vastly improved: one of the greatest benefits which stereo offers to drama is that it frees us from the absolute necessity to hold effects so far back as to separate them from the rest of the action. Unfortunately, the need for compatability with mono often makes it impossible to take this advantage.

Loudness is only one element in the make-up of a sound, and one which is nothing like so important as its *character*, the evocative quality which makes it visual in effect. This is true even of effects for which loudness appears to be a particularly important part of the sound—for example, a car crash.

But, in fact, analysis of a car crash shows that it consists of four separate elements: skid, impact, crunching metal, and broken glass falling to the ground. In a real crash the second of these is the loudest part: so loud, in fact, that if this were peaked exactly to the loudest permissible volume for no appreciable distortion the rest of the sound would be much too quiet and decidedly lacking in dramatic effect. So the whole sound has to be reorganized to ensure that no part is seriously louder than any other. But, even more important, during this recomposition certain of the characteristics have to be modified to create the right mood for the sound to fit into its context. The effects man is a good way along the road to mastering his craft when he realizes that a dizzy blonde driving into a brick wall makes a different noise from a payroll bandit doing exactly the same thing. For the former we would try to create (or select) a sound which is funny; for the latter, one which is vicious and retributive.

The various stages of the crash would be made up as follows:

(i) The skid. This is essential for a dramatic effect. A crash without a skid is just a noise which is half through before we can decide what is going on. But the scream of tyres is an absolutely distinctive noise which pulls the listener to the edge of his seat. A skid may or may not happen in real life: whether or not it happens in radio depends on mood. The skid is nemesis, doom closing in on the bandit and preparing to take him. But the dizzy blonde crash has no skid, or only a tiny and rather silly one: she is overtaken by events and does not find out until afterwards what went wrong.

(ii) A pause. The listener, having been drawn to the edge of his seat, must be given half a second to hold his breath and ... wait for it. ...

(iii) Impact. A hard, solid thud: very difficult to get just right, but fortunately not so important as the other sounds.

(iv) Crunching metal. In a real crash this usually sounds like a couple of dustbins being banged together, a ludicrous enough sound for the dizzy blonde, but not sinister enough for the bandit. A more purposeful and solid sound, and one with less of the empty-tin-can quality, is needed.

(v) Broken glass: like the skid, this is an identifying sound, and also one which clearly puts an end to the sequence of noises. For the listener it plays an essential part in the dying away of sensation, but it must be followed by one further dramatic element:

(vi) A period of silence.

The car crash provides a good illustration of the general principles which lie behind the creation of sound effects. No drama sound effect should be simply the noise which would naturally accompany the action being played, unless it is merely included as part of the counterpoint of sound and silence, i.e. for variety of backing. Rather, it must be related to the dramatic content.

This applies just as much to the more important actuality sound effects that are used in film. They must be recorded and treated with creative care if they are to work, not just adequately but really well.

Unrealistic and surrealistic effects

Effects which are intended to be funny are very different from normal dramatic effects. The latter may be exaggerated, but this is done in a subtle way, by slightly emphasizing the characteristic qualities and cutting away the inessentials; but in the comic effect the same process of emphasis of character is carried to its illogical extreme. A whole canon of what are called "cod" effects is created by this method, and in a fast-moving comedy show every sound is deliberately overdone—even including the way a door is opened in radio comedy programmes such as the old "Goon Shows".

In fact, the cod "door opens" is typical of the way all of these sounds are created. An ordinary door opening may or may not produce a slight rattle as the handle turns, but for dramatic purposes this characteristic is seized upon; indeed, if it were not for this, it would be difficult to find any readily identifiable element in the otherwise rather quiet sound—a faint click would be meaningless. But for a cod door the volume and duration of this identifying characteristic is exaggerated beyond all normal experience—though not so as to obstruct the action.

Such a method of codding effects only works if the normal spot effect makes use of some slightly unreal element; where the natural sound cannot be conveniently exaggerated, other methods have to be found. For example, little can be done with the sound of a "door shuts", which in any case has to be toned down slightly to prevent over-modulation. So other methods must be examined: for example, the creation of completely different and totally unreal sounds. These might include such cod effects as a "swoosh" exit noise (created, perhaps, by speeding up the change of pitch in a recording of a passing jet plane). Or an object (or person) being thrown high into the air might be indicated by the use of a glide up and down on a swannee whistle (this is a whistle which has a slide piston to govern the pitch). The swannee whistle is only one example from a rich field: that of musical spot effects. The villain in a comedy show may be dealt a sharp tap on the Chinese block; or in a children's programme, Jack and Jill may come tumbling down a xylophone arpeggio.

As with dialogue, timing can be used to make noises comic. Typical of this is the way many a crash ends. Don Quixote being thrown from his horse by a windmill was my own earliest experience of this: after the main pile of "armour" had been thrown to the ground and stirred around a little there followed a slight pause, and then one last separate piece of "armour" was dropped and allowed to rock gently to rest. (For this effect a pile of somewhat bent metal-based "acetate" records was used: these were threaded at intervals along a piece of string—except for the last "single". Any similar pile of junk might be used.) The timing of such a sequence is its most vital quality; the essence of its humour could almost be written out like music—and, indeed, an ear for music is very useful to an effects operator.

Just about the ultimate in this line of effects was reached when in a "Goon Show" the script demanded "a 16-ton, 1½-horsepower, 6-litre, brassbound electric racing organ fitted with a cardboard warhead". Here anything but sheer surrealism was doomed to remain stickily on the starting-line. The first stage in the creation of this sound was to dub together a record of an electric organ playing a phrase of music first at normal speed, then at double, and finally at quadruple speed. Three spot-effects enthusiasts dealt with gear-changes and backfires, engine noises and squeaks, and hooters, whistle, and tearing canvas—mostly produced by rather unlikely looking implements. And the whole effect was rounded off by a deep, rolling explosion.

Spot effects

A radio studio will need a supply of "sounds" readily available. At the BBC certain items are kept permanently in each drama studio; and others may be obtained from an Aladdin's cave of sound-making equipment, a spot-effects store.

The studio equipment includes a spot door, a variety of floor surfaces, a flight of stairs, a water tank, and perhaps a car door. (It is difficult to find an adequate substitute for this last, though a reasonable sound can be got with a rattly music stand and a stout cardboard box. Place the stand across the top of the box, and bang the two down on the floor together.)

A well-filled store may take on the appearance of a classified arrangement of the contents of an upper-crust rubbish tip. The shelves will be loaded with stacks of apparent junk, ranging from realistic effects such as telephones, clocks, swords, guns (locked away in a safe), teacups and glasses, door chimes and hand-bells—none of which pretend to be other than they are—to musical sound sources such as gongs, drums, blocks, glocks, tubular bells, and the rest of the percussion section—which may appear as themselves or in some representational capacity—and then on again to decidedly unobvious effects, such as the cork-and-resin "creak" or the hinged slapstick "whip".

In this latter field ingenuity—or a rather tortured imagination—pays dividends. One can, for example, spend days flapping about with a tennis racket to which thirty or forty strands of cloth have been tied (to represent the beating wings of a bird) only to discover later that the same sound could have been obtained with less effort by shaking a parasol open and shut.

But whether or not such ingenious improvisations are beginning to be old-fashioned, there are certain basic qualities of spot effects which are at least as valid today as they were thirty years ago. Indeed, the acoustic requirements of effects are now, in the days of high-quality radio transmission, a great deal more stringent than they have been in the past. Good timing, however, is the most important quality of a well-performed spot effect—the more so because it is now likely to be a staccato interjection, the continuous background sounds being more often in the form of recordings.

For this reason, in the following descriptions of spot effects, I shall concentrate on the ways in which the commonplace bread-and-butter sounds should be organized and timed rather than elaborate on such matters as how to create a guillotine sequence in suitably squishy detail (slice through a cabbage!).

Most of these are described in the form of radio effects, but may equally apply to out-of-vision effects in television or to the film dubbing theatre. Here they will often be recorded and played in.

How spot effects are made

DOORS

The basic item of studio spot-effects equipment is a large square box on castors, generally having a full-size door set in it. The handle is allowed to be just a shade loose, so that it can be rattled a little as it opens. A variety of other items of door furniture may also be fitted, including a lifting-type latch, a bolt, a knocker, etc. There can be a sash window fitted in the back of the box.

The sound of opening has to be exaggerated somewhat, as the real-life sound may be too quiet to register. The sound of closing may have to be quietened down a little to avoid overmodulation. Close the door lightly but firmly. The characteristic sound is a quick double click. Being quiet does not mean slowing the effect down to "click–pause–click".

Bad timing can impede the flow of a programme. The sound of a door opening should generally come slightly ahead of the point at which it is usually marked in a script; this allows dialogue to carry straight on without any undue pause. If the scripted cue follows a completed line of dialogue, superimpose the sound on the last word, unless there is some good reason for leaving that word cold (e.g. to follow a direction to enter). If the door is going to be closed again, allow sufficient time for the

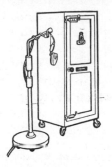

character to "get through" it. Also, the perspective of actor and door should match, and they should stay matched until the door is shut again, if he is supposed to shut it behind him.

There are, of course, types of door that have to be pre-recorded: prison-cell doors, castle gates, and so on. Sometimes heavy doors of this sort can be made up from a perfectly ordinary sound by recording it with reverberation and playing back at slow speed. Halving the speed doubles the size and weight of the door (but will not change the basic quality of it being a wooden door).

Such things as knocking are easy enough, provided care is taken to find a place where the door or frame sounds solid enough. Metal knockers, bolts, latches, lock and keys, etc., should be heavy and old-fashioned; they are best attached to the effects door or, if loose, held against it. The larger area of wood will act as a resonator for the sound and give it the true solid quality. Loose bolts, etc., should be screwed on to at least a small panel of wood.

One last note about doors: when in doubt, cut. Some scriptwriters seem to go mad on the mechanics of exits and entrances. An approach on dialogue is often quite as effective as door-plus-approach: it is better to keep doors, like all other effects, for the occasions when the sound has some actual significance in relation to the story, otherwise, when the time comes that it does, it will not be so easy to establish its importance.

FOOTSTEPS

What was a footnote when dealing with doors becomes a point of primary importance with footsteps. Are your footsteps really necessary? Go through a script with a blue pencil, if it appears to be full of feet. Make sure that every footstep that remains has a direct relevance to the action. In films this effect is often used merely to fill a silence, to reassure the audience that the sound has not broken down at a time when attention must be concentrated on the picture. There is no direct equivalent to this in the pure sound medium—and when footsteps are used here they will far too often draw the listener's attention in the wrong direction.

Such footsteps as remain may be created as spot effects or played in from a recording —the former is preferable, for the sound effect should tie in exactly with the mood of the moment. If the effect is created in the studio this means not only that the exact pace may be found easily but also that changes of pace and a natural stop can occur exactly on cue.

In the studio or not, the most satisfactory sound is obtained when the effects man (or girl) is walking about fairly freely, and not just treading the same few square inches of studio floor. And this leads to the major disadvantage of using a studio effect: that

263

an adequate amount of studio space is not ordinarily available, and if it is, more than half a dozen paces will be difficult to balance on a static microphone unless the effects man is walking in a circle.

A well-equipped drama studio will have a variety of surfaces available for footsteps: the most important are wood, stone, and gravel. Boards or stone slabs (laid out on top of the studio carpet) should be as hefty as is convenient, in order to give weight to their resonance—and the carpet will prevent them from ringing too much. The gravel effect can be obtained by spreading sand and gravel on the stone slabs.

On these surfaces long sequences of footsteps are a difficult matter: these will have to be done either by walking on the spot or by using pre-recordings. Walking on the spot is not really a very satisfactory way of creating footsteps, as it takes an expert to make them sound anything like real steps. Walking along, the foot falls: heel, sole; heel, sole. When walking on the spot it is natural to put the foot down sole first, so a special heel-first technique must be worked out: a fairly crisp heel sound, followed by a soft sole sound. This is not at all easy to get just right. Even when the foot action is the same, the two will still be readily distinguishable by the fact that the surface "ring" sounds different on every step when walking along, but will be monotonously the same when the foot keeps landing at the same place.

Walking or running up and down stairs are also better done with real steps: there is a very different quality for every step. But if the effect has to be simulated, the correct foot-fall is with the sole of the foot, going up, or sole–heel, going down. But again the result will not be right unless there is some variety of surface.

Some attention should be given to the footwear used. Leather heels and soles are best for men's shoes. High-heeled ladies' shoes are usually noisy enough without special care in their choice. If only one person is available for footstep effects, remember that it is easier for a girl to simulate a man's footsteps than vice-versa. It is not easy to get the right weight of step if shoes are held in the hand. The best way of getting two sets of footsteps is to have two people making the sound: one person cannot conveniently do the job—particularly as the two will not generally be in step. But two sets of footsteps will stand for three, and three will stand for a small crowd.

TELEPHONES, BELLS, BUZZERS

For electric bells and buzzers it is useful to make up a small battery-operated box which can be used to give a variety of sounds (or make up several boxes, each giving a different quality). The mobility of such a box will allow it to be placed at any appropriate distance, in any suitable acoustic, or against any surface which will act as a sounding board to it.

For telephones in radio a standard hand-set can be adapted, so that the bell may be worked by a press-button. In order to suggest that the ring is stopped by picking up the hand-piece it is usual to finish up with half a ring. For example, the ringing tone in Britain being buzz-buzz ... buzz-buzz ..., the ideal amount of ring is one which goes buzz-buzz ... buzz-b ... followed quickly by the sound of the hand-piece being lifted. As this last sound is much quieter than the ringing, two things can be done to make it clear: first, the rattle of picking it up should be emphasized a little, and second, the telephone can be brought closer to the microphone at the end of the effect. The first ring is fairly distant (e.g. partly in the dead side of a ribbon microphone). This is doubly convenient in that it may be interrupting speech, and it is better not to have a foreground effect in this case. The second ring will be closer, rather as though a camera were tracking in to the telephone, to become very close as it is picked up. The words following must, of course, also be in close perspective.

264

At the end of the conversation the action of replacing the receiver may be balanced at a greater distance: for one thing it is a sound which is naturally rather louder than picking up, and for another, it is an expected sound which fits neatly in the slight pause after the end of the telephone conversation.

Dialling is rather more of a performance than being on the receiving end of a phone call, simply because most dialling codes are much too long: for example, even the seven figures used for local calls in London can be a considerable embarrassment, and if there is any way of cutting this sort of hold-up from the script it should usually be adopted, unless dialogue can continue while the dialling is done.

The effect cannot be shortened by cutting down the number of figures dialled: for a

given location it should be assumed that this will be known by at least some of the listeners, and this is the sort of "mistake" which is quickly spotted and spoils the illusion. But it is as well to dial only low numbers. Even the British emergency 999 may well be cut to 444 to speed things up—radio cannot spare the time which is expected to be available in genuine emergencies!

For television, telephones are used so often that it is worth making up "specials"—a portable kit using real telephones, properly (and permanently) polarized so that they are fully practical, and linked together. This is necessary because good sound separation between the microphones picking up the two halves of the conversation may make it difficult for the parties to hear each other clearly without a telephone! Indeed, if one of the speakers does not appear in vision it is best to place him in an acoustically separate booth.

If both speakers do appear in vision at different times their voices are balanced on normal studio microphones, but that of the speaker who is at any particular time out-of-vision must have telephone quality distortion (see p. 347). The switching *can* be done manually, but this is risky, as the result of the slightest error may be very obvious. A better arrangement is therefore for the distortion circuit to be linked to the camera cut buttons so that the two ends of the conversation are automatically reversed on a cut. But note that when there are more than two cameras (i.e. one at each end) it is necessary to make sure that *any* camera which can possibly be used in the sequence is linked in to the switching system.

In the kit used by the BBC up to six telephones are connected through a box which is effectively a small telephone exchange which can produce either manual or automatic ringing tones at 17, 25, or 50 Hz, as required. Lights above each key show the condition of the associated line, showing "called" or "calling". (See p. 271.)

When the automatic button is pressed the selected telephone rings immediately, starting with the start of the first buzz; and it goes on automatically (using the proper ringing tone for the country represented) until either the operator's finger or the phone itself is lifted—when the ringing stops in the proper realistic manner. The use of such an automatic telephone also ensures that the bell itself is heard in the same acoustic and perspective as the actor.

Most "far end of the telephone" dialling, ringing, or engaged tone effects can be provided by the use of a buzzer, etc., on strong filter (see p. 349) or by the use of a recording. For the more complicated sequences which are less often required—e.g. a phone booth—a recording is necessary; and a few judicious cuts in the recording will tighten up the action.

PERSONAL-ACTION NOISE

I use this heading to include various sounds which are so individual in their application that it would be almost ludicrous to attempt to use recordings: sounds of a newspaper being folded, a letter being opened, or a parcel undone; or eating and drinking effects.

265

First, paper noises. Newspaper makes a characteristic noise, but as a spot effect it is as well to treat it in a fairly formalized way, e.g. shake slightly, fold once, and smooth the page. Opening a letter should be similarly formalized into two or three quick gestures, the last action, smoothing out the paper, being tucked under the dialogue (reading, or comment on contents) which follows. The balance will need to be fairly close to the microphone. The type of paper used should be thin but hard surfaced: thick brown paper crackles like pistol shots, airmail paper sizzles like a soda syphon, and duplicating paper provides a somewhat dull sound. With the right sort of paper, the effect will be simple but definite. And it is the same with undoing a parcel: a cut, perhaps, then two deft movements to smooth away the paper, and a final slower crinkling noise trailing into the speech which follows.

Many sounds, such as an orchestral conductor tapping his baton, can be made quite realistically (using a music stand); similarly for the chairman's gavel and block (though here it may be as well to soften the quality just a little to avoid sharp peaks, e.g. by binding a layer or two of electrician's tape round the face of the gavel). And again, the quality of surface struck is important: it will not do to hold a small block of wood up in the air; it should be lying on something solid.

Pouring a drink is also inevitably a spot effect. The sound of pouring is itself not a very definite one, and for all but the longest of long drinks will be over too quickly to establish itself properly; so a clink of bottle on glass will help. But even without this clink it is important to use the right thickness of glass. Health salts do fine for fizzy drinks. A pop-gun may be a shade less acceptable as a champagne cork than the real thing—but it is a degree or two more predictable!

If "tea" or "coffee" is to be poured out into a cup, the effect can be confirmed by placing a spoon in the saucer afterwards—and again the right thickness of china for the occasion is essential.

Sometimes a scene is set at a meal table. For this the complete noise-making set consists of knife, fork, and plate, and cup, saucer, and spoon. It is a good idea to give the noises a rest from time to time—and the right points to choose for this depend on the mood and pace of the script. At any point where the tension rises, stop the effect; as the mood relaxes again, the knives and forks get back to work. It takes only a little of this noise to suggest a lot: listen to a recording of a tea-party for six and you will find that it sounds like crockery noises for twenty.

SHOTS

A rifle shot is one of the simplest sounds you can meet. Basically, it is an N-wave like that from a supersonic aircraft: a sharp rise in pressure is followed by a relatively gradual drop to as much below normal pressure. Then there is a second sharp rise in pressure, this time returning it to normal, after which nothing—of the original sound, at any rate. The length of the N (its duration in time) depends on how long the object takes to pass a single point. For a supersonic airliner this is short enough—for a bullet the whole thing is practically instantaneous. All there is, is amplitude and brevity. A rifle shot travels at something like twice the speed of sound, and that from a smaller gun at about the speed of sound. But whatever the speed, any loudspeaker would have a hard job to match the movement, however simple it may be. It is perhaps fortunate that what happens after the double pulse is a little more complicated.

In fact, the very size of the initial pulse is itself, in recording or broadcasting, unacceptable; everything must be done to discriminate against it. One way of doing this is to fire (or simulate) the shot on the dead side of the microphone; another is to take it outside the studio door—or into some small room built off the studio—and the door can then be used as a "fader".

Very often a script will call for loud shouts and noisy action when shots are being fired, which will clearly make it a little easier to deal with the sheer loudness of the effect than if the microphone has to be faded right up for very quiet conversation. The balance used will vary from case to case, and experiment will always be necessary to check this, so that in each particular case the shot is as loud as the equipment can comfortably handle.

But experiment will also be necessary to judge the appropriate acoustics for the shot: for the sound to be picked up is a picture of the acoustics in their purest form. Shots recorded out of doors are all bang and no die-away, which means that at the level at which they must be replayed they sound like a fire-cracker. So always check the acoustic when balancing a studio shot, and watch out for colourations and flutter echoes which may not be noticeable on a more commonplace sound.

A third element in the sound is (or may be) a ricochet: this is the whining noise which is made by the jagged, flattened, spinning scrap of metal as it flies off some solid target. And whereas the previous sound is just a noise of the purest type, the ricochet is a highly identifiable and highly characteristic sound. Even if in reality ricochets are rarer than they might appear from Westerns, they should certainly be used in practically any outdoor context, i.e. anywhere where there is actually the space for a ricochet to take place.

At the BBC the complete range of techniques is used at one time or another; of the following the first two may not be so easily available, but will be worth examining by those with a lot of gunplay to find.

(i) A gun. For this, a modified revolver is better than a starting pistol, which some times tends to sound a little apologetic. But the regulations must be conscientiously observed, and, needless to say, care used in handling the gun. Even blanks can inflict burns. Guns for BBC radio are modified to allow the gas to escape from a point along the bottom of the barrel, and not from the end. The microphone balance adopted for a gun is generally that for a maximum ratio of indirect to direct sound.

 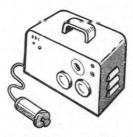

(ii) An electronic gunshot generator. This consists of a white noise generator which when triggered into action can produce "bangs" with a variety of decay characteristics, ranging from staccato to reverberant. And, in the BBC design, several settings have associated circuitry to produce some very acceptable ricochets.

(iii) A slap-stick: a flat stick with a hinged flap to clap against it. Depending on balance and acoustic conditions, this may sound like a gunshot (though not a good one), the crack of a whip, or just two flat pieces of wood being clapped together. Narrow strips of thick plywood are as good as anything for this.

(iv) A long, fairly narrow piece of wood, with a string attached to one end. Put the wood on the floor with a foot placed heavily on one end, then lift the other end off the ground with the string and let go. The quality of the sound depends more on the floor surface than it does on the type of wood used. A solid floor is best—stone or concrete.

(v) Cane and chair seat. The sound quality again depends on the surface struck. Padded leather gives a good crisp sound.

267

(vi) A piece of parchment on a frame, with an elastic band round it: the band can be snapped sharply against the resonant surface. This method is included as an example of the kind of improvisation which the effects man might invent.

 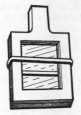

(vii) Recordings of real bangs or of any of the above. The apparent size of an *explosion* can be increased by slowing down a recording. A sharp clap may become a big, rumbling explosion if dubbed down to an eighth or a sixteenth of the original speed.

If the gun itself is used in radio there is no problem in taking it well away from the action. But for television this may not be possible: particularly if the gun is to be fired in vision, perhaps several times, with realistic flashes and smoke and perhaps with dialogue before, between, and after. In this case two microphones are used. The close (dialogue) microphone has a limiter set for 2 dB below 100% modulation; the second is distant and is balanced for a high proportion of reverberation, and may also have echo added.

But for television gunshots out-of-vision or for radio the BBC uses its own design of generator which is linked direct to a studio loudspeaker, which, in turn is balanced acoustically. As they can hear the sound the actors are able to react satisfactorily.

The basic sound is provided by a white noise generator. This passes through a gate (operated by the "trigger", a push button) and a low-pass filter. The gating circuit allows the white noise passing through to rise sharply from zero to a predetermined peak, and this is automatically followed by an exponential fall which eventually shuts off the white noise once again. A low-pass filter set for 5 kHz cut-off gives a quality simulating the close shots of a revolver or automatic; set to remove all but the lowest frequencies, it gives distant heavy gunfire—a "cannon" quality.

A machine-gun effect can be obtained by using an impulser relay which operates the gate at regular intervals for as long as the button is pressed. In this case the exponential decay is made faster in order to keep the shots separate and distinct.

Ricochets are produced by a separate pulsed oscillator, the output from which is rich in harmonics and falls in frequency with time. This oscillator works from the same initial trigger action, but delayed a little. (See diagram, p. 287.)

Similar devices can produce door-squeaks, bells, pizzicato strings, steam and motor-cycle engine noises, and many other sounds.

CREAKS, SQUEAKS, SWISHES, CRASHES, AND SPLASHES

Creaks and squeaks offer rich opportunities for improvisation. Over a period of time the enterprising effects man can assemble an array of squeaky and creaky junk just by noticing the noises when they happen and claiming the equipment which makes it. Wooden ironing boards, old shoes, metal paper punches, small cane baskets; anything goes in a collection of this sort.

But there are two rather more organized ways of producing creaks and squeaks:

(i) String, powdered resin, and cloth. The resin is spread in the cloth, and this is then pulled along the string, which is tied to something rigid. If it is attached to a resonant wooden panel the sound becomes a creaky hinge. Varying pressure varies the quality of sound.

(ii) A cork, powdered resin, and a hard surface, e.g. polished wood, a tile, or a saucer. Place some resin on the surface and slowly grind the flat of the cork into it. Again, the squeak will vary in quality with pressure and speed, and with the type of surface and resonator, if any.

The swish of a javelin or arrow may be simulated by swishing a light cane past the microphone. In real battles the arrows must have bounced off stone walls and parapets, making an undramatic clatter. An arrow landing in wood is, however, more satisfying aurally, so convention demands that all the best misses land in wooden panelling and tree-trunks. For this, throw a dart into a piece of wood close to the microphone. Proximity makes the sound grow bigger—so the twang of an elastic band will do well enough for the bow.

Crashes are another reason for hoarding junk—ranging from empty tin cans up to pretty well anything which makes a resonant noise when dropped. But glass crashes demand a little care. For these, spread out a heavy ground sheet and place a stout cardboard box in the middle. Sprinkle some broken glass in the bottom and place a sheet of glass across the open top of the box. Give this sheet a sharp tap with a hammer, and as it shatters it should all fall inside the box. Have a few odd pieces of glass in the free hand to drop in immediately afterwards. Not difficult—but it may still be just as well to pre-record such a crash, if only to save the worry of having broken glass around on the take (and the same goes for footsteps in broken glass). And an additional reason for pre-recording is that successive crashes may not be predictable in quality and volume.

One of the fittings for a well-equipped drama studio will be a water tank. If convincing water effects are to be obtained this must be filled pretty full, to avoid any tinny resonance of the space at the top of the tank. For any but the gentlest water effects it may be a good idea to protect the microphone—which may have to be pretty close—by hanging a gauze in front of it.

HORSES' HOOVES

I include horses' hooves as an example of a highly specialized spot-effects technique which dates back a long way but which is still valid today. For coconut shells really are as good as the real thing, if not better—and certainly they are a great deal easier to fit to dialogue.

The secret of a good sound lies not so much in the shells (one shell sawn neatly across the middle) as in the surface. Start with a tray about three feet across and perhaps three inches deep. Fill the bottom with a hard core of stones and put gravel and a mixture of sand and gravel on top. For a soft surface place a piece of cloth or felt on top of this at one end of the tray, and bury a few half bricks at the other end to represent cobbles. This tray will give all the qualities of surfaces ordinarily needed for horses' hooves. But for horses' hooves (or human footsteps) in snow a tray of broken blocks of salt may be used.

There are three basic actions to simulate: walking, cantering, and galloping, and the rhythm is different for each. When a horse is walking, the rhythm goes clip, clop ... clip, clop ... With a shell in each hand use them alternately, but with alternate steps from each shell move forwards, digging in the "toe" of the shell, or backwards, digging in the "heel". The sequence is left forward, right back (pause), left back, right forward (pause) ... In this way a four-legged rhythm is obtained. For the canter the same basic backwards and forwards action is used, but the rhythm is altered by cutting the pauses to give a more or less even clip, clop, clip, clop, clip, clop, clip, clop. In galloping the rhythm alters to a rapid clipetty clop ... clipetty clop ... 1, 2, 3, 4, ... 1, 2, 3, 4, ... But there is now no time for the forward and backward movements.

For jingling harness a bunch of keys and a piece of elastic will do the trick: the keys hang between the little finger and a solid support to the side of the tray, and will jingle in rhythm with the horse's movement.

A special spot-effects microphone will be needed for hooves. This should not be too close; and the acoustic should match that used for dialogue.

OBSOLESCENT EFFECTS FOR WEATHER AND FIRE

At one time rain effects were regularly produced by gently rolling lead shot (or dried peas) around in a bass drum; sea wash was produced similarly, but rather more swooshily, while breakers could be suggested by throwing the shot into the air and catching it in the drum at the peak of the swoosh. Nowadays a recording of the real thing is more likely to be used, but the technique may still come in handy where no decent recordings are available. In fact, a bass drum is a useful item in a spot-effects store—a noise produced by something placed on top of it is given a coloured resonance which may be particularly useful in over-emphasizing the character of a sound for comic effect. For example, brontosaurus' footsteps can be made by grinding coconut shells into blocks of salt on a bass drum.

A bright, crackling, spitting fire may be simulated quite successfully by gently rolling a ball of crinkled cellophane between the hands (and if it is a major-disaster type fire, falling buildings can be added by crumpling the occasional wooden matchbox close to the microphone).

A wind machine consists of a weighted piece of heavy canvas hung over a rotating, slatted drum—but again it is easier to use a record of wind, except where the noise is wanted for an orchestral work such as Ravel's *Daphnis and Chloe*, where the ability to control pitch is valuable. But wind comes in many qualities, and its tone should suit the dramatic context. A good recorded effects library has gentle breezes, deep-toned wind, high-pitched wind, wind and rain, wind in trees, wind whistling through cracks, and blizzards for the top of Mount Everest or the Antarctic. A wind machine produces just one sound: wind. And the same goes for thunder sheets.

The recorded sound picture

There are two distinct types of actuality sound recordings: those which create a *sound picture* in themselves, and those which are selective of some particular *sound element* pretty well to the exclusion of all others. These two general categories are not only different in content but are based on totally different concepts of sound programme work. The sound picture is the *complete* picture, a programme item in its own right. But the true recorded sound effect is, like the spot effect, heightened reality; it is the distilled essential quality of the location or action. It is a simplified, conventionalized sound, the most significant single element of the complete picture.

A sound picture of a quiet summer countryside may have many elements: there will certainly be plenty of birdsong of one sort or another, and perhaps the lowing of cattle a field or two away, with

in the distance a train whistle. A beach scene may ha
(shouts and laughter), the squawk of seagulls and distan
surf on shingle, and, beyond that, the popping exhaust of
boat. As pictures in their own right these may be delightful
tive, but how would they fit into a play?

In either case it is easy enough to imagine dialogue to m

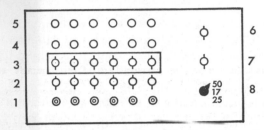

TELEPHONE CONTROL UNIT for operating and interconnecting telephone:
television plays. 1. Input sockets for up to six lines. 2. Keys to select mode of o
(manual or automatic) for each line. 3. Line keys: down–select, up–cancel. 4. I
lamps: "line called". 5. Indicator lamps: "line calling". 6. Ringing switch fo
operator: up—automatic ringing; down—manual ringing. 7. "Auto-dial"
When "on", this permits extensions having dialling facilities to ring each oth
matically; in addition normal dialling tone is heard when a receiver is raised. In a
forms of operation the switch is left "off". 8. Ringing frequency selection. This apparatus is similar to several used in BBC television studios; but for most purposes a simpler
arrangement for interconnecting telephones will be adequate.

scene—but, significantly, it is the speech we have to fit to the sound
effect, and not the other way round: in the countryside picture the
cows would play havoc with an idyllic love scene, and the distant
train whistle would add a distinctly false note to Dick Turpin's ride
to York. Similarly, the beach scene is fine—if we happen to be on
the sand and not in the boat. And suppose we want to move about
within this field of action? With a sound picture we are severely restricted: the only view we ever have is that seen by the artist from
the point at which he set up his canvas; we cannot stroll forward and
examine one or another subject in greater detail unless he has chosen
to do so for us. But if we ourselves are given paints and canvas instead of a finished picture we can recompose the scene in any of a
hundred ways. The true sound "effect" is the pigment, not the
painting.

Now, in a play or in any other programme where recorded effects
are to be combined with speech, the final composition of the mixture
will at many points be very different from that of a sound picture
which has no speech.

For example, the beach scene: the first sound to be heard may be

271

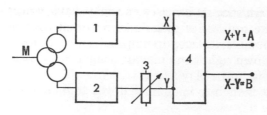

SPREADER CIRCUIT. The monophonic input (M) is split equally between paths X and Y. 1 and 2. Delay networks producing differential phase shift. 3. Spread control fader. 4. Sum and difference network producing A and B components from the X and Y signals (see p. 287).

a surge of surf on shingle, and, as this dies, the hoarse cry of a gull; then, more distantly, a shout and answering laughter. The second wave does not seem quite so close, and from behind it emerges the distant exhaust note of the motor boat for a few moments. Then the first words of scripted dialogue are superimposed at a lowish level upon this picture, and gradually faded up to full. From here on the composition of the effects will alter again. Staccato effects, such as gulls and shouting, must be, in general, rather more distant, and will be timed in with the speech, being brought up highest at points where the dialogue is at its lowest tension, or where characters move off-microphone, or where there are gaps in the dialogue (other than dramatic pauses). The motor boat, too, may go completely or be missing for long stretches, appearing only as a suggestion in such a gap. These various individual elements can be peaked up much more readily than the waves themselves, which cannot be subjected to sudden fluctuations in volume without good reason.

When using effects in this way avoid those which have become radio clichés. Because of a certain programme called "Desert Island Discs", which starts with seagulls, seawash, and a record of "The Sleepy Lagoon", it has become practically impossible to use seagulls on the British radio. Another warning concerns authenticity in such matters as the location of birds and railways. There are so many experts on the sounds of these things that it is as well to try to get the region right—and in the case of birds the time of year as well.

The use of recorded effects

As the aims differ, when recording a sound picture or sound effects, so also must the recording methods. For effects, the backgrounds must not be obtrusive, nor must the acoustics be strongly assertive on effects which are of a continuous nature; the levels must not be subject to sudden high peaks, and there must be no unexpected changes of character.

A suitable microphone placing for an effects recording may not be the most obvious one. For example, a microphone placed inside a

272

modern, closed car may not pick up any clearly recognizable "car" sound. And so for a car recording—even for an interior effect—the microphone must be deliberately placed to emphasize the continuous engine noise. The mechanical noises associated with gear changes, on the other hand, should not be emphasized (except for starting and stopping), as the staccato quality of this may interfere with the flow of the script.

An effects sequence, like the composite sound picture, is best constructed from individual elements. Take, for example, a sequence with dialogue in which a car stops just for a short while to pick up a passenger. The elements of this are as follows:

(i) Car, constant running.
(ii) Car, slows to a stop.
(iii) Tick over.
(iv) Door opens and shuts.
(v) Car revs. up and departs.

Of course, a recording could be found which has all of these in the right timing and in the right order. But:

(i) Supposing that there is any considerable amount of dialogue before the cue to slow down, it will certainly make the timing more flexible if the slowing is on a separate disc or tape. The cue to mix from one to the other should be taken at a point in the dialogue which is some ten seconds or so before the actual stop, or there will be too marked a change in engine quality. And since the sound of a car stopping is lacking in identifiable character, a slight brake squeal or the crunch of tyre on gravel will help to clarify the mental image. The overall level of effects may well be lifted a little as the car comes to a halt.

(ii) The tickover may well be part of the same recording as the stop. But the microphone balance for a good clear tickover is so different that it may be just as well to record it separately. Fade in the tickover just before the car comes to rest—this is the point at which the engine is slipped out of gear and begins to idle.

(iii) Doors opening and slamming—obviously these must be timed to fit in with dialogue. Since a real car door shutting is very loud indeed compared with sounds such as the door opening and the tickover, it needs a separate recording and separate control.

(iv) Departure: again, this could be on the same recording as the tickover, but timing is more flexible if the two are separate and the departure can be cued very precisely.

(v) Extraneous noises, such as shuffling on seats, footsteps, etc., may well be omitted.

(vi) Additional sounds—e.g. another door, a motor horn, or the characteristic sound of the meter of a London taxi being set— may be played in at will.

This example of a car sequence is only one of a multitude of such sequences—and each one should be thought through as fully as this if the result is to blend into the landscape of sound.

The best way of putting together such sequences will obviously depend a lot on the facilities available. At the BBC the tried and trusted way over many years has been to use effects records and a bank of turntables. Tape cassettes are now also being used in a similar way. The flexibility of such a technique is beyond question, and it is necessary to pre-record only the most complex sequences.

An alternative method, using two tape reproducers, is to pre-record into short tailor-made sequences and assemble these in the form of two insert tapes, which can then be used to mix from one to the other at the points where flexibility of timing or of the level of individual components is required. But if only one tape reproducer is available, then all the tailoring must be done on a single tape by editing—trimming the tape to fit the dialogue by cutting between points at which the level and quality is the same—and it will be best to record the effects sequence specially for the programme in which it is to be used.

Changing the speed of a recorded effect

The range of sound compositions available from a given set of effects recordings can be increased if the reproducers have more than just a single standard replay speed. The best sort of turntable for disc effects will have a good range of speeds. In the very earliest days of disc reproduction speeds were not standardized, and a governor was used to regulate the replay: for effects, this old-fashioned sort of design still has its points.

Nowadays, of course, turntables usually have only certain specific speeds available, with a fine adjustment control on some transcription models. While not so versatile by a long way, these can still often be used very successfully for changing the quality of an effect.

274

In musical terms the changes of pitch obtained by switching from 33⅓ to 45, and again to 78, may appear somewhat irrational; but in terms of changing the quality of sound effects this does amount to a certain degree of versatility. Tape speeds, too, can usually be lifted or dropped an octave. And although this is rather a drastic speed change as such transformations go, an otherwise unavailable effect can sometimes be created in this way.

Equipment designed to operate at given fixed speeds can sometimes be modified to provide speeds that are continuously variable between, say, half and double the nominal speed. This is done by powering the drive motor from a three-phase variable-frequency oscillator.

When the speed of an effect is changed the first difference in quality that presents itself is a change of *size*: slow down the two-stroke engine of a motor lawn-mower and it becomes the lazy chugging of a motor boat—or a small motor boat becomes a heavy canal barge. In the same way, water effects are increased in scale by slowing down the recording—just as filming a model boat in slow motion can provide some sort of substitute for the full-size real thing. (As a by-product, it may sometimes happen that reducing the speed will get rid of some unwanted rumble or resonance in the bass.)

Speeding an effect produces the reverse change of quality, e.g. mice talking, and so on. These points should be borne in mind not only to extend the range of already available material but also when planning new recordings. The use of these methods can sometimes save a lot of work.

A change of speed also changes the apparent size of the room in which an effect was recorded: the characteristic colourations go up or down in pitch with everything else. This means that recordings made out of doors may be more conveniently speed-changed than those with indoor acoustics attached. A good subject for drastic transformation is wind. Record a good deep-toned wind and double its speed, and you get a high, stormy wind; double its speed again, and the result may be used for a biting, screaming Antarctic blizzard.

There are times when it seems to be a very good idea to vary the speed of effects while they are being played, but the results often sound weird. Nearly every sound contains some colouration which is essentially fixed in frequency—for example, do not bring footsteps to a halt by slowing down the last couple of steps, unless you are prepared to accept a sudden apparent enlargement of the feet (this

275

may be partly compensated for by lowering the volume) and a deepening of the tone quality of the surface.

The effects of speed transformations are considered further on p. 362.

The effects library: contents

The contents of an effects library will fall into a variety of general classifications.

First, and most important, there will be crowd effects—a crowd being anything from about half a dozen upwards. It may seem odd that the very first requirement among recorded effects should be the human voice in quantity, but the fact remains that the illusion of numbers, the "cast of thousands", is often essential if a programme is to be taken out of the studio and set in the world at large. The classifications under this general heading are many and various: chatter, English and foreign, indoor and outdoor; the sounds of fear, apprehension, agitation, surprise, or terror; people shouting, whispering, rioting, laughing, booing, applauding, or just standing there and *listening* ... for the sound of a crowd which is silent except for the occasional rustle, shuffle, or stifled cough may at times be as important as the noise of a football crowd. A subdivision of crowd effects is footsteps ... in this case a crowd being anything from two feet upwards.

Then there are transport effects: cars, trains, aircraft, boats, and all the others (such as horses), all doing all the various starting, carrying on, and stopping things that are associated with them, and recorded both with the microphone stationary and moving with the vehicle (interior and exterior recordings).

Another important group that has links with both of the above is "atmosphere of location" recordings. Streets and traffic (with and without motor horns), railway station, airport, or harbour atmosphere of various types and places; all these will be needed, as well as the specific identifying noises of London, Paris, and New York; also the atmosphere of a schoolroom, courtroom, museum, shop, or concert hall, and the distinctive sounds of many other locations.

The elements—wind, weather, water, and fire—provide another vital field. Then there are the sounds of all branches of human activity: industrial sounds, sport, domestic effects from the ticking of clocks to washing up, and the sounds of war. There are animals, birds, babies; and dozens of other classifications of sound, such as bells, sirens, atmospherics, electrical sounds, etc.

The effects library: disc or tape

An effects library may be built up using disc or tape—or both.

The disc effects library. One or more copies of a wide variety of records is kept (these may be purchased from a variety of commercial sources, or, as at the BBC, specially pressed). The records from such a library get a great deal of use in the process of selection and rehearsal, but it is simplest to accept this fact and replace them when they are worn out, rather than dub them to a special programme-effects tape—provided that sufficient turntables are available. Disc has the tremendous advantage in a large library that it is easy to spot through a dozen different recordings which are nominally suitable to find out which is best and which just will not do at all. It is possible to go to the studio with two or three specimens of each sound: one the likely best bet, and two others which are sufficiently different in character to provide alternatives in case, on adding the sound to dialogue, the first turns out to be wrong in mood, level, or timing. A different disc can be readily substituted at any point in a production without involving any dubbing and editing as with tape. But some expertise in gram-playing is needed for programmes with complex effects.

The tape effects library. When tape is used there are two conflicting requirements. One is for the storage of a wide selection of effects; the other is for immediate accessibility, both for sampling and for rapid setting up in the studio. To store a very large number of effects normal (but small) spools may be used, with many recordings each identified by a separate spacer or some other marking on the tape. Such a store is, however, inconvenient for operational use and is likely to hinder a thorough search for the exact sound. It might perhaps be used by dubbing the sounds required in sequence on to a programme tape (or alternate effects on to two tapes). But the result is inflexible: if even one effect proves unsatisfactory or is dropped, the system is disrupted much more than if each effect were handled individually.

Small *tape cassettes* are much more satisfactory than normal spools. No time is spent in lacing up, and they can be automatically reset to the start. But for a store of substantial size a very large number of cassettes is required. A possible compromise is to hold permanently on cassette those effects which are most in demand; complementing this with effects transferred to cassette from the larger library (tape or disc) or specially recorded either in the studio or on location.

It may be noted that cassettes are particularly suitable for short running effects which start abruptly on cue: in other words, they provide a very convenient tape equivalent to what I have previously described as studio spot effects. As a result, the designers of the various types of automatic effects reproducing machines that use tape as a medium have tended to emphasize the "spot" facility rather than continuous running as their major advantage.

Automatic replay devices

Of a very large range of possible effects playing machines using tape and with some degree of automatic operation, I will describe three which are representative of different approaches to the problem. None require manual threading of tape; all set themselves up automatically at the start of the tape. As it happens, none of those described here can automatically set themselves up at a given point within a recording (this is in marked contrast to the ease with which this can be done by most manually operated systems—both tape and disc). Instead, several of the machines can be used to re-record with the given feature at the start of a section of tape. All reproduce the required effect almost instantaneously on pressing the start button or key.

Note that all of these can also be used for standard spot announcements, jingles, or radio commercials.

The continuous-loop cartridge. Loops of various lengths are used— say of ten, twenty, or thirty seconds. This allows sounds of various durations to be recorded (and, in principle, steady continuous sounds). When the replay button is pressed the loop is played through until the starting-point is reached again, when it automatically stops to await further replay. The cartridge is engaged by being pushed into the slot: when pressed fully home it is immediately

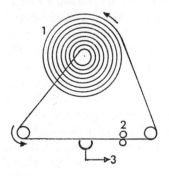

ENDLESS TAPE. This is lubricated with graphite so that it slips easily when on the spool, 1. 2. Drive roller. 3. Output from reproducing head.

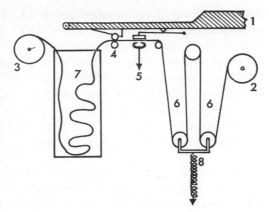

MELLOTRON EFFECTS CONSOLE: one key (1) and its associated tape. The effect required is selected in advance from those available in the store (rolls 2 and 3); the storage rollers do not move when an effect is being played. When the key is pressed the pinch roller holds the tape against the capstan (4) which draws it over the reproducing head (5). The tape is transferred from two deep loops (6) to the storage bin (7). When the key is released the pulleys and spring (8) draw the tape rapidly back into its original loops. (The Mellotron has a keyboard like a harmonium.)

ready for replay. To disengage the cartridge a "reject" button is pressed: the cartridge emerges partly from the slot and may now be removed by hand.

Reset time depends on the length of tape that remains to be played through after the required effect has been reproduced. This is the reason for having a range of cartridges of different durations, rather than using a single length of loop for all purposes.

The keyboard effects console. Looking rather like an electronic organ (or harmonium), this type of replay machine has a tape associated with each key, which is played for as long as the key is pressed. On the machine to be described here, the Mellotron, each key has the tape physically below it, and pressing the key presses the pinch roller down against the tape and drive capstan, which is already turning as long as the machine is switched on. The key also mechanically operates a pressure pad to hold the tape against the reproducing head.

At any particular time six feet of tape lies between two storage rollers, which remain static during replay of the effects on the section lying between them. When the key is pressed a spring-loaded loop of tape in front of the head is drawn over the reproducing head and dropped into a tape storage box on the other side. When the key is released the tape is drawn rapidly back to the starting position by the return spring. So again, the reset time depends on the duration of the effect, but this time in a different way: the starting position is resumed in a fraction of the replay time, and the shorter the replay, the faster the reset. This means that repeated staccato sounds, e.g. hammer blows or (using pairs of adjacent keys) left foot, right foot sequences of footsteps can be run in any rhythm, and if

279

necessary (and given an adequate sense of timing by the operator) synchronized with picture.

The six feet of tape allowed for each effect recorded on the Mellotron is replayed at $7\frac{1}{2}$ ips, with a facility to vary this between 6 and 10 ips—giving at normal speed a usable eight seconds only. (Longer continuous sequences can be put together, but not always very successfully when the sound is supposed to be smooth and continuous. So this is a disadvantage of this particular design.) A non-standard tape width of $\frac{3}{8}$ inch is used: this permits three normal "half-tracks" to be accommodated side by side, any one of which can be selected by sideways movement of the replay head. Also, the total length of tape under each key and the associated storage spools is sufficient for six effects tracks to be recorded along the length of the tape; so that each key has 18 effects available to it. As there are 70 keys the machine holds a total of 1260 effects—a number which sounds a lot, but may be found to be curiously limited when actually used.

Even apart from the difficulty of what to do when the exact sound required is not present (despite the large number available), there are problems in the use of those that are. For example, footsteps produced in the way described are always going to fall in exactly the same way on to exactly the same surface, so that whereas rhythm may be varied, the quality of sound produced remains constant.

There are a number of other operational inconveniences and difficulties in the particular machine described here (as it was originally designed), but given the choice of effects of a particular operator it could be useful. It could, for example, be programmed to contain a large number of subtly different laughter and applause tracks— which might be a convenience for some users, if not the BBC!

The programme effects generator. This rather indeterminate title was adopted by the BBC designers of another type of replay machine, one which uses single-spool tape cassettes in a way which is different from either of the above. The basic assumption was that the most versatile arrangement was one which permitted a number of individual cassettes to be plugged into a bank of reproducers; that the cassettes should be very small and of inexpensive construction, so that they could be large in number; that fast resetting was required; that variable-speed replay (in practice ranging from less than half to double the nominal speed) should be available on at least one channel; and that another channel should be equipped to record (but stock-effects cassettes have a simple device to prevent their being wiped and re-recorded by accident).

280

PROGRAMME EFFECTS GENERATOR (BBC). When the special cassette (1) is pressed firmly down the metal loop (2) at the end of the tape is located over a hook (3) on the head of the lacing lever (4). The lacing lever then immediately carries the tape over the reproducing head (5) and between the drive capstan (6) and pinch wheel (7) to a point beyond them (at 8). The lacing head then stops and the pinch wheel closes on the tape, which is now ready to run. When the RUN button is pressed and the tape is re-played, a slack loop falls into a random store (9). This store will hold the 18¾ feet of tape that is replayed from the cassette in 30 seconds. When a REJECT button is pressed, the tape rapidly rewinds, the lacing lever returns to its original position and the cassette pops up. Several other facilities are available, including (on one unit in a bank) provision for making recordings.

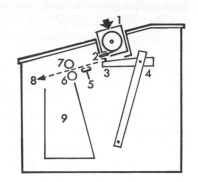

Standard quarter-inch tape and a normal 7½-ips replay head is used, but the cassette and replay machine are of special design, owing to the adoption of a single spool system. A metal loop is attached to the end of the tape. As the cassette is pressed fully home this loop is automatically drawn out and threaded, so that it is ready for re-play, with the drive motor already running. Pressing the replay button gives the near-instantaneous start that is usual for this type of equipment (and in which it scores marginally over disc). Resetting can be made to be automatic, so that it happens either as soon as the replay button is released or at the end of the tape, and takes a tenth of the previous running time: thus after a run of 5 seconds it resets in half a second; after 30 seconds a further three is required to return to the start.

A limitation imposed by the size of the cassette is that only 30 seconds of standard play tape can be accommodated. However, the use of double or long-play tape would extend this to more useful durations for continuous running effects (in this context it is worth noting that continuous backgrounds are in general of a character which is less likely to be affected by print-through than are many short staccato effects). Alternatively, very long continuous running effects sequences can be taken from standard effects tape (or transferred to them).

Although there is automatic muting when the tape is not running at speed, each channel also has its individual fader, as well as bass and top-response controls and a pre-hear (pre-fade listen) facility.

And although each tape can be replayed only from the start, this can be changed simply by re-recording to a second cassette. Re-recording can also be used to build up rapid but individually tailored effects sequences.

Sound effects for television and film

All of the effects that have been described here will work well out-of-vision on television. Recorded effects will more often be preferred to spot effects, which in turn will more often be recorded in advance and played in from quarter-inch tape: this helps to limit the number of open microphones and produces more predictable results in a situation where the director has many more elements to watch and listen to at the same time. However, in-vision sound effects will still be produced by some practical props. These need the same care in balancing that they would be given in sound radio, but here in more adverse conditions.

Often an effect which can be picked up satisfactorily on a speech microphone will sound much better if given its own close effects microphone. For example, a studio discussion about radioactivity using a geiger counter could have a small "personal" microphone hidden near the loudspeaker of the counter. In this actual example a recorded effect could not have been used successfully because the rates would not have varied realistically; because the people present would not have been able to react properly to the rates; and because a visual counter was sometimes shown in close-up, working synchronously with the clicks. The effects microphone made it possible to vary not just the volume but the *quality* of the sound at appropriate points in the discussion, so that the clicks could be soft and unobtrusive at points where they were not central to the discussion, and hard and strong when they were the centre of interest.

This is an extreme example of one use for effects, but there are many others: for example, where clear, crisp action noise enhances an otherwise quiet sequence.

As for sound radio, recorded effects are used to suggest atmosphere. Effects plus a camera track in over the heads of six extras may convince the viewer that he has seen a shot of a crowded bar; or film may establish a street scene and the sound may continue over a shot in the studio set showing a small part of the street.

Television introduces an extra dimension to sound effects which radio never had, the ability to jump easily between different viewpoints—say, between interior and exterior of a car or train. For

282

fast-cut sequences it is convenient to use a twin track effects tape with interior on one track and exterior on the other. The operator simply fades quickly from one to the other on each of the appropriate cuts. Pre-recording of effects sequences is in any case useful for complex scenes in television, for which little rehearsal time is available in the studio itself.

Footsteps in vision

Where footsteps are to be heard in the studio, the television or film designer must help sound by providing suitable surfaces. Rostra, in particular, cause problems. Stock rostra are generally 6 feet × 4 feet with a folding frame supporting a 1-inch wooden surface. Such a surface will give a characteristic hollow wooden sound to footsteps. An action area on rostra should therefore be felt treated to reduce this to reasonable proportions: a suitable treatment would be to "felt and clad", i.e. to surface the rostra with a half-inch layer of felt with hardboard on top. On this, footsteps will be audible but will no longer have the objectionable drumming sound. If little or no footsteps are to be heard a further soft layer of rug or carpeting is needed.

For outdoor areas the use of sufficiently large areas of peat will not only deaden the surface but may also deaden the acoustic locally. But certain materials which are commonly found out of doors cannot be used in television studios.

Sand cannot be used, as it spreads too easily, gets in technical equipment, and makes an unpleasant noise when a thin layer is ground under the feet. Sawdust is a convenient substitute. For similar technical reasons salt and certain types of artificial snow cannot be used: again substitutes may be found which do not cause sound problems.

Rocks are rarely used in studios, because they are too heavy and inconvenient. Wooden frames covered with wire netting and surfaced with painted hessian are used instead; or alternatively, fibreglass mouldings or expanded polystyrene may be used. Unfortunately, neither of these has a satisfactory sound quality, so that any climbing, rubbing, or bumping must be done with the utmost care by the performers—and then only at points which have been specially arranged not to resonate, perhaps by using peat or sawdust either as a surface layer or packed in sandbags. Falling "rocks" of expanded polystyrene must have recorded sound effects exactly synchronized—which will be easier if the action is seen in big close-

283

up, with the rocks falling through frame, rather than wide-angle. (But film gives a better guarantee of achieving realistic effects, as individual elements of the sound can be laid on the track.) Expanded polystyrene can sometimes squeak when trodden or sat on (particularly when small pieces are ground against the hard studio floors). Problems of this sort can be so difficult to overcome that it is always worth considering filming or pre-recording on location.

Sidewalk *paving stones* are often simulated by fibre-glass mouldings, as these are light and convenient to hold in stock. When laid in the studio they should stand on cloth or hessian to stop any rocking and to damp the resonance somewhat. If, in addition, performers are wearing rubber-soled shoes and there is recorded atmosphere the results should be satisfactory. But if synchronous footsteps are to be heard there is no satisfactory alternative to the real thing, despite the inconvenience and weight.

Stone floors can be simulated by the use of a special half-inch simulated stone composition sheeting laid on underfelt. But stone steps that are actually constructed of wood are very likely to cause trouble if the sound effect is required (and often if it is not). If a close effects microphone with good separation can be used for the footsteps there is some chance of improvement, as heavy bass cut can then also be used.

Wind, rain, and fire in vision

The sound effects for wind, rain, and fire create no problem: recordings are used as in radio. It is when they must be combined with visual effects that the trouble starts: the usual problem is that the device which makes the right picture sometimes makes the wrong noise, which must therefore be suppressed as much as possible, to be replaced perhaps by the proper recorded effect.

Wind is generated by machines varying in size from the very large aircraft-propellor-type fans about eight or nine feet in diameter, through medium sizes three or four feet in diameter and which can be moved round on a trolley, down to small machines about eighteen inches in diameter, which can be set on a lamp stand and used for relatively localized effects.

The large and medium sizes are both very noisy and push out a large volume of air over a large area of studio (if they are used indoors); windshields are needed for any boom or other microphones that may be used. The largest size may be used for the controlled single shots of a film, but is inconvenient for use in the television studio.

The smallest size is most convenient for studio use, especially when running at relatively low speed, when the noise produced actually sounds like wind. At higher speeds, however, blade hum is heard. The visual effect is localized and controllable (so that microphones may be avoided).

Rain, when produced in the television studio, may be far too noisy: it should be arranged for it to fall on soft material in a tray with good drainage. Also, if it is being used in the foreground of the shot the feed pipe may be close to the ideal microphone position, making balance on a boom difficult.

Another problem is that it takes a little while to get going and even longer to stop completely, to the last drip. This may be overcome either by slow mixes to and from effects (including recorded effects) accompanying the transition to and from the rain scene or by discontinuous recording and subsequent videotape editing.

Fire—including coal and log fires—in television studios must be provided by gas (with visual flicker effects added by lighting.) Unfortunately, gas does not burn with a sound appropriate to other flames, so again recorded effects have to be used (though usually at a very low level). The hiss of the gas tap can be prevented by leaving the tap fully open at the burner, controlling the flow instead from the tap at the studio wall.

Sound effects on film

In film, effects are used in the dubbing (see p 488) to maintain a continuous background of sound, or to define a particular quality of near silence. But in addition, effects of the "spot" type are made easier by the process of synthesis that is used to create films from many individually directed short scenes, within each of which the sound element may be given greater care than in the continuous take of the television studio. And a live action effect which is recorded synchronously as a scene is filmed may be enhanced in a number of ways:

(i) It may be changed in volume at the dubbing.
(ii) A second copy of the effect may be laid in synchronism on a second track, so that it can be changed in quality and volume to reinforce the original sound.
(iii) The timing may be altered, e.g. for an explosion filmed from

285

a distance the noise can be resynchronized visually, and not left trailing behind as in the original recording (which is out of synchronization because of the time taken for the sound to reach the microphone).

(iv) The original effect may be replaced or overlaid by a totally different recording, again in exact synchronization with picture.

Even if a particular staccato sound works well on the speech microphone, it may work even better if recorded wild-track (i.e. without picture) and given its own special balance. But when neither work well, some other spot sound simulating the proper noise may be tried.

For example, take the case of a bulldozer knocking down a street sign. In the main synchronous recording the dominant noise will be the engine and machinery noise of the bulldozer: the impact of blade on metal will hardly be heard against this. So a second version of the noise of impact is simulated, e.g. by using a brick to strike the metal, and recorded separately and without any bulldozer engine noise. This is then added in the dubbing.

If the bulldozer is knocking down a wall the sound is complicated still further, as the dramatic importance of three sounds may be the inverse of their actual volumes: impact noise may once again be the most important; then the sound of falling masonry; then the bulldozer engine and mechanical noise. In this case several recordings of the principal event could be made with different microphone types (but preferably highly directional) and positions (on either side of the wall), with additional "dramatic" sounds recorded separately to be incorporated at the dubbing stage.

Obviously if this much effort is to be worthwhile, the sound effect being created must be one which really adds to the dramatic experience of the audience. But a surprisingly large number of scenes do benefit from this treatment.

Commercials (and many documentary features) now make great use of punctuating sound effects. E.g. an item of equipment built up stage by stage by stop-action techniques has a series of parts suddenly appearing in vision: each time this occurs there may be a staccato noise in the sound which might be a recorded "plug-in", or something tapped on a metal surface, or indeed any other sound which may be felt to be relevant. Cash-register noises accompanying messages about the amazingly low price of a product have been overdone: such music may delight the man who pays for the commercial more than the customer in the shop. But there is a vast potential for non-representational, comic, or "cod" effects in commercials.

Many really good ideas used in television commercials are adaptations of original advances first seen in "serious" films or television (this is true in Europe to a greater extent, perhaps, than in America). But advertising films are a particularly suitable showcase for both the novel and the best of established techniques; they also have more care (and money) lavished on them than much other television. So those who are open to a rapid extension of their knowledge of what can be done with sound given time and all the talent that money can buy should watch commercials with close attention: it may be that the reverse journey—carrying unusual techniques back to "legitimate" film or television productions—may also be taken with advantage.

Stereo effects

Effects can be created in true stereo as, for example, spot effects played to the main microphones in a stereo sound play. But more often they are taken mono and steered to their appropriate position on the sound stage, by use of the pan-pot.

But the monophonic recorded-effects library can also be used in other ways. For example, certain types of sound can be fed through a spreader. This is a device which distributes a mono sound like wallpaper over the whole of the sound stage. Rain or crowd scenes can be treated in this way. For other sounds, movement may be added by panning a mono effect. Or for a static sound spread may be added in the form of stereo echo.

In an example illustrating all of these, a horse and carriage may be heard to pan through a spread crowd, until a shot is heard from a

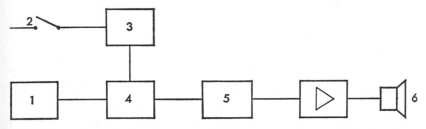

GUNSHOT EFFECTS GENERATOR. 1. White noise generator. 2. Push button. 3. Impulser relay. 4. Gate. 5. Low pass filter. 6. Loudspeaker. The special equipment includes only items 1–5. An existing good quality studio amplifier and loudspeaker unit is used in combination with it. (See p. 268.)

particular point, its reverberation echoing over the whole of the sound stage. . . . But note that in stereo sound drama there is a danger of lingering too long on movement that is meaningless in mono: for the sake of compatability this should be avoided.

Similar devices can be used for effects in stereophonic film.

9

HIGH LEVEL SOURCES

RECORD players and tape reproducers usually have amplifiers directly associated with them. These amplifiers not only raise the signal volume to a level which is less likely to be affected by hum and cross-talk but also have the special function of changing the frequency response to compensate for the deliberately introduced "recording characteristic". It is this equalization which makes it convenient to feed tape and disc output to the control desk at "high level", i.e. at a level which is about the same as that of the output of the desk itself. For similar reasons, videotape sound and film optical and magnetic tracks are fed at high level.

Outside sources must necessarily also be distributed at this same high level, so these, too, are dealt with in this chapter, as are telephone circuits when used as programme sources.

In this chapter we shall be dealing with these various sources not as recording media and communication links but as programme sources in their own right, comparable to the microphone, and requiring their own operational techniques.

The techniques for tape and disc replay which are described here are valid equally for monophonic or stereophonic sound; they are valuable to television and in the film dubbing theatre, and vital to radio. In radio, in particular, many programmes consist of a sequence of records or recordings. Such programmes range from the most banal to some of the most creative and imaginative material that can be heard in the sound medium.

Each small segment of this type of programme is collected, selected, or pre-recorded individually. The creative process is spread out in time, and each element may have lavished upon it all the care that it demands for perfection—within the limits of human fallibility and commercial pressures. So far, the technique is very similar to that of film making and indeed the final putting together of the programme has much in common with the film dubbing

289

session. With a sound production there often comes a stage where all the pre-recording is complete, and all the "insert" material is taken back to the studio to be re-recorded into a complete programme, using "live" links.

In order to match levels, mix in effects, introduce fades, and avoid abrupt changes of "atmosphere" and so on, tapes where possible should be *played in*, not cut in; each insert must be controlled afresh, so that it will be fully integrated into its new setting—and particularly in terms of the relative levels at the beginning and end of each insert. The subtler points of mixing from one sound into another will be considered in the next chapter; here we shall be more concerned with the operation of the reproducing decks and turntables themselves. And perhaps the most important aspect of this is good timing, for where successive sounds are linked by mixing it is unlikely that faults of timing can be put right by editing; and on a radio transmission there is no calling back miscues.

In broadcast automation systems tape replay is controlled by cueing systems which sense tone (or silence). In one example each recording has, superimposed at the end, a 25-Hz signal which provides two cues. As the sensing amplifier detects the beginning of the 25-Hz tone it starts the next tape in the playback sequence; and at the end of the 25-Hz signal it stops the first playback. But should that system fail, or should a playback break down in the middle, another sensing system will take over. In this a second amplifier is used to listen for any period of silence: this, too, will cue the next channel to start.

These devices are capable of cueing the routine transmission of a large number of items of a random nature very effectively; but in this and the next chapter the older, manual techniques will be described. These are the techniques which are still used for most creative production work—in fact, to build the programmes or items which can subsequently be broadcast automatically—and they are also the techniques which, in their most developed form, the automatic equipment must try to simulate, or against which it must, in the final resort, be judged.

"Live-and-insert" programmes

The linked actuality programme is a typical example of what might be termed the "live-and-insert" type of work. Here "on-the-spot" recordings in the form of sound effects and interviews are collected and arranged in a sequence that helps to tell a story. Unless

290

a concentrated effort is made to ensure that each collected item leads into the next—i.e. unless a certain amount of stage-managing is done at the time—linking narration will almost certainly be necessary.

Another type of programme which is very similar in construction is the illustrated report, in which summary, comment, and discussion in the studio are mixed with extracts from recordings of the events that are being dealt with (parts of the talk and discussion may also have been recorded in advance).

Disc-jockey shows, whether of "pops" or "serious music", may also be regarded as "live-and-insert" programmes. In this case we can be sure that exquisite care has been exercised at the time of recording the "inserts"; their arrangement in the form of a programme deserves equal care.

These are just a few examples of the technique, and there are many more which combine both tape and disc with live narration. The script of such a feature might look like this:

1.	TAPE	(BELLS, *Actuality: Peal from beginning. 15″ and fade under.*)
2.	NARRATOR	Bells. Bells to proclaim to the world that a new cathedral stands ready for the praise of God.
3.	TAPE	(HYMN, *Actuality. Lose bells behind. Fade singing on end of first verse, and out before start of second.*)
4.	NARRATOR	But this is a story which began one quiet night (*Begin to fade in grams*) in 1940.
5.	GRAMS	(NIGHTINGALE. *Fade in drone of* BOMBERS *until nightingale drowned out. Add some distant* ANTI-AIRCRAFT FIRE. *Hold bombers behind speech.*)
6.	NARRATOR	The bombers swept across the quiet countryside to the city. In the centre of the city, the old cathedral ...
7.	GRAMS	(BOMB *screams down and explodes.*)
8.	NARRATOR	... a glory of Gothic architecture. Windows of richly stained glass, set in delicate traceries ...
9.	GRAMS	(BOMB, *tinkle of* BROKEN GLASS.)
10.	NARRATOR	... carvings and statuary that were the life-work of countless medieval craftsmen ...
11.	TAPE	(*Prerecorded effects sequence: 2* BOMBS, *begin to fade in* FIRE: *hold this, but gradually lose record of bombers.*)
12.	NARRATOR	... the hammer beam roof a triumph of human ingenuity ... (*Effects sequence continues: several* FALLING TIMBERS *followed by* CRASH *as roof falls in.* FIRE *up to full, and fade to silence.*)

291

13. NARRATOR   With the cathedral had gone many other buildings. The centre of the city was largely a wasteland. Rebuilding could not be started until after the war. But nothing could stop people dreaming of the future ... and planning for it in practical terms.

14. TAPE   (*Interview, as edited. Quick fade in on atmosphere.*)
At first there was quite a lot of opposition to the idea of a new cathedral: well, of course, people said houses first and the new city centre, shops; the cathedral could come later ...

This script begins to show signs that it might need every possible technical facility. So far it requires two tape insert machines, a bank of turntables, and a microphone. Given such resources, the results might be very effective—but remember that it is the subject which provides the greatest strength, not just the techniques; and among the techniques the most important is the cheapest: good timing.

It would even be possible to get results (though of a more disjointed nature) without any facilities for playing-in at all, provided a certain amount of rewriting and simplification were done: all the narration and inserts could be recorded separately and cut together in sequence afterwards.

Preparing tape inserts

Each insert must first be considered as though it were a programme in its own right: it must go through all the processes of rough and fine editing that are needed to give it point and clarity of expression. One can often afford to be more drastic at this stage than would be possible in editing a complete programme. For anything which does not quite come off may be cut out without necessarily being completely lost; the essence of confused or muddled actuality can generally be tied into the script in a way which makes it both lucid and concise.

Heavy background effects should preferably be long enough before and after speech for fades (or, alternatively, a loop or an effects record can be used to cover the ends and provide the fade).

Indeed, it is not a bad idea to allow a second or two of atmosphere at the end, if not at the beginning, even in cases where this is not heavy. And there is no reason why the intake of breath before the speaker's first word should not be left on the tape. At normal listening levels neither atmosphere nor breath will be particularly noticeable, but their absence might be. Special care is needed when recordings of speech are interpolated between music recordings or gramophone records, on which the background of studio atmosphere may be very low indeed.

292

All the various pre-recorded segments of the programme should be made up into a single insert tape (omitting only the items which have to be mixed or crossfaded from a separate replay machine). Short spacers, one or two seconds long, will give a visual indication of where one insert ends and the next begins.

If atmosphere has been left on the front of the inserts some sort of mark will be necessary to indicate the point at which the tape should be faded full in. (The end of the spacer only indicates the point at which the fade-in starts.) On professional machines which have no pressure pads a mark with a (yellow) wax pencil can be used. But in cases where pressure pads would wipe wax marks away, a felt marker pen is equally effective.

At this stage of a production a convenient form of script is one which gives the narration in full but the inserts in cue form (and also showing their duration)—something like this·

NARRATOR ... spoke on his return to London Airport.

TAPE *Insert 10. Dur: 27"*
In: What we all want to know ...
Out: ... or so they tell me (laughter)

NARRATOR The minister stressed the need for unity between the two countries and then said:

TAPE *Insert 11. Dur: 30"*
In: It's all very well to be critical ...
Out: ... there's no immediate danger of that.

Note that on this script there are two different types of cue-in from the narration. The first needs about the length of a normal sentence pause. But the second piece of narration ends with what we may call a "suspended cue", which demands to be linked closely to the sentence which follows. In the first case the fade-up of atmosphere may follow the cue; in the other it will need to be tied under the last words of the cue. In the second case the timing will also depend on the pace of the first sentence on the tape. For instance, "It's (pause) all very well..." would sound ludicrous if tied too close to the cue "... and then said:".

I have been assuming that what is wanted here is the simplest form of fade, but there are various circumstances in which more complex joins between narration and insert might be needed for the most tidy (or most artistic) effect. How such fades and mixes can best be arranged will be considered in more detail later.

But at this stage the thing to note is the importance of marking up the script to indicate in some sort of bold private shorthand all the peculiarities of each individual cue. The purpose of a rehearsal is to

293

examine these in detail, and unless the programme is being assembled by a trial-and-error method, or in short sections, cues will come up so thick and fast on the actual "take" that some quick visual reminder of what is needed for each one should be kept at hand in all but the simplest sequences, and used as a musician uses a sheet of music. This marked-up script is in a very real sense your score—and there is no real virtue in trying to play it from memory.

The main things to mark on the script are as follows:

(i) Location of material.
(ii) Any peculiarities of timing.
(iii) Volume control settings and type of fade in.
(iv) Duration (or other means of noting in advance when the out-cue is coming up).
(v) Type of fade out.

These notes will provide an indication of what is likely to be needed for satisfactory work; however, when the tape is being played in there is no obligation to hold exactly to what you have worked out. But by using this method you will have a standard to work from, something to try to improve on; you will not be still at the stage of trying to do the job completely by ear.

Playing tapes in

First, it is necessary to check how long the tape takes to come up to speed. There are two conditions that one may start from:

(i) Motor switched off. In this case the reproducer may take as much as a second or so to run up, as the flywheel attached to the drive motor has to be set in motion. Check this run-up time by using a recording of pure tone; set the start of the tone back at various distances from the head, and then switch on. If the setting is too close the tone will be clearly heard climbing to its true pitch; whereas if it is set back a long way there will be no appreciable wow. Find the point at which for pure tone a very slight slide-in is just noticeable, and this will be the amount of setting-back needed for speech and nearly all music. (A slight wow-in is quite undetectable by the ear in all but the rarest of cases. In singing, the voice hits true pitch not at once, but by what might be termed a method of successive approximations; and the same is true of many instruments. The ear accepts this readily.)

294

(ii) Instantaneous start—by means of pause control, etc. The drive motor is left running, but the idler pulley is lifted from it. (But do not leave running for very long periods in this condition, as the motor may get very hot.) Here mechanical considerations no longer apply, and the set-back distance can be decided purely on the grounds of what is most convenient for timing. Tight cueing is the best safeguard against last-second changes of pace in a "live" cue, so a setting allowing only a few inches of tape—say, half a second's worth—is reasonable.

In either of these two cases you will establish a standard run-up time, and it is worth while practising with this and getting the feel of the timing. Set up the tape, start it, and fade up. And remember not to start fading up until the run-in is complete: there must always be that pause—however short it may have been made—between starting the tape and the beginning of the fade-in. This pause must certainly be observed if you are not coming in at the start of the tape; otherwise you will either get a wow (if only on atmosphere), or for the "instantaneous" start we might hear the tape jerk into motion. So do not get trigger-happy; remember that it is as much a fault to flick the fader open too quickly as it is to be too slow off the mark.

Do not rely entirely on the remembered timing to give the delay between start and fade: get into the habit of checking as it happens —watch as tape runs up to speed and fade up as the marker passes the replay head (or whatever reference point you may be using). In this way you can use a variety of different machines without being thrown by differences in run-up time (different specimens of the same model sometimes vary in this respect).

With many reproducers it will be possible to do the whole operation with one hand; and it may prove to be no disadvantage later if you make a practice of doing it this way. The free hand may come in useful for other operations which have to be carried out at the same time.

Two tape replay machines

When a very long radio programme—one extending to severa reels of tape—has to be reproduced, the changeovers are made visually. Tape number two is set up in the normal way, and as the trailer to tape one passes a certain point, No. 2 is run and faded up. With practice, the operation can be managed as neatly as if the two tapes were edited together with jointing tape.

But this is, after all, a purely routine use of a second reproducer. For constructive work it is the facility of *mixing* from one to another which is of greater value, and this is used for the many cases where, for one reason or another, a simple cut gives an ugly result.

A typical problem is that presented by two speech tapes with different background effects, where we wish to go from one to the other without a cut or fadeout. Assuming for a moment that the change-over point is internal to both tapes (i.e. before the end of tape one and after the start of tape two), there are a number of ways of doing the mix, depending on the degree of pause between words on each of the two tapes. In the simplest case there is a full sentence pause or paragraph pause on both tapes. Here we have the option of retaining the whole of this natural pause—and if we have the same voice on both tapes with merely a slight change of background effect we shall certainly want to do this, unless the pause is excessively long.

In preparing to make the mix, first examine the length of the pauses in both cases (and if in doubt mark their beginnings and ends). Having found the start of the pause on tape two, set back the normal run-up time from this (so that the tape is actually set up before the end of the unwanted material). Now, watch—or listen to —tape one carefully as the cue comes up, and at a predetermined point in the last words that are wanted, start tape two. There will now be a fraction of a second during which the two machines are running together, but with the second still faded out. In this way the start of the pause arrives on both reproducers at the same time.

At this point, in order to maintain the fullest continuity, we can do a crossfade which keeps the atmosphere running throughout the pause. For this we simply have to fade tape two in to full (or nearly full) before we start to fade the other one out, i.e. we make the cross by doing the two fades in sequence, and not together. (If the two fades were made simultaneously there would be a dip in atmosphere; whereas if we complete the fade-in before starting the fade-out there is merely a slight "bump" in the atmosphere. Of the two, the latter is preferable when complete continuity is required.)

In this simplest case we have retained the timing of the pause that preceded the speech on the second tape. But there is considerable latitude of choice: by varying the time of entry of the second tape the pause can be lengthened or shortened. And if one or other of the originals has no pause, it should still be possible to arrange a tidy mix; for example, if there is no pause at the out-point of the first tape, then the second can be cued in and faded up early.

With mixes of this sort one could cut in blank tape or a spacer at the end of what atmosphere there is, to ensure that as much of this as possible is kept, while unwanted words are lost. But there is rarely any advantage in this; for if the fade is mistimed to the extent that the clipped end of the effect passes across the head while the fader is still open the cut away may still be noticeable.

But there will be times where there is no real pause available on either side, and then it becomes necessary to find some matching atmosphere from somewhere else on the tape and tack it on. A good place to look for this is not sentence pauses—these should be left at a natural length, and in any case may contain a breath—but in mid-sentence hesitations. If the required atmosphere is cut from one of these it will probably contain no intake of breath, and its absence from the original position will not be apparent.

In all of these cases care must be taken to match levels (this is one of the reasons why it may be necessary to mix, rather than edit) and one of the commonest ways of doing this is to edge one side of the join in or out a few dB to avoid a sudden "doorstep" effect on the voice. The same technique can be used where heavy atmosphere is cut off close to the last (or first) word. This edging away must not occupy the duration of more than a word or half a word, and the way it is done depends very much on the delivery of the sentence. As with all the other elements of these mixes, a good sense of timing is needed for the best results.

Disc and tape cassette inserts—getting organized

There are many occasions when disc may be used: gramophone records of music, effects records, and direct recordings ("acetates") are the three main types. And with disc there is no arrangement directly comparable with the insert tape, so it is much more important to be able to find a place on a disc very quickly; to be able to put the disc on the turntable, locate the right groove, and the right part of that groove, and set the record up ready for playing in, all in a matter of a few seconds. There are special quick-start techniques for playing discs in accurately, but in all matters of cueing and timing there is no difference between tape and disc.

In a complex programme there may be many cues, which creates extra problems of storage and location of material; for instead of one or two carefully edited tapes, there may be a dozen or more discs, some of which may have to be used several times at different places in the programme. Fifty cues in a half-hour radio programme is quite normal. If the disc-player is not to spend the greater part of

297

his time searching for the right records, some simple system of quick identification is necessary.

Start by numbering the spaces in a record rack, and then as the sequence of discs is established start numbering these as well. Then put the records in the rack; and except for the times when they are actually needed for playing, keep them there. Then, at all stages of the rehearsal and recording (or transmission) the right record will always be available at once, even if there are some which are wanted several times. In any case, discs should be treated with care, and returning them to a rack immediately after use will help with this. It should be possible to handle a disc—including putting it in and taking it out of the rack—without touching the grooves. Hold it with two hands by the outer edge, or single-handed by supporting it at the label with the fingers and at the rim with the thumb.

For numbering discs, use a soft blunt wax pencil (of the same type as that used for marking edit points on tape), and write on the smooth part of the record just outside the label, so that the number can later be rubbed off with a paper tissue. If you do not expect the rack(s) to be more than half full, number only alternate spaces (also with the wax pencil), and then if extra discs have to be put in there will be spaces for them without too much renumbering.

It is worth making a rule of getting discs numbered as early as possible in rehearsal, even if changes are expected. It does not really matter if your final sequence of numbers runs something like 1, 2, 4A, 4B, 4C, 5, 8, 8A, 9, ... at least you know where everything is all the time.

And, of course, always mark the numbers on the scripts at the same time as they go on the records. This system of numbering does not clutter the script as much as writing in the manufacturer's full serial number, etc.

Where *tape cassettes* are used, the handling problems are a little simpler, but the organization of the work is much the same.

Groove location

Given a suitable design of pick-up, a fairly steady hand and some means of identifying the groove, it is not at all difficult to place the stylus within one or two revolutions of a required sound on a coarse groove disc, or within two or three on a microgroove record.

It is, of course, a great help if there is a handle on the side of the business end of the pick-up. Many high-quality record players have a raise/lower handle working at or near the pivot, but this is not the same thing; it does not offer the facility of "spotting" the stylus from place to place on the disc in the same convenient way—and since it is this very facility which lends disc a marked operational superiority to tape (in certain circumstances) it is a pity not to be able to guide the stylus into the right groove in one simple movement. Whether there is a handle on the side or not, the pick-up head should not be held (i.e. gripped between finger and thumb) but *supported* and *lowered* into the groove. Nowadays stylus assemblies are usually highly compliant, but damage can still be caused by clumsy handling. It is presumably to discourage the hamfisted that handles are not fitted as standard equipment. However, such a modification is not difficult and can generally be made in such a way as to have a negligible effect on performance. It is also useful to have a design of pick-up on which it is possible to see the stylus without getting down on hands and knees.

Another advantage of disc lies in the fact that you can see the modulation of the groove. A point source of light reflected in an unmodulated part of the record shows up as a characteristically smooth-edged radial line. As the modulation of the groove becomes heavier, the light is more diffused, and the reflection is smudged at the sides of the radial line. The progress of a symphonic work can be "read" as easily as the volume markings in the score. (The same method can also be used to check records for flaws or damage.)

On certain records—particularly coarse-groove shellac records—it is convenient to mark the groove with a wax pencil. But this requires care. The pencil should be sharpened to a V-tip—not to a point, but a knife edge—and touched gently into the groove behind the stylus. To be on the safe side, mark just *after* an out cue and just *before* an in cue—so that the mark does not have to be played through with the fader open. (This means that cues out are easier to mark than cues in.) For immediate identification the mark should extend for the greater part of a revolution. A soft wax pencil (of the type recommended for marking tape) can be used, but this may sometimes result in a partially clogged groove—and a squeak as the stylus drags through it. A wax pencil of medium hardness is less likely to give a squeak, but more care is needed not to damage the groove.

This form of record marking is certainly the most convenient for the old shellac records, but whether it is to be recommended for vinyl (from which most present-day records are pressed) or for "acetates" (direct recordings) depends on the skill of the operator and the views of the owner of the records. But in any case it is not recommended for microgroove; these are far too fragile. Another disadvantage is that the marks are, for all practical purposes, there for the life of the record.

For the accurate location of particular places on a record, BBC studios are equipped with record players which have optical groove-locating units. On these a mirror is fixed beneath the pivot and throws the image of a scale on to a ground-glass screen. This device works very well indeed, as the magnification of the scale is such as to make it a very sensitive measure of position; indeed, it will also show any "swing" in the record due to the grooves not being accurately centred on the hole, a condition which can cause "wow" on sustained notes of music.

Unfortunately, however, unless such specialized equipment can be made up, the best thing of this type that can be suggested for practical use is some sort of protractor type scale, fixed below the arm. Since this has to be fairly close to the pivot, it can at best only be coarse-reading. But even this is better than nothing.

The type of locator which sits on the spindle and extends in an arc round in front of the pick-up head (the other end being held in the hand), although not very satisfactory for quick operational work, is useful for scripting disc programmes where selection work has to be done on a record player away from the studio (as when radio programmes are being devised in an office or at home). The groove-locating unit is portable, can be carried around

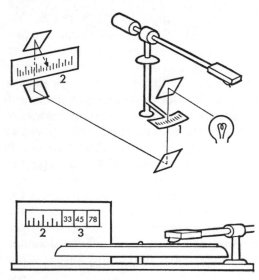

OPTICAL GROOVE LOCATOR: this projects the image of a scale (1) fixed to the pick-up pivot on to a ground glass screen (2) indicating the exact position of the needle on the radius of the disc. This is accurate to within the error produced by groove-swing (which can also be seen very clearly). The display includes a panel which illuminates the speed chosen (3). (As used in BBC disc reproducers.)

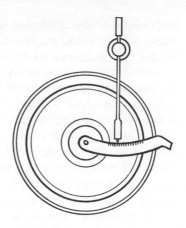

with the records, and so simplifies the job of explaining the programme.

But a simpler device that serves the same purpose is an ordinary ruler, provided it is used accurately. It is perhaps best to use a decimal system, and to add additional information, e.g. "start 1·35″ in, on the trombone solo; out at 1·45″, after three drum beats". This is more valuable than "about an inch and a half in" or something like that; and quicker to find than "seven bars after letter D (in the score); play 17 bars". But none of these is as simple as being able to write "g.l.u. 97–122".

All these are for the almost universally used pivot-mounted pick-up arms. Where parallel tracking arms are used, calibration above the track is a fairly simple matter. (But parallel tracking, though superficially attractive, has not proved itself in practice.)

Setting up records

Given the facility, and ability, to find the right groove on a record, the next step is to find the exact place on that groove and set up to bring the record in at that point. Accuracy is important: to get a clean start in the middle of a work it may be necessary to fade up within a fraction of an inch of the start of a note. For real accuracy of timing the disc is stopped in preparation for the cue, and then, on cue, the disc is set in motion and faded up, as with tape.

Having found the place roughly, lift the stylus back a few grooves and run up to the point again, switching off the motor before reaching it, and bringing the turntable to halt as the in-cue passes under the stylus. Indicate the start of the required sound by putting a mark

301

opposite it just outside the label. For this, use the soft wax pencil again. Check the mark by running the disc again: the sound should start just as the mark is opposite the stylus.

With most modern forms of stylus mounting no noticeable harm is done if the record is spun slowly backwards under the stylus: in this case the exact point can be found in the same way as for tape, and the disc can then be spun back to the set-up point.

The only way to find out if damage is done to a disc by spinning back is to experiment—using scrap discs! If wear is noticeably accelerated, or if there is an occasional tendency to dig in, then this easy way is out of the question, and rather complicated ways of setting up have to be devised.

For example, on a speech record, note the previous words and pause (if any) and set up at the appropriate place. Suppose we have on the disc, "... so far, so good. But the difficulties start..." with the last four words given as our cue into the insert. After listening carefully we may mark up the disc and write on the script something like, "so far, so good/$+\frac{1}{2}$" meaning "set up at the mark about half a revolution after the cue word". This will allow sufficient space to run up to speed and catch the "But" right on the nose. (With a shade more care in marking up and starting the record the "But" can probably be cut as well, so as to come in clean on "the difficulties start...".) Similar methods can be used for music, marking the set-up cue on the script in some sort of musical (or pseudo-musical) notation in the way that I have used words above.

If the disc is being played from the start, or if there is no sound definite enough to be used as a cue, it will be necessary to count the revolutions from the run-in groove, taking care to start from the same "first" groove each time (it is easy enough to make a mistake on direct-cut discs, which have a segment in which the cutter has been gently lowered into the coating). Some people are able, with coarse-groove records, to lift a stylus back one groove without damaging the groove wall (i.e. without putting a click on the record).

The distance to be set back depends on the same considerations as apply for tape: convenient settings are $\frac{1}{4}$ revolution for $33\frac{1}{3}$ r.p.m., $\frac{1}{3}$ for 45, and $\frac{1}{2}$ for 78.

An additional facility that may be provided on or fitted to some players is a "mute". This interrupts the output for perhaps a quarter of a revolution, more than enough to run up to speed. But if sound then cuts in abruptly there may be an audible click. It is better for the output to rise rapidly but not instantaneously (i.e. taking not less

302

than a hundredth of a second). Mutes are more common on record players set for "instant" start than on tape decks, but may also be used on the latter.

BBC effects discs now have a burst of tone at the start of each band of modulation. This tone rises quickly to a maximum volume and is then cut off abruptly; used in conjunction with a quick-start device, and with or without a mute, this makes for rapid operation.

Quick-start techniques for disc

If a disc is to be cued in with the same accurate timing as tape, it is no good having the disc running and lowering the stylus more or less into the right place. Inaccurate enough with 78's, this is a completely hopeless method for LP's. But using the methods of marking and setting up that have already been described, records can be brought in from a standing start dead on cue.

Quick-start techniques fall into two categories, depending on the type of drive employed by the turntable.

(i) Rim drive. The turntable gets up to its full speed quickly after the motor is switched on. Set up with the drive disengaged and then re-engage with the motor switched off. On cue, simply switch on, pause while the turntable and disc together run up to speed, and as the mark passes the stylus, fade up. But remember not to leave the turntable standing with the drive engaged for long periods: this can cause a "flat" on the rubber idler wheel.

(ii) Centre drive. Quick starts are not so easy here, as the essence of the design is that the turntable acts as a large flywheel (to even out any short period speed variations). This flywheel is generally driven by a motor which is small in relation to the power that would be needed to get the turntable very quickly up to speed. For this reason a variety of techniques have been devised for overcoming this difficulty.

(a) The spin start. This is a sort of "assisted take off" method. The disc is set up in the normal way and left with the motor switched off. At the appropriate time— i.e. about a second, or less, before the cue—the motor is switched on with one hand and the turntable is flicked into motion with the other; and then the first hand is used to fade up.

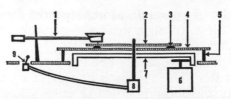

QUICK-START DEVICES. Form of drop-start mechanism in which turntable and motor assembly can be lowered away from the record. When a record is set up the pick-up 1 is at rest in groove of the record 2 which in turn is supported by rubber studs 3 on aluminium plate 4. This rests on tripod 5 when motor/turntable assembly 6 and 7 is dropped away by raise/lower cam 8 operated by lever 9. (In other designs there is no aluminium plate and the record itself is raised and lowered on a moving tripod. But the latter type of player cannot be used for 7-inch discs.)

(b) The drop-start. Here the record is stopped but the turntable left running. The disc, with the stylus resting in the groove, has to be lifted away from the turntable, and then lowered on to it on cue.

At the BBC several special devices have been invented to make drop-starts easy for the operator, and although they are not essential to the method, there is no doubt that they have helped to make many complicated disc programmes relatively easy to get on the air. Indeed a number of fast-moving gramophone programmes have evolved through this factor.

The first of these devices is mechanical, and uses two press buttons. One of these operates a lever which lifts the disc from the turntable on a tripod: when pressed fully, this lever passes a catch, and the disc is held suspended above the turntable. Pressing the second button clears the catch so that the disc falls to the turntable and is very soon up to speed. If both buttons are pressed the disc can be lowered gently instead of being dropped.

The second device is an improvement on this in that the control of the tripod simply rests on a cam operated by a quadrant lever. (In a later development the lever is replaced by a switch, and the "drop" is motorized—the tripod being fixed and the turntable dropping away from it.) This is the device currently used by the BBC.

Fortunately for those who cannot run to such sophisticated "plumbing", it is not at all difficult to extend the method to ordinary turntables. Simply set up the record with the motor off, then switch on and carefully lift the disc by fingertip a fraction of an inch above the turntable, which in a few seconds will run up to speed. Then, slightly anticipating the cue, drop the disc on to the turntable and fade up. Some form of drop-start is, I would say, preferable to the spin-start.

Prefade and overlaps

For professional disc work, as for tape, it is valuable to be able to "prefade" (i.e. listen before fading up) while the studio loudspeaker is being used to monitor the rest of the programme. It is usual to have a separate headphone feed from each turntable for this purpose; but if this is not possible, some arrangement may be made whereby the record-player output is disconnected from the mixer (or recorder) with the volume control for this source faded out, and fed to headphones instead; the programme input feed being restored after the circuit has been used to monitor the setting up.

Separate circuits are indispensable, however, for overlap change-overs.

An "overlap" is made by starting to record each new disc half a minute or more before the old one is due to run out; the extent of the overlap is indicated by "scrolling" (i.e. by momentarily increasing the cutter's rate of travel towards the centre of the disc). To replay an overlap, the second disc is set up near to the start on a recognizable cue, and started as this comes up on disc one. The two are now running almost in synchronization. To complete the job, the speed of disc two is varied slightly by hand, or by the speed regulator: listening to this disc on prefade, it is brought into step with disc one. When the two are synchronized number two is faded in and number one out.

An alternative method of replaying an overlap is to convert it into a butt change-over by setting up for a drop start just before a pause, and changing over during that pause. This method is not satisfactory for continuous music or absolutely continuous speech, unless the timing of the drop can be made perfect.

Butts and cuts

Butt change-overs on disc work in much the same way as with tape. And the ability to negotiate these cleanly is especially useful when playing orchestral works which are split up on 78-r.p.m. discs. Many records that are old but interesting, and perhaps even historic, still exist in this form. For their replay it is important to be able to time their start accurately, though not necessarily using quick-start techniques.

If the disc is set up several revolutions before the start of the first note on the record a little practice will show at what point on the previous side the new record should be started to give time for it to

305

run up to speed and for the "surface" to be eased in before the start of the music. It may prove necessary to fade in gently; sudden changes in the quality of surface noise remind the listener of its presence.

When playing records of orchestral works on 78's, use a score to check the timing of change-overs. It is not always clear, if one is not absolutely familiar with a work, whether there is a single beat or two, or more, between one disc or the next. It can also happen that a note is repeated to round off a side. A decent pause must be left between movements, and if the surface noise on the run in and run out of the two records is not sufficient, or is unpleasantly heavy, a "blank" (i.e. unmodulated) record can be used to lend continuity of background. These rules should be followed whether the old records are being used for broadcast or for transcription to tape (but note that the latter is one of the many things which, under British copyright law, cannot be done without permission from the record publisher—who will demand a good reason, and probably a nominal payment).

One thing which can be done on a disc, and which is utterly impossible on tape, is a jump cut, i.e. the disc is faded out, and the pick-up is lifted by hand to a new in-cue. A mark on the disc or the g.l.u. is used for guidance. After a quick prefade check, the disc is once again faded up.

Jump cuts are only practicable for 78-r.p.m. coarse-groove discs, and are used only if no duplicate copy is available. Nowadays, with the vastly increased use of tape, jump cuts are rarely seen; but at one time they were quite common. The operation was generally completed well within two seconds. Loss of background atmosphere was inevitable.

Another type of cut is the "pot. cut" ("pot." = potentiometer, or fader), in which a word or two is cut during replay by simply fading out momentarily. The fades out and in must be very sharp, and the timing must be memorized carefully if the results are to be clean—though listening on prefade may help. This can be done with sound recorded in any medium.

Repeating grooves

There is one other event which the disc-player must always be prepared for, and this is the repeating groove. If this occurs during a radio transmission the cure may have to be as violent as the effect: quickly fade out, jump the stylus on a groove, and quickly fade up.

306

This is not the time for artistry: a gentle fade out on the repeated phrase is good for a laugh, but it is not much good for the programme. It may be possible to cure the repeat in another way, without fading out or lifting the stylus from the groove. When a repeating groove occurs the stylus will generally require very little persuasion to return to its original path, or at worst to jump forwards. To do this, rest a pencil across the pick-up arm or head at an angle to the horizontal of not more than 45°. This will "squeeze" the stylus towards the centre of the record, but at the same time it will increase the playing weight momentarily, and prevent skating. If no pencil or similar object is available the same thing can be done, very gently, by hand—remembering not to push forward too hard.

Occasionally the tendency to jump grooves may be repeated—due perhaps to a sticky pick-up mounting. The pencil treatment may cure this too, but may have to be held in contact for the whole duration of the record.

Recorded sound in the television studio

Disc and quarter-inch tape are played into television programmes in precisely the same way as they are for sound radio—with the obvious proviso that sometimes the cue is visual instead of verbal. For example, if a character in a play puts a record on, the sound assistant's action must synchronize with picture.

It should be added here that when radios, television sets, record players and tape machines are used as props by actors in television programmes they are never "practical"—obviously, the sound gallery will want to retain control so that the most suitable sound balance can be maintained at all times, and also so that there will be perfect sound cueing in and out. This means that careful rehearsal is necessary for exact synchronization.

Since the actors rehearse in advance without cameras, there is a tendency for them to slide in to sloppy visual habits—and particularly with tape recorders. Everyone who has ever used a tape recorder knows that to spool fast backward or forward and always land on the right word without any cueing aids is virtually impossible; but actors, assisted by the sound gallery, do it all the time; and rarely with even a hint of awareness that the writer is asking them to be just a little lucky in their guesswork.

Writers generally show more awareness with radios and television sets, though here too, all too often we hear half of a previous sentence and then go straight in to the item that is required for the

307

plot. This is one of those places where technique all too easily becomes noticeable—and if it is added to clumsy programme construction it makes it much worse.

Occasionally such items are read live from a microphone in a distant part of the studio, but as control of sound quality (by filtering) is easier if it is pre-recorded this is usually preferred. Where it is necessary for cueing the actors the sound is fed at low level to a studio loudspeaker.

Pre-recordings using the studio itself are sometimes used for out-of-vision sound. This may allow the correct perspective to be obtained or, more often, it is used simply to fix one element in an otherwise all-too-flexible medium. Music is often pre-recorded where complicated song and dance numbers are to be performed—and frequently in a different acoustic and with a close balance, both of which create matching problems.

Nevertheless, with all of these timing is relatively easy. It is less so when the sound arrives with a film or videotape insert.

Videotape and film sound in television

Videotape machines are allowed a 10-second run up. Though the speed pick-up is almost instantaneous, time has to be allowed for the picture to stabilize, and then (generally) to be locked to the same picture scan as the studio, so that a dissolve is possible or a cut is clean without a picture bump. Telecine machines move into action more lumberingly but stabilize picture quicker; they are normally run from the figure 10 on the leader. This means 10 "35 mm-feet", i.e. ten measures of sixteen frames, and is the same for both 16-mm and 35-mm film. It is equivalent to about 7 seconds, to which an extra second is added for reaction and run-up time. There is no sound or picture before 0, as this defeats the object of the exercise: you might just as well have run off some other figure—as in fact you can if the machine is always stable in less than 10 feet.

This makes exact cueing difficult: it is generally done on word counts in the first instance (two words per foot, or three words per second for a fairly fast speaker with no pauses), and corrected after each rehearsal. This method of successive approximations goes for nothing if the performer suddenly produces a performance on the "take" with radically different (and usually slower) timing. The director has either to make sure this will not happen or to outguess the performer.

308

Even where the rest of the material is ad-libbed, the film or video-tape cue is generally scripted and learned, or perhaps written out on cue cards and held near the camera; or run on one of the systems for unrolling cue script close to or optically superimposed in line with the camera lens. Alternatively (with very practised performers), a cue to run is agreed, and then the performer, watching a monitor showing the videotape or film run-up out of the corner of his eye, exactly matches his introduction to the time available for it.

All of these systems break down occasionally, so there is a tendency to allow them to influence programme material—to allow a "soft" start rather than one that crashes in with important picture and sound from the first second as a disc or quarter-inch tape would.

What this means for the sound man (who has nothing to do with the cueing) is that he has to be prepared to do either a straight-forward match of sound to sound, as he would with quarter-inch tape, or a first-aid rescue job.

The easiest line is to follow the picture: fade in if the picture fades in or mixes; or do a quick mix if the picture cuts (on a miscue, a planned mix may be changed to a cut). But this assumes that no essential sound information is going to be lost by waiting for picture; sometimes it is best to anticipate by fading up the new sound in advance of a delayed cut. On an overlap of different voices it may be best either to clip a few words of the incoming speech or, more likely, to hold the first word or two at low level behind the last words of studio. Neither is elegant, but the latter makes it easier to make sense of what is said subsequently and is therefore preferable.

Where "hard" cues are needed within a recorded programme because the insert just has to start with a bang and exact cueing cannot be guaranteed, the whole of this clumsy procedure is thrown overboard, the cue made loose, and the two parts subsequently edited together (which means that the sound change will probably have to be resynchronized with the cut: see page 460 for the video-tape editing techniques that are used for this).

In other circumstances the cueing is predetermined by cue dots. When switching from one reel of film to the next cue dots are shown in the top right-hand corner: the first being the cue to run film and the second to switch over sound and picture together. This is not a procedure that concerns the sound man; it is done by a film projection-ist. Cue dots in the top left of frame are used in television for continuity purposes, giving exact synchronization to everybody on "stand-by", "run", and "fade-up" cues.

Outside sources

Another type of high-level source is the line incoming from another studio. Contact between the two studios may take a number of forms. Sometimes there are, in fact, two lines: the programme circuit, which may be one- or two-way, plus a control line which is effectively a telephone between the control points at the two ends.

Consider first the case of a one-way "music" line (i.e. broadcast quality line) plus control circuit.

Often it is possible to prove the line fully before the programme goes on the air. In such a case contact is first established on the control circuit, and the distant contributor is asked to send line-up tone and to identify the programme line. Both of these can be checked with the channel fader open, so that the level of the incoming material can be accurately set and its quality is known.

In the event that the line is not available until the programme of which it is to form part is on the air, the line can only be fully tested to the last switching point prior to the active part of control desk. But the routine can be checked right up to the channel fader input if the desk has "pre-hear" (sometimes called "pre-fade") on the channel used. (If this facility were not available it should still be possible to listen to the circuit in the sound-control area at the last point before it is plugged through to the control desk. Headphones or a small loudspeaker could be used.)

The control line may be made double-purpose: as well as being used for general communication between the two points before, during, and after the contribution, the return circuit may have cue programme fed to it at all other times. Several other switching arrangements could also be made—for example, for the producer's talkback circuit to be superimposed on cue programme. In each of these cases the cue feed and the results of any other switching are checked by the contributor as part of the line-up procedure.

What happens at the contributor's end is again a matter for local arrangement: it depends, for example, on whether the contributor is on his own in a "self-operated" studio or not. If there is a separate, manned control point the cue programme may terminate there and the contributor be given a cue to start by the operator. Or it may be fed to the studio (for the contributor to hear on headphones or a "deaf-aid" earpiece: either of these should be preferred to a loudspeaker, which might cause colouration). In this case the feed might be for just the beginning and end of the contribution, or it might be left open all the way through. Obviously, the latter will be necessary in the case of an interview.

An apparently simpler arrangement is for there to be not three channels of communication but two: a music line in each direction, instead of a single music line and a two-way telephone circuit. However, this will be a more expensive arrangement (unless, instead, telephone circuits are used for contributions to a broadcast—of which more later).

The system using two music lines will therefore be used only if there is a need for high-quality sound to be transmitted both ways (as when the programme is being simultaneously broadcast or recorded at both ends), or when the facility is in any case available on stand-by. The arrangements prior to and during the broadcasts are broadly similar to those already described, except for the obvious proviso that it is not possible for a line to be used for control purposes when it is on the air.

A further possible arrangement is for there to be two-way programme lines with a completely independent control circuit. This, the most versatile arrangement, is also, of course, the most expensive.

Clean feed and multi-way working

So far, "cue programme" has been mentioned without any indication being given as to what point in the control desk this is derived from.

Normal cue programme consists of the output of the mixer studio fed to all participants; but if, say, a speaker at the New York end of a transatlantic discussion were fed the full programme from a mixer in London he would hear his own voice coming back, delayed by the time it takes for a telephone signal to travel some 6000 miles by line or very much more if the signal goes by satellite. The delay is only a fraction of a second, but is enough to make speech decidedly uncomfortable. If the return signal is loud enough it becomes impossible to carry on without stuttering. (Moon circuits, however, involve delays of several seconds.)

The alternative to this is "clean feed", an arrangement whereby contributors hear all of the programme except their own part. Clearly, special circuit arrangements must be made in the control desk for this to be possible. For two-way working using clean feed a way of doing it is for the outside source line to be added to the studio output after the main gain control, the "clean" feed being taken through a parallel fader just prior to the main control.

311

Equally, however, the same could be done at an earlier stage in the mixer, at a group fader—though this would mean that only those channels which were selected to the group being used could be included in the clean feed, which might mean that the full range of the mixer could not be used. If the studios are far apart—at continental distances—the time delay problem makes the use of clean

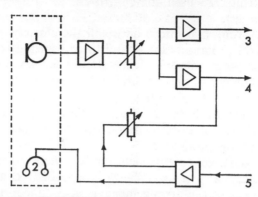

"CLEAN FEED" CIRCUIT. For Multi-Studio discussion a speaker in the studio can hear a distant source on headphones without also hearing his own voice. "Clean" cue is also provided. 1. Microphone and 2. Headphones or "deaf aid" for speaker in studio. 3. Clean feed to distant studio. 4. Combined studio output. 5. Incoming line. This arrangement is essential for both radio and TV when studios are linked by satellite, as this introduces a relatively long delay to any sound that is returned to its point of origination. Note also that if headphones are replaced by a loudspeaker, this could easily wreck the arrangement unless it is carefully placed for minimal pick-up on the studio microphone and kept at low level.

feed essential; if they are close together clean feed may be used for comfort and convenience (some people are put off by hearing their own voice on headphones); a third use is to provide an "actuality" feed of an event to which various broadcasters add their own commentary. The actuality sound is fully mixed at the originating control desk, at which the commentary for the "home" audience is added through an independent channel which is added to the mixer output after the master control (or after the appropriate group fader, if the clean feed is taken from this point). This arrangement is similar to the provision of mixed music and effects tracks in film dubbing: there, too, commentary may be added separately by the user, perhaps in a language different from that of the original production.

A very complex use for this form of clean feed was in a World Cup football series, where picture and sound were recorded on videotape and a synchronized 1-inch sound tape. Ten commentaries

312

in different languages could be recorded at the same time and then recombined individually with the actuality sound in replay of the tapes.

A totally different arrangement of studios and feeds has its application in an "independent evidence" type of programme where a compere questions two people in separate studios who cannot hear each other (e.g. to examine the reactions of various partners who knew each other well: brother and sister, secretary and boss, or husband and wife). Three studios are required: one for the compere, who, listening on headphones, hears the full programme output, and two remote studios in which the victims sit, and are fed nothing of the other person's answers, and only that part of the questioning which is directly addressed to them. Various ways of arranging this can be devised; in the BBC layout the switching was done by two assistants, one in each of the two remote studios.

Telephone circuits used in radio and television programmes

Telephone circuits are not normally used in broadcast programmes for several reasons:

(i) The speech quality of the carbon microphone generally used in telephones, though very satisfactory for communication purposes, is below that normally required in broadcasting. Distortion and noise levels are relatively high, and the frequency response is not flat. Nor are telephone lines designed to the same sound-quality standards as are those intended specifically for broadcasting.

(ii) The bandwidth is relatively narrow: 300–3000 Hz in America and 300–3300 Hz in Britain. This contains more than enough of human speech to permit full intelligibility, but, again, less than is required in broadcasting.

(iii) The telephone system cannot reasonably be expected to guarantee the same standards of freedom from interruption that are required on lines used for broadcasting.

(iv) Connection by automatic equipment at any given time cannot be guaranteed: junctions, overseas circuits—or the number itself—may be engaged.

Clearly, since broadcasting is geared to different technical standards, telephone circuits will not be used except for very good reasons—which should not normally include the economy of opera-

313

tion that is a major criterion for a telephone system. Valid reasons are:

(i) Extreme topicality. With no time to arrange high-quality lines or to get a recording or the man himself to the studio, this is the only way of obtaining his contribution. The justification here is that the same programme value could not have been obtained in any other way.

(ii) Extreme remoteness. Here physical inaccessibility is the problem: the speaker may be in a distant country from which high-quality lines are not available or would be so prohibitively expensive or inconvenient as to limit the availability of information; or in a place which is cut off from outside other than by telephone (or a variant of it). For example, the speaker may be aboard a boat, train, or aeroplane; or in an area which has been struck by natural disaster.

(iii) Audience participation. Here the justification is that the ordinary citizen in his own home may without elaborate pre-planning be invited to take a direct part in the proceedings of which he is normally only a passive witness.

Any of these may be used to justify the remote voice being heard with telephone quality. They cannot, however, excuse a change in quality of the studio voice, which is what would happen if a normal two-wire circuit, which carries both the "transmit" and "receive" elements of the connection, were used on its own for both sides of the conversation. In practice, a feed is taken from the telephone circuit through an amplifier to the studio sound-control desk, where it is mixed with normal studio output to add the full frequency range of the voice at the "near" end of the conversation.

Obviously, for the studio sound to mask the telephone quality version of the same voice the latter must not be mixed in at too high a volume. Special measures may be necessary to avoid this, for it is all too likely that, tapping directly from the telephone circuit so close to the studio, the volume of the distant voice will be reduced by losses on the line, and may therefore be low in comparison with the near voice. For a long-distance call this will depend on the line quality and the distance between the last signal amplifiers and the studio. (This means that in certain studio situations it may be better not to use the local exchange, but instead to have a low-loss line installed to a point which is nearer the "centre" of an area system.)

314

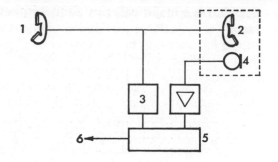

BROADCASTING LIVE TELEPHONE CONVERSATIONS. 1. Remote telephone. 2. Studio telephone. 3. Constant volume amplifier. 4. Studio microphone. 5. Mixer. 6. Studio sound output.

But the most important measure that may be employed is a constant-volume amplifier or (essentially the same thing) a combination of amplifier and limiter. This will ensure that incoming speech is as loud as that originating locally. Note that the gain of a simple limiter should not be set too high (say, a maximum of 8 dB), or line noise may be boosted to an objectionable level during pauses in the conversation. However, if a noise gate is also incorporated in the circuit (and assuming that there is adequate separation between speech and noise level) the gain of the limiter can be substantially increased (see page 435).

The line may be specially provided for programme use, and have its own number independent of that listed for the studio and office complex, or it may be routed through the local switchboard. In either case it is advisable that rather than go directly in to the studio proper the line should terminate at a control point which is under the supervision of the sound man. He may then switch it either to a control telephone, which may be used for engineering tests or production purposes, or to the performer in the studio and, in parallel, the control desk.

In this system the control phone is used to establish the call, which is then checked for quality before transmission: in particular, it is essential to establish that no cross-talk is intelligible. When the circuit is finally switched through to the studio it must be arranged that the control telephone microphone is out of circuit, or noise from the control point will also be heard.

As the call is switched to the studio it is also fed in parallel via the "receive" amplifier to the control desk and to a separate loudspeaker or headphones to "pre-hear" the incoming circuit, so that if the circuit is faded down it may still be monitored.

It should be arranged that the call will remain connected as long as it is routed through to the studio, even if the studio telephone is not picked up, and will not be disengaged at the end of the conversation by putting the studio phone down. It is finally disconnected by switching back to the control phone when this is down (and therefore open-circuit) or by the other party replacing his receiver.

Special services may sometimes be arranged; in particular, "fixed time" calls may be booked in advance. Or it may be that if timing pips would normally be superimposed on a call made with the assistance of an operator these may be suppressed by special request.

From the point of view of the engineers of the telephone service there are two rules that must be observed:

(i) No equipment from which there is any possibility of a dangerous high-voltage signal arising should be connected to the line.

(ii) No abnormally high signals should be transmitted as these would inconvenience other users of the system by inducing abnormally high cross-talk levels.

The way in which calls are used in programmes will normally be subject to some code of practice which is agreed with the Telephone administration. Whether the following are regarded as rules or merely as suggestions for such a code will depend on factors such as the arrangements between the broadcasters and the telephone service concerned, and regulations imposed by the licensing authority. So this may vary from country to country and also with the method of use (recording or live broadcast) and to a lesser extent the type of programme. Some are formulations of common courtesy or common sense; others are designed not to bring into disrepute or draw complaints to co-operating organizations whose service is inevitably seen at a technical disadvantage; yet others are designed to limit intrusion:

(i) Obtain the consent of the other party before a broadcast is made.

(ii) Avoid the use of party lines.

(iii) Do not, in the context of any call, broadcast any criticism, or any comment that may be interpreted as criticism of the telephone service.

(iv) If calls become unintelligible or subject to interference do not persist with their broadcast, but bring them to an end as quickly as possible.

(v) Immediately abandon calls which are interrupted by the operator or by a crossed line. (Someone should ring as soon as possible to explain to the other party what happened.)

(vi) Do not broadcast telephone numbers (or permit them to be broadcast) except by prior arrangement. Special measures may have to be taken to avoid exchange congestion and the blocking of emergency calls: this may prove expensive.

(vii) Do not involve operators or other telephone service staff in the broadcasting of a call. (In Britain the Post Office requires that no reference should be made on the air to Post Office approval having been given either to the transmission or to the equipment used for it.)

Where a conversation is recorded the same result must be achieved as if the item were live—but obviously editing may be used in this case to help achieve it.

In order to ensure that quality is as high as possible, speakers at both ends should be asked to speak clearly but without shouting, not too fast, and with the mouthpiece by the mouth and not under the chin. Broadcast sound should not be audible at the position of the telephone. And if there are parallel extensions at the telephone subscriber's end these should not be used by others listening in to the call, or this, too, will reduce the quality.

10

FADES AND MIXES

THE fade is one of the simplest operations. But as much as anything else, it is the way that fades and mixes are carried out (and more particularly the way they are timed) that distinguishes the polished, finished recording from the one which sounds amateur—in the worst sense of that word. Not every fade consists of a slow, steady movement in or out. A fade has to sound right and not just look smooth. Everything from disc-jockey shows to high drama on film or television depends on a sensitive hand on the sound fader. A good fade has the qualities of a well-played piece of music. A good operator does not wait for a cue and then act on it; he anticipates, and to the onlooker cause and effect will often appear to coincide—but it is, after all, the purpose of rehearsal to ensure that they do.

A more complex form of fading is the mix. Where no mixer is available, it may be that linking music, etc., can be cut in by editing the tape; but I would regard a simpler mixer—with two faders—as the very mimimum for creative programme work.

The film sound recordist working on location will often have a small portable four-channel mixer. The sound supervisor in a television studio will generally have literally dozens of faders beneath his hands.

An alternative to mixing is superimposition; but this has no place in professional work.

"Smooth" fades

What constitutes a smooth fade?

We know that the ear detects changes of volume according to a logarithmic scale (the decibel scale). This means that a linear potentiometer faded out at a steady rate would produce very little drop in volume at first, followed by a much quicker fall away at the lower end. But if, on the other hand, a logarithmic potentiometer were

318

divided up into arcs of equal length, each would represent an equal number of dB. So, for a steady fade-out of an even sound source to sound smooth, a fader which is logarithmic over the greater part of its range should be used.

Over the greater part, but not all; for at the lower end of a fade, as the listener's interest is withdrawn from the sound, the ear will accept a more rapid rounding off. The fade is, in fact, a device for establishing a process of disengagement between listener and scene: once this process is accepted, it only remains to get rid of the tail-end as quickly as possible. Taking this extra condition into account, it seems that the ideal fader should be logarithmic over the upper two-thirds of its arc, with a gradually increasing rate of attenuation at the lower end, until at the bottom stop there is complete cut-off. The best faders designed for professional use work in just this way. Several such types are described in Chapter 2: see pp. 62–67.

The fade in radio

In describing the use of the fade I will deal first with the most extreme case: its use in radio. Types of programme in which fades are used are still an important part of broadcasting in Britain and many other parts of the world. Television and film fades will be dealt with later.

When we talk about the fade, the first thing that springs to mind is the use to which it is put in dramatic productions: the convention is that each scene starts with a fade in, and ends with a fade out. Narration, on the other hand, is cut off almost square—so that there need never be any difficulty in distinguishing between story and storyteller. The type and rate of fade, and the length of pause, each have their own information to give to the listener; so the man taking on the job of creating a sound picture must start out by deciding just what it is that he is trying to convey. The means at his disposal are much more slender than those available for film—which can employ cuts, fades, dissolves, and wipes, plus all the elements of camera technique: pans, tracking shots, and so on. A lot has to be conveyed in sound radio by slight variations in the technique of fading.

When a situation calls for a scene change the simplest form that this can take is a slow fade to silence over about ten seconds, a pause of two or three seconds, and an equally slow fade in. Such a fade implies a complete discontinuity of time and action.

Faster versions of this simple fade will imply shorter lapses of time or smaller changes of location. For instance, the "Maybe its down in the cellar, let's go and see if it's there ... well, here you are, have a look round" type of fade can consist of a very quick out and

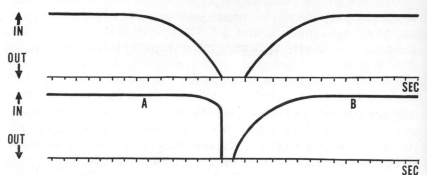

FADES IN DRAMA. *Above*: Simple fades between scenes: smooth fade out, smooth fade in. *Below*: Fades between narration and scene. Slight edge out at end of narration (A) and smooth fade in (B). (For these diagrams, the base line represents silence and the upper limit is normal volume.)

in, just enough to establish that a slight time lapse has taken place (and not just a move off microphone and on again).

Moving off and on, perhaps helped by small fades, is used for still smaller changes of location—say, from one room to the next. In general, it is convenient to assume that a microphone is static within the field of action, although this itself may be moving, such as a scene in a car. Any departure from this convention must be clearly signposted with dialogue or effects, otherwise the listener will be confused. Even a scene that starts near a waiting car which then moves off, may create a moment of confusion during which it is not clear whether the microphone is with the car or not. But the use of suitable dialogue pointers will ensure that the listener has some guide as to what is going on.

The deliberate misuse of pointers can be very funny, as in the hoariest gag in the medium—the one which goes:

FUNNY MAN Quick, drive to Tunbridge Wells.
EFFECTS (*High-powered car departs and fades out.*)
  (*Pause.*)
FUNNY MAN He might have waited for me to get in.

To a limited extent, moves on and off microphone are interchangeable with fades. Tests carried out in the United States showed that listeners found that a fade gave just as good an impression of moving off as did actual movement. However, it only works this way

320

round: if a move is used to represent a fade the change in acoustic perspective usually shows, and makes the effect sound rather odd. Actors sometimes helpfully offer to do what is called a "self-fade" (i.e. a move representing a fade); but such a device can hardly be expected to work except in acoustically dead conditions.

Occasionally quite complicated faking has to be worked out in the studio; for example, where a fade is combined with increasing artificial echo to suggest a move off in reverberant surroundings.

There is one case where a fade is definitely preferable to moving off. This is when outdoor scenes are being re-created in the studio. Open-air scenes are—or should be—characterized by lack of reverberant sound, and when played indoors in a confined "dead" area, moves off microphone will inevitably show up the reverberation from the open studio. A fade, on the other hand, may result in temporary loss of studio atmosphere, so it may be necessary to cover this with some light background effects mixed in from a record.

Depth of fade

How deep should a fade be? Obviously, if a scene has a good curtain line it must not be faded very much; or if the first line of a new scene contains important information a quick fade-in is necessary. In both cases we have to ensure that the adjacent fade is of the conventional slow-fade type, otherwise the impression of a scene change will be completely lost—the result could easily sound like a pause in the conversation.

But apart from such special cases, most fades fall into one of two main groups, or programme types. First, there are the full-scale dramatic productions: these tend to have long, deep fades, taken almost to inaudibility before being cut off. Second, there are feature programmes in the form of narration and actuality recordings (or narration and dramatic scenes presented in a documentary style): in these partial fades are common, as against the complete fades which are to be found in plays.

Schools broadcasts in Britain (supplied by transcription to most other parts of the world) generally have relatively light fades, whether they are dramatic or documentary in style. Part of the cause lies in the listening conditions in classrooms; the radio set may be poor, and the room boomy. The producers of these programmes make a point of listening under the same conditions as school audiences from time to time—and as a result tend to prefer a high-

321

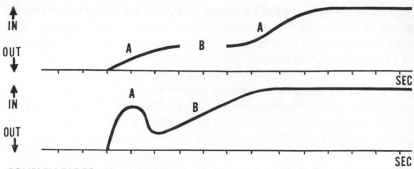

COMPLEX FADES. *Above*: (A) Speech. (B) Silence. Do not fade in on silence. *Below*: Complex fade to accommodate quiet effect at start. At (A) fader is open for "Door Opens" then taken back for fade-in (B) on speech.

intelligibility type of construction, with low dynamic range and background effects held well down so that they do not interfere with speech.

Average listening conditions in many parts of the world may be expected to be poor, either because crowded short or medium wave transmissions are heard by many at the limit of their range, or because car or small "transistor" radios are largely used by the audience. If this is the case, a form of presentation that uses fairly shallow fades will be necessary.

Complex fades

Difficulties arise when a scene starts off with some such stage instruction as "Enter Wilberforce". The trouble is that it is not really possible to establish a location clearly, and the entry of the first speaking character into it, in just a few seconds. To make it quite clear what is going on, it is necessary to fade in on effects of other people talking, and *then* "Enter Wilberforce". But such a "radio script" will probably have to be reinterpreted; and here the likely solution is simply to forget the instruction and rely on the text, acoustics, and effects to establish the situation instead.

It is better, in fact, to go to the other extreme with fades, exits, and entrances, and be very deliberate about them. And this often means breaking a fade up into several parts, for there is not much point in fading during a pause. This may seem obvious, but in practice it is often ignored. So, if Wilberforce has two lines to speak during his approach, most of the fading in should be done while he is doing the talking and not during the intervening line.

322

This is true of any fade-in: it is better to hold it momentarily if there is a pause in the speech. It may even be necessary to reset, jumping up or down in level between lines from different speakers, if the overall effect of the fade is to be smooth. A graceful fade during a pause, or an actor stalking menacingly up to a microphone in silence means nothing in radio terms.

"Door opens": this is another instruction which may head a scene. If such an effect is to be clear it will have to be recorded at getting on for normal level, and the fader will then have to be taken back a little for the fade-in proper. But, in general, a short spot-effect of this sort is not really recommended for the start of a scene.

The fade with effects

If you adopt a convention in radio whereby each scene opens and closes with a fade it is pretty obvious that some sound is required for the fade in each case—and this usually has to be an unimportant throw-away line from one of the characters. Dramatically this is rather weak construction—starting and ending every scene with a line which is deliberately weak—so ways are constantly being devised for getting round it. One of these shows itself up as the often-repeated instruction "fade out on laughter". But this itself can become a cliché if over-used.

A much better way of closing a scene quickly is possible when background effects are being used. As the scene comes to a close the speech is faded down and the effects are lifted to swamp the line. Then after the effects have been peaked for a few seconds they too can be slowly faded out.

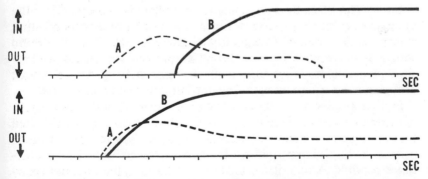

FADES WITH EFFECTS. *Above:* Establishing effects (A) before speech (B), on separate faders. *Below:* Fading up effects (A) with speech (B), and then holding them back to avoid an excess of distracting backing sound.

323

Similarly, a continuous background of sound may be used for a fade-in—such effects are very useful indeed for establishing new localities—and here again the sound may be peaked for a short while, and then faded gently down as the dialogue is brought up.

Another way of handling a fade in is to bring up speech and effects almost together, though here again the effects should be slightly ahead of speech—sufficiently so for it to be clear to the listener what they represent. Otherwise they may distract his attention from the first words that he should be hearing. The more complicated the background effects, the more likely it is that they will need to be established first, though the final decision will necessarily depend on the story. And in either case they will nearly always have to be dropped to a lower level behind the main body of the scene than they are at the beginning and end. The level may in fact have to be unrealistically low (this is one of the ways in which mono differs from stereo, where the spread background can be much louder without interfering with intelligibility).

Effects behind and between scenes

It is a good idea to vary the levels of effects behind a long scene almost continuously—just enough to prevent the sound from becoming dull. When doing this, tend to have the backing lowest behind speech which it is important to "get over" for the plot, and loudest when dialogue is inconsequential, or there is reference to the backing sound, or when characters are pitching their voices against it. (Although in any case actors should be encouraged to sharpen the tone of their voices, if in similar natural circumstances they would do so.)

Effects can often be peaked as a bridge between two parts of the same scene: different conversations at a party can merge into and emerge from a swell of background chatter. In film terms, this is the equivalent of a number of different camera treatments, such as a slow pan or a tracking shot from one group to another; or one group moving off and another group on before a static camera.

Note how easy it can be, when constructing a scene for radio, to imagine that you are being more precise in terms of movement than in fact you are. Fortunately it is not usually very important if the listener has a different picture from you. Nevertheless, it is sometimes possible to be a little more precise and to give the impression of a tracking shot, by peaking effects and then gradually changing their content; you can, for example, move from general party chat-

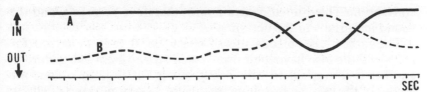

MIXING EFFECTS. Background effects (B) can often be varied continuously and can sometimes be peaked to bridge scenes, as fader for speech (A) is dipped.

ter to a relatively quiet "balcony scene"; and the best way of doing this is by means of an effects mix.

One should beware of over-use of background effects. Used for occasional scenes, the result is to enliven a production. Used for every scene, the result may be tedious—the more so if they are too loud. Some relief from distracting backings is necessary now and then. Do not be too "busy".

Fades in television and film

The techniques of fading so far described apply particularly to sound radio. For television and films the rate of fade and timing of any pause is normally set by the picture: in the simplest case a fade of picture is matched exactly by fade of sound. This is made slightly more complex if there is a low-level but significant sound during the fade; this sound may be emphasized disproportionately. Similarly, if there is an effect of little significance, but which would be too loud, this can be reduced. Minor variations of this sort will normally be fairly obvious both in the television studio and in the film dubbing theatre.

Hardly less obvious are the uses that can be found for effects and music during fades of the picture. For example, to bridge a time lapse in a party scene, it may be appropriate to peak the chatter background up, rather than fade it out. This will firmly imply that action and location are unchanged during the time lapse (if the new scene then turned out to be a different party a deliberate incongruity would have been introduced). A change of scene from one noisy location to another might be made by peaking effects against the fade and mixing while the picture is faded out. This will work best if the two sounds are characteristically different.

This is a technique which should be used only with calculated and deliberate intent. It is self-conscious in that it draws attention to technique as such—at least for as long as it takes to establish a

325

convention. The dramatic reason must therefore be strong, and the sound important to the action.

The rather less obvious use of effects as already described for fades in radio also have their uses. When mixing from one picture to another it is normal to mix backgrounds (or fade in or out the louder of the two) to match picture. Here a slight peaking of effects to bridge the mix may be readily accepted.

Location cuts

More interesting—because more open to the creative use of sound —is the picture cut from one location to another. The simplest case, however, uses a straight cut with dialogue (or strong action) to carry it. For example:

Vision:	Sound:
Midshot oilman: turns on last words to see distant figure striding out towards burning rig	*Effects: Burning oil rig* OILMAN: Sure it's easy. When you've stayed alive as long as this boy has the hardest job is working out what to write on the paper.
Paper in manager's hands: fast tilt up to C. S. face	MANAGER: Two and a half million! . . .

Here the effects behind the first scene must disappear very fast. They should not be cut in the physical sense of cutting tape or film sound, or there will be a click as they go. Anything just short of this will be satisfactory. If the scenes are staged in a television studio the background to the first shot will perhaps be on back-projection with effects from sound tape or disc (or the whole action of the first shot might be on film). The effects would be whipped out *on* the cut. This is difficult to time accurately, and there is a danger of trailing slightly behind, and so damaging the dramatic effect.

An alternative is to introduce a recording cut at this point. If this is a physical cut in the videotape the sound will have to be dubbed. (This is due to the displacement between the sound and picture recording heads, see p. 456). Videotape machines are now engineered to avoid a click as the audio condition is switched on or off.

Another television technique which avoids the use of a fader is to stop the recording at the end of the first scene, run the tape back, and switch sound and picture to record again, on cue. The same sharp, but click-free change of effects will be achieved.

If both of the shots in the sequence above are on film a quick fade will be used. The first effects track will probably be laid (see p. 483)

326

to overlap into the next scene. The dubbing mixer (p. 488) will then rehearse the cut using the picture and footage counter until he can fade on the cut and not a few frames after.

The next example uses a variety of techniques to cover three shots:

Vision:	Sound:
Through archway to cathedral tower; tilt down to low angle, boys walk through arch and past camera.	*Effects: Singing of distant choir; chatter, footsteps.* COMMENTARY: In the shadow of the mediaeval cathedral this group's interest in electronics complements traditional activities like choral singing. . . . RUGGER PLAYER: Break!
Wide shot, football field, cathedral, and old school buildings in background; pan left as ball and players cross diagonally towards camera; when centred on science block, zoom past and in to windows.	COMMENTARY: . . . and Rugby football. Perhaps rather surprisingly, the work we're going to see started not with physics, but here in the chemistry lab.
Wide high shot, inside laboratory; various experimental groups, with two boys and glassware dominating foreground.	BOY: Oh, no! If we've got to do this, it's set all wrong. . . .

In this story the picture has been shot with the commentary in mind (indeed, the second shot would have been meaningless otherwise). The music was recorded separately; but chatter and footsteps, football effects and laboratory sound were all recorded in sync. with the picture. The chatter and footsteps track was, however, displaced a few frames because the approach matched better with the tilt down when this was done.

The music was held low from the start and chatter and effects faded in to dominate it with the tilt down.

The shout "break" cued the cut to the football field and killed the music. The football effects which continued on the same track had therefore been brought up to their full volume before the picture cut. With the first zoom the effects dipped sharply to a level matching that of the laboratory, so that a quick mix on the cut was all that was required.

The key device here was that of sound anticipating picture. Here the result was natural—rather like someone hearing a noise in a street and turning to see where and what it was. It can also be used for strongly dramatic cuts. More noticeably to the viewer, the anticipation of sound can be used stylistically, as when the football fan has been talking about the big match, lapses into a daydream during which we hear the sounds of the crowd distantly as though in his thoughts, followed by a cut to a crowd scene at the match and the roar of the crowd at full volume.

The whip pan

The whip pan generally implies a spatial relationship and as such may offer interesting possibilities for the use of sound (this refers to the whip pan proper and not the flashing blur that is sometimes cut between static scenes to give an illusion of pace in moving from location to location).

Here is another example:

Vision:	Sound:
Low angle through rigging to flag on mast	*Music: military band starts playing*
Low angle, figurehead of Nelson, band crossing R–L	COMMENTARY: And the martial music, the uniforms, the disipline, and the impressive reminders of a glorious past,
Closer shot figurehead . . . whip pan R, tilting down	all tell us that this school trains its boys for the sea . . . .
Cut in to matching whip pan to boys turning capstan	*Effects: capstan, footsteps, creaking ropes*
Closer shot, pairs of boys on spokes of capstan, passing through shot	Their project, too, is suitably nautical.
M.S. boy; in background, boat being hauled up slipway	BOY: With two of our boats at school we had a problem. . . .

In this case the whip pan was not a single shot of the two objects: the figure-head and the capstan were in fact separated by about half a mile. But they were all part of the same general location which was being suggested by a series of atmospheric detail shots rather than a wide shot which would have been relatively dull.

Sound has an important part to play in this. The sync. music from the second shot was laid back over the first (mute) shot and also carried on through the whip pan, through dropping sharply during the camera movement. On the capstan shot the associated effect (which had been recorded wild-track) was allowed to dominate, and the music eventually faded out under the boy's speech. The capstan noise, which was relevant to what he was saying and to subsequent shots, was held low behind him.

The use of sound in these various ways is suitable to both television and film. So, too, is the use of music links between scenes. Indeed, the music "bridge" is a device common to radio, television, and film.

Theme, background, and linking music

Few things about radio or television plays attract so much controversy as the use of music. This is because to be really effective—and indeed, to get a return on the cost and effort of using specially

328

composed music—it will often be reasonably loud. And in the home many people like speech loud and music soft (the cinema audience, however, is less likely to complain). Most people agree that where it succeeds, music helps to create works of the highest quality; but at worst it may merely be used to smudge a little elegance over a scene that would have been as effective with good natural sound.

In so far as television shows works which are the product of, or derived in style from, the older traditions of the film industry, music is still definitely "in". But with financial economy as the keynote of modern television, simpler styles have been evolved, artistically justified and found to be effective. An increased use of well-recorded effects is linked with this. Effects are cheaper, and can serve many of the purposes that music was formerly used for. So it follows—even more than ever it did—that music must be selected with the utmost care (and rejected if the perfect fit is not forthcoming), and it must be integrated into programmes with considerable delicacy.

The ideal, for those with sufficient resources of money or talent, or both, is specially recorded music; but links or background music may be found in the "mood" record catalogues. However, mood music remains rather out of fashion in Britain for straightforward dramatic productions, although links are still used in plays where there is a strong element of fantasy, whimsy, or pastiche (and in light entertainment), or where some binding element is needed for a programme which would otherwise be too fragmentary. But it is much easier to lose tension and coarsen the texture with music than to enhance it. So the number one rule about music is: when in doubt, don't.

One should, of course, avoid popular and recognizable music unless it is to be featured as itself—and remember that all but the most out-of-the-way records are likely to figure as "popular" and "recognizable" to some people in most audiences.

Signature tunes or theme music must be in harmony with or provide a counterpoint to the qualities of the programmes they punctuate; in fact, at the start of a programme they must help to define the mood of what is to follow, and at the end, sum up what has gone before. But another criterion which might well be applied to choosing this, or any other sort of linking music, is "fadeability". Whatever other quality it may have, it is important that there are points at which it can be got in and out tidily, and this in a piece of the right duration.

Clearly there is no necessity to use the same section of a work at both the beginning and end of a programme (if, indeed, the same

329

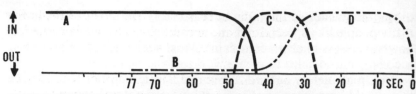

PREFADING MUSIC. The prefade time is the number of seconds from the scheduled end of programme (in this case 77 seconds). (A) Last item of programme. (B) Closing music playing but not faded up. (C) Announcer. (D) Music faded up to close programme.

work is used at all). As the ideas have progressed in the intervening time, so it is reasonable to have a piece at the end which is a fairly complex development of that heard at the start. For some works this rather conveniently means that the end of the record can be used for the end of the programme. But it is not so common for the start of a record to provide a good crisp opening signature; more often it is necessary to disregard any introduction and start clean on the main theme.

For the close of many radio programmes *prefaded* music is used: this is a device which is used to ensure that a programme space is filled exactly, to the last second. (The term "prefade" here means "not yet faded up". Another word for this is "deadroll".)

In the case of a typical prefade (that used for the BBC's Radio Newsreel) it is known that the duration from a certain easily recognizable point to the end of the record is exactly 1' 17". So the record is started exactly 1' 17" from the end of the programme. It is usually arranged that no more than about 15" to 30" is actually needed; and this last remaining part of the record is faded up under the announcer's last words—or a little earlier if a suitable phrase presents itself to the disc player, who should be listening on headphones.

Obviously, vocal music is not usually suitable for prefading, and is therefore rarely used for a closing signature tune.

Mixing from speech to music

To examine the manner by which music and speech may be linked together I will deal first with a few of the ways in which it can be done in a disc-jockey show. The treatment of music in dramatic or magazine programmes will be similar in many respects—subject to the rule that in such cases music should not be obtrusive, i.e. it should be at a much lower level than featured music. In practice, this means that almost every fade or mix is different and must be judged according to the individual needs of the situation. And for this the factors to be taken into account include not just the immediate context, but the mood, pace, and style of the programme as a whole.

Within a single programme, many different types of fade may be used. Taking a typical case of a "pop" vocal with a short instrumental introduction, here are some of the ways in which the transition from speech to music may be arranged.

(i) *"Straight"—or nearly so.* But remember that the "intro." on the record is now no longer an introduction: it has become a music link between the preceding speech and the vocal which follows, and its level can often be altered with advantage to match the speech better. After this has been done, the record may be faded (up or down) to a suitable overall level. The first notes of the intro. can sometimes be emphasized to give "bite" to an unusual start.

(ii) *Cutting the introduction.* The first word of the vocal follows the cue fairly quickly, as though it were a second voice in a briskly conducted argument (the exact timing being determined by the pace and inflection of the cue). It may be necessary to edge the record in a little.

(iii) *Introduction under speech.* Here the start of the music is timed and placed at an appropriate point under the cue, which must be specially written. The intro. has to be played at a fairly low level, so that it does not distract from the intelligibility of the speech; and there may be a break in the cue in which the music may be heard on its own for a few seconds—i.e. it is *established.* The fade-up generally starts just before the final words and is then lifted to be at or near full volume for the start of the vocal, which should follow the cue after no more than a breath pause.

A similar range of fades could be listed for the transition from music back to speech.

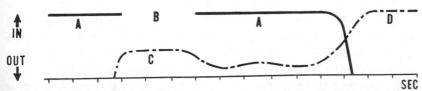

MIXING FROM SPEECH TO MUSIC. Intro. under speech (A). During the pause (B) the music (C) is started and then dipped behind continuing announcement. It is finally lifted on cue to its full volume (D).

Joining music to music

A link from one piece of music to another can be complicated—or very simple. The simplest case is, of course, the *segue* (pronounced "seg-way" and meaning follow-on), in which the new number follows either after a very short pause or in time with the previous piece. Sometimes an announcement may be spoken over the intro. at a convenient point, or over the join—though starting an announcement at exactly the same moment as the new number can be confusing, and as a general rule is best avoided unless the continuity between the two pieces of music is perfect.

In some cases it may be better to avoid endings and introductions by *mixing* from one number to another. Each two- or three-minute number on a "pop" gramophone record is, naturally, written and recorded as though it were a complete programme in itself. It has, like any other complete and individual work, a beginning, a middle, and an end. But in a fast-moving record programme it may be only the middle that is wanted, or the intro. (or ending) may be too "big" (or weak) to go into the programme without throwing it out of shape.

A mix from one record to another can be very tricky, and unless the cross is just right, the result may sound ugly. If the rhythm is strong in both pieces perfect timing is essential. But the mix may be easier if the music reaches a point where its form is not too definite, e.g. where one number can be faded on a long sustained note and the other brought in on a rising arpeggio or glissando. But—and this is a big but—whereas this sort of programme can be great fun to put together, and will certainly earn the applause of those who know what went into its making, it may not necessarily give the average listener a vast increase in listening pleasure. So do not mess discs around just for the sake of doing so.

Key sequences

A segue or mix is only possible if keys are the same or suitably related. Indeed, it may be that keys which are nominally the same may not be close enough in pitch without a slight adjustment of the playing speeds. Expert musical knowledge is not necessary for this; though a reasonably good sense of relative pitch is essential.

In any record programme it is a good thing to give an occasional thought to the key sequence (this also can be done by ear): a lively variety of keys will help to give vitality to the overall picture. The question is, how to get from one key to another. In a single piece of music this is generally done through a progression of related keys. This may not be possible when linking together several pre-recorded items, so, unless a deliberate dissonance is wanted, some other means of softening the transition must be found. There is a story of a music-hall conductor who, whenever he was faced with the problem of a quick modulation, simply wrote in a cymbal crash and immediately led off in the new key! The cymbal crash—a sudden loud noise of indefinite pitch—was designed to make the listeners forget the key that had gone before. In radio work a slightly more subtle means to the same end is used—the announcement.

With an announcement between two items, even a very short one of five seconds or so, difficulties over pitch tend to disappear. The ear will not register a dissonance if the two sounds are spaced out and the attention distracted by speech. Happily this means that programmes can be compiled according to content, with suitable contrasts of style and pace between items, and without worrying too much about keys.

But there is one special case of a linking announcement which does take key-change very much into account, a technique adopted by a disc jockey who, taking up the key at the end of each record, "doodled" on the piano until the end of his spoken comments and then finished up in the right key for the next record. The adjustment of levels between live piano and record requires even more care than usual, if the transition is to sound smooth.

The methods outlined above apply particularly to record programmes, of course; but the same principles apply where live or pre-recorded music has to be linked together.

Adding speech to music

Where speech is added *to* music, e.g. as in the case of theme music with announcements or introductory comments superimposed, the voice will normally be chosen for high intelligibility. The music can therefore often be given its full value and dipped only just in time to accommodate the first word. Similarly ensuring only that the last word is clear, the music will be brought up close on the tail of speech. Also, in anything longer than a breath pause in speech, the music will be peaked up. This is called a "newsreel" commentary and music mix after the old style of filmed newsreel in which the inconvenience of synchronized speech—or even sound effects—was avoided.

At the end of a programme an up-beat finish may demand that

music, applause, and speech all fight each other: here, similar techniques may again be used. But in neither case should it be forgotten that for many of the audience disengagement will be accelerated only by what at home just sounds like a loud and not particularly pleasant noise.

An alternative, and much more relaxed, way of mixing music and speech is to employ gentle music fades before and after the speech.

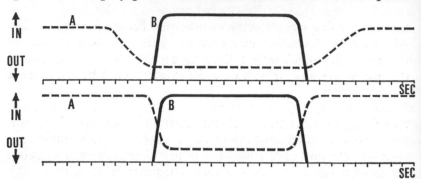

FILM MUSIC AND COMMENTARY. *Above*: normal cueing. Music (A) is gradually adjusted in volume so that commentary or other speech (B) is clearly audible when it starts. After the speech ends, the level is adjusted gently. (Alternatively the music may be written or chosen specially to give this effect.) *Below*: "Newsreel" cueing. Music (A) is held at high volume until a moment before speech (B) starts, and is raised to high level again immediately speech ends. Adjustments are rapid.

This has the doubtful virtue that it does not excessively distort the musical levels—doubtful, I say, because film music (or supporting music in radio and television) does not have any prior right to be considered as a work of art separate from the completed work, any more than does, say, a series of individual frames from the picture—however well composed.

Editing music into programmes

In the absence of suitable equipment it is often possible to introduce music links into a programme without using a mixer—by editing. But before inserting the music it will usually be necessary to copy the original recording in order to get the level of the in and out points exactly right.

There are a number of points to keep in mind when inserting music links into a non-musical programme. First, remember to keep the music level low, unless a shock effect is wanted. Often a slight fade-in will make the start sound smoother.

If the fade-in adopted is a long, deep one, it may be cut as close

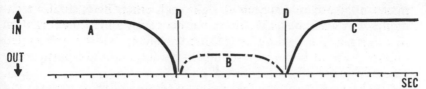

MUSIC LINK EDITED BETWEEN SPEECH. (A) End of one scene. (B) Music link. (C) Start of next scene. (D) Tape edits.

to the preceding speech as the reverberation on that speech allows. Alternatively, the fade-in may be in two parts: a very sharp fade-up to a certain point below the full required level followed by an edge-in the rest of the way. In this case the music cannot be cut quite so close to speech.

The fade-out may be equally complex. At the end of a long deep fade the tape can be cut very close to the following speech. The result may actually sound to the ear like a slight overlap. But do not slice into the end of the music fade to "improve" on this effect— the result would be an obvious join. The other method, a two-stage fade (slow and then sharp) is more tricky to get just right, as the ending must be timed perfectly according to the music, and the last sound heard must be at such a level that the lack of reverberation is not noticeable.

Superimposition

There remains one final method of adding sounds together— superimposition. If a second recording is made on a tape which already has a recording on it (i.e. where the initial recording is not wiped by the erase head) the result will be a composite sound consisting of a high-quality superimposed foreground mixed with background remnants of the first recording. The high-frequency bias which accompanies the second audio signal will act as an inefficient erase current and partially wipe what was already on the tape. One way to control superimposition is to vary the strength of the erase current.

But because the quality of the initial recording is impaired, superimposition is not regarded as a valid professional technique.

335

11

ECHO AND DISTORTION

"Echo" is something of a misnomer for a studio technique which serves to extend reverberation without (it is hoped) introducing any actual echoes, but the name has stuck. It is used on occasions when more reverberation is wanted than the built-in acoustics of a studio can supply, or (for music) when a multi-microphone close-balance technique has been adopted.

Two satisfactory methods are the echo chamber and the reverberation plate: both produce a random decay of sound by a system of multiple reflections; and the main technical design problem in each case is the removal or avoidance of distinctive colourations.

As an example of a typical echo chain I will describe the layout adopted by the BBC. The following are the standard facilities which are available for all but simple radio talk studios.

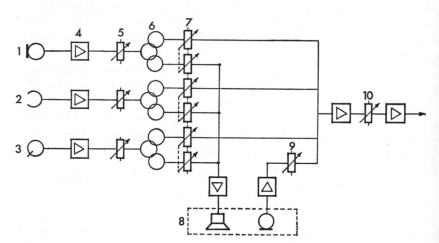

SPLIT FEED SYSTEM FOR ECHO. 1 Microphone. 2. Tape reproducer. 3. Gramophone pick-up. 4. Preamplifiers. 5. Source faders. 6. Hybrid transformer giving independent feeds. 7. Echo mixture switches (ganged). 8. Echo chamber. 9. Echo fader. 10. Main control.

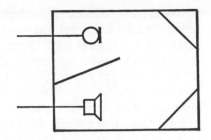

ECHO CHAMBER. A U-shaped room is often used to increase the distance the sounds must travel from loudspeaker to microphone.

After passing through its pre-amplifier and fader the output from each of the sources (microphones, tapes, grams, etc.) is split and the second leg is fed to the loudspeaker in the echo chamber (or to the input of the echo plate). But for each source there is also an echo mixture switch, which is used to control the proportion of the two feeds. In its central position both are fed at full volume; turning one way, the echo feed is reduced to zero; turning the other, the "direct" is cut down instead (a two-pole, nine-position switch is used). The output from the echo chamber microphone is returned to the control desk as an additional source with its own individual fader.

The echo chamber

The echo chamber itself may be a room with "bright" reflecting walls, perhaps with "junk" littered about at random, in order to break up the reflections and mop up excess mid-range reverberation. Or it may have a wall most of the way down the middle, so that sound has to follow a U-shaped path. Or a disused stone staircase can be used.

A humid atmosphere will give a strong high-frequency response; a dry one will absorb top. An echo chamber linked to the outside atmosphere will vary with the weather.

The shape and size of the room controls the quality of reverberation which is produced, and where space is limited small rooms have to be used, often resulting in an unpleasant timbre. Echo chambers seem to have distinctive—and sometimes difficult—personalities. Another disadvantage of the echo chamber is that, once laid out, its reverberation time is fixed. If this is about two seconds it may be suitable for music but less satisfactory for drama: a little echo goes a long way on monophonic speech. If, however, only a touch of echo is used on speech, it will be noticeable only on the louder sounds; a situation which corresponds well with what we observe and in real life. In this case the rather overlong reverberation time will

337

be apparently reduced. (Another way of dealing with this would be to replay a tape through the echo chamber and re-record, with both machines running at half speed—or at double speed for doubling the apparent reverberation time.)

One reason for some of the problems met in using echo rooms is that they are often made rather small, i.e. about 4000 cubic feet or even less. As a result there is broadly spaced colouration, due to the natural room resonances in the lower middle frequency range. These and any other peaks in the response are emphasized by the many reflections that there will be in a given time in a small volume.

Another element to add to the cost of these rooms is that, like radio studios, they need to be isolated from structure-borne noise. Otherwise—even at best—whenever alterations are being carried out, even in distant parts of the same building, the echo chamber will be out of commission unless all noisy work is stopped; at worst it could resonate to every footfall in the rooms above or around.

An advantage of echo chambers is that their decay is natural: in particular, as the sound continues to reverberate in three dimensions, the wave gets broken up into reflections that reach the microphone at progressively shorter intervals until, long before the decay is complete, the reverberation is apparently continuous.

If an echo chamber is used to simulate a large hall, in addition to having the appropriate reverberation time there should be a reduced response at high frequencies to correspond to the long air paths, and suitable delay before the "first reflection". If the shortest direct path between echo loudspeaker and microphone is too short to give such a feeling of spaciousness, tape delay can be used to lengthen it.

The reverberation plate

Another device—more versatile than the echo chamber because its reverberation time may be varied—is the reverberation plate. In principle, this plate is rather like the sheet of metal that used to be used in the theatre to create a thunder effect, except that, instead of being shaken by hand and delivering its energy directly to the air, it has two transducers. One of these vibrates the plate, rather as the coil vibrates the paper cone in a moving-coil loudspeaker; and the other, acting as a contact microphone, picks up the vibrations. (It is possible to make an electronic thundersheet by using a suspended metal plate and a contact microphone or adapted gramophone pick-up.)

338

Reverberation plates have a tinned steel sheet suspended in tension from a tubular steel frame at the four corners. To reduce the metallic quality of the resonance to proportions that are acceptable for most purposes a minimum size of 2 square metres is combined with a maximum thickness of half a millimetre. This thickness of

REVERBERATION PLATE. I. Metal Sheet. 2. Tubular steel frame. 3. Damping plate, pivoted at 4. (Here the spacing is shown as being set by the hand-wheel, but many damping plates are motor driven from a point on the sound control desk.) D. Drive unit. M. Contact microphone.

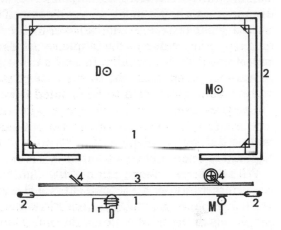

steel plate has good transverse vibrational properties (other metals are internally damped too quickly). Unlike the echo chamber, these natural resonances at low frequencies do not thin out to sharp peaks at the lower frequencies, but are spread fairly evenly throughout the audio range.

Colouration may also be caused by any irregularity in the flatness of the sheet. In the early days of production this was a major problem, as steel sheet rolling mills did not work to the very close tolerances that are required. Samples had to be held in suspension for several days before tests for suitability could be carried out, and many had to be discarded at this stage. In addition it was established that the contact microphone and the brass rod from the drive unit must be of low weight and have to be spot welded to the sheet (the use of bolts or rivets will not do).

A moving-coil-drive unit is anchored to a bridge across the frame and a piezo-electric contact microphone is used to pick up the sound (see p. 159); the two are asymmetrically placed on the plate. The frequency characteristic of the plate itself, the two transducers and their amplifiers are ingeniously arranged to give a response that is suitable overall. For normal reverberation this has its maximum duration at mid-frequencies, with some roll-off in the bass and rather more at higher frequencies (15 dB at 10 kHz), thereby simulating the h.f. absorption of the air of a room of moderate size. To achieve this, some damping has to be applied: without it, the response of the plate would rise to very high values in the extreme bass.

To produce this damping, and to control the reverberation time, a thin, stiff, porous foil is rigidly held at a controlled but variable distance from the plate: 0·8 mm of a compressed glass-fibre material is used (light textiles would move with the air and thicker fibrous materials give an unsuitable frequency characteristic). The mechanism of absorption depends on the fact that although there is little acoustic radiation from the reverberating plate, standing waves are set up near the surface, with the result that if the damping plate is in the way, energy is absorbed and the reverberation time thereby reduced. (It is interesting to note that this mechanism differs from that used in normal sound absorption, in that no great thickness is required to absorb low frequencies.)

With the broadest separation of the damping plate (120 mm) there is a reverberation of 5·3 seconds at 500 Hz, dropping to 1·5 seconds at 10 kHz: this is similar to the response that may be found in excessively reverberant large spaces such as some cathedral interiors. The narrowest separation between the plates is as small as 3 mm: this gives a reverberation of 0·3 second. In the simplest version, the separation can be varied manually by turning a wheel at the top of the outer box; but the damping plates may also be motorized, with push-button control and a reverberation time indicator on the control desk: this allows experimental changes to be made at any time during rehearsal. During a take any change would normally be made with echo faded out—though, in fact, the motor noise is not loud.

It is an advantage of reverberation plates that their two-dimensional structure allows the wave to radiate outwards and break up, producing reflections that arrive in increasing numbers as reverberation continues and dies away. This effect is not actually so marked as with three-dimensional reverberation, but cannot easily be distinguished from it.

With a plate, having a short direct path between the transducers is unavoidable, so, once again, to simulate a large hall tape delay can be introduced into the echo feed.

There may be difficulties in finding a suitable place to stand the plate: it needs to be kept fairly quiet as it picks up noise from the air. In particular it cannot be kept in the control cubicle, as with very high loudspeaker levels howl round may occur at 200 Hz. The studio lobby is a reasonable place if there is room; or some separate quiet room—perhaps with other plates for other studios (they do not affect each other).

With the plate, as with an echo chamber or any other room, the nature of the decay process means that there is likely to be some colouration. As I have already indicated, within limits this is desirable in that it gives a sense of shape and size to a sound; but it is very easy for these limits to be exceeded and for the colouration to assert itself unpleasantly. The positioning of the two transducers on the plate will give some degree of control over this. Incidentally, there may be quite a significant signal taking the direct path between the two transducers (a condition which can be avoided in the chamber), and this means that there is a limit to the porportion of echo that can be mixed with a sound if the plate is being used. But this is a restriction which is very rarely of importance—and far outweighed by the convenience of being able to vary the reverberation time.

Tape delay and water-tank reverberation

Other systems have also been invented: for example, tape delay systems in which a sound fed on to a tape loop is reproduced by a number of heads spaced out around it. This magnetic artificial reverberation machine suffers from the disadvantage that there are

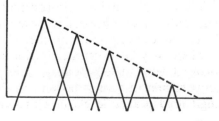

ECHO WITH COATED WHEEL OR TAPE LOOP. I. Input to recording head. 2. Output. 3. Erase circuit. 4. Output mixer. 5. A feed from the last head may be used to continue the sound at progressively lower levels.

APPARENT REVERBERATION FROM TAPE LOOP OR FEED-BACK ECHO. A hard mechanical quality is generally obtained.

341

too few simulated "reflections", so that the effect, lacking the natural colour and warmth of room acoustics, tends to sound mechanical and dehumanized. But this does have its applications in *musique concrète* transformations (see p. 369), as well as for "pop" gimmicks.

Another device is the water-tank artificial reverberation machine (sometimes used in conjunction with the magnetic machine), in which the sound is modulated on to a 80-kHz carrier and fed via a piezo-electric element to produce pressure waves in the water-tank. A second contact element picks up the direct "sound" and its many reflections, and after demodulation the signal is returned to the control desk. A disadvantage of the water-tank system is that standing waves are set up at low frequencies.

A relatively inexpensive device uses a system of springs as the reverberating element.

Stereo "echo"

Echo mixture switches are included in both mono and stereo channels of a stereo mixer.

On the stereo channel there will generally be separate switchable echo feeds from the A and B signals. These may be fed to separate A and B echo devices (e.g. springs) or combined as a single A + B

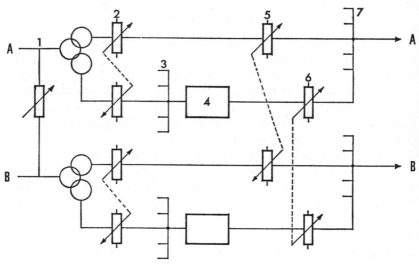

STEREOPHONIC ARTIFICIAL REVERBERATION—using separate echo devices (e.g. spring systems) on A and B channels. 1. Width control. 2. Echo mixture switches. 3. Echo feeds from other sources in the same group. 4. Echo devices. 5. Channel offset control. 6. Echo fader. 7. Group star-mixer.

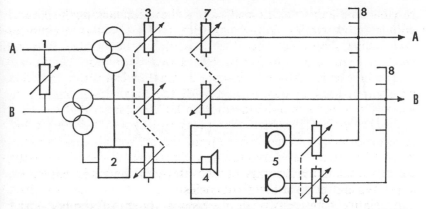

STEREOPHONIC ARTIFICIAL REVERBERATION—using echo room. I. Width control. 2. Echo selection (A, B, or A + B). 3. Echo mixture switch. 4. Echo room loudspeaker. 5. A and B echo microphones. 6. Echo fader. 7. Channel offset control. 8. Group star mixers.

signal to be fed to an echo chamber. The echo chamber, although having only one loudspeaker, will have two microphones the output from which will reappear on the mixer as new A and B sources.

Monophonic sources in stereo will often require stereo echo, as the balance usually has to be very close and dead to avoid "tunnel" acoustic reverberation.

Using "echo"

Reverberation is added by an echo chamber in direct proportion to the volume of sound fed into it. If an actor works close to the microphone and whispers, this will, for the same setting of the echo fader, produce just as much reverberation as there would be with the actor standing ten feet away and shouting. So the first thing to remember about using echo in drama is to watch perspective effects: these will have to be re-created from scratch. As an actor moves in towards the microphone the echo fader will have to be faded down.

However, if there are other voices or sound effects in a different perspective to be taken at the same time a more complex set-up will be necessary; and a particularly useful arrangement has a second bi-directional microphone, with a strong echo feed, suspended above the main working microphone, which itself has little or no echo. Then, as the actor moves in close to the lower microphone he moves out of the field of pick-up of the upper one. In this way perspectives can be emphasized without constant resort to the echo fader. This refine-ment is more likely to be of use in radio than in the visual media

343

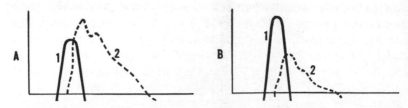

ECHO MIXTURES. With separate control of direct (I) and echo (2) feeds, a wide range of effects is possible. In (A) reverberation dominates the sound, and in (B) tails gently behind it.

where there are restrictions on the ideal placing of microphones.

When echo is wanted on only one voice, as, for example, in a conversation between two people, one of whom is at the bottom of a well, control over this can be exercised with the echo-mixture switch. With the echo fader left at a pre-determined setting, the mixture switch is snapped in and out between alternate voices. And so, although the output fader for the echo chamber remains open all the time, only one of the voices is being fed in and being given the echo treatment. Similarly, if different amounts of echo are wanted on alternate voices, the mixture switch can be alternated between two different mixture settings.

If in either of these two cases the echo fader is used instead of the echo mixture switch the timing of the operation is different: the fader must not be taken in or out until the new voice has begun speaking. This ensures that the full duration of any pause has the proper amount of echo, or none, as the case may be, and that the mechanics do not become obvious. A third way of controlling echo in such a complex situation is to place the two speakers on separate microphones, dead-side-on to each other or sufficiently separated that there is little spill. This permits completely independent control of the echo feeds from each.

For television music artificial reverberation is essential (unless ambiophony is used). Serious music shows all artificial techniques to their greatest disadvantage: sometimes, to get rid of (or mask)

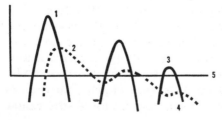

THE EFFECT OF LEVEL. I. Loud direct sound. 2. Audible reverberation. 3. Quiet direct sound. 4. Reverberation now below threshold of hearing 5.

the colourations of individual echo sources several different types are used either mixed together or in series. To produce a suitable delay between the direct sound and its "first reflection" the signal may be fed first to a tape recorder and delayed by the time it takes

ECHO ON TWO VOICES. If differing amounts of echo are needed on two voices which are taking part in a conversation, it helps if opposing microphones and voices are placed dead-side-on to each other. This layout might be adopted in a radio studio; in a television studio there will normally be more space available, making separation easier.

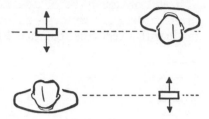

for the recording to pass to the replay head. Additional clarity can be gained by reducing the high frequencies on their return from the echo chamber. (Both of these measures simulate what might occur in the natural acoustics of a large hall.) Additionally, echo of different reverberation times may be applied to singers and orchestra.

On the whole, it is probably a good idea to feed sound through the echo chamber at a fairly high level: this means that the echo

ECHO FOR PERSPECTIVE. The use of a second bi-directional microphone, suspended above the main and having a stronger echo feed, helps to create perspective on crowd scenes.

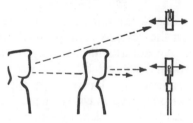

return fader can be held relatively low and ensures that "atmosphere" from the echo chamber is not too noticeable as it is faded in and out—and also that extraneous noises are less likely to be audible.

All of this complex equipment and technique is very much for the studio. Away from the studio, however, satisfactory results can be obtained from less orthodox methods. One tape I have heard gave a highly convincing picture of a journey into a crypt; and it turned out later that after opening the creaking door (ironing board) the scene had been played to a microphone underneath a kitchen sink.

"Acoustic" foldback through the studio

An arrangement which is related to the echo chain is that for acoustic foldback through the studio. Effects—spot effects or those recorded on tape or disc—should wherever possible sound in a similar acoustic to the main action. And in certain cases, usually where lively acoustics are being used, it is possible to route pre-recorded sound effects through the studio via a loudspeaker and fairly close microphone.

It will obviously be of advantage to do this in cases where the pre-recording is very dry—an outdoor recording, perhaps, or one made with a very close balance. Passing the sound through the studio

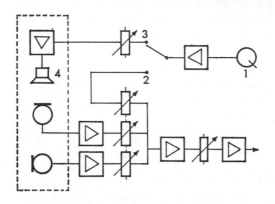

"ACOUSTIC" FOLDBACK. Tape or disc reproducers 1, which are normally fed direct to the mixer via switch contact 2, may sometimes be switched via 3 to provide an acoustic feed to the studio loudspeaker 4.

will add the same recognizable acoustic qualities which are present on the voices working "live" in the studio.

An additional advantage is that actors have something to work to, and will pitch their voices against the sound or react to it in a realistic way. However, headphones would be just as good for this purpose, and in cases where there is no value in changing the acoustic of the sound, would ensure that the overall quality would not be reduced.

The trouble with this technique is that, unless very high-quality equipment is used, the loudspeaker/microphone combination can introduce distortion. There will not usually be room for the loudspeaker at the same microphone as the actors, so a specially placed microphone will often be necessary. A close balance should generally be adopted.

The acoustic effects chain will start with a switch at the output of the reproducer which diverts the signal from its normal path and sends it via a separate fader on the control desk to a loudspeaker in the studio. The gain of the loudspeaker amplifier should be set at such a level that most of the range of the input fader is in use. These two controls are used in combination to set the sound level in the studio; what comes out of the studio is governed by the position of loudspeaker relative to the microphone, and the settings of the

346

microphone faders on the mixer. A little experiment will be necessary to find the optimum settings for the various elements in the chain—if a satisfactory result can be obtained at all.

There are certain things which common sense decrees to be impossible. For example, this technique will not improve the match between effect and studio if the effect is already brighter than it should be and the studio is dead. Passing it through the studio will only make it hollow-sounding as well as mis-matched.

If such methods are tricky for the professional with high-quality equipment, they are likely to be decidedly unsatisfactory where such equipment is not available. In particular, the technique provides no adequate substitute for proper mixing facilities. Importing a portable gramophone or tape reproducer into the studio is permissible for high quality programmes only where a deliberately distorted sound is wanted: e.g. for public-address announcements, or for a gramophone record playing *within* the action of a scene.

"Telephone" conversations

One of the simplest methods of distorting sound is restriction of the frequency range by means of filters. A microphone that is used in conjunction with such circuitry is called a filter microphone, or in BBC jargon a "distort" microphone. Its most frequent use in plays is to simulate the far end of a telephone conversation.

In a full-scale studio "telephone conversation" set-up it is usual to have two microphones, one normal and the other with a filter in circuit. In radio, these two can be placed in different parts of the same studio, the idea being that they should not be separated so much that the actors cannot hear each other direct. This arrangement avoids the necessity of wearing headphones—which can be awkward when holding a script.

In such a set-up it is particularly important to avoid "spill", which in this case means pick-up of the "far" voice on the normal microphone; otherwise the effect of telephone quality will be lost. If the "near" microphone is directional (e.g. a ribbon), and it is placed with its dead side towards the "far" voice, the pick-up of direct sound will be effectively prevented. But discrimination against reflected sound presents more of a problem, so it sometimes helps to use the deadest part of the studio for the filter microphone. As spill from the full-range to the filter microphone will not noticeably change the quality of the "near" voice, it does not really matter very much whether the second microphone is directional or not.

347

The two microphones are mixed together at the control desk (in some studios the filter controls are also conveniently built in to the desk) and the relative levels are judged by ear. When this sort of distortion is being introduced into a programme, meters will be even less use than usual in matching the two voices, as the narrow-band input will contain less bass, and therefore less power, for similar degrees of loudness.

But in any case, equal loudness from the two voices will not gener-

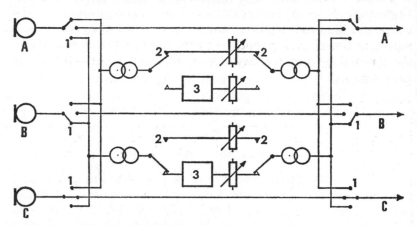

TELEPHONE EFFECTS SWITCHING UNIT for use in television. I. Pre-selector switches. 2. Switch linked to video cut buttons: any sound routed through this will automatically be switched in and out of the "distort" condition (bass and treble filters 3) as the pictures are cut. In this example, microphone A is undistorted only while B is filtered and vice-versa; and microphone C remains undistorted whatever the picture.

ally be required. At normal listening levels there is very little difference in intelligibility between full-range speech and the narrow band used to simulate telephone quality; a fairly considerable reduction in the loudness of the distorted speech may be tolerable in the interests of creating a feeling of actuality.

In a television studio the microphones should be well separated in space. Then, as the picture cuts from one end to the other, the normal distort arrangement can be reversed, without spill in either direction. It is useful to have the selection linked to the vision cutting buttons so that sound and picture changes are synchronized. But it is best to avoid cutting during a word as this sounds unpleasant and draws attention to the technique being used (see p. 265).

Note that as distorted sounds must be held at a lower level than "clean" sound great care must be taken not only in balance, but also before that, in studio layout. If the two performers cannot be acoustically completely separated, because both must appear in vision and must therefore be in the same studio, it should be arranged for the two sets to be as far apart from each other as possible. If they are not, colouration can affect both artists (distant, reverberant but otherwise undistorted sound is superimposed on the telephone quality speech). Also, if one performer speaks more loudly than the other his voice is likely to be heard over the quiet speaker's microphone. It may help for the speakers (in their separate sets) to be facing towards each other in the studio layout, as this will mean that cardioid boom microphones will be directed away from each other. On the other hand the use of wide shots will make matters worse, as boom microphones will have to retreat from the speaker, thereby making it more likely to hear the distant voice as the channel gain is raised.

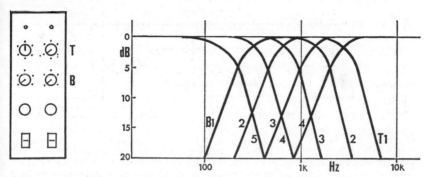

EFFECTS UNIT MODULES in BBC control desk (each module contains two units: these are the same as the portable effects unit also described). Four degrees of bass cut-off (B1–4) and five degrees of treble cut-off (T1–5) are provided. In BBC-TV control desks one pair of units is used in conjunction with a camera channel switching unit for reversing telephone effects.

Degrees of filter

For filter effects BBC radio uses an effects unit which provides sharp bass and top cut at various set frequencies. These units are available as standard features of most modern control desks.

Now, telephone circuits may have a band-width of some 3000 Hz with a lower cut-off at about 300 Hz, but this should not necessarily be copied when simulating telephone quality. The selection of suitable settings for bass and treble filters should, as always in such cases, be made by ear. And the degree of cut that seems most appropriate will vary from one play to another—or even between different "telephone" conversations in the same play.

quality between male and female speech; and between different examples of each. If the fundamental of a male voice is at 110 Hz, then a cut at 220 Hz will give a small but appreciable change of quality. For a female voice with a fundamental an octave higher, a 440-Hz cut will clearly be more suitable. In fact, 440 and 880 Hz are more often used: the loss of bass is stressed for dramatic effect.

Indeed, the need for dramatic emphasis may take us still farther into the realms of distortion, and we may place the "far" microphone against a reflecting surface, or clip some sort of baffle to it. A piece of hardboard might be used for this.

A telephone conversation is one situation where the visual media have more flexibility than radio: in the former the device can be used with ease to change location, in radio this is more difficult.

Filtered speech: mixing, cutting, or superimposing

When background effects are added to a "telephone conversation" they may make a considerable difference to the necessary balance between voices. The degree of distortion and its volume relative to the undistorted speech must depend on both the loudness of the effects and their quality. In particular, background sound which is toppy in quality will tend to blot out quiet speech; whereas if the backing is fairly woolly or boomy the shriller telephone effect will have little difficulty in cutting through it. In either case, the mix must be very carefully monitored to check that intelligibility is reasonably high—unless, of course, the script requires otherwise.

A fairly complicated scene may require varying degrees of intelligibility—as for example in a radio script like this:

Two quite different mixes will be required for this; besides which the balance and pitch of the near voice will change on the cue "door

EFFECTS	(*Loud party chatter background; phone dialling close, ringing heard on line: it stops.*)
GUEST	Hey, is that you, Charlie?
CHARLIE	(*On distort, barely audible against the party chatter*) Yes. This is Charlie.
GUEST	Say, this is a great party; why don't you come on over?
CHARLIE	What are you at, a football game or something?
GUEST	What am I what?
CHARLIE	I'm in bed.
GUEST	Hang on, I'll shut this door. *Door shuts; chatter down.*) S'better! Now what was all that about a football game? It's three in the morning.
CHARLIE	(*Now more distinct*) Yeah. It's three in the morning. I'm in bed.

shuts". An additional point that is worth thinking about in this case is that the backing should also change in quality: heard through a real door, such effects would become muffled and muddy, as well as being reduced in volume. Some degree of top cut might well be introduced at this point.

Incidentally this is one of the few cases where the amateur's technique of superimposition may easily achieve results which are as good as those which can be obtained with a mixer. If the backing effects are recorded first and the "telephone" conversation is then superimposed the change in the frequency response of the first recorded signal should give a pretty good imitation of a "party-in-the-next-room" sort of effect.

There are many other uses for filters or "distort" besides telephone quality: railway station and airport announcements, for example. And when these effects are created in the studio, it may turn out that a "crackle" background or a touch of echo will help.

Yet another interesting case is that of the radio play (or recording) which includes the effect of a radio announcement (or a tape recorder). A convenient convention which is frequently adopted is that the reproducer in question produces little better than telephone quality. Essentially, this implies a sort of caricature process—whereby one type of distortion, reproduction of sound through a single loudspeaker is having to be represented by another, limitation of frequency range.

AUDIO RESPONSE CONTROL. Octave filter with slide controls marked in decibels. *Above*: desk control panel. *Below*: A. Typical response curves for a single selector. B. Response obtained by setting adjacent selectors at −14 dB and +14 dB. For even more precise control see filter illustrated on p. 368.

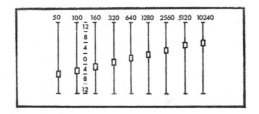

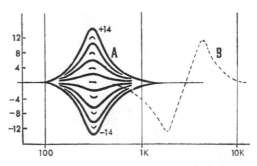

In the absence of specially designed equipment it may be found that a second tape recorder, using the internal speaker at a suitable distance from the studio microphone will do very well for either Public Address or radio announcements. It will probably be best to set the tone control to minimum bass.

Equalization

Nominally "equalization" means restoring a level frequency response—for example, to the output of a microphone that has inherently or by its position an uneven response. It can be used to match microphones of similar quality—e.g., in a television studio, where a boom microphone is generally taken as the standard and all others matched to it (see p. 190). In a film-dubbing theatre, quality variations can be reduced; and the intelligibility of voices recorded in difficult conditions or heard against strong sound effects can be improved (pp. 486, 488).

A particular use for equalization is in popular music (p. 213) and radiophonics (p. 368) where it may often be the second step in the creative distortion of sound for a particular effect—the choice of microphone and its position being the first step. Here the result will be judged by the balancer as that which he finds most satisfying in the final mix: his aim will not necessarily be to "equal" any natural response, so the term "equalization" is itself less appropriate—if shorter—than "response selection" or "response control". Within the range of possibilities that this implies, "tone control" includes changes in bass and treble response; and "midlift", or "presence" various peaks in the upper middle response. (*Mid*lift is perhaps not

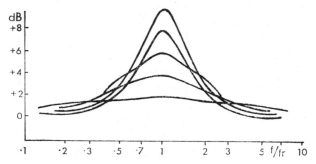

MIDLIFT. Response curves for a midlift tone control unit. In a typical unit centre frequencies $f_r = 2, 3, 5, 8$ Hz (approx) may be selected; also five degrees of lift, as shown. The effect is very similar to the production of *formants*, i.e. the selective amplification that occurs at characteristic frequency ranges in musical instruments (and the human voice) due to cavity or structural resonances.

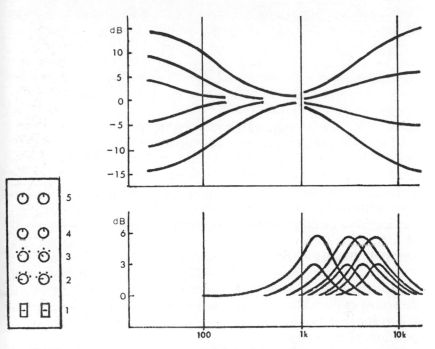

RESPONSE SELECTION AMPLIFIER CONTROL MODULE as mounted on BBC desks (two units in single module). I. Bypass switch. 2. Mid-lift selection (1·4, 2·8, 4·0, 5·6 kHz). 3. Presence control (3 and 6 dB lift). 4. Bass lift and cut control. 5. Treble lift and cut control. *On the right, above:* typical response curves for bass and treble controls. *Below:* presence peaks. Modern BBC–TV desks have seven RSA modules (fourteen units), an octave filter, four effects unit modules (sharper bass and treble filter units) and a telephone effects switching unit.

the best name for a peak that is normally introduced only in the treble range.)

If we take response selection a stage further we reach the shaping filter (see pp. 351, 368) in which the whole frequency spectrum is split into bands of an octave or less. In practice, the bands are overlapping peaks, arranged so that if all the controls are set at zero their sum is a level response. The sharpness of cut-off between bands depends on the characteristics of the particular filter. In a shaping filter, selection of the desired effect is made by setting the slides for the various component bands to form what appears to be a graph of the new response. In fact, the actual response achieved may differ from this: it depends on the design of the filter and the size of the fluctuations set. The true arbiter—once again—must be subjective judgment.

353

12

SHAPING SOUND

OVER the years, the primary aim of audio engineering has been to approach ever closer to the ideal of perfect fidelity in sound recording and reproduction. But as our technical grasp of the means of eliminating distortion in all its forms has been extended, so also has our ability to use and control distortion for creative purposes. And so we have now reached the stage where some form of distortion of the sound as picked up by the microphone may be introduced into a recording quite deliberately and intentionally. In such cases recording, editing, and dubbing may become part of the process of composition, of creating music.

Two types of music which will illustrate this are *musique concrète* and the special brand of popular music on gramophone records known colloquially as "pop". So different in style, these two do in fact have a great deal in common. Certainly, both have been dismissed with mild contempt by many people with a serious regard for conventional music. But in both fields there has been a great deal of careful thought along much the same lines, and at least a fair degree of achievement.

Among the differences between the two it is hardly necessary to point out that one has helped to build a multi-million dollar industry, whereas the other has been more noted for the massive apathy with which its novelties have been greeted by the general public—which must be at least partly due to the association between *musique concrète* and "advanced" modern composition.

Techniques based on *musique concrète* have been used, often with considerable effect, in the theatre in London; and what are called "radiophonic" effects have been used in many BBC radio and television productions. There is a growing awareness that whatever the musical merits of a "new sound", there is great scope for musically organized sound effects and "treated" musical sounds to enhance dramatic effects in a variety of media—including commercials.

354

Besides this, the BBC's Radiophonic Department has noted that precise control over sound means that it can be specially designed to cut through noise: for the BBC one application of this has been in short-wave broadcasting to other countries, for programme signature tunes and so on. They have also found that the formal organization of any sequence of sounds will have some resemblance to music, but more or less so depending on the musical sense of the person making the arrangement (and, not surprisingly, it will be more so if the sounds themselves have some recognizably musical quality); and that if the starting-point is noise, or a series of noises the effect will often be comic. Comedy—and comedy timing—is relatively easy to achieve.

Progress has been made in a number of different directions: electronic music in Germany and Italy; "tape-music" and "electronic tonalities" in the United States, and "animated sound" in Canada (this last follows experiments in the field of sound-track drawn on film which briefly made an appearance in Russia round about 1930); and, of course, the *musique concrète* produced in France.

Distortion and sound conventions

It must be remembered, when we are talking about distortion, that practically every sound we ever hear in mono—however high the quality—is a rearrangement of reality according to a certain special convention. Monophonic sound is distorted sound in every case except the one where the effective point source of the loudspeaker is being used to reproduce a sound which is itself confined to a similarly small source.

Thus, every balance (even a single voice)—i.e. every carefully contrived mixture of direct and indirect sound—is a deliberate distortion of what you would hear if you listened to the same sound "live". But this distortion is accepted so easily as the conventional form of the medium that very few people are even aware of it, until they are required to make a conscious direct comparison between mono and either live sound or good stereo (the relationship between the latter two is a complex study in itself.)

Perhaps distortion would be better defined as "unwanted changes of quality", rather as noise is sometimes defined as "unwanted sound"; and whether mono would then qualify as distortion would depend on the requirements of the listener.

Anyway, we must accept that, using the term in the broader sense, distortion is for ever with us: that sound is continuously being

355

moulded to one end or another; and that the listener is constantly being required to accept one convention or another for its use.

A point which immediately presents itself concerns listening conditions: the use of good equipment is much more important when we are listening to "new sounds" than it is for conventional music.

When a listener with good musical imagination hears instruments he knows and musical forms which he understands, he will be able to judge the qualities of writing and performance in spite of bad recording and bad reproduction. And although they may reduce his enjoyment, noise and distortion will be automatically disregarded. The musical elements will be identified according to the listener's previous knowledge and experience, and so in his imagination he will reconstitute the original musical sound without too much difficulty.

But, obviously, this will not happen on the first few hearings of a piece of music in which the new sound is produced by what, in other situations, would be regarded as distortion. Thus we reach the novel situation in which any imperfections produced by the equipment are, for the listener, indistinguishable from the process of musical composition, and indeed become part of the music. Many items of concrete or electronic music are highly effective (although perhaps an acquired taste), but one may wonder how many people have been put off by the diabolical noises for which their own equipment may be responsible; or which may have been produced by the poor acoustic properties of some theatre, or by a sound system over which even a symphony by Mozart sounds like *musique concrète*.

Differences between the various forms

When a composer sets pen to paper he knows that he has a large number of independent variables at his command. He specifies each instrument and the way in which it is to be played; the pitch of each note and its duration; and the relationship in time and pitch between successive notes and between different instruments. But however much is specified, there is always room left for interpretation by the performer.

This leads us to the first and most obvious difference between conventional music and taped new forms, for an electronic or concrete composition exists only in its final state, as a painting or carving does. It is not performed, but merely replayed. In this one respect, at least, *musique concrète* is like electronic music (from which it otherwise has certain fundamental differences).

356

At times there have been valiant attempts to combine the synthetic media with live music, or live action. But for the most part the result has appeared laboured, as though attempting to justify charging an audience for admission.

Musique concrète is made by recording the ready-made timbres of some particular group of sound sources, transforming them in various ways, and then cutting and assembling them in a montage. And the primary difference between this technique and that of electronic music lies in the sound source. Electronic music starts, as might be expected, with electronically generated signals such as pure tones, harmonic series, or coloured noise (noise contained within some frequency spectrum). This basic divergence in technique produces results which are characteristically different—although in theory the concrete sounds could be imitated by electronic synthesis, and, indeed, an oscillator is a valid "concrete" sound source.

One characteristic quality of *musique concrète* is that the pitch relationship between the fundamental and the upper partials of each constituent sound remains unaltered by transformation (unless any frequency band is filtered out completely, or certain rather exotic types of transformation are introduced). This in itself is both a strength and a restriction: it helps to give unity to a work derived from a single sound or range of sounds, but it severely hampers development.

In electronic music, on the other hand, where every sound is created individually, the harmonic structure of each new element of a work is completely free. Where *musique concrète* has restrictions, electronic music offers new freedoms—and this is the essential difference between the two. And although it is yet to be established that either electronic or concrete music will have any real lasting importance as forms in their own right, the two techniques really do have a proven value in extending the range of sound comment—that is, in providing radiophonic effects (to use the BBC term).

This is the field in which sound effects take on formal musical qualities in structure and arrangement; and musical elements (whether from conventional or electronic sources) complement them by taking on the qualities of sound effects. Radiophonics does not in general attempt to assert itself as an art form in its own right; it is always an element in a larger picture, and indeed rarely even moves into the foreground of the audience's attention.

The BBC's workshop is alone among the organizations of its kind in Europe (France, Germany, and Italy) in that in its early years it has had no single established composer regularly working with it.

357

This has the advantage that it tends to prevent the group from latching too firmly on to any one particular musical style. One extremely valuable attribute for anyone working in this field is, I would say, a strongly self-critical sense of humour.

The construction of musique concrète

Musique concrète is built up in three distinct phases—selection, treatment, and montage.

The first characteristic of the form lies in the choice of basic material: a concrete sound is one which from the start is complete in itself. In the early days of *musique concrète* the emotional associations of the original sound were incorporated into the music. There was a later reaction away from this idea, for the lack of an immediate mental association can lend power to sounds. The basic materials may include tin cans, fragments of human speech, a cough, canal boats chugging, or snatches of Tibetan chant (all these are in an early work called *Étude Pathétique*). Musical instruments are not taboo; for instance, one piece uses a flute—both played and struck. And there are other things besides the natural sound qualities of an object which may affect a recording: such things as differences in the balance or "playing" of a sound help to extend the range of sound materials enormously.

This preliminary sound recording may be considered analytically in terms of a variety of qualities:

(i) The instantaneous content of the sound, its frequency spectrum or timbre (this may contain separate harmonics, bands of noise, or a mixture of the two).
(ii) The melodic sequence of such sound structures.
(iii) The dynamics or envelope of the sound (by this is meant the way in which the sound intensity varies in time).

The second stage in building *musique concrète*, and the second characteristic of it, is treatment of the sound materials to provide a series of what may be termed "sound-subjects". The bricks from which the work is to be constructed must be fashioned from the raw

LINE AND BAND SPECTRA. Instantaneous content: here the sound is composed of individual tones superimposed on a broad spectrum band of noise.

materials selected. A wide range of technical operations is now available, and in France the *Groupe de Recherche de Musique Concrète* has distinguished between various types of manipulation:

(i) Transmutation of the structure of sound—that is, changing the instantaneous sound content in a way which will affect its melodic and harmonic qualities, but leave its dynamics unaffected. Included in this category of manipulation are transpositions of pitch (which may be continuous or discontinuous) and filtering (to vary the harmonic structure or colouration).

(ii) Discontinuous transformations of the constituent parts of a sound by editing. An individual sound element may be dissected into attack, body, and die-away; and particular sections subjected to reversal, contraction, permutation, or substitution. This form of manipulation will vary the dynamics of the sound, though on any given scrap of tape the instantaneous sound content will not be altered.

(iii) Continuous transformation in which the envelope of a sound is varied without editing, by the use of faders, by adding reverberation, or by using some more out-of-the-way technique.

Here is an example of what a complex operation might involve. Starting with, say, a recording of a piano note, it might be decided that the effect required by the composer could be obtained by replaying through a frequency filtering network, at the same time varying the speed of the re-recording machine, the result being edited by chopping a piece out of the middle and placing it at the end, and then joining the ends together to form a tape loop which is played backwards, twice, through an echo chamber. The result of this (or any other arbitrarily selected series of manipulations) might sound horrible or, just possibly, it might be exactly what the composer wanted.

The third phase in the manufacture of *musique concrète* is that of construction; the sound-subjects are put together piece by piece, like the shots of a film. There is no such thing as a live concert-hall performance by suitably qualified "concrete" musicians; the music must always be played from tape or disc through a suitable loudspeaker system.

Several techniques are available for construction. The simplest methods are the editing of a single tape by cutting and joining pieces together (montage), and dubbing and mixing in the same way that

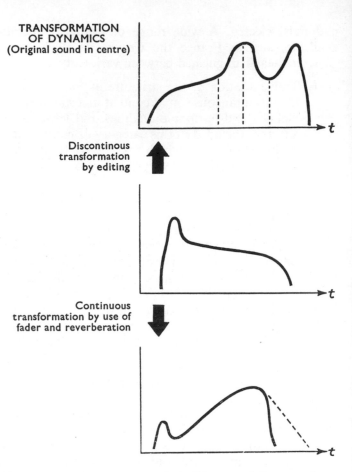

TRANSFORMATION OF DYNAMICS (Original sound in centre)

Discontinous transformation by editing

Continuous transformation by use of fader and reverberation

sound-effects sequences are put together. More satisfactory, however, are track laying systems, which will be described later.

So much for the construction of *musique concrète*; in these three stages the work is complete. All that remains is replay. And once again it must be stressed that the conditions under which the tape is heard will go a long way towards conditioning the reaction of the audience. Indeed, one composer, Pierre Henry, has attempted to cut down on this element of chance by specifying that his compositions should be heard in a large hall, and should be played very loud.

Early ideas on musique concrète

Musique concrète started out quite simply as the transformation and arrangement of recorded sounds, usually short, sharp, isolated

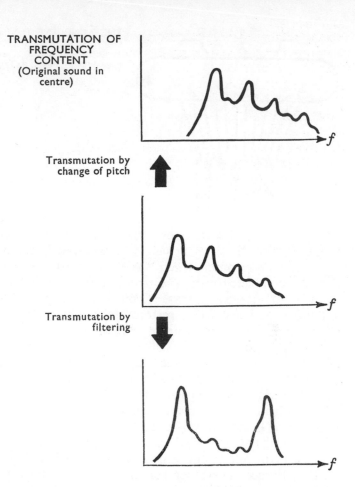

TRANSMUTATION OF
FREQUENCY
CONTENT
(Original sound in
centre)

Transmutation by
change of pitch

Transmutation by
filtering

noises or fragments from longer ones (because short sections are easier to handle), according to musical principles.

The first musical element to be exploited was that of rhythm, when Pierre Shaeffer put together his "Railway Study" in 1948. He constructed it with immense labour, not on tape (not at the time conveniently available) but on disc, using locked grooves to provide rhythmic repetitions. The effect is very much the same as may be obtained with tape loops, where the joint provides the bar line.

Later, melodic elements were brought under control to a much greater degree by means of the *phonogène*, a device with a piano type keyboard also invented by Schaeffer. Each key engaged its own individual capstan, one of a series of twelve of different diameters located round a tape loop. By using a two-speed motor, any note on

361

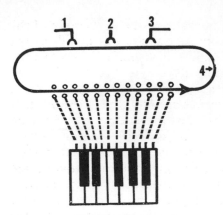

THE *PHONOGÈNE*. This has twelve keys, twelve spindles, and a 2-speed motor. 1. Recording head. 2. Erase head. 3. Reproducing head. 4. Tape loop.

an equal-tempered scale over a range of two octaves could be reproduced immediately. The *phonogène* was used in conjunction with a second tape recorder which was continuously variable in speed; this gave complete freedom of pitch transposition.

The rhythmic element was, of course, lost in most of these transmutations, and had to be restored by dubbing and cutting. And there is the further complication and limitation, which any recordist can easily discover for himself, due to the almost completely inextricable interrelation between tape speed, pitch, and timbre.

One of the most immediately engaging compositions that dates from the early days of experiment is an item about two minutes long called *Bidule en Ut*—whose title implies the use of a "doh–re–mi" scale. I have heard two versions of this work (both, of course, from the same original), one of which was in a presentation album pressed by the experimental group which has sponsored most of this type of work in France. The other version was issued on a gramophone record. And an odd thing about this second version is that its pitch (and therefore duration) is different; and the title has also been changed slightly in translation to become *Trifle in C*. If this story has a moral it must surely be that if you finally decide that you do not like the key you started out in you can change the whole thing afterwards to a completely different pitch. And it will subsequently be impossible to tell which is the original and which the translation.

Transposition of pitch by changing the tape speed

When a sound is originally being made its creator generally has a fair degree of control over various characteristics of the sound—its pitch, timbre, duration, and envelope (i.e. the way in which the

362

attack and decay are related in intensity to the main body of the note). Naturally it is usually possible to exercise a greater degree of independent control of these variables if a musical instrument is chosen as the sound source, rather than some "concrete" sound effect. (This leads to what at first sight may appear to be a rather surprising result: that musical sources are often preferred to other sounds. After its adventurous early history *musique concrète* soon showed tendencies to return to the conventional in this one respect at least.) But once this original recording (or series of recordings) has been made, all of these formerly independent variables are locked together, and it is not at all easy to treat them separately.

Suppose you play a $3\frac{3}{4}$ ips recording at 15 ips. You have achieved your first objective—the pitch has gone up two octaves. But the duration has come down to a quarter, the attack and decay characteristics have changed so that the sound may now be a great deal more percussive than before. The timbre has changed to something like that of an instrument a quarter of the size; and so on. Everything changes together.

One way of achieving some degree of control over the final result is to change the quality of the original sound material before recording—i.e. having seen what is wrong with a transposition, go back to the beginning and try to compensate for this in the creation of the sound. This can sometimes improve matters, but the method is less effective than one would wish. Speed transformations will so easily swamp all but the most emphatic differences in the raw material.

It has often been said that some of the most successful results in *musique concrète* are obtained when the composer does not try to impose his will too strongly on the source material, but instead listens to it together with its most effective-sounding transformations and then lets these suggest their own arrangement—a sort of sonic equivalent of that branch of modern art which is called *objets trouvés*.

When treating actuality sound, e.g. a foghorn, any background sound recorded with it (and which cannot be filtered out) will be treated as well. Such a background may be hardly noticed with the ordinary sound, because it is natural, but treatment may make it vividly apparent where open air sounds cannot be recorded without the background. It is much better, therefore, to synthesize the effect (or something recognizably like it) if this is possible, or to use sounds which can be recorded with a very close microphone, so that they are loud in comparison with "atmosphere"; this holds for both exterior actuality sounds and those recorded in the controlled

363

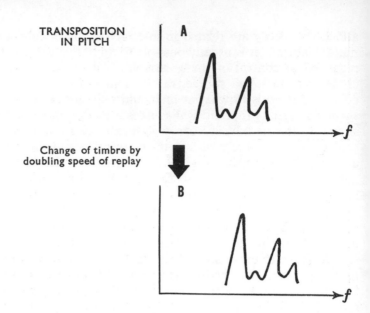

TRANSPOSITION
IN PITCH

Change of timbre by
doubling speed of replay

A

B

conditions of the studio. Similar problems arise with any surface noise that there may be on discs.

Coming back to conventional music sources (and popular music), a fairly simple example of pitch change is that of the double-speed piano mixed with normal piano. On the first recording the piano is played with slow deliberation, to avoid the appearance of a totally inhuman virtuosity when the tape is speeded up. The music should be preceded by a spoken "One, two, three, four" to give the tempo on replay. This initial recording is then played back at double speed, and a conventional piano accompaniment added. After this, further playbacks and dubbing-in, perhaps with other instruments such as the celeste, can be used.

But it should be noted that the double-speed piano sound on which the whole composition is based is no mere variation on this instrument's ordinary quality. It sounds like a new instrument, and must be treated as such in the musical arrangement.

Pitch transposition and vibrato

One sound source which usually gives pretty disastrous results when subjected to a speed change is the human voice, and particularly the singing voice. The basic reason for this is a quality which I have not already mentioned: vibrato. This is a cyclic variation in

364

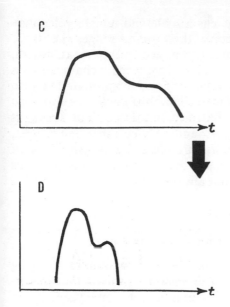

Replay at twice the original speed changes both timbre (A and B) and dynamics (C and D) of a sound.

Change of dynamics by doubling speed of replay

pitch which gives colour and warmth to a singer's sustained notes. (And the technique is copied on orchestral instruments such as the violin.) Analysis of voices which are generally considered beautiful suggests that pitch variations of as much as 8% may not be excessive (a semitone is about 6%). But the really critical quality of vibrato is the number of these wobbles which occur in a second. The acceptable range is narrow: it seems that to create an attractive sound the vibrato rate must fall somewhere between about 5 and 8 Hz.

These characteristics of vibrato are more or less independent of the pitch of the note sung—though cases have been observed where a sudden drop of pitch is accompanied by an *increase* in the vibrato rate, and vice versa.

Outside the limits of 5–8 Hz the effect resembles wow or flutter: the vibrato range can be taken as dividing the two. Clearly, only small speed changes will be possible without taking the vibrato outside its normal range. If this is exceeded a vibrato which did not previously call attention to itself may suddenly become both obvious and ugly. Doubling the speed of a sustained note automatically produces a characteristic effect: it sounds like a small, vibrant-voiced animal (which, it must be admitted, does have its uses both for records and for musical television shows using puppets).

And although it is possible to avoid the worst of this by keeping the changes small, it is as well to remember that difficulties may crop

365

up in other directions. For whereas a male and female voice may differ in fundamental by an octave, the *formant* ranges (i.e. those parts of the vocal sound which are emphasized by the throat, mouth, and nasal cavities and which are used to give the main characteristics of speech) are, on average, only a semi-tone or so apart, and vibrato ranges are also little separated. Small changes of pitch therefore tend not to change the apparent sex of a voice, but rather to de-sex it. As an illustration of some of the odd-sounding effects that one can get, try listening to the voice quality produced by playing 33's of languorous male singers at 45 r.p.m.; the effect sometimes becomes that of a vibrant female ... but not always.

Special equipment for transmutations

Is it possible to make radical changes in pitch without introducing a host of awkward side effects? The answer to this is that in certain circumstances it can be done—but at a cost. Some years ago in Germany the *Zeitdehner* ("time-stretcher") was invented, an ingenious device which permits frequency and duration to be altered independently of each other. The time-stretcher is like a normal replay machine except that, instead of the tape being drawn across a single replay head, it passes round a capstan into which several replay heads are fitted. This capstan can be rotated so that the heads "chase" the tape (and thus reduce the pitch of replay without affecting duration). Or it can be rotated in the opposite direction, lifting the pitch.

The disadvantage of this sort of arrangement is that there is bound to be some sort of discontinuity at the moment when one replay head takes over from another; a characteristic form of distortion is created. It may, however, be possible to remove some of the evidence of the method used by judicious editing.

Another device for changing pitch independently of duration is the ring modulator. By means of this, a fixed number of cycles per second can be added to (or subtracted from) all frequencies present (e.g. components f_1, f_2, f_3, become $x + f_1$, $x + f_2$, $x + f_3$; whereas simple alteration of speed multiplies all frequencies by a common factor). Alternatively, frequencies can be inverted ($x - f_1$, $x - f_2$, and so on) so that high frequencies become low ones and vice versa. By means of this type of transmutation certain curious qualities of consonance and dissonance can be obtained. These are of a type which do not occur naturally (i.e. in conventional music) but

366

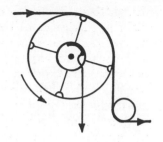

ZEITDEHNER (TIME-STRETCHER).
Head assembly can rotate either way:
*If sense is opposite to that of tape, pitch
increases; if heads chase tape, it decreases.*
Signal is fed from whichever head is in
contact with tape, via commutator and
brushes, to a second recorder.

which have been made a feature of the development of electronic music.

Modulators are regularly used in telephony, so that narrow-frequency bands containing the main characteristics of speech can be stacked one above the other on a line capable of carrying a broad band. In their modulated form some of the speech bands may be transmitted in an inverted form—and it is in fact possible to bring them back down to normal frequencies but still have them inverted. For example, a band of speech might be inverted so that what was 2500 Hz becomes zero, and vice versa. The most important effect of such a manipulation is to invert the three most important bands of formants, so that the speech is translated into a sort of upside-down jabberwocky language—which curiously enough it is actually possible to learn.

But this is only one very pedestrian example of what can be done with modulators: if both signals are complex the results may be a great deal more complicated. For example, in the field of sound effects, a filtered human voice can be used to modulate a train siren to make it talk. (This is a technique that has been used in Disney cartoons.) Or, in electronic music, two relatively simple sound structures can be combined to make a much more complex form. After use of a modulator it may be necessary to filter to get rid of unwanted products.

Both the *Zeitdehner* and ring modulator have been used at the Cologne and Milan studios, where the emphasis has been on electronic music, but the devices are equally suitable for the treatment of sounds obtained from "concrete" sources.

Unless such remarkable devices as these are used, there is only one circumstance in which a pitch change can be made without everything else going haywire at the same time, and this is when an absolutely steady note can be made into a loop. But it is surprising how rare a really steady note is!

367

Filters

Filtering is another form of transmutation which requires special equipment. A simple filter which is used to give telephone quality cuts off only at the top and bottom; a hiss filter may give various degrees of roll-off from certain specific frequencies; a hum filter gives a narrow band cut-off at the mains frequency and its harmonics. All of these can be used for radiophonics, but they are decidedly blunt instruments. Far more versatile is a filter which will divide each sound into narrow intervals (of, say, an octave, a half octave, or less) so that the frequencies which lie in these bands can be attenuated at will.

One filter (used in the BBC's Radiophonic Workshop) divides up into intervals of about a minor third. It has a face panel of slides labelled in Hz, starting with 94, 113, 136, 163, 196, ... and so on, so that a band of four of these intervals nominally amounts to rather more than an octave. Each slide is marked from 0 to -60 dB, below which it cuts out completely.

A "shape" can be imposed on a sound by making a pattern with the slides across the face of the filter. But such shapes are often somewhat disappointing: after all, the effect of many items of medium-quality equipment is to impose a "shape" on the signal passing through it—and, indeed, quite severe frequency distortion can and does go practically unnoticed by 99% of the general public. Speech, for example, is judged by intelligibility, and a couple of broad dips of up to 30 dB will produce a reduction in intelligibility of only about a half of 1%. So when filtering bands out of a sound, it is as well to remember that the mind of the listener reinstates them; it infers their presence from what is left. So filtering must be pretty drastic if it is to have any dramatic effect.

But there is one form of frequency distortion which is more effective than selective filtering, and this is selective emphasis of particular frequencies. The worst fault a microphone can have is a sudden sharp peak in the response, for this is noticeable where a dip would not be. Now in engineering terms there is no basic difference between

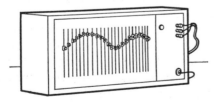

SHAPING FILTER. In this design the slide faders may be at, say, third or half octave intervals and the band between successive slides is attenuated according to their volume settings. The shaping shown here would have very little effect on the intelligibility of speech.

this sort of distortion which produces peaks in the frequency response and that which produces dips. So a filter such as that described above can be used to provide peaks almost as easily as dips. A peak of 15 dB, for example, is obtained by increasing the gain by 15 dB before feeding the signal into the filter and then setting all the slides 15 dB down except where the peak is wanted.

This effect, which certainly can be dramatic, is one of the principal weapons in the armoury not of *musique concrète*, but of its commercial big brother: pop music with the modern sound.

Artificial reverberation techniques

The addition of reverberation is a powerful tool in transforming sound. The equipment (echo chambers and reverberation plates) and the basic techniques have already been described (see p. 336). And passing mention has been made of an artificial reverberation machine which uses a loop of tape (or coated wheel) with a number of replay heads spaced along it. This last device is one which can be used either for an orthodox reverberation effect or, in a modified form, to create entirely new sound envelopes.

To create the smoothest possible reverberation, a multi-track system with staggered recording heads (having progressively increasing attenuation) may be employed. With this design the number of "reflections" is the product of the numbers of recording and (full-track) output heads. It is usual to place the earlier heads fairly close together in order to avoid amplitude flutter—if "pure" artificial reverberation is what is wanted. As an added refinement the last replay head may be used to feed the signal back into the recording head at an appropriately lower level, so that the process may continue beyond the duration of one circuit of the loop.

If the number of "reflections" are cut down and the loop speed is reduced the effect becomes first a flutter echo and then a series of individual echoes. For freak effects the positions of the output heads and their relative volumes can sometimes be altered. A number of records have been made using this arrangement for "gimmicks": individual sounds, words, or phrases are switched through the device and recombined with the original sound.

In the early days of *musique concrète* it was realized that the output volume need not be set to give the envelope of an exponential decay of sound (i.e. to simulate reverberation). There is no reason why the output settings should not take any series of values; they may even progressively increase. And, in fact, from any initial short sound element a wide variety of envelopes can be created—for example, one which has its loudest point at the middle instead of at the start. When this was done in Paris the device used was called a *morphophone*.

Feedback, echo, and delay techniques

A much simpler way of getting a reverberation effect—of a sort— is direct feed-back. If the output from the replay head is mixed back into the input signal the apparent reverberation time will depend on the amount of attenuation in the replay circuit. The quality of the reverberation will depend strongly on two factors, the tape speed and the spacing between the two heads: playing the tape at 15 ips with a three-inch separation (i.e. with a built-in delay of a fifth of a second) produces a marked flutter effect.

It is possible to start with a staccato sound such as a tap on a water glass and let the signal go round and round indefinitely, using a fader to keep the level constant. This is a game that will quickly show up any peaks in the frequency response of the circuit; with a good professional recorder it is about half a minute before the characteristic of the system completely swallows the original sound. It is worth experimenting with a control unit in the circuit if possible; the bass and treble filters may improve the character of the result.

Both of the above techniques, using tape-loop or feed-back, have one thing in common—their mechanically repetitive quality, which compares very unfavourably with the warmth of random decay processes (for all the more normal purposes). In the case of feedback echo, there will simply be a gradual build-up of a single pattern of colouration as the sound dies away. And another limitation here is that the proportion of direct to indirect sound is governed by the straight-line decay law: the ratio of direct sound to first echo, and first echo to second echo, and so on is constant. Of course, all this may well fit in with the desired effect.

A second and slightly more complex form of this delay technique may be used if only a single echo is required. A second recorder is needed: the direct sound is split, one leg going to a record/replay machine which supplies the delayed signal (the duration of the delay again being determined by the speed of the tape and spacing of the heads). The other leg is passed through a small amplifier and recombined with the recorder output. (The purpose of the amplifier is to avoid feed-back on the loop, and any other suitable means may be used.) If a flutter effect is required, instead of a single echo, feedback

370

may be introduced into the echo leg of the circuit before it is recombined at some suitable level with the original sound.

There is one type of delay which produces an entirely different effect: this is where the original sound and the "echo" are equal and are almost, but not quite, synchronized. Instead of an echo effect a completely new sound quality is created. What happens depends on the phase relationship between the sounds; certain frequencies are reinforced and others are cancelled. Thus, for frequencies where an integral number of cycles occur during the delay the output is doubled; but at intervening half-cycles the two are 180° out of phase, and the output falls to zero. Sound engineers are well acquainted with this form of distortion, as they constantly have to watch out for it when setting up microphones close to each other. Another example occurs in short wave radio, where the signal sometimes has a continuously varying "whooshy" quality, as signals from the same transmitter, but arriving by different sky routes, drift in and out of phase. Similar effects can be obtained by mixing the output of two gramophone records or tapes playing almost in sync.

Pure tones and white noise

In creating electronic music, the composer has complete control of his resources. Unlike the composer of *musique concrète*, who starts off by selecting from the timbres that can be produced by relatively conventional means, he synthesizes every first and last detail of the sound. With no performer to get between him and the final product, he has the whole responsibility for the work, and more freedom than any other composer—subject only to the limitations of time, patience, and, of course, his equipment.

The basic equipment for producing electronic sound includes generators for producing pure tones and combinations of tones, which are normally required in quantity: perhaps as many as a dozen sine/square wave generators may be needed at once, though for the most part these need not be of high quality.

Tone generators are available in a variety of designs—and some which are sold as do-it-yourself kits are not at all expensive. It is useful, however, to have at least one with a high degree of accuracy in calibration. After all, if musical instruments are off pitch it is only one performance that is affected, and the score itself remains unaltered; but in the case of electronic music the composer is playing for keeps—the first "realization" will in all probability be the only complete evidence of his intentions.

One of the most characteristic sounds of early electronic works has been the use of short bursts of tone at various frequencies, sounding like a series of pips, beeps, and bloops. If a work is assembled from a series of short lengths of tape to give this effect, variations in attack and decay can be introduced by varying the angle at which the tape is cut. A 90° cut gives the strongest effect of a click at beginning or end; other angles of cut soften this. So the electronic composer may use a pair of scissors for editing tape instead of the usual 45° slot in the editing block.

White (and coloured) noise is another type of sound which is peculiar to electronic music (and radiophonic sound, since this incorporates electronic techniques). It can be produced in several ways—for example, by amplifying the output from a noisy valve. In fact, special valves can be bought for this purpose. A simpler way of obtaining a good even source is to record the amplified output from a VHF set, choosing a frequency on which no transmitter is operating.

White noise is in itself not particularly useful; but in combination with a versatile filter it can be used to produce "colours" which can be of indeterminate pitch, or related to any desired musical scale by placing peaks at particular frequencies and troughs at others, or by using bands of particular widths. Electronic "wind" effects can also be manufactured in this way. The frequency analogy between light and sound can, incidentally, be extended so far as to assign colour-names to particular bands. For example, white noise with bass tip-up is "pink" noise.

One or two other things can be done with white noise: for example, a sinusoidal envelope (or any other waveform) may be imposed on the noise so that it becomes a series of "puffs" of sound. If this is speeded up sufficiently it is transformed into a tone which can be used musically—then on slowing down again the granular structure of the original sound may be observed. One electronic work includes a "dive-bombing" effect by a tone, in which something like this happens. The principle behind this sort of sound is, of course, very similar to that of the siren.

In another application white noise is used as the source of a very narrow band of sound: a particular frequency ±2 Hz, which amounts in practice to a sharply defined single frequency. For this the studios of Radio Milan use a wave analyser.

In view of the difficulties involved in creating electronic music; the mountainous task of assembling a work, not merely note by note, but harmonic by harmonic, it is not surprising that methods of

372

cutting down on the labour have been suggested—particularly for the cases where conventional harmonic structures are required. One line of attack is to use a sawtooth generator (very rich in harmonics) and filters.

Another, and even simpler, method is to use the colours provided by some sort of electronic organ. There is now quite a variety of these available: the Monochord, the Melochord, the Spinetta, the Ondes Martenot, and so on, besides the more conventional Compton and Hammond organs. In Germany there is a special instrument called the Trautonium—one of a group of instruments which can be used (and played, "live") to provide notes of *any* pitch, not just those corresponding to a keyboard.

The BBC Radiophonic Studios have their own home-made versions of the electric guitar and zither, an electric autoharp, harmonium, and piano (among other instruments, conventional and rare), and also have access to five of the BBC's main music studios which, beside several of the now standard electronic organs, have a specially designed Multicolourtone organ and a large conventional pipe organ.

Radiophonic treatment of tone sources

Where a work is being synthesised from such basic sources it is obviously a major task to treat and assemble them. Besides having many of the now conventional devices for treatment—including filters of many different kinds; a variety of tape recorders, some with variable speed facilities; square-wave shapers, ring modulators, vibrator devices, compressors and limiters, several types of echo equipment, and control desks with conventional operational facilities—the BBC has devised for itself a number of other useful instruments, which are described below.

Keying unit. This is a single-octave piano-type keyboard instrument with twelve inputs to separate circuits which can be adjusted to give three attack times: *sharp* (0·01 second, about the shortest time that does not give an audible click), *medium* (0·03 second), or *slow* (0·07 second), as a key is pressed; and decay times of between 0·2 to 5 seconds on release of the key. Alternatively it can be arranged for the note to be held when the key is released. The unit is most commonly used with a bank of signal generators which would normally be preset.

Metronomic switching unit. This gives facilities for cutting between sound sources at regular intervals—effectively, a single musical beat.

Related to this is a *sequencer*, which can be set up to sustain previously selected inputs for given periods of time.

Photo-sensitive faders. Normal faders rise and fall in discrete steps, generally 2 dB. These jumps will not be heard on most sounds, but can be on pure tone. Where this problem does arise the Workshop controls the fade by a light sensitive cell—this makes it very smooth and free from crackle.

Multitrack recorder. These are now regularly available with ten tracks on 1-inch tape, but were not when the BBC Radiophonic Workshop was set up. One (with eight tracks) was built specially. The technique for use is that the first sound (or a guide track) is recorded on the top track, and the next recorded to replay of the first, on the bottom track. When the operator is satisfied about the timing, this second recording is transferred to track two. The volume does not matter at this stage and is kept high. The third component is tried on the bottom track and then rerecorded to the third track, and so on until the whole tape is used. In the BBC version there is a separate erase head for only one of the tracks, the lowest; but all eight tracks have combined record and replay heads (which are stacked vertically one above the other). The capstan motor has a highly stabilized speed control which can also be varied to run at any speed from 0 to 40 ips. After the sounds have been assembled, they are reproduced through a control desk with a separate fader for each track—at which point they can be treated by normal echo and filtering devices and augmented by other sources (throvgh up to eleven other faders).

High quality recorders are required where much rerecording has to be done, otherwise wow, tape hiss, and distortion are liable to build up. The workshop also has facilities for recording to magnetic film tracks and for synchronizing radiophonic sound to picture.

Stereophonic work has been done using mono techniques and the normal means of conversion to stereo (i.e. by the use of panpots and spreaders).

Aspiring radiophonic composers should note that all this equipment (in two studios) is fully occupied creating sound for radio and television productions and was not designed for the creation of electronic music except in the most exceptional circumstances. They may possibly be luckier with the British Society for Electronic Music or some of the music laboratories in France, Germany, or Italy; or at Bell Labs. or the University of Illinois which among other American University centres have facilities for computer music, i.e. computer control of electronic sources. The rules by which the computers operate to create their music must of course be written and programmed by humans, for whom a knowledge of both music and, perhaps, mathematics may be an advantage.

New laws for music

Electronic music is a law to itself. And not just because it "sounds different". It really can be fundamentally different from conventional music: "impossible" scales and harmonies can be devised. But before we can begin to examine the freedom the composer is allowed in this new medium, and in particular his freedom to create new harmonic structures and scales, we shall have to take a look at the concept of scale as we know it, and the restrictions that this imposes.

In conventional music, played on conventional instruments, everything is derived from one fundamental relationship, that of the harmonic series in which the partials are all integral multiples of the fundamental. Almost the whole body of musical composition as we know it is restricted to forms and scales derived from this harmonic structure. All stringed and wind instruments produce harmonic series of this sort quite naturally; and most percussion instruments are constructed or used in such a way as to fit in with this arrangement of partials.

All of the scales that have ever been devised for conventional music have one thing in common—the interval of an octave, in which the frequency of the upper note is exactly twice that of the lower. If the two notes are sounded together on orchestral instruments the combination sounds pleasant because of the concord between the fundamental of the higher note and the first harmonic of the lower; and there are also many other harmonics in common. If, however, one of the notes is shifted slightly off-pitch these various concords will be lost—they are present only when the frequency of the two fundamentals can be expressed as a ratio of small whole numbers.

But—and this is important—if there had been no harmonics present this sense of concord or discord would have been lost, unless the fundamentals had been themselves fairly close together. If we start instead with two pure tones at the same frequency, and then increase the pitch of one of them, the first effect that we hear is a "beat" between them. As the difference becomes greater than 15 Hz (twice or three times this at high frequencies), the beat is replaced by the sensation we call dissonance. This increases to a maximum

and then falls away again, until as the frequency ratio approaches
5 : 6 it is no longer apparent. For pure tones dissonance occurs only
within this rather narrow range. (There is just one proviso here:
that the tones are not exceptionally loud. If they are, the ear begins
to generate its own harmonics.)

Some experimenters with electronic music, noting all this, have
concluded that our conventional concept of scale is merely a convenient special case, and that if only we could create harmonic structures which were not based on the conventional 1, 2, 3, 4, ... series,
completely new scales could be devised. And, indeed, they have
been.

Stockhausen's "Study II"

The way in which electronic music can be based on a totally new
concept of scale is made easier to explain by the fact that one complete score has been published, showing everything that had gone
into the making of a particular work: Karlheinz Stockhausen's
"*Study II*". When the tape of this is played to a listener with perfect
pitch, or even good relative pitch, it seems immediately that "something is wrong"—or at the very least, that something is different.
And indeed, by all conventional musical standards, something is;
the arrangement of musical intervals is such as could never
have been heard before the introduction of electronic sound
synthesis.

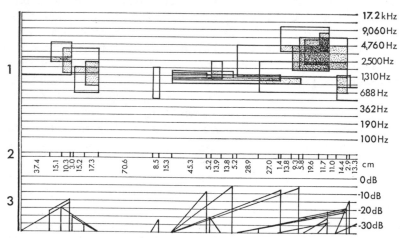

ELECTRONIC MUSIC. Score of the type devised by Stockhausen to show the structure
of his "Study II". I. Pitch: showing the groups of tone mixtures used. Each block
represents a group of five tones (see opposite) 2. Intervals of tape measured in cm.
Tape speed: 30 ips (76·2 cm/sec). 3. Volume: dynamics of the tone mixtures.

376

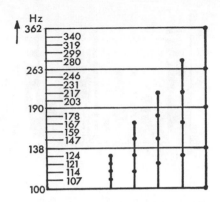

TONE MIXTURES. Five typical mixtures used in Stockhausen's "Study II". 193 were used in all.

Now, in order to accommodate as many small-whole-number relationships as possible, the conventional scale is based on a division of the octave into twelve equal (or roughly equal) parts. Each note in the chromatic scale is roughly 6% higher in frequency than the one before, so that the product of a dozen of these ratios is two—the octave. But Stockhausen, in his "*Study II*", dispenses with the octave completely, and takes instead a completely new scale based on an interval of two octaves and a third, i.e. the interval between a note and its "normal" fifth harmonic, or, to put it another way, the interval between any two notes whose frequency ratio is five. This large interval he subdivided into twenty-five equal small intervals, which means that each successive note on his scale is about 7% higher than its predecessors. So it is only to be expected that very few of the intervals based on this scale will correspond to anything in the previous musical experience of the listener.

Now, if music written to this scale were played on almost any conventional musical instrument (violins and trombones are examples of instruments which *could* be immediately adapted to playing in it; others, such as trumpets and woodwind instruments would have to be specially made), almost any combination of notes attempting either harmony or melody would be dissonant because of the harmonics present. The only feasible way of attacking the problem is to use completely synthesized sound derived from electronic sources. But the labour involved in this is bound to be immense.

Stockhausen, having devised his new scale, proceeded to construct new timbres in which the partials would all fit in with each other on the new scale. He limited himself to five basic sound groups, each composed of five tones. The most compact of these contains a group of five successive frequencies or "notes" from the new scale. The

377

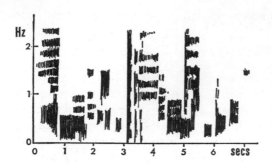

quality of this first group could be described as astringent, as it consists of a series of dissonant pairs. The next group contains members spaced two notes apart, and the internal dissonance has now almost gone; in the other groups, whose members are spaced at three-, four-, and five-note intervals, it has gone completely, and the difference in character between them depends solely on the width of their spectrum. (Before use, each of the 193 basic groups were replayed through a reverberation chamber and re-recorded, in order to blend the sound.)

Using these basic tones, Stockhausen proceeded to experiment with different shapes, durations, combinations, sequences, and so on —and the final work lasts just long enough for the composer to explore and scout around a variety of the possibilities that have occurred to him.

Animated sound

The use of optical sound tracks for animated sound has been going on intermittently almost as long as film has carried sound. Animation, in this sense, means photographing drawings or inscribing them directly on to the sound track either frame by frame, in convenient lengths of track, or continuously (using rotating wheels with cog patterns).

Attempts to simulate actual waveforms are less interesting than experiments using common graphic forms. Sometimes sound was constructed by filming series of rectangles, triangles, ellipses, etc., pitch being controlled coarsely by using different-sized versions of the shape filmed, and finely by varying the distance of the camera. Volume could be controlled by exposure, and double exposure could be used to add one sound to another. Other graphic material has included lettering, fingerprints, and facial profiles. Light slits

378

linked to simple and complex pendulum systems have also been tried.

Animated sound for animated (and other) films achieved what have been their most popular successes under the hand of Norman McLaren in Canada. He made no attempt to imitate natural sounds, but used easily drawn shapes which again, by repetition, produced a pitch. A range of tone colours was drawn and filed away for use as required. Some quite simple drawings were very rich in harmonics; so that strident or harsh as well as simple sounds could be selected.

Volume would be controlled by varying exposure or the area of card exposed. Frame by frame exposure was used, sometimes being extended over several frames to produce a continuous or mandolin quality. For silence (or a pause) black card was photographed. Reverberation was sometimes produced by photographing diminishing series of similar images—though this is tedious in comparison with rerecording using normal echo.

The most interesting part of the technique was the use of tone contouring masks. A tone colour would be selected and over it

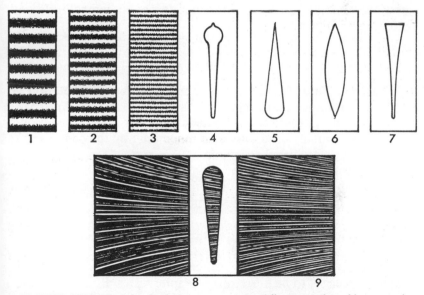

ANIMATED SOUND. 1–3. Cards from a set giving different pitches. More complex patterns of density give richer tone colours. 4–8. Masks (to be superimposed on tone cards) giving dynamic envelopes of a particular duration. Long durations are obtained by adding together cards that are open at the ends. 9. A card giving a range of pitches of a particular tone colour. Those sounds are all photographed directly on to an optical film track. A wide range of similar techniques have been employed, using both variable density and variable area.

would be superimposed a cut-out having an attack, a mid-note dynamic contour and a decay. At times, fascinating (and in their content very appropriate) sounds were produced: blips, clunks, and splinges, tone colours squirted in blobs or squeezed out like toothpaste: the difficulty in describing them illustrates the degree of success that was achieved in getting away from orthodox sound.

Since then (the early fifties) another development has been the use of drawn animation techniques to control the various parameters of musical sound independently. "Oramics", named after the English composeress who has developed the method, uses the full width of 35-mm picture area with, in fact, many film paths running synchronously, to create a range of sounds that can simulate existing musical sound or explore new paths virtually at will.

Separate tracks are drawn for such parameters as volume, vibrato, duration, reverberation, pitch (or more complex functions) which interact together to define and produce a sound.

When the tracks are played together through the machine reading them the score is realized—but if the composer feels that he can improve on it in any detail he can simply go back to the point in question, visually identify and rub out the offending squiggle and write in a modification.

Notation

It has been said that there are as many systems of notation as there are electronic or concrete composers. Since there is little scope for interpretation, there is little practical use for a published score: notation is normally used only as a mnemonic by the composer or as a guide to his technical assistants.

This second use presents one slight difficulty, for the medium is one in which two distinct groups of people must learn to speak a common language and possess a knowledge of each other's problems.

How is the music to be written down? In conventional notation harmonic content and, in fixed-pitch instruments, scale as well, are determined by the instruments written for; while many other details are left imprecise, to be filled in by the interpreter. But in the radiophonic forms there is so much more to be described; and while for any particular work certain basic facts or rules of composition may be stated which remain true for the whole work, so that no reference need be made to them in the detail of the score, different works are likely to have different sets of variables.

CLASSIFICATION OF SOUND

The dynamics or envelopes of sounds: classifications devised by *musique concrète* composers and engineers as a first step towards a system of notation. The terms shown here could represent either the quality of an original sound or the way in which it might be transformed.

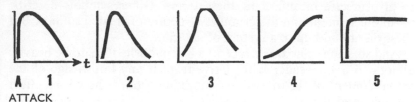

A 1 2 3 4 5

ATTACK

1. Shock—bump, clink, etc. 2. Percussive—tapping glasses, etc. 3. Explosive—giving a blasting effect. 4. Progressive—a gradual rise. 5. Level—full intensity from start.

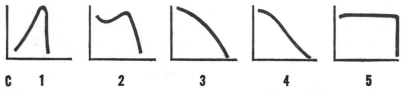

B 1 2 3 4 5

INTERNAL DYNAMICS

1. Steady—an even quality. 2. Vibratory or puffing. 3. Scraping—or tremulous. 4. Pulsing—overlapping repetitions blending together. 5. Clustered—subjects placed end to end.

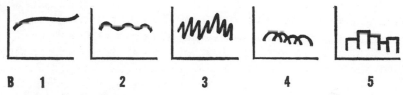

C 1 2 3 4 5

DECAY

1. Reversed shock. 2. Accented. 3. Deadened. 4. Progressive. 5. Flat—cut off sharply.

Works based on electronic synthesis will usually require representation throughout a very broad frequency band, and therefore for these the conventional stave will probably have to be discarded (as with Stockhausen's "*Study II*"). Whereas for music based on concrete sources (or any other work in which harmonic content is determined by stating the source), it may perhaps be retained where those with a musical training find this desirable.

In Paris a certain amount of work has been done in the way of writing down some of the more essential characteristics of concrete sounds. A note can be described in terms of its qualities of attack

381

and decay, the pitch and volume of the body of the note and its reverberation, and variations in these within the duration. Symbols have been suggested for such subjective qualities of sounds as "fatness", "thinness", and "hollowness", and attempts have been made to give precise meanings to these terms. Other symbols describe harmonic content and the granular structure of treated sounds. But these do not add up to a system of notation.

And so, each score or extract which is published has to be heavily annotated if the reader is to derive from it any knowledge of the actual content of the music, or—more important—how each effect was achieved.

13

CHECKING QUALITY

DURING rehearsal, recording, or broadcast, the ear should be constantly searching out the faults that will mar a production; certainly there are plenty of things to watch out for—here are just a few that affect sound whether in radio, television, or film:

1. *Production faults:* e.g. miscast voices, stilted speaking of the lines, uncolloquial scripts, bad timing.
2. *Faulty technique:* e.g. poor balance and control, untidy fades and mixes, misuse of acoustics.
3. *Poor sound quality:* e.g. distortion, resonances, and other irregularities in the frequency response, lack of bass and top.
4. *Faults of the equipment or recordings:* wow and flutter, hum, excessive tape hiss, noises due to loose connections, poor screening, or mis-matching.

Of these, the faults in the first group are certainly the most important. They are also, perhaps, the easiest to spot. And as for techniques: the ability to see faults here comes with the practice of the techniques. But the various things that can be wrong with the quality of a sound—objective, measurable things—appear, somewhat surprisingly, to be the most difficult for the ear to judge in other than subjective "I-know-what-I-like" terms.

Quality and the ear

The quality of sound which the ear will accept—and prefer—depends almost entirely on what the listener is used to. Very few people whose ears are untrained can judge quality in reasonably precise and objective terms. Given a choice between qualities, listeners are generally prepared to state a preference, but experiments in the United States have indicated that as many will prefer medium quality as prefer the best.

There was a demonstration of this at an Audio Fair in Britain when a manufacturer of loudspeaker enclosures invited members of the public to judge and compare the quality of three different stereo speaker systems (without being able to see which was playing or being told the prices until afterwards). To a trained ear there can surely have been little doubt about the order. A large number of people, most of them presumably audio enthusiasts, took part in the tests. And their votes split very evenly between the three systems.

At first sight the results of such experiments may appear rather depressing for the high-quality-sound enthusiast. Even among people who claim to like hi-fi (a term which covers any sound equipment from medium quality upwards) the real preference is often for a box which sounds like a box, and the sort of quality which turns a living-room into one corner of a great concert hall is found to be somewhat disturbing.

This is an attitude which must be respected; but it must nevertheless be true that quality and enjoyment will often be closely related. The high-quality performance of a musical work gives more *information* to a listener who is new to it; and it is often a technically superior disc which first "sells" music content, and interests a listener in something new.

The difference between a good loudspeaker and a poor one boils down to this: that the good one allows more of the original conception of the sound to reach the listener. So, potentially, it permits greater enjoyment of the programme—or, at any rate, a more sophisticated enjoyment of it. On the technical monitoring side it would appear obvious that a high quality speaker is essential.

High-quality sound is not—as with, say, wide-screen film—an advance which imposes a new set of limitations. Different degrees of quality may be acceptable to the same person when applied to different programme ends. For example, high quality may be best for brilliant modern music (or for any orchestral music listened to as a concert); medium or low quality can be satisfactory for ordinary speech, where the primary reason for listening is usually to hear what is said; and "mellow" quality is often felt to be less obtrusive when music is required for a companionable background noise. On high-quality equipment these different types of programme are all available at the appropriate levels of quality; on poor equipment they are all debased to the same indifferent standard.

So it is undoubtedly worth persevering with the education of one's ears, and allowing other people the opportunity of listening to sound which is of rather better quality than they are used to.

Nevertheless, any organization that is conscious of cost must decide what is to be the practicable economic upper limit to the audio frequency range to be offered.

Tests have been carried out by the BBC in which the audio frequency range was restricted to 7 kHz, 10 kHz, and 12 kHz. Sounds heard within the test material included tubular bells, brass, cymbals and triangle, snare and military drums, maraccas, hand-claps, and female speech. The listeners were all under 40 years of age, both male and female and included a number of people who were experienced in judging sound quality. The results of the tests suggested that:

   (i) Only a few critical observers will hear restriction to 12 kHz.

  (ii) Many inexperienced listeners can detect restriction to 10 kH; experienced listeners will do so readily.

 (iii) A filter at 7 kHz could be detected even by inexperienced observers.

In fact the BBC broadcasts up to 15 kHz on VHF/FM.

Loudspeakers

The main obstacle to good sound has nearly always been the loudspeaker. It is, in principle, fairly easy to get good middle range and high-frequency response, but efficient production of bass requires either a fairly large surface area to push the air, or a horn with an equally large aperture. The reason for this is one that we

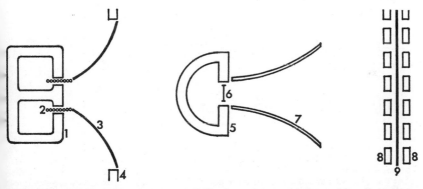

LOUDSPEAKER TYPES. Moving coil (*left*): the most commonly used for all purposes (bass, treble, and wide range). 1. Permanent magnet. 2. Moving coil. 3. Cone. 4. Baffle or enclosure. Ribbon unit (*centre*): Sometimes used for treble. 5. Permanent magnet. 6. Ribbon (seen in plan view). 7. Acoustic horn. Electrostatic (*right*). 8. Perforated fixed electrodes. 9. Diaphragm.

385

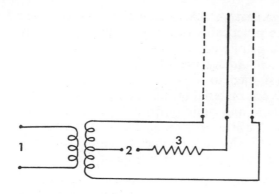

ELECTROSTATIC LOUD-SPEAKER. 1. Signal input. 2. UHT. 3. High resistance. Push–pull operation allows the driving force to be applied evenly over a large area of diaphragm, to produce relatively large excursions. One full-range electrostatic loudspeaker has two bass units on either side of a single middle and high frequency unit, with a cross-over at 200–300 Hz.

have already met: just as sounds of long wavelengths do not "see" small objects, slipping instead round the sides, so too will small surface areas be unable to move a mass of air efficiently at low frequencies.

One apparent alternative to this is to have a relatively small area driving the air but to boost the bass so that the inefficiency of the coupling is compensated for in advance. But there is a limit to this, as the excursions of the diaphragm get so big that this in itself is a complication, as is the extra power that is required from the amplifier.

Most loudspeakers use a stiff diaphragm working as a piston. This is operated by an electro-mechanical device which is usually very similar in principle to those used in microphones—except, of

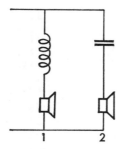
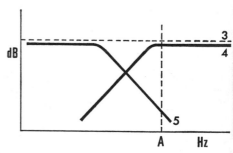

LOUDSPEAKER: SIMPLE CROSS-OVER NETWORK. 1. Bass unit. 2. Treble unit. The total power (3) is divided evenly between the two units (4 and 5); for each it falls off at 6 dB/octave beyond the cross-over point. This is a very satisfactory type of network provided that there are no severe irregularities in the response of the cone itself that are close enough to the cross-over point to make a significant contribution even though attenuated. For example a very severe fluctuation in the bass cone output at A will still affect the overall response: the answer is to make the cross-over point lower (if the response of the high frequency unit permits) or to use a more complex dividing network with a steeper cut-off at the cross-over point.

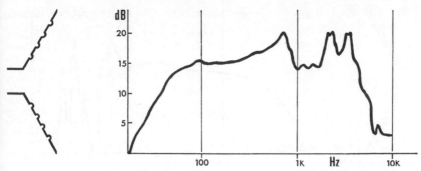

LOUDSPEAKER CONE WITH STRAIGHT SIDES of corrugated paper felt. The performance diagram shows axial frequency response with output in dB (arbitrary scale).

course, that it converts an electrical signal back into physical movement. The most common type is the moving coil; but electrostatic, ribbon, and other types are also sometimes used (the ribbon particularly for high frequency units).

It is not easy for a single diaphragm to respond equally well to all frequencies: sometimes the signal is split and fed to separate loudspeakers covering two (or even three) different parts of the frequency range. When the sound is divided up in this way there is no need for a sharp cut-off as one loudspeaker takes over from another, so long as the acoustic output adds up to a full signal. But careful relative positioning of the two units is necessary, so that there is no phase cancellation at the switch-over frequencies.

With the low-frequency unit a cone of paper may be used as the diaphragm. This has to be corrugated concentrically in order to stop

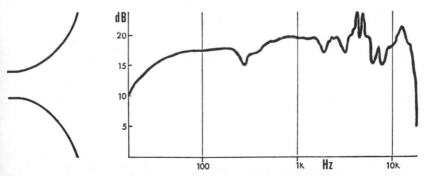

LOUDSPEAKER CONE WITH CURVED PROFILE (paper felt)—a shape which gives good results. The response curve shows the axial output of a wide-range 8-inch cone. Note that the fluctuations in high frequency response are greater than at other points in the audio chain.

387

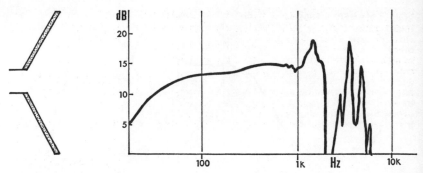

LOUDSPEAKER CONE: EXPANDED POLYSTYRENE SANDWICHED BETWEEN ALUMINIUM FOIL. Experiments with these materials have not been very successful. The material acts well as a rigid piston at low frequencies but lacks sufficient internal damping to reduce resonances at 1 kHz and above. Even for a bass unit a smooth response to beyond 1600 Hz is required.

unwanted harmonics from being formed (these may include a subharmonic which is actually below the main frequency at which the cone is being driven). Although simple cones of this type work well, cones or pistons of expanded polystyrene between thin aluminium foil surfaces have also been tried. These are more rigid, but lack adequate internal damping: they ring like a wineglass at certain frequencies. Latterly, combinations of plastics have been adopted: these can be tailored to produce the best compromise between stiffness and damping. The cone, of whatever construction, must also be of low mass or its inertia may affect the response.

A problem with a cone—or any other diaphragm—is that as it radiates the wanted signal from the front, a second signal, in the

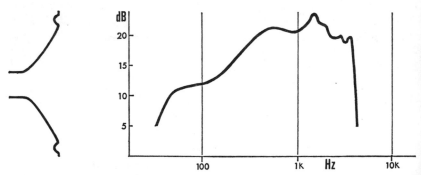

LOUDSPEAKER CONE: BBC DESIGN, 1967; at which time it was claimed to be better than any other commercially available cone of equal size (12 inches) or larger used in a bass unit (with cross-over at 1600 Hz). The material used is Bextrene (a polystyrene/synthetic rubber compound), with a PVC surround.

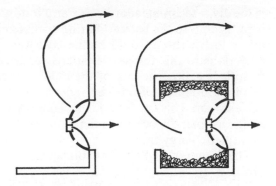

opposite phase, is being radiated from the back; and if there is nothing to stop it, some of this back-radiation will leak round the sides and join with the sound from the front. The long-wavelength low frequencies will be most affected by this: as the two signals combine, they will still be partly out of phase and will therefore partly cancel a signal that is already weaker than it should be because the cone is too small for effective low frequency work.

There are several partial cures for this. One is to house the loudspeaker in a baffle of relatively large area. The size of this will determine the limiting wavelength, below which cancellation will still occur: a baffle about 30 inches square is about the minimum for a moderately good low frequency response. A second technique is to turn the space behind the cone into a low frequency resonator with a port which radiates some of the power. It can be arranged that by phase change this will now boost the response in the region in which it previously fell off. But this bass reflex loudspeaker (as it is called) is bulky, may be subject to cabinet colouration in the bass, and below its resonant frequency cuts off even more sharply than before. In fact it has a characteristically recognizable quality—which

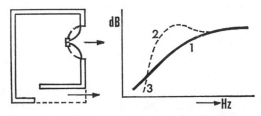

BASS REFLEX LOUDSPEAKER: this uses the internal cavity and a port at the front as a Helmholz resonator with a low frequency resonance peak. Added to the normal bass response of the loudspeaker (1) it can be used to lift the bass for about one octave (2). But below this (3) the cut-off is more severe.

is hardly a recommendation for any loudspeaker. Yet another idea is to try to lose the back radiation completely. Simply feeding it out into another room would be the best way, but as there are usually objections to this the next best answer is generally adopted: to try to stifle it within the box of the loudspeaker in such a way that the diaphragm is not affected by reflections or by the "stiffness' of the enclosed air. This can be done reasonably well; but, again, the bulkier the cabinet the better, as the more volume there will be to lose the unwanted energy in.

The design of high-quality loudspeakers is undoubtedly a difficult problem to which there have been many other ingenious part-solutions attempting, in particular, to get round the difficulty of the sheer size that is naturally associated with the longer wavelengths of sound. But this is a very big subject, and one that is beyond the scope of this book.

Monitoring arrangements

The best distance to place a loudspeaker for monitoring pro-grammes is probably about 3–6 feet. Closer than this the sound has a somewhat unreal quality owing to standing waves close to the cabinet; at a greater distance than 6 feet the acoustics of the listening room begin to take over. It is desirable that these acoustics should be more or less the same as those of a domestic living-room. But it is important to produce a well-blended signal and to know whether some minor fault is due to the studio or listening room; and the only way to be sure is to sit rather closer to the loudspeaker than one does when listening purely for pleasure at home. This is, however, possible only for mono.

For monitoring stereo the listener should be at the apex of an equilateral triangle (or, perhaps a little closer). The speakers will be about 8 feet apart and the listener therefore 6 feet or more from them. The producer will sit immediately behind the balancer. In a studio layout the ideal arrangement is one in which the balancer and producer do not see directly in to the studio as they face the sound stage, but can do so (to sort out positioning or other problems) by simply turning round.

For four-channel stereo two additional loudspeakers will be placed behind the listener. Where direct sound is heard on all four speakers (and especially for monitoring balance) the four should be a balance set of the same type. But for most normal listening it is not normally essential to have rear speakers which are as powerful or of

390

such high quality as those at the front. Indeed, since the total power is now being split four ways, if a room were being equipped afresh, all four loudspeakers could be of a matched set which could be (individually) less powerful than would be desirable for mono or two-channel stereo.

Listening for faults

Several of the points raised so far have a wider application than the present context, and I shall be returning to them again in the next chapter. Here I want to go on to deal more specifically with some of the things which mar the technical quality of sound.

This book is not concerned with the technicalities of equipment, such things as circuit details and so on, except when these are directly relevant to operational techniques. But a limited degree of technical knowledge and understanding of the sound medium is certainly of value, if only to indicate why the things we do have the effect that they do, or to trace an effect—wanted or unwanted—back to its cause.

As we monitor a sound for quality our first concern must be to recognize faults when they occur—and this is the reason why most of the main headings of this chapter are the names of forms of distortion or faults. Once the fault and the conditions in which it occurs are observed we are a long way towards a cure (though there is no pretence that the details given here are exhaustive—particularly where defects of components may be the cause).

Also, various faults can occur in recording which may pass unnoticed at the time. Methods of correcting faults in recordings are indicated wherever these are feasible.

Noise

Noise, for our present purpose, may be regarded as random sound of indefinite pitch. There are plenty of other forms of "unwanted sound", but these can each be treated separately.

All irregularities in the structure of matter cause noise: the separate particles of iron oxide in magnetic tape, tiny roughnesses in the wall of a record, the granular structure of carbon in a resistor, the random flow of individual electrons through a metal or across the vacuum of a thermionic valve; all of these are bound to produce some level of noise in a recording or broadcast. The only question is, how low can it be kept in relation to the signal? For most purposes a ratio of 55 dB or more throughout the chain may be regarded as reasonably good; and, as will be seen later, this provides an adequate range of volumes even for programme material which in real life would demand wider dynamics.

Noise becomes serious when components before the first stage of amplification begin to deteriorate; at a later stage, when there are more drastic faults (e.g. a "dirty" fader or a "dry" joint); or where there are long lines or radio transmissions broadcast in unfavourable circumstances.

One form of noise which does have definite pitch is *hum*. This nuisance is caused by the mains frequency (and its harmonics) getting into the audio signal. The second harmonic is generally the most serious component except in certain types of hi-fi loudspeaker cabinet which provide a high output at low frequencies, so most hum filters concentrate on getting rid of 100 (or 120) Hz. More elaborate hum filters take out narrow slices of a wide range of harmonics without affecting the music.

Mains hum may be caused by inadequate smoothing of the power supply when it has been rectified from A.C. to D.C., or by lack of adequate screening on the wires carrying audio signals—particularly at low level, and in high-impedance circuits such as those from electrostatic or crystal microphones before the first amplifier. (All electrostatic and some crystal microphones have head amplifiers; but crystal pick-ups may not have an amplifier close to the head—so that here the lead will require screening.) Magnetic microphones can be directly affected by nearby electrical equipment, such as mains transformers or electric motors.

Earthing faults may cause hum: either the simple lack of an earth or (at the other extreme) the connection of an item by separate paths to a common earth, thereby causing an earth loop, which like any other loop can pick up signals from wiring or equipment carrying mains.

Distortion

If at any point in a broadcast or recording chain the volume is set too high for any stage that follows, the peaks of the waveform will become flattened, or distorted. The new frequencies introduced are harmonics of the original frequencies present. In musical terminology, new overtones are produced—but a great deal of it at precisely those frequencies which are already present in much sound, and most music. The introduction of harmonic distortion is therefore to some extent masked by sound already present; and where it is not is made more acceptable by its pseudo-musical relationship to the wanted sound.

Small amounts of distortion may be more acceptable than a high noise level: 2% harmonic distortion will not generally be noticed; and 1% represents a reasonable limit for high quality.

Where unduly high distortion occurs it may be due to actual equipment faults. For example, it will occur if the moving parts of a

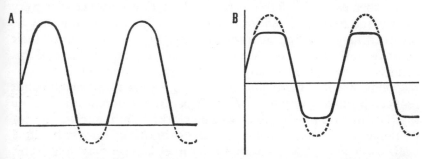

HARMONIC DISTORTION: the dotted portion of the signals is flattened. A. Bottom-ming causes each alternate peak to be clipped. B. Both peaks are flattened, as excessive swings in each direction cannot be followed by some item of equipment. In both cases the distortion produced includes tones which are exact multiples of the frequency of clipping.

transducer have worked loose or are in the wrong place, e.g. a ribbon or moving coil hanging out of the magnetic field. It will occur if for some reason a valve is working in the wrong condition, or if too much or too little bias is used when recording on magnetic tape.

Intermodulation distortion is less tolerable than harmonic distortion: it occurs when two frequencies interfere with each other to produce sum or difference products. High quality sound equipment is designed to avoid the production of intermodulation effects which occur in the audio range.

Distortion may arise right at the start of the chain, at points that are—in theory—under the control of the balancer. Some air pressures (perhaps caused by wind, or due to explosive consonants in close speech) may be such as to move a microphone diaphragm outside its normal working range.

Or the output of the microphone may be at too high a level for the first pre-amplifier. Amplifier stages have a linear response to changes in volume (i.e. their output is proportional to input) only over a limited range. The sensitivity of professional microphones is

393

related to the volume of expected sound sources in such a way that they mostly feed signals to the mixer at about the same range of levels. But there are notable exceptions in such sound sources as the bass drum, brass, and the electric guitar, the loudspeaker from which may be set very high. If the preamplifiers are of fixed gain, a 12 dB attenuation (or perhaps a great deal more) will be required between microphone and amplifier. Alternatively, a microphone of low sensitivity may be selected; or a microphone may be used that has a head amplifier that can be switched to accept different input levels.

Another example of this form of distortion may occur in very close piano balance. Used for pop music in this way, pianos may be regarded as percussion instruments, deriving a great deal of their effect from the attack transient. The brief, very high volume of this transient may not be apparent from a meter which takes time to respond—but it is there, and is liable to distort if the signal is not reduced again by perhaps 6 or 12 dB before preamplification. Note that in this case the amplifier will be working on the lower part of its range for the main signal, and the overall signal must be lifted again later in the chain—where the same damage may still occur. There has therefore been controversy as to the value of this technique.

The deliberate distortion of frequency response due to the selection of particular microphones and their placing, together with the changes that can be made for subjective reasons, is dealt with in another chapter.

Loss of high frequencies

Most of the links in an audio chain are capable of distorting the frequency response; and this is usually worse at the higher end of the scale. High frequencies can be lost in a variety of ways, and whether or not anything can be done about it depends on whether or not there is a frequency at which the signal is totally extinguished.

When a signal passes along a line the capacitance between the two wires carrying it provides a path whereby the high frequencies are selectively lost, but the damage can be repaired by boosting the high-frequency response from time to time—and the signal-to-noise ratio is substantially maintained because high-frequency noise is first reduced and then boosted in the same proportions.

But the amount of high frequency loss depends on distance, and with long lines one has to make a compromise somewhere. Taking a particular quality of line, we may decide that 8 kHz, say, is all that can be economically maintained; and then install equalizers at the various distances where the signal-to-noise ratio has fallen, say, from 55 to 40 dB at this frequency.

Nor is this a complete cure, because at every stage where the frequency response is corrected a little of the noise on the line is boosted, and at the same time the many stages of distortion and subsequent correction inevitably begin to make the top end of the

RESTORING HIGH FREQUENCY LOSSES. (A) top can be boosted and effectively restored. (B) h.f. extinction at two frequencies: top cannot be restored effectively.

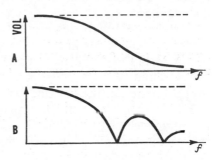

frequency spectrum erratic, so that eventually the signal begins to get lost even below our nominal 8 kHz.

In a building the size of a broadcasting studio centre there is a danger not only of high frequency losses due to capacitance, but also induction of programme signals, hum, etc., from other lines. One way in which this is kept at least partially in check is by the use of standard impedances for as much of the equipment as possible. The BBC has adopted a standard of 600 ohms.

If a low impedance system had been adopted, the resistance and capacitance of the wiring itself would have been significant, simply because there is so much of it.

The exact matching of impedances is important when *power* is being transmitted, e.g. to a loudspeaker, as mismatching produces power losses. Where the significant part of a signal is its *voltage*, mismatching may matter less. Low in to high may go; high in to low may not: this is the rule. If a high-impedance input such as a crystal pick-up is fed to a low-impedance input there will be loss of bass; if the output from a magnetic pick-up or microphone is fed into lower than its rated impedance there will be loss of high frequencies.

Even more important, do not feed a high-level signal (e.g. from a tape deck or a record player) to a low-level input (such as that for a microphone) without appropriate attenuation or there will be severe overloading, with consequent distortion.

Magnetic tape

One of the major occupations of the sound recordist is to ensure that he has, on the one hand, a good overall signal-to-noise ratio, and on the other, no appreciable distortion. The proper control of levels, and the correct lining up of equipment, are both intended to make the best use of the region between the two. The recordist also requires a smooth and level frequency response throughout the audio range.

For the ability to achieve these results he is dependent on a medium which is remarkably complicated to make: it is fortunate that most of the problems can safely be left to the manufacturers to worry about. Briefly, magnetic tape consists of a strong plastic support material (the backing) and a coating of finely divided iron oxide dispersed in a further plastic binding material. (A more recently developed magnetic recording medium is chromium dioxide: this promises a still better performance than has been obtained with the material for which the following details are given.)

The particular form of iron oxide used is the ferric oxide, Fe_2O_3. This is chemically the same as jeweller's rouge, but in its physical form and magnetic properties it is different (jeweller's rouge is non-magnetic). By a complex process of manufacture acicular (needle-like) crystals are formed: these are about one micron long (i.e. a twenty-fifth of a mil), and have to be dispersed as evenly as possible throughout the binding material without being broken into smaller fragments. Then, when the coating has been applied to the backing and while it is still in the form of a liquid emulsion, these crystals have to be orientated magnetically so that they are lengthways along the tape.

The oxide concentration in the coating will be between 20% and 40%, and its sensitivity as a recording medium depends on both concentration and orientation. The thickness of the coating, too, has an effect: as the thickness of the emulsion (or the concentration of oxide) increases, low-frequency sensitivity will increase, but high-frequency sensitivity will go down. In thick coatings, self-demagnetization is troublesome at high frequencies.

The range of levels available between that at which distortion (measured as 2% third harmonic distortion) will be produced and that at which there is appreciable noise should be above 50 dB. The noise in question is that which is generated as a recording is made: when wiping a tape it will be possible to erase the tape to a much lower noise level—say, 70 dB below the same distortion level.

Modulation background noise depends not only on the degree of dispersion of the oxide throughout the emulsion, but also on its surface quality; tapes for BBC use are improved by surface polishing.

In fact, to record the full range of audio frequencies efficiently it is necessary to add a high frequency bias (upwards of 50 kHz) to the signal. The most important result of this will be to reduce distortion and noise at low and mid-range.

To get the most satisfactory signal-to-noise ratio the bias level must be set with care. As bias amplitude is increased from zero, the percentage distortion decreases as the strength of the recorded signal goes up. The recorded noise level also rises, but not so fast as the programme signal: these two both reach a maximum together, but as the bias strength increases beyond this point the signal-to-noise ratio continues to improve.

In the case of one good-quality recorder the signal-to-noise ratio is 52 dB at maximum output, and this rises to 54 dB as the bias is increased by just enough to reduce output by 1 dB. But if the bias is increased still further the output decreases sufficiently for the percentage distortion to become more of a nuisance. So the optimum bias setting is chosen as that at which the output has increased to a maximum and then dropped away again by 1 dB.

Faults in manufacture *can* occur—otherwise there would be no reason for pen-testing every inch of professional tapes. Unevenly coated tapes show marked deterioration after a few recordings. But the risk of this or, for that matter, the risk of "drop-out" is, nowadays, remote. Recorded tapes showing such faults should, of course, be returned to the manufacturer; but for most other cases where there is a slight flaw such as a drop-out, making a simple joint (and removing the flawed scrap of tape) will save time and trouble and leave the tape substantially perfect.

Videotape has to be of a higher standard than quarter-inch sound tape; where faults occur these will generally be apparent on the picture first.

A recording head which has become permanently magnetized will itself magnetize the crystals of iron oxide more in one direction than the other when it is used for recording. At high levels it will therefore over-record on half the cycle, and introduce distortion. This tendency will be cured by the use of a tape head demagnetizer (or "degausser"), effectively a mild steel horseshoe magnet with a fairly small gap, energized by mains voltage. The gap of the demagnetizer is drawn along that of the recording head and removed to a distance before the energizing current is switched off. A degausser such as this may also be used to remove clicks and bumps from a tape (which may be caused on some equipment by switching on and off). However, degaussing a tape will also remove atmosphere as well as the click. (On quarter inch and 16 mm separate magnetic film tracks, editing is preferable; but this is more difficult on videotape.)

High frequency losses on tape

Severe loss of high frequencies will occur if the tape is not in close contact with recording or replay head. This, for a gap of one micron (a twenty-five-thousandth of an inch) has been shown to produce a loss of nearly 4 dB at a frequency of 12 kHz (recorded at $7\frac{1}{2}$ ips).

On some recorders, pressure pads are used to ensure that contact is complete; professional machines are engineered to ensure that the back-tension on the feed spool is sufficient to deal with this (but not enough to stretch the tape). If either of these devices fails, and the tape buckles away from the head, the gap produced may cause noticeable losses.

And if there is a really marked loss of top ... well, it could be that the tape was recorded or replayed with the wrong side of the tape against the head. And to record through no more than the thickness of the backing (about 1–1·5 mils) is sufficient to ruin the quality completely.

Losses—on a somewhat smaller scale—can also be due to magnetic dust from the tape coating collecting in crevices around the gap of a tape head, which should therefore be cleaned regularly. (Such crevices are minimized in the manufacture of tape heads by filling the gap with a shim of material which is harder than the metal of the head. Wear is thereby kept even.)

Where the high frequency losses are progressive, measures may be taken to equalize for them. But where complete extinction at some frequency occurs no amount of boosting can restore it.

Again the tape head provides an important example of this: if the wavelength to be replayed is an integral multiple of the gap width the two opposing half-cycles of the signal will exactly cancel each other out. Clearly, such a signal cannot be restored in the reproducing amplifier. However, this does not imply that nothing can in this case be done, as the gap-width of the recording head is not directly related to scanning loss (recording is achieved at the trailing edge of the gap). So scanning by a replay head with a narrower gap might extract a signal.

398

A replay head scans a slightly greater length of tape than would be suggested by the size of the gap (say 0·65 mils for an actual ½-mil gap); but for a recording head the effect of high-frequency bias is to narrow the effective gap width (say 0·75 mils for an actual 1-mil gap). So, if a separate head is provided for monitoring the tape on replay, its gap width should be half that of the recording head.

These are details which are of importance when considering the specifications of a new deck or when deciding on a tape speed, but which at other times may be forgotten. However, the matter becomes of more than passing importance when the gap of the recording head is not at right angles to the direction of tape travel. This fault ("azimuth misalignment") is one of the most common causes of poor frequency response on tapes recorded on machines of which the alignment is not checked as a matter of routine.

The gap of a tape head is very much narrower than it is long; and it follows that if the line of the gap is only a very little out of its true 90° to the direction of travel, then the head will, in effect, be scanning a much broader segment of the tape. Whether it is in fact the head that is out of true or the tape that is being pulled along at a slight angle, a tape which has been recorded in this way will suffer a serious loss in top response when replayed on any correctly adjusted replay head.

If this fault is suspected when a tape is played back on a second machine, try varying the angle at which the tape is traversing the head by pushing the point of a pencil between the tape and the deck. If it is possible to achieve some improvement in top response by doing this, then there is an azimuth fault (which could, remember, be on the replay machine).

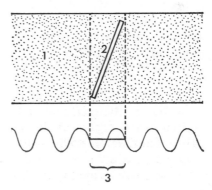

AZIMUTH MISALIGNMENT. I. Tape.
2. Misaligned recording or reproducing
head. 3. Extinction wavelength.

399

Correction can be made by:

(i) copying from the original recorder (and head) to another machine;

(ii) replaying on a machine with a variable azimuth setting; or

(iii) replaying only part of the full recorded track width: e.g. replay a full-track recording half-track, or a half-track recording quarter-track. Either of these measures will improve the effective frequency response, but the signal-to-noise ratio will go down by about 4 dB.

Another example of extinction at high frequencies is provided by the ribbon microphone, where the length of the ribbon in certain of the older (and larger) types was sufficient to reduce the high-frequency response of a signal reaching it at an acute angle to the line of the ribbon. "Tilting" such a ribbon was at one time commonly used as a means of discriminating against sibilance (a voice defect which seems to be less of a nuisance than it has been in the past, now that microphones with a smooth response in the upper middle frequency range have come into general use: an extended *flat* frequency range seems to mean that sibilance is less apparent than before).

Frequency correction

Correction of a whole range of faults, such as noise, distortion, and unsatisfactory frequency response, is often attempted by means of filter circuits.

In some cases frequency correction of one sort or another may help; in others we may tip out the baby with the bathwater. For speech the results will depend on whether the main body of the fault lies in the same frequency band as that required for maximum intelligibility; for music, whether a limited frequency band is acceptable.

Frequency correction units are closely related to the type of tone controls available on pre-amplifier/control units, and the two are for many purposes interchangeable.

Minimum requirements are:

(i) bass and treble tone controls giving at least $\pm$ 10 dB at 100 Hz and 10 kHz, and preferably more (see p. 352);

(ii) a variety of top cut filters, with or without variable slope;

(iii) hum filters for 50, 60, 100, and 120 Hz, and

(iv) an "in/out" switch so that each degree of correction can be compared directly with the original.

Use of these controls is simple: it is merely a matter of personal preference—but bearing in mind intelligibility and clarity, on the one hand, and the need to preserve as much of the original voice or music quality as possible, on the other.

However, the above controls are practically useless for certain types of frequency distortion. For example, sibilance combined with a sharp peak in the microphone response somewhere below 5 kHz would hardly be affected.

Tape bases

For the everyday user, the material of the tape base may be of more direct interest than the coating. This is because tape is available with three widely used backing materials and four thicknesses. The materials are:

(i) "Acetate" (Cellulose Triacetate or Diacetate) This is very widely used professionally, though less in Britain than Continental Europe. If it is given a sharp tug it will snap rather than stretch (extending perhaps 0·5%, which is tolerable in speech). This makes repair easy: a simple splice is usually sufficient. However, it also tears easily and is damaged by excessive humidity.

(ii) PVC (Polyvinyl Chloride). Favoured by the BBC, this is much stronger than an acetate backing but when damaged may stretch too much for adequate repair. It is also sensitive to heat (particularly temperatures above 80° C).

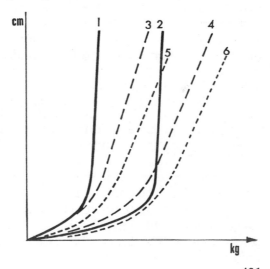

TAPE BASES. Extension (stretch) compared with load. 1. Acetate 18μ. (double play). 2. Acetate 37μ. (standard play). 3. Polyester 12μ. (triple play). 4. Polyester 18μ. 5. PVC 25μ. (long play). 6. PVC 37μ.

401

(iii) Polyester. This is stronger still, but more expensive; it is there-fore most suitable for the thinner backings. Like PVC, it is liable to stretch extensively before breaking.

The four thicknesses are:

(i) Standard play ($1\frac{1}{2}$ mil; 37 micron).
(ii) Long play (1 mil, 25 micron).
(iii) Double play ($\frac{3}{4}$ mil, 18 micron).
(iv) Triple play ($\frac{1}{2}$ mil, 12 micron; polyester only).

Standard play is normally used for professional work as it is best able to stand up to rough treatment—including fast rewind. It is also less subject to printing (see below).

Two speeds now used professionally are:

(i) 15 ips for high quality music recordings.
(ii) $7\frac{1}{2}$ ips for other good quality recordings (but mainly for broad-cast speech).

Several other speeds below this are available: $3\frac{3}{4}$, $1\frac{7}{8}$ and $\frac{15}{16}$ ips. They are adequate when intelligibility is required but technical quality (and particularly a wide frequency response) is unimportant.

Tapes are usually wound on spools with side flanges; though in Central Europe tapes are often wound on cores (i.e. without flanges). Apart from presenting the obvious possibility of disaster—dropping the whole thing on the floor—these are also subject to uneven spooling in fast rewind. For users who find this a problem acetate tapes with a matt backing surface are provided: this gives a more even wind, presumably by maintaining a steady tension without slippage. These are used by Continental broadcasting organizations but not by the BBC, where spools with flanges are preferred.

Printing

This is a tape storage fault in which the strongest effect occurs soon after recording—although sheer length of time in storage will certainly add to it.

Printing increases with temperature, and if this is too far above the optimum 55° F, the effect can be serious—so tapes should not be stored on top of radiators. Other causes are electrical fields (keep away from the magnets of loudspeakers, microphones, etc.) and physical shock. The distance between successive magnetic layers on the spool also comes into it: the thinner backing of extended and

402

TAPE PRINT-THROUGH. Printing depends on the thickness of the tape base layer, as well as temperature and physical shock. 3. Layer with original signal. 2 and 4. Adjacent layers with printed signals. 1. Wavelength of original and printed signal.

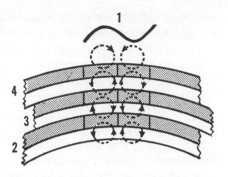

double-play tape produce a higher print level. In the type of tape where the iron oxide is distributed throughout the bonding material (impregnated tape) printing tends to be much heavier—but this sort of tape is now rarely encountered.

If caught within, say, a fortnight of its occurring, much of the printing effect may be removed by a partial "wipe" using only a very light erase current. Naturally it does not improve any part of the signal, but the erasure is more marked on the small printed signal than on the main body of the recording (the print being reduced by perhaps 16 dB, as against 3 dB off the main signal). But after a fortnight the fixity of the print increases very rapidly, and this method becomes relatively ineffective. And then the only method of correction is to cut out the most audible effects of printing from the pauses and replace them with similar lengths of tape recorded with studio "atmosphere"—not very satisfactory.

Printing is a common problem with sound on videotape. It does not occur, however, with magnetic film stock, of which the backing is much thicker.

Damaged tape—and accidental erasure

Where a tape has spilled and wound round the spindle and become crumpled, speech recordings are often still playable, while music recordings are not. The smoothing effect of a tight wind may help, and so may backing the worst parts with jointing tape, but where the output is still breaking up after these measures the only answer is surgery: first cut out the damaged parts, and then edit to restore continuity (or revise your programme to incorporate a link at that point).

Just about the worst way in which a tape can be damaged is described rather graphically as "bootlacing"; here the tape is

403

stretched until it resembles a piece of string. For this and many less serious cases the only answer again is surgery.

The ultimate tape fault is accidental erasure. There is no cure whatsoever for this disaster, other than to understand how it happens and make sure it doesn't. The most obvious way of accidentally wiping is to switch a replay to record by mistake. Most machines have some sort of safeguard against this, usually by requiring a double operation. If it is a shade too easy to reach the record condition on a given machine it may be worth while devising some modification to the recorder which will prevent this.

A second menace which just occasionally destroys a recording is the strong magnetic field of, say, a ribbon microphone or a moving-coil loudspeaker, or some other item of equipment of this sort. Usually only a small part of a spool of tape is actually reduced in level, but this is quite as bad as if the whole lot had gone, and a great deal more tantalizing: the electric field has taken a "bite" from every turn of the spool.

A few experiments with a spool of used tape will indicate if there are any danger-spots in a studio. When tapes are to be sent through the post or carried in public places the simplest safeguard (apart from screening the tape) is to make a copy.

Inconstant pitch

Variable speed is a fault which afflicts battery tape recorders when the batteries are failing. Each take starts off at something close to the correct speed, but the tape soon slows down to fluctuate about whatever speed the battery is able to sustain. Any brief break in recording will be followed by another "surge" of speed. Faulty motors may produce the same effect, even when the batteries are sound.

Speed correction may be required for a variety of other reasons, e.g. to match music pitches exactly. One system employs an oscillator which is plugged in to replace the mains supply. The drive frequency can then be varied by manual control by $\pm 20\%$.

It is only possible to correct tape-speed faults if these are slow and regular enough to be adjusted by manual control. If you can, compare the recording with one of the same voice at the correct speed. A methodical way to go about the job is to prepare a cue sheet, taking four or five words at a time every ten or fifteen seconds; then check the amount of correction needed at each of these points. This will provide you with reference points to work to. It will be necessary to stop and reset every time you reach a point at which the machine stopped during the recordings (or, alternatively, if spacers are cut in, these will give a chance to reset while still running). These methods are suitable for speech only.

Another fault which involves fluctuation of pitch is "wow"; this will be considered later in the chapter.

Magnetic film

The coating on 35- and 16-mm magnetic film is the same as or very similar to that on $\frac{1}{4}$-inch tape. The difference is in the backing, for which thick acetate (cellulose triacetate) is used.

A thickness of about 5 mils is necessary because of the sprocket holes, which easily become worn, thereby reducing the strength of the film. (But note that if at any time the sprocket holes or the film are broken, they can usually be repaired quite easily by using a guillotine tape joiner: see p. 475.)

This thickness of acetate is relatively stiff, and as a result high tensions are required to maintain adequate contact between film and heads; which in turn causes rapid wear and low life both for film and for heads. Dropout may also be caused at joins, either by the flexing of tape joins or by the loss of contact at an overlap join.

Other bases (e.g. polyester) could be thinner, a great deal more flexible, would have a longer life and would not be subject to surface coating faults. However, film editors prefer the acetate based magnetic stock, which can be handled very much like that used for picture.

Standards for the positions of tracks on the magnetic film vary. The BBC records centre-track on 16-mm film and edge-track on 35-mm. In both cases the track width is 200 mil—only a little less than that for full-track $\frac{1}{4}$-inch tape.

The 35-mm edge-track position corresponds to that used on 35-mm combined magnetic film, except that the presence of a picture limits the latter to 100 mil.

Various further arrangements of magnetic sound and picture apply to film stereo systems.

Film sound problems in television

The first problem of film sound is quality: the optical sound, particularly of old films, can be noisy, low quality, or both. When replaying them on television, the simplest thing is to put in a filter at

5 kHz and to forget it. More recent films have combined magnetic track and have reasonable quality, unless in the process of wear and tear of an ageing print the sound track has actually got worn or torn (or magnetically damaged). Momentarily the picture may go out of sync at a point where a join has been repaired: this will last as long as it takes for the repair to pass from the projector gate to the sound head, where with a click it will right itself. On intermittent projectors the "loop" which absorbs the intermittent movement may be lost, also causing a slight loss of sync.

More serious are synchronization problems of films with separate magnetic film tracks (see p. 489).

Stereo tape recordings

In tape recording, a defect of quality peculiar to stereo is *crosstalk*. This is measured as the level at which tone which has been recorded on one track can be heard on the other. It may vary for different frequencies: the levels regarded as acceptable within the BBC are −38 dB at 1 kHz, rising to −30 dB at 50 Hz and 10 kHz. These figures compare very favourably indeed with what is practicable in disc reproduction.

If stereo recordings are made with the same tape and recording conditions as mono, there will be a poorer signal-to-noise ratio. This is because part of the tape—a track along the centre line—must remain unused to allow physical separation of the A and B information. Two standards are used for the width of this guard track:

(i) Narrow guard track. This is roughly one eighth of the full width of the tape. Only 1 dB of signal-to-noise ratio is lost on tapes of similar quality, but crosstalk may be higher than with the other standard.

(ii) Broad guard track. Nearly a third of the track is unrecorded, but the effective loss is even greater: the signal-to-noise ratio drops by 3·5 dB. Crosstalk is low, but if other standards are to be maintained a more sensitive tape is required than for mono.

For stereo the BBC uses a tape which can be recorded 6 dB higher than that used for mono (the upper limit being that which can be recorded without exceeding acceptable distortion). In practice only 4 dB of this is used: this more than compensates for the loss due to the presence of a broad guard track, and allows something in hand for the less controllable conditions of stereo.

Four-channel stereo tape recordings employ the same configuration that has previously been used for twin-track stereo recorded in both directions along the tape (see p. 46).

Records

Discs, either specially cut "acetates" (as they are sometimes called—although in fact the material used is cellulose nitrate) or commercially pressed gramophone records, may be important to the tape recordist for a variety of reasons. Radio stations, of course, use records as an important source of programme material (although in Britain the amount of this use is severely limited by agreement with record companies and unions).

Sometimes valuable tapes are transferred to disc. The direct-cut recording produced is only processed if there is a need for many replays—if, say, twenty or more copies are wanted. The main reason for having a disc cut is so that the recording will be readily available and playable in situations where tape replay may not be available. There is also something of an illusion of greater permanence about a disc: certainly the recording is more irrevocable. But actual permanence is another thing; this varies with materials and other factors.

"Acetates" are particularly fragile, and under heavy playing weights the groove rapidly breaks up. At one time, when this was the standard form of recording at most radio studios, recordings played under a tracking weight of about 1½ oz. were reckoned to have a life of about a dozen playings. Often a disc was well on its way towards the end of its useful life before it ever got on the air. Also, if the original blank was not in prime condition (e.g. if the castor-oil plasticizer was beginning to dry out) the initial recording was likely to be a great deal rougher and the subsequent process of wear accelerated.

Nevertheless, "acetates" can make—and stay—very good recordings. Cut by the hot-stylus method, which helps to smooth the wall as the cutter moves on, and subjected to no more than medium to low playing weights a microgroove direct-cut disc can survive very many replays without appreciable signs of wear—although it will always be very susceptible to physical damage to the grooves.

Direct-recorded discs may be used either as an end product in themselves or as the first stage in the production of a master from which gramophone records can be made—but in the latter case there is one difference in procedure, in that the disc is very definitely

407

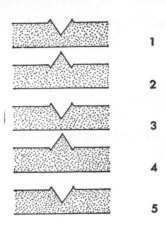

PROCESSING DISC RECORDS. The five stages of processing: 1. Original recording. 2. Master. 3. Mother. 4. Stamper. 5. Record. Note that any shoulders which are thrown up by the cutter stylus are faithfully reproduced at each stage.

not monitored on recording or at any other time; whereas otherwise it must be.

From the cellulose nitrate original recording, records are produced by a four-stage process. First the surface is made conductive by blasting it with a finely divided metal (e.g. gold) and a copper "master" is grown on to this electrolytically. Then the two are stripped away from each other. In the second stage a "mother" is grown, again electrolytically, on this; and the signal is now once again in the form of a groove. A "stamper" is then produced (with ridges instead of grooves), and this will press a thousand or more records.

If only a small number of records is required (say, up to fifty) two of the stages can be cut out, and after plating with a harder surface material the master can be used as a stamper.

Stereo reproduction from disc

In describing how the signal is picked up from discs I will give two examples from the more general case: stereo.

A stereo crystal pick-up uses a mechanical system to flex two piezo-electric crystals which are set more or less at right-angles to each other and equally inclined to the vertical. Information inscribed in the "A" wall causes the "A" crystal to flex but leaves the "B" crystal almost undisturbed. In practice about 15 dB of separation is achieved at middle audio frequencies.

Within the playing head of a moving coil pick-up there is a magnetic field parallel to the groove. Within this field are two coils

408

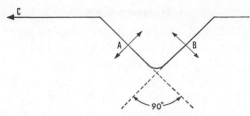

GROOVE ON STEREO DISC. Movement of the stylus due to wall A (closest to the centre of the disc, C) provides information for Channel A. The wall at right-angles to it gives the information for channel B.

which are at right-angles to each other, but which are so placed that both of their planes lie along the line of the field when they are at rest. Movement of the stylus by the "A" wall causes them to pivot so that lines of force may cut the "A" coil. Movement of the stylus along the "A" wall produces an electrical output from the "A" coil. Little of this signal is transmitted mechanically to the "B" coil, so a good channel separation—25 dB at middle frequencies—can be achieved.

However, the design of the moving coil pick-up requires finer engineering than the crystal pick-up, and this is reflected in the relative prices.

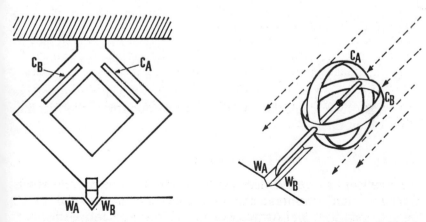

STEREOPHONIC PICK-UPS. Left: using piezo-electric crystals. Crystal A (C_A) is twisted more than crystal B as the needle follows undulations in Wall A (W_A) on the disc. This provides moderately good stereo separation at low cost. Right: using moving coils. Coil A (C_A) in the magnetic field (M) responds to signals in Wall A (W_A) of the disc. This provides good separation, but the signal is small and manufacturing costs are relatively high.

Noise on discs

Noise on discs may be due to minute irregularities in the groove wall—or dust. The materials from which both direct recordings and gramophone records are made (basically these are cellulose nitrate and polyvinyl chloride, respectively) do not conduct electricity. They therefore hold static charges which attract dust. Fingerprints can also cause noise; the fat helps to hold dust and the acid bites into the surface.

Both types of record need to be kept absolutely clean; and there are several methods offered commercially. But neither type of disc will suffer from actually being washed, perhaps with a little mild detergent in the water. Dusty direct recordings can be washed under a tap, shaken, and left to dry.

A rather less obvious cause of noise in discs is the shoulder of cellulose nitrate that is thrown up as a record is cut. As the cutter stylus ploughs its way through the surface of a disc a rough edge of material on either side of the furrow is pressed upwards and outwards. This shoulder is, of course, faithfully reproduced when records are pressed. If either gramophone records or direct recordings are stacked flat on floors or shelves in heavy piles, these shoulders will tend to be squashed downwards into the groove and their ragged edges will be "played", along with the rest of the signal which is impressed into the groove wall. The shoulders are much less pronounced in modern recordings which are cut by hot stylus techniques, and in any case the raised rim on some records gives an additional measure of protection.

One form of treatment which helps to prevent the formation of static charges on records utilizes the roughness of this shoulder to hold a conductive material. When something rubs against a disc it is the shoulders which make the contact and develop most of the charge, so there could not be a more appropriate way of dealing with it than this.

Distortion on discs

It has been suggested that, for minimum wear, a one mil stylus tracking at half a gram is a reasonable ideal for disc materials based on polyvinyl chloride. As playing weight increases above this, permanent deformation and then fracture of the groove wall will occur. This is indicated in extreme cases by a crackling noise on replay.

The ability of l.p. styli to track and extract a signal from a kink in the groove which is of the same order of size as the stylus tip is quite remarkable, in view of the fact that it is being thrown from side to side under forces which are enormous in comparison with the area of contact.

As the stylus moves towards the centre of the record, the recorded wavelengths of the high frequencies close up and become progressively more difficult for the stylus to track. This gives an imperfect match in quality when changing over from the inner edge of one disc to the outer edge of another. Wear too is more rapid towards the centre of the disc than at the outer edge.

Another characteristic of records is "pinch effect". This is caused by the different actions of cutter and replay styli: the cutter is chisel shaped and produces a groove of which the cross-section *along the radius of the disc* is constant. But the replay stylus has a rounded tip and simply rides between points on the lateral cross-section of the groove, and this means that as the modulation twists the groove to its greatest angle the stylus is squeezed upwards to ride higher in the sharper angle of the walls. With two such "bumps-up" to each cycle recorded in the groove, this means that the second harmonic of the recorded signal is being produced in the vertical plane. For mono records played with mono equipment, pinch effect is not serious with the light compliant stylus mountings of today. But for mono records played on stereo equipment it introduces a spurious stereo signal which, as it is out of phase with the main signal, should be suppressed.

For the mono replay of all discs (whether mono or stereo) the BBC uses stereo heads with the leads paralleled to produce an A + B mono output. This ensures that stereo discs are not accidentally damaged, and assures maximum playing life for all records.

Hill-and-dale recordings, i.e. those in the vertical plane, are subject to mechanical distortion effects which are different from those which affect lateral recordings. This is a reason why stereo is recorded with each channel at 45° to the vertical: the two forms of distortion are split evenly between the two channels.

There are also very slight distortions of the reproduced waveform due to the use of a pivoted tracking arm. But if the head is mounted correctly these are not worth bothering about.

Damage to discs

The most common cause of damage to records is scratching. This may be due to grit which is scraped against the surface, or it may be caused by an overweight pick-up shooting across the record, or by a stylus being accidentally ground into a disc. Whatever the cause, the effect is irreversible, as is groove wear.

A device was once invented which copied and "declicked" records; but, on the whole, the simplest way of dealing with bad clicks on records that cannot be replaced is to copy to tape and nip out the worst clicks by editing. Fortunately clicks occupy an extremely short space of time (or length of tape). Tight editing can produce copies which are hardly distinguishable from unscratched originals.

But the best way of dealing with damage is prevention, not cure. It is hardly necessary to handle records with gloves, or with a pair of tongs. You should pick up and hold discs by rim and label. Never lay records on or against flat surfaces—even soft surfaces may harbour grit—nor should they be left out of their bags any longer than is necessary. Old heavy and uncompliant l.p. heads should be avoided. So should autochangers—although, with the advent of lightweight pick-ups and records with raised rims, the worst risks have been reduced.

A badly worn or chipped stylus can do serious damage. At worst the effects are visible on the disc—it changes colour, becoming grey as the stylus grinds through it. And if the stylus seems to be gathering up scraps of purple dust or fluff from a direct-cut disc, beware! This is the colour of finely carved cellulose nitrate.

Stereo discs will be damaged if they are played by a mono stylus, or by too great a playing weight, or by a cartridge with inadequate vertical compliance. Stereo records should only be replayed on equipment which has been designed for the purpose (even if only a mono output is required, a compatible head must be used). The first sign that an unsuitable stylus or head has been used on a stereo record is degradation of the stereo information.

Heat affects discs less than tapes—at any rate, as far as the recorded signal is concerned—so discs are preferred for despatching BBC transcription programmes to tropical countries. But heat will make PVC soft, so that a record may warp if left lying on a radiator, on shelves above an amplifier, or in a closed car which is left in the sun. A record standing on edge on a hot surface will be flattened along the rim enough to make the first few grooves bump so much as to be unplayable.

Wow

Wow is a slow rhythmic variation in pitch due to non-musical causes, which may afflict either tape or disc recordings. It can be described in terms of the percentage variation of speed (and there-

412

fore of recorded pitch) which occurs in a single cycle of the wow. The smallest change of pitch which can be distinguished by most people is less than one twenty-fifth of a semitone at middle frequencies; for low frequencies the interval is much greater. Consequently, we may expect wow to be a great deal more apparent on middle range notes than those which are low in pitch.

The ability of the ear to detect wow depends not only on the amplitude and frequency but also on the character of the instrument

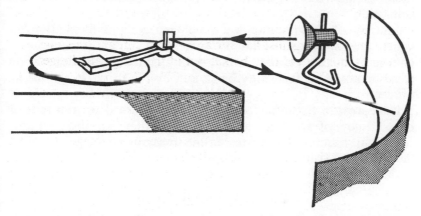

WOW IN RECORD PLAYERS. Device for measuring "wow" in disc (see also optical groove locating unit, p. 300).

and type of note played. With the human voice and many stringed instruments the tones produced are not of fixed pitch, and there is, therefore, a subjective tendency to blame the performer, instead of the mechanics. But on wind instruments (which mostly produce notes of fixed pitch) and on the decay tones of plucked and struck instruments wow may be more painfully obvious.

If notes are sustained on fixed-pitch instruments over a period long enough for wow to produce a variation of more than about 0·25%, the effect will begin to be appreciable; and if it reaches 1% the results will be, to most ears, excruciating. But this also means that passages of moderate pace can take rather more wow than slow ones. Briskly played passages will stand even more distortion, because the ear tolerates a certain inaccuracy of pitch on notes which are held for only a very short space of time.

One cause of wow in record reproduction is a faulty turntable. This can be detected easily enough by the use of a stroboscopic disc. Another cause may be eccentricity of the groove on the pressing.

413

This may be due to the hole not being in the centre of the disc, or being larger than the spindle; or it may be due to the disc being warped, or physically deformed.

To check whether a fault lies with the disc or the turntable: first note the way in which the cycle of the wow is related to the position of the label, and then stop the turntable and turn the disc through 180° relative to it. If the wow is now examined again it will immediately be obvious whether the wow originates with the turntable or the record (provided that the record is tight on the spindle).

Flutter, a related fault, is a much more rapid fluctuation, in which the speed variation is sufficiently rapid to impose a change of quality on any sound—and again, most noticeably on steady notes. This fault may be caused by the drive spindle being off centre.

Once wow or flutter have actually been recorded on to a tape or disc, I know of no means of curing it. If they are observed at a recording session it is a waste of time to carry on.

Tape *v*. disc for studio use

Much of this chapter has been concerned with the technical qualities and defects of the two main recording media, tape and disc. In comparing the two the balance of advantages favours tape for all normal recording purposes—its standard high quality and relative ease of fine editing are only two of its more obvious advantages. But all studios should have both disc and tape *reproducers* available—and preferably several of each.

Nevertheless, there are purposes for which tape does not have all the advantages, because no tape system available today is anything like so versatile as disc when working against time.

There may be many reasons why an item cannot be put on the air live, and it takes vital seconds to spool tape back to the start, or spool on to check an alternative in-cue; and one cannot visually spot the start or finish. All these things can be done instantaneously with disc.

In addition to their primary use in the form of gramophone records, discs are still used for mood music and sound effects libraries, transcription material, and historical archives. And the user must always be on the watch-out for signs of wear, producing a poor signal-to-noise ratio.

Picture and sound quality in television and film

Television and film are nearly always conceived primarily in terms of picture: it is important therefore that the needs of sound restrict this as little as possible.

Nevertheless, it is essential for film or television that despite the presence of the camera and the constant attention that is paid to picture, sound quality should be high. It goes without saying that the reader of this book shares this view, but as the problems of practical film and television production pile up, it may appear that only the sound man appreciates the point. However, he may rest assured that the experienced director will—given time to think—agree with him.

It is the sound man's responsibility to any production to obtain the best sound that he possibly can in whatever circumstances he is presented with. And if the quality of sound falls below that which might reasonably be expected—and nothing can be done about it—he must warn the director. In extreme cases, where sound is not suitable for use he must say so. When he *has* said so the responsicility then becomes the director's.

However, the sound man must be sensible in his judgment of what is good, barely acceptable, or totally unsatisfactory; and this must reflect the director's intentions for the sound, which he has a right to know about—if, indeed, the director has made up his mind. A director is also within his rights to ask for sound to be taken with the intention of making a decision later on how it might be used, if at all. The sound man is not within his rights to refuse to record on the grounds of low quality though he may protest strongly: the director may still be able to use the sound at low level behind another high level track, or as a guide track for post-synching or for other use in dubbing. Indeed, there are some circumstances in television where on important material poor quality sound is unavoidable and therefore simply has to be used, though perhaps with an apology to the viewing public if the reason for this is not obvious.

A subjective scale for quality check

The BBC operates a system for checking programme quality (for our purposes, sound; but in television, picture is also checked). Observations are made on general sound quality; background hum, noise, or hiss; change of sound level at programme junctions; and interference. In this last category is talkback induction which can sometimes be heard on radio as it is transmitted, but much more often on television because of the continuous stream of instructions and information that is being fed from the gallery to the studio floor.

Sampling is done for periods of five minutes on a wide range of material, including the programmes as they are transmitted (both before the transmitter and off the air); studio output (but taking in to account conditions which may exist early in rehearsal before all adjustments have been made); material incoming from other areas by landline, radio link, or satellite: and all recordings.

These are two subjective scales which are used:

Scale 1: Assessment of degradation

    1.1. Imperceptible
    1.2. Just perceptible
    1.3. Perceptible but not disturbing
    1.4. Somewhat objectionable
    1.5. Definitely objectionable
    1.6. Unusable

Scale 2: Assessment of quality

    2.1. Excellent
    2.2. Good
    2.3. Fair
    2.4. Fairly poor
    2.5. Poor
    2.6. Very poor

14

CONTROLLING VOLUME

ONCE again we return to the kingpin of the whole studio system: the monitoring loudspeaker. For although the balance engineer has a meter to check his levels, the control of programme volume is another field in which most of his work must bo done by ear.

Odd how the cartoon image of a man with headphones and a meter still persists! Both these devices have important uses, but they cannot be regarded as a substitute for a high-quality loudspeaker. Indeed, meters can easily prove misleading, as they indicate peak volume, not loudness. And some instruments, such as bagpipes, harpsichords, clavichords, and virginals, sound very loud compared with the meter reading. So does much pop music. Balance of these against less noisy music and speech can and must be judged by ear —and this is only a particular case of a general rule: meters are a guide, but ears must be the judge.

Not only must levels be set correctly for the various technical processes which the signal undergoes; individual passages may also have to be compressed (restricted in dynamic range) so that they are neither too loud nor too quiet in comparison with the rest of the programme. Controlling and compressing is one of the sound man's most important jobs; and one which is not undertaken solely for technical reasons.

Volume control is a job in which there are few really dependable short cuts: an automatic volume control, for example, would ruin Ravel's *Bolero*. Nevertheless automatic devices have become increasingly sophisticated in recent years, to the extent that some are capable of controlling certain specific types of programme material with a reasonable degree of adequacy. A disadvantage is that different control characteristics are required where several types of output are heard in succession, and that for some types of music in which subtle dynamic control by the performers is important to the artistic effect (this includes some light music and jazz as well as most

417

serious music), no compressor will do an adequate job unless it can be specially set for the individual item. As a result no radio station with a reasonably wide range of programme material can expect to be able to apply automatic level control for its whole output without introducing some degree of degradation; and the greater the compression, the greater that degradation will be.

The most common fault in automatic control is a lack of "intelligent anticipation"—and even if the element of anticipation were introduced (say, by feeding all programme material to a tape loop which produced a 30-second delay) systematic errors would still result as common solutions were applied to different problems.

The uses for compressors and limiters include short-wave radio where a continued high-signal level is necessary to overcome "static" and other noise; certain other types of "high intelligibility" radio where a limited range of output is broadcast to a maximum service area for a given transmitter strength; and certain purposes within programmes themselves, e.g. as an element of pop music balance, or to even up the two voices of a telephone conversation which is used as programme material (see p. 315).

For the purposes of this chapter, however, the main theme will be the manual control of volume using the ear, the eye (for meter, script or score, and to observe events in the studio), and genuine intelligent anticipation. Most of what follows applies almost equally to radio, television, and film sound.

Programme meters

Although a meter cannot be used to judge such things as the balance of one voice against another, or speech against music, it is nevertheless an essential item of studio equipment. Its uses are:

   (i) to check that there is no loss or gain in level between studio, recording room, and transmitter (see p. 86);

  (ii) to provide indications of levels which would result in under- or over-modulation at the recorder or transmitter;

 (iii) to compare relative levels between one performance and another;

 (iv) to check that levels meet the prescribed values for good listening.

There are several types of meter which can be used to line up equipment or check for overmodulation; but a "peak programme meter" (PPM) seems to be the most satisfactory instrument for the above functions. As its name suggests, it indicates not average levels but peaks. Essentially the PPM is a special type of voltmeter which is arranged to read logarithmically over its main working range. It has a rapid rise characteristic (the BBC version has a time constant of 2·5 milliseconds; this gives 80% of full deflection in 4 milliseconds: the ear cannot detect distortion of such short duration) and a slow die-away (time constant, 1 second; giving a fall of 8·7 dB/second). The circuit for this is complex but, transistorized, may now take up little space, so that it can be used even for portable recorders (though expensive ones). A "modulometer" is essentially similar to a PPM in operation, though the scale may be different.

A simpler type of meter than the PPM is the American VU meter, the face of which shows two scales; "percentage modulation" and decibels. This meter reads programme volume directly. It is fed through a dry rectifier and ballast resistance, and draws from the programme circuit all the power needed to operate it. For cheaper models the ballistic operation may allow the needle to peak substantially higher on programme than on steady tone. However, the more expensive, studio quality VU meter will overshoot by only a small amount when a pulse signal is applied (in which it compares favourably with a PPM). But the time constant of 300 milliseconds will prevent transient sounds from being registered at all.

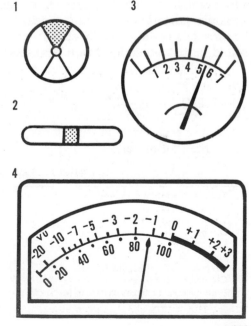

VOLUME INDICATORS. Devices for measuring programme volume include 1 and 2. "Magic Eye" methods, 3. Peak programme meter, and 4. VU meter. In the BBC peak programme meter, 6 represents 100% modulation and each division is 4 dB. The VU meter scale includes dB (above) and percentage modulation (below).

419

Also, though it may have a linear calibration in percentage modulation (the rectifier characteristic should ensure this), more than half the scale is taken up with a range of 3 dB on either side of the nominal 100% modulation. Since little programme material will remain consistently within so narrow a range, the needle is generally either registering only small deflections or flickering bewilderingly over the full range of the scale.

For maximum volumes, continuous sounds (including most music) may read "100% modulation" on the VU meter; however, for staccato sounds such as speech a true maximum volume is given by an indicated "50%", as the meter does not have time to register a full swing to the 100 mark on the louder individual constituents of speech.

"Magic eyes", which are used on some cheaper items of equipment, register peaks instantaneously. For maximum volume the glow of the "eye" should just close together on peaks, but not overlap. However, each peak comes and goes so quickly that they are wearing to watch and are not used professionally.

Programme volume: relative levels

A peak programme meter can be used to suggest or check levels. For example, if ordinary talk or discussion is allowed a normal dynamic range with occasional peaks up to the maximum, then newsreaders (who generally speak very clearly and evenly) usually sound quite loud enough with peaks averaging about 6 dB less.

A whole system of such reference levels can be built up; and the following are some specimen PPM peak levels for speech and music that experience indicates are "about right" for listeners hearing radio programmes under reasonably good conditions (the values shown are peak levels in dB relative to the maximum that may be fed to the transmitter).

PPM PEAK LEVELS

Talk, discussion programmes	0
News and weather	−6
Drama: narration	−8
Drama: action	0 to −16
Light music	0 to −16
Serious music	0 to −22 or lower
Harpsichords and bagpipes	−8
Clavichords and virginals	−16
Announcements between music (depending on type of music)	−4 to −8

Even if such a list is adopted as a general guide, it will not solve all the problems posed by junctions between speech and music or, on the larger scale, between programme and programme. For radio stations with a distinctive "personality" in the American style (i.e. a restricted range of programme material) there are only a limited number of types of junction, and it is fairly easy to link item to item (although for BBC listeners in Britain, where a single service includes news, comedy, light and serious music, religious services, magazine and discussions programmes, and so on, problems of matching between successive items can become acute).

A slight complication to this question of matching was suggested by the results of a BBC survey on listeners' preferences for relative levels of speech and music. Taking a large number of pieces in different styles (but excluding modern pop music) and with different linking voices, the results were:

Speech following music to be (on average) 4 dB down;
Music following speech to be (on average) 2 dB up.

At first sight these results appear to present a contradiction, but in fact this is easy enough to resolve: it simply means that announcements linking music items should be "edged in" a little.

In this experiment the listeners were giving the music and speech their full attention. And here there is a second inference from these results: that if you are listening to music deliberately and consciously you will probably set your loudspeaker volume fairly high, with the result that announcements may appear unpleasantly loud. Had they been using the music for background listening only, it is unlikely that the people taking part in the experiment would have wished for a similar balance between music and speech.

Maximum volumes

When a broadcast or recording is being made the balancer monitors at a fairly loud listening level, and is, of course, giving it his full attention. This is true in the television studio and film dubbing theatre too. So it must always be remembered that the state of affairs at the listening end may be very different.

Some further experimental results will underline this: tests were made on the maximum sound levels preferred by BBC studio managers, musicians, and members of the public. It was found that studio managers preferred louder levels than the musicians, and very much louder than the general public:

PREFERRED MAXIMUM SOUND LEVEL
(dB, referred to 2×10^{-5} N/m²)

| | Public | | | Studio managers | |
	Men	Women	Musicians	Men	Women
Symphonic music	78	78	88	90	87
Light music	75	74	79	89	84
Dance music	75	73	79	89	83
Speech	71	71	74	84	77

These figures were obtained in 1948, before the advent of FM broadcasting. But the picture has probably been affected very little by this.

The figures for the public correspond reasonably well with what they would hear in real life in a seat fairly close to the players. Musicians, who in real life would be much closer to the sound sources might reasonably be expected to choose higher levels. But the studio managers (sound balancers) chose unrealistically high levels. Why?

Part of the reason for the diversity of these results is that people professionally concerned with sound are extracting a great deal more information from what they hear, and the greater volume helps them to hear the finer points of fades and mixes, etc., and check technical quality. (Musicians, on the other hand, draw on a vast fund of experience of musical form and instrumental quality, and are listening for performance, often disregarding technical quality almost completely.)

Loudness and listening conditions

These preferred maximum levels refer specifically to the case where the listeners, like those concerned in creating the programme, want to listen attentively and have reasonable conditions for doing so. But there are very many occasions when this is not the case. For example, part of many people's early evening listening may be done while driving or working in the kitchen. In such cases, where the listeners' attention will be limited, and background noise may be high, speech may be peaked 8 dB higher than music. If, when listening to a programme controlled in this way, you decide that a particular item of music appeals to you and you turn it up, you will find that the announcement following it appears unduly loud. As a general rule, the listener can do little to combat the levels as transmitted.

Linking together speech items of varying intelligibility presents a special problem—particularly in the case where an item containing a great deal of noise and distortion has to be matched to good studio quality. Here, the least unsatisfactory solution will be found if the noisy item is matched for loudness at the beginning and end, and lifted for intelligibility in between: the item must be slightly faded in and out.

There is a further way in which listening conditions may vary. On the one hand, we have listeners with the increasingly popular, small transistor portables, which demand a high-intelligibility type of programme; and, on the other hand, wide-range hi-fi, demanding not only high-quality transmissions but also a wide dynamic range. The two sets of requirements are largely incompatible. In the United States there are different radio stations tailored to fit the two audiences and Britain and many other countries have gone most of the way in following this lead.

But where different types of programme material still form part of the same service, what is the solution? Unfortunately there can be no rule-of-thumb answer. It is a question of judgment; of trying to imagine what the audience will hear when listening to your programme for the first and (almost certainly) only time. Remember that your own ideas are considerably coloured by long acquaintance with the material: familiarity breeds acceptance.

Dynamic range—and the need for compression

The ear can take an enormous range of volumes of sound. At 1000 Hz the threshold of pain is 110 dB or more above the threshold of hearing—that is, a sound which is just bearable may be over a hundred thousand million times as powerful as one which is just audible. But for a recording or for a broadcast such a range is simply not practicable. Some sort of compression of the signal is usually necessary: the question is, how much?

In inexpensive equipment there may be only 40 or 50 dB between the noise and distortion levels, and the user will want to keep well above the noise for the most part. Professional equipment will generally have a better signal-to-noise ratio, but in broadcasting there are many more links in the chain. In general, a signal-to-noise ratio of at least 50 dB throughout the chain is regarded as desirable.

Also, as we have seen, much depends on listening conditions. For example, for an orchestral concert which is being heard on a good FM receiver, a fairly wide dynamic range is desirable—but nothing like the 60 or 70 dB which may separate the loudest and quietest passages in the concert hall. A relatively narrow range is suitable for listening under domestic conditions: indeed, only 45 dB separate the average listener's preferred maximum listening level and the noise level of a quiet living-room. A recording or broadcast which is to be heard under such "average" conditions must take this into account. BBC practice for broadcast concerts is to keep peak levels generally within a range of 22 dB, with quieter passages not exceeding half a minute at a time. Popular music is kept to a very much narrower range, and so is speech.

Gramophone records, it is true, have a wider dynamic range than broadcast concerts, in order to cater for those who can listen under ideal conditions; but an adequate signal-to-noise ratio must still be maintained for the quieter passages.

An AM transmitter has to be protected by limiters against sudden overmodulation. FM transmitters and receivers will also run into distortion at some level, and in Britain the maximum frequency deviation is set at 75 kHz; this means that radio engineers and receiver manufacturers can work to the same standard, above which distortion may be expected.

The maximum level that may be recorded on tape is subject to similar considerations: go over the top and harmonic distortion sets in. At the lower end of the scale the signal is competing with tape hiss—noise due to the grain structure of the oxide coating on the tape. Between these two the range that is available for recording depends on the grade of tape.

Another way of looking at this business of compression is in terms of listening conditions: if a programme has to be replayed rather quietly (and it is generally true that other people will not wish to listen to a work as loud as will its creator!) careful compression will ensure that it is all still audible.

Controlling a programme

As has already been seen, the control desk is essentially just a very high-quality mixer unit, with logarithmic faders for each source, for groups, and for the main gain, marked off in "stops" which are each, in BBC practice, equivalent to $1\frac{1}{2}$ or 2 dB (over the main working range). This allows the operator very convenient means of checking and correcting his levels. He will have a script or full score to guide

MANUAL CONTROL OF PRO-GRAMME VOLUME. Method of compressing a heavy peak to retain the original dramatic effect and at the same time ensure that the signal falls between maximum and minimum permissible levels 1 and 2. Steps of about 1½–2 dB are made at intervals of say, ten seconds.

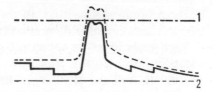

him, and during the rehearsals he can use this to note his settings and other information that will be useful on the "take".

Having set his main gain at a suitable average level for the type of programme, and adjusted his loudspeaker to a comfortable volume, he can carry on and listen under conditions which are reasonably close to those of a domestic living-room. He will judge divergences from his average level on the grounds of relative loudness and intelligibility (sometimes these two factors do not suggest the same results, as we have seen), and he does not have to worry about his meter too much except to watch for very quiet or loud passages. (When recording, the effects of any particularly high peaks can be checked on the tape, to see whether there is appreciable distortion. On a broadcast, too, an occasional peak may be risked rather than reducing the effective service area of the transmitter by under-modulating a whole programme; the limiter will deal with any peaks which are big enough to damage equipment.) On speech programmes the sound man will also check his levels on the meter from time to time to see that he is maintaining the same average volume. The ear is not reliable for this—it tires. At the end of the rehearsal of a record programme, say, it is worth checking the levels of the first few records again, to see if one's judgment of the appropriate level for them has changed; and it usually has.

Compression of music

Overmodulation on music must be avoided not by "riding the gain" but by careful preparation—gradually pulling back on the gain control for half a minute or so before the peak is due. During the rehearsal, the appropriate setting for handling the peak will have been noted on the score, and after the loud passage there is a slow return to the average level. Each operation should consist of one or more steps of about 2 dB. A similar procedure may be used to lift long periods of low level.

Often it will be found best to vary the level continuously through-

425

out a programme, so that all the elements of light and shade fall within the acceptable dynamic range.

Such techniques as these are most likely to be necessary when recording orchestral works, but (and this depends on the nature of the music and the quality of the recorder) control may also be needed with smaller combinations or groups, or even a solo instrument, such as a piano.

There is one other possible way of dealing with the control of orchestral music, and this is to leave it in the hands of the conductor. It has even been known for a conductor to have a meter on his desk as he rehearses and records; but this technique has not been generally adopted. On the whole, it seems preferable that the conductor should concentrate on the performance, bearing the limitations of the medium in mind if he can, but leaving the control to the balance engineer.

However, music programmes which are specifically designed for background listening may have some measure of compression built in by the arranger; and also, of course, smaller musical forces will be employed.

The farther the microphone is away the easier it is to control music: studio or concert hall acoustics smooth out the peaks. The balancer who adopts a bright "tight" balance will have more work to do without necessarily earning the thanks of listeners—many of whom prefer a well-blended sound for classical music, as BBC listening tests have shown.

Control of music affects the reverberation just as much as the main sound. The effect may be disconcerting: the microphone moves closer, but the perspective remains the same! The two may be controlled more effectively by using two microphones, one close and one distant, and working between them on changes of music volume. This can be done in stereo too, with two co-incident pairs, one almost over the conductor's head with a double cardioid pick-up; the other on double figure-of-eight and so placed (farther back) that the various parts of the orchestra are reasonably co-incident. Alternatively there may be reverberation microphones facing away from the orchestra: they are controlled independently of the main pair to achieve the best effect as the acoustic volume of the music varies.

Compression: scripted speech and effects

In controlling speech the problems are somewhat different, as are the methods employed for dealing with them. In real life speech and noises might occupy the full range from the threshold of hearing to the threshold of pain. This would be quite intolerable on tape, even if it could be recorded.

The BBC regards something like 16 dB as being an adequate range for peak values of speech in radio plays—the average being about 8 dB below the maximum permissible. The main effect that this has on speech is that scenes involving shouting have to be held back, possibly making them sound rather distant—which is fine if this fits in with the picture that is wanted. But for cases where close shouting must be mixed in with more normal levels of speech it is up to the actors to hold back on volume, and "project" their voices.

This upper limit makes even more difference when it comes to loud sound effects—a gunshot, for example, or a car crash. Even a sharply closed door is too loud.

It is therefore fortunate that radio and television drama have established a convention in which such effects are suggested by character rather than by volume. Volumes have to be controlled; they have to be evened out and held back—which explains why extremely unlikely-looking methods for making sound effects often produce the best results.

Compression: unscripted speech

Studio interviews and discussions for radio and television also benefit by careful control, particularly if one speaker is much louder than the others, or where a speaker habitually starts off with a bang every time he speaks, and then trails away. Here, control is a matter of intelligent anticipation: whenever your "needle-bender" opens his mouth to speak, drop the fader back—sharply if he does so in a pause, but rather more gently if someone else is speaking. Do not worry too much if one or two pieces of "intelligent anticipation" misfire: a slight dip in level is a great deal more acceptable than the risk of a sudden unexpectedly loud voice booming forth. Laughter is another thing to look out for if the general level is being held well up. But edge the fader up again as quickly as possible after the laugh.

This sort of control, if carefully carried out, should be completely unnoticeable: the way *not* to do it is to miss the first high peak and *then* haul back on the controls. No control at all is better than bad control.

Do not discourage speakers from raising their voices, unless they actually ask for advice; even then the best advice is, "Be natural."

A natural but controlled programme is much superior to one in which voices are never raised and the programme meter never has any bad moments. It is sometimes said that the sound engineer's idea of a perfect programme is pure tone at a constant level—because it never does anything it should not. Speakers who never do anything they should not sound just as dull and uninteresting as that pure tone.

A good programme depends on variety of pace and attack. It should not be necessary to hold the overall level back in order to accommodate possible overmodulation. But if much editing is envisaged it would be better to deal with the more violent fluctuations of level after the editing session, otherwise there may be difficulty even in the case that we have been considering so far, a studio in which extraneous noise is kept at a low level.

A completely different situation arises when recordings are made on location, whether for radio, television, or film *when subsequent editing is envisaged* (as nearly always is the case when filming). In this case a level should be set so that background remains constant throughout a sequence. If absolutely necessary some control can be exercised by slight movement of a directional microphone held by hand.

Copying

The first basic rule of copying, which applies whatever the source —disc, radio, or tape—is this: always copy electrically; never acoustically. That is to say, unless a marked change in the quality of the sound is wanted, there should be wires all the way from the source through to the recorder; loudspeaker and microphone should form no part of the chain. (There are honourable exceptions to this rule: these are the "echo chamber"—i.e. an acoustic feed through a highly reverberant room—and certain special cases where an acoustic feed of effects through the studio loudspeaker is required in a dramatic production. These are considered elsewhere.)

When copying tape material from one machine to another it is as well to make the usual level tests to ensure that the loudest passages fully modulate the second tape. The signal-to-noise ratio certainly cannot be improved; but the test will ensure that there is no great loss. If the intention is to re-record only part of an item and cut this back on to another part of the original (as may be done sometimes in copy editing) any differences or distortions will be highlighted, unless every care is taken.

428

However, when working with two good-quality machines of the same type, or where the machines have been lined up to the same standards, it should be fairly easy to copy at "zero gain" (i.e. to produce a copy which is at the same recorded level as the original).

To calibrate for this, the most accurate method is to replay a reference tone (or some other steady sound) from one machine and record on the other. Use the same grade of tape, by the way. Increase the gain of the replay machine gradually in steps during the copying, and note the settings. Then transfer the copy to machine one and replay. It is now possible to compare the original and re-recorded signals directly (by meter or by ear) and determine the setting which produces zero gain.

Also, before doing any copying, it is worth checking to see if any internal controlling is needed, or whether fades in and out may be introduced with advantage at the beginning and end; it may be possible to kill two birds with one stone.

Compressors and limiters

The terms "compressor" and "limiter" are sometimes used as though these were entirely different devices. In fact, as will be seen, they are not: there may be considerable differences in design between two different types of compressor, either of which, with minor modifications (or simply by switching to a particular setting) can be used as a limiter.

Essentially, a compressor works like this:

Below a predetermined level (the threshold or onset point) the volume of a signal is unchanged. Above this point the additional volume is reduced in a given proportion, e.g. 2:1, 3:1, or 5:1. For example, if the threshold were set at 8 dB below the level of 100% modulation and 2:1 compression selected, it would mean that signals which previously overmodulated by 8 dB were now only just reach-

TYPICAL COMPRESSOR/LIMITER. A. Attenuation meter (scale: 0—24 dB). B. Threshold setting, —24 to +16 dB relative to nominal O dB setting. C. Compression control 1:1 (i.e. no compression), 2:1, 3:1, 5:1, and Lim (20:1, i.e. acting as limiter). D. Decay time control: 0·1–3·2 seconds.

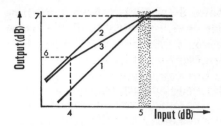

LIMITER AND COMPRESSOR. 1. Limiter used for overload protection. 2. Limiter used for programme compression. 3. Compressor. 4. Lowest level of programme interest. 5. *Shaded area*: Range of expected maximum level. 6. Lowest acceptable level in output (defining lower limit or required dynamic range). 7. Maximum permitted level.

ing full modulation. Similarly if 5:1 had been chosen, signals which previously would have overpeaked by 32 dB will now only just reach 100%.

What this means in practice is that the overall level may be raised by 8 dB or 32 dB, so that relatively quiet signals are now making a much bigger contribution than would otherwise be possible.

Suppose now that the compression ratio were made large, say 20:1, and the threshold level raised to something very close to 100% modulation (since there would now seem to be little point in leaving it at 8 dB below, unless a signal about 150 dB above normal levels were expected). The result of this would be that the compressor is now acting as a limiter. And in this condition it can be used *either* to hold individual unexpected high peaks *or* to lift the signals from virtually any lower level in to the usable working range of the equipment (though not without causing problems with high level signals which are being excessively compressed, and background noise which will be lifted as well—of which, more later).

It will be seen that the effect of a 2:1 compressor with a threshold at 8 dB below 100% modulation will be to compress only the top 16 dB of signals while leaving those at a lower level to drop away at a 1:1 ratio. An interesting variation on this would be to place two limiters together, working on a signal in parallel but with the threshold set at different levels. If one is set for 2 dB below 100% and the other for (say) 24 dB below, but raised in level, the effect will be to introduce a variable rate of compression which is greater at the

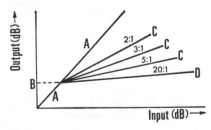

COMPRESSION RATIOS. A. Linear operation, in which input and output levels correspond. Above a given threshold level (B), various compression ratios (C) reduce the output level. In the extreme case (D) the compressor acts as a limiter holding the maximum output volume close to the threshold level (but still permitting a small proportion of any high peak to pass).

lower end of the range than towards the top, where something approaching the normal dynamic range is used until the upper limiter operates. A further variation is that the lower limiter could have a weighting network to arrange that quiet high- or low-frequency signals were lifted more than those whose power was primarily in the central (500—4000 Hz) part of the audio range.

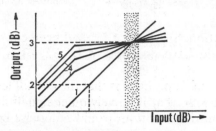

INCREASING THE VOLUME OF LOW-LEVEL SIGNALS by the use of a compressor. With the compressor out of circuit (1) only a small proportion of the input range goes in to the desired narrow dynamic range (2–3). With increasing degrees of compression (4) more can be accommodated, and with a limiter (5) most of all. In these examples the choice of threshold setting has been governed by arranging for the expected maximum level to produce full modulation. The greater the compression, the less the effect of overmodulation beyond this expected level.

In the past, the main purpose for limiters was to protect equipment from excessive signals. The final power-amplifying tube in an AM transmitter was at particular risk: already a very large and expensive piece of equipment, it was undesirable to increase its capacity and cost much beyond that required for the nominal full modulation. The difficulty was that once this level was reached, only a few decibels were required to raise the power passing through the valve to double its normal maximum level, or even more.

Compressors and limiters work by sampling the signal at a particular point in the chain, and if it is above a designated level, deriving a control signal which is fed back through a side chain to reduce the overall volume at an earlier point in the main programme chain. It is usually arranged that this control signal operates with a fast attack and slow decay—though both "fast" and "slow" may have a very wide range of actual durations in different circumstances.

A typical modern compressor/limiter reduces the power of a signal by earthing it momentarily at intervals of 250 kHz. At 6 dB above the onset point the selection of a 2:1 compression ratio means that half the power must be removed from the signal—i.e. to reduce it by 3 dB. It is arranged, therefore, that the control switch spends half of each successive 4 microseconds open and half closed. (Such

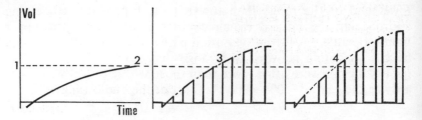

SIGNAL CHOPPING reducing the power of an audio signal. When signal (2) does not exceed compressor threshold (I) the compressor remains inoperative. For higher signals (3 and 4) progressively more of the power is removed. Note that the chopping frequency is high compared with the highest audio signal and that it operates over the whole waveform, not just on the peak.

a high rate of switching will of course have no audible effect on the signal, but will simply achieve its aim of reducing the total power transmitted.) Similarly, a signal 12 dB over the threshold will have to be reduced by 6 dB, so that the switch must be closed for 3 microseconds of every 4; while for signals at or below the threshold it will not operate at all.

In the feed-back side chain there are controls for varying the compression ratio and decay time, and also a circuit for driving a meter which shows the degree of attenuation at any moment.

Other systems have also been used for compressing and limiting signals: but a necessary criterion for any is that it should not operate selectively on that part of the wave which exceeds the threshold level (which would introduce harmonic distortion), but should reduce the whole wave in proportion. Perhaps the simplest way of doing this is to rectify part of the excess signal, store it in a capacitor and use it to provide a DC control bias until such time as the charge has been allowed to leak to earth.

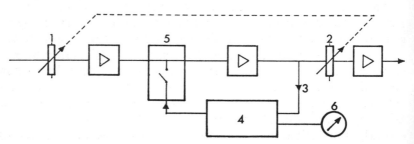

SIMPLE COMPRESSOR/LIMITER. I and 2: threshold level control (ganged). From the main programme chain a sample signal (3) is fed to a side chain (4) having compression ratio and recovery time controls, then to a control element (5) operating on the main programme chain. The degree of attenuation is shown on a meter (6).

432

COMPRESSION BY A COMBINA-
TION OF TWO LIMITERS, low level
(1) and high level (2) in parallel. The
resulting compression characteristic
is different from that of a normal compressor which would give a straight
line from 3 to 4.

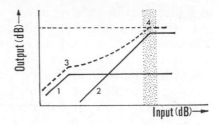

But over the years successively more ingenious variations have
been played on this theme.

Compression: attack and decay times

Early limiters were operated by the first half wave of the overload
signal—which meant that this first half wave itself got through
undiminished. For a very low frequency such a signal could send a
considerable amount of power to the transmitter, so that, for
example, someone kicking a table supporting a microphone could
produce a bump big enough to cause damage. It was therefore
necessary to provide additional protection in the form of a trip
which would stop the signal reaching the transmitter in extreme
cases—which meant in effect that overloading would put the transmitter off the air until the mechanism operating the trip had had
time itself to recover.

Later designs such as that already described were more sophisticated in that they were capable of chopping the signal and sampling
it for a shorter period: this means that an attack time of something
of the order of tens of microseconds can now be achieved. This,
however, introduces a new problem, since such a very sharp change
of level is liable to introduce an audible click.

The answer is to delay the whole signal for about half a millisecond and then make a gradual change of level over the same
period—in advance of any sudden heavy peak. This eliminates the
click as the background changes level, but cannot affect the fact that
if the background *is* there, it *is* suddenly going to change level—and
that this is bound to be in some degree objectionable. The particular
quality of unpleasantness will, of course, also be affected by the rate
of decay of the control signal.

Early limiters had gain-recovery (or control signal decay) rates of
the order of seconds: this allowed a reasonable time for the overload condition to pass so that it would not be "pumped" by too
rapid a train of high level signals. The more sophisticated limiters

433

(e.g. that described above) have a selection of decay times available (e.g. 100, 200, 400, and 800 milliseconds, and 1·6 and 3·2 seconds). The fastest of these can hold isolated brief excessive peaks without having a severe effect on the background; but they will not be so satisfactory for a rapid series of short peaks: any background will be given an unpleasant vibrato-like flutter.

However, if there are only occasional peaks, and they are not too big—say, of not more than about 3 dB or so—the recovery time will probably not be critical, and something like half a second will probably be adopted: it is only at high levels of compression that the exact choice of recovery time becomes important. One very satisfactory type of limiter which is used for gain reductions of up to 16 dB has automatic variations built in: varying, in fact, between about 30 milliseconds and 10 seconds according to the level and duration of the overload signal.

Discrimination against noise

A major problem with limiters and compressors working on high gain is that background noise is going to be lifted as well, unless something is done to prevent it. In particular, when there is no foreground signal to regulate the overall level (that is, during a pause), the noise is liable to rise by the full permitted gain. Such noise will include ventilation hum and studio clocks; movement and other personal noises; traffic or other more distant sound; electronic or line noise—and so on. Even where such sounds are themselves not raised to an objectionable level certain consonants at the start of subsequent speech will not be powerful enough to trigger the compressor; the most unpleasant result being the excessive sibilance at the start of certain words (though this can be avoided by high-frequency pre-emphasis in the input to the limiter: this is sometimes called "de-essing").

One device that can be used to discriminate against noise is a *noise gate*. In this, when the sound level falls below a second, lower threshold setting the gain is allowed to fall to a parallel but lower input/output characteristic: this might, for example, be 8 dB below that which would apply without a gate. At this setting, a device which could not previously have been used for more than 8 dB compression on a particular signal without the background noise becoming excessively loud in the pauses could now be used for 16 dB compression.

Noise gates are often made fast-operating, so that in even the

434

COMPRESSOR/LIMITER WITH NOISE GATE. 1. Range of maximum expected input level. 2. Corresponding maximum output level. 3. Lowest level of interest. 4. Lower end of designed dynamic range. 5. Gating level: if level of signal drops below this, the input characteristic falls from level A to level B.

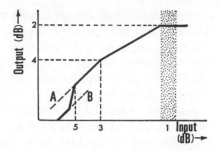

slightest pauses between the syllables of a word the noise is sharply reduced. But for such an operation to be successful, the device has to be set up with care: the gate must be *below* all significant elements of speech, but *above* all of the basic noise. Indeed, if both of these conditions cannot be met the result could be unpleasant, with either the speech or the noise wobbling up and down on the edge of the gate. But in any case any extraneous staccato sound of a higher volume or a rise in the background to an unexpectedly high level will fool the gate; as also (in the opposite sense) would a very quiet passage at the start of a piece of music.

In the "automatic level control" which is available on one type of high quality portable recorder used for professional sound radio and film location work, yet another type of limiter is used: one which avoids most of the rise and fall of background noise which is heard with other limiters. A short delay is introduced before the control signal begins to decay. The duration of this delay can be adjusted to allow for different lengths of pause between syllables or words as spoken by different individuals or in different languages, but is normally 3 seconds—after which the "memory" is erased and a new level of adjustment selected. (This same recorder has a separate circuit for the control of very brief transients, which do not therefore affect the basic level.) Obviously, such a device still has limitations: there would undoubtedly be many cases where a human operator would adjust the level (for example, on a change of voice); so it will probably only be used where it is inconvenient to employ a human operator. Like the fast-operating gate, the device can all too easily be fooled by unexpected events.

The use of limiters and compressors

We have already accepted that the purpose of control is three-fold: to avoid overmodulation, to maintain a good signal-to-noise ratio at the lower end of the dynamic range, and—within these extremes

435

—to ensure that all dynamic expression is appropriate to the nature of the programme.

Clearly, considerable advances have been made in automatic control of the first two of these variables: it is the third that remains the problem. It has proved difficult enough to design a device which will discriminate quickly between speech and music—and even then it is nothing like so fast as the human brain—so it would be much more difficult to discriminate quickly (if at all) between different types of music or different situations in which speech is used (though there has been some success in recognizing the tonal structure of certain irritating and insistent types of commercial). And yet a human operator would unhesitatingly apply totally different measures of control in such apparently similar situations. So—I will emphasize once again—heavy automatic control should only be applied in those situations where systematic errors do not become too obvious, or where very strong advantages outweigh the disadvantage of artistic ham-fistedness.

Short wave radio, and commercial radio stations determined to obtain the maximum service area from a given transmitter power, form a special case. Here control is used only to ensure that the average level is as high as possible consistent with a distortion of peaks that is not excessive.

How acceptable this is to the listener depends on conditions in the main service area. If a broadcast is intended to be heard a long way from the transmitter and likely to have to compete with heavy static and possibly even jamming by unfriendly natives, the intending listener will welcome a heavy use of the limiter.

If the main service area is the town round the transmitter and there is little or no interference the listener will find all but the lightest touch of the limiter objectionable; if he is listening on a car radio and the signal is subject to moderate interference and fading he would welcome more.

A completely different use for compressors and limiters is that adopted in pop music balance. Here the technical possibilities are being used as creatively as the musical instruments themselves: the use of compression is assumed in the composition of the music. Similarly, compression can also be used in other ways (see Chapter 11: "Shaping Sound").

Controlling stereo

Where the stereo broadcast is on FM, control is easy. It can be shown that the deviation (i.e. size) of the signal does not exceed the greater of the A and B channels, so all that is necessary to avoid overmodulation is that these do not exceed their normal limits. The same will be true for recordings on magnetic tape, where the A and B channels are kept separate. BBC stereo equipment has a double-reading peak programme meter on which both A and B signals can be seen, in addition to a combined A+B PPM.

In broadcasting, however, several problems may arise:

(i) In a large network some of the transmitters may be in mono.
(ii) Some of the listeners to the stereo broadcast will have mono receivers.
(iii) Some of the items on the stereo service may be broadcast in mono only.

For practical purposes it is assumed that the average level for A+B will be 3 dB higher than A or B on its own; accordingly, the stereo and mono parts of the system are lined up with a 3 dB difference in level. Unfortunately, however, this is not a complete answer to the problem of relative levels.

There would be no difficulty if the signals added together simply, so that the maximum volume of A+B really were always no more than 3 dB higher than the separate maximum volumes for A+B, but in fact this happens only for identical sources (e.g. for tone, or for a signal in the centre of the sound stage). If A and B are both at the same volume but are different sounds the sum will vary from +0 dB to +6 dB. So where A and B are at maximum volume, the A+B signal may be overmodulating by 3 dB. This should therefore be controlled for the benefit of mono systems.

On the other hand if the signal is being controlled primarily on the A+B signal, the stereo signal can overmodulate. This will happen when A+B is at its maximum and all of the signal is in the A or B channel, which will then be 3 dB over the top. So again there is a case for control.

Fortunately these control problems only occur in this mixed mono and stereo situation: controlling stereo for a single medium is much simpler.

15

TAPE EDITING

"EDITING" can mean various things: cutting and rejoining a tape with a *temporary* or *permanent* joint; *copy editing*, in which selected sections from originals are copied in a required sequence on to a make-up tape; *mixing*, where the combined output of two tapes are fed to a third recorder; and *dubbing*, where several magnetic film tracks and other sound sources are combined in a final mix of film sound.

But, principally, "editing" does mean physically cutting recorded material—and here again there are several forms that it can take.

Rough editing is assembling the main body of a programme or sequence in the right order and taking out the longer stretches of unwanted material.

Fine editing is tightening up this assembled material to provide for the best continuity of action and argument, at the same time deleting where possible the fluffs and other minor irrelevancies that distract the attention and reduce intelligibility; and *reclamation* is the process of checking stock the sound on which is no longer required, examining joints and removing spacers, so that it is ready for re-use.

All of these apply to quarter-inch sound tape, to video tape, and to film sound.

Four reasons for editing

Editing is generally undertaken for one of four reasons:

(i) Getting the programme timing right. The duration must be adjusted to fit the scheduled space. In radio or television this is often the overriding consideration. If a programme is badly planned and turns out to be seriously overlength the editing process may result in what is virtually a different programme. However, if only a small amount of fining down is necessary

438

most people seem to agree—afterwards—that the programme is improved by it.

(ii) Shaping the programme: giving it a beginning, a middle, and an end, and ensuring that the pace and tension varies, and does not drop too low. Awkward parentheses, repetitions, phrases, whole sentences, or paragraphs will have to go if they obstruct the flow of the argument.

(iii) Cutting fluffs, etc. Some minor faults lend character to speech; too many will make it difficult to follow. Mistakes in reading a script do not often sound like natural conversational slips.

(iv) For convenience of assembly: to combine film or material recorded on location with studio links, to allow material of different types to be rehearsed and recorded separately, or to pre-record awkward sections.

Whether editing is used in a positive and constructive way, or whether the major part of the creative effort goes into the actual recording, is a matter of temperament. Some people regard the need for editing as an admission of defeat, and use it only for dealing with overruns or particularly bad errors; others prefer to place a greater reliance on the impromptu and follow this with selective editing.

But techniques which aim to avoid editing presuppose either that the broadcast has a well-rehearsed and perfectly timed script or that those taking part are capable, in an unscripted programme, of presenting their material logically, concisely, and coherently (or that they are under the guidance of an expert interviewer or chairman who will ensure that they do). In fact, such self-control under the stress of a recording session is rare except among experienced broadcasters; and even when a sound recording or film is made in familiar surroundings, the presence of the microphone (even more than the camera) produces an unreal situation with (very often) stilted and uncharacteristic reactions on the part of speakers. One purpose of editing is to restore the illusion of reality, generally in a heightened form.

Naturally this process of editorial selection imposes a considerable responsibility on the producer, which is not met if the result distorts the character or the intention of the speaker. If the speaker heard a playback he should recognize it as the essence of what he said (within the limits of what was needed for the programme, which should have been made clear to him) and feel pleased that he had expressed himself so clearly.

439

Record with the editing session in mind

Nearly all recordings will benefit from, at the very least, a little tidying up: and this should be borne in mind when recording. But do not expect the razor blade to accomplish the impossible: it will make things a lot easier if right from the start of the first recording you are constantly checking in your mind what might be needed in the editing.

There are lots of things to watch for: just what these are, depends on the type of programme. For example, if a fluff occurs in speech, will it be possible to edit, or would a retake be advisable?

In film the fluff may occur at a point when a cutaway (in vision) was in any case intended, or can easily be arranged. In this case the fluff may simply be left for the editor to remove, or if this sounds awkward the retake may be taken in sound only ("wildtrack"). If a retake in vision is necessary the director will have to decide whether to go again from the start of the scene, whether to vary the framing of the picture (usually, if possible, to a closer shot or to a different angle), or whether the same framing can be continued after an earlier cutaway. The sound recordist should also (and generally without being asked for it) supply background atmosphere at the same recorded level in sufficient quantity to be cut in to any gaps that may be introduced in the editing at points where there are more pictures than synchronous sound. This saves time and effort later, at the film dubbing session.

In a radio discussion between several people, the director should be asking himself whether the various voices have identified themselves, each other, and the things they are going to talk about sufficiently clearly. If not, he should record a round of names and subject pointers in each voice so that these can be cut in where necessary. Watch for continuity of mood: if the point you are likely to join up to ends with a laugh, try to start the new take with something to laugh about (which can be cut out). Discreetly discourage phrases such as "as I've just said", and retake if they are not clearly editable. And so on.

When editing radio programmes, "pauses" may be required. So, if possible, get everybody to sit still and record 10 seconds of atmosphere (for, even though atmosphere for pauses can generally be picked up quite easily from hesitations between words at other points on the tape, it is better to be safe). If you are going to record atmosphere for this purpose it is best to do it while your speakers are still there: after they have gone the sound may be slightly different. If much editing is going to be required, don't be too clever in your control of levels; this can make for difficulties with the background atmosphere. And if the background is heavy, record a spare track of perhaps 20 seconds. (Longer periods than 20 seconds can perhaps be dealt with by making a loop of tape or, at a film dubbing session, a loop of magnetic film.)

At a recording session for serious music it is again useful to record a few seconds of atmosphere at the end of each item in order to have something to join up to the start of the next piece. Music retakes should be recorded as soon as possible after the original, so that the performers can remember the exact intonations at the link point, and also so that the physical conditions of the studio should be as close to the original as possible. An orchestra quite literally warms up; its tone changes appreciably in the earlier part of each session in a studio.

In describing the techniques used I shall deal first with editing on ¼-inch sound tape, then videotape (with which sound tapes may be used as an accessory). Electronic editing (copy editing) can be used for both. Then I will describe film sound editing techniques.

Editing equipment: quarter-inch sound tape

There are basically two different types of tape splicer: those which give "temporary" and those which give "permanent" joins.

In permanent jointing the tape is overlapped by a quarter of an inch and stuck together. This means that a small part of the tape is permanently lost with each cut. The advantages of permanent over temporary jointing are negligible, except perhaps for reclamation.

Here I shall be dealing only with "temporary" techniques, where there is no overlap, and no tape is lost when a joint is made. In the

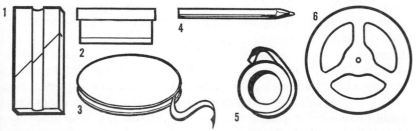

EQUIPMENT FOR TEMPORARY JOINTS. 1. Splicing block. 2. Blade. 3. Leader tape. 4. Wax pencil. 5. Jointing tape. 6. Spare spool.

event of an unsatisfactory temporary joint it should always be possible to get back to the starting-point and try again. This allows experiment and is a valuable—indeed, often necessary—facility.

Temporary joints may be made on blocks that have complicated systems of clamps, slicers, and cutting grooves: on some, jointing tape half an inch wide is used, and the tape has to be trimmed and "waisted" to make a satisfactory joint. But BBC engineers who do a great deal of editing find that with very simple tools they can work with speed and accuracy.

For "temporary" jointing the following tools are needed:

(i) A simple block with a channel to take the tape. The channel should be lapped slightly so that the tape once smoothed into it with the fingertip is gripped firmly for a length of about five inches. It will also have a cutting groove at 45°. The block should be fixed firmly to the near edge of the tape deck. (It may be screwed or bolted on, or fixed with adhesive.)

(ii) A fairly sharp stainless steel razor blade. Use the one-sided type to avoid cut fingertips; I say only "fairly sharp" for the same reason. But as soon as the blade begins to get blunt it will tend to drag on the tape so that the two butt ends may not match properly.

(iii) A soft wax pencil for marking edit points. Yellow is the best colour for showing up on the tape.

(iv) A roll of quarter-inch jointing tape—nominally quarter-inch, that is, for that available nowadays is slightly narrower. This allows for a little inaccuracy in use without overlapping the edge of the tape, so avoiding the necessity for trimming.

(v) As an optional extra: leader and spacer tapes—coloured and uncoated. It is useful if you have some which you can write on for purposes of visual identification. The BBC uses three colours as standard: white for leaders, yellow for spacers, and red for trailers.

One item which is not on this list is "non-magnetic scissors". Of course, these can be used instead of a razor blade, but few people actually do; and generally their work seems to be a shade slower. A non-stainless razor blade could cause trouble by becoming magnetized, but in practice this just does not seem to happen.

Dusting powder is often recommended, and French chalk is sometimes specified, although in fact almost any fine absorbent powder will do as well. But nowadays it hardly seems worth bothering with this for most "temporary" joints (at one time the adhesive on jointing tape was more oozy than it is today). It is, of course, important that tape should not be sticky, or layers will "pull" as they come off the spool, drag on pressure pads, and clog the heads. And for tapes that are to be broadcast it is better to be safe than sorry—particularly in hot climates.

Many freelance contributors to radio programmes prefer to do their own editing before submitting their tapes to programme editors.

There are many good reasons for this, so in the following I assume that the editing may be undertaken either on recorders of professional quality or on cheaper domestic equipment. With skilful editing there should be no difference in the result.

Preparing to cut

First, play the tape up to the point at which the cut is to be made, and then switch from the normal "replay" condition to one in which the tape can be spooled by hand with the tape still in contact with the head. The appropriate condition for this will vary from machine to machine. In some cases there is a "pause" control, in others it will be "replay/off", and so on. Sometimes the best way will be to pull against the spool clutches or brakes (but only if these are fairly loose and there is no risk of stretching the tape). The exact point can then be checked by hand (suggestions for finding this in difficult cases are given later in the chapter). When in doubt about a mark, set up the tape with the mark at the replay head, switch to "replay", and run. If the machine has a quick enough start it should be quite clear whether the mark is correct or not. Alternatively, pull quickly up to speed by hand.

Always mark the cut in the same way, e.g. along the lower edge of the tape. This is the quickest way of ensuring that a scrap of tape which is transposed, or cut and then reinstated, is put back in the tape the right way round.

Most recorders in the low- to medium-price ranges have pressure pads, and the head assembly is fitted with a protective cover which completely surrounds it. If much editing is to be undertaken, remove this cover and store it away somewhere. It will then be possible to get at the replay head (if necessary by lifting the pressure pad) and mark the tape at the point you intend to cut.

But for owners of these less-expensive machines who do not want to remove the cover, or who are in the habit of checking each mark by pulling the tape backwards and forwards after it has been made (so that it might be erased by the pressure pad), there is an alternative, almost equally convenient method. For this, measure the tape distance from the replay head to the first rigid guide pillar to the right of the assembly, and put a notch on the editing block at the same distance to the right of the cutting groove. The tape can then be marked at the guide pillar.

Making a joint

A "temporary" joint is made like this:

(i) Locate and mark the joint, as already indicated.
(ii) Switch the recorder to whatever condition allows the tape to be lifted from the heads, and place it coated side downwards in the editing block.

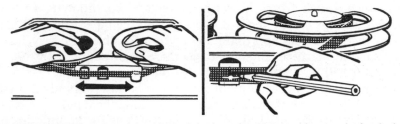

TAPE EDITING I. *Left*: moving the tape backwards and forwards over the heads, by hand, in order to find the exact point. *Right*: marking the tape with a soft wax pencil, exactly at the playback head gap.

(iii) Cut. The razor blade should be sharp enough not to drag when drawn lightly along its guide channel. It should not be necessary to apply pressure (or, if the block is made of a relatively soft alloy, it will be damaged by the steel blade).
(iv) Then, if a fairly long piece of tape is to be taken out, replace the take-up spool by a "scrap" spool and wind off to the new "in" point. Mark this, cut again, and swap the take-up spools.
(v) Now place the two butt ends of the tape together in the block (and a little to one side of the cutting groove) so that they are just barely touching each other. Check that the tape is clean on either side of the butt.
(vi) Cut off an inch (or perhaps a little more) of jointing tape, taking care not to fingerprint the tacky side any more than is absolutely necessary, and lay it along the tape, using one edge of the channel to steady it and guide it into place.

(vii) Run a finger along the tape to press the joint firm. This is the point at which the joint may be dusted with French chalk (dip a finger in the powder and run it along the tape again).

Checking the joint

After a joint has been made, place the tape back on the heads, and spool back a foot or so (again, this can usually be done by hand against the braking effect of the clutch plates without any adverse effect on the mechanism).

Then play through the joint checking that:

  (i) it is properly made;

 (ii) the edited tape makes sense—and that you have in fact edited at the point you thought;

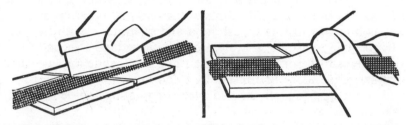

TAPE EDITING 2. *Left*: cutting the tape. *Right*: placing the jointing tape across a joint, so that the two sections become butted together.

 (iii) the timing is right: that the words after the joint do not follow too quickly or too slowly on those before;

 (iv) the speaker does not take two breaths;

  (v) neither the perspective nor volume of voice takes an unnatural jump;

 (vi) there is no impossible vocal contortion implied;

 (vii) the tone of voice does not change abruptly, e.g. from an audible smile to earnest seriousness;

(viii) the background does not abruptly change in quality; nor is any "effect" or murmured response sliced in two.

 (ix) (for stereo edits) no "flicker" has been introduced by an imperfect butt.

It is worth studying this list of possible errors with care, not because you will not notice them once they are made (they will probably shout at you) but to bear in mind both when recording and when selecting suitable points at which to cut. After a little practice,

445

very few of your joints will have to be remade. In fact, occasional very minor faults can be tolerated, as few people will notice them unless they are watching out for them. However, they *should* only be tolerated if a remake, or a repair by the insertion of a section of tape from somewhere else in the recording is impossible.

Remaking a faulty joint

You may need to cut down a gap that is too long; or insert a pause or breath or even an "um" or "er" to cover an abrupt change of subject or mood; or you may have to reinstate part of what was cut. The great advantage of "temporary" over permanent joints is that this may be done without damage to the tape.

After marking any new point at which you propose to cut, undo the joint. To do this turn it over and "break" it; you will be able to get a grip of one of the 45° points of the butt and pull it away from the jointing tape. If it is a fresh joint and separates cleanly you will often be able to use the same piece of jointing tape a second time; so, having cut the other side to the right point, slide the two butts together in the block and reseal by smoothing along the joint with your fingertip. Strip off the old piece of jointing tape completely and start afresh.

Freelances should note that faulty or awkward-sounding edits are most likely to be noticed by the employer or a member of his staff.

Rough editing: sound radio

In rough editing the objective is much the same in sound radio, television, and film: it is simply to assemble the material in its intended order, so that the effect (logical or artistic) can begin to be seen. I will deal first with the case where sound only has to be considered.

In the first instance, as you cut your programme into rough shape, you may perhaps start by putting spacers in to indicate where you will be inserting a studio link.

Remember that you can *transpose*. This is of considerable importance when several unrelated subjects have arisen in an unscripted discussion. The factors which governed the order of recording may not hold for the finished programme. You will want to start with a bang: start with something which may not be of vital importance, but which engages the listener's attention and gives him a sense of "being there". The middle should, while progressing logically, have light and shade: there should be variety of pace, of speech lengths and rhythms, and of mood. And the tension should build to an effective "curtain": something which will contain in a few lines the essence of all that has preceded it, or which will suddenly offset and illuminate it.

As you select material, feed it on to your make-up tape in programme order, with transpositions and retakes in their proper place. At this stage try to cut at "paragraph pauses". And if you have specially recorded any fades of background noise you will, of course, need to cut or transpose these to their proper places at the beginning and end of the section. Rejoin the unwanted material after each cut, by feeding it on to a reject spool (this should be kept until the programme is complete, after which the tape is ready for re-use).

Even at this stage exercise a fair amount of care where you cut: do not cut in the middle of a breath, or cut too close to the first word when there is a heavy background. And except when only small cuts are being made, it is always safest in a discussion programme or interview to switch from one voice to another at the join. If you do come back in on the same voice, check that voice quality, mood, and balance are sufficiently similar: it is easy enough for the listener to get the impression that a completely new voice has entered the conversation and to start asking "Now, who is this?" instead of listening to what is being said.

It will often be possible to rough edit without bothering to mark the tape. Choose a particular point to the right of the heads, one at which it is convenient to take the tape between finger and thumb. Then lay this part of the tape in the block, appropriately offset, i.e. so that your thumb is at the same distance from the cutting groove as it was previously from the replay head. With very little practice it is possible to get quite expert at this, rough-cutting to an accuracy of less than a quarter of an inch.

When an additional replay machine is available the rough editing stage can be done by copy editing. In this way the original tapes can be kept intact, which will be of advantage if you want to arrange the same material differently for another programme later. Other reasons for copy editing may be that the material on another track is valuable, or simply that you do not trust your own editing and want to insure against possible mishaps!

To copy edit a tape, the selected programme material is re-recorded to a make-up tape in the appropriate order, taking a little more at the beginning and end of each insert than is absolutely necessary, and remembering to check for any controlling that may be needed. The inserts are then cut together on the make-up tape in the normal way.

Fine editing: sound radio

After your rough editing you must consider how much more needs to be done. Think of this in terms of the following:

(i) The shape of the programme as a whole.
(ii) The intelligibility and conciseness of individual contributions.
(iii) The character and personality of the speakers.

The first of these considerations may mean that you have to make severe internal cuts in one section and not in another; you may have to cut out repetitions or verbal embroidery. Try to keep the theme of what remains tight and unified.

Here are some of the other things you may wish to cut:

(i) Heavy coughs, etc. These hold up the action and may cause the listener to lose the thread. But if the speaker has a frog in his throat (and this section of the recording cannot be cut) it will not do any harm to leave in the cough which clears it— just for the psychological satisfaction of the listener!

(ii) Excessive "ums" and "ers" (or any other vocal mannerism which runs to seed). They should be cut if this actually improves intelligibility—which it generally will if they appear in the middle of a sentence. But about one in ten actually *improves* intelligibility by breaking the flow at a point where it needs to be broken. So be careful. Some speakers use these noises as an important integral part of their vocal sentence: it may not look good written down, but it sounds right on the tape. Other speakers seem to express quite a bit of character in these punctuating noises. In these cases, do not cut. An "er" which is moulded into the preceding or following word often cannot be cut, anyway.

(iii) Excessive pauses. In real life these can stand to be a great deal longer than on a tape, because we watch the speaker's face as he thinks. On a tape a pause is just a pause, unless it lends real dramatic emphasis to its context. But pauses should not be cut down to nothing if the result sounds like a series of impossible vocal contortions. To see what I mean, record the sentence "You (pause) are (pause) a (pause) good (pause) editor" and then cut the pauses out completely. The result will sound like a case of hiccups. How much gap you need to leave depends on how much the mouth would have to change in shape during the pause. (This goes for "ers", too.)

(iv) Superimpositions. Two people talking over each other are irritating. But this sort of thing needs great care in editing: it will generally be necessary to leave a partial overlap, or take out part sentences before and after.

(v) Fluffs, where the speaker has gone back on himself. Again an edit will generally improve intelligibility. But take care here, as well; the first word of the repeat will often be overemphasized, so try to find some place to cut after (or in the middle of) this word.

There will, of course, be many other types of editing to do. Each different speaker presents a new set of problems and decisions as to whether to cut or not.

For example, when you start recording someone "off the cuff" it is a common thing for the piece to start off slowly and gather speed and interest as it progresses. This is completely wrong for the start of a new voice in a programme tape, where the listener's attention and interest must be caught in the first few words. If you cannot come in after this "warm up" period it may be necessary to tighten up the opening sentence: this matters a great deal more than hesitations at a later stage, when the voice and personality are accepted by the listener.

In certain cases, particularly where the recording is of importance as a "document", no editing should be done at all (with the possible exception of cutting down really excessive pauses), and the greatest care should be exercised if any condensing is to be attempted. If in doubt, resort to a studio link.

In any case do not go mad with your razor blade. It is very useful to have good ideas about where to cut; but just as important, perhaps, is to know where *not* to cut.

Finding the exact point

There are two places to cut at in a "sentence" pause. One is after the word (and its "studio" reverberation) has finished and before the breath; the other is after the breath and before the next word. For most purposes it is best, and safer, to choose the latter. You retain the full natural pause which the speaker allowed, and you can cut as close as you like to the new word (which helps to mask any slight change in "atmosphere").

449

Cutting between the words of a sentence can be a great deal more difficult, however, as words sound very different when they are wound through slowly by hand. But certain characteristics of speech can soon be recognized: e.g. the "s" and "f" sounds. And the explosive consonants "p" and "b", as well as the stopped "k", "t", "g", and "d" are easy to pick out (though not always as easy to distinguish from each other) because of the slight break in sound which precedes them on the tape. Often enough in a spoken sentence the words may be run together to such an extent that the only break may be before such a letter—perhaps in the middle of a word.

Do not assume that because a letter *should* be there it *will* be. Complete vowel sounds may prove to be absent. The personal pronoun "I" is typical of many such sounds. In the sentence "Well I'm going now" it may be missing completely. If you try to cut off the "well" you may even find the "m" was a vocal illusion, no more than a slight distortion of the end of the "l" sound. Similarly, in "It's a hot day", spoken quickly, there is probably no complete word "hot". Nor is it possible to isolate the word from "hot tin roof", as the first "t" will be missing and the one that is there will be joined on to the following vowel sound in such a way as to have no separate existence. Before going in for a lot of fine editing it is worth doing a little research into what the beginnings and ends of words sound like at slow speed, and where words blend into each other and where they do not.

In cutting between words, cut as late in any pause as possible. When searching for the right pause on a tape do not be misled by the tiny break in sound which often precedes the letter "t" and similar consonants. You can often cut *in* to a continuous sound (e.g. where several words have been run together), provided that the cut is at an angle, but do not attempt to cut *out* of one, unless you joint straight on to a sound of equal value (one for which the mouth would have to be formed in the same shape).

It is very difficult to insert missing "a's" and "the's"; these are nearly always closely tied with the following word, so that unless the speaker is enunciating each word clearly and separately, it is necessary to take this in combination with the sound which follows. The letter "s", however, is relatively easy to insert or (sometimes) remove. I quote these few cases as examples of the verbal surgery in which the tape editor sometimes finds himself involved when trying to make a difficult transition. Experience gained in this kind of editing is a great time-saver later on, as you can quickly locate each cut.

450

These principles apply equally to videotape and film sound editing; though in the latter case the cut will normally be made at discrete points defined by the frame interval.

Editing music

There are various reasons why we may wish to edit music: to cut out a repeat, or one verse or chorus; to cut in a retake; to cut everything up to a certain point so that we hit a certain note "on the nose"; to condense or extend mood music to fit the action of a play, and so on.

Editing music is one of the more skilled tape-cutting jobs—in which most of the skill lies in making sure you are marking the right part of the right note. So before getting down to work in earnest, practise on scrap tape until you can be sure that you are finding the right point every time. (Remember also when handling music tapes that any damage due to spillage or stretching, etc., will be more noticeable than on speech tapes.)

The important thing in music editing is not that the *next* note after each of the two points marked should be the same, but that the *previous* one should be—that is to say, when cutting between two notes it is the quality of the reverberation which must be preserved. This means that any retake must start *before* the point at which the cut is to be made: there is nothing so painfully obvious as a music edit where a "cold" retake has been edited in, resulting in a nasty clip on the reverberation to the previous note. It might be supposed that if the new sound is loud enough the loss may be disguised, but this will not be so unless the "in" is cut so close as to trim away part of the start of the note (and this "attack" transient is particularly important to the character of a sound).

So unless we are cutting on pauses in the music which are longer than the reverberation time of the studio, our first requirement for a successful joint is that the volume and timbre preceding both the "out" and "in" points on the original tape should be identical.

But it may be possible to make an exception to this rule when cutting mood music to fit behind speech and effects: if the level of the music can drop low enough the whole business may often be treated fairly casually. For preference, choose a rest to cut out on and something rather vague to come back to, but if in doubt the edit point can be "dipped" slightly. But you cannot take such liberties with "foreground" music. For example, if you are trimming linking music to length, any internal cuts must be made with the same

451

care that would be given to featured music. And speech over music is often practically impossible to edit, as an untidy join in the music generally coincides with a slight gap in the speech. Unless you are very lucky a perfectly good speech joint will sound obviously edited.

When everything up to a certain point in a piece of music is cut, in order to create a new starting-point—e.g. when you want to come in on a particular theme—the effect of the "tail" of reverberation under the new first note is often unimportant. Except in the case when this "tail" is loud, and contrasts strongly in quality with the first wanted sound, it seems to be accepted by the ear as a quite unexceptionable part of the timbre of the note. However, for this particular case a sharp manual fade-in often sounds better than a cut. And for getting out of a piece of music at a point before the end (where there is no pause) there is no alternative to a fade.

Since, in music editing, finding the exact places to cut at two similar but separate parts of the tape is often the main difficulty, a couple of hints on this may be of use—particularly if you are not cutting at a clearly defined point. It will often be possible to identify the two places to cut in each case by: (a) measuring off the distance on the tape from a more easily located point a little earlier, or (b) marking out the rhythmic structure of the music with a wax pencil on the back of the tape. (Of these two the second is possibly the better guide, as the "easily located" note may not have been played exactly on the beat.)

Complex editing problems

Editing staccato effects and absolutely regular continuous effects presents no problems. But effects which are continuous yet progressively changing in quality can be very difficult to edit, as can speech with heavy but uneven effects behind, or speech in heavily reverberant acoustics.

Rhythmic effects are fairly simple, as they can be treated rather like music; and so, possibly, in its different way can reverberant speech. But with the more uneven type of noise it may be difficult to find two points which are sufficiently similar in quality, and in this case we have once again to resort to mixing.

Typical of the type of problem which seems as though it ought to be simple, but is not, is editing applause. A burst of applause lasting, say, ten seconds is very difficult to cut down to five without a slight "blip" at the join. But to do this with two copies of a disc is very easy, as indeed it is when crossfading from one tape to another.

452

Sometimes the change of quality behind a speech edit can be covered by mixing in some similar, but heavier, effects afterwards, using an effects disc or tape, or a loop. Even so, a change of quality can often show through unless the added effects are substantially heavier than the earlier backing, or are peaked at the point of the join.

But there is just one case where the untidy effect of a succession of sharp cuts in background noise has come to be tolerated. Over the last few years a sort of convention has arisen whereby "man-in-the-street" interviews are cut together by simple editing, with breaks in the background appearing as frank evidence of the method of assembly.

The technique is used both for sound and film work, purely as a matter of convenience, but its frequent use has helped to invest such editing methods with an air of quick-fire actuality.

Why cut at an angle?

It is always recommended that tape should be cut at an angle. The figure of 45° is often mentioned as being suitable, and most editing blocks make provision for such a cut (though a 90° cut is sometimes offered as an additional facility, without actively being recommended for use).

What is so magical about 45°? Is the 45° cut superior to those at other angles? The simple answer to this is that provided the tape is actually cut at a reasonably sharp angle and not straight across, the exact angle is not vital.

But a 90° cut has the disadvantage that any sound on the tape, even atmosphere, starts absolutely "square" at the point of cut; and any sound which suddenly starts at full volume *sounds* as if it starts with a click. Excellent examples of this are time signal pips or "beep" tones: the very words "pip" or "beep" suggest the effect I mean. To demonstrate this for yourself record a pure tone (which contains one frequency) and cut in a short length of spacer at 90°. Then try the same thing with angled cuts.

The effect of a 45° cut can be expressed in quantitative terms as follows:

It can be demonstrated that if a fade in or out exceeds 10 milliseconds in duration there will be no click. (In fact this is over twenty times more than is actually needed in most circumstances.) This duration corresponds to 0·15 inch of 15 ips tape. As a 45° cut on full track tape extends 0·25 inch along the tape there will therefore be no click. Similarly, 10 milliseconds corresponds to 0·075 inch of 7½ ips tape. A half-track recording fades in or out over 0·1 inch for a 45° cut, so again there will be no click.

The standard angle of cut provided on some joiners used for magnetic film sound is 10°. A recording on separate magnetic film track is 0·2 inch wide: a cut therefore fades in over about 0·018 inch. As 35-mm film travels at 18 ips this represents a period of 1 millisecond; for 16 mm the corresponding duration would be 2·5 milliseconds; both of these should be quite long enough to avoid a noticeable click.

Tape recorded at 7½ ips full track is the most convenient for editing when using cine spools. Lower speeds give lower quality and less precision in marking, and higher speeds make it more difficult to pull the tape over the heads by manually rotating the spools against the clutch or brakes. Using the larger NAB spools (10½ inches diameter) 15 ips is a convenient recording speed for editing.

Tape reclamation

To reclaim tape that has not been edited is a simple matter. Leader, spacers, and trailer are removed and replaced by well-made joints. Heavily edited tape and short off-cuts should not, however, be re-used.

In principle it should then be technically possible to re-issue used tapes without further ado. But this assumes that you have no objection to the earlier material falling in to the next user's hands (which, apart from anything else, may cause copyright complications). And it also assumes that the technical condition of the recorder that is about to be used is satisfactory. If it is not, and particularly if the erase circuit or head is faulty, it may leave background "chatter" from the previous recording to mar the new one. A bulk eraser is the safest answer, of course, and is essential with certain battery recorders which have no erase head anyway.

The bulk eraser provides a wash which is incomparably quicker than playing the tape through. The spool is placed on the eraser, which is simply a device for providing a strong alternating field. The spool is given one or two complete turns to ensure that all parts of the tape get the full benefit of the field, and then it is lifted off and drawn right away from the eraser before the current is switched off.

In BBC practice reclamation also includes the removal of all temporary joints, replacing them by cemented joints. The machines used by the BBC are equipped to locate joints at high speed, and have other aids to fast working such as the application of heat to speed up the drying out of the joint.

Permanent joints: tape and film

The more complex "permanent" tape editing blocks are very similar to those formerly used regularly for film editing, from which the permanent jointing method is derived. The method has little

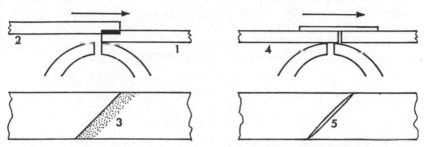

LAPPED AND BUTT JOINS. The overlap on a lapped join must be so arranged that the first part (1) of the tape or film past the head lies on top of the second part (2), so that contact is quickly regained as the second part drops on to the head. If the join is angled (3), the temporary loss of contact is less important as its effect is spread over a length of tape. If, however, a butt join is made (4) there is no loss of contact at any time unless the butt is imperfect (5). Again, the effect of any slight gap or overlap will be minimized by angling the join.

to recommend it for editing recordings on either $\frac{1}{4}$-inch tape or magnetic film, as there will inevitably be a point at which the coating lifts from the head during subsequent use, resulting in slight drop-out (which is, however, minimized by using an angled cut).

The tape is cut in the normal way (at an angle) and the coating is removed from the last quarter of an inch of tape on the left-hand side of the joint (i.e. the butt end which is attached to the feed spool). This can be done by applying the jointing compound and then wiping away with a paper tissue, to expose a short length of transparent backing. (If there had been any programme signal to edit the cut on this part of the tape should have been a quarter inch to the right of the edit point.) Some more of the jointing compound is applied to the exposed part of the tape coating, and the backing of the other butt end of tape is pressed on to it, and held under pressure

455

long enough for the joint to dry out. Heat may be applied to speed this process. Points to note:

    (i) The coating should appear to be continuous after the joint has been made.

   (ii) Experience will indicate the right amount of compound to use. (At first attempts the joint may be bumpy, or just not permanent!)

 (iii) The most suitable type of block will be that in which the tape is held by clamps, and not the type I have advocated for temporary joints. Jointing compound can too easily get stuck in corners.

 (iv) The tape should always be lapped so that the new section of tape is farthest from the head on normal replay. Otherwise the edge of the new section of tape will strike against the head and may bounce away momentarily.

Bonding agents for acetate, PVC, and polyester-based tapes are obtainable. In the case of acetate or PVC this may be of the solvent type (different compounds for the different bases). There is also one of the adhesive type which can be used for any type of base (a "universal jointing compound").

Sound problems in editing videotape

The main problems in editing videotape arise from the fact that the sound and picture are not recorded exactly beside each other: the sound is three-fifths of a second ahead of the picture.

This means that if the tape is cut straight across, the part before the cut will include three-fifths of a second of sound associated

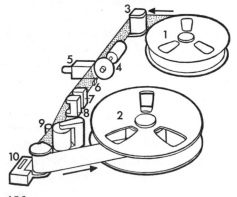

VIDEOTAPE RECORDER. 1. Feed spool. 2. Take up spool. 3. Master erase head. 4. Drum motor and rotating recording head. 5. Tape guide (tape held in position by suction). 6. Control track recording head. 7. Sound and "cue" track erase heads. 8. Sound and "cue" sound recording heads. 9. Drive capstan. 10. Tape timer.

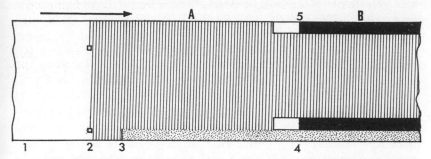

VIDEOTAPE (2 inches wide) visualized during recording, and as seen from the backing side of the tape (i.e. with recording heads on far side). 1. Unrecorded videotape. 2. Video recording heads (two of four set at 90° to each other on a rotating disc). Each line recorded on the tape represents a group of lines in the television picture. 3. Control track recording head. 4 "Cue" track recording head. This can also be used as an additional sound recording head. 5. Main sound recording head. As the picture and sound recording heads are displaced by $9\frac{1}{4}$ inches the sound is not directly related to the picture lying alongside it., e.g. the sound at B belongs to the picture not at B but at A, which trails $9\frac{1}{4}$ inches to the left. A physical cut across the tape at B would include more sound than picture: in terms of dialogue, one or two more words would be heard after the picture had gone.

with picture which has now been removed. Similarly the part of the tape after the cut will be deficient in sound: if it were joined to blank tape, as the picture came up the first 0·6 second would be silent; there would be no background atmosphere. And worse, if the picture were of a person who had been speaking during that time he would be seen mouthing unheard words before the sound suddenly arrived at full volume.

This situation arises because it is not practicable to record sound on a videotape at the same point as the picture. The video signal is recorded in a complex manner, with a system of four heads rotating in a vertical plane against the moving tape which is formed by suction in to a quadrant of a circle as it passes the recording head drum. This video recording occupies the greater part of the 2-inch width of the tape.

As you look at the uncoated side of the tape, it moves from left to right; it moves from the left spool over the recording heads and is taken up on the right. After the tape has passed the video recording system, three other signals are recorded lengthways along the tape. First, there is a control track along the lower edge: this is used subsequently to control the speed of replay, and also contains an edit pulse on each frame which indicates to the editor where he must cut (obviously, he must cut between similar points in the frame). Then at $9\frac{1}{4}$ inches from the video heads (and shortly

457

after the sound erase head) the tape passes over the sound recording head. This displacement may be occupied by about two spoken words, or, perhaps on the average, rather less.

There are, in fact, two sound recording tracks. One along the top edge records programme sound; the other lies between the control track and the video signal area, and is called a cue track. In principle it is designed for recording information of one sort or another which may later be of use but which is not to be broadcast. While possibilities for its use are many, in practice they seem to be few, so that programme staff often forget its existence. It is worth remembering: it is there, can be, and is used. However, in the following I will restrict myself to considering the sound on the upper edge track.

Videotape: finding the point to edit

There are, in fact, two points to be found in marking up videotape: the picture cut and the sound cut. If picture and sound are to change together the marks will be separated by 9¼ inches. However, it may be that a sound overlap is desired: in this case the sound mark may perhaps be at the same place as that for picture, making a simple physical cut all that is necessary, or the mark may have to be made at some third point.

Very conveniently, simple cuts often work perfectly satisfactorily. As a person looks up, or turns his head, and opens his mouth to speak, the movement from start to finish may well take, near enough, just that three-fifths of a second. If, in addition, the shot

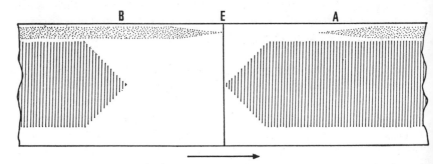

VIDEOTAPE SOUND-AND-VISION EDITING WITH FADES. A. Fade-out. B. Fade-in. E. Tape join. Note that as sound and picture are displaced by 9¼ inches there must be a gap of at least 0·6 seconds in both sound and picture if a simple edit is employed. (The fades are represented symbolically.)

from which we are cutting has atmosphere which closely matches that of the new scene, we have a simple cut which will work. We must, of course, watch that we do not cut in to a breath or some intermittent background sound. There may be a range of several frames where a picture cut may be satisfactory; we can then find the exact point in the sound (usually just before the word) by rocking the tape slowly over the sound head just as for the $\frac{1}{4}$-inch sound tape. The preferred sound cut point can then be marked on the tape with a thick felt marker pen (thick, so that it can clearly be seen when travelling at normal tape speed).

If there is any danger that the cut will not work satisfactorily; if, for example, there is a cut in the picture at about this point (as there often will be), the picture cut is checked by running the tape at normal speed. As the sound cut mark goes past the video head the tape editor will tap (perhaps with his marker) on the corner of the machine; another person—the director perhaps—will watch the monitor and note whether the tap came the right or the wrong side of the picture change. If on the wrong side, another sound cut point is tried, if there is room; if there is not the edit must be managed some other way.

The straight cut may also be timed accurately on the picture, with merely a check on sound. The picture is played through, "tapping" the preferred cutting point. When this is agreed, the machine is played up to the agreed frame and then stopped. The picture will disappear at the right point, but the tape will run on a few inches—experience will show how far. A mark is made at this (now offset) point, checked; and the tape cut.

Naturally this procedure must be undertaken at both "out" and "in" points. Each editor will have his own system for marking the various points to indicate whether they are for sound or vision, in cues or out cues, and whether they are the first, second, or whatever numbered attempt.

Another case for the straight cut is when two scenes have fades of sound and vision (normally these will have been made to fade together) with at least 0·6 second of black in between. The black will lie before the cut but the sound recording will trail 0·6 second towards it. The new picture will start at this cut but the sound recording will fade up 0·6 second later. This will not, of course, work if the pace of a programme demands shorter fade-outs, or where sound bridges the link in a manner that makes the cut awkward (though sometimes if it is a sufficiently similar sound, there will be no problem from this).

459

Many simple cuts will work; but many will not. If they do not, the answer may be to dub the sound using ¼-inch tape.

Videotape cuts with sound dubs

The usual case for a dub is where the sound and picture must change at the same time. For this to be achieved the first 0·6 second of the new sound must be dubbed on to the last 0·6 second of the old picture. The cutting points are found as I have already described, and then the "new" sound is copied on to ¼-inch tape. The appropriate section of it is then recorded on to the "old" picture by running the tape from a point 10 seconds or so ahead of the video cut mark and then—as this is about to pass over the video drum—starting the sound replay. Then, just as the mark reaches the video head the videotape machine is switched to the "audio only" recording condition for about one second: it has to be switched off again so very quickly in order to stop the new recording from running over on to useful tape.

The same sounds will now be heard at two separate places on the videotape, over different pictures. The edit will be made by cutting at the same point in both of these two sound recordings: this will in fact be at the point in the sound previously decided upon, i.e. just 0·6 second in to the newly recorded sound. Note that if there is speech in vision in the first half second of the new picture, lip-sync. will automatically be restored when the cut is made.

Before this sort of operation is undertaken, a fair amount of the original sound should be copied to the ¼-inch tape as an insurance against accidents.

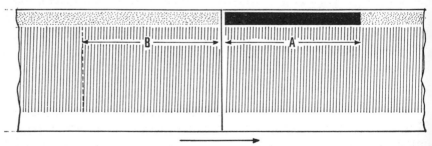

DITING VIDEOTAPE WITH SOUND DUB—so that sound and picture change togethe he sound corresponding to section B of the picture has been copied to ¼ inch tape and the e-recorded parallel to picture section A. When the tape was cut, the dubbed sound becam esynchronized with its original picture. Electronic editing (in which each required sequenc : copied from the original tape to assembly tape) is in principle simpler and uses up less tap ut more capital equipment is required, and the picture is slightly degraded.

Once the sound has been transferred in this way all of the sound editor's tricks of the trade are open to the videotape editor—provided that when he dubs the edited sound back over picture he is not doing so in a way which makes any loss of synchronization noticeable. This sort of complex editing job must be done over a cutaway shot—perhaps one specifically cut in from another part of the tape.

Often when complex editing is done on a sound tape it will be tacked on to a straight copy of the previous 20 seconds or so of unedited sound. The videotape and sound tape can then be run together, with 20 seconds to get them exactly in synchronization, after which the edited material is heard and can be timed against the following picture.

This will show how much of the picture can be eliminated; and cuts may now be made without regard for the sound currently recorded on it. The edited sound is then played again as before, at first in sync., then continuing against the edited picture; but this time, while the early parts of sound on videotape and sound on $\frac{1}{4}$-inch tape are still running together, the videotape machine is switched to its "sound only" recording condition.

A more awkward type of edit occurs when new sound must be overlaid over the start of the picture which follows an edit. The trick is to stop the recording before erasing wanted sound, and also to stop the sound-erase head from leaving a gap of an inch in the atmosphere as the machine stops. This latter is sometimes accomplished by slipping a piece of card under the tape at the erase head as the machine is switched off. An alternative is to cut the picture very carefully (it will probably have to be within a shot) at the point where the new sound must end, join on some unwanted tape, dub, and then reassemble the original picture. But as well as being time-consuming, this could easily distort the tape at the point of the cut, resulting in a twitch in the picture.

Editing videotape

Much of the above assumes that the tape will be physically cut. I will describe the technique for this briefly and then indicate some alternatives.

The tape, having been marked, is rough cut rather more than a frame to the safe side of the mark. The nearest edit pulse on the safe side of the mark is then found by one of two methods.

The simplest method is of an "iron filings" type. A special

461

"developer", a fine magnetically permeable powder suspended in a volatile liquid is spread along the control track. As the liquid evaporates a tiny dot is seen: this is the frame pulse. Also to be seen are the lines transversely across the tape that have been recorded by the video heads. (These correspond not to individual lines of the picture but to batches of them; there is no question, therefore, of developing a picture too.) Using a microscope to line up each in turn on the cutting edge of the editing block, the two rough-cut ends of videotape are re-cut, but this time at exactly the same place in the frame.

The alternative method is electronic, and requires more elaborate equipment. The control track is scanned electronically and the edit pulse centred by lining up a blip and a curved scan in the centre of a small cathode ray tube. For each section of tape in turn this gives the cutting point on the block. There is little to choose between this method and the last.

In both cases the tape is then butted carefully together, backing side up and joined with a thin, strong strip of jointing tape which is sealed transversely across the videotape.

Cutting tape is costly, as videotape is expensive and more than a few cuts makes it unsatisfactory for further high quality programme use. The alternatives conserve tape but use more high-capital machinery or facilities.

The most attractive alternative is to copy-edit. Two machines are required, the first of which is used for marking up and replay. After the first section has been copied the second is chosen, and then both machines are set back ten seconds from the cutting point, marked and run up together. It is checked that the cut will be in the right place; if it is, the machines are set back again, run up, and this time the second machine is switched to record at the editing point. In this way a second segment of programmes is cut on to the first without physically cutting tape. Sound and picture cuts are automatically coincident—but sound levels can be controlled during the dub (as they can be with the method previously described).

This whole process—except for control of sound levels—can be automated. A system has been devised whereby the programme is recorded on to special rehearsal quality recorder (having 1-inch tape and a "helical scan" video recording system). The director can find his own edit points on this tape and electronically mark the ins and outs and the order of the required material on the control track. This is then fed through a computer to control the copying of the main recording. The only problem—a small one, perhaps, for some purposes—is the lack of sound dubbing or mixing facilities: these must still be done by the skilled human hand.

Other editing and programme assembly techniques use mixers, sound dubbing studios, or television studios in combination with the videotape recorder. Mostly they are expensive in time or equipment, but may be worth it for a programme result that might otherwise be almost impossible.

When considering different systems of sound and picture editing it is worth noting that it is easier to maintain sound quality through successive copyings than it is picture quality. For this reason if two alternative systems produce in one case a second generation sound and picture and in the other case first generation picture with third generation sound, the latter will always be preferred as providing the best final overall programme quality.

Multitrack sound used with videotape

Sound tapes 1-inch wide carrying twelve tracks have been used in conjunction with videotape. Ten tracks are used for sound and one for a control track used for synchronization with the videotape. The remaining track, and the cue track on the videotape are used for a system using spoken figures and pulses of tone which will enable the same point to be identified in both tapes for editing purposes.

This system has been used by the BBC for multilanguage commentary coverage of the Olympic Games. Other possibilities for its use may be where very complex sound has to be assembled and dubbed to an existing picture.

New techniques are developed in the video field quickly, and are quickly replaced or revised as new machines are provided to do existing jobs more economically. Video recording techniques of various types are confidently seen by many as being "the future". But in the meantime we still have 2-inch videotape and 16-mm and 35-mm film as the standards.

Stereo and editing

The principal additional rule for editing stereo sound is that any cut and rejoin must not introduce a confusing change of position or one that is contrary to any convention that is being observed.

Interesting or amusing results can be obtained from editing in stereo; e.g. a tune composed from stereo recordings of ships' sirens.

463

In television, interest in stereo has not been great; colour has come first, though slowly: its promotion will continue to occupy manufacturers for many years. In any case in contrast to the effect that stereo has had on radio and records, a big sound adds little to the small picture except for specialized purposes (e.g. music) where the sound itself may be dominant. However, should it be necessary stereo could easily be recorded on videotape (using the cue track for the second channel). Editing presents no additional complications, other than that a twin-track stereo sound recorder would be required for sound dubbing.

16

FILM SOUND EDITING

THE standard professional film gauge is 35 mm. However, throughout the world there must today be much more 16 mm shot, edited, and shown to the public than there is 35 mm. The reason for this is television. In Britain, the BBC alone keeps about a hundred cutting rooms permanently in business. This is a gigantic output of film by any calculation—and by far the greater part of it is 16 mm.

Nearly all of the techniques described in this chapter apply equally to 16 mm and 35 mm, but in view of the vast increase in the use of 16 mm where slight differences do exist I have described the method used for this gauge.

I shall completely disregard the older methods of joining film, those involving the overlap of part of a frame (or on 35 mm, the frame bar) and the use of cement to join the two. This has now been completely superseded by butt joining, for which by far the most convenient method is the guillotine type of tape joiner—this requires no precise registration of pre-perforated tape. The advantages of using this type of joiner for the magnetic track will be described in detail; but equally great advantages are found with the picture. Indeed, the joiner has facilitated (in Europe) a new type of film-making based on the freedom to experiment during editing. (Cement joins are, however, still used to join cut negative or reversal camera master.)

Another sweeping decision (and one which may offend many experienced editors who still swear by them) will be to disregard almost all editing and viewing machines that are based on intermittent action, the normal film projection method which claws up each successive frame, pins it firmly in the gate for a forty-eighth or a fiftieth of a second, illuminates it, and then moves on jerkily to the next frame. In projectors this system is good enough, but in the cutting room it is arguable that such equipment is outdated.

In this book we are concerned with good sound quality. Now that equipment exists which will permit editors the better to judge such quality it should be used. The equipment I favour has systems of prisms rotating with the film, and reflecting light in such a way as to project an image which is static on the screen. These include viewing tables for the selection of shots and picture-synchronizers for its assembly. Both have facilities for running sound with picture; the synchronizer normally has provision for several rolls of sound to run together.

At this point I will go back a little in the order of events and describe how the picture and sound got to the cutting room.

Film: sound and picture as shot

It will be recalled (p. 98) that synchronous film sound can be recorded directly on the same film as the picture. This normally takes the form of a magnetic stripe running down the side of the picture, a system which has to a considerable extent taken over from optical sound tracks for projection, and completely taken over for recording on film at the time of shooting.

A displacement between sound and picture of rather less than a second for 35 mm and rather more for 16 mm is dictated by the amount of film transport mechanism required to guide the film and smooth its flow between the intermittent movement at the camera or projector gate and the flutter-free motion required at the sound head.

Since optical sound came first, this has the position closest to the gate. On the 16 mm gauge, provision for magnetic sound recording and replay was subsequently made at a different position (with the result that projectors could be modified to have the two heads

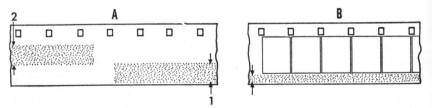

RECORDING ON 16-MM FILM. A. Separate magnetic film. 1. Edge track (200 mil) used in US and Canada. 2. Centre track (200 mil) used in most other parts of the world. The full width of the film is coated, and can therefore be used for either system. B. Combined magnetic film with 100 mil edge track recording. The oxide coating occupies the space formerly used for optical sound. Sometimes the coating is applied to the surface of the film (in which case a narrow strip will also be applied to the edge close to the sprocket holes in order to ensure even winding); sometimes it goes into a groove in the film, so that the surface of film and magnetic track is flat.

permanently in position on the same film path). For 16-mm film, optical sound is $25\frac{1}{2}$ or 26 frames ahead of the picture, and magnetic sound 28 frames ahead; for 35-mm, optical sound is recorded $19\frac{1}{2}$ or 20 frames ahead of picture.

For television news, 16-mm striped stock is often used. In principle, the film, once it has been developed, can be transmitted immediately, with its own sound and without any danger of loss of sync. in the rush. (The film negative is used: after this has been scanned electronically in telecine, the blacks and whites are switched by the simple electrical device of phase reversal to give the normal positive picture.) But difficulties begin to pile up as soon as the film has to be edited.

The sound displacement on 16-mm striped film is gross. On few occasions, and particularly on news, would a picture cut precede a sound cut by well over a second: unlike the comparable case with videotape, the pause is not a convenient and natural one. It is, however, rather less than the length of a reaction shot—so a reporter's nod may bridge the gap. Even so, the result is often still awkward and untidy. The better alternative, if time permits, is to transfer all sound to separate magnetic film stock and edit on that.

The alternative and preferred system of film sound recording employs twin-track $\frac{1}{4}$-inch tape, of which one track is used for sound and the other for a sync. pulse (pilot tone). This tape will never be edited: it is used as a master for transfer to magnetic stock (one or more copies, as required); for the transcript of unscripted dialogue (these are valuable in editing); and for finding extra wanted sound if this solves a problem at the dubbing session (at this the tape may be played in directly as an unsynchronized sound source).

Sound transfer

Film sound transfer has (apart from the normal business of maintaining sound quality from one generation of recording to the next), one major concern: to provide separate sound which is absolutely synchronous with the film when run together, sprocket hole to sprocket hole. In transferring from stripe (or in making a new copy from existing magnetic stock) the problem could in principle be solved simply by interlocking the two films mechanically. But when transferring $\frac{1}{4}$-inch tape to film this would not work unless sprocketed tape were used (this does exist but is not widely used professionally). The alternative that must be employed is an electrical interlocking system, with a recording speed control derived from the sync. pulse on the sound track of the original tape. Since this in turn was generated at camera speed, picture and separate magnetic sound are accurately synchronized.

So satisfactory is electronic synchronization that it is generally used even in cases where mechanical systems would be feasible, e.g. in multichannel dubbing suites, and in film projectors used in television.

Film and equipment in the cutting room

The film editor has delivered to him:

   (i) Film negative.
  (ii) Film positive ("rush prints") of the good takes.
 (iii) The original sound tapes.
 (iv) Sound transfers of the good takes (on the same gauge as the original film).
  (v) Documentation on film and sound, provided by cameraman and sound recordist; and perhaps also laboratory and viewing reports on the rushes.
 (vi) A shot list.
(vii) A script, or (sometimes) a transcript of the sound.
(viii) (Alternatively or additionally) a cutting order: this may have shot descriptions taken from the shot list and dialogue copied from the transcript.

To this list may be added: whenever possible, the presence of the director.

Film editors may have a creative talent but this should be subordinate to that of the director. It follows that creative editing devised in the cutting room takes the form of suggestions to the director (perhaps in the form of a trial cut), and whether the director accepts these depends on how well they follow or fit in with his overall artistic intention. Apart from such experimental work, editing in the absence of the director must be according to established techniques for cutting pictures (or pictures and sound) together, of which the editor must be the master: these will follow either the generally accepted conventions of film editing, or some style agreed with or expected by the director. But as a general rule, progress towards a final result will be faster if a director is present for some part of the editing.

468

The cutting room will have the following equipment:

A viewing machine. On this picture and sound can be run together or separately. It should provide a projected picture and sound reproduction of moderately good quality.

FILM VIEWING BENCH. The simplest and most convenient form of bench for viewing 16-mm film to give normal playing speeds and picture of sound or medium quality (i.e. the best, short of projection in a theatre). 1 and 2. Picture feed and take-up plates. 3 and 4. Sound feed and take-up plates. Lacing is simple, with drive spindles on either side of the sound and picture heads (which are in the centre). The sound path has additional, tensioning rollers. It is not necessary to have rolls of film as shown here; the machine requires only enough head or tail of film to be held by the drive rollers. Typically the film can be run at normal and "fast" speeds, and either forwards or backwards. In addition to the heads shown there will normally be a further group to the right of the picture column, to replay combined magnetic or optical sound.

An assembly bench. This has two canvas-lined bins into which film (and more important, the film sound) can fall without coming to harm, and between them a flat platform wide enough to hold the synchronizer. This platform has a frosted glass illuminated plate, against which film may be seen and identified (this is more useful for 35 mm than for 16 mm, for which, as will be seen, alternative provision must be made). On either side of the bench and outside the bins are supports for the rolls of film which will allow it to pass across the bench from left to right. On the left-hand side is a "horse", several uprights with holes, so that rolls of film can be supported freely on spindles which are passed through the centre of the plastic cores on which film is generally wound. On the right is a take-up spindle on to which a number of split spools can be fitted, and which

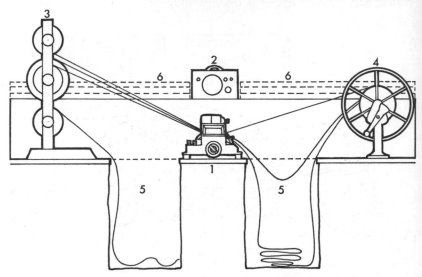

EDITING BENCH. 1. Picture synchronizer. 2. "Squawk box". 3. Horse, supporting rolls of film and spacer. 4. Winding spindle with "split" reels fitted. Bins, lined with canvas, to hold excess film that has not been wound up. 6. Racks for small rolls of film awaiting insertion in to the film. A tape joiner will be on the bench, but will not be fixed; and also a supply of wax pencils and felt marker pens. This editing bench does *not* give (*a*) full picture detail, (*b*) high quality sound, (*c*) normal or constant running speeds for picture or sound. Where these are important they must be checked on other equipment.

has a handle which may be wound to take up film. (There is a similar spindle on the left, which may be used in place of the horse for large or unevenly wound spools.)

The synchronizer. This has, perhaps, four sprocketed wheels all rigidly mounted on the same axle so that they are always mechanically synchronized. Each wheel is one foot in circumference, so that for each revolution 1 foot (16 frames of 35 mm or 40 frames of 16 mm) of film passes through the synchronizer. There is a rev-counter showing feet of film. (Sometimes, in BBC practice, this uses the 35-mm measure for 16-mm film: i.e. the counter is calibrated in "35-mm feet", which means that 16 frames equals one digit on the counter. "35-mm feet" are a finer measure in dubbing than 16-mm feet.) There is also a disc which gives a number to the separate frame positions on the circumference of the wheels (on 16-mm equipment

470

these run 1–40). For 16 mm there should be internal provision for the projection of a small (nearly 3-inch) image of the picture: this is provided on the front film path and sometimes on the second one as well. On all but the picture tracks there are sound replay heads which may be lowered or turned so that they do not press against

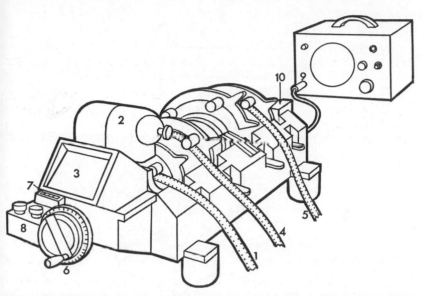

SYNCHRONIZER. Picture synchronizer with "squawk box". 1. Track one (picture) passes below lamp (2) which projects a picture via a system of rotating mirrors on to the screen (3). 4 and 5. Two of the three sound paths. These pass over the sound heads, which are on the centre line behind the frame through which the lamp is projected. Each path passes over a wheel with 40 sprockets and which has a diameter of one foot. The wheels are fixed to a common axle which is turned by hand at the front (6). A disc attached to this indicates the frame within each foot, and a nearby digital counter (7) shows the number of feet from the point at which the counter was set at zero. The reproduced sound signal is fed through a simple low-level mixer (8) to the loudspeaker input (9). Power is fed to the projector lamp through a transformer (10) which also has a switch on the far side. Other picture synchronizers have different numbers of sound paths; or may have two picture heads.

the film if the path is being used to measure a length of picture (the head would scratch the film). The sound signals from the replay heads are fed through a small, simple low level mixer which is built into the equipment.

A small amplifier and loudspeaker. This is the "squawk box", to which the output of the synchronizer is fed. A small battery powered transistorized unit is often used for this but any amplifier and loudspeaker system will do.

471

A tape joiner (guillotine splicer). This is used to cut film (with a stainless steel blade) and then hold the two ends in position while tape is stuck across the join. The tape recommended for joining the film is similar in appearance to transparent plastic domestic tape but is of polyester; it is very thin, very strong, and has a non-oozing

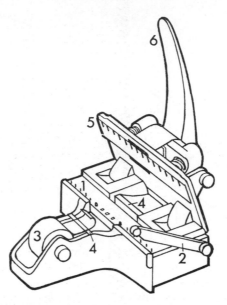

TAPE JOINER. The film (picture or magnetic track) to be cut is placed on the lower plate (1) and located precisely over the sprockets which stand along one edge. The knife is brought down on the film. The cut end is then moved to the centre of the plate and the film that is to be joined with it butted to it. Again, the sprockets hold the two ends precisely in position. A strip of adhesive tape is drawn from the roll (3) and placed across the butt and stuck also to the bars (4) on either side of the base plate. The upper head (5) is then brought down on to the film and the arm (6) pressed down. This causes two guillotines to cut the tape on either side of the base plate, and a punch to perforate the adhesive tape at the three sprocket holes nearest the centre of the plate. (For clarity, the second, angled knife which is sometimes used for sound cuts has been omitted from this diagram. Where it is supplied, it is fitted to the right-hand side of the main knife.)

adhesive. It is also comparatively expensive. The tape and joiner is used for picture as well as sound: the clear base permits normal projection. As there is no overlapping of the film, and the tape is much more flexible than the film itself, joins held slackly are liable to appear to "break" to an angle at the line of the join. The join will, however, hold in normal use with greater reliability than a cement join unless there is any way in which butted film can catch on a projection in defective equipment, or if it is replayed on certain old

472

types of machinery for which it is unsuitable. In the latter case matters may be improved by taping the film on both surfaces and (this being impracticable with the magnetic track) double backing the sound join, to stop it bending so easily. Tape joins can, of course, be undone easily for remaking edits, and for many other purposes, without the loss of frames. The only regular maintenance required for the joiner is a change of blade after a very long period of use.

Wax pencils. White or yellow, and also red and black are useful colours for writing on film "cel".

A trim bin. This is for hanging up sections of picture and sound that have been cut. Sound trims, in particular, are valuable and may be needed later for overlapping sound in order to crossfade between scenes.

Blank spacer film. This is for inserting in the sound assembly where no sound is available (or in the picture assembly where a shot is missing; or where "opticals"—visual mixes, freeze frames, etc., which require film laboratory work—are to go in later). Spacer is also used to protect the ends of rolls of assembled film. Note that spacer is made opaque by coating one side of the film support by a suitable material. Allowing this to run on the sound head will cause unnecessary wear, so it is usual to cut spacer in to sound with the coated side away from the head. Rough and smooth sides can most easily be distinguished by touching them with the tip of the tongue.

Leader film for picture and sound. This is printed with start marks and 35-mm footages counting down from twelve to three, after which the print is black to the point at which the film starts (which is where zero would be on this count). Sometimes a frame of tone at 1000 Hz (for 16 mm) or 2000 Hz (35 mm) is cut in on the sound leader at "3" (or at "4" in BBC practice, to allow greater latitude in fading up sound at the start of a programme). As it passes through the projector or telecine prior to this being switched, the presence of the tone confirms that sound is live on the replay itself. Some leaders have pulses printed on the optical track, but this is little use in television, where magnetic sound is used on almost everything except old films and commercials.

A waste bin—specifically for inflammable film waste. It should be made of metal and have a lid which will exclude the air in case of a fire in the bin. (As a further safety measure all technical equipment should be on a single circuit with a readily accessible isolator switch.)

In addition to all of these other items of equipment, there will be an adequate supply of plastic cores and split spools; perhaps a fast re-wind bench; and spare lamps, and so on.

The mechanical operation of most of this equipment is fairly obvious or self explanatory; and its use closely follows the routine described for other editing jobs. These are rough assembly (p. 446) and fine editing (p. 448). It is not the purpose of this book to describe the cutting of picture: the literature on this is vast and exhaustive.

The cutting of sound is, however, very much our business. And here, many of the principles of cutting ¼-inch tape carry over virtually without modification; but extra problems (and possibilities) arise from the combination of sound with picture.

Cement joiners are obsolete and should no longer be used in editing. The lapped join necessitates the loss of a frame on each piece of film joined—and this was permissible only when it was essential. The value of trims is shown below: for many purposes they should be complete, without loss of frames for out-of-date technical reasons.

Picture and sound in the cutting room

Film picture available to the editor includes:

  (i) Film shot with synchronized sound:

   (*a*) lip-sync. sound,
   (*b*) synchronized effects or music,
   (*c*) material where picture and sound are related, having been shot at the same time; but for which there is no need to maintain perfect sync.

  (ii) Mute or silent film, for which no directly useful sound could be recorded in sync., or for which a blimped camera could not conveniently be used. Sometimes this may have been shot to playback or wildtrack commentary or other sound (see below).

  (iii) Library film for which suitable sound may or may not exist, or only in a technically imperfect form (e.g. optical track).

Film sound available to the editor includes:

  (iv) Sync. material as in (i) above.
  (v) Wildtrack commentary or dialogue which will be played over pictures which do not show the speaker's mouth.

(vi) Wildtrack effects which will be synchronized to action in mute film (e.g. a gunshot) or sync. film for which the effects recorded at the time were inadequate (e.g. too distant). This includes wildtrack speech which it is hoped can be fitted to lip movements of speakers shot on a silent camera (this is not advisable, but sometimes inevitable).

(vii) Location atmosphere tracks.

(viii) Library sound effects: atmosphere or music recorded originally on disc or tape but selected and transferred to magnetic film stock.

The editor will later have the advantage of all the extra sound that can be provided in a dubbing theatre: out-of-vision commentary, post-synchronized dialogue, spot effects, recorded effects, specially composed music and recorded music. Some of these, particularly post-synchronized dialogue, must be recorded separately and early; much of this may be left to the day of the final mix.

To the dubbing theatre the editor will take a cutting copy of the film and as many rolls of sound as the dubbing mixer needs for separate control of the levels and quality of the various constituent parts of the final sound. But in the first instance the editor will work with one picture and one sound track.

If at this or any other stage a magnetic sound track is broken, it can often be repaired quite easily by using the tape joiner. Broken or torn sprocket holes may also be repaired by similar means: in this case the tape is not guillotined after being put on the back of the

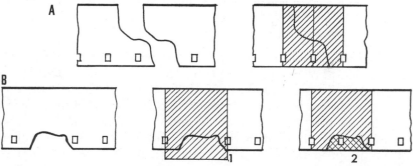

REPAIRING BROKEN FILM WITH A TAPE JOINER. A. A simple butt and rejoin. B. Torn sprocket holes with film missing: for picture the damaged section is simply taped on both sides, turned over again and the sprocket holes punched through. For sound film the tape is stuck to the upper (uncoated) surface only but is cut with a razor blade or scissors a little way from the edge of the film (1) before the guillotine is brought down. The loose edge is then doubled under, on to coated side of the film (2), but will not reach as far as the recorded track.

475

film, but is cut by hand, broad enough to be folded over on to the other side, just far enough to cover the damaged holes, which are then repunched using the guillotine. It is essential that the editing tape does not extend far enough across the coated side to cover any of the track or catch on the replay head.

Cutting picture and sound together

The editor's first responsibility (in practice usually undertaken by his assistant) is to synchronize the rushes. This means running film and sound, finding the frame where the clapperboard closed and

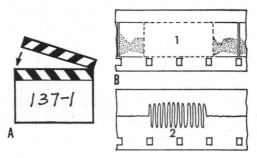

SYNCHRONIZATION OF SEPARATELY RECORDED SOUND. A. Clapperboard. In addition to the scene and take number there will be other information on the board. B. Simple "blip-sync.". In this case after the camera and sound have both started to run (so that the camera has a picture) a light is flashed to blank out the picture (1) for the same duration as a buzz (2) is recorded on sound. More complex systems have provision for varying the marking, so that scene numbers from one to ten (but not take numbers) are allocated in rotation. This still lacks the precision of identification given by the clapperboard, but is more than compensated for by the increased operational flexibility, and reduction in film stock used.

using a wax pencil to mark it with a boxed X and the corresponding frame of sound with three bars, III; then writing the shot and take number ahead of this in both picture and sound. For convenience of continuous replay the spacing is then adjusted so that this picture and sound follow in the same synchronization as that of the preceding shot. If preferred, intervening mute film shots and wildtrack sound may be cut out at this stage and wound on to separate rolls: all of the good takes of sync. material can then be seen in the sequence in which they were shot.

Alternatively, after marking sync., the film takes may be broken down immediately into single slates of picture and sound together. Or—yet again—the assistant, using the cutting order, may reassemble the shots in the intended order of the film.

The editor will then make a rough cut—almost invariably at this stage cutting sound and picture parallel (making a "straight" or "editorial" cut). A methodical editor (or his assistant) will mark the sound trims with wax pencil so that they can easily be identified later.

At the fine cut, as further sound and picture is trimmed away, sound overlays (where the sound from one shot runs over the next) may now be allowed, but the cut in picture will be marked on the

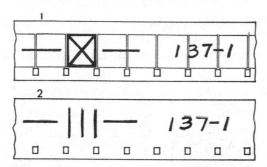

SYNCHRONIZATION MARKS on picture (1) and separate magnetic sound (2). In the conventional clapperboard system these will be marked at the picture and sound of the board closing, and in the case of electronic synchronization, with the flash on the picture and the corresponding buzz on sound.

sound track. Before any complex non-parallel cut is made, the editor will satisfy himself that he can easily find sync. again both before and after the region of the cut: he will then be able to satisfy himself that the same number of frames have been cut from both picture and sound. Most of this work will be done in the synchronizer, with only occasional excursions to the viewing machine to check points where better quality of picture or sound is required, or where the editor wishes to view or hear at normal speed.

Sync. marks will follow the editor's private code of letters or symbols, the same one being marked on corresponding frames of sound and picture. It is essential for an editor to be able to hold synchronization with both accuracy and the sort of confidence that does not waste time unduly: an automatic part of this will be a quick check on sync. after every cut is made.

Fine-cut trims often require to be carefully marked and kept—and although there is a limit to the time that can be spent on this sort of detail, they should certainly be kept with or close to the rest of the trims of the associated shot. Note also that some very methodical editors like to number every cut separately (in addition to putting the shot numbers on the trims). This is because there may be

477

many more cuts than shots: each shot that is used may be cut two, four, six, or even more times.

At this point it is worth taking a look at two different types of edge numbers.

When handling picture, the editor is helped by the fact that professional film stock is edge-numbered: to do this, the manufacturer

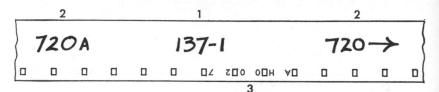

IDENTIFICATION MARKS ON A MAGNETIC SOUND TRIM. 1. The number on the clapperboard: scene 137, take one. 2. Numbers identifying position in the cut film: here the numbering system will depend on the editor. And in this case the figures and letters refer to the points at which the film is cut. Note that the scene (137–1) may appear in the film in several different places or not at all. 3. "Rubber numbers" which can be printed on both picture and sound after the rolls have been fully synchronized; using these, sound and picture trims can always be matched (however, the numbers are repeated at intervals of 40 frames on 16 mm, so that on very short trims they may not be present). The letters identify the roll; the numbers, 16 mm feet within the roll. All of these systems are optional; editors often use none of them. But for films of more than a few minutes duration they are very useful both in any subsequent recut and in tracklaying prior to the dub.

optically exposes the edge of the film to serial numbers at intervals of one foot. These numbers are later used by negative cutters when the edited film is ready to be printed, as those on negative will necessarily correspond to those which are printed from them on the rushes. Only in exceptional circumstances do the neg-cutters ever have to look at the picture to "eye-match" negative and print.

As the negative arrives in the cutting room, the editor's assistant logs the edge numbers of each roll. As a result, any length of film which is not too short to have a single complete edge number on it can later be identified without too much difficulty, even if the editor has omitted to mark on it what part of what shot it is.

This idea can be extended to sound by using an inexpensive service called "rubber numbering".

Rolls of picture and sound are synchronized in the normal way, and the synchronization is checked by the editor, possibly when he and the director view the rushes with sound in the theatre. After this the film is run, again with the sound and picture rolls in synchronization, through a machine which stamps a new set of corresponding numbers on the two. The rolls themselves are numbered AA, AB, AC, and so on, and then each foot is given a serial number

AAOOO1 and so on. Each group of letters and numbers is split in to three pairs which appear between successive sprocket holes: this is a position which is used for nothing else, not even the picture edge numbers (which are still needed for their original purpose of correlating the cutting copy picture and the original negative).

It is clear that the rubber numbers will serve two purposes:

(i) They will provide a rapid means of finding the original synchronization between sound and picture. But where during the editing the cutting copy sound is deliberately displaced relative to the picture this will have to be marked clearly on both tracks, so that the rubber numbers do not cause any confusion later.

(ii) They provide an easy check on the identity of trims—including this time, the sound trims. But this should be in addition to the normal marks giving such things as the shot and cut numbers.

Over a long period of editing it is possible to wear magnetic track enough to lose sound quality noticeably—and particularly on musical items. To avoid this, two transfers from the original tapes can be made at the same time and given identical rubber numbers. One of these can then be held in reserve until the editor lays tracks prior to the dub.

Since rubber numbers are printed on to cutting copy, the show copy (which is printed from the original negative) will not have these numbers; nor will the final mix of the sound which is made at the dubbing session. The transmission film can therefore be numbered as a new roll or rolls without risk of any confusion by double numbering.

Cutting unsynchronized elements together

At the rough assembly, spacers will have been cut into both tracks of the film, so that at some places where there was picture the sound had a spacer inserted in to it, and at some places where sound ran on, there was no picture. Indeed, even after the first rough cut, some of these spacers may still have been left in. Also, at some points where sound and picture were running side by side, one or the other will have been marked for later deletion or perhaps even replaced by spacer. There could be several reasons for this.

Firstly, the usable (or wanted) lengths of sound and picture may be different from each other even within the same sync. take. The film may have been shot with this intention, or there may be some imperfection in sound or picture only, or it may be that continuity of action does not coincide with continuity of sound.

Secondly, where mute film and wild track sound have been shot for a particular sequence they are unlikely to be exactly the same length. The good director will often have been able to plan picture and sound to be the same length as it is finally to be cut together; but the pictures may turn out to be very good or very bad, so demanding a longer or shorter use of the visual element. (The experienced documentary director normally has an excess of mute film to choose from; and perhaps an excess of good sound to cover.)

Where unsynchronized picture and sound differ in length, matching will sometimes just be a matter of making the longer one equal to the shorter with a parallel cut. Sometimes picture will be longer than the sound intended to cover it: in this case the picture will usually be allowed to run its proper length, and the sound filled out with matching atmosphere or effects (this will be done when the tracks are laid, i.e. when the sound is prepared for the dubbing; for the present spacer will probably be left in). But if sound (e.g., commentary) is longer than the picture it is intended to cover, things are a little more complicated. If the difference is small, the number of frames of overrun can be counted and the same number removed at some point in the commentary track: there must, of course, be no important lip-sync. or synchronized effects between the two points where the cuts are made and it must be checked that looser points of synchronization (e.g. in commentary or out-of-vision dialogue referring to the picture) are not seriously affected.

Cuts may also be made by removing lengths of sound or picture (including spacing that has been inserted to hold sync.) and having found another suitable length from the other track simply measuring one against the other by hand, marking, and cutting. The film base is virtually unstretchable and it is easy to check that the lengths are the same, frame for frame, by matching the sprocket holes by eye.

A useful method for cutting sound to match a shorter picture involves looping the sound back on to another path through the synchronizer. The first thing to do is to mark sync. before and after the sequence affected, noting the last frame at which synchronization is essential at the front and the first which follows. The unwanted length of picture (or spacer) is then removed and the film rejoined. Picture and sound are now in sync. at one end only. The excess sound on the unsynchronized side is now looped back on to the next sound path through the synchronizer and the second sync. mark is located to coincide with the corresponding mark on the film. The length of sound in the loop is that which has to be cut, and by running the film and sound backward and forward between the two sync. marks and using both sound heads in turn a suitable sound cut can often be found. Before the cut is actually made the remaining sound can be heard against the picture it will accompany and the words before and after the cut can be heard in sequence.

This is only a particular case of a more general idea: obviously (given two picture heads in the case of 16 mm) it can be done the

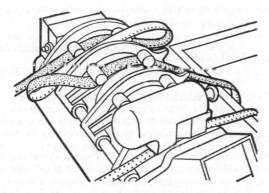

LOOPING BACK. Here sound and picture are synchronized on both sides of the picture synchronizer; but at the join there is an excess of sound, and this has been taken up in a loop between two of the sound paths. Picture and sound can now be rolled backwards or forwards together until suitable points for cutting the sound are found. If some of the sound in the loop is still required to be overlaid at the picture join, it will be marked and retained for reinstatement on another track when additional tracks are laid prior to the dub.

other way about, looping picture back instead to match a sound track that is shorter.

In another example, it may be desired to cut both sound and picture by the same amounts, but not at the same point. In this case neither is cut; but both are looped back the same amounts so that two picture paths and two sound paths are used as the film is run backward and forward to find matching lengths to cut. If required, the effect of using shorter or longer (but still equal) loops can also be investigated before making the cut.

These looping techniques are still very useful, although they are now used rather less than they were before the advent of the tape joiner (which permits experimental cuts to be remade without harm).

481

Note that a short cut in picture can often be accommodated by making *several* shorter cuts in sound (perhaps hesitations or inessential words) which add up to the same length.

Remember, too, that picture can be opened out for sound by the use of freeze frame or slow motion—both of which can be processed from existing film by film laboratories, and that sound can be opened out for picture by the insertion of effects or atmosphere either on the track or later on at the dub.

Opening out sound (in particular, wildtrack commentary) to match picture is a common and often desirable device, as it is better to have more picture than words; but lengthening picture to match sound is an exceptional measure—and one which should have a better reason than solving an editing problem.

In all cases, the timing of speech—both in its spoken rhythm and in its cueing—must remain comfortable and natural.

Film sound cutting in detail

Here, much of the technique is identical to that used for ¼-inch tape (see p. 449). The mechanics of choosing the place are just the same; joining the magnetic film is governed largely by the same principles (with one exception that will be noted below); and the things to listen for in checking a join are precisely the same (see p. 445).

Here are a few additional points to note:

Words, syllables, or pauses can often be transferred from rejected takes, replacing the same number of frames as are inserted. If this results momentarily in an apparently inappropriate mouth movement it is still worth considering whether this may be preferable to inappropriate words. (This is a real question: sometimes it is, but very often it is not—it depends on the individual circumstances.)

A change of sound that happens with a cut is much more natural and acceptable than an unexplained change at another point.

Short gaps in background atmosphere that are created by lengthening the picture (e.g. with a cutaway that needs to be seen for longer than the master action it replaces) should be filled in with sound as closely matching it as possible. This is preferable to leaving it to the dub and hoping; it takes a lot to obliterate a dropout of atmosphere, particularly where there is a continuous steady noise such as machinery hum or the whine of distant jet aircraft.

This will be made worse by the fact that, unlike ¼-inch tapes, film sound is now only rarely cut at an angle, so that the beginning and ending of a high-level continuous sound are emphasized by the plop that abrupt starts and stops in such a sound must always make. These plops, remember, are not due to a physical cause such as the dropout associated with a lapped join; nor are they to be confused with recorded noise such as may be made with a magnetized blade; they are due to the sharp change in waveform the edge of which, analyzed, contains noise at all frequencies (see p. 453).

Tape joiners are available with angled blades in addition to the straight ones, but as many editors prefer to work with exactly parallel cuts in sound and picture they get little use. As they also add to the cost and do (very slightly) get in the way of cutting with the other blade they are not much in demand. Most editors seem to think that it is not worth bothering to use one blade for picture and the other for sound, unless there is a possibility that mechanical stress during projection will cause the joins to be noisy (this may be discovered by experiment or experience). However, I would strongly recommend that the angled blade should be used for cases where cuts are made in the middle of a word or any other loud sound where two points which do not match are to be joined together. Better still is to use an angled cut always.

Track laying

When the fine cut is complete, the constituent parts of the cut sound are separated on to several tracks. For so long as the sound continues at the same level and quality (whether of the main or background sound) it is retained on the same roll; but at points where these change, the sound is switched to another roll. If by simple adjustments of level and tone quality settings the sounds can then be matched, a parallel shift from one roll to the next is all that is necessary. But if there is a more drastic change that is not immediately explained by an equally strong change of picture, then extra sound must be found for the dubbing mixer to fade in on or out of, or both. These fades will generally be made quickly, but it is better to have too much than too little to fade on, or the sound may be heard starting or finishing at low level. Such chopped off sounds will appear unnatural as they do not occur at a cut.

During the editing, extra tracks which had to be synchronized with action could not be cut in because of other synchronous material already present; these were marked and put to one side. At the track laying they can now go in on their appropriate rolls.

Music may also be laid: where this is dominant it will already have been arranged for the picture cuts to be related to it. The precise manner in which picture and music should be co-ordinated is a complex study; but note particularly that a strong rhythm demands that some (but not too many) of the cuts will be made on the beat; similarly, individual strong notes may cue a cut. The recording of special music is described in Chapter 7 (see also p. 74).

As many of the sound effects as possible will be accurately laid by the editor; this includes both library effects which should be selected and transferred for this purpose, and wildtracks which were shot for the purpose during filming.

Some continuing sounds may be formed as loops: lengths of recorded track which are made up with the end joined back on to the beginning. Loops which have strong distinguishing features must be long, so that the regular reappearance of such a feature does not become apparent. (If it is likely to, it could perhaps be trimmed out, though this would shorten the loop still further.) Also, in joining the ends of loops together care must be taken to find points where volume and quality are matched.

The editor prepares a chart with a column showing the main points of the action, and opposite this the sound on each roll, showing the cuts in and out of sound with symbolic indications of fades and mixes and clearly marked footages, together with notes on loops and tape and disc effects that may also be used at particular points.

Commentary that has been prerecorded will also be laid; but many directors prefer to cut the film completely before the final version of the commentary is settled. The exact length and value of each picture will then be known.

Shot listing and commentary writing

A shot list giving footages is usually made for other reasons besides commentary writing. It can conveniently be combined with a script of the dialogue as finally cut and notes of other important sound: in this case it will be laid out to look like the standard film or television script with picture on the left of the page and the corresponding sound on the right. A draft of this may be derived from the cutting order (or shooting script) by rewriting it to include the changes introduced in the editing; this can then be checked in detail by running the film (the completed cutting copy) on the synchronizer before the tracks are laid.

PRODUCTION SCIENCE FAIR - FINAL CONTEST   REEL Nº 3

PRODUCER/DIRECTOR ALEC NISBETT   EDITOR   PAGE (1)
PLOP ON 4   PLOP ON 4

ACTION	1 PLOP ON 4	998 2	3	4 COMM	LOOPS, ¼" TAPE, DISC, ETC.
SCHOOL EXT. BOYS THRU 17	17 16	CHOIR 17	BOYS CHAT 17	2	LOOP OF LAB BUZZ AVAILABLE AS REQ'D
RUGBY FOOTBALL 28	RUGBY FX 28		----(21) 28		
LAB	(32)------		LAB SYNC (CUT AT 40) 42	28½ 41 42½	
79 SCI. MEETING	80 TEACHER V/O 84	(77) ----- -19 CHAT FX	79 84 RICHARD V/O (104 GAP)		
THERMISTOR INTRODUCED 105	105	105	105		
R EXPLAINS	(109)-------------		R. SYNC		
235½ UP TO LOFT	BOYS FX		235½	236	
246 UP LADDER	246 255	246 SYNC FX		246 252	
279 VARIOUS JOBS (IN WORKSHOP) COVER WITH LOW CHAT+HUM		279		289 294 312	279 LOW CHAT + LAB HUM 312

DUBBING CUE SHEET (N.B. the original on which this was based has provision for six sound rolls). The action column does not list every picture cut, but only sequences within which sound should remain roughly the same. In some cases sound has been laid to several feet beyond a picture change but will be faded out quickly on the cut (this is represented by the shallow V). Fine points are discussed or decided by consultation on the spot. For example in this case it was not made clear on the chart, but the choir was taken behind the boys' chatter between 3 and 17 and was faded quickly after 17 although it was originally laid as far as 32. The Rugby football sound (at 16) preceded the cut at 17 and, in effect, killed the sound on tracks 2 and 3. "V/O" means "voice over". At 80–84 the teacher's voice was to be heard over background chatter and effects and from 84–105 this in turn was taken to low level while Richard's voice was heard (out of vision) talking about what is happening at this point in the story. "Hum" and "buzz" are terms used here to indicate "low-level background sound". The commentator's voice has been recorded in advance and has also been laid (on track 4).

Footages should be noted not only at cuts in the picture but also at important points within the action of a shot (e.g. when a detail of importance first appears in vision). Footages at the start and finish of dialogue should also be noted; and also those of important effects or dominant music.

Commentary can then be accurately written to picture: for a fast-speaking commentator allow about three words per second (or, measuring by footages, two per 35-mm foot or 5 per 16-mm foot). Where a speaker is slower or more expression is wanted these figures must be reduced. It is better to write too little than too much and have to rush the words; and in any case strong or exciting pictures will often be better without any words at all.

The audience's primary need from a commentary is that it should interpret the picture: in the short term this is a more effective use of the medium than when the reverse is attempted. The worst possible case is when pictures and words do not agree, either because the commentator wants to talk about something else or because he wants to continue about something which is no longer in the picture. In these cases an even averagely interesting picture will demolish the commentary entirely: the words will simply not be heard.

It is the same as with the words and figures on a cheque: commentary and pictures must agree, or the value will be lost. Only if the commentary satisfies this primary rule may it go on to give additional information.

There is one particular danger that is encountered when part of a commentary is recorded in vision, either in the studio or on location, and another part (using the same voice) is dubbed on later in the confined acoustic of a commentary box: there may be a series of abrupt changes of acoustic. Short links should if possible be planned in advance, and recorded at the location; if at this stage doubt still exists as to the best form of words, a variety of versions should be recorded. If the same voice must appear successively in location sound and as dubbed sound, one possibility is to allow a period of time, a music link or a burst of some sound effect to intervene; the change may then be less noticeable.

If it is obvious from the picture that the dubbed voice is not that filmed on location the change in quality may be an advantage: the commentator finishes speaking in vision, turns, and walks in to the action; and his dubbed voice takes over: here, at least, a clear convention has been adopted, and the change of acoustic actually helps.

But nothing is more clumsy than a rapid succession of different acoustics on the same voice when this has no apparent reason. At best it is mildly distracting (and certainly destructive of artistic unity); at worst it is actively confusing, with the viewer having moments when he is not sure whether the new sound is the same voice or a completely new and unexplained character.

This is a trap for the documentary director that is often met, and all too easy to fall in to.

Post-synchronization

Post-synchronization is a specialized job which must be done well to be really effective. It is often done very badly even by professional actors.

In particular, many continental films have been shot on location and the dialogue then badly rerecorded later. English audiences (which are very sensitive to accents) often prefer to have foreign films in the original, as a result, getting the worst of all worlds: a picture which can claim only part of the visual attention because of the sub-titles, and "original" dialogue which flaps slackly towards and away from lip-sync. It is perhaps fortunate that the former deficiency must to some extent distract attention from the latter.

Good post-synchronization has to be done phrase by phrase using (for foreign language originals) words that give reasonable approximations to the original mouth movements (thereby making films much more difficult and unrewarding to translate than operas). A loop of film should be played round and round again until the best match is obtained; then the next phrase is taken with the next loop.

Any final trimming that is necessary to match lip movements perfectly must be done as the whole is finally cut together. Obviously, this means a lot of hard work for the editing team, but now that tape joins can be used it is possible to use the same cutting copy for both purposes rather than having to resort to "duping".

Post-synchronization of spot effects is—for a few talented individuals—a well paid job in the film industry. These experts are capable of seeing through a reel of film a couple of times, then collecting together a pile of odds and ends which they manipulate in perfect timing to movements both in and out of picture, giving it a convincing simulation of the casual sounds of live action. The best spot operators are well worth their apparently high rate of pay:

they save days of special recording and editing. The techniques of producing the sounds themselves were described on pp. 261 to 270, but the greater skill lies in the timing of effects to picture.

A complementary technique is shooting picture to playback of prerecorded sound. This is regularly done for musical production numbers (miming), where the quality and the integrity of the sound is of primary importance. It also permits action (such as dancing) to be combined with song in a way which would be difficult if not impossible in real life. In miming, the illusion is, however, easily shattered by the sudden change of acoustic between dialogue and song, emphasizing and making awkward a transition that should be smooth.

In documentary work, close shots such as hands indicating detail are often shot to playback of the master sound take. In this case exact synchronization is unlikely, but a good match between sound and picture is fairly easily found by the editor.

The dub

For a documentary the first part of the dubbing session may be spent in commentary recording (though if time permits it is usually better that it should be pre-recorded at a separate session and laid accurately to picture by the editor).

Although the commentator has the picture and footage counter in front of him (sometimes relayed by closed-circuit television from the screen in the main theatre), he will not often be able to look up from his script when he is actually speaking or about to speak. Except for rare specialists, commentators will have to rely on signals (by hand cues or by using a cuelight: see p. 92).

The mix itself may have to be undertaken in several successive stages, first combining music and effects, then adding dialogue, and then commentary. Or in simple cases the whole dub can be completed in one go. Sometimes a separate music and effects track ("M and E" track) must be recorded so that commentary or dialogue can be recorded in foreign languages. If this is done at an intermediate stage of the original dub, time (and expense) will be saved later.

A useful device for dubbing is a spot tape-replay device using $\frac{1}{4}$-inch tape which may be started accurately on cue, will replay to the end of a loop and then automatically set itself up for the next cue. A still more complex device—possibly too complex—has piano-style keys which cue different sounds (see p. 279). For playing in

488

effects and atmosphere the BBC is fortunate in having a first class library of recorded sound on tape and disc, together with a skilled band of operators; this can make editing for and dubbing in a BBC theatre easier and quicker than in some commercial studios.

But the greatest aid to fast dubbing is the facility to stop when a fault has been made, run back and rerecord from any point. The dubbing mixer goes back to ten or fifteen feet before the error, runs up, switches to record at a suitable point and carries on, incorporating the revised sound level or change of quality, fade or mix. This facility is called reverse interlock, or more colloquially, rock'n'roll.

If dubbing seems time consuming and fraught today, it should be compared with the days when only optical tracks were available, and every take was fed into a sound camera until finally a satisfactory result would be greeted with a happy cry of "print that one". The term "print" is still often used for sound, meaning a recording which may be used.

The editor is normally present throughout the dub, in order to deal with any problems that may arise, and to interpret his dubbing chart which, accurate as it may be, remains only a guide. The director, too, should be present.

For the big-screen film, stereo—potentially—can add much to the finished product; in practice, however, the results are spectacular but gimmick ridden. Indeed, apart from film music there is little approaching true stereo to be heard on film.

The sound for stereophonic films is still largely recorded and edited monophonically; then at the dub the various sounds are apportioned between the final film tracks by the judgment of the dubbing mixer. The process is extremely laborious and is far from being as convincing as true stereo.

After the dub

The film editor's responsibilities continue after the dub. If the film is to be a television programme it will normally be transmitted with the film and sound on separate tracks. The editor will cut a leader on to the start of the final mix. With the show print of picture (prepared by cutting and assembling the negative to match the finished cutting copy—sometimes on two rolls—and then printing) the sound is despatched for transmission.

Synchronization of picture and separate magnetic sound may be

489

lost temporarily or permanently during transmission, due to any of the following:

(i) Runaways. Picture and sound are linked electrically and not mechanically: it can happen on some systems that the sound becomes synchronized at double the speed.

(ii) Wrong start marks. If the editor has put proper leaders on this is not likely. But sometimes wax or other marks are used and there may be confusion if there are several marks (or if a wax mark has transferred itself to the inside of the next wind).

(iii) Unauthorized removal of picture. While a film is laying in a library or film vault it may by error or stupidity get into the hands of unauthorized people who remove sections of film or break the film and repair it, losing some frames (in neither case correcting the sound to match).

(iv) Faulty editing: a shot or sequence has got out of sync. and this has never been put right; or the new faults have been introduced when opticals have been put in after the dub, or when other changes or corrections are made at a late stage, and when there is no time for a further technical review of the finished product.

(v) Faulty negative cutting: frames may have been omitted or inserted in error, or the wrong section of film used. (This, too, would normally be noticed at the review of the show print.)

(vi) Lost loop of the picture (when played on intermittent projector), or slippage of film or track due to damaged sprocket holes.

(vii) Wrong sound track played.

Some problems of loss of synchronization can only be cured by stopping the film, adjusting the picture or track by what appears to be the right amount, checking it, correcting again if necessary, rechecking, and starting again. For an organization with network breaks to meet this may result in a disastrous delay—particularly if the breaks contain commercials. (But if the film and track have been "rubber-numbered," resynchronization is easy.)

These faults may all affect film specially prepared for television showing: in an organization with a large film output most of them will occur at some time, and everyone who handles film should be constantly on their guard to prevent them.

If the film is to be projected in the normal way (or is a television commercial) a combined sound track will be required. The show

490

print is made on magnetically striped stock, which is then recorded with the final sound mix. Alternatively (and particularly for commercials) an optical track may be printed. These measures ensure that whatever misfortune in handling may occur later to the film it cannot be shown out of synchronization, except for the second or so after a break and rejoin where frames have been lost, or if the "loop" is lost in an intermittent projector (though using "flying spot" telecine machines—in which the film runs continuously and smoothly—will also avoid the latter possible fault). Nor is such a film likely to be shown with the wrong sound.

17

COMMUNICATION IN SOUND

JUST how important is technique?

This is a question which is fundamental to a book which is about this very subject. The mechanics of programme work must be seen in their true relationship to the full process of creation, and they should be given neither too much deference nor too little. Obviously I think technique *is* important, otherwise this book would not have been written. But technique is a means to an end, not an end in itself: and its major object must be to concentrate the audience's attention upon the content, and to do so in a particular way, with particular emphases. In such a supporting role technique is indispensable.

When combined with picture, in television or film, it should always support, occasionally counterpoint, and rarely dominate; its most effective role is to extend, strengthen, and more closely define the information which comes first through vision.

It is relatively easy for the skilled professional to make technique serve the programme; and work is very rarely, if ever, done merely to display the operational ingenuity of those involved. But for the newcomer much of his work must necessarily also serve as exercises in handling sound. To the novice, technique is a vital need; perhaps even his most vital need—since he may have no lack of ideas, but little or no knowledge of the means of expressing them. And what he does need to learn are the techniques, not merely of construction, but also of self-criticism and correction. Once he has mastered the techniques he must learn to apply them—to make them serve the needs of each successive production. The medium itself is *not* the message.

The final result should be more than just a collection of sounds which have been strung together; it should have a unity, a shape of its own—whether the sound is on its own, or supporting picture.

492

Production qualities

What makes a good production? The answer to this question is of importance not only to the writer or to the man who is directing a programme but to everyone in the studio. It concerns them all in two ways: first, so that they can see their own contribution in perspective, and to know in what ways this must be subordinated to the whole; and secondly, as the programme's first audience.

Over the years people in daily contact with a medium become intensely sensitive to virtues or defects which even the director himself may be unsure of; and this front-line audience can be of immense value to him in cross-checking his calculation or intuition.

The things which matter most in any programme are the ideas within it (its content) and the way these are presented to the audience (its form). Some subjects are better for sound than others, because they make contact more easily through the listener's imagination. Others are more suitable for television or film, demanding the explicitness or possibilities for visual imagery which these give.

Many subjects can be treated adequately in any medium— adequately but differently, because the medium will dictate certain possibilities and impossibilities; or it will present alternatives, where one path presents only difficulties, while another luxuriates in opportunities for attractive or artistic results. To this extent at least the medium does condition and reflect itself upon the message.

But so far as technique is concerned there is one major condition which in conventional (if not in modern experimental) terms, must be fulfilled: that whatever the choice of subject, it must be presented in such a way as to create interest and maintain it throughout the production.

Sound and the imagination

The greatest advantage of the pure sound medium lies in its direct appeal to the imagination. A child once said that he liked sound better than television "because the scenery is better". Of course the scenery is better: it is built in the mind of the listener. It is magic scenery, which can at times seem so solid that you feel you could bang your head against it; but in a moment it may dissolve into an insubstantial atmospheric abstraction. It is scenery within which not only people can stand but also ghosts. Ideas, emotions, impressions can be conjured up as easily as the camera can show reality.

Well, perhaps not quite so easily, because sound does require a greater contribution from the listener. To compel this involvement—and to deserve it—the material coming from the loudspeaker must maintain a high level of interest throughout. And if this drops for one moment the imagination will be turned off like an electric-light switch, and all real communication will be lost. The magic scenery is built and painted by the artists and craftsmen in the studio; but it is illuminated by the imagination of the listener.

The ways in which the imagination can be stimulated are many. To some extent these depend on form, which depends in turn on techniques. Apart from this, what is done, rather than the way it is done, is a matter for individual judgment or intuition.

What makes a programme interesting?

In our analysis of the qualities of any programme, we should perhaps take "interest" as our starting-point: because the one factor that all successful productions have in common is the ability to engage and retain the listener's interest.

For a start, it is clear that interest depends on previous experience. What we know we like; what we do not know leaves us relatively indifferent: this is true even of most people who regard themselves as being "interested in anything". For very few people indeed are interested in subjects which cannot be explained in terms of things which are already understood.

The reason for this is simple enough: any reference to something which is within the listener's experience can call up an image in his mind. When we are listening to somebody talking we soon begin to forget such superficial qualities as accent and voice timbre (unless we are forcibly reminded of them at any point); we do not listen closely to the actual words, but go straight to the meaning. The words we forget almost the moment they are spoken; the meaning we may retain. This meaning, together with its associations in the listener's mind, forms an image which may be concrete or abstract, or a mixture of the two. And if it is possible to present a subject in terms of a whole series of such images a considerable amount of interest may be aroused.

When a radio or television producer starts work he must bear in mind not only what he wants to say but also who he wants to say it to. This is not merely a matter of the listener's intelligence, but also of what sort of background he has, what sort of things he is likely to have learned at school and in later life; what sort of places he knows and people he has met; what sort of emotions he is likely

494

to have experienced, and so on. It is also related most powerfully to the things he would *like* to do, consciously or not—ranging from taking up a life of meditation and prayer to winning a thousand pounds for saying that the Eiffel Tower is in Paris.

In practice many programmes develop a distinctive personality according to the characteristics of the audiences at which they are aimed, and may be further modified in style according to the time of day at which they are transmitted.

But, all in all, the dominant factor in programme appeal is the previous background and knowledge of the listener; and failure to take proper account of this is one of the most serious mistakes any producer can make—if his aim is communication. (I am not really concerned here with works of art where the artist is *not* interested in communication. And I am certainly not decrying them. But if they are works of importance to anybody but the artist himself, teachers and critics will busy themselves with explaining and relating until in the end communication between artist and public will be established, just as though it had been intended in the first place.)

In a study that was made of a number of BBC educational broadcasts in 1950, intelligibility was the main issue, but a few sidelights were thrown on "interestingness".

It was noted that while too many main "teaching points" (say, six or more in a fifteen-minute programme) were definitely bad for a programme, the presence of what sometimes seemed to be an unduly large number of subsidiary points did not seem to result in the confusion that might have been expected; and also whereas long, complex sentences with difficult vocabulary (for this particular audience) and lots of prepositions (used as an index of complexity of construction) did appear to have a slightly adverse effect on intelligibility, the presence of a large number of adverbs and adjectives did not.

It seems reasonable to conclude that an apparent excess of facts, figures, and descriptive terms is no disadvantage, because although they may not be assimilated themselves, they help to maintain interest during the necessary gaps between the teaching points. Apart from any other function they may serve, these are the things which provide "colour"; they are part of that vital series of images which the listener's imagination needs. And remember here that what is true for educational programmes is also true in the broader sense for a much wider range of programmes (on the larger canvas we can take "adverbs and adjectives" to include any descriptive, or even simply amusing, piece of illustration in sound or picture).

For the particular audience of this survey (listeners to Forces Educational Broadcasts) concrete subjects were preferred to abstract ones; and, when ideas were being explained, concrete examples—references to people, incidents, and actions—were preferred to high-flown "clever" metaphors.

This, too, must surely be a fairly general requirement. For apart from the genuine "absent-minded professors" of this world—the people for whom the world of the mind is more real than the world of reality—there can, I think, be very, very few people for whom abstractions (except those dealing with the emotions) are more telling than are concrete references. Indeed, one danger was noted in the study: that well-developed illustrations can sometimes be so effective as to attract the attention away from the main point.

Obviously, this business of creating interest in the audience can be something of a struggle; but there need be no reason to regard it as a mystery.

If there's no picture—where is everybody?

Some problems in communication apply to one medium more than another. Before we turn to the more general case, let us consider one or two that apply particularly to the pure sound medium.

We have established that the real advantage of sound lies in its direct appeal to the imagination; and that the really successful programme has one quality above all else—the ability to conjure up an unbroken succession of powerful images in the mind of the listener. These are not just imagined visual images, there to replace concrete visual evidence which the eye is being denied: they are a great deal more. Nevertheless, we must now recognize that some of the main limitations and disadvantages of sound do stem from the confusion which can be caused by the lack of exact pictorial detail.

In our ordinary life we take this detail for granted in so many ways: when we take part in a conversation with half a dozen other people we are never in any doubt as to who is talking at any time; our eyesight combines with our faculty for judging direction aurally, and no thought is necessary. Indeed, we would have no difficulty in coping with almost any number of people; the ears locate and the eyes fix on the speaker immediately.

Without vision, the number of voices that we can conveniently sort out is reduced very considerably. In the case of stereophonic sound, half a dozen people, spread out and not moving around too much, should be fairly easy to place; but with more people (or with more movement) the picture will become confusing. When this happens the imagination will fail to do its stuff; the voices will no longer appear as identities. And instead of a mental picture of a group of individuals, we merely register the sound as a quantity of depersonalized speech coming from various points in space.

In monophonic sound the picture is even more restricted: we only have room for three or four central participants in any scene at any one time, and even then the voices and characters must be very clearly differentiated. Further voices may come and go, provided that it does not matter if they do so in a fairly disembodied sort of way; the butler who comes in to say "My Lord, the carriage awaits" does not count as an extra character to confuse the ear; he is hardly more than a sound effect. But the basic group must be small.

It must also be remembered that the moment a character falls silent, the audience "loses" him. Leave him out of a conversation for half a dozen or more lines and he becomes invisible, so that when he speaks again his sudden re-entry into the middle of things can come as a shock; he seems to leap in from nowhere.

From this we already have one considerable restriction on subject and treatment. So beware: any feature which involves many-voiced scenes is going to sound terribly vague. And a discussion programme involving half a dozen speakers should not be embarked upon if it really matters that the listener should be able to sort out who is who —he will probably identify only about two or three speakers clearly. The extreme case is an open debate: this will be merely a succession of voices; though it may help a little if each speaker in turn is named. (For clarity this must generally be done even when a voice has been heard before.)

Often, of course, it will not matter that voices are not identified individually by the listener; but the producer must know what effect he is aiming for—and getting. If the voices are not pinpointed, and especially if this is permitted without the producer being aware of the fact, then the audience will be living in a place of shadows when the artist thinks he is communicating a world of imagined substance. There is a great deal of difference between the two.

The next difficulty with sound is a related one: that of establishing location. This must be fixed as early as possible, and then constantly reaffirmed by acoustics, effects, references in the text—anything to prevent the scene slipping back into a vague grey limbo and becoming once again no more than a set of voices from a box.

On the other hand, it is often a positive advantage that the listener is not burdened by irrelevant pictorial detail in cases where this is not wanted. During a television talk the eye is captured by the picture but may wander within it. It may wander to the clock on the mantelpiece behind the speaker: it may be distracted by the shape of a lampshade, or the pattern on the wallpaper. With sound only, the speaker becomes part of the atmosphere of the listener's own living-room.

These weaknesses and strengths must be seen before the treatment of a subject is chosen; it is important to allow for the frequent reiteration of locale in the scene of a play, or the formal disregard of surroundings in a straight talk.

It is obviously going to be impossible to establish one picture, and one only, in the mind's eye of every single listener. So it is wise to avoid subjects which require precise pictorial detail, or treatments where the impact of a thing that is seen has to be explained in dialogue—in fact, any stories which depend heavily on visual information. Let us take as an example of this, the first meeting of boy and girl in a crowded room: eyes meet, fall, and meet again ... it needs a Shakespeare to express verbally the magic of such a moment; and even in *Romeo and Juliet* the visual element adds immeasurably to the impact. Suppress it, and the shape of the whole scene is altered.

And this example also illustrates another point: that direct emotional effects are best expressed visually. The close-up of the human face, and most particularly the eyes, can touch the audience directly. In terms of pure sound, using only the voice, parallels with this are not so easy to find.

The emotional link between screen and viewer can be very strong indeed. Vision is the dominant faculty, and it must be either fully engaged or completely suppressed if the audience is to identify itself with the actor. With film or television the link is simple, direct, and semi-hypnotic. In sound only, this link has to be established indirectly (but no less firmly) through the imagination. The results may be quite as effective, but they are a great deal more difficult to achieve.

The time factor

As a medium, sound has a great deal in common with print. Both printed and spoken word can be presented as straight argument (or narrative) or as dialogue, and the forms in which they can be illustrated also seem to be related: these are the sound effect, the picture or diagram. And further, because of the restriction to a single channel of communication, neither medium can engulf the senses without first making an extremely strong appeal to the imagination.

498

The analogy is so good that it is worth considering where the differences lie: the more so as there will inevitably be a tendency to assume that what can be done in print can also be done in sound.

The great difference lies in the dimension of time. With the printed page, the time element is left in the hands of the reader. He can read at any speed he likes. He can read a novel in a few hours, or take weeks over a textbook. He can read one paragraph quickly and the next slowly. He can stop and go back when the meaning of something is not clear at first reading. In the process of reading the eye can afford to run on ahead in order to see how a sentence is shaped, and to take in its meaning as a whole.

For the radio (or television) audience the time relationship between successive elements of story is fixed absolutely. Similarly, once a listener has decided *when* he is going to play a record he has virtually no further control over any other aspect of time: for technical reasons (the interrelation of speed and pitch) he may not play the record faster or slower than was originally intended; nor should he be expected to jump on or back, or to stop and start as with a dictating machine.

So it is important to remember that ideas must be presented in a clear logical sequence. And it is not only the order of the arguments which must be clear: the style in which they are presented must itself be lucid and lively. If possible (that is, if the subject matter does not militate against it, and sometimes even if it does) speech should be grammatical, as well as vivid in expression. Realistic dialogue, with its broken sentences, repetitions, fractured logic, and other inconsistencies, is often regarded as essential to modern writing. But if used carelessly it can also confuse the listener; and when this happens he will hear not meanings but words and (particularly) any imperfections in the way they are spoken. The most frequent complaint about this sort of dialogue is inaudibility. (This is not to say that it should never be done, only that it should be done for good reason; and the degree of communication calculated.)

Going to the other extreme, in the "radio talk" (a single speaker with a prepared script) good delivery is still important. For some listeners, a bad speaker, obviously reading, and doing so from material written in a flat literary style which makes no concession to colloquial speech, will seriously diminish enjoyment. The listener may well ask, "Why bother to present this in sound at all, when it is so obviously designed for print?" But this may be a minority view, for it has been shown that the quality of delivery has very little effect on intelligibility, and that it does not worry the majority of listeners any more than would any other relatively unimportant fault of technique. For example, many of the film-stars of the 'thirties now seem curiously stilted when we see revivals of their films; but this never prevented huge audiences from adoring them in their day. Only if a programme is thrown completely out of balance (as, for example, by speech that is too fast) is faulty or "unrealistic" delivery found to be upsetting.

It is reasonable to demand that the basic "message" of a piece should be understood in a single hearing—for both sound and television are basically "one-shot" media. By all means include deeper layers of meaning for the benefit of the people you hope will be shouting for an encore—or for whom your main points may be old hat. But a good basic assumption to start from is that no one will ever hear your creation twice.

If you find yourself donning a weak smile and saying to a fairly baffled audience, "You'll probably see what I'm getting at if we hear it through again", then you may take it that you are almost certainly on the wrong lines. Only if you recognize this, is it at all likely that anyone will *want* to hear you twice. Of course, there are many important exceptions to this; and it is always tempting to assume that one's own work is such an exception. This is almost invariably a major error. So: aim to make a major impact at the very first hearing.

Understanding and remembering

Since control over the rate at which ideas are presented is completely in the hands of the creator of a programme, he must be particularly careful not to use this power in such a way as to impair intelligibility. There are two ways in which a producer may be tempted to disregard this need. The first of these is the quest for "pace"—but as we shall see later, pace is not achieved by overcondensing vital information.

The second factor which may influence a producer is a more subtle one: it is his wish to present a subject in a tidy, well-shaped sort of way—in itself an unexceptionable aim. But, being by nature and education a fairly literate sort of person, he all too often falls into the trap of assuming that what looks well shaped in the form of a script will also appear as a neat construction in its finished form, once such minor details as logical presentation and colloquial speech values have been attended to.

Unfortunately, this may not be the case. For the producer must also study one further vital factor: the rate at which new ideas are being presented. To take an extreme case: on the printed page, a concise elegant argument can be presented neatly, tautly, as finely shaped as a mathematical theorem—and the eye will dwell on it until it is understood. In a broadcast, such a construction is out of the question.

In order to ensure at least a moderate degree of intelligibility in this constantly progressing medium, the argument must sometimes be slowed down to what in literary terms will often seem like an impossibly slack pace. The good magazine programme, play, or documentary may appear in script form to have a much looser construction than a well-written article or short story: there may perhaps be an apparent excess of illustration and "padding".

This is necessary because it seems that the brain will accept and retain material which is new to it only if that material is presented at no more than a certain speed. Even if a listener is intellectually equipped to follow a concise complex line of argument he will need time—more time than it takes to present the bare bones of the argument—if it is to sink in. He needs time to turn it over in his mind.

There is a clear analogy with the teaching process here. But learning—in the sense of the *permanent* retention of fact and argument—may not be the immediate result. *Repetition* plays an important part in learning; if something which is clearly understood in the first place is repeated after a few days, and once again after a few weeks, then there is a reasonable chance of it being retained for a long time. Nevertheless, radio or television may help in the learning process, for although very few individual items will be given a second hearing by the audience, their content may be related to what he has read somewhere or heard in a previous programme, or knows already. In such a case the content of the programme stands a much better chance of being understood and making some impact.

Clearly, learning is very much a matter of chance, or perseverance on the part of the audience. But the *immediate* effectiveness of any particular item is, or should be, more predictable: the producer must calculate his effects: he must allow sufficient time for the audience to take each point as he makes it. Certainly, this will affect the amount that remains in the mind after a programme is over, or the following day—but that is only half the story.

If there is a logical argument or a narrative line involved a single failure may render the whole programme incomprehensible, or considerably change its meaning. In the action of a play, for

501

example, an understanding of points made early on is often essential to being able to follow developments at a later stage. Fail to establish a single important plot point and the play fails as a whole.

This is a matter of vital importance to a broadcasting organization such as the BBC, and it is perhaps not surprising that a number of experiments have been carried out to determine the intelligibility of programmes and the rate at which fact and argument can be absorbed.

One of these tests was made with news bulletins to determine how many items and how much detail could be recalled by an attentive listener immediately after the end of the news. The answer was that only a small proportion was retained.

Anyone with a tape recorder can very easily prove this for himself. Record ten minutes of news and then, before playing it back, try to write down all the items of news in as much detail as possible (the exact words are not important here; the gist of them will do). Playback will confirm what will by then be pretty clear, that by far the greater part was missed. (News on radio is the most convenient for this.)

Another way of trying this experiment is in a group, as a sort of party game (and if no recorder is available, one person should take down the subject matter and timings for particular items on a piece of paper). After listening to the news bulletin, try to reconstruct it by discussion and without help from the running order. And, incidentally, if a recorder *is* available it may be instructive to record the discussion as well as the original news; and then play them both back together; this will make it doubly clear just how vague one's memory is.

These experiments are called aural assimilation tests. Marks are awarded for major and minor points that are recalled, and are subtracted for errors. Many tests of this sort have been carried out, and the marks have always been very low. The ear is a very inefficient way of taking in ideas.

The other main enquiries were into the intelligibility of educational and current affairs broadcasts. One series of five-minute programmes was studied exhaustively. This was "Topic for Tonight" which used to be in the BBC Light Programme. The aim of the programme was to be simple and straightforward; to be understandable without too much difficulty by the greater part of the Light Programme's mass audience.

Getting on for a third of Britain's adult radio audience listened to this programme every week. It was respected and enjoyed by the

502

vast majority of listeners. It was, on the whole, listened to attentively and thought to be interesting and informative.

The enquiry, which was very thorough, showed that for the average case hardly more than a quarter of the talk sank home. Each talk was divided up into main and subsidiary points and marks were allocated according to their importance. Individual talks scored between 11 and 44%. The average was 28%.

It was quite clear that, simple as these talks already (mostly) were, they could with profit be simplified still further. If this could be done without giving an appearance of talking down—always to be avoided at all costs—the intelligibility could be increased a great deal. Direct faults in presentation were found in some cases: such things as taking too much background knowledge for granted; the use of unfamiliar words, or jargon, or flowery analogies or abstractions; poor logical construction or unnecessarily complex sentences.

One of the major conclusions from this survey was that the presentation of the relatively more important points should be better organized. Major points should be emphasized and repeated in such a way that it is quite clear which, out of all that is said, is the important part to grasp (and a summary at the end would improve things still further).

This particular survey was carried out for a specific programme aimed at a specific audience. But I think that the results are likely to be true for almost any type of programme (and not just serious ones) and for any audience, provided account is taken of possible differences in background knowledge, literacy, and intelligence.

The communication of ideas

Experience, together with the above experiments, seems to suggest this working rule: that *not less than three or four minutes of programme time should be devoted to any point of importance.*

This is very much a generalization, but if it errs, it is on the side of allowing too little time: these are pretty definitely *minimum* times for points of average complexity. Of course, for a fairly simple point it may be possible to get away with spending less than three minutes; and, on the other hand, a particularly complex point may need much longer to establish fully. But in this latter case it may be advisable to break the argument down into stages.

In a seven-minute item, for example, I would say that it is possible to make two major points. The rest of the seven minutes must be spent in supporting and linking those points. There may be many

503

minor points, but if a further major point is introduced, then it is likely that one of the three will be lost. To take an extreme case, if the seven-minute piece is made to consist of seven important points, then nearly all of them will be lost, and the listener may be left with a frustrating feeling that he has missed something. Or, alternatively, he may, perhaps, remember just one of the points which happens to appeal to him, plus the thought that this was part of a pattern which included half a dozen other points which on first hearing seemed plausible. But one cannot in this highly condensed case have an exact or predictable control over what the listener picks out and takes away with him. It may, in fact, be something totally unsuitable from the point of view of the producer, writer, or speaker.

One can point to Sir Winston Churchill as a broadcaster who triumphantly mastered the technique: a study of recordings of his wartime speeches will show how he took each point in turn and attacked, analysed, and presented it in a variety of ways before moving on to the next. Despite a "difficult" voice and an almost complete refusal to make any concession to radio (oratory is one of the "don'ts" of the medium) the results remain masterpieces.

So all broadcasters who want to get something over to their audience must follow these rules; they must, in fact, imitate the methods of a schoolteacher—though not too overtly, for unlike the teacher, they have no captive audience. But a good teacher, at whatever level, will aim to lay out his subject in just the way I have described. In the classroom his pace is subject to immediate correction by his pupils; with the constant reminder of their presence he is on the whole more likely to stick to the correct pace than is the man who talks to an invisible audience, who may feel himself under pressure to "get on with it" because everyone about him is behaving as though air time is valuable (which it is) and because he feels he has more to say than time to say it.

This rule about good layout is most clearly valid for programmes which seek to educate and inform; it is also true for most of those whose outward purpose is solely to entertain, and in particular those with a narrative element; stories, plays, and so on. I say "outward purposes", because most writers, whether serious or comic, are at heart moral people (in one sense or another), and whatever they write will express something of their philosophy of life. And at this deeper level, the level of the writer's basic philosophy, whether homespun or sophisticated, whether noble or just plain anti-social, the same rule once again applies: time is necessary for communication.

504

Pace

The term "pace" has already crept into this discussion: let us attempt to define it a little more precisely.

To maintain interest, a story or an argument must be kept moving at a fairly brisk rate. So the secret of pace is *to allot just sufficient time to each point for it to be adequately understood—and then move on.* Pace is impossible without intelligibility. It is perhaps odd that it should depend to such a degree on *not* going too fast. But there it is: pace is a sort of shaping of the programme in time, and it provides the basic foundation on which the finer details must be built.

When we talk of "lack of pace", we are often thinking of another, secondary, defect which frequently afflicts amateur work· this fault is a sort of superficial slackness which has as its origin the lack of an adequate sense of timing. But it is the other more subtle fault, lack of organization in the underlying shape, which is more likely to mar professionally produced shows that are slick enough to all outward appearance.

To sum up: in the construction of almost any successful programme we must have a series of basic units each occupying a few minutes. Each of these should contain one major point and sufficient supporting detail to help establish it as clearly as possible. There may also be material which will retain the attention of the listener in between the major points that are to be made, but which may not be of direct importance to them, and which must not actively draw the listener's attention away from them.

Quite apart from anything else, this sort of construction will give "light and shade" to a piece—that is to say, some variation in the pressure of attack. And that again is absolutely essential to a feeling of pace in the final product.

All this will very considerably affect the choice of form for the presentation of a particular subject. An argument which is by its nature concise may have to be filled out by extra material: illustration perhaps, repetition in a different way, anything. Or a cut may have to be made if an extra point seems to be creeping in which may be interesting enough to distract the listener from the main line that is being followed, but which cannot be allowed its own full development.

It must be recognized that certain types of sound or television programme, or film simply do not work: these are the ones which contain too much argument in too little time. The cool, swift logic of a mathematical theorem, or a solid, indigestible, encyclopaedic mass of essential detail are both death to clear, intelligible construction in sound.

Of course, there are exceptions to all of the rules; but these are not always those which appear to be so. Often the programmes which seem to succeed despite breaking all the rules that have ever been thought up are in reality the ones which stick most closely, but subtly, to the ideal form.

GLOSSARY

As well as short definitions, some indication of the context in which terms may be used is given. Unless otherwise indicated, the term is in international use; where usage in Britain and America differs, both forms are given. Certain expressions which seem to have originated in BBC usage are so indicated. No attempt is made here or elsewhere in this book to enter into a study of basic electrical theory, or to describe equipment or circuits in detail.

A   "A" SIGNAL. In stereo, the signal to be fed to the left-hand loudspeaker of a two-speaker system.

ABSORPTION COEFFICIENT. The fraction of sound which is absorbed on reflection at any surface. (It therefore takes values between 0 and 1, and unless otherwise stated, is for a frequency of 512 Hz at normal incidence.) *Soft absorbers* depend for their action on such things as the friction of air particles in the interstices of the material. This friction increases with particle velocity, and the absorption is therefore greatest where particle velocity is greatest, i.e. at a quarter wavelength from the reflecting surface. Soft absorbers (glass wool, fibre board, etc.) in layers of the order of an inch in depth are poor absorbers at low frequencies and are fair to good at middle and high frequencies. If the outer surface is hard (e.g. painted) and unperforated, the high frequency absorption will deteriorate. *Membrane and vibrating panel absorbers* are, in effect, boxes with panels and cavities which can be tuned to resonate at particular frequencies or broad frequency bands. They readily remove sound energy from the air at their resonant frequency and this is then mopped up within the absorber by various forms of damping. Such absorbers may be efficient at low and middle frequencies. *Helmholtz resonators* respond to narrow bands and if damped internally remove them selectively.

ACETATE. (*a*) Cellulose acetate, a material used as a tape base (i.e. the backing on which the magnetic oxide coating is carried). Tends to break rather than stretch when subjected to excessive stress. As a break can be mended easily and cleanly, whereas tape which has been stretched beyond its elastic limit can only be cut out of the tape, acetate backings offer some insurance against mis-handling. (*b*) Direct-cut lacquer discs. At one time such discs were made of cellulose acetate on glass. The term is still used colloquially for the cellulose nitrate on aluminium discs of today.

ACOUSTIC REPRODUCTION OF EFFECTS, ETC. (from tape or disc). A feed of prerecorded sound to a loudspeaker in the studio instead of directly

507

to the mixer. The sound picked up by the studio microphone will depend on the characteristics of the loudspeaker and microphone, and the studio acoustics and balance. It may well be very different from the original sound even if a close balance is used (often the loudspeaker is balanced at a separate microphone). Acoustic reproduction techniques may be used either to modify the sound or to provide cues when no other method (headphones, cue lights or hand signals) is possible. In the latter case volume should be kept as low as practicable, otherwise there may be a noticeable change of quality due to acoustic colouration. See FOLDBACK.

ACOUSTICS. The study of the behaviour of sound. The acoustics of a studio depend on its size and shape, and the number and position of absorbers. The *apparent acoustics* of a studio depend on the effect of the acoustics on the indirect sound reaching the microphone, and also on the ratio of direct to indirect sound. Thus, apparent acoustics depend on the microphone position, distance and angle from the sound source (i.e. the balance) and also on the level of sound reproduction. Besides this, the actual acoustics of the studio may be modified close to the microphone by the placing of screens, etc.

ACTUALITY. Recording of the actual sound of an event, as distinct from a report, interview, or dramatized reconstruction.

AMBIENT NOISE. In any location, from quiet studio or living-room to busy street, there will be a background of sound. In a particular location the ear automatically adjusts to and accepts this ambient noise in all except the loudest (or quietest) case. In a monophonic recording, however, noise at a natural level will generally sound excessive. One purpose of microphone balance is to discriminate against such noise, where necessary. Unexplained noises in particular should be avoided. (See ATMOSPHERE.)

AMPLIFIER. A device for increasing the strength of a signal by means of a varying control voltage. At each stage the input (to the grid of a valve, etc.) is used to control the flow of current in a circuit which is carrying much more power. Precautions (feedback) are necessary to ensure that the degree of amplification does not vary with frequency. In successive stages the magnification of the signal (i.e. ratio of output to input) may be much the same, so that the rise in signal strength will be approximately exponential. Relative levels may therefore conveniently be measured in decibels (q.v.).

AMPLITUDE MODULATION (AM). A method whereby the information in an audio signal is carried on the much higher frequency of a radio wave. The envelope of the amplitude of the radio wave in successive cycles is equivalent to the wave form of the initial sound. Historically, AM is the method which was used first and such transmissions now crowd the short, medium and long wave bands. This crowding restricts the upper limit of the frequencies which can effectively be broadcast without the transmitter bandwidth overlapping an adjacent channel (the limit may be 8 or 10 kHz). The random background of radio noise which a receiver is bound to pick up at all frequencies also appears as minor fluctuations in the amplitude of the carrier wave, and cannot be distinguished electrically from the audio signal. For high quality transmission AM has largely given way to FM (frequency modulation).

ARTIFICIAL REVERBERATION ("echo"). Simulation of the natural die-away of sound that occurs in a room or any other enclosed space (e.g. in a cave, down a well, etc.). Such techniques are used when the available studio acoustics are not reverberant enough. Multi-microphone techniques for music need "echo", as the studios used for this are normally much less reverberant than those used for natural balance. The technique is used to permit different treatment to be applied to each microphone output: after separate control of individual instruments or groups, their sound is fed at appropriate levels to the echo chamber, or plate, or whatever other device may be used.

ATMOSPHERE. The background sound at any location. This may not be undesirable, in that such atmosphere lends authenticity and gives listeners a sense of participation in an event. Even so, it may be advisable to discriminate against background sound in the main recording, and record atmosphere separately for subsequent mixing at an appropriate level (which may not be held constant). When proper monitoring conditions are available at the time of recording (or broadcast), separate microphones may be set up and the mixture again judged by ear. *Studio atmosphere* is the ambient noise which may at times be obtrusive even in a soundproofed room—particularly if omnidirectional microphones are used for other than close balances. The slightest movement, the flow of air for ventilation or even heavy breathing, may create problems for the balancer. (See AMBIENT NOISE.)

ATTENUATION. Fixed or variable losses (usually in an electrical signal). As with amplification it is convenient to measure this in decibels (q.v.). (See FADER.)

AUTOMATIC RADIUS COMPENSATION. See COMPENSATION.

AXIS (of microphone or loudspeaker). Line through centre of diaphragm and at a right angle to it. It is usually an axis of structural symmetry in at least one plane, and thus an axis about which the polar response is symmetrical. Also, it is generally the line of maximum high frequency response.

AZIMUTH. The angle which the gap of a recording or reproducing head makes with the line along which the tape moves. This should be exactly 90°. Misalignment may be due to incorrect setting of the head, or to the tape transport system not being parallel to the deck, and may be corrected by adjustment to either. Adjustment of a reproducing head may be made using a standard recording of high frequency tone (i.e. one recorded with a correctly adjusted head). Maximum output, which may be judged by ear or by meter, occurs when alignment is correct. If there is a separate recording head this may then be adjusted by recording tone with it and checking for maximum output from the reproducing head. Alternatively, satisfactory adjustment can usually be made using speech or music recordings. Azimuth misalignment produces a recording (or reproduction) which is apparently lacking in top. Although it is a common fault, many owners of cheaper tape recorders may not be aware of its presence, since tape which is replayed on the same head as was used for recording does not exhibit faults which would be at once apparent if the tape were replayed on most other machines.

B "B" SIGNAL. In stereo, the signal to be fed to the right-hand loudspeaker of a two-speaker system.

BACKING. The base on which the magnetic oxide coating of tape is carried. It gives strength and permits flexibility, and although it has no screening effect its thickness ensures that the physical separation of successive layers of the magnetic coating is sufficient to maintain printing at a low level. Materials are acetate, PVC, and polyester.

BACKING TRACK. Prerecording of the accompaniment to a singer (etc.) who then listens to a replay on headphones as he contributes his own performance. At this stage the two are mixed to give the final recording. The performer's (and other musicians') time is saved, and adequate separation is achieved without the use of separate studios. *Back tracking* is a related technique in which a preliminary recording by the same artist is used as the accompaniment.

BAFFLE. A small acoustic screen which causes a local variation in the acoustic field close to the microphone diaphragm. A baffle of hardboard, card, etc., when clipped to a microphone sets up a standing wave system at the diaphragm, distorting the sound. In ribbon microphones, gauze baffles are used as an integral part of the design to improve the response. A baffle may be used round a moving coil or electrostatic loudspeaker in order to reduce the flow of air around the edge of the speaker at low frequencies—an effect which causes serious loss of bass.

BALANCE. Placing of a microphone to pick up an adequate sound signal, discriminate against noise, and provide a satisfactory ratio of direct to indirect sound. This is the responsibility of a *balance engineer* or (in BBC radio) a programme operations assistant.

BALANCE TEST. Consists of one or a series of trial balances which should preferably be judged by direct comparison.

BAND. Separately recorded section of a disc, of which there may be several on a side. By extension, the term may also mean an individual section of a tape recording which is bounded by spacers. Locations may be indicated on a script in shorthand form, e.g. "S2B3" = side 2, band 3.

BASS. Lower end of the musical scale. In acoustics it is generally taken as the range (below 200 Hz, say) in which difficulties (principally in the reproduction of sound) occur due to the large wavelengths involved. Loudspeakers which depend on the movement of air by cones or plates (e.g. moving coil or electrostatic types) become inefficient in their *bass response* at wavelengths greater than their dimensions. This is due to too small a piston attempting to drive what is at these frequencies too pliant a mass of air. Certain systems of mounting (or cabinets) extend the bass response by means of a resonance in the octave below the frequency at which cut-off begins, but this results in a sharper cut-off when it does occur (e.g. bass reflex and column resonance types). *Bass Lift* may be resorted to, but this requires a more powerful amplifier (most power is concentrated in the bass of music, anyway) and a loudspeaker system which is capable of greater excursions without distortion. The most efficient way of producing bass is an acoustic exponential horn, preferably with a low rate of flare. This ensures that coupling between the moving element and the air outside is good, up to wavelengths approaching the diameter of the mouth of the horn.

BASS TIP-UP. This occurs with directional microphones when they are situated in a sound field which shows an appreciable loss of intensity in the distance travelled from front to back of microphone. The operation of the microphone depends on the pressure gradient and this becomes exaggerated at low frequencies. At middle frequencies the effect is masked by the phase shift which occurs in this path distance in any case; and at high frequencies the mode of operation is by pressure and no longer by pressure gradient.

BEAT. If two tones which are within about fifteen cycles per second of each other are played together the combined signal is heard to pulsate, or beat, at the difference frequency. Two tones may be synchronized by adjusting the frequency of one until the beat slows and finally disappears.

BIAS. A carrier frequency with which the audio signal is combined in order to reduce distortion during the tape recording process. Its importance is greatest in recording low frequencies. It is generally of the order of 50 – 100 kHz and is produced by an oscillator which is associated with the tape recorder amplifier unit. It mostly vanishes from the tape soon after recording, by a process of self-demagnetization. (However, a little of the bias signal can still be heard if recorded tape is pulled slowly over the reproducing head.) The bias oscillator also supplies the erase head.

BI-DIRECTIONAL MICROPHONE. One which is live on the front face and back, but which is dead at the sides and above and below. The polar response is a figure-of-eight in both the horizontal and the vertical planes.

BOARD, CLAPPERBOARD, SLATE. In film, a means of marking the start of each shot with scene and take numbers. It is held open for mute scenes (those shot without sound); for sync. takes the scene and take number are identified on sound and then the board is clapped in vision so that sound and picture can subsequently be matched.

BOOM. A telescopic arm (attached to a floor mounting) from which a micro-phone is slung.

BOOMY. Subjective description of a sound quality which has resonances in the low frequencies, or a broad band of bass lift. Expressions with similar shades of meaning are tubby or, simply, bassy.

BRIGHT SURFACE. Strongly reflecting surface, particularly of high frequencies.

BROADCAST CHAIN. The sequence: studio—continuity suite—transmitter—receiver, together with any other intermediate control or switching points, through which a signal passes.

BULK ERASER. See ERASER

BUTT CHANGEOVER. A changeover in mid-programme from one tape or disc to another, the second being started as the cue on the first is about to come up. The crossover from one reproduction to the other should not be noticeable.

C   CANCELLATION. Partial or complete opposition in phase, so that the sum of two signals approaches or reaches zero.

"CANS". Headphones.

CAPACITANCE. The ability of an electrical component (or components) to store static charges. Charges present in a conductor will attract opposite charges to nearby but not electrically connected conductors; changes of charge will induce corresponding changes of charge in nearby conductors. A signal may therefore cross between one component and another, between which there is no direct path. Capacitors are used in electronics for coupling, smoothing, and tuning purposes. In lines, capacitance is the mechanism whereby the signal is gradually lost (capacitance between the wires or to earth). Capacitance varies with distance between plates (or other components): this variation is used in electrostatic microphones and loudspeakers. *Stray capacitances* form the mechanism whereby audio signals or mains hum is transferred unintentionally from one component to another nearby.

CAPSTAN. Drive spindle of tape deck: the tape is driven between this and an idler pulley which presses against it when the machine is switched to record or replay. The diameter of the spindle and the motor speed, determine the speed of the tape. It is possible, by fitting a sleeve of twice the diameter of the spindle to double the top speed of replay (sleeves of other diameters may be used to produce other speeds, a device which has been used in radiophonic work). If the rotation of the spindle is eccentric there will be a rapid fluctuation in tape speed, causing a flutter in the signal.

CAPSULE. (a) Removable pick-up head. (b) A condenser microphone capsule is the diaphragm assembly.

CARBON MICROPHONE. Microphone in which the audio signal is produced by varying the resistance of a button of granular carbon to which a polarizing voltage is applied (a diaphragm presses on the carbon button). Extensively used as a telephone microphone, and at one time (in a slightly different design) in radio work. Not now used for high quality work, though the quality is better than early systems of sound reproduction, etc. were generally capable of handling.

CARDIOID MICROPHONE. Microphone with a heart-shaped polar diagram (arrived at by adding omnidirectional and figure-of-eight responses together, taking into account the phase reversal at the back of the latter). Some microphones consist of the two component types together in a single case, and working in parallel. In electrostatic (condenser) microphones (q.v.) the combination occurs in the principle of construction. (See PRESSURE GRADIENT.)

CASSETTE, CARTRIDGE. A fully encapsulated tape system which does not need to be laced up. It employs a special tape which is narrower than the $\frac{1}{4}$-inch type that does have to be laced up and is fed from spool to spool. On half-track tape the recording configuration is the same as on $\frac{1}{4}$-inch, i.e. the top track is played from left to right, and then the cassette is turned over so that the other track may be played in a similar manner. The stereo cassette recording layout is different from that on $\frac{1}{4}$-inch tape: and A and B information is carried on tracks 1 and 2 and can therefore be reproduced on a mono replay machine, which will scan both tracks to produce an A+B signal. 4-channel stereo tapes are also compatible with both 2-channel stereo and mono replay systems as the primary A and B frontal information remains on tracks 1 and 2, while that for the rear speakers is on tracks 3 and 4. Cassettes (or cartridges) are also used for endless tape loops, in this case often employing $\frac{1}{4}$-inch tape. (To avoid confusion it would probably be best to use the term cartridge for the endless loop system, and cassette for the encapsulated double-spool system.)

CCIR CHARACTERISTIC. In tape recording, the pre-emphasis and subsequent equalization standard used in Britain and Continental Europe.

CEMENTED JOINT. (Permanent joint). A method of editing tape in which the two ends are overlapped and fixed together by an adhesive or bonding agent. As there is a slight step in the tape, this type of joint is marginally more likely to cause a momentary loss of signal on subsequent re-use than is the temporary joint which leaves the surface smooth and substantially continuous. Cement is used for joining film negative and reversal camera masters, but not in modern film sound and picture editing.

CERAMIC MICROPHONE OR PICK-UP. This is similar in principle to a crystal design, but has a barium titanate element. It is less sensitive to temperature and humidity.

CHANNEL. Complete set of (professional) recording equipment. Recording room (or part of recording room which can operate independently to record a a programme). (See also MICROPHONE CHANNEL.)

CINÉ SPOOLS. See SPOOLS.

CLEAN FEED. A cue feed back to a programme source which includes all but the contribution from that source.

CLEAN SOUND. Actuality sound of an event, without superimposed commentary.

CLOCK. See VIDEOTAPE CLOCK.

COATING (Emulsion). The layer of finely divided magnetic material, bonded in plastic and polished to allow smooth flow over the tape heads, that carries the magnetically recorded signal. Ferric oxide and chromium dioxide are both used as the recording medium, the latter having the better performance (thereby permitting lower tape speeds, narrower tracks, etc.).

COCKTAIL PARTY EFFECT. The means whereby a listener can concentrate on a single conversation in a crowd. Depends largely on the spatial spread of sound, a quality which is lost in monophonic recording—so that if a cocktail party type of background sound is recorded at a realistic level it is not only unpleasantly obtrusive but also seriously impedes intelligibility of foreground speech.

COD EFFECTS. Effects which are exaggerated for comic effect.

CO-INCIDENT PAIR. In stereo this is a pair of directional microphones or a double microphone with two directional elements mounted close to each other (usually one above the other) and crossed at an angle (often 90°), which is used to pick up the A and B signals. This technique avoids the phase distortion effects produced by using a spaced pair.

COLOURATION. Distortion of frequency response by resonance peaks. Marked acoustic colouration in a studio may be due to the coincidence of dimensional resonances, to wall-panel resonances, or to frequency-selective excessive absorption of sound. Some mild acoustic colouration may, however, be beneficial. Colouration is often exhibited by microphones and loudspeakers, and in these is generally regarded as unwanted. Nevertheless, many people, preferring what they are already used to, "like a loudspeaker to sound like a loudspeaker", i.e. to exhibit cone and cabinet resonances, rather than the disembodied perfection of a smooth frequency response. Colouration may also be caused by loud sound spilling to a microphone set for a quiet source.

COLOURED NOISE. See NOISE.

COMMAG. Combined magnetic film sound, i.e. with the sound on a magnetic track running beside the picture, and recorded 28 frames ahead of it.

COMOPT. Combined optical film sound: the sound track is recorded beside the picture, but advanced from it by 19½ or 20 frames (35 mm) or by 25½ or 26 frames (16 mm). See OPTICAL SOUND.

COMPATIBILITY. In stereo, the requirement that a broadcast can also be heard in mono without additional equipment. Stereo gramophone records are also compatible (but may be damaged by unsuitable mono equipment). Special measures may be needed for the *artistic compatibility* of stereo recordings or broadcasts.

513

COMPENSATION. Control of levels, e.g. between the voices of a duologue, in order to place them in a suitable sound-volume relationship. Compensation is an imprecise term, and may also refer to other forms of adjustment of imbalance. *Automatic radius compensation* (variable diameter equalization) is a technique used in cold-cutter disc recording. The increased damping of the cutter, due to the more cramped waveform at the centre of the disc, means that progressively more high frequency pre-emphasis has to be fed to the recording head.

COMPLIANCE. The ease with which a stylus can be displaced sideways: the ratio of displacement to applied force. It is the inverse of the (mechanical) stiffness of the system. Vertical compliance is also necessary in order to ride pinching up and down in the groove. Compliance is the acoustical and mechanical equivalent of capacitance and also enters into the theory of microphone and loudspeaker construction.

COMPRESSION. Controls of levels in order to ensure that (*a*) recorded or broadcast signals are suitably placed between the noise and distortion levels of the medium, and (*b*) the relationship between maximum and minimum volumes will be acceptable to the listener who in his own home may not wish to hear the greatest volume of sound that he would accept in a concert hall, and who may be listening against background noise. *Manual compression* seeks by various means to maintain as much of the original dynamics as is artistically desirable and possible, and will vary in degree with the expected listening conditions. The purpose of *automatic compression*, in short wave transmissions, is to bring peak volumes consistently to full modulation of the carrier. It is also used in the transmitter of radio microphones to prevent overloading at a point where volume cannot be controlled, and in pop music to limit the dynamic range of the voice or a particular instrument. Above a selected onset volume, say 8 dB below full modulation, compression is introduced in a ratio that may be selected: e.g. 2:1 3:1, 4:1, or 5:1.

CONDENSER MICROPHONE. See ELECTROSTATIC MICROPHONE.

CONE. A piston of stiff felted paper or possibly of plastic. It should be light and rigid. Paper cones are often corrugated to reduce any tendency to "break up" radially and produce sub-harmonic oscillations. Elliptical cones give a greater spread of high frequencies out along the minor axis: they should therefore be mounted with the major axis vertical.

CONSTANT IMPEDANCE FADER. See FADE.

CONTACT MICROPHONE. A device for picking up sound which is transmitted within a solid: an important application is in the reverberation plate.

CONTINUITY. Linking between radio programmes, including opening and closing announcements (when these are not provided in the studio), station identification, trailers and other announcements.

CONTINUITY SUITE. A centre through which programmes are routed or where they are reproduced to build a particular service ready for feeding to a transmitter (or for quarrying in continuities elsewhere). Continuity staff includes an announcer, who is immediately responsible for the maintenance of the service, and one or more engineers.

CONTROL. The adjustment of programme levels (in the form of an electrical signal) to make them suitable for feeding to recorder or transmitter; where necessary, this includes compression. Mixing involves the separate control of a number of individual sources. At a *control desk* there are faders (individual, group and main control), associated cue systems, echo and distortion controls (where required) and a variety of communications equipment. A *control line* between one location and another is a telephone circuit on which programme details may be discussed, and is so called to distinguish it from the broad band (i.e. high quality) "music line" along which programme is fed. A control line may, of course, be narrow-band, but for outside broadcasts it is safer to use lines of equal quality so that the two are interchangeable.

CONTROL CUBICLE (*BBC* radio). The soundproof room equipped with control desk, gramophone and tape reproducers and high quality loudspeaker, which is occupied by production and operational staff.

CONTROL ROOM (*BBC* radio). A switching centre.

COPY EDITING. The copying of selected extracts from recorded material into sequence on a main programme assembly tape. Subsequent fine editing will generally be necessary.

COPYRIGHT. The law in relation to the ownership of creative works, which is automatically vested in the author, composer, or artist. In Britain this extends to 50 years after the author's death (expiring at the end of the calendar year). For criticism or review, "fair dealing" provisions generally permit extracts which do not constitute a substantial part of the whole, without payment. Otherwise payment must always be made, the details being arranged by negotiation with the author or his agent. *Mechanical copyright* is, in Britain, a somewhat similar restriction which attaches to recordings, films, etc. Thus a gramophone record may have two copyrights, that of the composer (etc.) and that of the company which has made the recording, and the two may extend from different dates. Public performance of records, etc., is easy to arrange, and fees are small (usually paid through the Performing Rights Society) but copying, except of music recorded specially for the purpose (mood music), is permitted only with elaborate safeguards, and even so permission may be difficult to obtain. Radio broadcasts (or the sound part of television broadcasts) are also subject to copyright. However the BBC permits the recording of schools broadcasts to be made by schools provided that the records are only used for instructional purposes in class and that they are destroyed at the end of the school term. There is no copyright in events: e.g. an impromptu speech which makes no claim to be a work of art. Casual sound effects are therefore not copyright (though recordings of them are). Dramatic or musical performers are also protected; their permission must be obtained before a record is made of their performances. *However, recordings of copyright material can be made for private purposes* (the recording of records is not permitted even for private purposes), but "private" in this context is not clearly defined, and there is no doubt that many copyright owners would claim that the scope for private use is very narrow. Copyright laws are easily evaded and owners are justly concerned at the losses they undoubtedly sustain. Copyright laws vary considerably in detail from country to country—the above comments relate only to British law.

COTTAGE LOAF CHARACTERISTIC. See HYPERCARDIOID.

CRAB. Move camera or sound boom sideways relative to the performing area.

CROSSED MICROPHONES. See CO-INCIDENT PAIR.

CROSSFADE. A gradual mix from one sound source or group of sources to another. During this, both faders (or groups) are open at the same time. In sound the process is manual, and the rate of fade can be varied internally within the crossfade if this seems desirable for artistic effect.

CROSSOVER. The frequency at which a signal is split in order to feed separate parts of a loudspeaker. *Crossover Network*. The filter which accomplishes this.

CROSSTALK. In stereo, the breakthrough between channels, measured as separation (in dB) between wanted and unwanted sound. It is measured by recording tone or zero level on one track and then measuring output on the other. Outputs of −38 dB at 1 kHz rising to −30 dB at 50 Hz and 10 kHz are reasonable. Crosstalk also means breakthrough (or "induction") of signal between any other pair of lines, e.g. on a telephone circuit.

CRYSTAL MICROPHONE OR GRAMOPHONE PICK-UP. This generates a signal by means of a crystal bimorph—two plates cut from different planes of a crystal of Rochelle Salt and held together in the form of a sandwich. Twisting the bimorph produces a voltage (termed a piezo-electric voltage) between foil plates on top and bottom surfaces of the sandwich. The principle is well suited to use in a gramophone pick-up, as the frequency response is a fair match to the characteristic which is needed to reproduce gramophone records. This means that the output level after equalization is higher than it would otherwise be and smaller amplifiers are needed. The whole assembly can be very light in weight and may be cheap to produce. Crystals are widely used in inexpensive equipment in such a way as to obtain maximum output. Alternatively, at the loss of some output, a crystal assembly with a smoother response may be engineered. Rochelle salt is affected by temperature and humidity, so that in the past crystal microphones and pick-ups have not been used in the tropics. However, the crystal can now be effectively protected.

CUBICLE. See CONTROL.

CUE. Signal to start. This may take the form of a cue-light or a hand cue, or may be related to a pre-arranged point in a script. Headphones or, exceptionally a loudspeaker may also be used for cueing.

CUE MATERIAL. Introductory matter which is supplied with a recording for the scriptwriter to fashion into a cue for announcer or narrator to read.

CUE PROGRAMME. A feed for cueing purposes.

CUT (*Am.*). One of several separately recorded bands (q.v.) on a disc.

CYCLE. One complete excursion of an air particle when vibrating in a sound, or the corresponding signal in electrical or any other form.

CYCLES PER SECOND (c/s). Now written Hz. See FREQUENCY, HERZ.

D   DB. Decibel (q.v.).

DEAD ACOUSTIC. One in which a substantial loss is introduced at every reflection. For studio work this is the nearest approximation to an outdoor acoustic (in which little or no is sound reflected).

DEAD ROOM (anechoic chamber). Has very thick soft absorbers (3 feet or more) and is used for testing the frequency response of microphones and loudspeakers. Such an acoustic is unsuited to use as a studio because of its claustrophobic effect.

DEAD SIDE (of microphone). The angles within which the response of a microphone is low compared with the on-axis response. In figure-of-eight microphones this is taken to be about 50° – 130° from the axis; in cardioids, the entire rear face. In the dead region there may be rapid changes in response with only slight movement of position, and the frequency response is more erratic than on the live side(s). In a studio these effects may be masked by the pick-up of reflected sound on the live sides.

DEADROLL (Am.). See PREFADE.

DECAY CHARACTERISTIC (of studio). The curve which indicates how the sound intensity falls after a steady note is cut off. This will generally be slightly erratic. Plotted in decibels against time, decay should (roughly) follow a single straight line, and not be broken-backed.

DECIBEL (dB). A measure of relative intensity, power or voltage. Sound intensity is the power flowing through unit area and is calculated relative to a reference level of 2×10^{-5} N/m^2. The threshold of hearing at 1000 Hz is at about this level for many young people. However, the aural sensation of loudness is not directly proportional to intensity (I) but to the logarithm of the intensity. It is therefore convenient to measure differences in intensity in units which follow a logarithmic scale, i.e. decibels. Differences of intensity in decibels are calculated as $10 \log_{10} (I_2/I_1)$. Thus, a tenfold increase in intensity is equivalent to a rise of 10 decibels (i.e. 1 Bel). Doubling the intensity gives a rise of almost exactly 3 dB. In a circuit the power is proportional to the square of the voltage, so that (for a particular impedance) a power ratio may be expressed in decibels as $10 \log (V_2{}^2/V_1{}^2)$, or $20 \log (V_2/V_1)$. The decibel is also convenient in that it can be regarded (very roughly) as the minimum audible difference in sound level. A change in speech or music level of 2 dB or less will not ordinarily be noticeable to anyone who is not listening for it. Loudness levels are measured in *phons* (q.v.). For dBA, dBN, and PNdB, see NOISE.

DE-GAUSS or DE-FLUX. Demagnetize (e.g. a tape recording head, or scissors or blades used for cutting tape). Wipe or erase (tape) in bulk.

DIAPHRAGM. The part of a microphone upon which the pressure of a soundwave acts. In size it should be small enough not to suffer substantial high frequency phase cancellation for sound striking the diaphragm at an angle, and big enough to present a sufficiently large catchment area to the pressure of the sound wave. In microphones working on certain principles the diaphragm mass may be small. In such designs (e.g. the condenser microphones) there are minimal innertial effects and therefore a very good transient response.

DIFFERENCE TONE. A perceived frequency "heard" when two tones are played together, e.g. if 1000 Hz and 1100 Hz are played, 100 Hz may also be perceived.

DIFFUSION OF SOUND. The degree to which sound waves are broken up by uneven surfaces, and by the placing of absorbers more or less equally in all parts of the studio rather than allowing them to cluster in one particular part. A high degree of diffusion is desirable in a sound studio.

DIN (Deutsche Industrie Normen). German industrial standard. Most commonly met with as a film rating, but standards are also applied to tape equalization characteristics and items of equipment such as plugs and sockets.

DIRECT-CUT DISC. One which is made by cutting the groove, rather than by pressing in plastic material by means of a stamper. These are made of cellulose nitrate (which contains a castor oil plasticizer to soften it for easy cutting) but are often referred to as "acetates".

DISC. Record, either direct-cut or pressed. The latter are also called pressing, or, when commercially sold, gramophone records.

DISSONANCE. The sensation produced by two tones which are in the region of about a semitone or full tone apart. As the tones get closer together they beat together and finally become concordant; as they get further apart the dissonant sensation disappears, and for pure tones does not return with increasing separation. However, dissonances and concords also arise due to the presence of harmonics. The sensation of dissonance is sometimes described as unpleasant, but "astringent" would perhaps be a better antithesis to the sweetness of consonance.

DISTORTION. Unwanted changes of sound quality, in the frequency response, or by the generation of unwanted products. *Harmonic distortion* is most easily caused by flattening of peaks in the waveform. As the human voice and nearly all musical instruments possess a harmonic sound structure, this tends to mask the distortion unless it is very severe. 1% harmonic distortion is not usually noticeable. *Intermodulation distortion* is, however, more serious, as this includes sum and product frequencies which are not necessarily harmonically related to those already present.

DOLBY NOISE REDUCTION SYSTEM. This has been applied primarily in tape recording to provide an extra 10 dB signal-to-noise ratio to be used partly to reduce hiss, hum and rumble and also (by lowering recording levels a little) to produce less distortion and to lower the danger of print-through. In the professional system the signal is split by filters into four frequency bands as follows: 1. 80 Hz low-pass; 2. 80 Hz–3 kHz; 3. 3 kHz high-pass; 4. 9 kHz high-pass. Each band is separately compressed, so that very low level signals (40 dB down) are raised 10 dB, while signals from 0–20 dB down are virtually unaffected. The recovery time is 1-100 milliseconds depending on the signal dynamics. There are also limiters in each channel: these are simple peak choppers. An exactly matching network is used to reconstitute the original signal on playback. The principle of the system depends on the fact that noise which is similar in frequency to the louder components of the signal will be masked by it, while that which is widely separated in frequency from the louder components will be reduced in level: the improvement is therefore partly real and partly apparent. As the system produces a coded signal which must then be decoded it cannot be used to improve an already noisy signal. It is widely used in professional recording studios to improve the quality of tape recordings (this being particularly valuable for multi-track recordings) but it can in principle be used around any noisy component or link. The signal is, of course, unusable in its coded form: characteristically it sounds "bright, breathy, and larger than life". A simplified system for domestic tape recorders is used to reduce tape hiss.

DROP-OUT. Loss of signal due to a fault in tape coating.

DUBBING. Copying, to arrange for material to be available in convenient form, e.g. transferring music from disc to tape. Also, copying together and combining effects or music with pre-recorded speech. In film, the mixing of all sounds to a single final track (or the several stereo tracks).

DUSTING POWDER. A fine powder which will adhere to tacky points after a tape joint has been made, and ensure that the tape unwinds without pulling and does not drag as it passes over the heads and guide pillars.

DYNAMIC LOUDSPEAKER, MICROPHONE OR PICK-UP. See MOVING COIL.

DYNAMIC RANGE is the range of volumes in a programme. It may be measured as the range of peak values (i.e. the difference between the highest PPM readings at passages of maximum and minimum volume) or, alternatively, the range of average volume. It may refer either to the range of the original sound, or to what remains of this after compression.

DYNAMICS. The way in which volume of sound varies internally within a musical work (or in a speech or speech-and-music programme). It may refer to the variation of levels within the work as a whole, or from note to note, or in the envelope of a single note.

E   EARPHONE, EARPIECE. One side of a pair of headphones (q.v.), usually a telephone type (moving coil) receiver for placing close to the ear. Alternatively a transducer and ear-fitting of the hearing-aid type may be used.

ECHO. Discrete repetition of a sound, produced by a single reflected sound wave, or a combination of such waves whose return is co-incident in time and at least 0·05 second after the original sound. Colloquially, "echo" is used to mean the sum of such reflections, i.e. reverberation.

ECHO CHAMBER. A room for producing or simulating the natural reverberation of an enclosed space. Ideally, the walls (and floor and ceiling) should not be parallel. It has sound-reflecting walls and such treatment as is necessary to break up the sound, and produce a frequency response which is fairly flat. A reverberation time of about two seconds may be suitable.

ECHO PLATE. This is better known by its proper name, reverberation plate.

"EDGING IN ...", "TAKING THE EDGE OFF ...". A technique to ensure that, for example, programme inserts with heavy atmosphere or rough quality do not hit the listener with too much of a bang. Once the first word has been heard at a little below the volume of the preceding speech the level of the insert can be very rapidly adjusted to be the same as earlier speech (or higher, to compensate for any deficiency of intelligibility). Similar techniques can be used to smooth a wide range of transitions. Another example is the case where an outside source of unknown volume is inserted into a live programme. It is much better that the first word should be a shade too quiet rather than too loud, so the initial level is set at perhaps 4 dB below the expected setting, and adjustment made (as it can with practice) within the first half second. Edging in and out may also be used more formally in dramatic work, where it is the same thing as a slight fade.

EDGY. Subjective description of a sound quality which has colouration in the middle or high frequency response, in the form of sharp peaks. "Toppy" suggests a smoother, broader peak in the top response.

519

EDITING. The process of revising the contents of recorded material, usually by physically cutting and removing portions of unwanted material, or by transposing or inserting or cutting together material.

EDITING BLOCK. In its simplest form, a metal plate with a channel the width of magnetic tape running along the centre, with lapped edges to grip the tape, and a 45° cutting groove to guide a razor blade across it. More complex (but not necessarily more helpful) blocks are similar to film editing blocks (from which their design is derived).

EFFECTS. Simulated incidental sounds which would (*a*) occur in the location portrayed (usually *recorded effects*) or (*b*) as a result of action (usually *spot effects*—those created on the spot). A heightened realism is generally preferred to the random quality of naturally occurring sounds; but effects which are taken a stage further than this and are formalised into musical patterns are called *radiophonic effects* (*BBC*) or *musique concrète*. *Comedy* or "*cod*" *effects* are those in which some element, a characteristic natural quality of the sound, or a formal element such as its attack or rhythm, is exaggerated for comic effect. In this category are simple *musical effects*, in which a sound is mimicked by a musical instrument.

EIGENTONE (*German*). The fundamental resonance tone which belongs to any dimensional resonance of a room. Its wavelength is twice that dimension. It can form effectively only between parallel surfaces.

ELECTRONIC MUSIC. A work which is constructed from recorded electronic source materials by arranging them in a formal pattern (which may be beyond the range of conventional instruments or musicians).

ELECTROSTATIC LOUDSPEAKER. An application of electrostatic principles to the movement of air in bulk. This is done by means of a charged diaphragm (which may be several square feet in area) suspended between two perforated plates. As the alternating signal is applied to the outer plates, the diaphragm vibrates; and so long as the excursions are not too large the transfer of power is linear (the use of two plates rather than a single backplate helps considerably in this respect). The problem of handling sufficient power and transferring it to the air at low frequencies is not fully solved in any such speaker of convenient size (though baffles reduce the immediate losses). Electrostatic loudspeakers should not be placed parallel to walls, or standing waves will form behind them. With careful positioning, however, the quality of sound achieved is very clear. As with a number of other transducer principles this can also be applied in reverse, as a microphone.

ELECTROSTATIC (CONDENSER) MICROPHONE. In this, the signal is generated by the variations in capacitance between two charged plates, one of which is rigid and the other flexible, acting as a diaphragm in contact with the air. If the space between the plates is enclosed, the air vibrations can affect one side of the diaphragm only and the microphone is pressure operated (and substantially omnidirectional). If the backplate is perforated the diaphragm is operated by a modification of the pressure gradient principle. It can be arranged that the distance that sound has to travel through the back-plate (via an acoustic labyrinth) is the same as the effective path difference from back to front of the plate: in this case the pressure gradient drops substantially to zero for signals approaching from the rear of the microphone, and a good cardioid response is obtained. If two such cardioids are placed back to back, the characteristics depend on the sense of the potential between centre plate and the two diaphragms.

The doublet can become bi-directional, cardioid or omnidirectional, simply by varying the size and sense of the potential on one of the diaphragms. Condenser microphones have to be fitted with a head amplifier (a single stage is sufficient) in order to convert the signal into a form which is suitable for transmission by line. A further complication of design of both electrostatic microphone and loudspeaker is that a high polarising voltage has to be available.

ENCLOSURE. A loudspeaker cabinet. Its most important function is to improve bass response in some way. It may do this by acting as a box baffle and increasing the distance which rear-emitted sound has to travel before it can combine with and cancel forward sound, with which it is out-of-phase (and thus lowering the frequency at which this occurs). It may be a ported or bass-reflex cabinet, from which a low-frequency resonance is emitted more or less in phase with the forward output from the cone. In another design the box entirely encloses the rear of the loudspeaker; in this "infinite baffle" case the rear-emitted sound is supposed to be damped and absorbed entirely within the box. A variety of other enclosure designs is available.

ENVELOPE. The manner in which the intensity of a sound varies with time. Graphical representation of the envelope (or dynamics) of a single note may show separate distinctive features in its attack, internal dynamics and decay. The term may also refer to the envelope of frequency content, or of an imposed frequency characteristic, as in a formant.

E.P. (EXTENDED PLAY) RECORD. A 45 rpm 7-inch fine groove record which may carry more material than a coarse-groove 10 or 12-inch 78. (Pop singles contain the same amount as a 10-inch 78, whereas e.p. records contain perhaps double.) (See GROOVE.)

EQUALIZATION. The use of a filter network (a) to compensate for any distortion of the frequency response introduced by a transducer or other component (e.g. a landline), or (b) to compensate for a recording or transmission characteristic which has been employed to ensure an efficient, low-noise use of the medium (as in disc recording or FM transmission).

ERASURE. The removal of recorded signals from a tape so that it is ready to re-use. This is done automatically on most machines as the tape passes the erase head, which lies between the feed spool and the recording head. The erase head is similar in structure to the other heads except that the gap is much wider. The pure bias signal fed to it magnetizes the tape first in one direction and then the other until it approaches the end of the gap, when the magnitude of the oscillations dies down, and the tape is left demagnetized. With a *bulk eraser*, the tape as a whole is given a similar washing treatment, being physically removed from the region of the alternating current before switching off. (In very powerful bulk erasers it is not necessary to remove the tape to complete the wiping action.)

ESTABLISHING AN EFFECT. Allowing it sufficient time (and volume, which may be greater than that subsequently used) for it to register in the listener's mind. Introduced at the same time as speech, this might be puzzling or distracting.

ESTABLISHING A LOCATION (or any other "plot" point). May be helped by the above technique, but equally it may be a matter of supplying sufficient "pointers" in scripted speech. In visual media a wide shot is generally used before close shots. There must be continuity of background sound effects between a filmed wide shot and a closer sequence in the television studio.

521

EXPONENTIAL. An exponential curve is one which follows the progress of natural unrestrained growth or decay. If, in exponential growth, something has doubled in time t, it will double again in further time t, be eight times its original size at time 3t, and so on. Exponential growth will inevitably overhaul all other forms of regular growth (unless as happens in nature, some regulating factor intervenes). Exponential decay which halves in time t, halves again in a further time t, and so on. This must eventually become the slowest regular form of decay. A *logarithmic scale* (e.g. on a graph) is one in which the scale is gradually reduced according to the same principles. The spaces between 1, 2, 4, 16, 32 ... are all equal. This form of representation reduces an exponential growth to an apparently linear growth. However, the ear judges both changes of volume and changes of pitch by ratio; thus a logarithmic scale is is more relevant than any other to perceived sound. The doubling of sound frequency is equivalent to an interval of one octave. A tenfold increase in the intensity of a sound is equivalent to an interval of 1 Bel (10 decibels).

EXTINCTION FREQUENCY. Frequency at which there is complete loss of signal. It is a function of dimension of a component or of layout.

F   **FADE.** Gradual reduction or increase in the signal. This is accomplished by means of a *fader* (i.e. a potentiometer—or "pot" for short). A *constant impedance fader* is one which presents the same resistance to signals from all other sounds, whether it is open or closed. It therefore introduces a greater loss into the circuit when partly open than does a simple fader—and a pre-amplifier is needed. However, the operation of one fader does not affect the apparent output of any other source, as happens in the mixer composed of simple faders. A *logarithmic fader* is one in which the ratio of gain or loss between successive studs (or for equal degrees of turn) is constant. Such a fader may be marked off in a linear scale of decibels. All faders used in audio work should be logarithmic over their main working range.

FEEDBACK EFFECT. This is obtained when a tape is replayed on a separate head immediately following the recording head and the output mixed back into the input to the recorder. Each sound is repeated again and again in a series of echoes spaced at regular intervals. If the feedback is mixed in at a higher level than that of the original signal, a howl-round will occur; if at a lower level, it will gradually die away. If there is no gain or loss in the feedback circuit, the frequency characteristics of the system will soon swamp the original sound.

FIELD PATTERN (*Am.*). Polar response (q.v.).

FIGURE-OF-EIGHT. See BI-DIRECTIONAL MICROPHONE.

FILM INSERT. Filmed sequence played in to a television programme.

FILM LEADER. Section of film used at the head of picture or magnetic track showing a common "start mark" and footage marks at 16-frame intervals between "12" and "3" after which the leader is black until the first frame of the film. The same intervals (representing feet on 35-mm film) are used for all film footages. Television films with synchronous sound are usually run off "10".

FILTER. A network of resistors and condensers (inductances could also be used) which allows some frequencies to pass and attenuates others. The simplest form of filter (one resistor and one condenser) rolls off at 6 dB/octave above or below a certain frequency. There is an elbow in the curve at the turnover point: the nominal cut-off frequency (which may be calculated easily) is that at which the loss is 3 dB. For many audio purposes this gentle form of filter is quite as satisfactory as the sharper cut-off that can be obtained with a more complex network. The terms *bass-* and *top-cut filter* and *stop-* and *pass-band filter* are self-explanatory. An *octave* filter is one in which the signal is divided into octaves whose levels may be controlled separately. (Again, the simpler circuitry, providing smoother slopes at the boundaries may be just as satisfactory.)

FINE GROOVE. See GROOVE.

FLAT. (*a*) On a stylus, this is a surface of wear which appears on the two sides of the tip after some period of use. Seen under the microscope, the surface really is flat. These areas gradually become larger, the angles at their edges sharper, and the tip shape more like that of a chisel moving end-ways on in the groove. (*b*) On the rubber tyre of an idler wheel, a "flat" is an indentation which may form if the idler is left "parked" in contact with the drive spindle, or other surface. It causes a momentary flutter in recording or replay.

"FLICK" (*BBC*). Flash of about one second on cue light, as cue to start.

FLICKER. See WIGGLE.

FLUFF. (*a*) A small accidental error in operational work or in speech. (*b*) A quantity of fibrous dust gathered by a stylus moving in a record groove.

FLUTTER. Rapid fluctuation in pitch (having a warble-frequency of, say, 8 c/s or more) due to a fault in equipment such as an eccentric drive-spindle. The term is sometimes used to include all unwanted mechanical variation in pitch, i.e. including wow.

FOLDBACK. A feed of selected sources to a studio loudspeaker at suitable levels for the benefit of the performers. It may be used for outside sources, tape or disc; or from a microphone in a distant part of the studio to overcome problems of audibility or (in music) time lag. See ACOUSTIC REPRODUCTION OF EFFECTS, PUBLIC ADDRESS.

FOOTAGE. Length of film expressed in feet: either in terms of its own gauge or the equivalent for 35-mm film.

FOUR-CHANNEL STEREO. See STEREO.

FORMANT. A characteristic resonance region: a musical instrument may have one or more such regions, which are fixed by the geometry of the instrument. The human voice has resonance regions associated with the nose, mouth and throat cavities which are capable of more or less variation in size and shape, permitting the formation of the vowel sounds and voiced consonants. The range of the formant regions is not directly related to the pitch of the sound on which they act. If the fundamental is well below or low in the formant range, the quality of sound produced is rich, as harmonics are clustered close together within the formant; if the fundamental is relatively high, there are less harmonics in the range and the quality is thinner.

FREQUENCY. The number of complete excursions which an air particle makes in one second (formerly described as cycles per second, c/s or cps, now as Hertz, Hz). The only sound which consists of a single frequency is a pure (i.e. sinusoidal) tone. This corresponds to the motion of an air particle which swings backward and forward in smooth regular cycles (simple harmonic motion). The velocity of sound in air is about 1120 ft/sec (340 metres/sec), according to temperature. Frequency (f) and wavelength (λ) are related through the velocity of sound (c) by the formula $c = f\lambda$, so any frequency can be represented alternatively, but with a little less precision, as a wavelength. A complex sound can be analysed in terms of its frequency components, and plotting volume against frequency gives the *frequency spectrum*. A sound which is composed of individual frequencies (fundamental and harmonics or partials, or a combination of pure tones) has a *line spectrum*. Bands of noise have a *band spectrum*.

FREQUENCY CORRECTION. The change in the frequency characteristics of a signal which is required to restore it to its original form; but the term is sometimes ambiguously used to indicate the application of desired deliberate distortion of the response (often a peak in the upper middle frequencies). A *linear response* in any process is one in which the frequency distribution is the same at the beginning and end.

FREQUENCY MODULATION (FM). A method whereby the information in an audio signal is carried on the much higher frequency of a radio wave. The frequency of the audio signal is represented by the rate of change of carrier frequency; audio volume is represented by amplitude of frequency swing. The maximum deviation permitted for FM transmission is set at 75 kHz. Transmitter and receiver equipment is engineered to this standard, which is arbitrarily regarded as constituting 100% modulation. Overmodulation does not necessarily cause immediate severe distortion, as with AM, and limiters are not needed to avoid overloading transmitter valves. Noise, which appears as fluctuations of carrier amplitude, is strongly discriminated against, though it does produce phase-change effects which cannot be eradicated. Pre-emphasis of top (i.e. prior to transmission), with a corresponding de-emphasis at the receiver, helps to reduce the noise level still further. Unless two carriers on the same wavelength have almost the same strength, the stronger "captures" the area: there is only a small marginal territory between service areas.

FREQUENCY RESPONSE. Variation in gain or loss with frequency.

FUNDAMENTAL. The note associated with the simplest form of vibration of an instrument, usually the first and lowest member of a harmonic series.

"FX" (indication in script). Effects.

GAIN. Amplification: ratio of anode voltage to grid voltage in a valve. However gain may more conveniently be calculated in decibels.

GAIN CONTROL. A fader associated with an amplifier.

GAP WIDTH (*Am.*: Gap-height). The distance between poles of magnetic recording (or reproducing or erasing) head at the point of contact with the tape.

G.L.U. (*BBC*). Groove Locating Unit.

"GRAMS." (indication in script). Gramophones (a bank of record players).

GRID. A framework below the roof of a theatre or television studio from which lighting and microphones may be suspended. A television studio will normally have some of its microphone points in the grid.

GROOVE. Track on record which carries the audio signal in the form of a lateral displacement, or in the case of stereo a combination of two 45° displacements. *Coarse-groove.* The groove normally used for 78 rpm recordings. Approximate dimensions: width 6 mils, depth 2·5 mils; included angle 87°, with about 4 mils land between grooves, and a pitch of the order of 100 – 150 grooves per inch (*Am.*: lines per inch). *Fine groove, microgroove, minigroove.* The groove normally used for 33⅓ and 45 rpm recordings. Approximate dimensions: width, 2·5 mils; depth, 1 mil; included angle 85°; pitch 250 – 330 grooves per inch (varies according to modulation).

GROOVE RUN. See REPEATING GROOVE.

GROUP FADER. (*Am*: Sub-master fader). One to which the output of several individual faders is fed.

GUIDE TRACK. A second track on a twin track recorder which is replayed to artists to assist synchronization, but is not included in the programme.

GUN MICROPHONE Moving coil or electrostatic microphone fitted with an interference tube leading out along the axis. Sound enters the tube through a series of ports. That approaching off-axis reaches the diaphragm by a range of paths of different lengths, and mostly cancels out. The microphone is thus intensely directional except for sound of wavelengths substantially greater than the length of the gun.

H HALF-TRACK RECORDING. A recording occupying the upper 40% of tape (the tape moving left to right across the heads).

HARMONIC DISTORTION. See DISTORTION.

HARMONICS. A series of frequencies which are all multiples of a particular fundamental frequency. They are produced by the resonances of air in a tube (e.g. woodwind, brass, organ) or of a vibrating string, etc.

HEAD. Transducer which converts electrical energy into magnetic or mechanical energy, or vice versa. Thus we have a tape recording and reproducing heads and disc cutter and pick-up heads. The electromagnet used for erasing tape is also called a head.

HEADPHONES. A pair of electro-acoustic transducers (usually moving coil as in telephone receivers) held to the ears by a headband. Alternatively, devices similar to hearing aids may be used in a single ear (e.g. for listening to talk-back instructions during a programme). Earphones are most efficient and produce the best quality when the channel from transducer to ear is completely closed (as with moulded plastic ear-fittings). But as headphones are used solely for communication purposes, high quality is rarely of importance; and some degree of control of volume can be achieved with telephone receiver type phones by moving them a little off the ear. But with the ear-fitting, it is desirable to have a volume control in circuit.

HEARING. Essentially, the ear acts like an instrument for measuring frequencies and volumes of sound logarithmically (so that they appear linear in octave scales and decibels). The subjective aspect of frequency is pitch: judgment of pitch is not entirely independent of volume. The subjective aspect of sound intensity is loudness. Below about 1000 Hz the ear is progressively less sensitive to low volumes of sound; above 3000 Hz the hearing may also become rather less sensitive—but not necessarily following a smooth curve. The upper limit of hearing for young ears may be 16 kHz or higher, but with increasing age this is gradually reduced. No audio system needs to exceed the range 20–16,000 Hz (the signal may be cut off at this upper frequency). The acoustic part of the ear (the outer and middle ear) is relatively simple; essentially, it consists of a group of bones the purpose of which is to provide efficient coupling, i.e. matching of mechanical impedances, between a diaphragm which is in contact with the air and a second diaphragm which transmits sound to the liquid of the inner ear. The physiological construction of the inner ear is known, but the mechanism of aural perception is complex.

HERTZ (Hz). The measure of frequency (q.v.) formerly expressed as cycles per second. It is more convenient for mathematical analysis to consider frequency as an entity rather than as a derived function.

HIGH LEVEL MIXING. See MIXER.

HISS. High frequency noise.

HOWL-ROUND or HOWL-BACK. Closed circuit (wholly electrical, or partly acoustic) in which the amplification exceeds the losses in the circuit. In a typical case the loudspeaker is turned up high in a monitoring cubicle and the microphone in the studio faded up high for very quiet speech, and then if the acoustic treatment is inefficient at any frequency (or if both connecting doors are opened) a howl may build up at the frequency for which the gain over the whole circuit is greatest.

HUM. Low frequency noise, at the mains frequency and its harmonics.

HYPERCARDIOID. Cottage-loaf-shaped polar response of microphone, intermediate between figure-of-eight and true cardioid.

I   IDLER. On a record player, this is a wheel which transmits rotation from the drive spindle to the rim of a turntable, but has no effect on turntable speed. When switched off it usually disengages (this prevents the formation of flats in the rubber). On a tape deck, the idler presses the tape against the capstan when the drive is switched on (it does not transmit rotation in this case).

IMPEDANCE. A combination of d.c. resistance, inductance and capacitance, which act as resistances in a.c. circuits. An inductive impedance increases with frequency; a capacitative impedance decreases with frequency. Either type introduces change of phase. See MATCHING.

INDIRECT SOUND (in microphone balance). Sound which is reflected one or more times before reaching the microphone.

INDUCTANCE. The resistance of (in particular) a coil of wire to rapidly fluctuating a.c. currents. The field built up by the current resists any change in the rate of flow of the current; and this resistance increases with frequency.

INSERT TAPE. A spool containing one or more pre-recorded programme segments ready for insertion into a production.

INTENSITY OF SOUND. The sound energy crossing a square metre. Relative sound intensities, energies, or pressures may all conveniently be measured in decibels. See DECIBEL, WAVE.

INTERMODULATION DISTORTION. See DISTORTION.

IONOPHONE (*Am.*: Ionic Loudspeaker). A type of loudspeaker which has no moving parts. At the neck of an exponential horn, an r.f. coil ionises the air. Modulation of this with an audio signal causes the face of the ionised volume to vibrate. The sound is then transmitted to the air by means of the acoustic horn, the size (and any resonances) of which produces the only limitation on frequency response and quality of sound.

IPS. Inches per second. See TAPE SPEED.

J JOINT. Point on a tape at which two physically separate butt ends have been joined together (see editing).

JOINTING TAPE. A specially prepared, non-oozy adhesive tape, slightly narrower than magnetic tape, which can be used to back two pieces of tape which have been butted together.

JUMP CUT. A cut in replaying a disc, made by lifting the stylus and replacing it in a later groove (at which the cue has been checked in advance). There is a momentary loss of atmosphere while the replay is faded out. In film, the term is used to describe a cut between two separate parts of the same scene in the same framing: continuity of action may be lost.

K KC/S. Kilocycles per second. Now written kHz. See also FREQUENCY, HERZ.

L LANDLINE. See LINE.

LAZY ARM. Simple form of boom consisting of an upright and a balanced cross-member from which a microphone may be slung.

LEADER. White uncoated tape which may be cut on to the start of a spool of recorded ¼-inch tape, and on which may be written brief details of the contents of the sound recording. See also FILM LEADER.

LEVEL. Volume of electrical signal as picked up by the microphone(s) and passed through pre-amplifiers and mixer faders. At the BBC this volume is calculated in decibels relative to a *reference level* of 1 milliwatt in 600 ohms (also called *zero level*). Zero level corresponds to 40% modulation at the transmitter: 100% modulation is 8 dB (approx.) above this. To *take level* is to make a test for suitable gain settings, in order to control the signal to a suitable volume for feeding to transmitter or recorder. This test may sometimes be combined with the balance test. *Voice level* is the acoustic volume produced by a voice in the studio.

LIMITER. An automatic control to reduce volume when over-modulation occurs, e.g., to prevent dangerously heavy peaks of power reaching a transmitter which might be damaged by it. The most usual form of operation uses feedback: the signal is monitored by the limiter and any wave which exceeds a certain volume causes a corresponding increase in feedback, which reduces the signal. After a while, the operation of a recovery device allows the gain to return to normal. Limiters are necessary in AM transmitters, and in the input to disc recorders in situations where overmodulation may occur by accident. They are also used in pop music balance.

LINE. A send and return path for an electric signal. In its simplest form a line consists of a pair of wires. A *landline* is a line (with equalizing amplifiers at regular intervals) for carrying programme across country. (c.f. radio link, broadcast).

LINE-UP. Arrange that the programme signal passes through all components at the most suitable level. In a broadcasting chain this is normally at or about zero level (see under Level).

LINE-UP TONE. Pure tone, usually at 1000 Hz, which is fed through all stages of a chain. It starts at zero level, and should read the same on a meter at any stage. If the level of the tone drops (or jumps) between successive points in the chain, this may be due to a fault in the line or in other equipment.

LIP-RIBBON MICROPHONE. A noise cancelling microphone which is placed close to the mouth, the exact distance being determined by a guard which rests against the upper lip. The microphone's directional properties discriminate in favour of the voice; close working also discriminates against unwanted sound, and bass is reduced still further by the compensation which is necessary when working so close to a directional microphone.

LIVE ANGLE. Angle within which reasonable sensitivity is obtained. (See CARDIOID and BI-DIRECTIONAL MICROPHONES.)

LIVE SIDE (of microphone). The face which must be presented towards a sound source for greatest sensitivity.

LIVE TRANSMISSION. Broadcast, none (or little) of which has been pre-recorded.

LOGARITHMIC FADER. See FADER.

LOGARITHMIC SCALE. See EXPONENTIAL.

LOOP. Continuous band of tape made by joining the ends of a length of tape together. A tape loop may be used (*a*) to provide a repeated sound structure or rhythm (in radiophonics), (*b*) for an "atmosphere" track where this is regular in quality, (*c*) in tape delay techniques. Magnetic film loops are used for continuous "atmosphere" in film dubbing.

LOUDNESS. Subjective aspect of sound intensity. See METER, DECIBEL.

LOW LEVEL MIXING. See MIXER.

L.P. (LONG PLAYING) RECORD. 12 - or 10-inch fine groove record which plays at 33⅓ rpm. The amount recorded on each side depends on the groove spacing, which in turn depends on the amount of heavy modulation. For a full 12-inch record, thirty minutes per side is about the upper limit.

M "M" SIGNAL. The combined A + B stereo signal. Corresponds to the signal from a single "main" microphone. See "S" SIGNAL.

MAIN GAIN CONTROL (*Am.*: Grand Master or Over-all Master. Control) Final fader to which the combined outputs of all group (*Am.*: sub-master) or individual faders are fed.

528

MARKING UP. Detailed individual marking of scripts (usually at an early stage in rehearsal) with special cues, fader settings for microphones, grams. and tape, echo, etc.; details of which microphone is to be used for what, and so on. Records may be marked with a wax pencil (just outside the label) to indicate the angle at which required material starts, and also, possibly, with the sequence number of the record; the script is also marked with sequence number and with notes for quick groove location. Tape may be marked with a wax pencil to indicate point at which required recording starts, and so on.

MASTER. This is the second stage in the processing of a record. The direct-cut original is sputtered with a finely divided conductor (e.g. gold) and then a copper electroplate is grown. This is stripped away from the original and nickel plated. The master has ridges instead of grooves. In half processing (when only a small run is required) the master is also used as a stamper; otherwise, for full processing, a mother is grown, and then a stamper.

MATCHING. Arranging that the impedance presented by a load is equal to the internal impedance of the generator. Unless this is done there will be a loss of power, and the greater the mis-match the greater the loss. Often, when there is adequate gain in hand, some degree of mis-match is not critical. However, in the case of microphones and similar generators, the signal is low to start with and any loss will result in a poorer signal to noise ratio. Matching is done by means of a small transformer. Where a microphone impedance is strongly capacitative (e.g. in an electrostatic microphone) its output voltage is fed to the grid of a valve and controls the current in an external circuit.

MECHANICAL COPYRIGHT. See COPYRIGHT.

METER. Device for measuring voltage, current etc. In audio, several types of meter are used for measuring programme volume. The *VU (Volume unit) meter* is used on much American equipment. Over its main working range it is linear in "percentage modulation". It is not, therefore, linear in decibels, and this means that for all but a very narrow range of adjustments of level the needle is either showing small deflections, or flickering over the entire scale. The VU meter is not very satisfactory for high quality work where a comparison or check on levels (which are not always close to the nominal 100% modulation) is required. In Britain the *Peak programme meter* (PPM) is used by the BBC. It is linear in decibels over the main working range.

MICROCIRCUIT. See SOLID STATE DEVICE.

MICRON (μ). A thousandth of a millimetre; roughly a twenty-fifth of a mil.

MICROPHONE. Electro-acoustic transducer. A microphone converts the power in a sound wave into electrical energy, responding to changes in either the air pressure or the pressure gradient (q.v.). Principal response patterns are omnidirectional, figure-of-eight, cardioid; principal types, moving coil (dynamic), electrostatic (condenser), ribbon, crystal, and carbon (q.v.). *Microphone sensitivity* is measured in dB relative to 1 volt/N/M². See NEWTONS PER SQUARE METRE.

MICROPHONE BALANCE. See BALANCE.

MICROPHONE CHANNEL. The pre-amplifier, equalization circuit, fader, etc., in the mixer which are available for each microphone. It may also include individual facilities for "pre-hear", and feeds for echo, fold-back, and public address.

529

MID-LIFT. Deliberate introduction of a peak in the frequency response in the upper-middle frequency range (somewhere between 2 – 8 kHz say). A group of mid-lift controls may be calibrated according to the frequency of the peak (e.g. nominal values, 2, 3, 5, 8 kHz) and degree of lift (e.g. 0 – 10 in 2 dB steps). A mixer used for recording "pops" may have two controls for mid-lift (plus bass, treble and echo-send controls) for each microphone channel.

MIL. A thousandth of an inch.

MIX. Combine electrically the signals from microphones, tape and gramophone reproducers, and other sources.

MIXER. Apparatus for doing this. In *low level mixing* each source is fed directly to an associated fader without pre-amplification. Low level mixers are relatively inexpensive, but are now rarely used professionally except for pre-mixing the output from a number of audience microphones. *High level mixing* with a pre-amplifier preceding each source fader gives a better signal to noise ratio at the input to the fader, and permits the use of constant impedance faders. See also FADE.

MODULATION. Superimposition (of sound wave) on a carrier, which may be a high frequency signal (e.g. by amplitude or frequency modulation, q.v.) or (on a record) a smooth spiral groove which, when it carries no recorded signal is described as *unmodulated*. 100% *modulation* is the maximum permissible amplitude for any recording or transmission system.

MONAURAL SOUND. Alternative term for monophonic sound suggested by the analogy that listening with one microphone is like listening with one ear— which is not strictly accurate. The term is confusing and is tending to be dropped—except for the case of a single-ear hearing aid, which genuinely is a monaural sound system.

MONITORING. (*a*) Checking sound quality, operational techniques, programme content, etc., by listening to the programme as it leaves the studio (or at subsequent points in the chain, or by a separate feed, or by checking from a radio receiver). A *monitoring loudspeaker* in the studio is usually as good as the best that listeners might be using (but it must be remembered that adverse listening conditions might radically alter the listeners appreciation of sound quality— also he may be listening at a lower level from that at which the monitoring loudspeaker is set.) (*b*) Listening to other services for information. (The BBC monitoring service listens round the clock for news to services all over the world, and the BBC news is itself monitored widely.)

MONO (Monophonic Sound). Sound heard from a single channel. This is defined by the form of the recording or transmission, and not by the number of speakers. (A number of microphones may be used and their outputs mixed; several loudspeakers may be used, and their frequency content varied, but this is still mono unless there is more than one channel of transmission. Multiplex radio transmissions and the single groove of a stereo disc each contain more than one channel.) In mono the only spatial movement that can be simulated is forwards and backwards. There is no sideways spread; in particular there is no spatial spread of reverberation, or of ambient noise (see "COCKTAIL PARTY EFFECT"). The balance of sound in mono is therefore not natural but worked out in terms of a special convention. Working within, and recognizing the limitations of this convention, considerable artistry is possible. NB. In television, "mono" is used in a different sense, to mean monochromatic, i.e. black and white, as distinct from colour pictures.

MOOD MUSIC. Undistinctive background music which does not distract the listeners' attention from foreground interest, but which is intended to guide the attitude of mind which the listener directs towards this.

MOVING COIL MICROPHONE, LOUDSPEAKER OR PICK-UP. (*Am.*: Dynamic). These all use a small coil which moves in the field of a permanent magnet. In the microphone or pick-up this movement generates a current in the coil; in the loudspeaker the current causes movement which is transmitted to a cone (q.v.) which drives the air.

MULTIPLEX. Radio transmission carrying A−B stereo information on a sub-carrier above the A+B signal.

MUSIC LINE. Broad-band circuit for carrying programme (including speech), as distinct from a telephone line which may occupy only a narrow band.

MUSIQUE CONCRÈTE (*French*). A work in musical form constructed from natural sounds which are recorded and then treated in various ways. The source material may include sounds from musical instruments.

MUTE FILM. Scenes shot without sound.

N   **NARTB CHARACTERISTIC.** In tape recording, the pre-emphasis and subsequent equalization standards used in America and Japan.

NETWORK OPERATION. A broadcasting system involving many local stations and transmitters which may join together or separate at will.

NEWTONS PER SQUARE METRE (N/m^2). The unit of sound pressure. This replaces a unit formerly used, dynes per square centimetre: $1 N/m^2 = 10$ dynes/cm^2. A common reference level, $2 \times 10^{-5} N/m^2$ approximates to the threshold of hearing at 1 kHz. Microphone sensitivity is calculated in dB relative to 1 volt/N/m^2: this gives values which are 20 dB higher than those using the older reference level, 1 volt/dyne/cm^2. Characteristically, microphones have a sensitivity of the order of −50 dB relative to 1 volt/N/m^2 or −70 dB relative to 1 volt/dyne/cm^2.

NOISE. This is generally defined as unwanted sound. It includes such things as unwanted acoustic background sounds, unwanted electrical hiss (e.g. caused by the random flow of electrons in a valve, or the random placing and finite size of iron oxide particles in tape coating), or rumble, hum or unwanted electro-magnetic noise (background noise picked up on a radio receiver). In all electronic components and recording or transmission media the signal must compete with some degree of background noise, and it is vital in radio and recording work to preserve an adequate signal-to-noise ratio at every stage. In general, noise consists of all frequencies or a band of frequencies rather than particular frequencies (hum is an exception to this). *White noise* contains all frequencies in equal proportion. *Coloured noise* is a band of noise which exhibits some colouration. (The term is used by analogy with coloured light.) In radiophonics and electronic music such forms of noise are sometimes used deliberately. Acoustic noise levels are often measured in dBA (or SLA). 1 dBA = 40 dB relative to $2 \times 10^{-5} N/m^2$ at 1 kHz, and at other frequencies is weighted (electrically) to be of equal loudness. PNdB (perceived noise decibels) use a weighting function which can be used to place aircraft and other noises in order of noisiness. The analysis of sounds in PNdB can be complex; a simpler analysis uses an electrical network which gives adequate results in units which are designated dBN.

O   **OBSTACLE EFFECT.** Obstacles tend to reflect or absorb only those sounds which have a shorter wavelength than their own dimensions; at greater wavelengths the object appears to be transparent to the sound. For example, a screen which is 27 inches wide is substantially transparent to frequencies below 500 Hz, but will absorb or reflect higher frequencies. 15 kHz is equivalent to a wavelength of about 0·9 in.; a microphone containing parts of about this size will be subject to effects which begin to operate when this frequency is approached.

OFF-MICROPHONE. On the dead (i.e. insensitive) side of the microphone, or at much more than the normal working distance on the live side.

OMNIDIRECTIONAL MICROPHONE. One which is equally sensitive in all directions. In practice, there is a tendency for this to break down at high frequencies, with the top response progressively reduced for sounds which are further away from the front axis. In the apple-and-biscuit (*Am.*: eight-ball) microphone this effect is compensated for in the construction of the casing and partially reflecting screen. Modern microphones which have sufficiently small capsules do not suffer from the fault to a marked extent.

OPEN-AIR ACOUSTIC. See DEAD ACOUSTIC.

OPTICAL SOUND. A film recording system which is replayed by scanning a track of variable width (or, sometimes, density) by means of a lamp, slit, and photocell. Magnetic systems are to be preferred for all work up to and including the final sound mix. For finished film, optical sound retains certain advantages, such as convenience of handling (particularly for commercials) and economy (where cost of stock is important) which may be set against the higher quality promised by magnetic "stripe" sound. See COMOPT.

OSCILLATOR. A device which produces an alternating signal, usually of a particular frequency (or harmonic series). An audio oscillator produces a pure sine tone at any frequency in the audio range. *Square wave* and *sawtooth generators* produce waveforms of roughly those shapes (these correspond to harmonic series). Other oscillators (e.g. tape bias and r.f. oscillators) provide signals at higher frequencies.

OUTPUT (from a studio). This should consist of the completed programme, fully controlled and ready for feeding into the transmitter (or recorder). The output which may be monitored during a recording is the product of a replay head. This cannot be done on tape recorders that have only a single record/replay head or when cutting acetates for processing (in these cases the input to the head is monitored).

OUTSIDE SOURCE. A source of programme material which originates outside the studio to which it is fed, and appears on an individual fader on the mixer panel just as any local source does (except that no pre-amplifier is needed as it is fed in at about zero level).

OVERLAP CHANGEOVER. A type of changeover from one recording to the next in sequence which may be used when the two have half a minute or so of recording in common. The overlap is used to adjust synchronization before crossfading from one to the other; before changing over, the first recording is heard on the loudspeaker, and the second prefaded on headphones, or on a loudspeaker of different quality.

OVER-MODULATION. Exceeding the maximum permissible amplitude for recording or transmission. Distortion may be expected, and in certain cases damage to equipment or to the recording itself (though where this may occur limiters are used).

OVERTONE. A partial in a complex tone, so called because such tones are normally higher than the fundamental.

P PANNING or STEERING. Splitting the output from a monophonic microphone between stereo A and B channels. *Panpot*. Potentiometer (fader) to do this.

PARABOLIC REFLECTOR. A light rigid structure (of aluminium or other material) which reflects sound to a focus at which a microphone is placed. The assembly is very strongly directional at frequencies with wavelengths greater than the aperture of the reflector. It differs from gun microphone systems in that it is not degraded by interference from reflecting surfaces.

PARTIAL. One of a group of frequencies, not necessarily harmonically related to the fundamental, which appear in a complex tone. (Bells, xylophone blocks, and many other percussion instruments produce partials which are not harmonically related.)

PCM. Pulse code modulation (q.v.).

PEAK. A period of high volume.

PEAK PROGRAMME METER (PPM). A device used in Britain for measuring the peak values of programme volume. See METER.

PEAK UP. Lift the volume either of an individual component of a mix, or of the entire programme.

PERFECT PITCH. The ability to judge frequency absolutely, i.e. without comparing it with another frequency, and to do so instantaneously.

PERMANENT JOINT. Cemented joint in slightly overlapped tape. It is permanent only in the sense that it cannot be undone as a temporary joint can. Less obvious in a tape than the temporary joint.

PERSPECTIVE. Varying the levels and the proportions of direct and indirect sound in order to suggest variety of distance. This can be done by the actor moving on and off microphone. In dead acoustics the ratio of direct to indirect sound cannot be varied, as indirect sound must be kept to a minimum. In this case it may help if an actor "throws" his voice, simulating raising it to talk or shout from a distance. In television, sound and picture perspectives are often matched by the adjustment of boom microphone distance, or by placing a fixed microphone sufficiently close to the camera that as a performer moves towards the camera the sound also appears closer.

PHANTOM CIRCUIT. An electrical circuit which economizes on wires by using a go-and-return pair for one side of its own path. If another pair or the screening is used for the return path no additional wires are used.

PHASE. This is the stage that a particle in vibration has reached in its cycle. Particles are *in phase* when they are at the same stage in the cycle at the same time.

PHASE-SHIFT is the displacement of a waveform in time. If a pure sine tone waveform is displaced by one complete wavelength this is described as a phase-shift of 360°. If it is displaced by half a wavelength (i.e. through 180°) it has peaks where there were troughs and vice versa. If two equal signals 180° out of phase are added together, they will cancel completely; if they are at any other angle (except when in phase) partial cancellation will occur. Some electronic components introduce phase-shift into a signal, and the shift will be of the same angle for all frequencies. This means that the displacement of individual component frequencies in the wave will be different (depending on their wavelength) and distortion of the waveform will result. This will not normally be of importance, because the ear cannot detect changes in phase relationship between components of a steady note. Interference between two complex signals, which are similar in content but different in phase, results in a very serious form of distortion: the loss of all frequencies for which the two signals are 180° out of phase. Electrical cancellation may occur when two records are played slightly out of synchronization, or when a signal has to be sent by two different paths (this can make the transmission of stereo signals by landline difficult, when lines with very broad transmission characteristics are not available). It occurs in radio reception when a sky wave interferes with a direct signal, etc. In a studio, cancellation may occur when one of a pair of bidirectional microphones has its back to a sound source. Care must always be taken when there is any possibility of pick-up on two such microphones at the same time. A check can be made by asking someone to speak at an equal distance from both, fading both up to equal volume, and mixing. If the sound appears thin and spiky, or direct sound is completely lost, one of the microphones should be reversed. (Studio reverberation and random sound generally are not affected by cancellation.) Pairs of loudspeakers may also be out of phase. If a monophonic signal is fed to an in-phase pair the sound will appear to come from between and behind them: if they are out of phase the sound will appear to be thrown forwards to a point between speakers and listener. (Correct phasing of speakers is, of course, vital to true stereo reproduction.)

PHON. A unit of loudness. Phons equal decibels at 1000 Hz, and at other frequencies are related to this scale by contours of equal loudness.

PICK-UP. The electromechanical transducer of a gramophone. The movement of a stylus in the record groove gives rise to an electrical signal. A very large variety of principles have been applied to this: some of the most important include crystal, moving coil and variable reluctance (q.v.). The pick-up head may consist of a turnover cartridge having styli for coarse and fine groove records on the two sides.

PILOT TONE. See SYNC. PULSE.

PILOT TONE SYSTEM. Stereo broadcasting system in which the A−B signal is transmitted on a subcarrier, and a pilot tone is also transmitted to control phasing of the two signals.

PITCH. The subjective aspect of frequency (in combination with intensity), which determines its position in the musical scale. The pitch of a group of harmonics is judged as being that of the fundamental (even if this is not present in the series). The dependance of pitch on intensity is greatest at low frequencies. Increase in loudness may depress the pitch of a pure tone 10% or more at very low frequencies, although where the tone is a member of a harmonic series the change is less apparent. Pitch does not depend on intensity at frequencies between 1 − 5 kHz, and at higher frequencies increase in loudness produces a slight increase in pitch.

PLAYING WEIGHT. This is the effective weight which bears down on the stylus tip in the groove. It should be sufficient to maintain the stylus in contact with the groove, but not greater. Counterbalancing of the arm should ensure that the optimum weight for the type of pick-up is adopted. Styli with very high compliance can track at very low playing weights. Tracking at less than 0.5 gm. is possible for mono but little advantage has been found in going below 1 gm.; 0·5 gm. is suitable for stereo.

POLAR CHARACTERISTIC, POLAR DIAGRAM. (*Am.*: Field Pattern). The response of a microphone, loudspeaker, etc., showing sensitivity (or volume of sound) in relation to direction. Separate curves are shown for different frequencies, and separate diagrams are necessary for different planes. Such diagrams can also be used to indicate the qualities of reflecting screens or the radiation pattern of transmitter aerials, etc.

"POPPING". Causing breakup of the signal from a microphone by blowing the diaphragm right out of the gap (for example, in a ribbon microphone). This may occur when explosive consonants such as "p" and "b" are directed straight at the diaphragm at close range.

POT (POT'METER, POTENTIOMETER). Fader (q.v.).

POT-CUT. Editing a short segment of unwanted material out of a programme without stopping the replay, by quickly fading out and fading in again. Results in a momentary loss of atmosphere; tape editing is preferable if time is available.

POWER (of sound source). This is the total energy given out by a source (as distinct from intensity, which is energy crossing unit area). Power is the rate of doing work; and in an electrical circuit equals voltage times current.

PPM. Peak Programme Meter. See METER.

PRACTICAL. A "prop" in film or television which works partly or completely in its normal way, e.g. a telephone which rings, or an office intercom which is used normally.

PRE-AMPLIFIER. Amplifier in circuit between a source and the source fader. See MIXER.

PRE- AND POST-ECHO. An "echo" of a particular programme signal which, on a disc, may appear the groove before or after that which carries the signal. This is due to the gradual relaxation of molecular tensions which occurs after the record has been pressed, and causes plastic deformation of the groove walls. On tape it occurs one turn of tape before or after the normal signal, and is caused by printing (q.v.).

PREFADE, DEADROLL. Playing closing music from a predetermined time in order to fit exactly the remaining programme time, fading up at an appropriate point during the closing words.

PRE-HEAR. A facility for listening to a source either on headphones or on a loudspeaker of a quality which is characteristically different from the main monitoring loudspeaker. The source can thereby be checked before fading it up and mixing it in to the programme.

PRE-RECORDING. Recording made prior to the main recording or transmission, and replayed into it.

PRESENCE. A quality described as the bringing forward of a voice or instrument (or the entire composite sound) in such a way as to give the impression that it is actually in the room with the listener. This is achieved by boosting part of the 2 – 8 kHz frequency range. In fact, emphasis of a single component (or several, at different frequencies) in this band gives greater clarity and separation, although at the expense of roundness of tone. Presence applied to the entire sound (e.g. by a distorted loudspeaker response) achieves stridency but little else.

PRESSING. A commercial gramophone record or other disc which is made by stamping plastic material, usually polyvinyl chloride (PVC) in association with other components which vary from manufacturer to manufacturer. PVC-based pressings have low surface noise (provided they have not been played with a heavy pick-up) and are not breakable. They are easily damaged by scratching or heat. Formerly, shellac was used for pressing records, and having much greater elasticity was suitable for record materials when only very heavy (low compliance) pick-up heads were available. The shellac was combined with a large proportion of inexpensive filler (e.g. slate dust) which made them hard, served to grind the stylus to the shape of the groove, and also contributed the characteristic surface noise of 78s.

PRESSURE GRADIENT MICROPHONE. One with a diaphragm which is open to the air on both front and back, and which therefore responds to the difference in pressure at successive points on the sound wave (separated by the path difference from front to back). The microphone is "dead" to sound approaching from directions such that the wavefront reaches front and back of the diaphragm at the same time. (See FIGURE-OF-EIGHT and CARDIOID MICROPHONE.) A pressure gradient microphone measures the rate of change of sound pressure, i.e. air particle velocity. This is not quite the same thing as measuring intensity (as the ear does) but differs from it essentially only in phase, and since the ear is not sensitive to differences in phase, this does not matter. Pressure gradient operation begins to degenerate to pressure operation for wavelengths approaching the dimensions of the microphone. This may help to maintain the response of the microphone at frequencies such that cancellation would occur due to the wave-length being equal to the effective path difference from front to back of the diaphragm.

PRESSURE MICROPHONE. One with a diaphragm which is open to the pressure of the sound-wave on one side and enclosed on the other. If the diaphragm and casing is sufficiently small, the microphone is omnidirectional (q.v.).

PRESSURE PADS. Felt pads on spring loaded arms which press tape against the heads. On professional recorders these are not used, the feed spool back-tension (and curved path of the tape over the heads) being adequate to ensure satisfactory contact.

PRINTING. The re-recording of a signal from one layer to another in a spool of tape. The recorded signal produces a field which magnetizes tape which is separated by only the thickness of the backing. (Other factors which affect printing are temperature, time and physical shock.)

PRODUCER. The man with overall responsibility for a production. In radio he will also direct in the studio and in editing. In television and film, direction is likely to be a separate function.

PROGRAMME. (*a*) Self-contained and complete item. (*b*) The electrical signal corresponding to programme material, as it is fed through electronic equipment.

PUBLIC ADDRESS SYSTEM. A loudspeaker system installed for the benefit of a studio audience. The output of selected microphones is fed at suitable levels to directional loudspeakers.

PULSE CODE MODULATION. A highly efficient means of using available band-width. The audio signal is sampled intermittently and may be interspersed between the pulses for other audio signals or other information. The highest audio frequency available is half the sampling frequency. In principle the system could be used for combining sound with a video signal, but a single pulse at the line frequency gives a band-width of only 7·8 kHz, and also would result in an extended period of dual standards. However, if television is eventually changed to a new, sufficiently high line-standard, PCM sound should be introduced at the same time, as it conserves band-width.

PVC (Polyvinyl Chloride). Plastic commonly used in disc pressings and some tape backings and electrical insulators.

Q   **QUALITY (of sound reproduction).** The faithfulness with which the original sound (or a monophonic representation of this) is reproduced in terms of frequency response and lack of distortion.

QUARTER-TRACK RECORDING. One which occupies about 15% of the full width of the tape. The tape runs from left to right and the top track is recorded first, and then the third. To record the other two tracks the tape is turned upside down and once again fed left to right. For stereo, the first and third tracks are recorded at the same time, using a stacked head (one with both gaps in line). Quarter-track recording has a signal-to-noise ratio which is poorer than that of half or full track recording in proportion to the relative widths. 4-Channel stereo uses all four tracks recorded in the same direction.

R   **RADIO LINK.** A radio transmission focused into a narrow beam and directed towards an equally directional receiver placed in line of sight. Used in place of a landline.

RADIO MICROPHONE. Microphone and small transmitter sending a signal which can be picked up at a distance of up to perhaps several hundred yards (provided that the two are not screened from each other).

RADIO TRANSMISSION. A system for distributing audio information by modulating it on to a high frequency carrier at a particular frequency which is then amplified to a high power and broadcast towards the receivers by means of an aerial. Transmitter and receiver aerials act in a similar way to the two windings of a transformer; they are coupled together by the field between them. (The field at the receiver is, of course, very tiny: it diminishes not only as the square of the distance, but also by the action of other "receivers" along the path. In passing over granite, for example, a great deal of a medium-wave signal is mopped up. For VHF, which does not penetrate so deep into the ground, the nature of the terrain does not matter—but high ground will cast a "shadow".) This highly inefficient transformer action is improved if the receiving aerial is so constructed as to resonate at the desired frequencies of reception, and it will discriminate against other signals if it is made directional. It is important that the aerials should be parallel (both vertical or both horizontal). Systems of carrier modulation in use are amplitude modulation and frequency modulation (q.v.).

RADIOPHONIC SOUND. Sound effects which are formally arranged, as in *musique concrète* or electronic music, but which are not usually intended to be heard independently of other radio or television material.

RECORDED EFFECTS. See EFFECTS.

RECORDER. Tape (or disc) recording machine.

RECORDING. An inscription of an audio signal in permanent form, usually on magnetic tape or on disc (optical systems and magnetic wire have both largely been superseded by magnetic tape). The term *"record"* implies "commercial gramophone record", as distinct from any other pressing or other form of recording. Discs were formerly cut at 78 rpm and now at 45 and 33⅓ rpm. These speeds can be shown to be the most satisfactory for the groove and disc sizes with which they are commonly associated. See GROOVE.

RECORDING ENGINEER (*BBC*). Professional engineer whose job includes the technical recording of sound and the editing of tape, but not microphone balance and control.

RECORDING SESSION. Time booked in a recording studio.

RECORDIST. Member of a film crew who is responsible for sound. Also the name adopted by amateur sound recording enthusiasts.

REFERENCE LEVEL. See LEVEL.

REHEARSAL. Time spent in preparing a programme for a recording or transmission: working through the script or working up unscripted ideas.

REINFORCEMENT (in sound balance). The strengthening of direct sound reaching a microphone by the addition of indirect sound. This adds body without adding appreciably to volume, and makes a sound appear louder for a given meter reading. See RESONANCE, REVERBERATION.

RELATIVE PITCH. The ability to judge one pitch by reference to another. Total lack of this ability is "tone deafness".

REPEATING GROOVE. An occasion when a stylus jumps back a groove. This may be due to a fault in the groove wall, grit in the groove, an excessive resonance in the pick-up arm, or a sticky pivot. A *groove run* is a run on to a following groove, due to a scratch across the grooves or similar cause.

REPRODUCER. Tape or disc player.

RESISTANCE. The ratio of e.m.f. (electromotive force) to current produced in a circuit; the ratio of voltage drop to current flowing in a circuit element.

RESONANCE. A natural periodicity; the reinforcement associated with this. The frequencies (including harmonics) which are produced in musical instruments (e.g. vibrating strings or columns of air) are determined by resonances.

RESPONSE. Sensitivity of microphone, etc. See FREQUENCY RESPONSE POLAR CHARACTERISTIC.

RETAKE. Re-recording of part of a programme, to be cut in subsequently.

REVERBERATION. The sum of many reflections of sound in an enclosed space. This modifies the quality of a sound and gives it an apparent prolongation after the source stops radiating.

REVERBERATION TIME. Defined as the time taken for sound to die away to a millionth of its original intensity (i.e. through 60 dB).

REVERBERATION PLATE. A metal plate, held under stress, which is fitted with two transducers, one to introduce "sound" vibrations, and the other to detect them at another point on the plate. By this means the decay of sound in an enclosed space is simulated.

RIAA CHARACTERISTIC. Recording characteristic used on gramophone records.

RIBBON MICROPHONE (or Loudspeaker). The ribbon is a narrow strip of aluminium alloy foil suspended in a strong magnetic field. This is provided either by a powerful horseshoe magnet with polepieces extending along the length of the ribbon or (in a much smaller assembly) by ceramic magnets, which are made from a compressed magnetically orientated magnet powder. In this microphone the ribbon (which is corrugated for greater flexibility) is made to vibrate by the difference in pressure between front and back of the ribbon. If both sides are open to the sound wave, the resulting motion will be in phase with velocity, and not with amplitude of the sound wave. Vibration of the ribbon in the magnetic field produces an alternating current along its length. (See FIGURE-OF-EIGHT, PRESSURE GRADIENT.) In the loudspeaker the same principle is used in reverse, but is not suitable for handling considerable power, and so is used only in a tweeter. A flared (exponential) horn is provided to improve coupling.

RING. Undamped resonance.

S   "S" SIGNAL. The stereo difference signal A−B. The "S" does not stand for stereo (of which it is only part) but for "side" (bi-directional) microphone—used sometimes in combination with a "main" microphone to produce stereo.

SATELLITE. In this context, a stage in the transmission of audio or television signals from one part of the globe to another by two line-of-sight paths. Using a synchronous satellite (i.e. one for which the orbital speed is the same as the earth's rotational speed, so that the satellite remains stationary with respect to a point on the surface of the earth) there will be a delay of nearly a quarter of a second.

SAWTOOTH. See OSCILLATOR.

SCALE. Division of the audio frequency spectrum by musical intervals (i.e. frequency ratios). An octave has the ratio 1 : 2, a fifth 2 : 3, a fourth 3 : 4, and so on: common musical intervals are derived from series of ratios of small whole numbers. The *chromatic* or *twelve-tone scale* is a division of the octave into twelve equal intervals (semitones in the equal-tempered scale). On this scale most of the small-whole-number intervals will correspond (though not exactly) to an integral number of semitones, which may, of course, be measured from or to any point. Certain scales omit five of the twelve notes of the octave, leaving seven (plus the octave) into which most of the small-whole-number ratios will still fit—but it will no longer be possible to start arbitrarily from any point. Instead, the interval must always be measured from a *key* note, or a note simply related to it. Music which for the most part observes the more restricted scales is called *tonal*, that which ranges freely over the chromatic scale is called *atonal*. In *twelve-tone music* an attempt is made to give each of the twelve notes equal prominence.

539

SCENE. A single continuous film shot or any repetition of it.

SCREEN. A free-standing sound-absorbent or reflecting panel which may be used to vary the acoustics locally, or to cut off some of the direct sound travelling from one point to another in the studio. It may be moved about the studio at will. An object (such as a script) is said to be *screening the microphone* if it lies in the path of sound coming directly from a source.

SCREENING. A protection from stray electrical fields. It may take the form of an earthed mesh of wire surrounding a conductor carrying a low level signal. Valuable tapes (particularly videotapes) are screened, i.e. enclosed in a metal box, when sent on aircraft.

SCRIPT RACK. An angled rack on which a script may be placed in order to encourage a speaker to lift his head. The rack itself should be transparent to sound, though papers placed on it will not in any case be at such an angle that they can reflect sound into the microphone.

SEGUE. Musical term meaning "follow on".

SEPMAG. Separate magnetic film sound, i.e. on a separate spool, but recorded with frame-for-frame synchronization. See COMMAG, COMOPT.

SEPARATION. Degree to which each of several microphones discriminate in favour of the sources or groups of sources associated with the individual microphones, and against sound which is to be picked up by other microphones or which is unwanted. The purpose of separation is to allow individual control of the sources.

SHELLAC. Material that has been used in the manufacture of 78 rpm records. (See PRESSING.)

SIBILANCE. The production of strongly emphasised "s" and "ch" sounds in speech. These may in turn be accentuated by microphones having peaks in their top response.

SIGNAL. The fluctuating current which carries audio information (programme).

SIGNAL-TO-NOISE RATIO. The difference in decibels between the signal and noise levels. The quoted signal-to-noise ratio of any item of equipment is that available when the signal is as loud as it can be without significant distortion.

SINE TONE (Pure tone). A sound (or electrical signal) containing one frequency, and one alone. This corresponds to an air particle executing simple harmonic motion, and its graphical representation (waveform) is that of s.h.m. (i.e. a sine wave). In principle all sounds can be analysed into component sine tones. In practice this is only possible for steady sounds, or for short segments of irregular sounds; noise contains an infinite number of such tones. Sine tones are useful for studying frequency response and for lining up equipment.

SLUNG MICROPHONE. One which hangs by suspending wires or by its own cable from a ceiling or grid fitting (or from a boom or lazy arm).

SOLID STATE DEVICE. A circuit element such as a transistor (q.v.) or a complete microcircuit combining a number of circuit elements and their connections. It is characterized by small size, low power consumption, and high reliability.

SOUND. A series of compressions and refractions travelling through air or another medium, caused by some body or bodies (sound sources) in vibration. At any place it is completely defined by the movement of a single particle of air (or other material). The movement may be very complex but there are no physically separate components due to different sound sources; separate components may be isolated by mathematical analysis, but this does not mean that they physically exist. The brain acts as a mathematical computer which enables us to perceive the different components as separate entities. See HEARING, DECIBEL, LEVEL, FREQUENCY, WAVELENGTH, PITCH, PHASE, FORMANT SINE TONE, VELOCITY OF SOUND.

SOUND CONTROL ROOM.

SOUND EFFECTS. See EFFECTS.

SOUND PICTURE. Composite landscape of sounds containing a variety of individual *sound elements* at different volumes and perspectives.

SOUND SUBJECT (in *musique concrète*). A segment of "treated" sound material, which will be assembled with others into the finished work.

SPACED PAIR. Two separated microphones used to pick up stereo. Phase distortion effects will occur but may be tolerable.

SPACER. Uncoated tape, which may be yellow or other colours (other than white or red which are used mainly for leaders and trailers), cut into a spool of tape to indicate the end of one segment and the start of another.

SPILL. (*a*) To allow sound to be picked up on a microphone other than that intended, thereby reducing separation. (*b*) To unspool a quantity of tape by accident.

SPIN-START. Quick-start technique for disc, requiring no special equipment, in which the record is set up with the stylus in the groove and the motor switched off. On cue, the motor is switched on and the turntable boosted to speed by hand. This boost is sometimes not necessary for turntables with rim drive.

SPOOL. Reel for carrying tape. *Ciné spools* for tape are similar in design to 8 mm. film spools. The most common types are made of clear plastic in a variety of sizes between 3 and 7 inches in diameter. In fact, spools which are used for loading 8 mm. ciné cameras (the 3-inch size, of a more flexible plastic than that normally used for tape) are very suitable as "message spools" as they can be sent through the post with little protection. Metal spools are available in larger sizes, 7 and 8¼ inches. An *N.A.B. Spool* is that generally used on professional machines; the 10½-inch spool will carry 2400 ft. of standard play tape. It has a much larger hub size than the ciné spool but the large transcription tape decks are normally equipped to play either type. (A large hub is used in order that the tension does not vary so much as it would with a large diameter ciné spool. Some recorders can be switched to provide reduced tension when ciné spools are used.) Another design consists of a hub and a one-side-only backing plate, but this gives the operator less security against spillage than the double-sided spool.

SPOT EFFECT. A sound effect created in the studio. It may be taken on a separate microphone or on the same microphone as the main action.

SPOTTING. Reinforcement of a particular element in a stereo balance using a monophonic microphone. The balance is usually very close, to avoid "tunnel" reverberation effects and other problems.

STANDING WAVES. See WAVE.

STEERING. See PANNING.

STEREO (Stereophonic sound). A form of reproduction in which the apparent sources of sound are spread out. The word "stereo" implies "solid", but in fact the normal range of sound in two-channel stereo is along a line joining the loud-speakers—to which an apparent second dimension is added by perspective effects. This may be used to simulate the spread of direct sound of an orchestra or a theatre stage very well. And whereas each individual source may be fairly well defined in position, the reverberation associated with it is spread over the whole range permitted by the position of the loudspeakers. But even this range is small in comparison with the situation in a concert hall, in which reverberation reaches the listener from all around him. Systems have been devised for simu-lating concert hall reverberation in a small room by the provision of a third loudspeaker behind the listener: this carries a signal which may be derived from a two channel system (by combining, delaying and reverberating the signals) or from a third tape track. *Four-channel stereo* uses four independent sound channels (from 4-track tape or other systems). Two loudspeakers are in front of the listener and two behind in X-formation. On tape the recording system is compatible with 2-channel stereo in that the A and B frontal information is recorded on tracks 1 and 3, and the left and right rear information on 2 and 4 respectively. *Stereophonic sound in the cinema* uses a multi-track, multi-loud-speaker system, largely to ensure that members of the audience who are not ideally situated for two-channel stereo still hear sound which is roughly co-incident with the image.

STOPS. Stud positions on a stud fader, and the markings associated with them. Thus, to lift programme level "a stop" is to increase it by turning the fader (potentiometer) from one stud to the next. Intermediate levels are obtained if the potentiometer sweep arm straddles two studs.

STRAY FIELD. Unwanted a.c. field which may generate a signal in some part of the equipment where it should not be. The use of balanced wiring discriminates against this (equal and opposing e.m.f.'s act in the two wires), and so also, where necessary, does screening (surrounding parts which might be affected, by an earthed conductor).

STROBOSCOPE. Since a.c. electric lighting pulsates in intensity (at twice the mains frequency) such light can be used to illuminate a disc which has bars (or spots) on it. When the speed is at an appropriate setting these move a distance equal to their spacing in the time from one pulse of light to the next. The number of bars for $33\frac{1}{3}$, 45 and approximately 78 rpm, can be easily calculated—the European mains frequency being 50 Hz and the American, 60 Hz (this difference means that exact standardization for 78 rpm is not practicable). Stroboscopic indicators can also be devised for checking tape speed, but if the indicator used is on a guide pulley the number of bars depends on the diameter of the pulley as well as the speed of tape. Stroboscopes work best with neon tubes; and not at all in sunlight. When the dots move onwards the speed is too fast; when they move backwards it is too slow. Stroboscopes are very sensitive to the slightest deviation of speed from the normal.

STUDIO (sound studio). Any room or hall which is primarily used for micro-phone work. Its most important properties lie in its size and its acoustics—the way in which sound is diffused and absorbed, and the reverberation time (q.v.).

STUDIO ATMOSPHERE. See ATMOSPHERE.

STYLUS. The needle of a pick-up. Materials most used are diamond and sapphire. Other materials have been used, notably osmium alloy, but these are not as hard as sapphire. Wear depends on playing weight (and record material) and is most rapid in the earlier hours of playing, and in any case, different users will tolerate different degrees of wear before replacing: it is therefore difficult to set a precise lifetime on styli. However, if a sapphire is badly worn after 50 hours use, the corresponding diamond would last over 1000 hours. There is therefore a considerable saving to be made by using diamond styli. But this saving (on styli, if not on record wear) may in many cases be only theoretical, as incautious users may be prepared to change a sapphire no more often than the careful user changes a diamond. The cost of a diamond depends on the time spent and equipment used in polishing. For monophonic records, tip radii are 1 mil for fine-groove reproducing styli and 2·5 mil for coarse-groove. For stereo the standard is 0·5 – 0·6 mil, though 0·7 – 0·8 mil may be used for "combination" styli. Styli of eliptical cross-section (0·7 × 0·2) have the advantage of spreading across the groove, but not along it; but they are more expensive and may be expected to wear quicker. The tip radius of the cutter used is smaller than that of the reproducing stylus in each of these cases (and the included angle greater), so that the stylus tip rests at two points in the groove. A mono cartridge used on a stereo disc should have sufficient vertical compliance to ride the hill-and-dale (A—B) element of the recording without damage.

SUBHARMONIC. A partial of frequency f/2, f/3, f/4, etc., lying below the fundamental f. The subharmonic f/2 tends to be generated in the paper cone of a moving coil loudspeaker.

SUPERIMPOSITION. The recording of a second signal on a tape without passing the previous recording through the erase-head field. The h.f. bias on the new recording reduces the volume of the earlier signal. The method is not used professionally.

SWARF (*Am.*: Chip). The filament of cellulose nitrate which is thrown up when a disc is cut. This has to be carried away from the head by an air suction system. Care must be used in handling it as it is very inflammable.

SYNC. PULSE (PILOT TONE). A signal related to camera speed which is fed to a ¼-inch tape on which the associated sound is recorded. In the system adopted by the BBC, sound and synchronizing pulse each occupy a half track, so that a standard stereo stacked recording head can be used; but many other systems have also been devised. When the sound is subsequently transferred to magnetic film, the pulse controls the speed of rerecording.

SYNC. TAKE. Film shot with film and sound together, using a synchronous recording system.

T   **TAKE.** An individual attempt at shooting a scene (film) or sequence (radio or television) which may be tried several times.

TAPE. Magnetic recording medium consisting of a ferro-magnetic coating on a plastic backing (see COATING and BACKING). The standard width for the recording of sound programmes is ¼-inch and this may be recorded full, half or quarter track (q.v.). *Long Play* tape gives 50% more recording time on a spool than *standard play*, and *double play*, of course, gives double. Thinner tape is more susceptible to printing, and its use does not save money (for comparable quality); but it does save storage space, and permits fewer reel changes for a given spool size. *Videotape* is a similar medium, but is generally two inches wide; sound is recorded along one edge. Metric equivalents: ¼-inch = 6·25 mm, ½-inch = 12·5 approx., and so on. Cassettes generally use a narrower tape, 3·8 mm.

TAPE DECK. The mechanical part (plus heads) of a tape recorder or reproducer.

TAPE JOINER. Film joiner using a guillotine and polyester tape. As the film is not lapped, no frames are lost. This type has replaced the cement joiner.

TAPE RECORDING AMPLIFIER. Differs from an ordinary amplifier in that it includes an oscillator for bias and erase.

TAPE SPEEDS. Are all based on the early standard of 30 ips (inches per second) for coated tape. Successive improvements in tape, heads and other equipment have permitted successive reductions in speed to 15 and 7½ ips (used professionally for music and speech) and 3¾, 1⅞ and 1⁵⁄₁₆ ips (used domestically). Metric equivalents: 15 ips = 38 cm/s, 7½ ips = 19 cm/s, 3¾ ips = 9·5 cm/s and so on.

TELEPHONE ADAPTOR. A pick-up coil which may be placed in the field of the line transformer of a telephone. The signal generated is fed to a recorder or other equipment.

TELEPHONE QUALITY. A frequency band between 300 – 3000 Hz. Simulated telephone quality should, however, be judged subjectively according to programme needs.

TENT. A group of screens, arranged to trap (and usually to absorb) sound in the region of the microphone.

TIMBRE. Tone quality. The distribution of frequencies and intensities in a sound at any particular time.

TIME CONSTANT. For a capacitor, C farads, charging or discharging through a resistance, R ohms, (as in a PPM, limiter, etc.) the time constant t = CR secs. (Similarly, for an inductance of H henries and resistance, R ohms, t = L/R secs.)

TONE. Imprecise term for sound considered in terms of pitch (or frequency content). Pure tones sound of a particular frequency. See SINE TONE.

TONE CONTROL. Pre-amplifier control for adjusting frequency content of sound (usually bass or treble).

TOP. High frequencies in the audio range, particularly in the range 8 – 16 kHz.

TOP RESPONSE. Ability of a component to handle frequencies at the higher end of the audio range.

TRACK. (*a*) To move a camera or boom towards or away from the acting area. (*b*) An individual recording among several on a record.

TRAILER. (*a*) An item in the continuity (link) between programmes which advertises future presentations. (*b*) Uncoated tape, usually red, which is cut into a tape to indicate the end of wanted recorded material.

TRANSDUCER. A device for converting power from one form to another. The system in which the power is generated or transmitted may be acoustic, electrical, mechanical (disc), magnetic (tape), etc. Thus, microphones, loudspeaker, pick-ups, tape heads, etc., are all transducers.

TRANSFORMATIONS, TREATMENT OF SOUND (in radiophonics). Changes in sound quality, pitch or duration, by any continuous or discontinuous process that may be used to convert the content of a sound into any other sound form.

TRANSIENT. The initial part of any sound, before any regular waveform is established. The transient is an important part of any sound and in musical instruments helps to give identifiable character.

Transient responce. Ability of a component to handle and faithfully reproduce sudden irregular waveforms. See DIAPHRAGM.

TRANSISTOR. A semiconductor device which performs most of the functions of a valve (vacuum tube), but differs from it principally in that (*a*) no heater is required, so that the transistor is always ready for immediate use and no unproductive power is consumed, (*b*) it is much smaller in size, (*c*) input and output circuitry are not so isolated as in a valve, and (*d*) there is normally no phase reversal in a transistor, as the control voltage is used to promote flow of current, and not to reduce it. A range of designs and functions of transistors (as with valves) is available. The circuit associated with a transistor will be somewhat different from that for a valve. Transistors are more sensitive to changes of temperature than valves. Power transistors, which generate heat, need to be well ventilated.

TRANSMISSION, TRANSMITTER. See RADIO.

TRANSMUTATION. Changing the timbre of a sound, but not necessarily its dynamics. This includes transposition in pitch.

TRANSPORT SYSTEM (of a tape deck). The drive motor, capstan and idler, the feed and take-up motors and spool mountings, and the guide pillars and pulleys round which the tape passes to draw it over the heads.

TREBLE. Higher part of the musical range; say,1 or 2 kc/s and above.

TREMOLO. A regular variation in the amplitude of a sound, e.g. of electric guitar, generally at a frequency between 3 and 30 Hz. Sometimes confused with VIBRATO (q.v.).

TURN OVER. In filming, the director's instruction to run the camera.

TURNTABLE. The rotating plate of a record player. Besides supporting and gripping the record, it acts as a flywheel, checking any tendency to wow and flutter. It should therefore be well balanced, with a high moment of inertia (this is highest for a given weight if most of the mass is concentrated at the outer edge).

TUNNEL EFFECT. Monophonic reverberation associated with an individual source in stereo.

"TWEETER". High frequency loudspeaker which is used in combination with a low frequency unit or "woofer". The problems of loudspeaker design are different at the two ends of the audio spectrum and in some designs are easier to solve if handled separately. A single unit becomes progressively more directional at higher frequencies; a small separate unit for h.f. can maintain a broad radiating pattern.

TWIN TRACK. Two half track recordings on ¼-inch tape used for different purposes: to record the separate stereo channels, to record mono plus a guide track (for television), or to make individual recordings in opposite directions.

U   **UNDERMODULATION.** Allowing a recorded or broadcast signal to take too low a volume, so that it has to compete to an unnecessary extent with the noise of the medium (and has to undergo greater amplification on reproduction, risking greater noise at this stage also).

UNIDIRECTIONAL MICROPHONE. This may refer either to a cardioid (q.v.) or near-cardioid type of response (live on one face and substantially dead on the other), or a microphone with a more strongly directional forward lobe. See PARABOLIC REFLECTOR, GUN MICROPHONE.

V   **VALVE** (*Am.*: Vacuum Tube). An almost completely evacuated glass envelope within which electrons released by a heated electrode (the cathode) are collected by a second positively charged electrode (the anode). In this, its simplest form, the valve is a *diode* and it conducts electricity whenever there is a flow of electrons into the cathode (on every other half cycle of an alternating signal). In the *triode* a grid is placed in the path of the electrons and variation of voltage on this controls corresponding fluctuations in the flow of electrons, producing an amplified version of the signal on the control grid. Additional grids may be added (*tetrode, pentode* etc.) and these further modify the characteristics of the electron flow.

VARIABLE RELUCTANCE (pick-up). One of the more common principles applied to pick-up design. The stylus armature (mounting arm or shank) forms part of a circuit of magnetic flux between the poles of a permanent magnet. Movement of the stylus produces variations in the magnetic flux, which in turn generates a current in a coil (or two coils situated on paths which are favoured alternately, and operating in push-pull).

VELOCITY OF SOUND. In air at room temperature this is approximately 1120 ft/sec. It can be calculated roughly as $1087 + 2\,T$ ft/sec where T is the temperature in degrees centigrade. Humidity also makes a slight difference. In liquids and solids it is much faster than in air.

VHF (Very High Frequency). See RADIO.

VIBRATO. Rapid cyclic variation in pitch at a rate of about 5 – 8 Hz, used by singers and instrumentalists to enrich the quality of sustained notes.

VIDEOTAPE. See TAPE.

VIDEOTAPE CLOCK. Clock mounted on a board showing programme details. Shown in vision before the start of a television recording between about minus 30 seconds and minus 3 seconds, after which the picture fades to black. This is accompanied in sound by a countdown, "30 . . . 20 . . . 10–9–8–7–6–5–4–3" with reference tone between minus 20 and minus 10.

VOCAL STOP. A short break in vocalized sound which precedes certain consonants. These help in the exact location of editing points on tape, and sometimes provide a useful place to cut at. For example, in the words "to cut at" there are several stops: "/to/cu/ta/t". It would therefore be possible to cut in before "to" or "cut", but it would not be possible to remove the word "at" cleanly from the end. However, the same result might be achieved by cutting from stop to stop in "cu/ta/t". It is sometimes possible to lose the sound after a stop completely, e.g. when cutting "bu/" (for "but") on to the beginning of a sentence.

VOICE LEVEL. See LEVEL.

VOLUME CONTROL. See CONTROL, COMPRESSION, FADER.

VOLUME METER, VU METER. See METER.

VOLUME OF SOUND. See DECIBEL, LEVEL.

W   WAVE (sound wave). A succession of compressions and rarefactions transmitted through a medium at a constant velocity. See VELOCITY OF SOUND. In representing this graphically displacement is plotted against time, and the resulting diagram has the appearance of a transverse wave (like the ripples on a pool). This diagram shows the *waveform*. The distance between corresponding points on successive cycles (or ripples) is the *wavelength* (λ) and this is related to the frequency (f) (the rate at which ripples pass a particular point) and sound velocity (c) through the relation $f\lambda = c$. Wavelength (in feet) can thus be roughly calculated as 1120/f. As sound radiates out from a source it forms a *spherical wave* in which intensity is inversely proportional to the square of the distance. When the distance from the source is very large compared with the physical dimensions of any objects encountered this effect becomes less important; the loss in intensity is small and the wave is said to act as a *plane wave*. See BASS TIP-UP for illustration of this.

WAVE ANALYSER. An instrument incorporating a selective amplifier of narrow band-width. It operates like a very sharp pass band filter.

WEIGHTED and UNWEIGHTED. Different ways of indicating levels of noise or hum relative to signal, with particular reference to their bass content. Programme meters do not normally give any frequency information, and low frequencies will not sound as loud as a VU meter or PPM will indicate, as the ear discriminates against bass. For this reason, quoted noise levels are sometimes "weighted" against bass according to standard loudness contours. Weighted and unweighted measurements may differ by 20 dB or more at low frequencies.

WHITE NOISE. See NOISE.

WIGGLE or FLICKER. The momentary displacement of a stereo image which occurs when faders on the sound channels are not making contact on successive studs simultaneously.

WILDTRACK. Film sound recorded without picture.

WINDSHIELD (*Am.*: Windscreen). Shield which fits over microphone and protects diaphragm from "rattling" by wind, and also contours the microphone for smoother airflow round it.

WIPE (tape). Erase.

"WOOFER". Low frequency unit in Loudspeaker. See "TWEETER".

"WOOLLY". Sound which lacks clarity at high frequencies and tends to be relatively boomy at low.

WOW. Cyclic fluctuation in pitch due to mechanical faults in recording or reproducing equipment (or physical fault in a disc). The frequency of the variation is below, say, 5 Hz. See FLUTTER, VIBRATO.

Z   ZERO LEVEL. See LEVEL.

BIBLIOGRAPHY

Millerson, Gerald The Technique of Television Production. *Focal Press*, London, and *Hastings House*, New York (9th ed., 1972). A highly analytical study of the medium, including the contribution of sound.

Oringel, Robert Audio Control Handbook. *Hastings House*, New York and *Focal Press*, London (4th ed., 1972). A simple and useful introduction to the subject (a little fuller in this edition than in the first three.) There is a strong emphasis on American equipment.

Wood, A. B. The Physics of Music. *Methuen* (6th ed., 1962). A standard primer on the subject.

Hilliard, Robert L. (ed.) Radio Broadcasting *Hastings House*, New York and *Focal Press* London 2nd ed., (1975). Describes the job of the audio operator in relation to American local radio.

Robertson, A. E. Microphones. *Butterworth* (2nd ed., 1963). Describes the engineering principles behind many types of microphones.

Reisz, Karel, and Millar, Gavin The Technique of Film Editing. *Focal Press*, London and *Hastings House*, New York (1969). Concentrates largely on the general principles of picture editing.

Stockhausen, Karlheinz Study II (Score). *Universal Edition.* See this and the scores of other works of a similar nature for illustration of the problems (and purpose?) of the notation of electronic music.

Potter, Kopp and Green-Kopp Visible Speech. *Dover* (1967). Useful when considering how to record, treat and edit speech and song.

Alkin, Glyn Sound with Vision. *Butterworth* (1973). A substantial work on television sound—based on BBC practice.

Nisbett, Alec The Use of Microphones, *Focal Press*, London, and *Hastings House*, New York (1974). A concise handbook on microphones, balance and control.

INDEX

549

552

Intermodulation distortion, 293, 518
Interviewing, 173–175
— hand-held microphone, 174–175
Ionophone, 527

Joint (see Editing)
Jump cut, 306, 527

Key, musical, 332–333
Keying unit (radiophonics), 373

Landline, 528
Lanyard microphone (lavalier), 155–158,
195–198
Learning from radio or television, 500–
506
Level, 417–437 (see also Volume)
— reference (see Line-up, tone)
— relative, 420–421
— test, 86, 99, 527
— zero, 86, 527
Library, recorded effects, 255–256, 276–
278, 489
Lighting, and sound coverage, 82–84
Limiter, 62, 429–436, 527
Line, 528
Line-up, tone, 84, 86–87, 429, 527
— stereo microphones, 168
Lip-ribbon microphone, 152, 528
Listening conditions, 38, 111, 117, 248,
321, 356, 360, 422, 436 (see also
Monitoring)
— for stereo, 38–42, 390
Live transmission, 74, 87, 528
Logarithmic scale, 31–35, 522
Log (programme), 55–57, 90
Loop, tape, 126, 278, 290, 341, 369, 418,
528
— film (magnetic), 484–485, 487, 528
Loudness, 32–34, 211, 258, 417–437, 528
(see also Level, Volume)
— and listening conditions, 422–423
Loudspeaker, 220, 384–390, 417
— acoustic horn, 385
— baffle, 389
— cone, 387–388, 514
— crossover network, 386–387, 516
— electrostatic, 385–387, 520
— line source, 191, 251
— moving coil, 385–387, 531
— principles, 385–390
— ribbon, 385–387, 539
— stereo (positions), 38–42
— television use, 61, 191, 251–252
L.p., long playing record, 528

"M" Signal (see Stereo)
"Magic eye", 419–420
Magnetic film (see Film)

Magnetic tape (see Tape)
Mandolin, 235
Marking up, discs, 297–301, 529
— script, 294, 298, 301–302, 529
— tape, 443, 459, 529
Mellotron, 276
Melochord, 373
Membrane absorber, 119, 507
Meter (programme volume), 417–420,
426, 529
Metronomic switching, 373
Micron, 529
Microphone, 17, 20, 129–171, 529 (see
also Balance)
— ancillary equipment, 159–161
— bi-directional, 135, 139–142, 162,
164–165, 511
— — use, 172–174, 205, 208–210, 343–
345
— boom, 80–84, 160–161, 189–192, 247,
253
— carbon, 20, 130–131, 512
— cardioid, 135, 142–147, 163–167, 513
— — use, 191–192, 208–220, 218, 232,
238, 248
— condenser, 20, 130, 134, 144, 145–147,
152–153, 205, 329, 520
—constant-amplitude, constant-velocity,
20
— contact, 159, 338, 514
— cottage-loaf, 144, 163–165
— — use, 218, 220, 230
— crystal, 20, 130, 134, 139, 329, 516
— double moving coil, 145
— double ribbon, 144
— electrostatic, 20, 130, 134, 144, 145–
147, 152–153, 205, 329, 520
— figure-of-eight, 135, 139–142, 162,
164–165, 172–174, 208
— gun, 148–151, 195, 249, 253, 525
— hand, 154–155, 158, 194, 253
— highly directional, 136–137, 147–151,
533
— hypercardioid, 137, 142–147, 163–165,
526
— lanyard, 155–158, 195–198
— lip-ribbon, 152, 528
— low-quality "actuality" types, 198
— mountings, 153–154, 160–161, 193,
253
— moving coil, 20, 129–130, 134, 139,
143, 144, 145, 154–156, 191–192, 232,
531
— neck, 155–158, 195–198
— noise-cancelling, 150–153
— omnidirectional, 134, 137, 139, 154–
157, 174–176, 182
— personal, 80, 155–158, 192, 194–198,
218, 282
— polar response, 130, 134–137, 162–
167, 535
— principles, 35, 129